Cognition

Tenth Edition

To the memory of my parents:

Kenneth D. Reed (1919 – 2007)

Anita M. Reed (1921 – 2012)

Sara Miller McCune founded SAGE Publishing in 1965 to support the dissemination of usable knowledge and educate a global community. SAGE publishes more than 1000 journals and over 600 new books each year, spanning a wide range of subject areas. Our growing selection of library products includes archives, data, case studies and video. SAGE remains majority owned by our founder and after her lifetime will become owned by a charitable trust that secures the company's continued independence.

Los Angeles | London | New Delhi | Singapore | Washington DC | Melbourne

Cognition

Theories and Applications

Tenth Edition

Stephen K. Reed

San Diego State University

Los Angeles | London | New Delhi
Singapore | Washington DC | Melbourne

For information:

SAGE Publications, Inc.
2455 Teller Road
Thousand Oaks, California 91320
E-mail: order@sagepub.com

SAGE Publications Ltd.
1 Oliver's Yard
55 City Road
London, EC1Y 1SP
United Kingdom

SAGE Publications India Pvt. Ltd.
B 1/I 1 Mohan Cooperative
Industrial Area
Mathura Road, New Delhi 110 044
India

SAGE Publications Asia-Pacific
Pte. Ltd.
18 Cross Street #10-10/11/12
China Square Central
Singapore 048423

Copyright © 2022 by SAGE Publications, Inc.

Printed in the United States of America

ISBN: 978-1-0718-7068-6

Library of Congress Control Number: 2022902688

Acquisitions Editor: Jessica Miller

Content Development Editor: Chelsea Neve

Project Editor: Veronica Stapleton Hooper

Copy Editor: Karin Rathert

Typesetter: diacriTech

Cover Designer: Candice Harman

Marketing Manager: Victoria Velasquez

This book is printed on acid-free paper.

22 23 24 25 26 10 9 8 7 6 5 4 3 2 1

BRIEF CONTENTS

CONTENTS

PREFACE

I began writing the first edition of *Cognition: Theory and Applications* in 1979 when I was a visiting associate professor at the University of California, Berkeley. Cognitive psychology was then a relatively new field of study, and I was disappointed by the lack of cognition textbooks that could inform students about this emerging field. My goal in writing a textbook was to share my own excitement by introducing students to the research, theories, and applications of cognitive psychology. Eight revisions of that first edition show its continued development.

I had not planned to write a new edition when I retired from teaching in 2014. I instead focused on writing journal articles on integrating ideas in cognitive psychology. I referred to this project as searching for the big pictures (Reed, 2020a). When I ran out of ideas for big pictures, I returned to writing books (Reed, 2021) and enthusiastically began this tenth edition.

Both my new publisher (SAGE) and I approached the tenth edition as if it were a new book. It had been nine years since the publication of the ninth edition, and the time in between editions provided an opportunity to introduce changes. It also produced a need to extensively update the content, and my search for the big pictures provided a head start on adding new content to the tenth edition of *Cognition*.

Another head start was my recently completed book *Cognitive Skills You Need for the 21st Century* (Reed, 2020b). The motivation for that book was the World Economic Forum's *Future of Jobs Report 2018* based on interviews of some of the world's largest employers regarding the latest needed skills and human investment trends across their industries. The report indicated that by 2022, trending skills would include active learning and learning strategies, reasoning, analytical thinking and innovation, complex problem solving, and creativity. I discuss these skills (and many others) in greater depth in this new edition of *Cognition*, making it especially relevant and useful to instructors and students in cognitive psychology courses.

You do not, however, need to wait for graduation to apply these skills. Applications are tailored to align with student interests, and they are useful in our daily lives, as shown in the photographs of people performing these activities throughout the book. The emphasis on real-world applications and the visually appealing art program that brings them to life, along with the balanced coverage of classic and contemporary theories and research, reflects my attempt to maintain the best features of previous editions while introducing new features to substantially enhance that content.

CHANGES IN THE TENTH EDITION

The most visible change in the tenth edition is that it is in full color. I have enjoyed the task of finding colorful figures and photos to make this edition more engaging and informative than previous editions. As you might imagine, a delay of 10 years between the publication of the ninth and tenth editions also provided an opportunity to include extensive new material that has appeared in the past decade.

One of these changes was the addition of a new chapter on action. Many cognitive psychologists now believe that much of cognition—perception, memory, learning, language, decision making, and problem solving—occurs to support action. It now appears counterproductive to describe these cognitive processes without considering how we use them to support action. Another change was finishing the book with the chapter on "Expertise and Creativity." Placing that chapter after the one on "Decision Making" enables discussion of both decision making and problem solving within the context of expertise.

A frequent request by reviewers of previous editions was to include more material on cognitive neuroscience. We therefore relied on the expertise of contributing author Paul Merritt to help add that content to the book. Paul had an additional influence on content. Many of the students who enrolled in his cognitive psychology course at Georgetown University and Colorado State University were not psychology majors. I therefore attempted to make this book more user-friendly to those students by eliminating or rewriting material that appeared too difficult for a more general audience. The result is a text that undergraduate students will find very readable and accessible.

APPROACH

I have continued to use three criteria for selecting material. The first is whether the material makes an important contribution to cognitive psychology. The second is whether it is accessible to students. Will they understand it and find it interesting? The third is whether it can be easily integrated with other material in the book. There must be a clear flow of ideas to tell a coherent story.

Three themes appear throughout the book: research, theories, and applications.

1. Research

Research is the foundation of any field of science. Cognitive psychologists have developed many innovative research paradigms to make inferences about cognitive operations. Their measures include accuracy, response times, verbal reports, brain waves, and blood flow to identify cognitive operations and discover their locations in the brain. This book describes experiments in sufficient detail to help students understand these research paradigms. The detailed descriptions typically occur early in each chapter to provide a basis for understanding the remainder of the chapter. Most chapters have a chronological flow that illustrates how contemporary research has built on the findings of classical research.

2. Theories

Research would consist only of a collection of measurements if theories did not organize and provide interpretations of the findings. The chapters begin with the initial theories that established a foundation for cognitive psychology, such as the information-processing models developed by Broadbent for speech and Sperling for vision, Miller's description of short-term memory, the Atkinson and Shiffrin model of learning, levels of processing and encoding specificity, Paivio's dual coding theory, Rosch's work on categorization, variations of semantic memory models, Kintsch's model of text comprehension, Newell and Simon's theoretical framework for problem solving, and the Kahneman and Tversky study of heuristics in decision making. The chapters then show how these theories have evolved, either as others continued to develop the initial ideas or proposed competing theories. This emphasis on the evolution of theoretical understanding is a central feature of this book.

3. Applications

Although research and theories are key components of science, both can appear rather abstract without illustrations of how they are useful. Previous editions of *Cognition: Theory and Applications* have always included applications, but the applications received less emphasis than the theories. The tenth edition places more emphasis on applications by adding a section on applications at the end of each chapter. Identifying visual disorders, misusing cell phones, managing cognitive overload, improving learning strategies, creating better memory codes, identifying clinical imagery, understanding dementia, producing concept maps, assessing comprehension, designing helpful decision aids, resolving conflicts, and enhancing creativity are a few of the many examples.

ORGANIZATION

The 14 chapters in the book cover a wide range of topics, and instructors can expand on whatever topics interest them. The book is divided into three parts: Cognitive Components, Cognitive Representations, and Cognitive Skills.

Part 1 on Cognitive Components consists of chapters on pattern recognition, attention, working memory, long-term memory, and action. Theories of pattern recognition seek to specify how people recognize and store descriptions of patterns in memory. Theories of attention are needed to explain how we select perceptual information. Working memory enables us to combine information retrieved from long-term memory with information that arrives from the environment. But its limited capacity and fast decay rate make it necessary for us to enter into long-term memory any new information we want to remember over a long interval. Action is needed to put this information to use.

Part 2 on Cognitive Representations contains chapters on memory codes, visual images, categorization, and semantic organization. The first two chapters describe qualitatively different memory codes because our ability to remember depends on the kind of memory code that we create. The study of memory codes also has important implications for how efficiently people retrieve information from memory and perform spatial reasoning tasks. The next two chapters emphasize how knowledge is organized into categories and how categories are organized into hierarchies. This organization can be studied by measuring how quickly people make classification decisions and retrieve semantic information.

Part 3 on Cognitive Skills consists of chapters on language, decision making, problem solving, and expertise and creativity. Language involves not only the meaning of individual words but the combination of words to form sentences that are both grammatically correct and convey intended meanings. The study of decision making has often focused on how people combine information when evaluating alternatives. The term *risky decision making* is used to describe situations in which there is uncertainty regarding possible outcomes. The study of problem solving describes the skills needed to solve different kinds of problems, identifies general strategies, and examines the role of memory in problem solving. The concluding chapter on expertise and creativity discusses how people use prior knowledge in reasoning and solving problems. The final section of this chapter describes recent theoretical and empirical approaches to the study of creativity.

In addition to the organization of chapters into three parts, the material in each chapter is organized into manageable sections and subsections. You should review the outline at the beginning of each chapter for an overview of the topics. You should also study the Learning Objectives at the beginning of each chapter to preview some of the major theoretical constructs that you will encounter during your reading.

ACKNOWLEDGMENTS

I wrote the first edition of this book while spending a sabbatical year at the University of California at Berkeley. I am grateful to Case Western Reserve University and the Group in Science and Mathematics Education at Berkeley for providing financial support during that year. The Group in Science and Mathematics Education also furnished me with a stimulating environment, and the Institute of Human Learning provided an excellent library. Shortly after arriving at Berkeley, I had the good fortune to meet C. Deborah Laughton, a psychology editor at the time. She expressed confidence in the book long before it was deserved and, with the assistance of excellent staff and first-rate reviewers, helped in the development of the text.

I am grateful to Abbie Rickard, Chelsea Neve, Jessica Miller, Lara Parra, Veronica Stapleton Hooper, Karin Rathert, and all the others at SAGE, who have contributed to the Tenth Edition. Paul Merritt played a major role as contributing author by explaining the neuroscience of the cognitive components described in Part 1. I would also like to thank the following reviewers for their helpful suggestions:

Arlo Clark-Foos, University of Michigan
Mark Cushman, William Peace University
Un So Diener, John Brown University
Doss Kanessa, Troy University
Jane Dwyer, Rivier University
Catherine Evans, Radford University
Omar Garcia, Texas A&M University
Patrick Garrigan, Saint Joseph's University
John Geiger, Cameron University
John Gomez Varon, Fordham University
Joanna Gonsalves, Salem State University
Ralf Greenwald, Central Washington University
Robert J. Hines, University of Arkansas at Little Rock
Robert Hoople, Bethune Cookman University
Nora Isacoff, NYU, Columbia, and CUNY
Andrew Kelly, Georgia Gwinnett College
Meredith Lanska, CSU East Bay
Roxane Raine, University of Memphis
Christina Salnaitis, University of South Florida, St. Petersburg
Gary Starr, Metropolitan State University
Janet Trammell, Pepperdine University

Valerie Scott, Indiana University Southeast
Chris Wahlheim, UNC Greensboro
Chrissy Whiting-Madison, Rogers State University
Mark Yates, University of South Alabama
Diana Young, Georgia College & State University
Xiaowei Zhao, Emmanuel College

The comments of others are always welcome, and I would appreciate receiving suggestions from readers.

ABOUT THE AUTHOR

Stephen K. Reed is currently an emeritus professor of psychology at San Diego State University and a visiting scholar at the University of California, San Diego. He has also taught at Florida Atlantic University (1980–1988) and at Case Western Reserve University (1971–1980). His research on problem solving has been supported by grants from NIMH, the National Science Foundation, and the Air Force Office of Scientific Research. He is the author of numerous articles and books including *Psychological Processes in Pattern Recognition* (Academic Press, 1973), *Word Problems: Research and Curriculum Reform* (Erlbaum, 1999), *Cognitive Skills You Need for the 21st Century* (Oxford University Press, 2020) and *Thinking Visually,* 2nd ed. (Routledge, 2021).

1 INTRODUCTION

LEARNING OBJECTIVES

1. Explain the growth of cognitive psychology as a field of study, including the differences between behaviorism, the information-processing perspective and the early development of artificial intelligence.

2. Discuss the benefits of close cooperation between the fields of cognitive psychology, cognitive neuroscience, and artificial intelligence.

Cognition can be defined simply as the study of the mental operations that support people's acquisition and use of knowledge. Both the acquisition and the use of knowledge involve a variety of mental skills. If you glanced at the table of contents at the beginning of this book, you saw a list of some of these skills. Psychologists who study cognition are interested in topics such as how people recognize patterns, store information in memory, use language, solve problems, and make decisions.

The purpose of this book is to provide an overview of the field of cognitive psychology. The book summarizes experimental research in cognitive psychology, discusses the major theories in the field, and relates the research and theories to situations that people encounter in their daily lives—for example, reading, driving, studying, designing products, solving problems in the classroom, and making decisions.

Most students are surprised to learn how much of their everyday lives is driven by cognitive processes. One major area of interest to both students and cognitive psychologists is how to improve learning—a topic that will run throughout several chapters in the text. Another important area of interest is marketing applications of cognitive psychology. For example, manufacturers spend a great deal of time trying to make their products visually distinctive and therefore easier to

---

cognitive psychology The study of the mental operations that support people's acquisition and use of knowledge

find on a store shelf—a direct extension of research conducted in *visual attention*. Further business applications include manipulating pricing and discounts to influence *decision-making* in purchasing—in fact, a great deal of economics is based on decision-making research.

A great deal of law and public policy has also been formulated directly from research in cognitive psychology. In a dramatic instance of law extending from cognitive research, the New Jersey Supreme Court set down a decision outlining the only legal ways in which police officers can interrogate eyewitnesses that is based entirely on research regarding the fallibility of memory (*State v. Henderson,* 2011). In the 21st century, cognitive psychology research has had other wide-ranging impacts, from the operation of airport screening checkpoints to the safe operation of subway systems to the design of roadways and sidewalks. A section on the applications of cognitive psychology occurs at the end of every chapter.

In addition to the important ways in which cognition influences our everyday lives, how we live our lives has equally important implications for our cognitive functioning. We are learning more every year about how our diet, exercise, and sleep influence critical cognitive functions such as memory and our risk for cognitive decline as we grow older. Stress, anxiety, and depression are all influenced by our lifestyles, and these in turn can have negative effects on cognition. Similarly, both prescribed and recreational drugs can influence cognition in a variety of ways that are both positive and negative.

Cognitive skills are needed in a wide variety of professions that I discuss in my book *Cognitive Skills You Need for the 21st Century* (Reed, 2020b). The book begins with the World Economic Forum's *Future of Jobs Report 2018* that asked executives at some of the world's largest employers to report on the latest skills and human investment trends in their industries (www .weforum.org). The industries include advanced materials and biotechnology, consumer and financial services, healthcare, information and communication technologies, infrastructure and urban planning, mining and minerals, transportation, travel and tourism, and professional services. Skills that will be trending in 2022 include analytical thinking and innovation, learning strategies, creativity and originality, critical thinking and analysis, reasoning, and complex problem solving. I analyze these skills in greater depth in this text. Before delving into these topics, let's take a brief look at the history of cognitive psychology.

THE GROWTH OF COGNITIVE PSYCHOLOGY

It is difficult to pinpoint the exact beginning of any field of study, and cognitive psychologists would likely offer a wide variety of dates if asked when cognitive psychology began. James's *Principles of Psychology*, published in 1890, included chapters on attention, memory, imagery, and reasoning. Kohler's *The Mentality of Apes* (1925) investigated processes that occur in complex thinking. He and other Gestalt psychologists emphasized structural understanding—the ability to understand how all the parts of a problem fit together (the Gestalt). Bartlett's book *Remembering: A Study in Experimental and Social Psychology* (1932) contained a theory of memory for stories consistent with current views. There are some other important articles or books that seemed modern but did not cause a major shift in the way cognitive psychology is currently studied.

One book that had a major impact on psychological research was Watson's *Behaviorism* (1924). The book's central theme was that psychologists should become more objective by studying only what they could directly observe in a person's behavior. Watson's argument lent support to a **stimulus-response (S-R)** approach, in which experimenters record how people respond to stimuli without attempting to discover the thought processes that cause the response. The S-R approach is consistent with Watson's view because the stimulus and the response are both observable. Watson's book contributed to basing psychology on a more objective foundation of scientific observations. A limitation of the S-R approach, however, is that it does not reveal what the person does with the information presented in the stimulus.

By contrast, the information-processing approach seeks to identify how a person transforms information between the stimulus and the response. The acquisition, storage, retrieval, and use of information comprise separate stages, and the information-processing approach attempts to identify what happens during these stages (Haber, 1969). Finding out what occurs during each stage is particularly important when a person has difficulty performing a task because the psychologist can then try to identify which stage is the primary source of the difficulty. Information-processing models continue to have a major impact on our understanding of cognitive processes (Jarecki et al., 2020).

Information Processing Gathers Momentum

Changing allegiance from a behavioral to a cognitive perspective required taking risks, as Miller (2003) points out in his personal account of the early years of the cognitive revolution. Miller (1951) wrote in the preface to his own book on language (*Language and Communication*) that the bias of the book was behavioristic. In 1951, he still hoped to gain scientific respectability by swearing allegiance to behaviorism. His later dissatisfaction with behaviorism resulted in the 1960 creation, with Jerome Bruner, of the Center for Cognitive Studies at Harvard. The cognitive emphasis at the center reopened communication with distinguished psychologists abroad, such as Sir Frederic Bartlett in Cambridge, England; Jean Piaget in Geneva, Switzerland; and A. R. Luria in Moscow, Russia. None of these three had been influenced by the behaviorism movement in the United States and therefore provided inspiration for the cognitive revolution.

Ulric Neisser's 1967 book *Cognitive Psychology* provided a clear explanation of the information-processing perspective. He defined cognitive psychology as referring "to all processes by which the sensory input is transformed, reduced, elaborated, stored, recovered, and used." This definition has several important implications. The reference

PHOTO 1.1 Ulric Neisser's 1967 book *Cognitive Psychology* contributed to establishing the field of cognitive psychology.

Credit: Cornell University

---

stimulus-response (S-R) The approach that emphasizes the association between a stimulus and a response, without identifying the mental operations that produced the response to a sensory input implies that cognition begins with our contact with the external world. Transformation of the sensory input means that our representation of the world is not just a passive registration of our physical surroundings but an active construction that can involve both reduction and elaboration. Reduction occurs when information is lost. That is, we can attend to only a small part of the physical stimulation that surrounds us, and only a small part of what we attend to can be remembered. Elaboration occurs when we add to the sensory input. For example, when you meet a friend, you may recall many shared experiences.

The storage and the recovery of information are what we call memory. The distinction between storage and recovery implies that the storage of information does not guarantee recovery. A good example of this distinction is the "tip of the tongue" phenomenon. Sometimes we can almost but not quite retrieve a word to express a particular thought or meaning. Our later recall of the word proves the earlier failure was one of retrieval rather than one of storage. The word was stored in memory; it was simply difficult to get it back out. The last part of Neisser's definition is perhaps the most important. After information has been perceived, stored, and recovered, it must be put to good use—for example, to make decisions or to solve problems.

Neisser's *Cognitive Psychology* (1967) brought many of these ideas together into a single source; other books on cognition followed as cognitive research and theories began to gather momentum in the 1970s. For instance, research on categorization in the 1960s had focused on a concept identification paradigm in which categories were defined by logical rules, such as category members consist of all geometric forms that are either circles or large.

The predominant criticism of the concept identification paradigm was that real-world categories, such as clothes, tools, and vehicles, are unlike the categories studied in the laboratory. A dramatic change in how psychologists viewed real-world categories had to wait until the 1970s when Eleanor Rosch (Photo 1.2) and her students at the University of California, Berkeley, began to study the characteristics of real-world categories (Rosch, 1973). Her ideas and research were so important that they deserve the extensive coverage they receive in Chapter 9 on Categorization.

PHOTO 1.2 Eleanor Rosch made major contributions to our understanding of the organization of real-world categories.

Source: Photo of Eleanor Rosch available at https://en.wikipedia.org/wiki/Eleanor_Rosch#/media/File:Eleanor_Rosch.jpg, licensed by CC0 1.0 Universal (CC0 1.0) Public Domain Dedication

Cognitive psychology currently has widespread appeal among psychologists. Almost all psychologists studying perception, attention, learning, memory, language, reasoning, problem solving, and decision-making refer to themselves as cognitive psychologists, even though the methodology and theories vary widely across these topics. A caveat is that most of the initial contributions to the cognitive revolution were made by men because of the lack of women psychologists in academia during the time this revolution occurred. There are important exceptions, such as Eleanor Gibson's (1969) contributions to perception discussed in Chapter 2 on Pattern Recognition and Anne Treisman's (1960) theory discussed in Chapter 3 on Attention (Photo 1.3).

As a whole, the psychology field has also historically lacked racial and ethnic diversity. American Psychological Association data from 2015 showed 86% of psychologists in the U.S. workforce were white. In contrast, only 14% were from other racial or ethnic groups. Psychology is becoming more diverse as more racial and ethnic minorities enter the field, and cognitive psychology in particular is diversifying as it becomes more international, but more progress needs to be made.

PHOTO 1.3 Anne Treisman's theory of attention advanced the information-processing approach for studying cognitive processes. Here, she is pictured receiving the National Medal of Science from President Obama.

UPI / Alamy Stock Photo

Higher Cognitive Processes

The information-processing analysis of perception and memory was accompanied in the late 1950s by a new approach to more complex tasks. The development of digital computers after

World War II led to active work in artificial intelligence, a field that attempts to program computers to perform intelligent tasks, such as playing chess and constructing derivations in logic (Hogan, 1997). A seminar held at the RAND Corporation in the summer of 1958 aimed at showing social scientists how computer-simulation techniques could be applied to create models of human behavior. The RAND seminar had a major impact on integrating the work on computer simulation with other work on human information processing.

One consequence of the RAND seminar was its influence on three psychologists who spent the 1958–1959 academic year at the Center for Advanced Study in the Behavioral Sciences at Stanford University. The three—George Miller, Eugene Galanter, and Karl Pribram—shared a common dissatisfaction with the then-predominant theoretical approach to psychology, which viewed human beings as bundles of S-R reflexes. Miller brought with him a large amount of material from the RAND seminar, and this material—along with other recent work in artificial intelligence, psychology, and linguistics—helped shape the view expressed in their book, *Plans and the Structure of Behavior* (Miller et al., 1960).

The authors argue that much of human behavior is planned. A plan, according to their formulation, consists of a list of instructions that can control the order in which a sequence of operations is to be performed. A plan is essentially the same as a program for a computer. Because the authors found it difficult to construct plans from S-R units, they proposed a new unit called TOTE, an abbreviation for Test-Operate-Test-Exit. A plan consists of a hierarchy of TOTE units. Consider a very simple plan for hammering a nail into a board. The goal is to make the head of the nail flush with the board. At the top of the hierarchy is a test to determine whether the goal has been accomplished. If the nail is flush, one can exit. If the nail sticks up, it is necessary to test the position of the hammer to determine which of two operations, lifting or striking, should be performed.

The ideas expressed by Miller, Galanter, and Pribram were influenced by earlier work in two areas outside psychology. The work of Newell et al. (1958a) in the area of artificial intelligence identified strategies that people use to perform complex tasks such as playing chess. A second major influence came from linguist Noam Chomsky, who argued that an S-R theory of language learning could not account for how people learn to comprehend and generate sentences (Chomsky, 1957). His alternative proposal—that people learn a system of rules (a grammar)—was consistent with Miller, Galanter, and Pribram's emphasis on planning.

COGNITION'S RELATION TO OTHER FIELDS

Cognitive psychology is part of a broader field of study labeled cognitive science. Cognitive science is the study of intelligence in humans, computer programs, and abstract theories, with an emphasis on intelligent behavior as computation (Simon & Kaplan, 1989). It attempts to unify

---

artificial intelligence The study of how to produce computer programs that can perform intellectually demanding tasks

human information processing The psychological approach that attempts to identify what occurs during the various stages (attention, perception, short-term working memory) of processing the stimulus

plan A temporally ordered sequence of operations for carrying out some task

cognitive science The multidisciplinary study of cognition through such fields as psychology, philosophy, artificial intelligence, neuroscience, linguistics, and anthropology

views of thought developed by studies in psychology, linguistics, anthropology, philosophy, artificial intelligence, and the neurosciences (Hunt et al., 1989).

There are several landmarks in the development of the field (Nunez et al., 2019). The journal *Cognitive Science* began publication in 1977, and the Cognitive Science Society was formed in 1979. In 1986, the first PhD-granting cognitive science department was created at the University of California, San Diego. Don Norman played a major role in the creation of the journal, the Cognitive Science Society, and the first PhD-granting cognitive science department.

Nunez and his coauthors nonetheless argue that the field as a whole has lost impetus, focus, and recognition. Instead of becoming an interdisciplinary field, it has become a multidisciplinary field. A multidisciplinary field makes use of the theoretical perspectives of the different disciplines without integration. In contrast, interdisciplinary theories are more coherent and integrated. A multidisciplinary field refers to a collection of disciplines without cohesive interaction among them (Nunez et al., 2019).

PHOTO 1.4 Don Norman at the University of California, San Diego, helped establish the multidisciplinary field of cognitive science.

Don Norman.

Gentner (2019) agrees that the field has not converged on unified theories but argues that this is not a departure from the goals of its founders. She applauds the multidisciplinary approach to cognitive science and believes that it should be preserved and celebrated. Both the multidisciplinary and interdisciplinary approaches have made valuable contributions to cognitive science, as documented in the remainder of this chapter.

Cognitive Neuroscience

An exception to a lack of integration among fields within cognitive science is the field of cognitive neuroscience, which combines the methodology and theories of cognitive psychology with the methods of neuroscience. Throughout the text, we will examine the relationship between specific brain areas and cognitive functions. Much of this will focus on the **neocortex**, which consists of the four lobes of the brain shown in Figure 1.1. Processing of visual information occurs in the *occipital lobe*, which is the sole function located in this brain region. The *parietal lobe* is specialized for dealing with the body and spatial information (where things are in the world, including the body). Damage to this area can result in difficulty with movement as well as loss of attention. The *temporal lobe* is essential for understanding language and contributes to recognizing complex visual patterns, such as faces. The *frontal lobe* receives sensations from all the sensory systems and contributes to planning motor movements. Damage to this area can also interfere with memory.

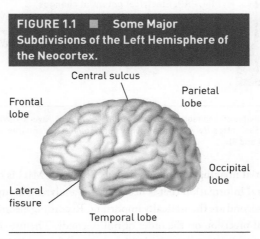

FIGURE 1.1 ■ Some Major Subdivisions of the Left Hemisphere of the Neocortex.

Central sulcus

Frontal lobe

Parietal lobe

Occipital lobe

Lateral fissure

Temporal lobe

Source: Garrett, Brain and Behavior 5e, Figure 3.8: Lobes and Functional Areas on the Surface of the Hemispheres.

---

neocortex Layers of the cerebral cortex that are involved in higher-order brain functions, such as perception, cognition, motor commands, and language

As technology has advanced, the ability of scientists to measure brain activity has also advanced. Positron emission tomography (PET) uses radioactive tracers to study brain activity by measuring the amount of blood flow in different parts of the brain (Posner & Rothbart, 1994). A more recent and widely applied method, functional magnetic resonance imaging (fMRI), uses magnetic fields to measure blood flow (Figure 1.2a). It is a popular method of neuroimaging in adults because it provides high spatial-resolution maps of neural activity across the entire brain. However, the loud noises and sensitivity to movement limit its use with infants (Kuhl & Rivera-Gaxiola, 2008).

FIGURE 1.2 ■ Functional Magnetic Resonance Imaging (fMRI) and Event-related Potentials (ERP) Provide Spatial and Temporal Measures of Brain Activity.

(a)

Expensive

fMRI: Hemodynamic changes
- Excellent spatial resolution
- Studies on adults and a few on infants
- Extremely sensitive to movement
- Noise protectors needed

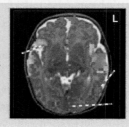

(b)

Inexpensive

EEG/ERP: Electrical potential changes
- Excellent temporal resolution
- Studies cover the life span
- Sensitive to movement
- Noiseless

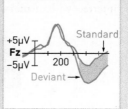

Source: From "Neural substrates of language acquisition," by P. K. Kuhl & M. Rivera-Gaxiola, 2008, *Annual Review of Neuroscience, 31,* 511–534. https://www.annualreviews.org/doi/10.1146/annurev.neuro.30.051606.094321. Figure 1 on page 514 (row 1 and 3)

A limitation of spatial imaging techniques such as PET and fMRI is that they do not provide the precise temporal information that is necessary for analyzing many cognitive processes in which fractions of a second are theoretically important. Recording electrical activity from the scalp provides temporal precision on the order of milliseconds. The use of these event-related potentials (ERPs) allows scientists to study the time course of mental operations. The vertical axis of the graph in Figure 1.2b displays voltage changes and the horizontal axis displays time in milliseconds (Kuhl & Rivera-Gaxiola, 2008).

---

positron-emission tomography (PET) A diagnostic technique that uses radioactive tracers to study brain activity by measuring the amount of blood flow in different parts of the brain

functional magnetic resonance imaging (fMRI) A diagnostic technique that uses magnetic fields and computerized images to locate mental operations in the brain

event-related potential (ERP) A diagnostic technique that uses electrodes placed on the scalp to measure the duration of brain waves during mental tasks

By combining PET and ERP studies, it is possible to take advantage of the more precise spatial localization of imaging techniques and the more precise temporal resolution of electrical potentials (Posner & Rothbart, 1994). Figure 1.3 illustrates how both techniques help scientists comprehend how people understand written words (Snyder et al., 1995). The red and yellow areas show increases in blood flow, indicating that the frontal and temporal areas of the left hemisphere are important for understanding the meaning of the words.

FIGURE 1.3 ■ A PET Scan Showing Changes in Blood Flow in the Left Hemisphere During a Cognitive Task. Brain Waves Show When Activation Occurs.

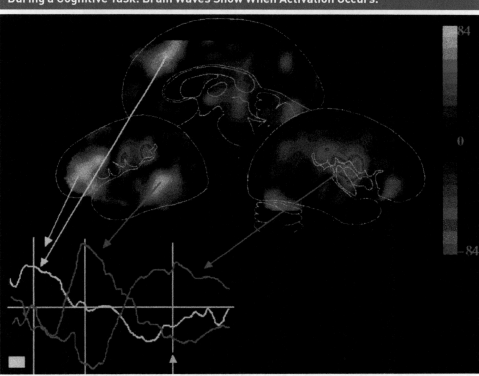

Source: From "Scalp electrical potentials reflect regional cerebral blood flow responses during the processing of written words," by A. Z. Snyder, Y. G. Abdullaev, M. I. Posner, & M. E. Raichle, 1995, *Proceedings of the National Academy of Sciences USA, 92*, 1689–1693. https://www.ncbi.nlm.nih.gov/pmc/articles/PMC42585/

The arrows connect PET blood-flow changes with the ERP waveforms recorded at the nearest overlying electrode on the scalp. The activation in the frontal part of the left hemisphere (yellow) leads the activation in the temporal part (red) by several hundred milliseconds. These findings imply that the earlier frontal activation is important for encoding the meaning of individual words and the later temporal activation may be more important for the integration of word meanings to understand phrases and sentences (Snyder et al., 1995). This hypothesis is consistent with the finding that damage to the temporal area of the left hemisphere often produces a language deficit that leaves the person unable to combine words to produce meaningful ideas.

Remarkably, it is possible to not only record ERPs but to directly change them (Widhalm & Rose, 2019). Transcranial magnetic stimulation produces a high-intensity magnetic field that passes through the scalp and causes neurons to fire. The effects of the stimulation are observed not only through changes in behavior but through changes in brain activity that reflect cognitive processes that contribute to that behavior (Widhalm & Rose, 2019). Figure 1.4 displays a brain stimulation system that navigates and targets transcranial magnetic stimulation on a 3D construction of the participant's brain. An EEG cap measures the electric field induced by transcranial stimulation and estimates its intensity on the cortical surface (Rosanova et al., 2012).

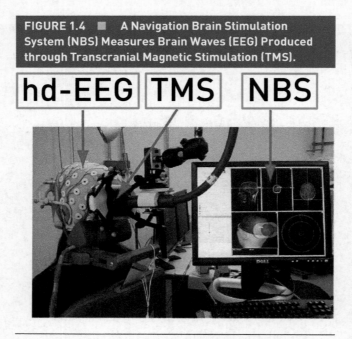

FIGURE 1.4 ■ A Navigation Brain Stimulation System (NBS) Measures Brain Waves (EEG) Produced through Transcranial Magnetic Stimulation (TMS).

Source: From "Combining transcranial magnetic stimulation with electroencephalography to study human cortical excitability and effective connectivity," by M. Rosanova, S. Casarotto, A. Pigorinni, P. Canali, A. G. Casali, & M. Massimini, 2012, *Neuromethods, 67*, 435–457. https://doi.org/10.1007/7657_2011_15

Cognitive neuroscience is particularly interesting to cognitive psychologists when it helps them evaluate cognitive theories (Yarkoni et al., 2010). For instance, we will see in Chapter 8 that one of the classic debates in cognitive psychology is the role of visual imagery in cognition. How do we know when people are using visual imagery to perform a task? Cognitive neuroscience has helped answer this question by allowing psychologists to study which part of the brain is active when

---

transcranial magnetic stimulation (TMS) A brain stimulation technique in which electrical pulses produced by a magnetic field cause neurons to fire in a focused region of the brain

people perform spatial reasoning tasks. Evidence for the use of visual imagery occurs when the same part of the brain is activated (the occipital lobe) as is activated during visual perception.

Artificial Intelligence

In their chapter on artificial intelligence (AI) in *The Cambridge Handbook of Intelligence,* Goel and Davies (2020) propose that, from an AI perspective, the construct of intelligence is not limited to humans or even animals but includes any type of intelligent system including computers. AI implements information-processing theories that describe intelligence in terms of the content, representation, access, use, and acquisition of information. It is helpful for exploring the benefits and limitations of different ways of representing and organizing knowledge in memory. It is also helpful for exploring how robots interact with the physical world through perception and action.

There are two major paradigms for designing intelligent computers, according to the authors. Engineering AI attempts to design the smartest possible intelligent systems regardless of whether the systems reflect intelligence found in people. The vast majority of AI research on robotics and machine learning falls into this category. In contrast, psychological AI attempts to design systems that think like people.

Goel and Davies (2020) describe a paradox in which tasks that are relatively easy for computers, such as producing logical proofs and playing chess, are difficult for humans. Tasks that are relatively easy for humans, such as perceiving, walking, and talking, are difficult for computers. The goal of general AI is to make computers proficient at a wide range of tasks, including those that are easy for humans.

There are at least three benefits of close cooperation between cognitive psychologists and people working on AI (Reed, 2019). The first is that computational programs in AI can serve as potential theoretical models in cognitive psychology. An early collaborative effort between a cognitive psychologist (Alan Collins) and a computer scientist (Ross Quillian) resulted in the hierarchical network model described in Chapter 10 to represent semantic organization in human memory (Collins & Quillian 1969). But it was human problem solving (Newell & Simon, 1972) that introduced many new ideas into cognitive psychology that is described in Chapter 13.

A second benefit is that AI and cognitive psychology share common interests, such as developing methods for categorizing patterns. In his book *The Master Algorithm: How the Quest for the Ultimate Learning Machine Will Remake Our World,* computer scientist Pedro Domingos (2015) explains different methods used in machine learning. Cognitive psychologists have developed similar methods to evaluate models of how people categorize patterns (Reed, 2019). The *Master Algorithm* asks how these different methods can be combined to improve performance, a challenge for both AI and cognitive psychology.

A third benefit of building bridges between AI and cognitive psychology is that the increasing impact of AI in our lives requires understanding how technology and people can work together. For instance, it is likely that robots will soon enter our lives as assistants in workplaces, shops, airports, healthcare, and classrooms (Wykowska, 2021). They will also serve as tools for

PHOTO 1.5 Alan Newell (left) and Herb Simon (right) at Carnegie Mellon University applied concepts in artificial intelligence to model human cognition.

Getty Images/Bill Pierce

FIGURE 1.5 ■ **An Experiment that uses Behavioral Measures, Evoked Potentials, and Eye Tracking to Record the Interactions between a Participant and the Robot iCub.**

Source: From "Robots as mirrors of the human mind," by A. Wykowska, 2021, *Current Directions in Psychological Science, 30*, 34–40. doi:10.1177/0963721420978609

generating new hypotheses, predictions, and explanations regarding human cognition. Robots offer the possibility of greater experimental control over initiating and responding to interactions with people (Figure 1.5).

Although AI is already having a major positive impact on our lives, it can also have a negative impact, which has raised concern about its ethical usage. Many of the questions raised in Figure 1.6 are concerns about the social consequences of algorithms (Rahwan et al., 2019). Do they disproportionally censor content? Do they discriminate against racial groups? Do weapons use appropriate amounts of force? Do competitors collude to fix prices? These types of questions are increasingly being asked in and out of courtrooms.

FIGURE 1.6 ■ AI Algorithms that Impact People's lives.

DEMOCRACY

NEWS RANKING ALGORITHMS
Does the algorithm create filter bubbles?
Does the algorithm disproportionately censor content?

ALGORITHMIC JUSTICE
Does the algorithm discriminate against a racial group in granting parole?
Does a predictive policing system increase the false conviction rate?

KINETICS

AUTONOMOUS VEHICLES
How aggressive is the car's overtaking?
How does the car distribute risk between passengers & pedestrians?

AUTONOMOUS WEAPONS
Does the weapon respect necessity and proportionality in its use of force?
Does the weapon distinguish between combatants and civilians?

MARKETS

ALGORITHMIC TRADING
Do algorithms manipulate markets?
Does the algorithm's behaviors increase systemic risk of market crash?

ALGORITHMIC PRICING
Do competitors' algorithms collude to fix prices?
Does the algorithm exhibit price discrimination?

SOCIETY

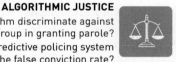

ONLINE DATING
Does the matching algorithm use facial features?
Does the matching algorithm amplify or reduce homophily?

CONVERSATIONAL ROBOTS
Does the robot promote products to children?
Does the algorithm affect collective behaviors?

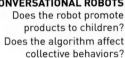

Source: From "Machine behavior," by I. Rahwan et al., 2019, *Nature, 568*, 477–486. https://doi.org/10.1038/s41586-019-1138-y

Cognitive Architectures

A landmark in the history of artificial intelligence was a book published by Alan Newell (1990) titled *Unified Theories of Cognition.* Unified theories should ideally be able to explain all aspects of cognition, including perception, learning, memory, problem solving, and decision-making. Such explanations require specifying interactions among the various components of cognition. Newell proposed a theory of how these components interact by developing a **cognitive architecture** called Soar (Newell, 1990).

Soar continues to be developed by the AI community (Laird, 2012), but its greatest contribution to cognitive psychology has been its influence on the development of ACT-R (Anderson, 1983)—a cognitive architecture for modeling human cognition. ACT-R assumes that cognitive architectures should be a theory of how behavior is generated through information processing that includes perception and action (Ritter et al., 2019). It has demonstrated how many aspects of cognition are intertwined, such as perception, memory, and problem solving. A manual, summer school, and workshops have supported building a community of cognitive scientists who have used the architecture to model cognition.

A limitation of ACT-R is its complexity; hence the need for summer school and workshops. Participants in a 2013 symposium on integrated cognition, sponsored by the Association for the Advancement of Artificial Intelligence, therefore met to develop a standard model of the mind based on a stripped-downed cognitive architecture. A standard model would be helpful because artificial intelligence, cognitive psychology, cognitive neuroscience, and robotics all contribute to our understanding of intelligent behavior but each from a different perspective. A standard model would provide a common framework for unifying these disciplines and guide practitioners in constructing a broad range of applications.

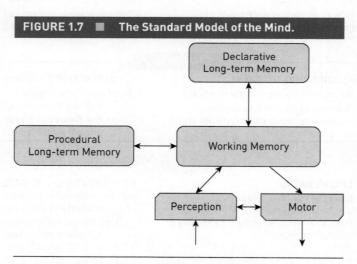

FIGURE 1.7   ■   The Standard Model of the Mind.

Source: From "A standard model of the mind: Toward a common computational framework across artificial intelligence, cognitive science, neuroscience, and robotics," by J. E. Laird, C. Lebiere, & P. S. Rosenbloom, 2017, *AI Magazine, 38*, 13–26. https://doi.org/10.1609/aimag.v38i4.2744

cognitive architecture An integrated system of cognitive components for modeling cognition

Figure 1.7 shows the components of the proposed standard model (Laird et al., 2017). Perception converts sensory stimuli into representations that can be stored in working memory or directly converted into actions by the motor component. Attention limits the amount of available perceptual information in both situations. Working memory provides a temporary storage space where perceptual information can be integrated with information from long-term declarative and long-term procedural memory. Declarative memory is the store for facts and concepts. Procedural memory contains knowledge about actions. The motor component uses the body to execute the actions.

You will learn much more about each of these components as you progress through the book, and the standard model will help relate these components. The authors of the standard model propose that it has the potential to provide a platform for the integration of theoretical ideas across different disciplines. I hope that including it in this text will help fulfill that goal.

SUMMARY

One reason for studying cognitive psychology is that cognitive processes influence many aspects of our lives. It differs from behaviorism by its emphasis on mental representations and procedures, such as replacing stimulus-response associations with hierarchical plans. Cognitive psychology is a member of a multidisciplinary field labeled "cognitive science," which also includes linguistics, anthropology, philosophy, artificial intelligence, and cognitive neuroscience. The interaction between cognitive psychology and cognitive neuroscience is the best example of an attempt to create an interdisciplinary field in which disciplines interact with each other. The objective of the standard model of the mind is to encourage more interdisciplinary interactions based on a shared cognitive architecture. The next five chapters discuss the components of this architecture—perception, working memory, long-term declarative memory, long-term procedural memory, and action.

RECOMMENDED READING

Readers interested in how major theoretical approaches influenced the history of psychology should read Heidbreder's (1961) *Seven Psychologies*. The book contains chapters on prescientific psychology, the beginning of scientific psychology, the psychology of William James, functionalism, behaviorism, dynamic psychology, Gestalt psychology, and psychoanalysis. *The Mind's New Science: A History of the Cognitive Revolution* (Gardner, 1985) and *How the Mind Works* (Pinker, 1997) provide very readable accounts of the evolution of cognitive psychology. The article "A framework for building cognitive process models" (Jarecki et al., 2020) demonstrates how information-processing models continue to influence the field. Chipman's (2016) introduction to cognitive science appears in the *Oxford Handbook of Cognitive Science*, which she edited. *Cognitive Skills You Need for the 21st Century* (Reed, 2020b) contains 20 short chapters on themes related to this topic. *How We Learn: Why Brains Learn Better Than Any Machine... for Now* (Dehaene, 2020) an overview of many issues discussed in this textbook.

Getty Images/JurgaR

2 PATTERN RECOGNITION

Describing Patterns
    Template Theories
    Feature Theories
    Combining Features
    Structural Theories

Information-Processing Stages
    The Partial-Report Technique
    Sperling's Model

Word Recognition
    The Word Superiority Effect
    A Model of the Word Superiority Effect

Scene Recognition
    Goal-Driven Scene Understanding
    Deep Neural Networks

Applications
    Brain Pathways
    Visual Disorders

SUMMARY

RECOMMENDED READING

LEARNING OBJECTIVES

1. Contrast feature and structural theories of pattern recognition.

2. Explain how Sperling's partial-report technique contributed to understanding characteristics of the visual sensory store.

3. Explain how the word superiority effect determines why a letter in a word is better recognized than a letter by itself.

4. Discuss the goals of understanding scenes and the applications of deep neural networks.

5. Describe how visual disorders have increased our knowledge of neural pathways.

The study of **pattern recognition** is primarily the study of how people identify the objects in their environment. Pattern recognition, which is discussed in this chapter, and attention, in the next chapter, play lead roles in the perception component of the standard model of cognition

---

pattern recognition The stage of perception during which a stimulus is identified

(Figure 2.1). We focus on visual pattern recognition in this chapter to provide continuity. Other chapters, such as the next chapter on attention, contain material on speech recognition.

Our ability to recognize patterns is impressive if we stop to consider how much variation there is in different examples of the same pattern. Figure 2.2 shows various styles of handwriting.

FIGURE 2.1 ■ The Perception Component of the Standard Model of the Mind.

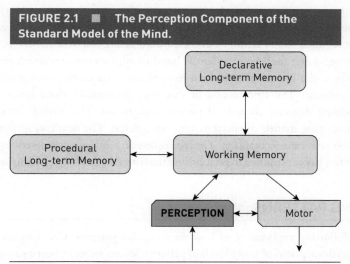

Source: Based on "A standard model of the mind: Toward a common computational framework across artificial intelligence, cognitive science, neuroscience, and robotics." by J. E. Laird, C. Lebiere, & P. S. Rosenbloom, 2017, *AI Magazine*, 38, 13–26.

FIGURE 2.2 ■ Variations in Handwriting.

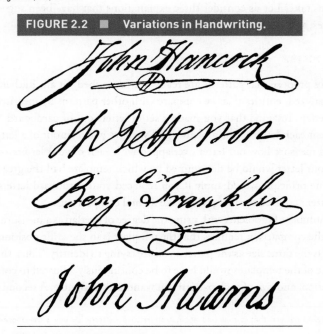

Source: istockphoto.com/DNY59

Not all people have the same style of writing, and some handwriting styles are much less legible than others. However, unless it is very illegible, we usually are successful in recognizing the words.

Our superiority over computers as pattern recognizers has the practical advantage that pattern recognition can serve as a test of whether a person or a computer program is trying to gain access to the Internet. If you have spent much time on the Internet you might have encountered a situation that required you to identify a distorted word before you were allowed to enter a site. The mangled word is easy for people to identify but difficult for computer search programs.

A large part of the literature on pattern recognition is concerned with alternative ways of describing patterns. The first section of this chapter discusses three kinds of descriptions that represent different theories of pattern recognition. The second section is about information-processing models of visual pattern recognition. The next two sections focus on word recognition and scene recognition. The last section on visual agnosia describes how studying brain disorders has contributed to establishing the neural basis of recognizing patterns.

DESCRIBING PATTERNS

Consider the following explanation of how we recognize patterns. Our long-term memory (LTM) contains descriptions of many kinds of patterns. When we see or hear a pattern, we form a description of it and compare the description against the descriptions stored in our LTM. We can recognize the pattern if its description closely matches one of the descriptions stored in LTM. Although this is a plausible explanation, it is rather vague. For example, what form do these descriptions take? Let us consider three explanations that have been suggested: (1) templates, (2) features, and (3) structural descriptions.

Template Theories

Template theories propose that patterns are really not "described" at all. Rather, templates are holistic, or unanalyzed, entities that we compare with other patterns by measuring how much two patterns overlap. Imagine that you made a set of letters out of cardboard. If you made a cutout to represent each letter of the alphabet and we gave you a cutout of a letter that we had made, you could measure how our letter overlapped with each of your letters—the templates. The identity of our letter would be determined by which template had the greatest amount of overlap. The same principle would apply if you replaced your cardboard letters with a visual image of each letter and used the images to make mental comparisons.

There are a number of problems with using the degree of overlap as a measure of pattern recognition. First, the comparison requires that the template is in the same position and the same orientation, and is the same size as the pattern you are trying to identify. Thus, the position, orientation, and size of the templates would have to be continuously adjusted to correspond to the position, orientation, and size of each pattern you wanted to recognize. A second problem is the

---

template An unanalyzed pattern that is matched against alternative patterns by using the degrees of overlap as a measure of similarity

great variability of patterns, as was illustrated in Figure 2.2. It would be difficult to construct a template for each letter that would produce a good match with all the different varieties of that letter.

Third, a template theory doesn't reveal how two patterns differ. We could know from a template theory that the capital letters *P* and *R* are similar because one overlaps substantially with the other. But to know how the two letters differ, we have to be able to analyze or describe the letters.

A fourth problem is that a template theory does not allow for alternative descriptions of the same pattern. You may have seen ambiguous figures that have more than one interpretation, such as a duck or a rabbit in Figure 2.3. The two interpretations are based on different descriptions; for example, the beak of the duck is the ears of the rabbit. A template is simply an analyzed shape and so is unable to make this distinction. By contrast, a feature theory allows us to analyze patterns into their parts and to use those parts to describe the pattern.

FIGURE 2.3 ■ An Ambiguous Figure that can be Perceived as Either a Duck or a Rabbit.

Source: "What an image depicts depends on what an image means," by D. Chambers & D. Reisberg, 1985, *Cognitive Psychology, 24*, 145–174. https://doi.org/10.1016/0010-0285(92)90006-N

Feature Theories

Feature theories allow us to describe a pattern by listing its parts, such as describing a friend as having long blond hair, a short nose, and bushy eyebrows. Part of the evidence for feature theories comes from recording the action potentials of individual cells in the visual cortex. By placing microelectrodes in the visual cortex of animals, Hubel and Wiesel (1962, 1963) discovered that cells respond to only certain kinds of stimuli. Some cells might respond to a line of a certain width, oriented at a correct angle and located at the correct position in its visual field.

---

feature theory A theory of pattern recognition that describes patterns in terms of their parts, or features

Other cells are even concerned about the length of the line. In 1981 Hubel and Wiesel received a Nobel Prize for this work.

Figure 2.4 shows the neural processing of visual information. Light is initially detected by photoreceptor cells in the retina to extract meaningful information about the visual world. This information is projected to the thalamus and areas of the primary visual cortex where the cells discovered by Hubel and Wiesel respond to features such as lines and simple shapes. These simple shapes are then combined in the ventral stream into more complex features to identify objects. We will learn more about visual features in the next section on perceptual learning and more about neural pathways in the last section on visual disorders.

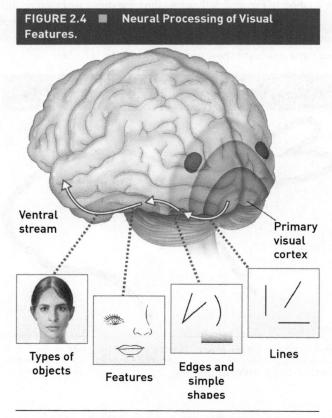

FIGURE 2.4 ■ Neural Processing of Visual Features.

Ventral stream

Primary visual cortex

Types of objects

Features

Edges and simple shapes

Lines

Source: Adapted from *INNATE: How the Wiring of Our Brains Shapes Who We Are*, by K. J. Mitchell, 2018, Princeton, NJ: Princeton University Press.

Perceptual Learning

Feature theories are convenient for explaining perceptual development, and one of the best discussions of feature theories is contained in Eleanor Gibson's (1969) *Principles of Perceptual Learning and Development*. Gibson's theory is that perceptual learning occurs through the discovery of features that *distinguish* one pattern from another.

Although most pattern recognition theorists make use of the feature concept, it is often a challenging task to find a good set of features. Gibson (1969) proposed the following criteria as a basis for selecting a set of features for uppercase letters:

1. The features should be critical ones and present in some members of the set but not in others to provide a contrast.

2. The identity of the features should remain unchanged under changes in brightness, size, and perspective.

3. The features should yield a unique pattern for each letter.

4. The number of proposed features should be reasonably small.

Gibson used these criteria, empirical data, and intuition to derive a set of features for uppercase letters. The features consist primarily of different lines and curves that are the components of letters. Examples of lines include a horizontal line, a vertical line, and diagonal lines that slant either to the right or to the left as occur in the capital letter *A*. Examples of curves include a closed circle (the letter *O*), a circle broken at the top (the letter *U*), or a circle broken at the side (the letter *C*). Most letters consist of more than one feature, such as a closed circle and a diagonal line in the letter *Q*.

A set of features is usually evaluated by determining how well it can predict **perceptual confusions,** as confusable items should have many features in common. For example, the only difference in features for the letters *P* and *R* is the presence of a diagonal line for the letter *R;* therefore, the two should be highly confusable. The letters *R* and *O* differ in many features, and so they should seldom be confused.

One method for generating perceptual confusions is to ask an observer to identify letters that are presented very rapidly (Townsend, 1971). It is often difficult to discriminate physically similar letters under these conditions, and the errors provide a measure of perceived similarity. Holbrook (1975) compared two feature models to determine how successfully each could predict the pattern of errors found by Townsend. One was the model proposed by Gibson and the other was a modification of the Gibson model proposed by Geyer and De Wald (1973). The major change in the modification was the specification of the number of features in a letter (such as two vertical lines for the letter *H*) rather than simply listing whether that feature was present.

A comparison of the two models revealed that the feature set proposed by Geyer and De Wald was superior in predicting the confusion errors made both by adults (Townsend, 1971) and by four-year-old children (Gibson et al., 1963). The prediction of both models improved when the features were optimally weighted to allow for the fact that some features are more important than others in accounting for confusion errors. Because the straight/curved distinction is particularly important, it should be emphasized more than the others.

---

perceptual confusion A measure of the frequency with which two patterns are mistakenly identified as each other

Distinctive Features

Children learn to identify an object by being able to identify differences between it and other objects. For example, when first confronted with the letters *E* and *F*, the child might not be aware of how the two differ. Learning to make this discrimination depends on discovering that a low horizontal line is present in the letter *E* but not in the letter *F*. The low horizontal line is a **distinctive feature** for distinguishing between an *E* and an *F;* that is, it enables us to distinguish one pattern from the other.

Perceptual learning can be facilitated by a learning procedure that highlights distinctive features. An effective method for emphasizing a distinctive feature is to initially make it a different color from the rest of the pattern and then gradually change it back to the original color. Egeland (1975) used this procedure to teach prekindergarten children how to distinguish between the confusable letter pairs *R-P, Y-V, G-C, Q-O, M-N,* and *K-X.* One letter of each pair was presented at the top of a card with six letters below it, three of which matched the sample letter and three of which were the comparison letter. The children were asked to select those letters that exactly matched the sample letter.

One group of children received a training procedure in which the distinctive feature of the letter was initially highlighted in red—for example, the diagonal line of the *R* in the *R-P* discrimination. During the training session, the distinctive feature was gradually changed to black to match the rest of the letter. Another group of children viewed only black letters. They received feedback about which of their choices were correct, but they were not told about the distinctive features of the letters. Both groups were given two tests—one immediately after the training session and one a week later. The "distinctive features" group made significantly fewer errors on both tests, even though the features were not highlighted during the tests. They also made fewer errors during the training sessions.

Emphasizing the distinctive features produced two benefits. First, it enabled the children to learn the distinctive features so that they could continue to differentiate letters after the distinctive features were no longer highlighted. Second, it enabled them to learn the features without making many errors during the training session. The failure and frustration that many children experience in the early stages of reading (letter discrimination) can impair their interest in later classroom learning.

Focusing on distinctive features might aid in distinguishing among faces, as it does in distinguishing among letters. To test this, Brennan (1985) used computer-generated **caricatures** that make distinctive features even more distinctive. For instance, if a person had large ears and a small nose, the caricature would have even larger ears and an even smaller nose than the accurate drawing. When students were shown line drawings of acquaintances, they identified people faster when shown caricatures than when shown accurate line drawings (Rhodes

---

distinctive feature A feature present in one pattern but absent in another, aiding one's discrimination of the two patterns

caricature An exaggeration of distinctive features to make a pattern more distinctive

et al., 1987). Making distinctive features more distinctive through exaggeration facilitated recognition.

Combining Features

Distinctive features are a key component of our ability to locate an object in our environment. If you ever waited for your luggage at an airport, you may have noticed many people tie color-ful ribbons to their luggage to help find their bags more easily because they "pop out" from the crowd. This phenomenon, as illustrated by the red flower at the beginning of the chapter, is a major prediction of feature integration theory (Treisman & Gelade, 1980).

According to this theory, all features across the entire visual landscape are represented simultaneously and pre-attentively. Thus one need only monitor the relevant feature to locate a distinctive item. Treisman and Gelade (1980) found that reaction times to find an object in a *single feature search* were independent of the size of the display, indicating that searching for a single feature is accomplished all at once. However, when two or more features must be combined in a *conjunction search*, each object in a visual scene must be examined for the combined features, which requires using attention. Returning to the airport example—if you have a standard black bag, you will now have to examine each black bag for size, shape, and so forth.

Many of the Treisman's experiments on feature integration theory explored the problem of how a perceiver combines color and shape, as these two features are analyzed by separate parts of the visual system. Figure 2.5 shows several demonstrations of how color and shape interact (Wolfe, 2018). In Panel A, it is easier to find the blue *O*, defined by the unique feature blue, than to find the red *X*. Finding the red *X* requires attending to the conjunction of red and *X* because there are also red *T*s and green *X*s in the display. Treisman found that it did not matter how many other letters were in the display, if people searched for a letter defined by a unique color or shape. The uniqueness made the letter pop out from the rest of the display, as occurs for the blue *O*. However, adding more red *T*s and green *X*s to the display would increase the time to find the red *X* because it requires attending to a conjunction of features.

Panel B illustrates another finding that is predicted by the attention requirements of feature integration theory. It is not immediately obvious that the left half of the display differs from the right half because attention is necessary for perceiving conjunctions of color and shape. The circles and diamonds switch colors, which you can observe by closely attending to the shape and color combinations. Another important implication of Treisman's theory is referred to as the "illusory conjunctions." Following a brief glimpse of the display in Panel C, observers may report seeing an incorrect combination of color and shape, such as a green square. Feature integration theory states that it requires attention to combine features such as color and shape. Insufficient attention, therefore, causes incorrect combinations of features.

FIGURE 2.5 ■ Visual Displays used to Evaluate Feature Integration Theory.

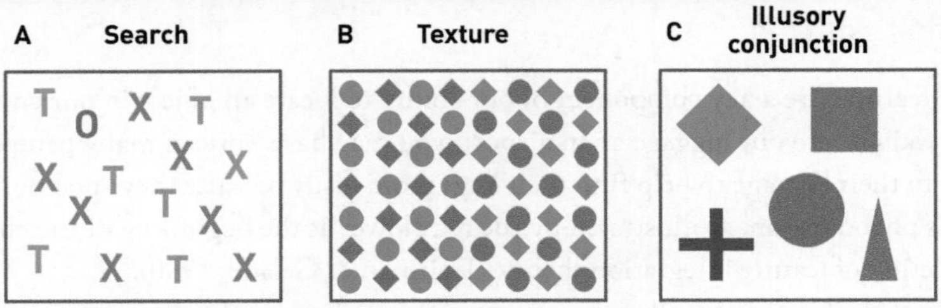

A   Search   B   Texture   C   Illusory conjunction

Source: "Ann Treisman (1935–2018)" by J. M. Wolfe, 2019, *Current Biology*, 28, R329–R341 (2018). https://doi.org/10.1016/j.cub.2018.03.009

Structural Theories

A limitation of feature theories is that descriptions of patterns often require that we specify how the features are joined together. Describing how features join together to create a structure is a guiding principle of Gestalt psychology. To Gestalt psychologists, a pattern is more than the sum of its parts. Providing precise descriptions of the relations among pattern features was initially formalized by people working in the field of artificial intelligence who discovered that the interpretation of patterns usually depends on making explicit how the lines of a pattern are joined to other lines (Clowes, 1969).

Structural Descriptions

Structural theories describe the relations among the features by building on feature theories. Before we can specify the relation among features, we have to specify the features. A structural theory allows specification of how the features fit together. For example, the letter **H** consists of two vertical lines and a horizontal line. But we could make many different patterns from two vertical lines and a horizontal line. What is required is a precise specification of how the lines should be joined together—the letter **H** consists of two vertical lines connected at their midpoints by a horizontal line.

Figure 2.6 illustrates shape skeletons for different animals that are based on structural descriptions originally proposed by Blum (1973) as a method for distinguishing among biological forms. Wilder et al. (2011) adapted Blum's methods to make predictions about how people would classify novel shapes into categories, such as *animal* and *leaf.* Their successful predictions support the argument that people use these kinds of descriptions to make classifications. The skeleton shapes of animals have relatively curvy limbs compared to the fewer, straighter limbs of leaves.

Moving from a two-dimensional world to a three-dimensional world creates additional challenges for identifying and describing the relations among features. Figure 2.7 illustrates the problem of identifying features by the relative difficulty of perceiving the three patterns as cubes (Kopfermann, 1930). The left pattern is most difficult to perceive as a cube, and the pattern in the middle is the easiest. Try to guess why before reading further. (Hint: Think about the challenge of identifying features for each of the three examples.)

---

structural theory A theory that specifies how the features of a pattern are joined to other features of the pattern

FIGURE 2.6 ■ Examples of Skeleton Structures of Animals.

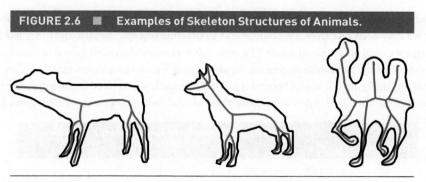

Source: "Superordinate shape classification using natural shape statistics" by J. Wilder, J. Feldman, J., & M. Singh, 2011, *Cognition*, 119, 325–340. https://doi.org/10.1016/j.cognition.2011.01.009

The theme of Hoffman's (1998) book on visual intelligence is that people follow rules in producing descriptions of patterns. The first of the many rules described in his book is to always interpret a straight line in an image as a straight line in three dimensions. Therefore, we perceive the long vertical line in the center of the right pattern in Figure 2.7 as a single line. However, it is necessary to split this line into two separate lines to form a cube because the lines belong to different surfaces. It is particularly difficult to see the figure on the left as a cube because you also need to split the two long diagonal lines into two shorter lines to avoid seeing the object as a flat pattern.

FIGURE 2.7 ■ Perceiving Cubes.

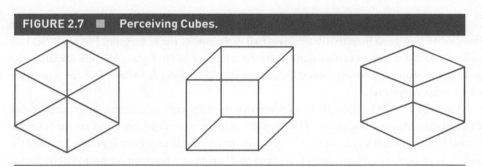

Source: Visual Intelligence, by D. D. Hoffman, 1998, New York: Norton.

The pattern in the middle is easy to perceive as a cube, which you may have recognized as the famous Necker cube. The Necker cube is well known because your perception of the front and back surfaces of the cube changes as you view it (Long & Toppino, 2004). It is yet another example that a structural description can change when the features do not change!

Biederman's Component Model

Descriptions of three-dimensional objects would be fairly complicated if we had to describe each of the lines and curves in the object. For example, the cubes in Figure 2.7 each consist of 12 lines (which you may find easier to count in the left and right cubes after splitting the lines than in the reversing Necker cube). It would be easier to describe three-dimensional objects through simple volumes such as cubes, cylinders, edges, and cones than to describe all the features in these volumes.

The advantage of being able to form many different arrangements from a few components is that we may need relatively few components to describe objects. Biederman (1985) has proposed that we need only approximately 35 simple volumes (which he called **geons**) to describe the objects in the world. Some objects contain the same geons, but the geons are arranged differently. The mug (d) in Figure 2.8 would become a pail, if the handle were placed at the top rather than at the side of the container. Add two additional geons, and the pail becomes a watering can (e).

FIGURE 2.8 ■ Different Arrangements of Geons Produce Different Objects.

(a) (b) (c) (d) (e)

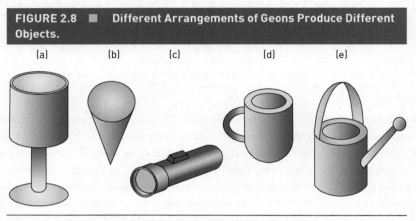

Source: Schwartz, Sensation and Perception 2e: Figure 5.25

Research by Biederman et al. (2009) established that it is easier to discriminate one geon from a different geon than to discriminate two variations of the same geon. For example, U.S. college students can more easily discriminate the middle object in Figure 2.9 from the left object (a different geon with straight sides) than from the right object (a variation of the same geon with greater curvature).

A question raised by these findings is whether there are cultural differences in people's ability to discriminate among geons. The distinction between straight lines and curves is fundamental in western culture, as we have already discovered, for discriminating among letters of the alphabet. In contrast, there is less of the need to discriminate between lines and curves by the Himba, a seminomadic people living in a remote region of Namibia. Nonetheless, the Himba also are more able to distinguish different geons from each other (the left two objects) than variations of the same geon (the right two objects).

If pattern recognition consists mainly in describing the relations among a limited set of components, then deleting information about the relations among those components should reduce people's ability to recognize patterns. To test this hypothesis, Biederman removed 65% of the contour from drawings of objects, such as the two cups shown in Figure 2.10. In the cup on the left, the contour was removed from the middles of the segments, allowing observers to see how the segments were related. In the cup on the right, the contour was removed from the vertices so observers would have more difficulty recognizing how the segments were related. When drawings of different objects were presented for 100 msec, subjects correctly named 70% of the objects if the contours were deleted at midsegments. But if the contours were deleted at

---

geons Different three-dimensional shapes that combine to form three-dimensional objects

the vertices, subjects correctly named fewer than 50% of the objects (Biederman, 1985). As predicted, destroying relational information was particularly detrimental for object recognition.

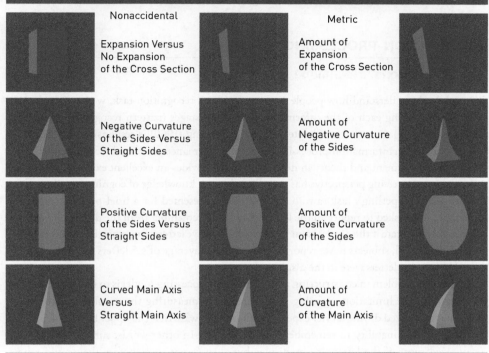

FIGURE 2.9 ■ **Discriminating between Different Geons (Middle and Left) is Easier than Discriminating between Different Variations of the Same Geon (Middle and Right).**

Source: "Representation of shape in individuals from a culture with minimal exposure to regular, simple artifacts" by I. Biederman, X. Yue, & J. Davidoff, 2009, *Psychological Science*, 20, 1437–1442. https://doi.org/10.1111/j.1467-9280.2009.02465.x

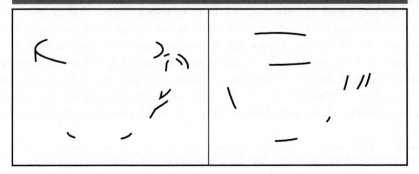

FIGURE 2.10 ■ **Illustration of 65% Contour Removal Centered at Either Midsegments (Left Object) or Vertices (Right Object).**

Source: "Human image understanding: Recent research and a theory," by I. Biederman, 1985, *Computer Vision, Graphics, and Image Processing*, *32*, 29–73. https://doi.org/10.1016/0734-189X(85)90002-7

In conclusion, structural theories extend feature theories by specifying how the features are related. Sutherland (1968) was one of the first to argue that if we want to account for our very impressive pattern recognition capabilities, we will need the more powerful kind of descriptive language contained in a structural theory. The experiments in this section show that Sutherland was correct. We now look at how pattern recognition occurs over time.

INFORMATION-PROCESSING STAGES

The Partial-Report Technique

To completely understand how people perform a pattern recognition task, we have to identify what occurs during each of the information-processing stages (pattern recognition, attention, working memory) discussed in Chapter 1. George Sperling (1960) is responsible for the initial construction of an information-processing model of performance on a visual recognition task. We discuss his experiment and theory in detail because it provides an excellent example of how the information-processing perspective has contributed to our knowledge of cognitive psychology.

Subjects in Sperling's task saw an array of letters presented for a brief period (usually 50 msec) and were asked to report all the letters they could remember from the display. Responses were highly accurate if the display contained fewer than five letters. But when the number of letters was increased, subjects never reported more than an average of 4.5 letters correctly, regardless of how many letters were in the display.

A general problem in constructing an information-processing model is to identify the cause of a performance limitation. Sperling was interested in measuring the number of letters that could be recognized during a brief exposure, but he was aware that the upper limit of 4.5 might be caused by an inability to remember more than that. In other words, subjects might have recognized most of the letters in the display but then forgot some before they could report what they had seen. Sperling, therefore, changed his procedure from a whole-report procedure (report all the letters) to a partial-report procedure (report only some of the letters).

In the most typical case, the display consisted of three rows, each containing four letters. Subjects would be unable to remember all 12 letters in a display, but they should be able to remember four letters. The partial-report procedure required that subjects report only one row. The pitch of a tone signaled which of the three rows to report: the top row for a high pitch, the middle row for a medium pitch, and the bottom row for a low pitch. The tone sounded just after the display disappeared, so that subjects would have to view the entire display and could not simply look at a single row (Figure 2.11). Use of the partial-report technique is based on the assumption that the number of letters reported from the cued row equals the average number of letters perceived in each of the rows because the subjects did not know in advance which row to look at. The results of this procedure showed that subjects

---

whole-report procedure A task that requires observers to report everything they see in a display of items

partial-report procedure A task in which observers are cued to report only certain items in a display of items

could correctly report three of the four letters in a row, implying that they had recognized nine letters in the entire display.

FIGURE 2.11 ■ **Sperling's (1960) Study of Sensory Memory. After the Subjects had Fixated on the Cross, the Letters were Flashed on the Screen Just Long Enough to Create a Visual Afterimage. High, Medium, and Low Tones Signaled which Row of Letters to Report.**

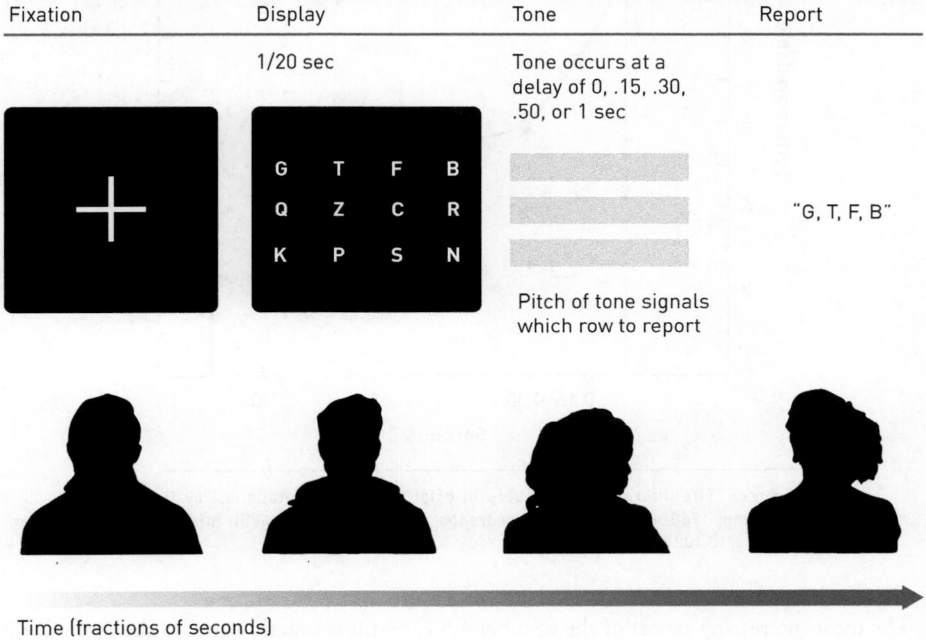

Fixation	Display	Tone	Report
	1/20 sec	Tone occurs at a delay of 0, .15, .30, .50, or 1 sec	

Pitch of tone signals which row to report

"G, T, F, B"

Time (fractions of seconds)

Photo credit: iStock/Vectorig

Source: "The information available in brief visual presentations," by G. Sperling, 1960, *Psychological Monographs, 74* (11, Whole No. 498). https://doi.org/10.1037/h0093759

It often happens that what is best remembered about a scientist's work is not what that person originally set out to investigate. Although Sperling designed the partial-report technique to reduce the memory requirements of his task and to obtain a "pure" measure of perception, his work is best remembered for the discovery of the importance of a visual sensory store. How did this come about? The estimate that subjects had perceived nine letters was obtained when the tone occurred immediately after the termination of the 50-ms exposure. In this case, subjects could correctly report approximately three-quarters of the letters, and three-quarters of 12 is 9. But when the tone was delayed until one second after the display, performance declined to only 4.5 letters. That is, there was a gradual decline from nine letters to 4.5 as the delay of the tone was increased from 0 to one second (Figure 2.12).

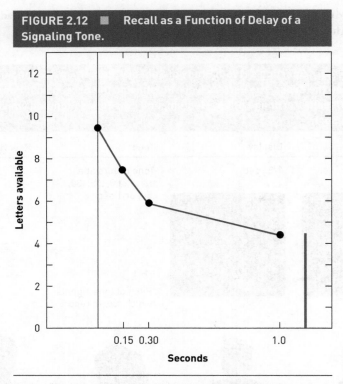

FIGURE 2.12 ■ Recall as a Function of Delay of a Signaling Tone.

Source: "The information available in brief visual presentations," by G. Sperling, 1960, *Psychological Monographs, 74* (11, Whole No. 498). https:// doi.org/10.1037/h0093759

The most interesting aspect of the number 4.5 is that it is exactly equal to the upper limit of performance on the whole-report task, as represented by the blue bar in Figure 2.12. The partial-report procedure has no advantage over the whole-report procedure, if the tone is delayed by one second or more. To explain this gradual decline in performance, Sperling proposed that the subjects were using a **visual sensory store** to recognize letters in the cued row. When they heard the tone, they selectively attended to the cued row in the store and tried to identify the letters in that row. Their success in making use of the tone depended on the clarity of information in their sensory store. When the tone occurred immediately after termination of the stimulus, the clarity was sufficient for recognizing additional letters in the cued row. But as the clarity of the sensory image faded, it became increasingly difficult to recognize additional letters. When the tone was delayed by one second, the subjects could not use the sensory store at all to focus on the cued row, so their performance was determined by the number of letters they had recognized from the entire display that happened to be in that row. Their performance was therefore equivalent to the whole-report procedure, in which they attended to the entire display.

In 1963, Sperling proposed an information-processing model of performance on his visual report task. The model consisted of a visual information store, scanning, rehearsal, and an auditory information store. The **visual information store (VIS)** is a sensory store that preserves information for a brief period lasting from a fraction of a second to a second. The decay rate depends on such factors as the intensity, contrast, and duration of the stimulus and also on whether exposure to the stimulus is followed by a second exposure. Visual masking occurs when a second exposure, consisting of a brightly lighted field or a different set of patterns, reduces the effectiveness of the VIS.

For pattern recognition to occur, the information in the sensory store must be scanned. Sperling initially considered scanning to occur for one item at a time, as if each person had a sheet of cardboard with a hole in it just large enough for a single letter to appear.

The next two components of the model were **rehearsal** (saying the letters to oneself) and an **auditory information store** (remembering the names of the letters). To remember the items until recall, subjects usually reported rehearsing the items. Additional evidence for verbal rehearsal was found when recall errors often appeared in the form of auditory confusions—in other words, producing a letter that sounded like the correct letter. The advantage of the auditory store is that subvocalizing the names of the letters keeps them active in memory. Sperling's auditory store is part of short-term memory (STM), a topic we will consider later in the book.

Sperling revised his initial model in 1967. By this time, evidence had begun to accumulate suggesting that patterns were not scanned one at a time but were analyzed simultaneously. This distinction between performing one cognitive operation at a time (**serial processing**) and performing more than one cognitive operation at a time (**parallel processing**) is fundamental in cognitive psychology. Sperling, therefore, modified his idea of the **scan component** to allow for pattern recognition to occur simultaneously over the entire display, although the rate of recognition in a given location depended on where the subject was focusing attention.

Sperling's model was the first that attempted to indicate how various stages (sensory store, pattern recognition, and STM) combined to influence performance on a visual processing task. It contributed to the construction of information-processing models and led to the development of more detailed models of how people recognize letters in visual displays.

---

visual information store (VIS) A sensory store that maintains visual information for approximately one-quarter of a second

rehearsal Repeating verbal information to keep it active in short-term memory (STM) or to transfer it into long-term memory (LTM)

auditory information store In Sperling's model, this store maintains verbal information in short-term memory (STM) through rehearsal

serial processing Carrying out one operation at a time, such as pronouncing one word at a time

parallel processing Carrying out more than one operation at a time, such as looking at an art exhibit and making conversation

scan component The attention component of Sperling's model that determines what is recognized in the visual information store (VIS)

WORD RECOGNITION

The Word Superiority Effect

Much of the research on pattern recognition during the 1970s shifted away from how people recognize isolated letters to how people recognize letters in words. This research was stimulated by a finding that was labeled the *word superiority effect*. Reicher (1969), in his dissertation at the University of Michigan, investigated a possible implication of the scan component in Sperling's 1967 model. If the observer tries to recognize all the letters in a word simultaneously (Alderman et al., 2010), is it possible to recognize a four-letter unit in the same amount of time as it takes to recognize a single letter?

To answer this question, Reicher designed an experiment in which observers were shown a single letter, a four-letter word, or a four-letter nonword. The task was always to identify a single letter by selecting one of two alternatives. The exposure of the stimulus was immediately followed by a visual masking field with the two response alternatives directly above the critical letter. For example, one set of stimuli consisted of the word WORK, the letter *K*, and the nonword OWRK. The two alternatives, in this case, were the letters *D* and *K*, which were displayed above the critical *K* (Figure 2.13). Observers indicated whether they thought the letter in that position had been a *D* or a *K*.

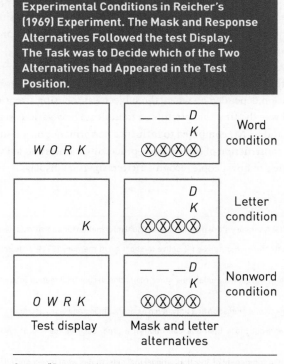

FIGURE 2.13 ■ Example of the Three Experimental Conditions in Reicher's (1969) Experiment. The Mask and Response Alternatives Followed the test Display. The Task was to Decide which of the Two Alternatives had Appeared in the Test Position.

Test display | Mask and letter alternatives

Source: "Perceptual recognition as a function of meaningfulness of stimulus material," by G. M. Reicher, 1969, *Journal of Experimental Psychology, 81*, 275–280. https://doi.org/10.1037/h0027768

This example illustrates several characteristics of Reicher's design. First, the four-letter word has the same letters as the four-letter nonword. Second, the position of the critical letter is the same for the word and the nonword. Third, both of the response alternatives make a word (WORD or WORK) for the word condition and a nonword for the nonword condition. Fourth, the memory requirements are minimized by requiring that subjects identify only a single letter, even when four letters are presented.

The results showed that subjects were significantly more accurate in identifying the critical letter when it was part of a word than when it was part of a nonword or when it was presented alone (the word superiority effect). Eight of the nine subjects did better on single words than on single letters. The one subject who reversed this trend was the only subject who said that she saw the words as four separate letters, which she made into words; the other subjects said that they experienced a word as a single word, not as four letters making up a word.

The word superiority effect is an example of top-down processing. It demonstrates how our knowledge of words helps us to more rapidly recognize the letters within a word. Top-down processing, based on knowledge stored in LTM, can aid pattern recognition in different ways. Top-down processing also helps us recognize words in sentences because the sentence constrains which words can meaningfully fit into the sentence.

A Model of the Word Superiority Effect

One of the great challenges for psychologists interested in word recognition has been to explain the reasons for the word superiority effect (Pollatsek & Rayner, 1989). A particularly influential model, the interactive activation model proposed by McClelland and Rumelhart (1981), contains several basic assumptions that build on the assumptions of Rumelhart's earlier model of letter recognition. The first assumption is that visual perception involves parallel processing. There are two different senses in which processing occurs in parallel. Visual processing is spatially parallel, resulting in the simultaneous processing of all four letters in a four-letter word. This assumption is consistent with Sperling's parallel scan and with Rumelhart's model of how people attempt to recognize an array of letters.

Visual processing is also parallel in the sense that recognition occurs simultaneously at three different levels of abstraction. The three levels—the feature level, the letter level, and the word level—are shown in Figure 2.14. A key assumption of the interactive activation model is that the three levels interact to determine what we perceive. Knowledge about the words of a language interacts with incoming feature information to provide evidence about which letters are in the word. This is illustrated by the arrows in Figure 2.14, which show that the letter level receives information from both the feature level and the word level.

---

word superiority effect The finding that accuracy in recognizing a letter is higher when the letter is in a word than when it appears alone or is in a nonword

interactive activation model A theory proposing that both feature knowledge and word knowledge combine to provide information about the identity of letters in a word

There are two kinds of connections between levels: excitatory connections and inhibitory connections. **Excitatory connections** provide positive evidence, and **inhibitory connections** provide negative evidence about the identity of a letter or word. For example, a diagonal line provides positive evidence for the letter *K* (and all other letters that contain a diagonal line) and negative evidence for the letter *D* (and all other letters that do not contain a diagonal line). Excitatory and inhibitory connections also occur between the letter level and word level, depending on whether the letter is part of the word in the appropriate position. Recognizing that the first letter of a word is a *W* increases the activation level of all words that begin with a *W* and decreases the activation level of all other words.

FIGURE 2.14 ■ The Three Levels of the Interactive Activation Model, with Arrows Indicating the Excitatory Connections and Circles Indicating Inhibitory Connections.

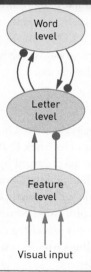

Source: "An interactive-activation model of context effects in letter perception: Part 1. An account of basic findings" by J. L. McClelland, & D. E. Rumelhart, 1981, *Psychological Review*, 88, 375–407. https://doi.org/10.1037/0033-295X.88.5.375

The interactive activation model was the first step for McClelland and Rumelhart in their development of neural network models of cognition. They referred to such models as **parallel distributed processing (PDP)** models because information is evaluated in parallel and is

excitatory connection A positive association between concepts that belong together, as when a diagonal line provides support for the possibility that a letter is a K

inhibitory connection A negative association between concepts that do not belong together, as when the presence of a diagonal line provides negative evidence that a letter is a D

parallel distributed processing (PDP) When information is simultaneously collected from different sources and combined to reach a decision

distributed throughout the network. A neural network model consists of several components (Rumelhart et al., 1986), some of which we have already considered in the interactive activation model. These include the following:

1. A set of processing units called nodes. Nodes are represented by features, letters, and words in the interactive activation model. They can acquire different levels of activation.

2. A pattern of connections among nodes. Nodes are connected to one another by excitatory and inhibitory connections that differ in strength.

3. Activation rules for the nodes. Activation rules specify how a node combines its excitatory and inhibitory inputs with its current state of activation.

4. A state of activation. Nodes can be activated to various degrees. We become conscious of nodes that are activated above a threshold level of conscious awareness. For instance, we become consciously aware of the letter *K* in the word *WORK* when it receives enough excitatory influences from the feature and word levels.

5. Output functions of the nodes. The output functions relate activation levels to outputs—for example, what threshold has to be exceeded for conscious awareness.

6. A learning rule. Learning generally occurs by changing the weights of the excitatory and inhibitory connections between the nodes, and the learning rule specifies how to make these changes.

The last component—the learning component—is one of the most important features of a neural network model because it enables the network to improve its performance. An example would be a network model that learns to make better discriminations among letters by increasing the weights of the distinctive features—those features that are most helpful for discriminating.

By 1992, the neural network approach had resulted in thousands of research efforts and an industry that spends several hundred million dollars annually (Schneider & Graham, 1992). The excitement of this approach can be attributed to several reasons. First, many psychologists believe that neural network models more accurately portray how the brain works than other, more serial models of behavior. Second, adjusting the excitatory and inhibitory weights that link nodes allows a network to learn, and this may capture how people learn. Third, the models allow for a different kind of computing in which many weak constraints (such as evidence from both the feature and word levels) can be simultaneously considered. Neural network models have continued to be developed into one of the most powerful learning methods in AI, as indicated by their application to recognizing scenes.

---

neural network model A theory in which concepts (nodes) are linked to other concepts through excitatory and inhibitory connections to approximate the behavior of neural networks in the brain

nodes The format for representing concepts in a semantic network

activation rule A rule that determines how inhibitory and excitatory connections combine to determine the total activation of a concept

SCENE RECOGNITION

Word recognition differs from letter recognition because words are composed of interacting letters. Similarly, scene recognition differs from object recognition because scenes are composed of interacting objects that are typically arranged in a meaningful spatial layout. Recognizing objects in scenes is often driven by accomplishing goals, as explained in the next section.

Goal-Driven Scene Understanding

Although our physical environment is usually stable, our goals can change and determine how we interact with the environment. Figure 2.15(A) illustrates four goals of scene understanding based on recognition, visual search, navigation, and action. Recognition determines whether a scene belongs to a certain category (a beach) or depicts a particular place (my living room). Visual search involves locating specific objects within the scene, such as sand, a bridge, or a lamp. Navigation determines whether it is possible to reach a particular location, such as crossing a stream. Action encompasses a broad set of activities, such as swimming, hiking, and watching television.

The four questions at the top of the figure are examples of questions we might ask for each of the different scenes (Malcolm et al., 2016). The first question "What is the scene?" requires scene recognition. It begins with gist—the perceptual and semantic information acquired from a single glance. Gist can include a conceptual understanding (a party), the spatial layout of the environment, and a few objects. It depends on the familiarity of stored representations, such as furniture is found in a living room. Unfamiliar scenes require more processing time than a brief glance to achieve scene understanding.

The second question "Where is X?" requires visual search using eye movements rather than a quick glance. Eye fixations focus on particular objects rather than the overall environment. They are required to answer the third question "How do I get from A to B?" Answering this question requires finding paths and potential obstacles that could block navigation, such as approaching objects. The last question "What can I do here?" determines actions, the topic of Chapter 6. Figure 2.15(B) shows scene properties that are needed to fulfill these goals. Low-level features, such as edges, establish the identity of objects. Object identities determine semantic categories and the actions that can be performed in those environments.

Deep Neural Networks

Computer scientists continued to develop the neural network models of the 1980s and connectionist models based on deep neural networks, which are some of the great success stories of AI (Sejnowski, 2018). **Deep neural networks** utilize the same principles as simpler networks but have added multiple layers of connections to fine-tune the weights of thousands of connections.

Figure 2.16 illustrates the application of deep neural networks to image recognition. The input begins with pixels from the image, and the output classifies the image as one of 1000 possible

---

deep neural networks Networks that learn by adjusting thousands of connections in multiple layers

FIGURE 2.15 ■ Goal-driven Scene Recognition.

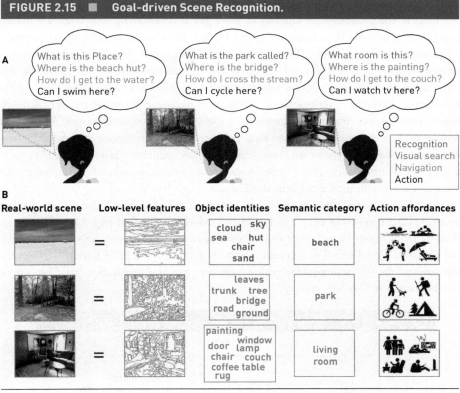

Source: "Making sense of real-world scenes" by G. L. Malcolm, I. I. A. Groen, & C. I. Baker, 2016, *Trends in Cognitive Sciences*, 20, 843–856. https://doi.org/10.1016/j.tics.2016.09.003

FIGURE 2.16 ■ Application of a Deep Neural Network to Classify Images.

ImageNet Challenge: Classify the images (1000 possible)

Gazelle   Model T   Rocking chair   Payphone   Jackfruit   Banjo

Deep Convolutional Neural Network

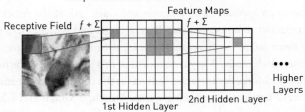

Source: "Comparing the visual representations and performance of humans and deep neural networks," by R. A. Jacobs & C. J. Bates, 2019, *Current Directions in Psychological Science, 28*, 34–39.

pictures. In between are many hidden layers in which each layer receives input from a small number of units in the previous layer to establish more global connectivity. The layers are hidden because, in contrast to the three layers in Figure 2.14, their function can be difficult to interpret.

The authors of this article, Robert Jacobs and Christopher Bates at the University of Rochester's Department of Brain and Cognitive Sciences, review evidence that people are still superior at recognizing images under adverse conditions. The authors list several reasons for our perceptual advantage over machines. We learn to recognize objects in perceptually rich, dynamic, interactive environments whereas networks are trained on static images. We can take advantage of three-dimensional features whereas networks are more limited to two dimensions. A disadvantage for people, however, is our capacity limits because we cannot visually perceive and represent all aspects of a scene. These limits can nonetheless occasionally be an asset when we learn to focus on the more discriminative features.

Artificial intelligence continues to improve and the use of drones illustrates how pattern recognition can be shared by people and machines (Morris & Chakrabarty, 2019). Drones are limited by small payload capabilities and onboard processing power so some of the computational demands are offloaded to a ground computer (Figure 2.17). Joint activity between the equipment and the operator requires sensing, planning, and communication based on coordination between people and machines.

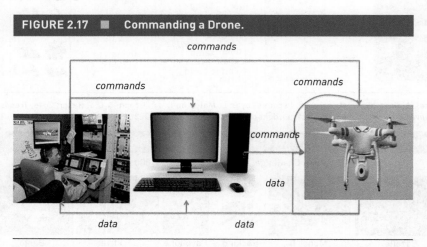

FIGURE 2.17 ■ Commanding a Drone.

Source: "Addressing autonomy in conceptual design" by R. Morris & A. Chakrabarty, 2019, *AI Magazine*, 40, 3–16. https://doi.org/10.1609/aimag.v40i2.2856

Figure 2.18 shows an application to a search and track task at the Ames Research Center in California. A controller monitors the search for a target and switches to a track mode if the target is found. At some point, the target may take evasive maneuvers that require the controller to switch back to the search mode. A key component of this interaction is the boundary between human and machine decisions. For instance, humans at the console may control the search phase and allow the drone to conduct the tracking phase. Although Morris and Chakrabarty (2019) focus on searching and tracking, they argue that many of the design principles apply to integrating human decision-making with various types of devices. An important decision related to the ethical use of AI discussed in Chapter 1 requires determining who should be tracked.

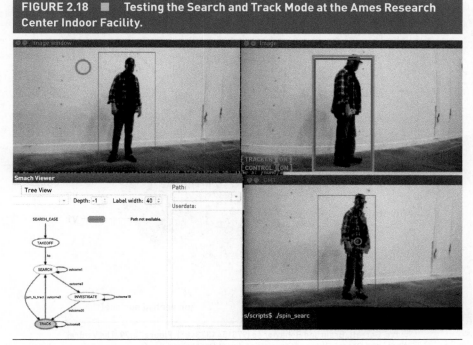

FIGURE 2.18 ■ **Testing the Search and Track Mode at the Ames Research Center Indoor Facility.**

Source: "Addressing autonomy in conceptual design" by R. Morris & A. Chakrabarty, 2019, *AI Magazine*, 40, 3–16. https://doi.org/10.1609/aimag.v40i2.2856

APPLICATIONS

Brain Pathways

People's remarkable ability to recognize patterns occasionally falls victim to various types of visual disorders, and studying these disorders has contributed to our understanding of visual perception (Haque et al., 2018). For example, patients with brain damage have revealed a dissociation between knowing what an object is and knowing where the object is located. Damage to one part of the brain results in an impairment of the ability to recognize visual stimuli, whereas damage to another part of the brain results in an impairment of the ability to indicate their spatial location.

These impaired aspects of vision are similarly impaired in visual imagery (Levine et al., 1985). A patient with object identification difficulties was unable to draw or describe the appearance of familiar objects from memory, despite being able to draw and describe in great detail the relative locations of landmarks in his neighborhood, cities in the United States, and furniture in his hospital room. A patient with object localization difficulties could not use his memory to perform well on the spatial localization tasks but could provide detailed descriptions of the appearance of a variety of objects.

Figure 2.19 illustrates the two pathways that support the localization and the identification of objects. The *where* pathway is primarily associated with object location and spatial attention. It is often referred to as the dorsal pathway because it is located in the dorsal (or upper) part of the brain. The dorsal pathway runs upward to the parietal lobes and has strong connections with the frontal lobe that coordinates limb and eye movements.

FIGURE 2.19 ■ Brain Pathways for Spatial (Dorsal) and Object (Ventral) Identification.

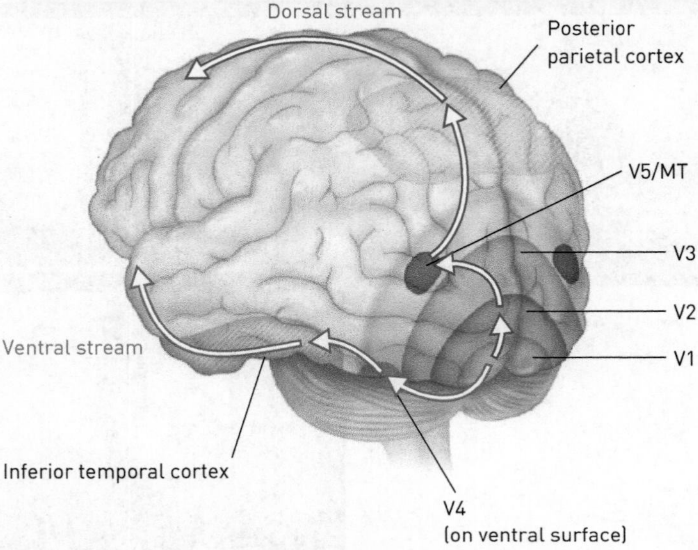

Dorsal stream

Posterior parietal cortex

V5/MT

V3

V2

V1

Ventral stream

Inferior temporal cortex

V4 (on ventral surface)

Source: Garrett, Brain and Behavior 6e (9781544373485), Figure 10.29: The Ventral "What" and Dorsal "Where" Streams of Visual Processing.

The other pathway, which results in object recognition, is known as the *what* pathway. It travels from the primary visual cortex in the occipital lobe and processes information such as shape, size, and color, as previously illustrated in Figure 2.4. It is primarily located in the temporal lobes and is often referred to as the ventral pathway because it is located in the ventral (or lower) part of the brain.

Figure 2.20 shows the approximate locations of specialized areas for object recognition. Some parts of the brain—the occipital face area (OFA)—respond more to faces than to other types of objects. Although this area is best activated by faces, it can also be activated by other objects, particularly if the person has acquired previous expert knowledge about those objects (Haque et al., 2018). The visual word form area (VWFA) is activated during reading.

Visual Disorders

Much of our knowledge of how the brain recognizes patterns comes from studies of patients with **visual agnosia**. Visual agnosia is a general disruption in the ability to recognize objects. Agnosia patients have normal visual acuity and generally show no memory deficits. The disability is also limited to a single sensory modality—for example, if you show a patient a set of keys, he will not be able to recognize them; however, if you hand him the keys to feel, he will easily identify them as keys. There are specialized forms of this disorder, such as an inability to recognize faces or familiar places.

---

visual agnosia An impairment in the recognition of visual objects

FIGURE 2.20 ■ Specialized Areas of the Brain. Areas Discussed in the Text Include the Parietal Lobe (SPL and IPL), the Temporal Lobe (MST and MT), the Visual Cortex (V1–V7), the Occipital Face Area (OFA), and the Visual Word Form Area (VWFA).

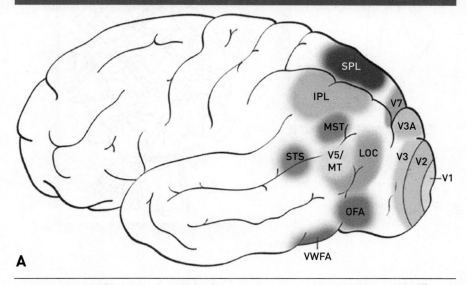

Source: "The visual agnosias and related disorders" by S. Haque, M. S. Vaphiades, & C. J. Lueck, 2018, *Journal of Neuro-Ophthalmology*, 38, 379–392. https://doi.org/10.1097/WNO.0000000000000556

Two general categories of agnosia disorders are **apperceptive agnosia** and associative agnosia (Farah, 2004). Apperceptive agnosia disrupts the ability of patients to group visual elements into contours, surfaces, and objects (Farah, 2004). Evidence from these patients demonstrates the pattern recognition is normally hierarchical—starting with simple cells in the primary visual cortex and then combining these features to form a perception of the whole object, such as the face in Figure 2.4. The fusiform gyrus in the temporal lobe is of critical importance to this process (Konen et al., 2011), as is the lateral occipital cortex (Ptak et al., 2014). It is the last stage of combining features that impairs people with visual agnosia.

Inadequate eye movements contribute to the failure to combine visual features (Raz & Levin, 2017). A patient with apperceptive agnosia identified an object as a bird from a visual organization test, shown in the left panel of Figure 2.21. He identified the circled fragment as a beak but ignored the rest of the picture. In the right panel from an overlapping-figures test, a patient hesitated in deciding whether the circled fragment was an arrow or the ear of a cat. His eye movements did not track the length of the object to determine its identity.

---

apperceptive agnosia An inability to combine visual features into contours, surfaces, and objects

FIGURE 2.21 ■ Object Identification Tests.

 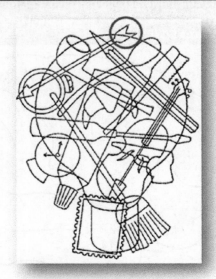

Taken from the *Hooper visual organization*

Taken from the *15-object test*

Source: "Neuro-visual rehabilitation" by N. Raz & N. Levin, 2017, *Journal of Neurology*, 264, 1051–1058. https://link.springer.com/article/10.1007/s00415-016-8291-0

Inadequate eye movements also occur in reading when patients perform shorter and delayed eye movements that limit their ability to integrate letters (Raz & Levin, 2017). A training task, shown in the right panel of Figure 2.22A, requires them to track letters in an alphabetical sequence. Another training task, shown in Figure 2.22B, provides practice in reading words. The number of letters in the words increases while the presentation time decreases as training progresses. To perceive the entire word, patients are trained to fixate on either the beginning or the end of the word depending on their particular deficit. Training tasks also exist for large visual fields. The person in the left panel of Figure 2.22A is searching for a square composed of four red dots.

In contrast to apperceptive agnosia, **associative agnosia** patients can combine visual elements into a whole perception but are unable to identify that perception. The most curious fact about these patients is they can accurately copy a line drawing but are unable to recognize what they have drawn! Essentially these patients can perceive the object but can no longer associate their perception with its meaning.

---

associative agnosia An ability to combine visual features into a whole object but an inability to recognize that object

FIGURE 2.22 ■ Training Eye Movements (A) and Reading Words (B).

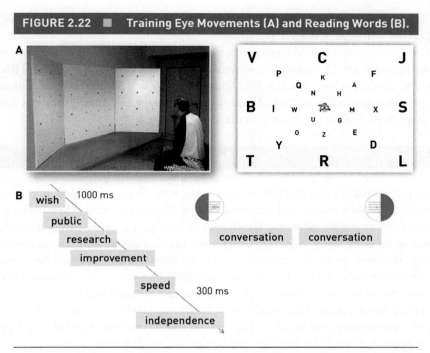

Source: "Neuro-visual rehabilitation" by N. Raz & N. Levin, 2017, *Journal of Neurology*, 264, 1051–1058. https://link.springer.com/article/10.1007%2Fs00415-016-8291-0

Face blindness provides an informative case study of how the "what" stream fails to connect to other parts of the brain. An area of the cortex known as the *fusiform face area* is responsive to recognizing that an object is a face, even for people with face blindness (Mitchell, 2018). Although the brain performs the initial stage of face processing perfectly well, it fails to communicate that information with the frontal cortex for people with face blindness (Figure 2.23).

FIGURE 2.23 ■ Disruptive Pathways Causing Face Blindness.

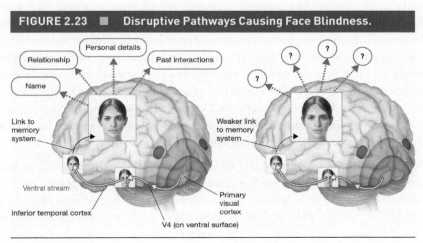

Source: Adapted from *INNATE: How the Wring of Our Brains Shapes Who We Are*, by K. J. Mitchell, 2018, Princeton, NJ: Princeton University Press.

The link to the frontal cortex is necessary to recall information such as the person's name, personal details, relationship, and past interactions.

The condition can be so debilitating that patients may not recognize close family members or even their own face. The famous neuropsychologist Oliver Sacks suffered from face blindness prior to his death. His book *The Man Who Mistook His Wife for a Hat* is based on a clinical case study of such a patient (Sacks, 1985). Interestingly, many patients suffering from this disorder can recognize the faces of loved ones after they hear them speak.

SUMMARY

Pattern recognition is a skill that people perform very well. Three explanations of pattern recognition are template, feature, and structural theories. A template theory proposes that people compare two patterns by measuring their degree of overlap. A template theory has difficulty accounting for many aspects of pattern recognition. The most common theories of pattern recognition, therefore, assume that patterns are analyzed into features. Perceptual discrimination requires discovering distinctive features that distinguish between patterns. Treisman's experiments on feature integration theory explored how a perceiver combines two features that are analyzed by separate parts of the visual system. Structural theories state explicitly how the features of a pattern are joined together. They provide a more complete description of a pattern and are particularly useful for describing patterns consisting of intersecting lines.

Sperling's interest in the question of how many letters can be perceived during a brief exposure resulted in the construction of information-processing models for visual tasks. Sperling proposed that information is preserved very briefly in a visual information store, where all the letters can be simultaneously analyzed. When a letter is recognized, its name is verbally rehearsed and preserved in an auditory store that is a part of short-term memory.

Recognition of letters in a word is influenced by perceptual information and the letter context. The finding that a letter can be recognized more easily when it is part of a word than when it is part of a nonword or is presented by itself has been called the *word superiority effect*. An influential model of this effect is the interactive activation model proposed by McClelland and Rumelhart. Its major assumption is that knowledge about the words of a language interacts with incoming feature information to provide evidence regarding which letters are in the word. Scenes are composed of interacting objects that are typically arranged in a meaningful spatial layout. Recognizing objects in scenes is often driven by accomplishing goals. Deep neural networks, used in scene recognition and many other complex AI tasks, utilize the same principles of simpler networks but have added multiple layers of connections to fine-tune the weights of thousands of connections.

Visual agnosia is a disruption in the ability to recognize objects. There are specialized forms of recognition disorders, such as an inability to recognize objects or familiar places. The "where" pathway is located in the upper parietal area and is primarily associated with object location and spatial attention. The "what" pathway supports object recognition and is primarily located in the lower temporal lobes. Patients with apperceptive agnosia are unable to combine visual features into a complete pattern whereas associative agnosia patients can, but these patients can not identify the pattern.

RECOMMENDED READING

Hoffman's (1998) book, *Visual Intelligence*, provides both a readable and scholarly analysis of how we construct descriptions of objects. Fallshore and Schooler (1995) argue that verbally describing faces can lower later recognition because verbal descriptions ignore configural information. Kristjansson and Egeth (2019) provide an extensive history of how feature integration theory integrated relevant research in cognition, perception, and neuropsychology. Experts provide an overview of the theoretical contributions of neural networks (McClelland et al., 2010). For a history of neural networks that has resulted in the exciting accomplishments of deep networks read *The Deep Learning Revolution* (Sejnowski, 2018). A very readable introduction to genetics and brain circuits is Kevin Mitchell's (2018) book *INNATE: How the Wiring of Our Brains Shapes Who We Are*.

Getty Images/MoMo Productions

ATTENTION

Attention Networks
The Alerting Network
The Orienting Network
The Executive Network

Bottleneck Theories
Broadbent's Filter Model
Treisman's Attenuation Model
The Deutsch-Norman Memory Selection Model

Capacity Theories
Example of a Capacity Model
Capacity and Stage of Selection
Multitasking

Automatic Processing
When Is a Skill Automatic?
Learning to Read

Applications
Training Drivers
Using Cell Phones
Coordinating Attention

SUMMARY

RECOMMENDED READING

LEARNING OBJECTIVES

1. Describe a hypothetical situation that shows how the three attention networks might influence reactions to a situation.

2. Analyze how the concept of a filter in Broadbent's model evolved in later models by Treisman and Deutsch-Norman.

3. Summarize the theory of limited capacity and how it differs from bottleneck theories in explaining interference, including successful and unsuccessful multitasking.

4. Apply Posner and Snyder's criteria of automatic processing to learning to read.

5. Explain how interactions between a driver and a passenger could make driving more or less safe, based on previous research.

The previous chapter on pattern recognition analyzed an important skill that is included in the perception component of the standard model (Figure 3.1). Another important perception skill is attention. In fact, it was impossible to avoid mentioning attention when discussing pattern recognition. Training children to attend to the distinctive features of letters (Egeland, 1975), looking at a cued row in a visual display (Sperling, 1960), tracking a person (Morris & Chakrabarty, 2019), searching for an object in a scene (Malcolm et al., 2016), and improving attention for patients with visual agnosia (Raz & Levin, 2017) combine pattern recognition and attention.

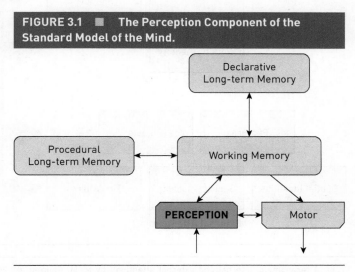

FIGURE 3.1 ■ The Perception Component of the Standard Model of the Mind.

Source: Based on "A standard model of the mind: Toward a common computational framework across artificial intelligence, cognitive science, neuroscience, and robotics," by J. E. Laird et al., 2017, *AI Magazine, 38*, 13–26. https://doi.org/10.1609/aimag.v38i4.2744

William James's famous book *The Principles of Psychology*, published in 1890, contains many fruitful insights about psychology, including how attention influences perception and memory:

Everyone knows what attention is. It is the taking possession by the mind, in clear and vivid form, of one out of what seem several simultaneously possible objects or trains of thought. Focalization, concentration of consciousness, are of its essence.

The primary goal of attention research is to understand which information is selected, how it is selected, and what happens to both selected and unselected information (Chun et al., 2011).

Chun and his coauthors partition research on attention into external and internal attention, as illustrated in Figure 3.2. External attention refers to attending to objects in the environment or to specific features of those objects. These objects occur in different sensory modalities at different spatial locations and at different points in time. All of these characteristics of objects can influence external attention. For example, in Sperling's (1960) partial-report procedure, viewers had to listen for a tone following a visual display in order to know which row of letters to report.

Internal attention refers to regulating our internal mental life (Chun et al., 2011). For instance, mind-wandering has traditionally been classified as a failure to regulate internal attention when unrelated thoughts distract us from focusing on a relevant task, such as reading this

FIGURE 3.2 ■ A Taxonomy of Attention.

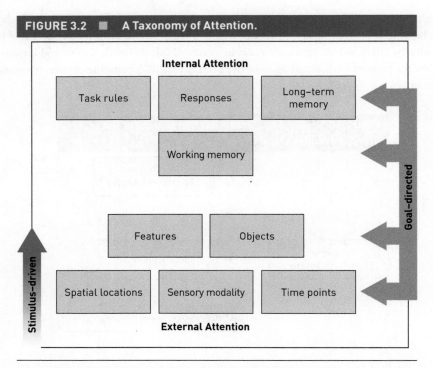

Source: From "A taxonomy of internal and external attention," by M. M. Chun et al., 2011, *Annual Review of Psychology, 62,* 73–101. https://doi.org/10.1146/annurev.psych.093008.100427. Copyright 2011 by *Annual Reviews.* Reprinted by permission.

book. A more inclusive perspective now considers "mind-wandering" as encompassing a broad range of phenomena (Seli et al., 2016). Mind-wandering, in this perspective, can be intentional, as when people purposively allow their thoughts to drift to enjoy an idle moment, deliberately neglect a task, or mentally escape an unpleasant situation. Much of internal attention is intentional and task related, such as managing information in memory, as we will see in Chapters 4 (Working Memory) and 5 (Long-Term Memory).

Shifting attention frequently occurs for both internal and external attention. Shifting external attention occurs when we enjoy an autumn day and look at the different colors of the leaves. The different colors may evoke memories of previous walks in the woods, motivating us to shift to our internal thoughts. Shifting *between* external and internal attention often occurs at a greater cost in both response times and errors (Verschooren et al., 2019).

This chapter discusses external attention and focuses on perceptual objects rather than on trains of thought. The first section idiscusses attention networks, their function, and location in the brain. The second section discusses theories that try to locate the stage at which selection of perceptual information occurs. Do we block off the sensory input before it reaches the pattern recognition stage, or do we make the selection after recognition? The next section discusses capacity theories of attention, which seek to explain how capacity or mental effort is allocated to different activities. Such theories propose that attention is limited in capacity, and when we try to attend to more than one event—studying while watching television, for instance—we pay the price of doing each less efficiently, unless we are able to automatically process the information. Applications—training drivers, (mis)using cell phones, and coordinating attention—are the topics of the final section.

ATTENTION NETWORKS

In order to fully account for the many disparate functions of attention, Posner and Petersen (1990) proposed an attention system in the brain comprised of three networks. The **alerting network** maintains sensitivity to incoming stimuli, the **orienting network** selects information from different sensory inputs, and the **executive attention network** monitors and resolves conflicts in thoughts, feelings, and responses (Posner & Rothbart, 2007). These networks are both functionally and anatomically distinct.

The Alerting Network

The alerting system is the most primitive system in our attention network and alerts us to potential danger (Photo 3.1). Imagine you are walking home from the library late at night, when suddenly all the power goes out on campus and you are plunged into darkness. Your heart will race, your pupils will fully dilate, and you will be hyperaware of your surroundings. This typical stress response occurs due to an increase in the stress hormone *norepinephrine* (Aston-Jones & Cohen, 2005). This release of norepinephrine enhances the effects of any type of warning

PHOTO 3.1 The alerting system directs attention to potential danger.

istock.com/Sitthiphong

---

alerting network Maintains sensitivity to incoming stimuli

orienting network Selects information from different sensory inputs

executive attention network Monitors and resolves conflicts

signal (Morrison & Foote, 1986). Sustained increases from stress or drug abuse (amphetamines are known to increase release of norepinephrine) can lead to increased states of vigilance and paranoia (Advokat et al., 2019).

Assuming we are in a normal state of arousal, certain stimuli will automatically capture our attention that in our evolutionary past would have been a threat to us (Franconeri & Simons, 2003). Rapidly appearing stimuli will almost always automatically capture our attention (Jonides & Yantis, 1988), and some such as cars and people are potentially threatening to us. Businesses capitalize on this attentional capture by using animate movement in advertising—hence the proliferation of people on the street corner dancing and throwing signs and the use of balloons at car dealerships—they convey movement that captures our attention. In fact, many have argued for abolishing digital billboards because of their propensity for distracting drivers (Belyusar et al., 2016).

The Orienting Network

The orienting network is involved in coordinating attention with sensory inputs from the visual, auditory, and somatosensory systems. This directing of attention can be overt—such as eye movements—or covert, by directing attention to target locations without any overt movements. Many of the brain areas involved in the orienting network are closely associated with the "where" pathway discussed in the previous chapter. It is part of the dorsal network located in the parietal lobe (Posner & Rothbart, 2007). The red area (OAN) in Figure 3.3 shows the location of this network.

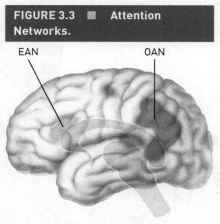

FIGURE 3.3 ■ Attention Networks.

EAN   OAN

Source: Schwartz, Sensation and Perception 2e, Figure 9.22: Attention Networks in the Brain.

A common test of the orienting network is a cueing task in which a cue, such as an arrow, directs a participant to a particular location or occurs at the location itself (such as brightening the location). These cues can be valid or invalid. When an invalid cue is presented, studies have shown the temporal parietal junction is involved in redirecting attention to the location where a target occurs (Corbetta & Shulman, 2002). This redirection of attention is shown behaviorally by longer reaction times to locate a target (Merritt et al., 2012).

From a practical perspective, the orienting network is involved in a great deal of our daily activities. Watching a football game, for example, requires directing attention to the location of the football. When a quarterback fakes a pass, this is similar to an invalid cue that can require time and cognitive resources to locate the true location of the ball. Similarly, magicians use *misdirection* to direct attention away from where they are moving or manipulating an object (Kuhn et al., 2008). Finally, designers of automobiles often fail to consider this allocation of attention in the layout of vehicles. Many cars will alert a driver to an impending collision by a beep and flashing light on the dashboard—directing their attention away from the road ahead. Visual aids on a windshield can also be a distraction (Photo 3.2).

PHOTO 3.2 Driving aids can distract attention.

istock.com/georgeclerk

The Executive Network

In general, the executive attention network has been tested using tasks involving some form of conflict. Consider a task (Stroop, 1935) in which you are shown words printed in blue, green, brown, purple, or red ink (Column A in Figure 3.4) and your objective is simply to name the color of the ink. If the words are names of colors that cause a competing response (such as the word **red** printed in blue ink), it is better to avoid reading the words because it makes the task much harder. However, people cannot completely avoid reading the words, as is revealed by the fact that they performed the task more slowly than when they had to name the color of squares (Column B in Figure 3.4).

The finding that it takes longer to process a stimulus when it has conflicting attributes is called the Stroop effect, named after its discoverer (Stroop, 1935). It is one of the most widely used paradigms in psychology because it can be used to study many types of conflicting attributes. The article has received more than 21,000 citations according to Google Scholar.

| FIGURE 3.4 ■ Stimuli Used in Experiment 2 by Stroop (1935). |

A.	B.
red	■
blue	■
green	■
brown	■
purple	■

Conflict tasks activate the midline frontal areas, such as the anterior cingulate, as well as lateral prefrontal areas (Botvinick et al., 2001; Fan et al., 2005). The yellow area (EAN) in Figure 3.4 shows the location of the executive attention network, which is involved in self-regulation of sensory input and affect when performing cognitive tasks. This has led to the belief that the executive attention network exerts a great deal of control over sensory, cognitive, and emotional systems within the brain.

The executive attention network is controlled primarily by the neurotransmitter dopamine (Posner & Rothbart, 2007), which has important implications for how various drugs influence the control of attention. Drugs used to treat attention deficit disorder, such as methylphenidate and amphetamine, are thought to control attention by modulating dopamine to increase the control over impulsive behaviors (Advokat et al., 2019). Unfortunately, when these and other drugs, such as cocaine, are used recreationally, their effects on dopamine may increase impulsivity and reduce the emotional and cognitive abilities of users. These drugs often have deleterious effects on working memory as well, an issue we will discuss further in the next chapter.

There is direct evidence that early attention has an impact in later life. A Canadian longitudinal study investigated how behavior in kindergarten influenced earnings 30 years later while controlling for child IQ and family background (Vergunst et al., 2019). Kindergarten teachers rated their students on six behavioral dimensions—inattention (easily distracted and lacking concentration), hyperactivity (fidgety and constantly moving), aggression (fighting and intimidating), opposition (disobeying and being inconsiderate), anxiety (worrying and being

Stroop effect The finding that it takes longer to process a stimulus when it has conflicting attributes

fearful), and prosociality (helping and showing sympathy). Measures of aggression and opposition were highly correlated so were combined into a single measure. For males, inattention had the greatest influence on later earnings, followed by prosociality and aggression/opposition. Hyperactivity and anxiety did not have a significant effect on their earnings. For females, only inattention had a significant effect on later earnings. The authors emphasized the importance of early monitoring and support for children who lack attention skills.

BOTTLENECK THEORIES

Our knowledge of attention has accumulated not only from neuroscience research but from information-processing theories of the stages involved in paying attention. The previous chapter described the first information-processing model of visual pattern recognition and attention proposed by George Sperling (1960). Several years earlier, Donald Broadbent (1957) developed an information-processing model of attending to speech. His model and subsequent adaptations are labeled "bottleneck theories" because they assume that a bottleneck exists as some stage in which the listener cannot simultaneously comprehend two simultaneous verbal messages. Bottleneck theories differ in the function and location of the bottleneck.

Broadbent's Filter Model

We occasionally at a party would like to eavesdrop on a nearby conversation as we listen to another conversation (Photo 3.3). The study of whether people can understand two simultaneous conversations began as an applied problem. Two pilots would occasionally simultaneously contact a control tower for instructions on landing their planes. Donald Broadbent, working at the applied psychology unit in Cambridge England, was assigned the task of studying this problem.

PHOTO 3.3 Listening among simultaneous conversations.

istock.com/Rawpixel

Broadbent simplified the task by asking enlisted men in England's Royal Navy to listen to three pairs of digits (Broadbent, 1954). One member of each pair arrived at one ear at the same time that the other member of the pair arrived at the other ear. For example, if the sequence were 73–42–15, the subject would simultaneously hear 7 and 3, followed by 4 and 2, followed by 1 and 5. That is

Left ear	Right ear
7	3
4	2
1	5

The pairs were separated by a half-second interval, and the subjects were asked to report the digits in whatever order they chose. They were able to report 65% of the lists correctly, and almost all the correct reports involved recalling all the digits presented to one ear followed by all the digits presented to the other ear. In other words, if 741 had been presented to the left ear and 325 to the right ear, the subject would recall either in the order 741–325 or in the order 325–741.

Another group was instructed to recall the digits in the actual order of their arrival: the first pair of digits, followed by the second pair, followed by the third pair. The time between successive pairs of digits varied from 0.5 to 2 sec. Figure 3.5 shows the percentage of lists correctly recalled as a function of the interval between pairs. Performance was better at the longer intervals; nevertheless, it was much worse than when subjects could recall the digits heard in one ear and then the other ear.

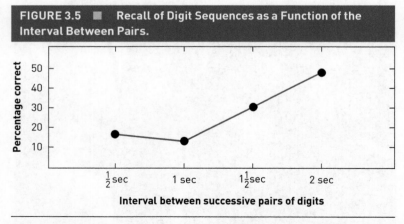

FIGURE 3.5 ■ Recall of Digit Sequences as a Function of the Interval Between Pairs.

Source: From "The role of auditory localization in attention and memory span," by D. E. Broadbent, 1954, *Journal of Experimental Psychology, 47*, 191–196. Original copyright 1954 by the American Psychological Association. Public domain. https://doi.org/10.1037/h0054182

To account for these findings, Broadbent (1957) used the **filter model**, which can be represented by the mechanical model shown in Figure 3.6. The mechanical model consists of a Y-shaped tube and a set of identifiable balls. The tube has a narrow stem that can accept only a single ball at a time (the **limited-capacity perceptual channel**), but upper branches (the *sensory store*) are wider and can accept more than one ball at a time. At the junction of the stem and branches is a hinged flap (the *filter*), which can swing back and forth to allow balls from either branch of the Y to enter the stem.

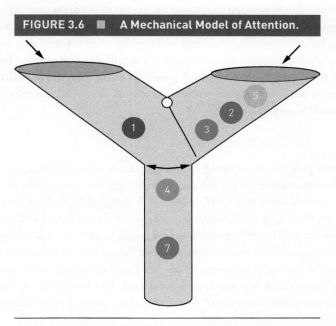

FIGURE 3.6 ■ A Mechanical Model of Attention.

Source: From "A mechanical model for human attention and immediate memory," by D. E. Broadbent, 1957, *Psychological Review, 64*, 205–215. Original copyright 1957 by the American Psychological Association. Public domain. https://doi.org/10.1037/h0047313

In this case, the balls represent digits, and the two branches represent the two ears. Two balls are simultaneously dropped, one into each branch. The flap door would be set to one side to allow one of the balls to enter the stem, while the other ball would be held in a sensory store. If the observer wanted to report all the digits entering one ear, the flap would stay to one side until all three balls from one branch entered the stem. This is illustrated in Figure 3.9 for reporting the left ear first. The

filter model The proposition that a bottleneck occurs at the pattern recognition stage and that attention determines what information reaches the pattern recognition stage

limited-capacity perceptual channel The pattern recognition stage of Broadbent's model, which is protected by the filter (attention) from becoming overloaded with too much perceptual information

flap would then be shifted to the other side, allowing the three balls from the other branch to enter the stem. If the observer were forced to report the digits as they arrived, the flap would have to be shifted back and forth to allow balls to enter the stem in the order in which they arrived.

The model accounts for performance on Broadbent's (1954) task by assuming that it takes time to switch attention (represented by the flap, or filter) from ear to ear. If the interval separating the pairs of balls is too short, the flap will not have time to switch back and forth, and performance will deteriorate as it did when the interval was one second or shorter (see Figure 3.5). The easiest case should be when the listener can report all the digits entering one ear before reporting all the digits entering the other ear. In this case, the listener can recognize all the digits entering one ear before recognizing the digits entering the other ear, and only a single shift of attention is required. But the shift has to occur *before* the information entering the unattended ear decays from the auditory sensory store. A limitation of the filter model is that the sensory store would have to last fairly long to operate as proposed; otherwise, the information would decay before it could be recognized.

Treisman's Attenuation Model

In the previous chapter, we encountered Treisman's feature integration theory that proposed attention is required to combine the features of a pattern. As a graduate student at Oxford University, she became interested in a listening task designed by Colin Cherry. She tested Broadbent's assumption that the listener can recognize information on only one channel at a time by presenting a different but continuous message to each ear and asking the listener to "shadow" or repeat aloud one of the messages (see Figure 3.7). Shadowing a message provides proof that the listener is following instructions and attending to the correct ear. The initial findings from shadowing experiments supported the filter model. As predicted, subjects were almost completely unaware of the content of the message played to the unattended ear (Cherry, 1953).

However, later research indicated that listeners occasionally could report information on the unattended channel. Moray (1959) discovered that subjects sometimes heard their own names on this channel, and Treisman (1960) found that the contextual effects of language would sometimes cause subjects to report words on the unattended channel and therefore shadow inappropriately. Following are two examples of the intrusions that occurred:

1. . . I SAW THE GIRL / song was WISHING. . .
   . . . . . me that bird / JUMPING in the street. . .

2. . . SITTING AT A MAHOGANY / three POSSIBILITIES. . .
   . . . . . .let us look at these / TABLE with her head. . .

---

shadowing An experimental method that requires people to repeat the attended message out loud

contextual effect The influence of the surrounding context on the recognition of patterns

FIGURE 3.7 ■ A Shadowing Task that Requires Repeating Aloud the Message in One Ear.

The farmer walked over to the barn to investigate the noise...

The man then called out to Steve...

"The farmer walked over to the barn to investigate the noise..."

Source: McBride, Cognitive Psychology 2e (9781506383866), Figure 4.2: An Example of the Shadowing Task From the Conway et al. (2001) Study.

The first line in each example is the message that the listener was asked to shadow. The second line is the unattended message. The words in capital letters are the words actually spoken by the subjects. The intrusions from the unattended channel—the word *jumping* rather than *song*—fit the semantic context better than the words on the attended channel. The contextual cues were not sufficient to cause subjects to change permanently to the unattended message in order to follow the meaning of the passage, but the results did raise some questions for the filter theory. If the filter completely blocks out the unattended message, how could subjects report hearing their names or shadow expected words on the unattended channel?

To answer this question, Treisman (1960) proposed a model consisting of two parts—a *selective filter* and a "dictionary." The filter distinguishes between two messages on the basis of their physical characteristics, such as location, intensity, or pitch. However, the filter in Treisman's model does not completely block out the unattended message but merely attenuates it, making it less likely to be heard. The recognition of a word occurs in the dictionary if the intensity or subjective loudness of the word exceeds its **threshold** (the minimum intensity needed for recognition). Thresholds have two important characteristics. First, they vary across words. Some words have permanently lower thresholds than others and thus are more easily recognized—for example, important words such as a person's own name and perhaps danger signals, such as *fire*.

threshold The minimal amount of activation required to become consciously aware of a stimulus

FIGURE 3.8 ■ Treisman's Attenuation Model.

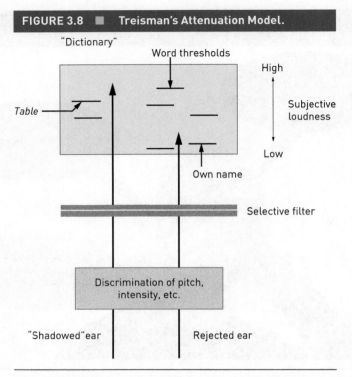

Source: From "Contextual cues in selective listening," by A. M. Treisman, 1960, *Quarterly Journal of Experimental Psychology, 12*, 242–248. https://doi.org/10.1037/h0026890

Second, thresholds can be momentarily lowered by the listener's expectations. For instance, if the words *sitting at a mahogany* are heard, the threshold for the word *table* will be momentarily lowered, making recognition of that word more likely.

The model proposed by Treisman was able to explain why usually very little is heard on the unattended channel, but occasionally some words are recognized. The **attenuation** of words on the unattended channel implies that they will be subjectively less loud than words on the attended channel. They will usually not be loud enough to exceed their threshold unless they have a very low threshold or their threshold is momentarily lowered. Figure 3.8 shows a schematic representation of this effect. The height of the arrows represents the subjective loudness of the two messages, and the height of the thresholds represents the loudness necessary for recognition of the word. Because important words such as a person's name have permanently low thresholds, they can occasionally be heard on the unattended channel, as was found by Moray (1959). A word like *table* normally has a high threshold, but its threshold can be momentarily lowered by expectations. This aspect of the model could account for Treisman's (1960) finding that words on the unattended channel were sometimes incorrectly shadowed if they better fit the context of the message on the attended channel.

---

attenuation A decrease in the perceived loudness of an unattended message

The Deutsch-Norman Memory Selection Model

We have previously seen that a frequent problem in constructing information-processing models is identification of the stage at which a performance limitation occurs. Constructing models of attention is no exception. The models proposed by Broadbent and Treisman placed the bottleneck at the pattern recognition stage. However, according to the models proposed by Deutsch and Deutsch (1963) and Norman (1968), the bottleneck occurs *after* pattern recognition. The problem is not one of perception but one of selection into memory after perception occurs. Because selection occurs later, these models are often referred to as late-selection models.

Let's apply a late-selection model to the task of listening to two different conversations (messages) in a shadowing experiment. The model assumes that words in both conversations are recognized but are quickly forgotten, unless they are important. Words on the attended channel are important because people have to shadow them. Words on the unattended channel are usually unimportant because the listener is asked to attend to another channel. Although recognized, they are quickly forgotten unless they are important—a person's own name, for instance. In the next section we will look at capacity theories before returning to bottleneck theories.

CAPACITY THEORIES

The models proposed by Broadbent and Treisman, Deutsch and Deutsch, and Norman stimulated many experiments and arguments regarding the location of the bottleneck. Some data seemed to support the assertion that the bottleneck was caused by the limitations of perception, whereas other data supported the assertion that the bottleneck occurred after perception (Johnston & Dark, 1986). Failure to agree on the location of the bottleneck has had two consequences.

First, it now seems reasonable to assume that the observer has some control over where the bottleneck occurs, depending on what is required in a particular task (Johnston & Heinz, 1978). However, as you can imagine, it would be more difficult to select information based on meaning than on pitch or location. This leads to the hypothesis that more mental effort (capacity) is required for late selection after pattern recognition than for early selection before pattern recognition.

Imagine that you are the first to arrive at a cocktail party and you carry on a conversation with the hostess. As long as there are no other conversations in the room, it will require little concentration or mental effort to follow what your hostess is saying. If she were not speaking in your native language, however, comprehension would be less automatic and would require more mental effort. You would also have to concentrate more to follow what she was saying if you were surrounded by many other conversations. If you wanted to eavesdrop on one of the other conversations while you were listening to the hostess, still more concentration or mental effort would be required.

We will look first at the capacity theory of attention proposed by Kahneman (1973) to see how a capacity model differs from a bottleneck model. Then we will review the theory proposed

---

late-selection model Proposal that the bottleneck occurs when information is selected for memory

concentration Investing mental effort in one or more tasks

mental effort The amount of mental capacity required to perform a task

capacity theory A theory proposing that we have a limited amount of mental effort to distribute across tasks, so there are limitations on the number of tasks we can perform at the same time

by Johnston and Heinz (1978), suggesting that attention is flexible. This theory is particularly interesting because it shows how a **bottleneck theory** can be related to a capacity theory.

Example of a Capacity Model

Capacity theories are concerned with the amount of mental effort required to perform a task. Kahneman's *Attention and Effort* (1973) helped to shift the emphasis from bottleneck theories to capacity theories. Kahneman argued that a capacity theory assumes there is a general limit on a person's capacity to perform mental work. His capacity model was designed to supplement rather than to replace the bottleneck models.

Both types of theories predict that simultaneous activities are likely to interfere with each other, but they attribute the interference to different causes. A bottleneck theory proposes that interference occurs because the same mechanism, such as speech recognition, is required to carry out two incompatible operations at the same time. A capacity model proposes that interference occurs when the demands of two activities exceed available capacity. Thus, a bottleneck model implies that the interference between tasks is specific and depends on the degree to which the tasks use the same mechanisms. A capacity model, in contrast, implies that the interference is nonspecific and depends on the total demands of the task.

A capacity model also assumes that variations in our alertness and emotional states influence our ability to perform tasks. Self ratings of attention, emotional states, and performance vary throughout the day, as illustrated in Figure 3.9 for a typical work day (Weiss & Merlo, 2020). Three studies involving 133 workers in a variety of occupations found that higher levels of negative affect

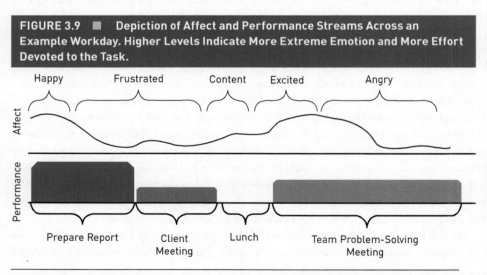

FIGURE 3.9 ■ Depiction of Affect and Performance Streams Across an Example Workday. Higher Levels Indicate More Extreme Emotion and More Effort Devoted to the Task.

Source: From "Affect, attention, and episodic performance," by H. M. Weiss & K. L. Merlo, 2020, *Current Directions in Psychological Science, 29*, 433–459. https://doi.org/10.1177/0963721420949496

---

bottleneck theory A theory that attempts to explain how people select information when some information-processing stage becomes overloaded with too much information

were associated with difficulty in maintaining attention and less time spent on a task. The opposite results occurred for positive affect. The results indicated that the relationship between affect and performance was mediated by the focus and allocation of attention (Weiss & Merlo, 2020).

Kahneman's model (1973) of the allocation of capacity to mental activities is shown in Figure 3.10. Any kind of activity that requires attention would be represented in the model because all such activities compete for the limited capacity. Different mental activities require different amounts of attention; some tasks require little mental effort, and others require much effort. When the supply of attention does not meet the demands, the level of performance declines. For example, we can usually drive a car and carry on a conversation at the same time if both activities do not exceed our capacity for attending to two different tasks. But when heavy traffic begins to challenge our skills as a driver, it is better to concentrate only on driving and not try to divide our attention between the two activities.

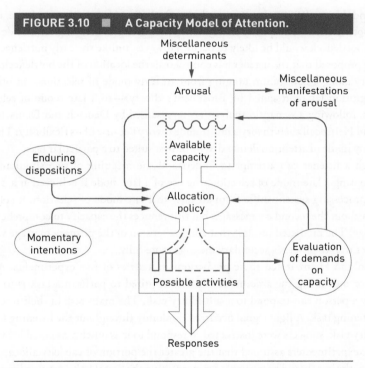

FIGURE 3.10 ■ A Capacity Model of Attention.

Source: From *"Attention and effort,"* by D. Kahneman, 1973. Englewood Cliffs, NJ: Prentice-Hall.

Kahneman's model assumes that the amount of capacity available varies with the level of arousal; more capacity is available when arousal is moderately high than when it is low. We have all experienced diminished capacity when tired. However, very high levels of arousal, such as

---

allocation of capacity When a limited amount of capacity is distributed to various tasks

arousal A physiological state that influences the distribution of mental capacity to various tasks

anxiety or euphoria, can also interfere with performance. This assumption is consistent with Yerkes and Dodson's (1908) law that performance is best at intermediate levels of arousal. The level of arousal can be controlled by feedback (evaluation) from the attempt to meet the demands of ongoing activities, provided that the total demands do not exceed the capacity limit.

The choice of which activities to support is influenced by both enduring dispositions and momentary intentions. Enduring dispositions reflect the rules of involuntary attention. A novel event, an object in sudden motion, or the mention of our own name may automatically attract our attention. The alerting network (Posner & Petersen, 1990), discussed previously, plays a major role. Momentary intentions reflect our specific goals or objectives at a particular time. We may want to listen to a lecturer or scan a crowd at an airport to recognize a friend.

Capacity and Stage of Selection

Johnston and Heinz (1978) demonstrated the flexibility of attention and the interaction between a bottleneck and a capacity theory. They used selective listening tasks to develop their theory, so a bottleneck would be likely to occur. However, unlike the early bottleneck theories, their theory proposed that the listener has control over the location of the bottleneck. The location can vary along a continuum ranging from an early mode of selection—in other words, before recognition (as represented by Broadbent's theory)—to a late mode of selection—in other words, following a semantic analysis (as represented by Deutsch and Deutsch's theory). Johnston and Heinz call their theory a multimode theory because of its flexibility: The observer can adopt any mode of attention demanded by or best suited to a particular task.

Although a listener can attempt to understand the meaning of two simultaneous messages by adopting a late mode of selection, the use of a late mode is achieved at a cost. As the perceptual-processing system shifts from an early to a late mode of selection, it collects more information about the secondary message, but this reduces the capacity to comprehend the primary message. The predicted result is that comprehension of the primary message will decline as the listener tries to process a secondary message more fully.

Johnston and Heinz tested these predictions in a series of five experiments. A common procedure for measuring the amount of capacity required to perform a task is to determine how quickly a person can respond to a subsidiary task. The main task in their research was a selective-listening task. A light signal occurred randomly throughout the listening task, and as the subsidiary task, subjects were instructed to respond to it as quickly as possible by pushing a button. The experimenters assumed that the greater the portion of capacity allocated to selective listening, the less should be available for monitoring the signal light, causing longer reaction times.

---

enduring disposition An automatic influence to which people direct their attention

momentary intention A conscious decision to allocate attention to certain tasks or aspects of the environment

multimode theory A theory proposing that people's intentions and the demands of the task determine the information-processing stage at which information is selected

subsidiary task A task that typically measures how quickly people can react to a target stimulus to evaluate the capacity demands of the primary task

One experiment used a paradigm in which subjects heard pairs of words presented simultaneously to both ears. Undergraduates at the University of Utah were asked to shadow words defined either by the pitch of a voice or by a semantic category. One set of stimuli used a male and a female voice, and the undergraduates were asked to shadow the words spoken by either the male or the female. These subjects could use an early sensory mode of selection because the two messages were physically different. Another group of undergraduates heard two messages spoken by the same voice. One message consisted of words from a category, such as names of cities, and the other message consisted of words from a different category, such as names of occupations. Subjects were asked to report the words from one of the categories and ignore the words from the other category. These subjects had to use a late, semantic mode of selection because it was necessary to know the meaning of the words to categorize them.

The multimode theory predicts that more capacity is required to perform at a late mode of selection. Use of the semantic mode should therefore cause slower reaction times to the light signal and more errors on the selective-listening task. The theory also predicts that listening to two lists should require more capacity than listening to and shadowing one list, which should require more capacity than listening to no lists. Reaction times for the subsidiary task supported the predictions. The average time to respond to the light signal was 310 ms (millisecond) for no lists, 370 ms for one list, 433 ms for two lists that could be distinguished by using sensory cues (pitch), and 482 ms for two lists that could be distinguished by using only semantic cues (categories). These results were accompanied by different levels of performance on the shadowing task. The percentage of errors was 1.4 for a single list, 5.3 for the two lists that could be separated using sensory cues, and 20.5 for the two lists that could be separated using only semantic cues.

Johnston and Heinz interpreted the results as supporting their view that selective attention requires capacity and that the amount of capacity required increases from early to late modes of selection. The first assumption received support from the consistent finding across experiments that reaction times were slower when the listener had to listen to two lists rather than only one. The second assumption received support from the consistent finding that reaction times were slower when the listener had to attend on the basis of semantic cues rather than sensory cues. This latter finding, when combined with the performance results on the selective-listening task, suggests that a person can increase breadth of attention but only at a cost in capacity expenditure and selection accuracy.

After reviewing much of the research on visual and auditory attention, Pashler (1998) proposed a general model that is very similar to multimode theory. As shown in Figure 3.11, the model has both an early (filtering mechanism) and a late (semantic analysis) stage of selection. The filter can prevent stimuli, such as those represented by S3 in Figure 3.11, from being analyzed to a semantic level. For example, imagine that you are asked to report words spoken by a female voice (S1) and ignore words spoken by a male voice (S3). The difference in pitch enables you to block out the words spoken by the male, without analyzing their meaning. Now imagine that you must listen to pairs of simultaneously presented words spoken by the same voice. Your task is to report the name of a city (S1) and ignore the name of a profession (S2). It is now necessary to understand the meaning of both words to know which name is a city. The success of semantic analysis for those stimuli that pass the filter (S1 and S2) is determined by whether the analysis exceeds the available capacity, as in Kahneman's model. This appeared to be the case in Johnston and Heinz's results, which produced a rather high error rate when listeners had to recognize both words.

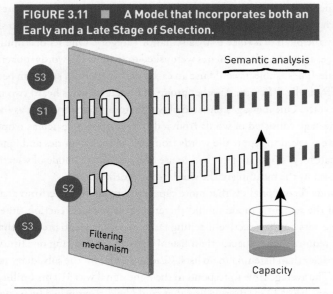

FIGURE 3.11   ■   A Model that Incorporates both an Early and a Late Stage of Selection.

Source: From *"The psychology of attention,"* by Harold Pashler, 1998, p. 227 (Cambridge, MA: MIT Press). Reprinted by permission.

There is a silver lining to the limited capacity of attention. If attention is as flexible as suggested by the multimode theory, a person at least has the choice of how best to use it. This choice becomes particularly relevant when we try to execute simultaneous tasks.

Multitasking

Capacity is a valued resource whenever we multitask (Photo 3.4). Although multitasking refers to the simultaneous execution of multiple tasks, most activities that require attention cannot be done simultaneously (Srna et al., 2018). You may believe that you are multitasking but may be rapidly shifting between tasks.

There is nonetheless evidence that a belief about engaging in multitasking improves performance. Imagine that you are asked to watch a video and type all that is said in the video. You will likely think of this activity as a single task if you classify it as transcribing. However, you will likely believe this activity requires multitasking if you consider watching and typing as two distinct tasks. To evaluate whether beliefs matter, some participants were told they would be transcribing the video while others were told they would be concurrently working on two tasks.

Participants who believed they were doing two tasks wrote more words and took higher quality notes (Srna et al., 2018). Consistent with prior literature that the amount of invested effort increases with the perceived difficulty of the task, the authors proposed that the perceived challenge of multitasking increased motivation to perform well. An additional factor is people likely perceive the ability to multitask as a desirable trait, which also increased their motivation to perform well.

PHOTO 3.4 Multitasking requires increased capacity.

istock.com/filadendron

Selective attention works against multitasking, so there are some situations in which a broader focus of attention is desirable (Amer et al., 2016). Tasks that depend on extracting and processing knowledge from a wealth of information benefit from this broader focus. These tasks include ones that involve insight, benefit from creativity, and require learning about the surrounding environment. The authors conclude that focusing attention is a double-edged sword—helpful in some situations but detrimental in other situations.

AUTOMATIC PROCESSING

A second silver lining to the limited capacity of attention is that, with sufficient practice, some tasks can become so automatic that they do not appear to require any of the precious capacity postulated by a capacity theory. Psychologists have used the term **automatic processing** to refer to such skills. One characteristic of automatic processing is that it occurs without conscious awareness. Indeed, some theorists have argued that much of what we do is determined not by deliberate choices but by features of the environment that initiate mental processes that operate outside of consciousness (Bargh & Chartrand, 1999).

Acquisition of automatic processing is often an advantage. It allows us to perform routine activities without much concentration or mental effort. However, automatic processing can also be a disadvantage. We may put so little thought into what we are doing that we make a silly mistake or fail to remember what we did.

---

automatic processing Performing mental operations that require very little mental effort

We begin by examining criteria that people can apply to determine whether they are using automatic processing. We then see how automatic processing is useful in performing complex tasks, such as reading.

When Is a Skill Automatic?

Posner and Snyder (1975) proposed three criteria to determine whether a skill is automatic. A skill is automatic if it (1) occurs without intention, (2) does not give rise to conscious awareness, and (3) does not interfere with other mental activities.

Learning to ride a bicycle is a familiar example that we can evaluate by using these criteria. Most of us have learned how to ride a bicycle, and perhaps we can still remember the early experience of wobbling back and forth for a few feet before stopping and having to start over. Balancing the bicycle initially required intention, conscious awareness of what we were trying to do, and mental effort that could interfere with our concentration on other activities. Once we learned how to balance, it became hard to imagine why we had had so much trouble initially. We could then ride a bicycle without consciously intending to balance, we had little conscious awareness of the movements we used to achieve balance, and we became more able to attend to the scenery or our thoughts because we no longer had to concentrate on balancing.

Another task that initially requires a lot of mental effort or capacity is reading a word. But, like riding a bicycle, reading a word eventually becomes a fairly automatic skill. As we learned earlier in the chapter, it becomes so automatic that it is difficult to stop, even when reading a word interferes with naming the color of its ink (Stroop, 1935).

The Stroop effect provides a partial answer to the question asked by Posner and Snyder (1975) at the beginning of their article: To what extent are our conscious intentions and strategies in control of the way information is processed in our minds? The fact that people could not avoid reading words illustrates that we cannot always adapt our thought processes to the strategies required by the task. Because automatic processes occur without intention, they may occur even when they are a nuisance. Fortunately, automatic processes usually are advantageous and allow us to perform complex skills that would otherwise overload our limited capacity.

Learning to Read

One of the most demanding cognitive skills that face the young child is learning how to read. Learning to read requires many component skills, some of which we considered in the previous chapter. The child must analyze the features of letters, combine the features to identify the letters, convert the letters into sounds for pronouncing words, understand the meanings of individual words, and combine the meaning of the words to comprehend the text (Photo 3.5). According to a theory proposed by LaBerge and Samuels (1974), the ability to acquire complex, multi-component skills such as reading depends on the capability of automatic processing.

PHOTO 3.5 Efficient reading requires acquiring automatic processing.

iStock.com/fizkes

Their criterion for deciding when a skill or subskill is automatic is that it can be completed while attention is directed elsewhere. The rationale behind this argument is that, unless at least some of the component skills can be completed without requiring capacity, the total demands of all the component skills will be simply too great for the individual to perform the task.

As we saw in the previous chapter, an initial component skill for successful reading is the ability to identify the features of a letter. The features must then be organized or combined to form a letter, a process that initially requires attention, according to LaBerge and Samuels. However, after sufficient practice in recognizing letters, the features can be combined automatically to form a letter, freeing some capacity for the other necessary component skills.

As an extension of their argument, words should require less capacity to recognize if we can recognize the word as a unit rather than as a string of individual letters. You may recall that almost all the people who participated in Reicher's (1969) experiment reported that they perceived a four-letter word as a unit rather than as four separate letters.

One consequence of perceiving a word as a unit is that it should cause us to attend less to the individual letters in the word. You can test your own ability to perceive individual letters in words by reading the following sentence. Read it once and then read it again, counting the *f*s.

FINISHED FILES ARE THE RESULT OF YEARS OF SCIENTIFIC STUDY COMBINED WITH THE EXPERIENCE OF MANY YEARS.

There are six *f*s in the sentence. If you counted fewer than six, please try again.

Most people find this a difficult task because they fail to detect the *f* in one of the words (*of*) even though it occurs three times in the sentence. One explanation of why we overlook this particular *f* is that it is pronounced like the letter *v*. Although this is a contributing factor, unitization also plays an important role (Schneider et al., 1991). Results obtained by Healy (1980) indicate that we often recognize frequently occurring words as units and therefore find it difficult to focus on their individual letters. Healy asked people to read a prose passage at normal reading speed but to circle the letter *t* whenever it occurred in the passage. She found that people were more likely to miss the letter when it occurred in common words than when it occurred in unusual words. In particular, they often missed the letter *t* in the word *the*, which is the most common word in the English language.

Healy's results are consistent with the theory advocated by LaBerge and Samuels. Because people encounter frequent words more often than unusual ones, they should be better able to recognize a frequent word as a unit. Less capacity should be required to recognize a frequent word because the reader does not have to pay as much attention to the individual letters. If less capacity is required to recognize a familiar word, the reader should have more capacity available for comprehending the meaning of the sentence.

Inspired by LaBerge and Samuels' (1974) theory, Kieffer and Christodoulou (2019) asked "How do executive functions and reading fluency interact in predicting reading comprehension?" Reading fluency, which refers to the accuracy and speed of reading, depends on automaticity as proposed by LaBerge and Samuels (1974). Comprehension also depends on executive functions such as shifting attention, updating working memory, and inhibiting irrelevant information. We will learn about these executive functions in the next chapter.

There is extensive evidence that both automaticity and executive functions influence reading comprehension, but less is known about their interaction. The hypothesis evaluated by Kieffer and Christodoulou (2019) is that executive functions are more critical for disfluent readers than for fluent readers because executive functions could compensate for the lack of fluency. The opposite result occurred—readers with higher reading fluency showed stronger relations between executive functions and reading comprehension. A theoretical implication is that the capacity demands of word recognition may be too great for disfluent readers to allocate additional capacity to executive functions. An instructional implication is that teachers need to evaluate how reading fluency interacts with executive functions to determine how both affect reading comprehension in their students (Kieffer & Christodoulou, 2019).

APPLICATIONS

You should now have an appreciation for the importance of attention in performing many cognitive tasks. The last part of this chapter discusses applications to driving and social interactions. We will first look at how to improve selective attention in both young drivers and older drivers, followed by the distracting effects of cell phones.

Training Drivers

One of the most important applications for improving selective attention is to assist young drivers. Per 100 million vehicle miles, a 16-year-old driver is almost eight times as likely to get into a fatal crash as a 45- to 64-year-old driver, and an 18-year-old driver is four times as likely. There is clearly a need for training programs that could provide needed experience.

Strayer (2016) developed a framework to describe the key cognitive processes that contribute to driver distraction. His acronym SPIDER refers to *scanning* the driving environment, *predicting* and anticipating potential threats, *identifying* threats that appear in the field of view, *deciding* whether action is necessary, and *executing* appropriate *response*s.

A team of psychologists at the University of Massachusetts designed a training program to improve scanning, predicting, and identifying threats (Pollatsek et al., 2006). The software requires dragging red circles to areas of the roadway that should be continually monitored and dragging yellow circles to areas that could contain relevant hidden information, such as pedestrians emerging behind hedges. The training required less than an hour to complete on a personal computer and involved both coaching and review tests.

The team then used the University of Massachusetts driving simulator (Fisher et al., 2002) to evaluate the success of the training. The simulator used a 1995 Saturn Sedan and a virtual world projected onto three screens surrounding the car. Participants controlled the vehicle in the same way that they would control a normal vehicle. A head-mounted eye tracker recorded where the drivers looked as they navigated through the virtual world.

The investigators studied a group of novice 16- and 17-year-old drivers on the simulator to measure whether they would attend to critical areas. Those drivers who received the training program fixated the appropriate regions 58% of the time, whereas the untrained drivers fixated appropriately only 35% of the time. A follow-up experiment revealed that there was no decrement in the training when the test on the driving simulator was given three to five days after training. A field study in the Amherst, Massachusetts, environment also showed that training transferred to real environments. The eye tracker revealed that trained drivers looked at critical areas 64% of the time, compared to 37% of the time for untrained drivers.

These findings show that even relatively brief training can enhance selective attention in inexperienced drivers. Brief training has also been proven effective for aiding older drivers (Pollatsek et al., 2012). Drivers over 70 years old are particularly vulnerable to crashes at intersections such as the one shown in Figure 3.12. A surprising finding is their failure has been attributed to the development of unsafe habits, such as following the lead car through the intersection without watching for oncoming traffic rather than physical decline. Older drivers monitored regions of potential threat less often than younger drivers.

A training study began by filming older drivers as they drove from their homes in their own vehicles while wearing head-mounted cameras. The drivers then received 30 to 40 minutes of instruction on where to look at intersections and why less careful scanning is a major cause of crashes. They were also evaluated in a driving simulator that provided feedback on their behavior at virtual intersections. Evaluation on both the simulator and the road revealed that, at the end of the training, the performance of the older drivers had substantially increased and was

FIGURE 3.12 ■ **A Dangerous Intersection for Older Drivers.**

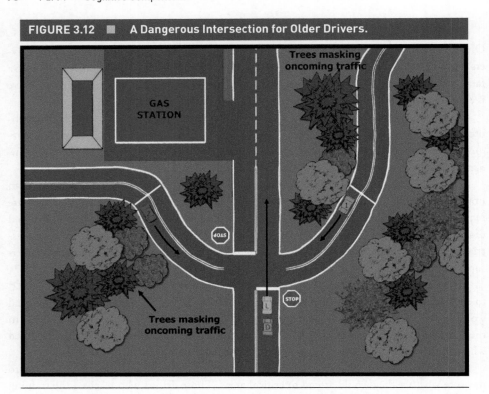

Source: Adapted from "Identifying and remediating failures of selective attention in older drivers," by A. Pollatsek et al., 2012, *Current Directions in Psychological Science, 21,* 3–7. https://doi.org/10.1177/0963721411429459

indistinguishable from that of younger drivers. Older drivers who received only 30 to 40 minutes of instruction without video feedback did not improve.

Using Cell Phones

The driving tests described in the previous section demonstrated that driving can be a challenging task for inexperienced and older drivers, even when they focus solely on driving. Driving with divided attention, as when the driver carries on a conversation while driving, is detrimental for everyone.

This concern is justified by accident reports. One study found that 24% of 699 individuals involved in accidents were using their cell phones within a 10-minute period preceding the accident (Redelmeier & Tibshirani, 1997). People who used cell phones while driving were four times as likely to be involved in an accident, an increase comparable to driving with a blood-alcohol level above the legal limit. It didn't matter whether they were holding the phone or using a hands-free device. This is an important finding because many legislatures assume that accidents would be reduced by using a cellular device that does not have to be held.

An experiment by Strayer and Johnston (2001) tested the hypothesis that conversing with someone on a cell phone while performing a simulated driving task would make it more difficult to perform the attentional demands of driving. The simulated driving task required participants to use a joystick to track a moving target on a computer display. At intervals ranging from 10 to 20 seconds, a red or green signal would appear on the display, and the instructions would indicate that participants should push a button for red signals. Participants either listened to a radio, carried on a conversation using a handheld phone, or carried on a conversation using a hands-free phone while performing the task.

The two independent measures were the probability of missing the red signal and the reaction time to press the button when the red signal was detected. Given the findings from accident reports that performance is not influenced by whether a handheld or a hands-free phone is used, these two conditions were combined and contrasted with performance while listening to the radio.

Figure 3.13 shows the results. The top figure indicates that participants missed 3% of the red signals when they did not talk on the phone or listen to the radio (single task) but missed 7% of the signals when talking on the phone (dual task). In contrast, listening to the radio did not interfere with detecting signals. The reaction-time data in the bottom figure also shows that

FIGURE 3.13 ■ **Probability of Missing the Simulated Traffic Signals (a) and Reaction Time to the Simulated Traffic Signals (b) in Single- and Dual-task Conditions.**

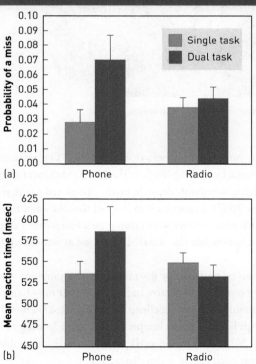

Source: From "Driven to distraction: Dual task studies of simulated driving and conversing on a cellular telephone," by D. L. Strayer & W. A Johnston, 2001, *Psychological Science, 12*, 462–466. https://doi.org/10.1111/1467-9280.00386

using a cell phone significantly delayed reaction time to a detected signal, but listening to the radio did not delay reaction time.

These results support the hypothesis that it is the *attentional* demands of using a cell phone that interfere with performance. Listening to a radio requires so little mental effort that it does not cause interference. Furthermore, the lack of difference between handheld and hands-free devices indicates that interference is caused by the mental demands rather than by having one less hand for driving.

PHOTO 3.6 Hands-free cell phones create distractions.

Getty Images/ martin-dm

Neurological research confirms these behavioral findings. The amount of attention allocated to a task can be measured by the amplitude of the P300 component of event-related potentials. Participants in a driving simulator, drove behind a simulated car that braked at random intervals (Strayer & Drews, 2007). Measurements showed that the amplitude of the P300 component was reduced by 50% when drivers were talking on a hands-free cell phone. These findings suggest the drivers did not encode the visual information as well when they were distracted by the conversation.

Processing language can be particularly distracting (and annoying) when you hear someone else talking on a cell phone. It is disruptive because you hear only half of the conversation. Performance on a visual monitoring task declined when participants heard only half of a cell phone conversation, perhaps because it was less predictable than hearing both sides of the conversation (Emberson et al., 2010). Talking on a cell phone while driving is dangerous, but listening to a passenger talking on a cell phone is also distracting.

Distractions while driving are a growing concern as automakers begin to sell cars that include automated steering and speed control mechanisms to ease the tedium of driving (Colias,

2020). As drivers do less behind the wheel, safety advocates are concerned that drivers will be tempted to indulge in distractions that could lead to accidents. In response to this concern, automakers are installing camera systems that monitor drivers' focus if their attention is straying. A spokesperson for the National Highway Traffic Administration says that they are researching whether these monitoring systems are effective in identifying and reducing inattention in drivers.

Coordinating Attention

Paying attention has more than personal consequences. It has social consequences. Gaze—where one looks, how long, and when—is an essential component of social interactions, including the establishment of eye contact (Photo 3.7). Establishing eye contact is a particularly critical in face-to-face meetings where gaze guides the flow of the interactions. Studying how humans look at other people is essential to understanding how they interact and acquire relevant information (Hessels, 2020).

PHOTO 3.7 Eye contact supports social interactions.

istock.com/gpointstudio

One aspect of social interactions is coordinating attention to obtain a shared focus (Battich et al., 2020). Coordinating attention plays a major role in our social lives by ensuring that we refer to the same object, develop a shared language, understand each other's mental states, and coordinate our actions (Photo 3.8). It requires coordinating senses that result in looking, pointing, and speaking to direct the attention of others (Battich et al., 2020).

PHOTO 3.8 Coordinated attention supports instruction.

Getty Images/miodrag ignjatovic

A relatively new approach to studying joint attention is the use of humanoid robots that have the advantage of maintaining excellent experimental control over the interactions (Chevalier et al., 2020). The child in Figure 3.14 is prompted by the robot Nao to look in the general direction in which a visual target is displayed. If the child does not respond to the prompt, Nao will increase the prompts by first moving its head and then pointing with its arm. Although much has already been learned in the research reviewed by the authors, it is still not fully understood how to integrate different nonverbal cues, such as the eyes, body posture, and pointing to direct human attention.

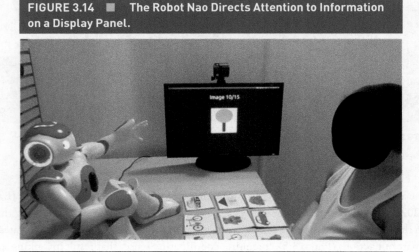

FIGURE 3.14 ■ The Robot Nao Directs Attention to Information on a Display Panel.

Source: From "Examining joint attention with the use of humanoid robots—A new approach to study fundamental mechanisms of social cognition," by P. Chevalier et al., 2020, *Psychonomic Bulletin & Review, 27*, 217–236. https://doi.org/10.3758/s13423-019-01689-4

Findings from this line of research are particularly valuable for improving the attention of children with autism spectrum disorder (ASD), who typically are deficient in this skill. In one study, 14 young children with ASD individually sat on a chair facing a robot that was standing between two display screens (Zheng et al., 2018). The children participated in four sessions over different days in which the robot directed their attention either to the left or to the right targeted display screen. The findings supported the hypotheses that the children would attend most often to the robot and least often to the nontargeted screen. This distribution of attention remained consistent across all four sessions, with relatively few instances of looking at the non-targeted screen.

Another study evaluated how children with ASD would interact with the social robot Probo to make a fruit salad (Simut et al., 2016). Each of the 30 children had one 15-minute session interacting with Probo (Figure 3.15) and one 15-minute session interacting with an adult. The robot and the adult did not differ in eliciting joint attention, verbal utterances, positive affect, or evading task behaviors. However, Probo did elicit more eye contact than the adult. The authors conclude that social robots have the potential to enhance *some* social skills among *some* of the children with ASD, but the research field is still in its infancy.

FIGURE 3.15 ■ A Child with ASD Interacts with the Robot Probo.

Source: From "Children with autism spectrum disorders make a fruit salad with Probo, the social robot: An interaction study," by R. E. Simut et al., 2016, *Journal of Autism Developmental Disorders, 46*, 113–126. https://doi.org/0.1007/s10803-015-2556-9

SUMMARY

The alerting network, the orienting network, and the executive attention network combine to account for the many different functions of attention. The alerting network warns us of potential dangers, such as approaching cars, and may release the stress hormone norepinephrine to increase vigilance. The orienting network directs attention and is closely associated with the "where" pathways in the superior parietal lobe. The executive control network aids in resolving conflicting demands and is influenced by the neurotransmitter dopamine.

Two characteristics of attention are selectivity and mental effort. Initial theories developed within the information-processing approach proposed that selectivity occurs at a bottleneck— a stage that can process only one message at a time. Broadbent's filter theory specified that the bottleneck occurs at the pattern recognition stage and represented attention by a filter that preceded this stage. Treisman modified the filter theory to allow for occasional recognition of words on the unattended channel. Unlike Broadbent and Treisman, Deutsch and Deutsch suggested that the bottleneck occurs after perception and determines what is selected into memory. Norman further developed the latter theory and argued that the quality of the sensory information is combined with importance to determine what enters memory.

Capacity theories emphasize the amount of mental effort required to perform tasks and are concerned with how effort is allocated. Capacity theories supplement bottleneck theories by proposing that the ability to perform simultaneous activities is limited when the activities require more mental effort than is available. Johnston and Heinz argued that a person has control over the stage at which selection occurs, but late modes of selection require more capacity than early modes. Multitasking is a good example of deciding how to allocate attention whenever we believe that we have sufficient capacity to simultaneously perform more than one task.

Automatic processing occurs when a task requires very little capacity to perform. Posner and Snyder proposed that a skill is automatic when (1) it occurs without intention, (2) does not give rise to conscious awareness, and (3) does not interfere with other mental activities. LaBerge and Samuels suggested that the acquisition of complex, multi-component skills such as reading depends on our ability to carry out some of the skills automatically.

Attending to critical parts of the environment can be enhanced by training both young and old drivers in simulators. Using cell phones while driving increases both the probability of failing to see critical aspects of the environment and the response time to react to those events. Coordinating attention is critical for social interactions. Robots are proving to be helpful in training coordinated attention, a skill that is often lacking in children with autism deficit disorder.

RECOMMENDED READING

Kahneman's *Attention and Effort* (1973) provides a comprehensive discussion of initial research on bottleneck and capacity theories of attention. Cowan's (1995) *Attention and Memory: An Integrated Framework* and Pashler's (1998) *The Psychology of Attention* followed. Schneider and

Shiffrin (1977; Shiffrin & Schneider, 1977) describe their research on the acquisition of automatic processing through extensive practice and presented a general theoretical framework for integrating a large number of experimental findings. Hasher and Zacks (1979) proposed a theory of *automatic encoding* that distinguished between two kinds of memory activities—those that require considerable effort, or capacity, and those that require very little or none. See Stanovich (1990) for an evaluation of LaBerge and Samuel's theory regarding the role of automaticity in reading. Bargh and Chartrand (1999) describe a theory for the pervasiveness of automatic processing in our daily lives. An analysis of mind wandering looks at its numerous forms (Seli et al., 2018). Evidence for improvement of multitasking with practice occurs for a variety of simultaneous tasks (Strobach, 2020).

4 WORKING MEMORY

Forgetting
> Rate of Forgetting
> Decay Versus Interference
> Release From Proactive Interference

Capacity
> The Magic Number Seven
> Individual Differences in Chunking
> Searching Short-Term Memory

Working Memory
> Baddeley's Working Memory Model
> Baddeley's Revised Model
> Central Executive
> Executive Functions

Applications
> Managing Cognitive Load
> Working Memory and Emotion
> Working Memory and Stress

SUMMARY

RECOMMENDED READING

LEARNING OBJECTIVES

1. Explain how research has helped resolve the controversy between decay versus interference theories of forgetting.

2. Describe how capacity constrains the effectiveness of short-term memory.

3. Delineate the purposes of the various components of working memory, including the central executive, visuospatial sketchpad, phonological loop, and episodic buffer.

4. Explain the relationship between working memory and everyday experiences, including learning and emotion.

The previous chapters on pattern recognition and on attention focused primarily on perceptual processing. Two other necessary components of cognition are working memory, discussed in this chapter, and long-term memory, discussed in the next chapter. The labels short-term memory and working memory have been used for a memory that is limited in both capacity (the

---

short-term memory (STM) A temporary memory store that is limited in both capacity and duration

working memory The use of short-term memory (STM) as a temporary store of information to accomplish a particular task

amount of information it can hold) and duration (the length of time the memory lasts). The fact that STM is needed when we perform most cognitive tasks reflects its important role as a **working memory** that maintains and manipulates information.

This chapter, like most of the other chapters, begins with classical studies in psychology in which the label "short-term memory" was frequently used to measure how much we can remember over a brief time period. Imagine that you looked up the phone number 1–739–8027–5924 and attempted to dial it without looking at it. It is difficult to remember so many numbers, even for a short interval. More recent studies typically use the label "working memory" to signify how short-term memory supports many cognitive activities. Now try to multiply 37 x 21 in your head. This task requires more than simply recalling numbers. It requires arranging numbers in working memory as you perform the arithmetic so you likely use both verbal and spatial representations. Figure 4.1 shows that working memory occupies a central position in integrating the other components of the standard model.

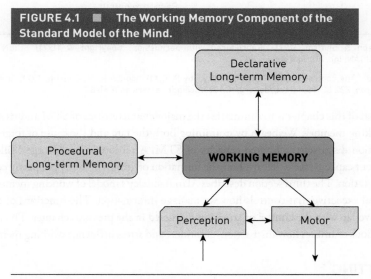

FIGURE 4.1 ■ The Working Memory Component of the Standard Model of the Mind.

Source: Adapted from "A standard model of the mind: Toward a common computational framework across artificial intelligence, cognitive science, neuroscience, and robotics," by J. E. Laird et al., 2017, *AI Magazine, 38*, 13–26. https://doi.org/10.1609/aimag.v38i4.2744

An early and influential chapter by Atkinson and Shiffrin (1968) emphasized the interaction among the sensory store, short-term memory (STM), and long-term memory (LTM). Figure 4.2 shows that STM can combine information from both the environment and from LTM whenever a person tries to learn new information, make decisions, or solve problems. When you add the numbers in your checking account, you are receiving information from the environment (the numbers in your account) and information from LTM (the rules of addition). Getting a correct answer depends on using both sources of information appropriately.

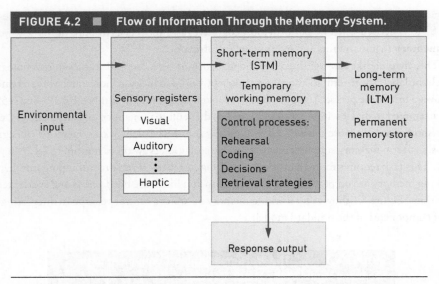

FIGURE 4.2 ■ **Flow of Information Through the Memory System.**

Source: "The control of short-term memory," by R. C.Atkinson & R. M. Shiffrin, 1971, *Scientific American, 225,* 82–90. https://doi.org/10.1038/scientificamerican0871-82

The goal of this chapter is to summarize the major characteristics of STM and its subsequent role as working memory. We begin by examining both the rate and the cause of forgetting. The second section discusses the limited capacity of STM. After looking at George Miller's (1956) insights about capacity, we will learn how the formation of groups of items can partly compensate for this limitation. The third section describes Alan Baddeley's model of working memory, including a central executive that controls how we manage information. The functions of the central executive overlap with the control of attention discussed in the previous chapter. The last section on applications examines how instruction, emotions, and stress influence working memory.

FORGETTING

Rate of Forgetting

Information in STM is lost rapidly unless it is preserved through *rehearsal* (Photo 4.1). Peterson and Peterson (1959) established that forgetting from STM is quite rapid by testing undergraduates on their ability to remember three consonants over a short retention interval. To prevent subjects from rehearsing the letters, Peterson and Peterson required them to count backward by 3s, starting with a number that occurred after the consonants. For example, a subject might hear the letters *CHJ* followed by the number 506. She would then count backward until she saw a light, which was a signal for recalling the three consonants. The light went on 3, 6, 9, 12, 15, or 18 seconds after the subjects began counting.

Figure 4.3 shows the results of this experiment. The probability of a correct recall declined rapidly over the 18-second retention interval. The rapid forgetting rate implies that we must rehearse verbal information to keep it available in STM. It also shows why it is very likely that,

PHOTO 4.1 Remembering the call number of a book may require verbal rehearsal.

istock.com/Ziga Plahutar

if we are momentarily distracted after looking up a telephone number, we will have to look it up again before dialing.

This rapid rate of forgetting can be very frustrating when we are trying to learn new information, but it can also be beneficial. There are many occasions when we need to remember something only briefly.

Think of all the phone numbers you have dialed. Most of these you dialed only once or twice and will never need again. If all these numbers were permanently stored in LTM, it could be very difficult to retrieve the few numbers that you constantly use.

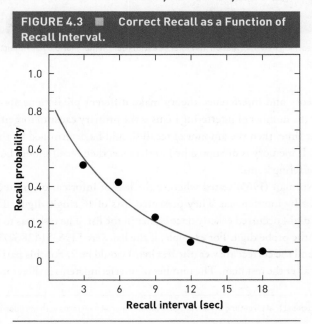

FIGURE 4.3 ■ Correct Recall as a Function of Recall Interval.

Source: From "Short-term retention of individual verbal items," by L. R. Peterson & M. J. Peterson, 1959, Journal of Experimental Psychology, 58, 193–198. https://doi.org/10.1037/h0049234

Decay Versus Interference

One question raised by Peterson and Peterson's findings is whether the loss of information from STM is caused by decay or interference. Try to remember the consonants *RQW* over a short interval without thinking about them. Because it's difficult not to think about them if you have nothing else to do, subjects in memory experiments are asked to perform some other task. An **interference theory** proposes that memory for other material or the performance of another task interferes with memory and causes forgetting (Photo 4.2). A **decay theory** proposes that forgetting should still occur even if the subject is told not to do anything over the retention interval, as long as the subject does not rehearse the material.

PHOTO 4.2 Learning new information may interfere with your memory for old information.

Getty Images/PeopleImages

The decay theory and interference theory make different predictions about whether the passage of time or the number of interfering items is the primary cause of forgetting. If memory simply decays over time, then the amount of recall should be determined by the length of the retention interval. If memory is disrupted by interference, then recall should be determined by the number of interfering items.

Waugh and Norman (1965) tested whether the loss of information from STM is caused mainly by decay or by interference. They presented lists of 16 single digits. The last digit in every list (a probe digit) occurred exactly once earlier in the list. The task was to report the digit that had followed the probe digit. For example, if the list were 5196351428627394, the probe digit would be 4, and the correct answer (the test item) would be 2. For this particular example, seven digits occur after the test item. The number of interfering items is therefore seven. Waugh

---

interference theory Proposal that forgetting occurs because other material interferes with the information in memory

decay theory Proposal that information is spontaneously lost over time, even when there is no interference from other material

and Norman varied the number of interfering items by varying the location of the test digit in the list. There were many interfering items if the test item occurred early in the list and only a few if the test item occurred late in the list.

The experimenters also varied the rate of presentation to determine whether the probability of recalling the test digit would be influenced by the length of the retention interval. They presented the 16 digits in a list at a rate of either one digit or four digits per second. Decay theory predicts that performance should be better for the fast rate of presentation because there would be less time for the information to decay from memory. Figure 4.4 shows the results. The rate of presentation had very little effect on the probability of recalling the test digit. Consider the case in which there are 12 interfering items. The retention interval would be 12 seconds for the 1 per second rate and 3 seconds for the 4 per second rate. Memory is only slightly (and insignificantly) better for the shorter retention interval. In contrast, the number of interfering items has a dramatic effect on retention. The probability of recall declines rapidly as the number of interfering items increases.

Waugh and Norman's findings support the contention that interference rather than decay is the primary cause of forgetting. Although some decay may occur (see Reitman, 1974), the amount of forgetting caused by decay is substantially less than the amount caused by interference. As Reitman and many others have shown, the extent of forgetting is determined not only by the number of interfering items but also by the degree of similarity between the interfering and test items. Increasing the similarity makes it harder to recall the test items.

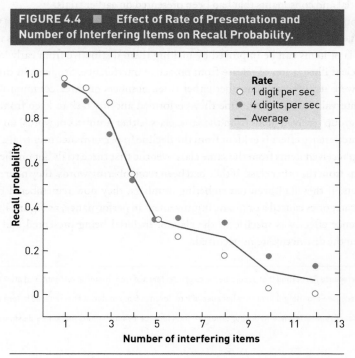

FIGURE 4.4   ■   Effect of Rate of Presentation and Number of Interfering Items on Recall Probability.

From "Primary memory," by N. C. Waugh & D. A. Norman, 1965, Psychological Review, 72, 89–104. https://doi.org/10.1037/h0021797

The finding that interference is the chief cause of forgetting is good news. If information spontaneously decayed from memory, we would be unable to prevent its loss. If information is lost through interference, we can improve retention by structuring learning to minimize interference. A phenomenon called *release from proactive interference* illustrates how interference can be reduced by decreasing the similarity among items.

Release From Proactive Interference

Psychologists have distinguished between two kinds of interference—proactive interference and retroactive interference. Retroactive interference is caused by information that occurs after an event. The Waugh and Norman (1965) study demonstrated the effect of retroactive interference—the number of digits that followed the probe digit influenced how well it could be recalled. Proactive interference, in contrast, is caused by events that occurred before the event that someone attempts to recall.

Keppel and Underwood (1962) had previously demonstrated the effect of proactive interference in the Peterson and Peterson STM task. They found that people initially performed very well in recalling three consonants after a short retention interval, but their performance deteriorated over subsequent trials. The reason is that the consonants they had tried to remember during the initial trials began to interfere with their memory for consonants during the later trials. People found it increasingly difficult to distinguish between consonants that were presented on the current trial and consonants that had been presented on earlier trials.

Reduction of this interference is called the release from proactive interference (Wickens et al., 1963). The study by Wickens and his colleagues was the first of many studies to show that the recall of later items can be improved by making them distinctive from early items. Figure 4.5 shows a clear illustration of release from proactive interference. Students in this particular experiment were required to remember either three numbers or three common words over a 20-second interval, during which time they performed another task to keep from rehearsing. The control group received items from the same class (either numbers or words) on each of four trials. The interference effect is evident from the decline in performance over trials. The experimental group received items from the same class over the first three trials but on the fourth trial received items from the other class. If they had been remembering words, they now remembered three numbers; if they had been remembering numbers, they now remembered three words. The shift in categories caused a dramatic improvement in performance, as Figure 4.5 illustrates. The interference effect was specific to the class of material being presented and was greatly reduced when the distinctive items occurred.

---

retroactive interference Forgetting that occurs because of interference from material encountered after learning

proactive interference Forgetting that occurs because of interference from material encountered before learning

release from proactive interference Reducing proactive interference by having information be dissimilar from earlier material

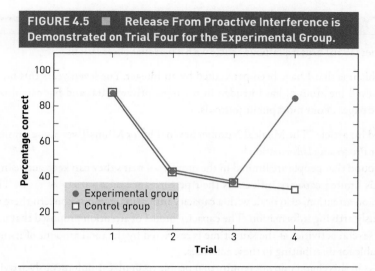

FIGURE 4.5 ■ Release From Proactive Interference is Demonstrated on Trial Four for the Experimental Group.

● Experimental group
□ Control group

Source: From "Characteristics of word encoding," by D. D. Wickens, in A. W. Melton & E. Martin (Eds.), *Coding processes in human memory.* Copyright 1972 by V. H. Winston & Sons. Reproduced with permission from Hemisphere Publishing Corporation, Washington, D.C.

Release from proactive interference also occurs when people are asked to remember more complex events (Gunter et al., 1980). The events consisted of television news items that people heard while they viewed a videotape of the same events. People heard three items during each trial and attempted to recall them after a one-minute delay. The control group received items from the same class (either politics or sports) over a series of four trials. The experimental group received items from the same class over the first three trials, but on the fourth trial, they received items from the other class. If they had been recalling sports events, they now recalled political events and vice versa. The results were very similar to the results shown in Figure 4.5. The proportion of correct responses declined for the control group over the four trials—87% on the first trial, 67% on the second, 55% on the third, and 43% on the fourth trial. The recall of the experimental group showed a similar decline over the first three trials but improved dramatically on the fourth trial, when they heard items from the different category. The experimental group recalled 82% of the items on the first trial, 67% on the second, 55% on the third, and 74% on the fourth.

The practical implications of these results are simply that, whenever possible, we should try to reduce interference by ordering material in an appropriate sequence. Items likely to interfere with each other should be studied at different times rather than during a single session. Reduction of interference through appropriate sequencing can partly compensate for the rapid forgetting from STM. Let's now look at how we can partly compensate for the limited capacity of this store.

CAPACITY

George Miller (1956) began a famous article with a personal observation:

> My problem is that I have been persecuted by an integer. For seven years this number has followed me around, has intruded in my most private data, and has assaulted me from the pages of our most public journals.

He titled his article "The Magical Number Seven, Plus or Minus Two: Some Limits on Our Capacity for Processing Information."

Miller found that people are limited in the number of items they can keep active in memory and that this limited capacity influences their performance on a variety of tasks. The previous chapter, on attention, also dealt with a capacity limitation, but our concern there was with simultaneously arriving information. The capacity model of attention proposed that our ability to carry on several activities at the same time is restricted by the total amount of mental effort that is available for distributing to these activities.

The tasks in this chapter do not require that people recognize simultaneously arriving information. There is no perceptual overload, and there is enough time to recognize each item and enter it into short-term memory (STM). The problem is that STM can hold only a limited number of items, which has a profound effect on the many tasks that require using it. The implications of this limitation are evident throughout this book—not only in this chapter but also in later chapters on text comprehension, problem solving, and decision-making.

The Magic Number Seven

The limited capacity of STM is demonstrated by a task that is often used as a measure of its capacity. It is called a *digit span* or more generally, a *memory-span task*. The task requires that a person recall a sequence of items in their correct order. Memory span is the longest sequence that a person can typically recall. An example of a memory-span task follows. Read each row of letters once without pausing; then shut your eyes and try to recall these letters in the correct order.

TMFJRLB

HQCNWYPKV

SBMGXRDLT

JZNQKYC

If you are like most other adults, you could probably easily recall a string of seven letters (rows 1 and 4) but not a string of nine letters (rows 2 and 3). It was this number seven that plagued Miller. The "magic number seven" kept appearing in two different kinds of studies: experiments on absolute judgment and those on memory span.

---

memory span The number of correct items that people can immediately recall from a sequence of items

In the **absolute judgment task**, an experimenter presents stimuli that vary along a sensory continuum, such as loudness. The experimenter selects different levels of loudness that are easy to discriminate and assigns a label to each. The labels are usually numbers that increase as the values on the continuum increase: If there were seven stimuli, the softest stimuli would be labeled one, the loudest seven. The subject's task is to learn to identify each stimulus by assigning the correct label. The experimenter presents the stimuli in a random order and corrects mistakes by providing the correct answer.

The experimenter is interested mainly in how many stimuli the subject can label correctly before the task becomes too difficult. The results vary depending on the sensory continuum, but Miller was impressed with the finding that the upper limit for a single dimension was usually around sevenn, plus or minus two. The upper limit was about five for loudness, six for pitch, five for the size of squares, and five for brightness. The average across a wide variety of sensory tasks was 6.5, and most of the upper limits were between five and nine.

It is important to point out that these results were not caused by an inability to discriminate adjacent values of the stimuli. All the stimuli would be easy to discriminate if the subject had to judge which one of two adjacent stimuli was louder, larger, brighter, or higher in pitch. The limitation was caused by the inability to keep more than about seven sensory values available in STM because of its limited capacity. The results represent performance during the early stages of learning, before the different sensory stimuli are stored in LTM. With sufficient experience, the upper limits can be increased, as is illustrated by a musically sophisticated person who can accurately identify any one of 50 or 60 pitches. However, that person is using LTM, which is not limited in capacity.

The upper limit found in the absolute judgment experiments corresponds very well with the upper limit found in memory-span tasks. Miller cited the results found by Hayes (1952), which indicated that the memory span ranged from five items for English words (*lake, jump, pen, road, sing*) to nine items for binary digits (0 0 1 0 1 1 1 0 1). The memory span for numbers or letters fell in about the middle of this range.

Miller's paper was important for drawing attention to how little the upper limit varies in performance on absolute judgment and memory-span tasks. His paper was also important for suggesting that recoding the information to form chunks can help one overcome the limited capacity of STM. **Chunks** consist of individual items that have been learned and stored as a group in LTM. You can demonstrate for yourself how chunking can increase the number of letters that can be recalled from STM. Tell someone that you will read 12 letters to him and that you would like him to repeat them back in the correct order. Then read the 12 letters grouped in the following way: *FB-IJF-KCI-AIB-M.* Next read to another person the same 12 letters grouped in a different way: *FBI-JFK-CIA-IBM.* You will likely find that the second person can recall more letters (the groups are now familiar abbreviations). The first person has to recall 12 separate letters, but the second person can recall 4 chunks, each containing three letters. Miller argued that the capacity of STM should be measured in chunks rather than in individual items. The 12 letters should be easy for the second person to recall because they take up only four "slots" in STM rather than 12.

---

absolute judgment task Identifying stimuli that vary along a single, sensory continuum

chunks A cluster of items that has been stored as a unit in long-term memory (LTM)

Individual Differences in Chunking

The power of chunking in aiding the recall of numbers is illustrated by the training of a dedicated participant (SF) over a one-year period (Chase & Ericsson, 1982). SF began with a typical memory span of seven digits, but after one year of practice, could recall a string of 80 digits (Figure 4.6). Pauses in his recall indicated that he organized the digits into groups of three or four and never formed groups larger than five digits. Because SF was a long-distance runner, he initially tried to encode many of the groups as running times. For example, he encoded 3492 as 3.492, a near world-record time for running a mile. He also showed evidence of using hierarchical organization—he combined digits into larger groups that usually consisted of three smaller groups. One interesting finding is that SF's ability to recall groups of digits didn't generalize to letters. When he was tested on recalling letters, his memory span immediately fell back to about six consonants.

Chase and Ericsson later taught another runner (DD) to use the grouping technique invented by SF. As shown in Figure 4.6, DD's learning curve was faster at the beginning of training but did not reach the spectacular digit span of SF and occasionally displayed dips (red triangles) in performance. Chase and Ericsson speculated that beyond a certain point, DD did not have the extensive prior knowledge to create chunks. Following nearly 30 years of essentially no practice on the digit-span task, DD was subsequently retested on four consecutive days and increased his average digit span from 10 to 19 digits over that period (Yoon et al., 2018). A retrospective analysis of this performance revealed that the vast majority of his chunks continued to be based on running times. DD had retired in 2014 as the cross country and track coach at Carnegie Mellon University.

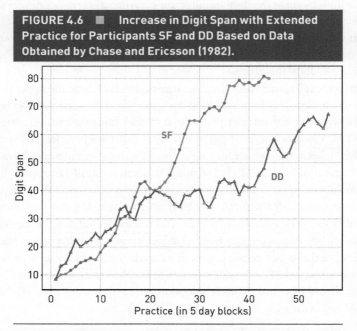

FIGURE 4.6 ■ Increase in Digit Span with Extended Practice for Participants SF and DD Based on Data Obtained by Chase and Ericsson (1982).

Source: From "Plateaus, dips, and Leaps: Where to look for inventions and discoveries during skill performance," by W. D. Gray & J. K. Lindstedt, 2017, *Cognitive Science*, *41*, 1838–1870. https://doi.org/10.1111/cogs.12412

Chunking is also helpful in performing challenging tasks outside the laboratory. The initial evidence for this conclusion came from the study of how chess players reproduce the pieces on a chessboard. The classic study of this task was begun by de Groot, a Dutch psychologist, during the 1940s and was later published in his book *Thought and Choice in Chess* (1965). The main conclusion of his study was that the difference in skill between chess masters and lesser players results more from differences in perception and memory than from differences in how they planned their moves.

Empirical support for de Groot's conclusion came from a series of clever experiments that required players of different abilities to reproduce a chessboard as it might appear 20 moves into a game (de Groot, 1966). Figure 4.7 shows two of the board configurations that were used in the study. The subjects were given five seconds to view the board. The pieces were then removed, and the subjects were asked to place the pieces back on the board to reproduce what they had just seen. When the subject was finished, the experimenter removed the pieces that were incorrectly placed and asked the subject to try again. The subjects continued to try to replace the incorrect pieces until they correctly reproduced the board or until 12 trials were completed.

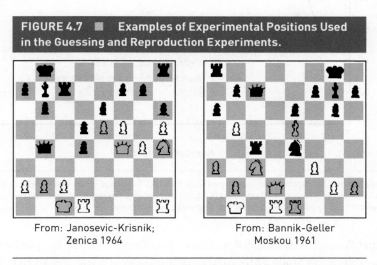

FIGURE 4.7 ■ Examples of Experimental Positions Used in the Guessing and Reproduction Experiments.

From: Janosevic-Krisnik; Zenica 1964

From: Bannik-Geller Moskou 1961

Source: From "Perception and memory versus thought: Some old ideas and recent findings," by A. D. de Groot, in B. Kleinmuntz (Ed.), *Problem solving: Research, method, and theory.* Copyright 1966 by John Wiley & Sons, Inc. Reprinted by permission.

The average performance of five master players and five weaker players is shown in Figure 4.8. The master players correctly reproduced approximately 90% of the pieces on their first attempt, compared with only 40% for the weaker players. To determine whether the results were caused by the masters' ability simply to guess where the pieces should be located, de Groot chose other board configurations and asked the players to guess where the pieces were located, without ever seeing the board or receiving any clues. Figure 4.8 shows that the master players were only slightly better at guessing where the pieces were located. The weaker players, in fact, did about as well at guessing as when they actually saw the board. De Groot argued that the master players depended on their ability to code the pieces into familiar groups. When the players viewed pieces that were placed randomly on the board, the master players no longer had an advantage over the weaker players, and the two groups performed about the same.

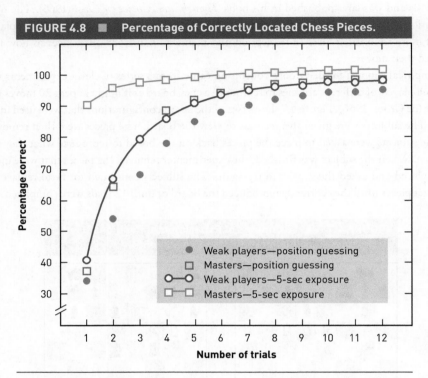

FIGURE 4.8   ■   Percentage of Correctly Located Chess Pieces.

Source: From "Perception and memory versus thought: Some old ideas and recent findings," by A. D. de Groot, in B. Kleinmuntz (Ed.), *Problem solving: Research, method, and theory.* Copyright 1966 by John Wiley & Sons, Inc. Reprinted by permission.

Chase and Simon (1973) extended de Groot's paradigm to identify the groups of pieces (chunks) that presumably produced the superior coding ability of master chess players. A master chess player, a class-A player, and a beginner were tested on de Groot's reproduction task. Chase and Simon assumed that pieces belonging to the same chunk would be placed on the board as a group. They measured the time between successive pieces and classified pauses greater than two seconds as indicating chunk boundaries. The latencies suggested that, for middle-game positions, the average number of chunks per trial was 7.7 for the master player, 5.7 for the class-A player, and 5.3 for the beginner; the number of pieces per chunk averaged 2.5, 2.1, and 1.9, respectively. More skilled players were more successful in reproducing the chess board because they had more chunks and more pieces per chunk. It is also noteworthy that the estimated number of chunks across the three skill levels fit within the range from five to nine proposed by Miller.

Searching Short-Term Memory

Our discussion of STM up to this point has emphasized the recall of material, as shown in the experiments asking for recall of three consonants, a string of letters or digits, a chessboard, or a group of words after a short delay. Psychologists have also been interested in how people try to "recognize" whether a given item is contained in STM. Imagine that you are shown four randomly chosen digits, perhaps 3, 8, 6, and 2. Then you are shown a test digit and asked to decide as quickly as possible whether the test digit was one of the four digits that you saw previously. To perform this task, you would need to store the initial set of digits in STM and then compare the test digit to the digits stored in STM to determine whether there is a match.

Perhaps you can think of instances in which you have to carry out this kind of comparison. For example, when you go shopping you may compare items on the shelves to the names of items you want to purchase and have stored in STM (Photo 4.3). People are fairly accurate at performing this kind of task for a shortlist, so psychologists have focused on response times rather than errors as a measure of performance.

PHOTO 4.3 Comparing an item on a shelf to a grocery list stored in STM.

istock.com/kali9

The digit-example task just described was invented by Saul Sternberg at Bell Laboratories to study how people encode a pattern and compare it with other patterns stored in STM. Sternberg first showed a sequence of digits (the **memory set**), which the subject stored in STM. Then he

---

memory set A set of items in short-term memory that can be compared against a test item to determine whether the test item is stored there

presented a test digit, and the subject had to quickly decide whether the test digit was a member of the memory set. When Sternberg (1966) varied the size of the memory set from one to six digits, he discovered that the time required to make the decision increased as a linear function of the number of digits in STM. Whenever the size of the memory set was increased by one additional digit, the response time was lengthened by 38 ms. Sternberg proposed that the test digit was sequentially compared with each item stored in STM and that it required about 38 ms to make each comparison.

One important issue concerning the scanning process is whether it continues after a match is found. Imagine you are shown the digits 5, 3, 7, and 1 and then given the test digit 3. Would you respond "yes" after matching the 3 in the memory set (a self-terminating search), or would you respond "yes" only after comparing the test digit with all digits in the memory set (an exhaustive search)? Most of us would probably say that we would respond "yes" as soon as we found a match. But Sternberg claimed that we scan the entire memory set before responding. This seems counterintuitive, so let's take a close look at the evidence.

Two aspects of Sternberg's data suggested that people were making an exhaustive search. First, response times for positive and negative responses were approximately the same. We would expect this finding if people always scanned the entire memory set. But if they responded as soon as they found a match, positive responses should be faster than negative responses because people would not always have to scan the entire memory set. Second, Sternberg found that response times were not influenced by the location of the matching digit in the memory set. We would expect this finding if people scanned the entire memory set, but not if they responded as soon as they found a match.

The trouble with an exhaustive search is that it would seem to be a very inefficient strategy to use. Why should comparisons continue once a match has been found? Sternberg's answer was that scanning occurs very rapidly but *checking* for a match takes considerably longer (Sternberg, 1967a). If we had to check for a match following each comparison, searching STM would be less efficient. But if we waited until after scanning the entire memory set to check whether a match occurred, we would have to perform the slower checking process only a single time.

WORKING MEMORY

Baddeley's Working Memory Model

We mentioned at the beginning of this chapter that STM is often referred to as a working memory because of its use in numerous mental activities such as text comprehension, reasoning, and problem solving. More than 45 years ago, Baddeley and Hitch (1974) began constructing a working memory model that is still evolving. Several characteristics of the Atkinson and Shiffrin (1968) framework influenced the development of the Baddeley and Hitch model

---

self-terminating search A search that stops as soon as the test item is successfully matched to an item in the memory set

exhaustive search A search that continues until the test item is compared with all items in the memory set

(Baddeley et al., 2019). One was the proposal of a limited capacity STM that influences a wide range of cognitive tasks. Another is the separation between memory structures and control processes that manipulate information in memory.

In 1992, Baddeley (1992) gave the Bartlett Memorial Address at the University of Cambridge, which gave him the opportunity to evaluate what was then the current status of the model. The model consisted of three components: (1) a phonological loop responsible for maintaining and manipulating speech-based information, (2) a visuospatial sketchpad responsible for maintaining and manipulating visual or spatial information, and (3) a central executive responsible for selecting strategies and integrating information (Figure 4.9).

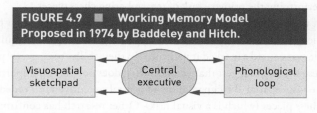

FIGURE 4.9 ■ **Working Memory Model Proposed in 1974 by Baddeley and Hitch.**

Source: From "Is working memory still working?" by A. D. Baddeley, 2001, *American Psychologist, 56*, 849–864. Copyright 2001 by the American Psychological Association. https://doi.org/10.103 7/0003-066X.56.11.851. Reprinted by permission.

Psychologists knew the most about the operation of the phonological loop, perhaps because most of the early research on STM used verbal material, as was illustrated in the previous sections of this chapter. Baddeley and others have proposed that the phonological loop has two components: a phonological store for holding verbal information and a rehearsal mechanism that keeps the information active in the phonological store. Baddeley et al. (1998) argued that the most important role of the phonological loop is in learning how to pronounce new words. The phonological loop stores unfamiliar words until they are permanently learned and stored in LTM.

As psychologists began to include more visual or spatial material in their study of STM, it became apparent that not all material is translated into a speech-based code. Let's take another look at the task of reproducing a chessboard in which chess players group the pieces into familiar chunks. We might speculate that chunks are based more on visual/spatial information than on speech-based information. Certainly, de Groot (1966) believed that perception played an important role in distinguishing good chess players from weaker players. Therefore, we might need a component of working memory that can store visual/spatial information, such as the visuospatial sketchpad.

---

phonological loop A component of Baddeley's working memory model that maintains and manipulates acoustic information

visuospatial sketchpad A component of Baddeley's working memory model that maintains and manipulates visual/spatial information

central executive A component of Baddeley's working memory model that manages the use of working memory

Baddeley (1992) reports a study on reproducing a chessboard that examined the relative contributions of the three components of his working memory model. As chess players of various abilities attempted to reproduce the board, they performed a secondary task that was designed to limit the use of a particular component. To prevent the use of the phonological loop to encode chess pieces, people had to continuously repeat a word aloud. To prevent the use of the visuospatial sketchpad, people had to tap a series of keys in a predetermined pattern. To prevent the use of the central executive, people had to produce a string of random letters at a rate of one letter per second. The rationale was that producing random letters requires people to make decisions about which letter to produce next, and this requirement will restrict their ability to make decisions about performing the primary task of remembering chess pieces.

The results of the study showed that suppressing speech had no effect on people's ability to reproduce a chessboard, but suppressing visual/spatial processing and requiring people to generate random letters caused a marked impairment in their ability to correctly place the pieces on the board. These findings suggest that verbal coding does not play an important role in this task, but both the visuospatial sketchpad and the central executive are needed to have good memory for the chess pieces (which is a visual task). Other research has confirmed that simply counting the number of pieces on the board or making decisions about moves is affected by secondary tasks that interfere with visual/spatial processing but is unaffected by secondary tasks that prevent subvocalization (Saariluoma, 1992).

Another component of Baddeley's model is the central executive. This is the decision-making component of working memory, and it also played a role in reproducing the chessboard. A possible reason is that although chunking is important in this task, pieces on the board do not come "prepackaged" into chunks; the chess player has to decide how to partition the pieces to form chunks. The central executive also plays a predominant role when people have to reach conclusions in a logical-reasoning task (Gilhooly et al., 1993). A secondary task that interfered with the central executive (generating random numbers) significantly impaired logical reasoning, but tasks that interfered with subvocalization or visual/spatial processing did not impair logical reasoning.

The central executive is also needed to determine whether to use the phonological loop or the visuospatial sketchpad when either is sufficient for remembering. For example, people who saw a hexagon, a star, and a circle could remember the shapes in a visual store or the names of the shapes in a linguistic store. The choice likely is influenced by individual differences in ability. Evidence supports the conclusion that the better the individual's imagery ability, the more likely he or she will use visual imagery as a memory tool (Pearson & Keogh, 2019).

A tremendous amount of research has also been conducted to discover the areas of the brain associated with working memory. The visuospatial sketchpad appears to involve primarily right hemisphere areas in which rehearsal of spatial locations activates areas associated with the orienting network, in particular, the inferior parietal lobule. The phonological loop appears to primarily involve the left hemisphere language and acoustic processing areas. As these investigations have progressed, it has become evident that the neural networks associated with attention and working memory overlap to a significant extent. The central executive component of working memory is most closely associated with the frontal lobes, much like the executive control network discussed in the previous chapter.

In conclusion, Baddeley's working memory model shows that more is involved in using STM than simply maintaining and operating on phonological codes. However, assigning the task of controlling attention to the central executive has created a dilemma for the Baddeley and Hitch (1974) model because it leaves their model without a place for integrating visual and verbal information. If visual information is in the visuospatial sketchpad and verbal information is in the phonological loop, how can the visual and phonological codes be brought together? Answering this question forced Baddeley to revise his model.

Baddeley's Revised Working Memory Model

Imagine that you stop to ask for directions and someone gives you a verbal explanation of how to reach your destination. You may try to mentally form a visual map from the verbal directions to help you remember. Your ability to integrate visual and verbal information can also support more sophisticated forms of reasoning, as we will discover in later chapters.

The placement of the central executive between the visuospatial sketchpad and the phonological loop in Figure 4.9 was no accident because Baddeley and Hitch initially thought that the central executive might function as a storage system where visual and verbal codes could be integrated. But the increasing emphasis on using the central executive to control attention left their model with no way of explaining how we can combine information from different modalities. For this reason, Baddeley (2000) proposed a revised model that contained a fourth component, the episodic buffer. The episodic buffer is a storage system that can integrate memory codes from different modalities. It explains how you could mentally form a visual map from verbal directions.

The episodic buffer also explains how you might remember the visual display in Figure 4.10 (Gonthier, 2021). Try to think of strategies that would you help remember it before reading further. The strategies listed below the diagram include a variety of visual and verbal codes. "Try to photograph the whole picture of your mind" is a visual strategy whereas "Remember three squares in the top half and three in the bottom half" is a verbal strategy.

Figure 4.11 shows Baddeley's revised model (Baddeley, 2000, 2001). The purpose of the new component, the episodic buffer, is to serve as a limited capacity store that can integrate information from both the visuospatial sketchpad and the phonological loop. The episodic buffer forms a model of the environment by combining memory codes.

You may have noticed another change between the Baddeley and Hitch (1974) model shown in Figure 4.9 and Baddeley's (2000) revision shown in Figure 4.11. The inclusion of LTM in the revision represents the attempt to develop a greater understanding of the interaction of working memory with LTM. For example, Baddeley and Andrade (2000) found evidence for the use of the visuospatial sketchpad in working memory when participants were asked to form a novel visual image. However, when participants were asked to form an image of a familiar scene, such as a local market, LTM became more important. The LTM strategy in Figure 4.10—imagine a tree with fallen fruit below—attempts to make a novel image meaningful by interpreting the colored squares as a familiar picture.

---

episodic buffer A component of Baddeley's working memory model that combines visual and verbal codes

FIGURE 4.10 ■ A Display used in a VisuoSpatial STM Task.

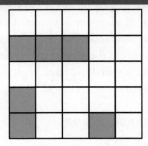

1. Chunking: memorize the three horizontal squares as a single line
2. Holistic encoding: try to photograph the whole picture in your mind
3. Relational encoding: remember that the horizontal line is one square from the top
4. Subdivision: remember three squares in the top half and three in the bottom half
5. Recoding: say to yourself *three in a line, two vertically below, one on the right*
6. Long-term memory: imagine a tree with a fallen fruit below
7. Visuo-spatial rehearsal: mentally redraw the picture (e.g., with eyes closed)
8. Others: count that there are six squares to remember

Source: Adapted from "Charting the diversity of strategic processes in visuospatial short-term memory," by C. Gonthier, 2021, *Perspectives in Psychological Science, 16*, 294-318.

FIGURE 4.11 ■ Baddeley's (2000) Revised Working Memory Model.

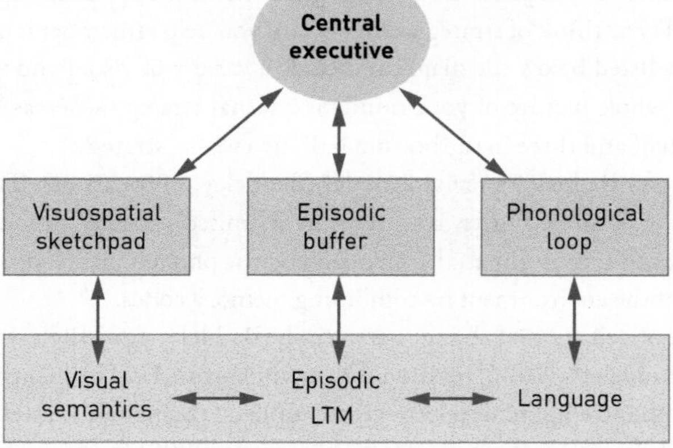

Central executive

Visuospatial sketchpad

Episodic buffer

Phonological loop

Visual semantics

Episodic LTM

Language

Source: From "The episodic buffer: A new component of working memory," by A. D. Baddeley, *Trends in Cognitive Science, 4*, 417–423. https://doi.org/10.1016/S1364-6613(00)01538-2

The success of Baddeley's models in distinguishing between verbal and visual/spatial codes raises questions about other types of memory codes. As shown in Figure 4.11, we can remember events by using phonological, visual, spatial, motoric, auditory, and other types of codes.

Representing all of these different modalities would require an explosion of components in Baddeley's model beyond the visuospatial sketchpad and phonological loop. According to Postle (2006), Baddeley's model (2000) is a victim of its own success. Demonstrating the importance of distinguishing between two memory codes also requires discriminating among many other types of memory codes.

Postle proposes that instead of adding more boxes to Figure 4.11, working memory should be viewed as directing attention to the many different kinds of memory codes stored in LTM. Working memory functions through the coordinated recruitment of brain systems that have evolved to accomplish sensory-, semantic-, and action-related functions. Neuroimaging studies have discovered different areas in the brain where such information is stored and will help psychologists better understand the relation between STM, working memory, and LTM depicted in Figures 4.9 and 4.11. We will look at how the brain recruits and coordinates these different systems, but first let's examine how the central executive manages attention and short-term memory

Central Executive

An important question raised by Baddeley's revised working memory model is, How is working memory related to STM? Psychologists now refer to "working memory" much more frequently than they refer to "short-term memory." Is "working memory" simply a new name for "short-term memory," one that reflects our dynamic use of STM as we carry out various cognitive tasks?

One promising answer considers STM to be a component of working memory that stores information but is separate from the central executive (Engle et al., 1999; Engle & Oransky, 1999). A critical feature of Engle's model is the prominent role given to the central executive and controlled attention as the primary function of the central executive. Engle and Oransky (1999) proposed that individual differences in measures of working memory capacity reflect differences in controlled attention and that these differences will be reflected only in situations that either encourage or demand controlled attention. Controlled attention is necessary for actively maintaining task goals in working memory, scheduling actions, maintaining task information during distraction, and suppressing task-irrelevant information.

This emphasis on controlled attention suggests that research should explore the relationship between the capacity model of attention discussed in the previous chapter and the allocation of attention in working memory (Barrett et al., 2004). Controlled attention is represented in the momentary intentions component of Kahneman's model (shown in Figure 3.7), and this control originates in the central executive component of working memory. Cowan's (1995) book *Attention and Memory: An Integrated Framework* was one of the first to make this important connection.

In contrast to the role of the central executive in controlling attention, the role of STM is to maintain the activated-memory traces. These are typically phonological or visual codes and therefore correspond to the phonological loop and visuospatial sketchpad in Baddeley's model. According to Cowan (1995) and Engle, working memory consists of the contents of STM plus controlled attention as managed by the central executive. Their proposal is consistent with correlational research that has found that the central executive is not influenced by whether the task involves verbal or spatial reasoning, but storage in STM does depend on the verbal/spatial nature of the task (Kane et al., 2004).

A dynamic-processing model of working memory (Rose, 2020) provides an integration of how working memory functions through the coordinated recruitment of brain systems (Postle, 2006). Dynamic processing means that the nature of the representations and processes involved in working memory fluctuate as our thoughts and actions change over time and across contexts. The main assumption of the model is that the brain retains information that is relevant for current goal-directed processing by either actively attending to a current representation or prioritizing representations for future processing.

Figure 4.12 illustrates how the brain accomplishes this task (Rose, 2020). Representations emerge from sensorimotor processing during perception or from the activation of associations stored in LTM. These representations are distributed throughout the cortex. The hippocampus and medial temporal lobe (MTL) bind together task-relevant features. The prefrontal cortex stores rules to regulate prospective actions related to goal-directed behaviors. It serves as an executive to manage various processes, such as the active maintenance of information and the retrieval of relevant associations needed for decision-making, performance monitoring, and updating. The colored regions in Figure 4.12 show the distributed nature of working memory for the decoding of faces (green), words (red), and motion (blue). Notice that some of these regions have previously appeared in diagrams of the brain in Chapters 2 and 3. The MTL is an exception that will become important in the next chapter on long-term memory.

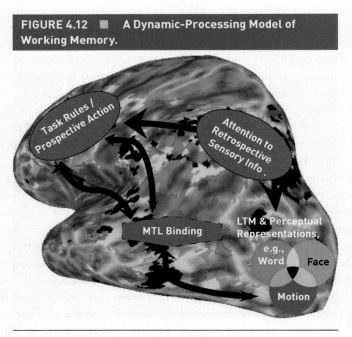

FIGURE 4.12 ■ A Dynamic-Processing Model of Working Memory.

Source: From "The dynamic processing model of working memory," by N. S. Rose, 2020, *Current Directions in Psychological Science,29*, 378-387. https://doi.org/10.1177/0963721420922185

The proposal that working memory consists of the contents of STM plus controlled attention fits nicely with a law relating processing to storage in working memory (Barrouillett et al., 2011). Storage in STM consists of maintaining memory traces while goal-directed processing includes updating the content of STM, retrieving information, and selecting responses. Both maintenance and processing require attention, so when attention is needed for processing, it is not available for maintenance. The consequence is that maintenance suffers as the demands on processing increase. The data in Figure 4.13 confirm this tradeoff between maintenance and processing. As processing becomes more demanding (as measured by cognitive load), maintenance declines (as measured by memory span). These results were obtained from a variety of processing demands, such as updating the content of working memory, selecting responses, and retrieving information from working memory. Such findings illustrate the combined power of data and theory for enhancing our understanding of cognitive psychology.

FIGURE 4.13 ■   Tradeoff between Maintenance and Processing.

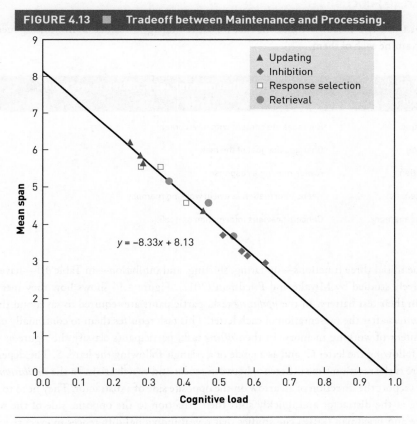

Source: From "On the law relating processing to storage in working memory," by P. Barrouillett et al., 2011, *Psychological Review, 118*, 175–192. https://doi.org/10.1037/a0022324

There have been many studies to evaluate whether training improves working memory as revealed in a literature review of 87 publications containing 145 experimental comparisons (Melby-Lervag et al., 2016). The training programs provided practice on standard measures of working memory, such as recalling a long list of stimuli or completing a distractor task interleaved with to-be-remembered stimuli (Figure 4.14).

The training programs caused short-term improvements in both verbal and visuospatial working memory (Melby-Lervag et al., 2016). However, these improvements were not sustained when retested after a delay of a few months. In addition, the improvements did not generalize to memory tasks that differed from the training tasks, including important real-world cognitive skills. The authors concluded that new approaches based on deeper theoretical analyses are needed for memory training to advance. This requires a better understanding of executive functions.

Executive Functions

Table 4.1 lists five executive functions that we use to manage information in working memory. Let's examine each of them.

TABLE 4.1 ■ Executive functions that manage information in working memory	
Updating	Replaces old content with new content
Shifting	Changes the goal of the task
Inhibition	Avoids making a response
Maintenance	Keeps information active in working memory
Disengagement	Cancels previous information or goals

The initial three functions—updating, shifting, and inhibition—in Table 4.1—have been extensively studied by Miyake and Friedman (2012). Figure 4.14 shows how they measured them in their test battery. In the *updating* task, participants are required to say aloud the last three letters after the presentation of each letter. This task requires them to continually update the content of working memory. In the *shifting* task, participants classify the figure as green or red following the letter C and as a circle or a triangle following the letter S. The dependent measure is the reaction time difference between repeat and switch trials. In the *inhibition* task, viewers report the direction of an arrow on the opposite side of a distractor. They need to avoid looking at the distractor and quickly shift their attention to the opposite side of the screen. Miyake and Friedman (2012) cite studies that reveal individual differences in executive functions can predict differences in clinically and societally important behaviors, such as controlling racial prejudice, staying faithful to romantic partners, and successfully implementing dieting and exercise goals.

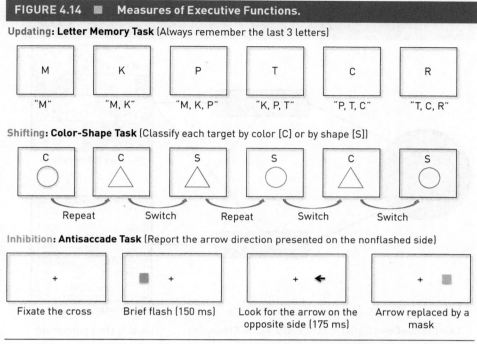

FIGURE 4.14 ■ Measures of Executive Functions.

Updating: Letter Memory Task (Always remember the last 3 letters)

M	K	P	T	C	R
"M"	"M, K"	"M, K, P"	"K, P, T"	"P, T, C"	"T, C, R"

Shifting: Color-Shape Task (Classify each target by color [C] or by shape [S])

Repeat   Switch   Repeat   Switch   Switch

Inhibition: Antisaccade Task (Report the arrow direction presented on the nonflashed side)

Fixate the cross   Brief flash (150 ms)   Look for the arrow on the opposite side (175 ms)   Arrow replaced by a mask

Source: From "The nature and organization of individual differences in executive functions four general conclusions" by A. Miyake & N. P. Friedman, 2012, Current Directions in Psychological Science, 21, 8-14.

One of our daily challenges is to ignore distracting stimuli that are physically attractive or associated with rewards. This challenge may appear to be unrelated to memory load but it is not. Investigators found that observers were better at avoiding distractions while maintaining only one number in working memory than while maintaining five numbers in working memory (Watson et al., 2019).

Two other key executive functions of working memory are maintenance and disengagement (Shipstead et al., 2016). Effective management requires the ability to maintain access to important information but to disengage or block outdated information. Maintenance requires people to keep attention focused on relevant information to avoid distracting emotions, thoughts, and events. Disengagement requires removing information about ongoing tasks so new information will have a greater influence.

Both of these executive functions apply to many tasks, as illustrated by the two very different tasks in Figure 4.15 (Burgoyne & Engle, 2020). The upper panel shows a working memory task that requires remembering letters while judging whether each equation is correct. It is a measure of working memory capacity. *Maintenance* is required to remember the letters (as indicated by the solid line) while *disengagement* plays a more minor role (as indicated by the broken line). The lower panel shows a fluid intelligence task that requires selecting the symbol that best completes the pattern. This task requires testing hypotheses, and disengagement plays a major role by discarding unsuccessful hypotheses.

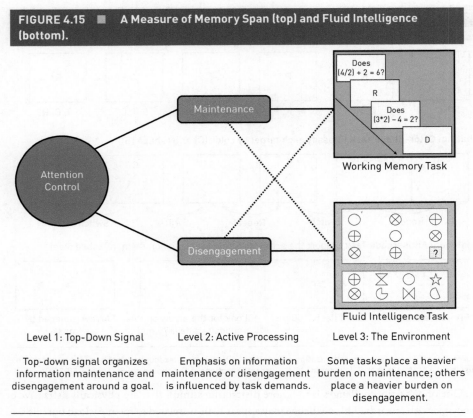

FIGURE 4.15 ■ A Measure of Memory Span (top) and Fluid Intelligence (bottom).

Level 1: Top-Down Signal

Top-down signal organizes information maintenance and disengagement around a goal.

Level 2: Active Processing

Emphasis on information maintenance or disengagement is influenced by task demands.

Level 3: The Environment

Some tasks place a heavier burden on maintenance; others place a heavier burden on disengagement.

Source: From "Attention control: a cornerstone of higher-order cognition" by A. P. Burgoyne & R. W. Engle, 2020, *Current Directions in Psychological Science*.

The strong correlation between working memory capacity and fluid intelligence is caused by the central role of executive functions in performing both types of tasks (Shipstead et al., 2016). Both rely on the ability to control attention and perform the mental work required to either maintain information or to disengage from that information. There is a difference, however, in emphasis (Engle, 2018). Maintaining information is more central in determining working memory capacity. Disengaging from irrelevant or wrong information is more central in determining fluid intelligence.

APPLICATIONS

Managing Cognitive Load

Table 4.1 lists five specific executive functions for managing information, but a general concern for all tasks is reducing cognitive load because of the limited capacity of working memory. From the instructor's perspective, reducing cognitive load requires creating instructional materials that do not overwhelm the learner (Sweller et al., 2019). From the learner's perspective, reducing cognitive load requires creating effective strategies for minimizing its influence (de Bruin et al., 2020). Let's begin with the instructor's perspective.

The limited capacity of working memory has serious consequences for designing instructional material, as documented in research by John Sweller and his colleagues. According to Sweller's cognitive load theory, efforts to combine instructional information can result in cognitive overload—too much information for our working memory to manage (Sweller, 2003).

Imagine for a moment that an instructor has to design a manual to teach technicians how to test electrical appliances to ensure that the appliances are safe. The instruction must explain how to perform four tests on an electric kettle using a meter that measures resistance. The instructor would most likely carefully write down the steps so the technicians could read each step and then perform it on the kettle and meter. The problem with this standard instructional approach is that it produces cognitive overload because of a *split attention effect*. The split attention effect occurs when people have to divide their attention between two sources, such as the instructions and a diagram.

The key to avoiding the split attention effect is to physically integrate the information, as illustrated in Figure 4.16. Notice that the steps are numbered and placed next to the appropriate part of the diagram. The reader does not have to continuously switch attention between the instructions and the apparatus.

FIGURE 4.16 ■ Integration of a Diagram with Text.

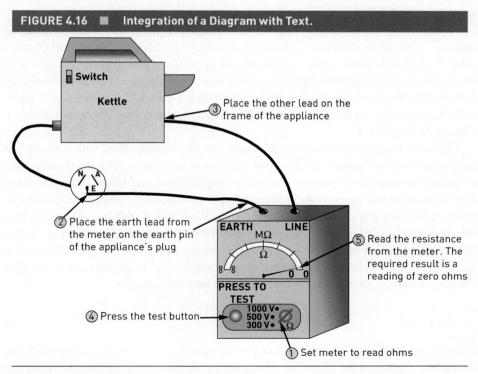

Source: From "Why some material is difficult to learn" by J. W. Sweller & P. Chandler, 1994, Cognition and Instruction, 12, 185–233. https://doi.org/10.1207/s1532690xci1203_1

Sweller and Chandler (1994) evaluated the effectiveness of the modified instructions in an experiment with first-year trade apprentices from a company in Sydney, Australia. One group received standard instructions, which they applied directly to the physical apparatus. A second group received modified instructions consisting of variations of the diagram and steps shown in Figure 4.16. The physical integration of the instructional steps and diagram reduced the instructional time from six minutes for the standard instruction to four minutes for the modified instruction.

More importantly, the modified instruction was much more effective. Technicians who received the modified instructions outperformed the standard group on both a written test and a practical test that included working with the physical apparatus. The better performance on the practical test was particularly impressive because the group who studied the modified instructions did not have any contact with the electrical apparatus until they did the practical test.

However, experience also influences the outcome. According to the *expertise reversal effect*, instruction that reduces cognitive load for the novice may increase cognitive load for the expert (Kalyuga et al., 2012). Adding text to a diagram can reduce cognitive load for the novice, but it will increase cognitive load for the expert if the expert can understand the diagram without the text. The split-attention effect, the expertise reversal effect, and many other instructional implications of cognitive load theory are all supported by extensive research (Sweller et al., 2019).

Now let's shift to the learner's perspective. Managing cognitive load became critical for students in 2020 when the corona crisis closed classrooms in schools and universities (Seufert, 2020). Students now had to make decisions for setting goals and planning, reflecting on what they had learned, and determining how to obtain help. These decisions were compounded by the tradeoff between maintenance and processing shown in Figure 4.13. Learners need to maintain information they are learning at the same time as they are processing how to manage cognitive load (Seufert, 2020).

Managing cognitive load requires generating and distributing effort, which necessitates coordinated decisions between the executive functions of working memory and the allocation of capacity discussed in the previous chapter. We may decide to invest little effort in learning either because the task appears easy or because it appears impossible (Scheiter et al., 2020). In either case, we face a problem when perceived effort is not a good indicator of learning. One remedy is to encourage learners to rely less on perceived effort as a measure of learning; another option is to train learners to make perceived effort more diagnostic of learning (Dunlosky et al., 2020). Let's next examine how working memory is influenced by emotion and stress before returning to learning strategies in the next chapter on long-term memory.

Working Memory and Emotion

Everyday activities are influenced by goals that are continuously updated based on available, often affective information. To pursue these goals, people need to use the executive functions of working memory to maintain goal-relevant information while ignoring distractions that may have an emotional basis. People with mental health problems are particularly vulnerable to impaired working memory in the presence of emotional material (Schweizer et al. 2019).

The relation between emotion and working memory is multidirectional (Mikels & Reuter-Lorenz, 2019). One direction occurs when affect influences working memory. A person who is anxious about giving a speech may find it difficult to focus on its content. This example illustrates MODE 1 in Figure 4.17. The influence of affect on working memory is very intuitive because we all have had experiences in which emotions determined how well we performed a task.

Another direction occurs when working memory influences affect. A fear of spiders may be diminished when seeing a spider if a person is focused on preparing the speech. In this case, performing the task (preparing a speech) impacted our emotions (fear of spiders) rather than our emotions impacting the task. MODE 2 in Figure 4.17 depicts the influence of working memory on affect (Mikels & Reuter-Lorenz, 2019).

FIGURE 4.17 ■ Relations between Affect and Working Memory.

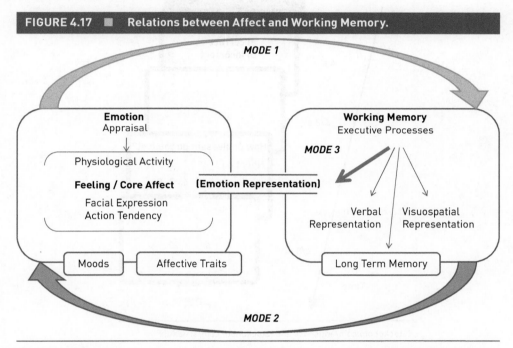

Source: From "Affective working memory: an integrative psychological construct" by J.A. Mikels & P.A. Reuter-Lorenz, 2019, Perspectives on Psychological Science, 14, 543-559. https://doi.org/10.1177/1745691619837597

MODE 2 is revealed in an fMRI study that demonstrated the effect of cognitive load on emotional reactions to pictures (Van Dillen et al., 2009). Figure 4.18 shows a typical trial. Participants viewed either an unpleasant or a neutral picture followed by either a complex ($24 - 2 * 6 = 14$) or a simple ($5 - 2 = 3$) equation that they had to judge as correct or incorrect. They rated the unpleasant pictures as less unpleasant following judgments of complex equations. The finding that a higher cognitive load attenuated affective responses was confirmed by fMRI measurements. The greater activation of cognitive brain circuits by the more complex equations decreased the activation of emotional brain circuits.

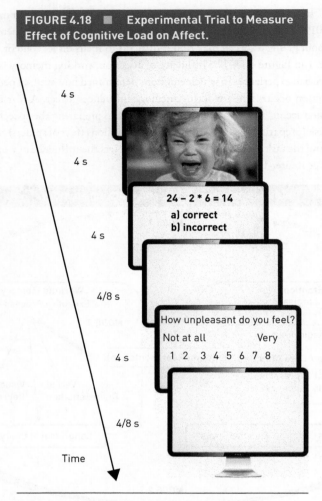

FIGURE 4.18 ■   Experimental Trial to Measure Effect of Cognitive Load on Affect.

4 s

4 s

24 – 2 * 6 = 14
a) correct
b) incorrect

4 s

4/8 s

How unpleasant do you feel?

Not at all   Very

1 2   3 4 5 6 7 8

4 s

4/8 s

Time

iStockphoto.com/antishock and iStockphoto.com/arnoaltix

Source: From "Turning down the emotional brain: An fMRI study of the effects of cognitive load on the processing of affective images," by L. F. Van Dillen et al., 2009, *Neuroimage, 45*, 1212–1219. https://doi.org/10.1016/j.neuroimage.2009.01.016

A subsequent study (van Dillen & van Steenbergen, 2018) revealed an interesting application of this finding. The investigators hypothesized that the reward-processing areas of the brain triggered by the reaction to food will partly depend on cognitive processes regulated in the prefrontal cortex. Pictures of high-calorie food did cause greater activation of reward-processing areas of the brain but only when cognitive load was low. As had occurred in the earlier study, cognitive load can turn down the emotional brain.

MODE 3 illustrates a third case in which emotional feelings are mental representations in working memory and therefore compete with other mental representations. Mikels and

Reuter-Lorenz (2019) refer to this mode as "affective working memory." It supports the integration of affective and cognitive processes as depicted by the bridge connecting emotion and working memory in Figure 4.17. Converging neural studies support the proposal that affective working memory actively holds a feeling in mind, as contrasted with merely passively experiencing the emotion. Research on math anxiety provides an example (Ashcraft & Krause, 2007). People with math anxiety waste working memory resources by attending to their anxiety.

Working Memory and Stress

If emotions influence working memory, it should not be surprising that stress has an impact. Acute stress responses occur due to activation of the hypothalamic-pituitary-adrenal axis in which the ultimate effects are the release of the hormone cortisol. Cortisol has been shown to reduce immediate short-term working memory capacity (Shields et al., 2015; Taverniers et al., 2010) but causes improvements in tasks measuring inhibition. Conversely, long-term chronic stress can reduce inhibition and its role in executive functions (Shields et al., 2015). In particular, combat stress (van Wingen et al., 2012), growing up in a high-stress environment (Evans & Schamberg, 2009), and the continued stress of caregiving (Mackenzie et al., 2009) have all been demonstrated to have significant negative effects on working memory.

Acute and chronic stress are thought to be the primary causes of both anxiety and major depressive disorders. Depression is one of the most common mental illnesses in the United States, with adults aged 18 to 25 suffering the highest rates. It appears that elevated cortisol levels are associated with these disorders, which unfortunately also results in severe working memory deficits in major depression (Hinkelmann et al., 2009). Rock and colleagues conducted a meta-analysis of 30 studies on depression and cognition in which they concluded that "current depression was associated with significant moderate deficits across all tasks within the domains of executive function, memory and attention" (Rock et al., 2013, p. 2034).

Unfortunately, the cognitive effects of depression are rarely targeted for treatment (Zuckerman et al., 2018; Pan et al., 2017). The primary treatment is pharmacotherapy, with various selective serotonin and norepinephrine inhibitors (Advokat et al., 2019). However, few drugs have been effective in treating the cognitive effects of depression. Two antidepressants—duloxetine and vortioxetine—have nonetheless demonstrated some success in treating working memory deficits in major depressive patients (Zuckerman et al., 2018; Pan et al., 2017).

In his APA award address for distinguished scientific applications of psychology, Steven Hollon (2020) argued that there is reason to believe that depression might be an evolved adaptation that serves to facilitate thinking about complex social issues until some sort of problem-solving resolution is found. Cognitive therapy works by attempting to make thinking

---

acute stress Symptoms that quickly develop but usually do not last long

chronic stress Emotional response to pressure suffered for a long period of time

meta-analysis A quantitative method to systematically evaluate the combined results of previous research

pharmacotherapy Medical treatment by using drugs

more efficient so as to facilitate the resolution of these conflicts. Although antidepressants can suppress symptoms, it is possible that they do so at the expense of failing to solve the underlying problems. Hollon (2020) proposes that this issue needs to be empirically resolved because medication is now so common and extended over time.

There has been increasing interest in how meditation is related to cognition and whether practicing meditation might improve cognition. Cognitive interventions, such as mindfulness meditation, have been used to reduce psychological stress and physical pain by modulating conscious access to information (Verdonk et al., 2020). Self-regulation of attention raises relevant information above the threshold of consciousness when it becomes relevant to the context. A review of research that measured the neurological components of event-related potentials demonstrated how the self-regulation of attention improved cognitive control, body awareness, and the regulation of emotion (Figure 4.19).

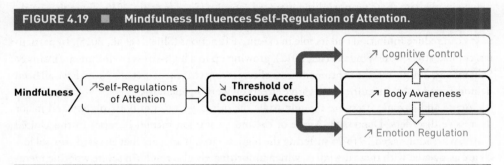

FIGURE 4.19 ■ Mindfulness Influences Self-Regulation of Attention.

Source: From "Toward a refined mindfulness model related to consciousness and based on ERP," by C. Verdonk et al., 2020, *Perspectives in Psychological Science*. Copyright 2011 by Annual Reviews. Reprinted by permission. https://doi.org/10.1177/1745691620906444

This interest stems from a series of research studies conducted by Tang and Posner (2009) on integrative body-mind training, a specific type of mindfulness meditation training developed in China. In their first major study, Tang and colleagues (2007) found that after only five days of 20-minute sessions, participants' executive control improved significantly compared to participants who were given standard relaxation training. The body-mind meditation group also had reduced cortisol release in response to stress and significant improvements in immune system responses. Figure 4.20 shows that the experimental (meditation) group released less cortisol than the control (relaxation) group when given a stressed-induced task. The difference between the two groups was even greater following additional training.

A review of research on the neuroscience of mindfulness meditation indicates that meditation training can induce long-term structural changes in brain areas associated with behaviors such as executive attention and emotion (Tang et al., 2015). The research also revealed that meditation can reduce the feelings of anxiety associated with stress and have protective effects on brain areas associated with cognition.

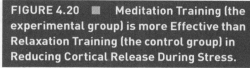

FIGURE 4.20 ■ **Meditation Training (the experimental group) is more Effective than Relaxation Training (the control group) in Reducing Cortical Release During Stress.**

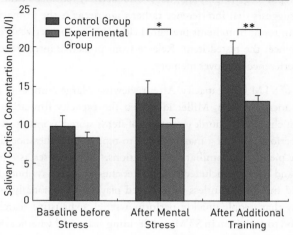

Source: From "Short-term meditation training improves attention and self-regulation," by Y. Y. Tang et al., 2007, *Proceedings of the National Academy of Sciences, 104*(43), 15152–15156. https://doi.org/10.1073/pnas.0707678104

Note: * indicates a $p < .05$ and ** indicates a $p < .01$ level of significance

PHOTO 4.4 Meditation reduces anxiety caused by stress.

Getty Images/Yuri Nunes / EyeEm

SUMMARY

Short-term memory has several limitations that distinguish it from long-term memory. First of all, STM results in rapid forgetting. Items that are not actively rehearsed can be lost in 20 to 30 seconds. Evidence suggests that interference rather than decay is the primary cause of forgetting. Interference can result from items presented either before (proactive interference) or after (retroactive interference) the tested item. Release from proactive interference illustrates how the reduction of interference improves memory.

Another limitation of STM is its capacity. After reviewing a large number of findings on absolute judgment and memory span, Miller identified the capacity limitation as consisting of approximately seven chunks. A chunk is a group of items stored as a unit in LTM. De Groot argued that the superior ability of a master player to reproduce a chessboard is a result of the ability to group the pieces into familiar configurations. Using pauses as a measure of chunk boundaries, Chase and Simon concluded that master chess players have both more chunks and larger chunks stored in LTM than less-experienced players. Occasionally, we need to search STM. Results show that people quickly perform a serial, exhaustive search by sequentially making a comparison to each item in STM and deciding at the end whether there is a match.

Baddeley's working memory model provides a more complete account of STM by proposing a phonological loop for maintaining and manipulating acoustic information, a visuospatial sketchpad for maintaining and manipulating visual/spatial information, and a central executive for making decisions. His subsequent revision of the model added an episodic buffer to integrate different memory codes, such as acoustic and visual codes. The primary function of the central executive is to control attention by updating, shifting, and inhibition. Disengaging from irrelevant or wrong information is central in determining fluid intelligence. The decline in memory span as processing demands increase shows the tradeoff between the maintenance and processing requirements of working memory.

An instructional consequence of a limited-capacity working memory is that instruction should be designed so it does not overload this limited capacity. Integrating text with diagrams is an example. Emotion can make it more difficult to focus on the content of working memory, and focusing on the content of working memory can reduce the influence of emotion. Both content and emotional reactions compete for its limited capacity. Applications of the neuroscience of working memory include treating stress and depression with antidepressants and using meditation training to reduce anger, fatigue, and anxiety while improving executive control.

RECOMMENDED READING

Baddeley's (2001) Distinguished Scientist Address to the American Psychological Association presented an impressive list of studies that fit within his working memory model. A meta-analysis contrasted different interventions for training executive function skills in typical and nontypical developing children (Takacs & Kassai, 2019). A related meta-analysis found that successfully trained skills often failed to transfer to other learning tasks (Kassai et al., 2019). The lack of transfer supports Doebel's (2020) argument that it is necessary to study how executive functions emerge to accomplish specific goals. One example is the combination of executive functions and automaticity to support reading comprehension (Kieffer & Christodoulou, 2019). Another example is the use of shifting to compare multiple perspectives and inhibition to reject faulty perspectives in mathematics and science classes (Vosniadou et al., 2018). A meta-analysis of fluid intelligence revealed that it correlated more highly with mathematics than with reading and with complex skills than with basic skills (Peng et al., 2019). Sweller et al. (2019) describe the history and broad impact of cognitive load theory. An entire issue of *Educational Psychology Review* was devoted to articles on synthesizing cognitive load and self regulation (de Bruin et al., 2020). Clinical models informed by cognitive neuroscience are aiding in understanding how cognitive control influences depression (Grahek et al., 2018).

5   LONG-TERM MEMORY

LEARNING OBJECTIVES

1. Explain how the Atkinson-Shiffrin model contributed to understanding memory.

2. Distinguish between episodic, semantic, and procedural memory.

3. Describe how neuroscience has advanced the understanding of memory.

4. Provide examples of techniques for improving the acquisition, retention, and retrieval of information.

What would life be like if we did not have a normally functioning long-term memory (LTM)? The movie *Memento* provides an answer. The story is about a man who, because of a brutal attack on him and his wife, is unable to store new events in LTM. His life's ambition is to seek revenge on his attacker, and he attempts to function by taking pictures of his world—his car, his motel, his friends, his enemies. Notes or pictures and tattoos on his body serve as external memories of his present life. The movie's audience shares his difficulty as both the man and the audience use flashbacks to try to make sense of his life.

Although it is difficult for most of us to imagine the struggles of a person with a severely impaired memory, we all have envied someone with an extremely good memory and wished that we could improve our own memory. For students, this is particularly true at exam time. If only they could remember everything that they studied, they would do so much better. The need to remember the material after the exam may seem less pressing, but even in this case, a good memory is quite beneficial.

One of the best ways to remember material over a life span is simply to spend considerable time studying it (Bahrick & Hall, 1991). Students who took college-level mathematics courses at or above the level of calculus had excellent retention of high school algebra for nearly 50 years. The performance of students who did equally well in a high school algebra course but took no college-level mathematics courses declined to near chance levels over the same period. Surprisingly, academic measures such as Scholastic Aptitude Test (SAT) scores and grades have little impact on retention (Bahrick & Hall, 1991; Semb & Ellis, 1994).

To retain information, we have to get it out of short-term memory (STM) and enter it into a more permanent store called **LTM**. This chapter summarizes some of the research on LTM—such as how we enter information into LTM and how it is tested. The first section describes ways in which information can be transferred from a temporary to a more permanent store by revisiting the Atkinson and Shiffrin model. The next section distinguishes among three components of LTM—episodic memory, semantic memory, and procedural memory. The final two sections discuss the neuroscience of LTM and applications regarding the acquisition, retention, and retrieval of information.

THE ATKINSON-SHIFFRIN MODEL

Transferring Information to Long-Term Memory

Let's return to the Atkinson and Shiffrin (1968, 1971) model introduced in the previous chapter. LTM has two crucial advantages over STM. First, the rate of forgetting is much slower for LTM. Second, LTM is unlimited in its capacity. Although there is a limit to the amount of information that we can maintain in STM, we will never reach the point where we cannot learn new information because LTM is full.

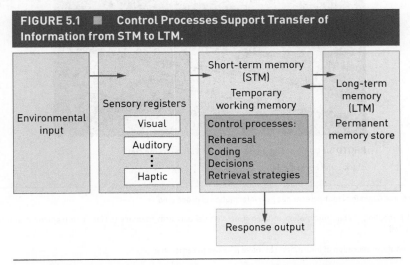

FIGURE 5.1 ■ Control Processes Support Transfer of Information from STM to LTM.

Source: "The control of short-term memory," by R. C. Atkinson & R. M. Shiffrin, 1971, *Scientific American, 225*, 82–90. https://doi.org/10.1038/scientificamerican0871-82

long-term memory (LTM) Memory that has no capacity limits and lasts from minutes to an entire lifetime

Nevertheless, it is not always easy to enter new information into LTM. Atkinson and Shiffrin proposed several control processes that could be used in an attempt to learn new information. As is shown in Figure 5.1, **control processes** are strategies that a person uses to facilitate learning. They include the acquisition strategies of rehearsal, coding, and imaging.

Rehearsal is the repetition of information—either aloud or silently—over and over until it is learned. You may have used rehearsal to learn your social security or phone number.

Coding attempts to place the information to be remembered in the context of additional, easily retrievable information, such as a mnemonic phrase or sentence. For example, many of us learned that the lines of a treble clef are E, G, B, D, F by remembering the sentence "Every good boy does fine." (Photo 5.1)

Imaging involves creating visual images to remember verbal information. This is an old memory trick—it was even recommended by Cicero in ancient Rome for learning long lists or speeches by attaching topics to mental locations, such as the coliseum (Photo 5.2). One could then visually navigate these imagined locations, which serve as reminders for the associated information.

PHOTO 5.1 Using coding to learn the lines of the treble clef.

istock.com/carloscastilla

---

control process A strategy that determines how information is processed

rehearsal Repeating verbal information to keep it active in short-term memory (STM) or to transfer it to long-term memory (LTM)

coding Semantic elaboration of information to make it easier to remember

imaging Creating visual images to make material easier to remember

PHOTO 5.2 Using locations as images in the method of loci.

istockphoto.com/sborisov

This list could be further expanded, but rehearsal, coding, and imaging are three of the primary ways of learning. Because there are so many control processes to study, Atkinson and Shiffrin (1968) chose to focus their research on only one—verbal rehearsal.

Verbal Rehearsal and Learning

Verbal rehearsal is usually considered a form of **rote learning** because it involves simply repeating information over and over until we think we have learned it. It can be useful when the material is rather abstract, which makes it difficult to use strategies such as coding or imaging. The task designed by Atkinson and Shiffrin (1968) required the learning of abstract, meaningless material and therefore encouraged the use of rehearsal.

The undergraduates in the experiment tried to learn associations between a two-digit number (the stimulus) and a letter (the response). The paired associates included items such as 31-*Q*, 42-*B*, and 53-*A*. Each pair was shown for 3 seconds, followed by 3 seconds before the next trial. Interspersed throughout these study trials were test trials, in which only the two-digit number was presented and the subject was asked to supply the letter that had accompanied it earlier. One of the variables in the experiment was the number of trials that occurred between the study and test trials. For instance, there are two trials between the study and test trials in the sequence 31-*Q*, 42-*B*, 53-*A,* and 31-. Some associates were tested on the very next trial and others after a delay that could last as long as 17 trials.

---

rote learning Learning by repetition rather than through understanding

Atkinson and Shiffrin interpreted the data from this experiment by proposing a model in which verbal rehearsal was used to learn the associates. They assumed that the students maintained a fixed number of items in STM and that these items were rehearsed whenever the student was not viewing a new item or responding during a test trial. The effect of rehearsal was to transfer information about that item into LTM. Atkinson and Shiffrin proposed that learning increased as a function of the number of trials over which the item was rehearsed. Once the item was no longer rehearsed, information about that particular item decreased as each succeeding item was presented for study. The predicted probability of a correct response, therefore, depended on both the number of trials in which the item was rehearsed and the number of intervening trials that occurred before the test trial.

Rehearsal and the Serial Position Effect

An easy way to test the claim that verbal rehearsal results in learning is to ask someone to rehearse out loud. The experimenter can then count the times each item is rehearsed and determine whether the probability of recalling an item is related to the number of rehearsals. A task designed by Rundus (1971) was exactly of this type. He presented lists of 20 nouns to undergraduates at Stanford. The words were presented one at a time for a period of 5 seconds each. Rundus instructed the students to study by repeating aloud words on the list during each 5-second interval. They were free to rehearse any word they desired as long as their rehearsal filled the intervals. After the presentation of the list, the students tried to recall the words in any order.

Figure 5.2 shows the results of the experiment. The probability of recalling a word depended on its position in the list. Words at the beginning and words at the end were easier to recall than words in the middle of the list. The U shape of the recall curve, which is called a **serial position effect**, is often obtained in recall experiments. The better recall of words at the beginning of the list is called a **primacy effect**, and the better recall of words at the end of the list is called a **recency effect**.

The curve showing the number of times each word was rehearsed illustrates that words at the beginning of the list were rehearsed more often than the other words. This is because there is time to rehearse several words between items on the list, and the initial items are the only ones available for rehearsal at the beginning.

The relation between the rehearsal and the recall curves reveals that the primacy effect can be explained by Atkinson and Shiffrin's theory. Because early words were rehearsed more often than the other words, they should have a higher probability of being retrieved from LTM. This explanation implies that the primacy effect should be eliminated if all the words on the list are rehearsed equally often. In fact, when subjects were instructed to rehearse each word equally often by rehearsing only the displayed word, the primacy effect disappeared (Fischler et al., 1970).

---

serial position effect The ability to recall words at the beginning and end of a list better than words in the middle of the list

primacy effect The better recall of words at the beginning of a list

recency effect The better recall of words at the end of a list

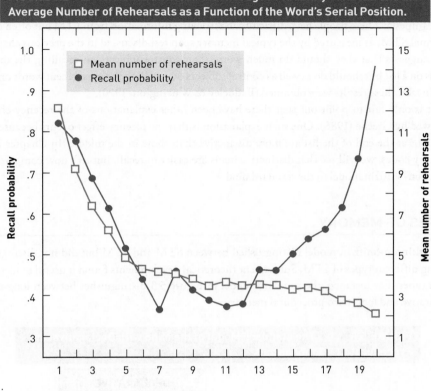

FIGURE 5.2 ■ **Relation between the Average Probability of Recall and the Average Number of Rehearsals as a Function of the Word's Serial Position.**

Source: "Analysis of rehearsal processes in free recall," by D. Rundus, 1971, *Journal of Experimental Psychology, 89*, 63–77. https://doi.org/10.1037/h0031185

Although the number of rehearsals can predict the primacy effect, it does not predict the recency effect. People were very good at recalling the words at the end of the list, even though they did not rehearse them any more than the words in the middle of the list. The recency effect is often explained by the proposal that the words at the end of the list are still in STM when a person begins the recall. The students in Rundus's experiment recalled the words immediately after the last item was presented; it is therefore reasonable to assume that the words they had just seen were still available in STM.

We learned from the Peterson and Peterson experiment discussed in Chapter 4 that information is rapidly lost from STM if people have to perform another task. If the recency effect is caused by retrieving the most recent items from STM, it should be eliminated if a person performs another task before recalling the items. Subjects in an experiment designed by Postman and Phillips (1965) had to perform an arithmetic task for 30 seconds before they tried to recall a list of words. The arithmetic task was successful in eliminating the recency effect, implying that the words at the end of the list had decayed from STM.

Another piece of evidence for the proposal that the primacy effect is caused by retrieval from LTM and the recency effect is caused by retrieval from STM comes from patients who suffer from amnesia. These people have difficulty in retrieving information from LTM but often have a normal STM, as measured by the typical memory span test discussed in the previous chapter. This suggests that they should do much worse than control subjects on recalling the initial words on a list but should do as well as control subjects on recalling the most recent words on the list. In fact, these results were obtained (Baddeley & Warrington, 1970).

It is only fair to point out that there have been other explanations of the recency effect, reviewed by Greene (1986). One such explanation is that the recency effect occurs because the positions at the end of the list are more distinctive than those in the middle. In Chapter 7 on memory codes, we will see that distinctive items are easier to recall, but let's now compare the Atkinson-Shiffrin model to the standard model.

TYPES OF MEMORY

The Atkinson-Shiffrin model distinguished between STM and LTM but did not distinguish among different types of LTM. Subsequent theoretical developments found it useful to identify these types. For instance, the standard model in Figure 5.3 distinguishes between long-term declarative and long-term procedural memory.

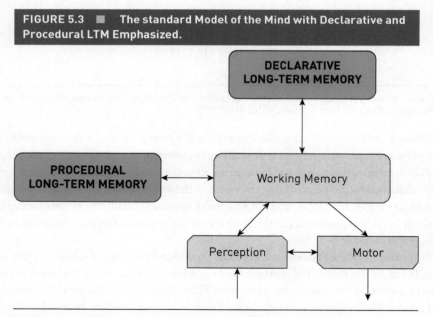

FIGURE 5.3 ■ **The standard Model of the Mind with Declarative and Procedural LTM Emphasized.**

Source: Based on "A standard model of the mind: Toward a common computational framework across artificial intelligence, cognitive science, neuroscience, and robotics," by J. E. Laird et al., 2017, *AI Magazine, 38*, 13–26. https://doi.org/10.1609/aimag.v38i4.2744

Declarative memory stores facts and concepts and can be further divided into episodic and semantic memory. Endel Tulving argued that it is important to distinguish between personal facts and general facts by proposing the personal facts are stored in episodic memory and general facts are stored in semantic memory (Tulving, 1972, 1985, 2002). **Episodic memory** contains recollections of personal experiences (Photo 5.3). It provides a record of what people have done, such as where and when they attended high school. **Semantic memory** contains general knowledge, such as a canary is a bird and the sum of 7 and 8 is 15. Episodic memory is therefore more autobiographical; it contains the kind of information we would record in a detailed diary. Semantic information is more general and contains the kind of information we would read in a book. The other emphasized component in Figure 5.3, **Procedural memory**, stores actions, skills, and operations for activities, such as typing.

PHOTO 5.3 Episodic memory records personal experiences.

istock.com/catscandotcom

The distinction between episodic memory, semantic memory, and procedural memory has been helpful in developing theories of LTM, as explained in this section.

---

declarative memory Memory for facts and concepts

episodic memory Stores specific events, including when and where they occurred

semantic memory Stores general knowledge not associated with a particular context

procedural memory Memory for actions, skills, and operations

Episodic Memory

Episodic memory differs from semantic memory because it stores specific events rather than general knowledge. This distinction is depicted in the hierarchical model shown in Figure 5.4. Semantic memory is context free. You know that 3 x 7 = 21. Episodic memory provides contextual detail that is depicted by the lower levels in the hierarchy. For instance, you may recall the name of the teacher and the grade level in which you learned the multiplication table. You *know* concepts but sometimes *remember* the details in which you used those concepts (Tulving, 1985; Umanath & Coane, 2020).

FIGURE 5.4 ■ Distinction between Episodic and Semantic Memory.

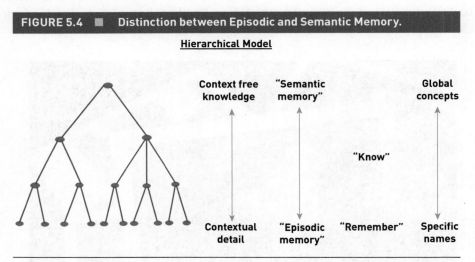

Source: "Levels of processing: Past, present . . . and future?" by F. I. M. Craik, 2002, *Memory, 10*, 305–318. https://doi.org/10.1080/09658210244000135

One of the remarkable characteristics of episodic memory is that there are a few people who remember almost everything that occurred in their lives. In the spring of 2000, a 34-year-old woman named Jill Price emailed James McGaugh about a memory problem. She revealed that she could recall on any date, as far back as 1974, the day of the week, what she was doing that day, and if anything of great importance occurred. It was a problem she said because her exceptional memory was nonstop, uncontrollable, and exhausting (McGaugh, 2017; Parker et al., 2006). Jill Price contacted James McGaugh because McGaugh's group at the University of California, Irvine comprises a prominent research center that has studied highly superior autobiographical memory, typically measured by the ability to associate dates and events.

In one study of this exceptional ability, researchers asked people with superior autobiographical memory and control participants to retrieve both autobiographical (the first time you drove a car, the last time you took a train) and semantic memories (examples of vegetables). Participants with superior autobiographical memories had faster and more vivid access to these memories but had only normal access to semantic memories (Santangelo et al., 2018). Brain scans using FMRI revealed that the superior autobiographical memory participants had increased connectivity of the prefrontal cortex with the hippocampus, a region well known to be involved in memory.

Personality differences also likely account for superior autobiographical memories. Individuals with this ability score high on a test of excessive-compulsive tendencies, within the range of people who are classified with obsessive-compulsive disorders. High-scoring participants provided more consistent autobiographical details when retested one month later (LePort et al., 2017). These findings suggest that people with highly superior autobiographical memory may have an implicit tendency to habitually reflect on previous events.

Episodic memory does more than help us recall the past; it also helps us imagine the future (Conway et al., 2016). Simulations of future events rely extensively on the retrieved details of specific past experiences that are recombined into novel events (Schacter & Madore, 2016). A link between past and future thinking is also established by a high correlation between how detailed people are in recalling the past and in imagining the future (MacLeod, 2016).

Remembering the recent past and imagining the near future occur within what Conway and his coauthors label the "remembering-imagining system." Details rapidly fade within several days within this system for both the remembered past and the imagined future. Detailed episodic memories can nonetheless influence future thinking by encouraging people to recall these details (Schacter & Madore, 2016) by using techniques such as those used in the cognitive interview procedure (Fisher & Geiselman, 2019) discussed later in this chapter.

Semantic Memory

Semantic memory, based on general knowledge, also influences future thinking. The clearest and least surprising difference between past and future thinking is that people think about the future more abstractly than they think about the past (MacLeod, 2016). Future thinking contains more common themes and less sensory detail than the past. Semantic memory influences the imagined future when it involves more general information such as goals (Schacter & Madore, 2016) and is unfamiliar rather than familiar (Wang et al., 2016). Realistic constraints also affect future simulations. Although it is fun to imagine how to spend a big lottery prize after buying tickets, it is important to remember that the probability of winning is extremely low (Conway et al., 2016).

The influence of both episodic and semantic memory on imagining the future has implications for well-being and mental health, as revealed in MacLeod's (2016) extensive review. A lack of specificity in future thoughts and past experiences has been found in a range of clinical groups, including schizophrenia, depression, post-traumatic stress disorder, bereaved partners experiencing grief, and autistic spectrum disorder. These findings emphasize the importance of semantic information in future thinking, possibly by providing a general framework within which episodic information is used to construct the future (MacLeod, 2016).

Another research area in which the distinction between episodic and semantic memory is helpful applies to variations in memory tests. Traditional tests of memory, such as recognition and recall, measure episodic memory. However, traditional tests are not the only way to evaluate a person's memory. Look for a moment at the word fragment in Figure 5.5. Can you identify the word? People are more successful at identifying very difficult word fragments if they are previously shown a list of words that includes the answers to the fragments (such as the word *METAL* for this example). The fact that the list is helpful suggests that people have a memory of some of the words on the list—indicating that this task could be used as a test for memory.

Source: "Amnesic syndrome: Consolidation or retrieval?" by E. K. Warrington & L. Weiskrantz, 1970, *Nature, 228*, 628–630. https://www.nature.com/articles/228628a0. Copyright 1970 Macmillan Magazines Ltd. Reprinted by permission.

You may believe that this memory test is less direct than the recall and recognition tests discussed in the previous section. Recall and recognition tests are called **direct memory tests** because they explicitly refer to a particular event in a person's past. The directions ask people to recall or recognize events that occurred earlier. In contrast, instructions for **indirect memory tests** refer only to the current task and do not refer to prior events (Richardson-Klavehn & Bjork, 1988). People performing the word-fragment task only have to identify the word, not judge whether they had previously seen the word during the experiment. One reason for distinguishing between these two types of tests is that what we learn about a person's memory depends on how we test it.

This point was strikingly illustrated in a study by Warrington and Weiskrantz (1970) at the National Hospital in London. They compared patients with severe amnesia with control patients who were closely matched for age and intelligence. The comparison involved four tests of memory for word lists. The recall test required a verbal recall of the words. The recognition-memory test required a yes or no decision regarding whether a test word was on the list. The word-fragment test required the identification of a word fragment. The correct word appeared on the list, and the fragments were difficult to identify if subjects had not previously seen the list. The initial-letters test contained the first three letters of a word that had appeared on the list, and the subjects had to generate a word that began with those three letters.

The amnesic subjects did significantly worse than the controls on both the recognition and recall tests. However, they did not differ from the controls on the word-fragment or initial-letters tests. They were just as likely as the controls to successfully use the words that they had seen on the word list. The lack of difference on these two tests occurred even though the amnesic patients often did not remember that they had seen the word list and approached the tests as a kind of guessing game (Warrington & Weiskrantz, 1968). But the influence of the word list on their answers indicated that they still had a memory of many words on the list.

According to this distinction, direct memory tests, which require recall or recognition of material that occurred earlier in the experiment, measure episodic memory (Schacter, 1987). Subjects are asked to recall items (such as a list of words) from a particular time and place.

---

direct memory test A test that asks people to recall or recognize past events

indirect memory test A test that does not explicitly ask about past events but is influenced by the memory of those events

Indirect memory tests, such as word identification or word completion, measure semantic memory. These tests depend only on our general knowledge of words and do not require that we associate the words with a particular time and place.

Procedural Memory

Others have argued that indirect tests differ from direct tests because they depend more on procedural memory (McKoon et al., 1986). Procedural memory is memory for actions, skills, and operations, whereas both episodic and semantic memory are concerned with factual information. Factual information seems more susceptible to forgetting than procedural information, as evidenced by amnesic patients who have difficulty recalling facts but do well at learning and retaining motor skills (Warrington & Weiskrantz, 1970).

An example of a skill that depends on procedural memory is the improvement in reading speed that occurs when rereading the same passage. Musen et al. (1990) studied improvement in reading speed for both amnesic patients and those without amnesia and found that amnesic patients increased their speed as much as those without amnesia when rereading the passage. However, amnesic patients were markedly impaired in their ability to correctly answer multiple-choice questions about the content of the passage. Once again, there were no differences between groups for an indirect test of memory (improved reading skill) but large differences for a direct (multiple-choice) test of memory.

The next chapter on Action describes how procedures support the execution of many different types of actions.

NEUROSCIENCE OF LONG-TERM MEMORY

Early Investigations

The exact nature of how memories are represented in the brain remains somewhat of a mystery, but neuroscientists are making steady progress in understanding the neurobiology of memory. Let's start with a brief history, beginning with the story of Karl Lashley.

Karl Lashley spent some 33 years in his search for the *engram*. The engram is a hypothetical construct in which memories are contained within the brain (Lashley, 1950). Lashley's research was conducted by lesioning the brains of rats to examine their degree of memory loss. Unfortunately for Lashley, he was never able to find a single locus in the rat brain in which memories resided. However, Lashley was correct in thinking that there are locations of the brain critical to memory.

Lashley would further contribute to our understanding of the neurobiology of memory through his doctoral student, Donald Hebb. Hebb (1949) introduced the idea that memories are formed via changes in the connections of neurons (Photo 5.4). This process is often referred to as *Hebbian learning* (Hebb, 1949) and forms the cornerstone of modern theories of memory, such as the consolidation of learning.

---

procedural memory Memory for actions, skills, and operations

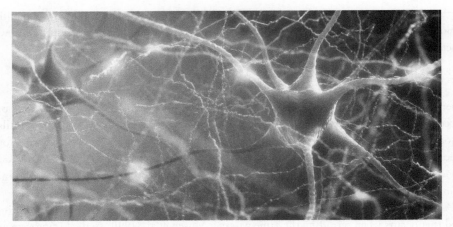

PHOTO 5.4 Electrical pulses across interconnected neurons.

istockphoto.com/ktsimage

Following their work, a history-making accident led to a dramatic change in our understanding of memory. Henry Molaison (widely known as patient H. M.) suffered from intractable seizures for much of his life. In 1953, Molaison underwent neurosurgery to treat his seizures in which his left and right medial temporal lobes were removed. Following his surgery, Molaison suffered from severe anterograde amnesia in which he was no longer able to form new memories. He also suffered a temporally graded retrograde amnesia in which he had little to no memory of the previous one to two years, with diminished memories up to 10 years prior (Scoville & Milner, 1957).

Remarkably, while Molaison was unable to explicitly remember anything following his surgery, he was still able to learn motor skills. Molaison's STM was also normal. These discoveries demonstrated several remarkable pieces of evidence regarding human memory. First, STM and LTM are accomplished in distinct regions of the brain, with the medial temporal lobes and the hippocampal complex critical to the formation of longer-term memories. Second, there are different pathways in the brain for long-term memories that require conscious retrieval from episodic memory rather than the performance of motor skills (Squire & Wixted, 2015).

Encoding and Retrieval

One of the other significant contributions from studies of Molaison's brain is understanding the role of the medial temporal lobe complex in memory (medial means toward the middle). A particularly important structure is the hippocampus, located in a central region of the brain where it can bind together diverse information (Photo 5.5).

The medial temporal lobe also occupies surrounding regions including the perirhinal, entorhinal, and parahippocampal areas shown in Figure 5.6. The amygdala interacts with the

---

anterograde amnesia Inability to form new memories

retrograde amnesia Partial loss of previous memories

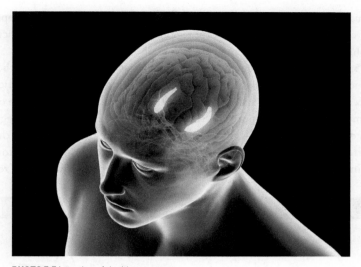

PHOTO 5.5 Location of the hippocampus.

Getty Images/ SEBASTIAN KAULITZKI/SCIENCE PHOTO LIBRARY

FIGURE 5.6 ■ Regions of the Medial Temporal Lobe.

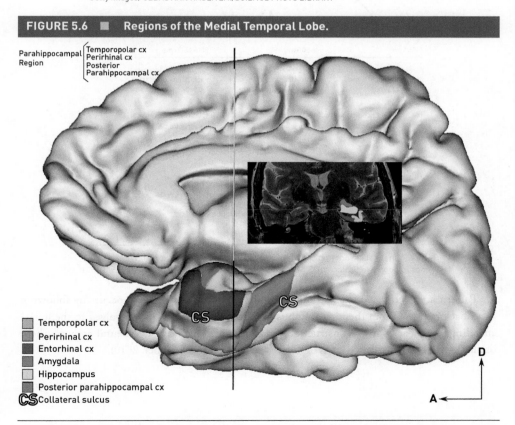

Parahippocampal Region
- Temporopolar cx
- Perirhinal cx
- Posterior Parahippocampal cx

- Temporopolar cx
- Perirhinal cx
- Entorhinal cx
- Amygdala
- Hippocampus
- Posterior parahippocampal cx
- **CS** Collateral sulcus

Source: "Self-awareness and the medial temporal lobe in neurodegenerative diseases," by C. Chavoix & R. Insausti, 2017, *Neuroscience & Biobehavioral Reviews, 78*, 1–12. https://doi.org/10.1016/j.neubiorev.2017.04.015

hippocampus in the processing of emotional memories (Phelps, 2004). The hippocampus is reciprocally connected to numerous cortical regions through the cortex. Of particular importance are connections to the frontal and parietal lobes.

Figure 5.7 illustrates the sequence of brain activities that are triggered when reminders such as a photograph, a song, or a familiar smell bring back vivid episodic memories (Staresina & Wimber, 2019). During the first 500 ms, a memory cue—a scene of a kitchen in this example—activates memories in the hippocampus. The activation triggers pattern completion during the next 500–1500 ms of a prior encoding that occurred in the posterior parietal cortex and sensory cortices. Pattern completion adds information from memory (such as eating a bagel for breakfast) and gives rise to the subjective experience of recollection.

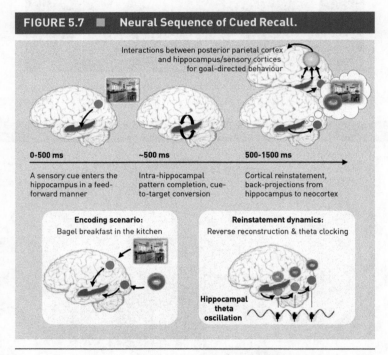

FIGURE 5.7 ■ Neural Sequence of Cued Recall.

Interactions between posterior parietal cortex and hippocampus/sensory cortices for goal-directed behaviour

| 0-500 ms | ~500 ms | 500-1500 ms |

A sensory cue enters the hippocampus in a feed-forward manner

Intra-hippocampal pattern completion, cue-to-target conversion

Cortical reinstatement, back-projections from hippocampus to neocortex

Encoding scenario:
Bagel breakfast in the kitchen

Reinstatement dynamics:
Reverse reconstruction & theta clocking

Hippocampal theta oscillation

Source: "A neural chronometry of memory recall," by B. Staresina & M. Wimber, 2019, *Trends in Cognitive Sciences, 23,* 1071–1085. https://doi.org/10.1016/j.tics.2019.09.011

Pattern completion occurs by reinstating the original experience. It occurs by following a feedback pathway from the hippocampus back to the cortical regions involved in the initial encoding. This backward reconstruction is accompanied by a burst of neural activity (theta oscillations) in the reactivated areas of the cortex (Staresina & Wimber, 2019).

---

pattern completion A partial activation of a memory trace activates associated information

Consolidation

The process by which memories are created and stored by individual neurons is referred to as **consolidation**. At the most basic level, memory consolidation resembles Hebbian learning in that the connections between neurons are strengthened through a process known as **long-term potentiation**. The neuron transmitting a neural impulse is referred to as the *presynaptic neuron,* and the neuron receiving the neural impulse is referred to as the *postsynaptic neuron* (Figure 5.8)

FIGURE 5.8 ■   The Synapse between a Presynaptic and a Postsynaptic Neuron.

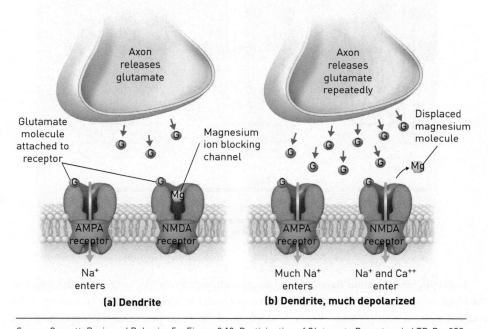

Source: Garrett, Brain and Behavior 5e, Figure 2.12: Participation of Glutamate Receptors in LTP. Pg. 355.

The strengthening of connections between two neurons results from the simultaneous activation of the presynaptic and postsynaptic neurons. Long-term potentiation alters neurotransmission that results in a stable memory trace (Cooke, 2006). The initial synaptic consolidation occurs relatively quickly—within hours of an experience; over the longer-term, memories undergo a process known as systems consolidation (Dudai, 2004).

consolidation The process of stabilizing a memory trace following initial acquisition

long-term potentiation Strengthening of synapses that result from the simultaneous activation of presynaptic and postsynaptic neurons

Standard consolidation theory proposes that all declarative memories are temporarily held in the hippocampus and gradually transferred to the cortex over time to become fully independent of the hippocampus. The encoding of perceptual, motor, and cognitive information initially occurs in specialized areas of the cortex. The hippocampus then integrates these distributed experiences and combines them into a coherent memory trace (Frankland & Bontempi, 2005). As indicated in Figure 5.9, successive reactivation of the neural connections between the hippocampus and the cortex strengthens the combined memory trace. Continued strengthening of the cortical connections enables the new memories to become independent of the hippocampus.

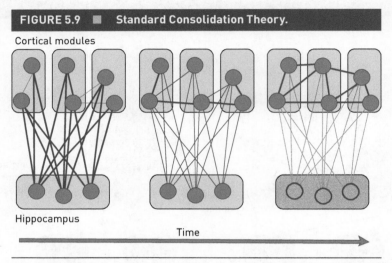

FIGURE 5.9 ■ Standard Consolidation Theory.

Cortical modules

Hippocampus

Time

Source: "The organization of recent and remote memories," by P. W. Frankland & B. Bontempi, 2005, *Nature Reviews Neuroscience, 6,* 119–130. https://doi.org/10.1038/nrn1607

However, investigations have shown that only semantic memories are truly independent of the hippocampus and stored entirely in the cortex (Nadel & Moscovitch, 1997), leading to the establishment of **multiple trace theory**. Multiple trace theory proposes that the hippocampus is critical for the retrieval of episodic memories and that each time memories are retrieved, they are strengthened and potentially altered through *reconsolidation.*

The strengthening of episodic memories by reconsolidation occurs through contextual binding that integrates a memory with the context in which it occurs. The hippocampus receives information from various regions of the brain, including the ventral "what" pathway and the dorsal "where" pathway that was discussed in Chapter 2. It also receives emotional information from the amygdala. The process of pattern completion combines this information into a single episodic memory that is eventually stored entirely in the cortex.

---

multiple trace theory Episodic memories continue to be more dependent on the hippocampus than semantic memories

Memories can be strengthened during sleep by a method referred to as **targeted memory reactivation**. The method involves presenting learning-related stimuli during sleep to reactivate memories and facilitate consolidation (Paller et al., 2021). Figure 5.10a illustrates the method. Before sleep, participants learn new information that is associated with a specific stimulus, such as the sound of a cat. During sleep, the associated stimulus is played to reactivate the memory without disrupting sleep. Following sleep, memory is tested to determine whether the reactivation improves memory retrieval. As indicated in Figure 5.10b, the presentation of either an associated odor (Rasch et al., 2007) or an associated sound (Rudoy et al., 2009) reduced the amount of forgetting during sleep.

FIGURE 5.10 ■ Targeted Memory Reactivation Paradigm.

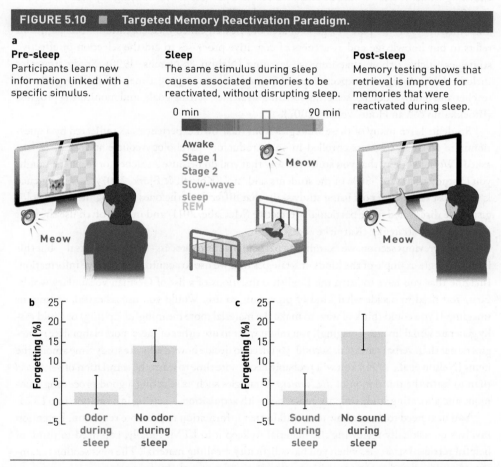

a

Pre-sleep
Participants learn new information linked with a specific simulus.

Sleep
The same stimulus during sleep causes associated memories to be reactivated, without disrupting sleep.

Post-sleep
Memory testing shows that retrieval is improved for memories that were reactivated during sleep.

Source: "Memory and sleep: How sleep cognition can change the waking mind for the better," by K. A. Paller et al., 2021, *Annual Review of Psychology, 72,* 123–150. https://doi.org/10.1146/annurev-psych-010419-050815

---

targeted memory reactivation The presentation of stimuli during sleep to reactivate and consolidate memories

A meta-analysis of studies of 91 experiments revealed that targeted memory reactivation improved memory across multiple domains, including spatial learning, associative learning, language acquisition, and skill learning (Hu et al., 2020). This effect was most clearly evident during Stages 2 and 3 of non-rapid eye movement (NREM) sleep. It was not effective during REM sleep or during wakefulness. The authors conclude that these studies show the most promise for using targeted memory reactivation for boosting language acquisition and for facilitating skill learning.

APPLICATIONS

Learning while we sleep would be an added bonus, but most of our learning depends on acquiring effective strategies to learn while we are awake. The control processes discussed by Atkinson and Shiffrin (1971) are part of a general area of research called metacognition. **Metacognition** refers to our knowledge and awareness of cognitive processes to aid the selection of effective strategies, such as those that improve learning (Nelson & Narens, 1990). Study strategies include determining the expectations of the teacher, managing time, interacting with the teacher and fellow students, selecting learning strategies, setting goals, and monitoring progress (Broekkamp & Van Hout-Wolters, 2007).

Students learn many of these strategies from their own experiences, as indicated by a questionnaire given to students enrolled in an introductory psychology course at UCLA. When asked "Would you say that you study the way that you do because a teacher (or teachers) taught you to study that way?" 80% of the students said "no" (Kornell & Bjork, 2007). A consequence is that most students report using study skills that differ from the ones that cognitive psychologists have discovered to be particularly effective (McCabe, 2011) and in fact, often use the least effective study strategies (Karpicke et al., 2009).

In the previous section, we examined a particular control process—verbal rehearsal—but this is only a single example of the kinds of strategies that we use to acquire and retrieve information. Imagine that you have to learn the English translations of a list of German vocabulary words. First, you need to decide what kind of processing to use. Would you use rehearsal, coding, or imaging? If you could think of ways to make the material more meaningful (coding) or could easily generate visual images (imaging), you might want to use either of these more elaborative strategies rather than verbal rehearsal. Second, you need to decide how to allocate study time among the items (Nelson et al., 1994). You will probably need more time to learn the translation of *der Gipfel* than to learn the translation of *die Kamera*. Strategies such as selecting a good processing technique and allocating study time are concerned with **acquisition**—getting information into LTM.

You next need to decide how to maintain that information to promote **retention**. Retention involves occasionally reviewing the material to keep it in LTM. Finally, you need to think of helpful **retrieval** strategies when you have difficulty recalling material. The next sections examine strategies related to the acquisition, retention, and retrieval of information.

---

metacognition Awareness of how our cognitive processes can improve information-processing strategies

acquisition Storage of information in long-term memory (LTM)

retention Maintaining information in long-term memory (LTM)

retrieval Recalling information from long-term memory (LTM)

Acquisition

Acquiring good acquisition strategies depends on our ability to judge how well we have learned the material. For example, determining which kind of processing is most effective requires that we recognize that we learned more from some strategies than from others. We saw that Atkinson and Shiffrin included three acquisition strategies in their model—rehearsal, coding, and imaging. They chose to study rehearsal, but is this the most effective one? As will be shown in the next two chapters, elaborative strategies such as coding and imaging are typically more successful than rehearsal.

Can people who do not know this research choose a good acquisition strategy by using their ability to judge that one strategy is more effective than another? A potential hurdle is that judgments of learning are often inaccurate if they are made shortly after studying an item because learning may only be temporary. Judgments of learning are also often based on variables unrelated to learning, such as font size (Rhodes & Castel, 2008). We may be very confident that we have learned some material immediately after studying it, only to discover that we can't later recall it (Atkinson, 1972a, 1972b). For this reason, it is best to delay judgments of learning until we are more certain that learning is relatively permanent. For students, this often involves testing one's own memory after studying to accurately assess learning.

Accurate judgments of learning are useful not only for helping us select effective acquisition strategies but also for helping us determine which items need more study. Dunlosky and Nelson (1994) found that delayed judgments helped students identify which individual items they had learned. The problem with immediate judgments is that items are still in STM, making it difficult to predict how easy it will be to later retrieve the items. Several decades of research have now produced extensive evidence that delayed judgments of learning are more accurate (Rhodes & Tauber, 2011). Similarly, students report that rereading or restudying material repeatedly is an effective study strategy (Karpicke et al., 2009) because they falsely believe they are learning due to the ease with which they are able to process this recent information (Rhodes & Castel, 2008).

Let's return to the serial position effect as an example of how our ability to easily retrieve information immediately after studying it can be a poor indicator of our ability to later retrieve it. When people begin recalling a word list, they typically recall the words at the end of the list first. These words are still available in STM and are therefore easy to recall. But people incorrectly believe that these words will also be easy to retrieve later (Benjamin & Bjork, 1996). The strong recency effect for immediate recall becomes a *negative* recency effect (depressed recall of words at the end of the list) for delayed recall (Craik, 1970). The recall of words from STM aided immediate recall but reduced delayed recall when it was necessary to rely on LTM. Benjamin and Bjork (1996) use these data to illustrate how **retrieval fluency** can be a misleading indicator of which items are best learned. Retrieval fluency—the ease with which an item can be recalled—failed to predict learning because those items that were easy to retrieve during immediate recall were difficult to retrieve during delayed recall.

---

retrieval fluency The ease with which an item can be recalled

The effectiveness of delayed judgments of learning is consistent with the neuroscience evidence presented in the previous section. A group of neuroscientists asked participants in a learning experiment to judge their degree of confidence in having learned each of the studied items (pictures of faces, scenes, and objects). The data supported the hypothesis that hippocampal activation is more critical when making memory judgments following a delay. Stronger activation of the hippocampus was associated with higher confidence ratings of learning for delayed judgments of learning but not for immediate judgments of learning (Kelley et al., 2020).

Another aspect of acquisition is the allocation of study time. Recall the example of learning German vocabulary words referred to at the beginning of this section. If you were listening to a tape that presented the words in a predetermined order, you would have no choice of which words to study. But if you had a choice, you would likely spend more time studying those words that you thought you hadn't learned.

A strategy that typically works well for students is to allocate more study time to the more difficult items (Photo 5.6). There is extensive evidence that students do, in fact, spend more time studying difficult items, with the exception of young students, such as those in first grade (Son & Metcalfe, 2000). However, these studies provided students with ample time to study. Imagine that you were behind in your reading and had to prepare for an exam but did not have time to learn all the material. What would be the best strategy in this case? Son and Metcalfe (2000) found that under high time pressure, people spent more time on the judged-easy items, whereas under lower time pressure, they focused on the judged-difficult items.

PHOTO 5.6 Spend more time on difficult items when there is sufficient time.

istockphoto.com/Zinkevych

Retention

You next need to decide how to maintain the information that you learn. Periodic review minimizes forgetting (Pashler et al., 2007), but students typically focus on whatever is due the soonest rather than developing periodic reviews of material they are trying to learn (Kornell & Bjork, 2007). Periodic retrieval of information through self-testing is a particularly effective learning strategy (McDaniel et al., 2009; Roediger & Butler, 2011), but surveys of students show that most of them study by rereading rather than through self-testing (Karpicke et al., 2009).

The benefits of self-testing were evident in a 2006 study by Roediger and Karpicke. Their research aimed to investigate the testing effect under educationally relevant conditions by using prose materials and free-recall tests without feedback. A second purpose of their research was to determine whether self-testing supports long-term retention. One group studied the text and then restudied it while a second group tested themselves on recalling the passage (without feedback) rather than study it for a second time. Members of each group were then tested either after five minutes, two days, or one week.

Figure 5.11 displays the findings. Restudying the material produced better recall on the five-minute retention test. However, opposite results occurred on the delayed tests. The self-testing groups recalled more of the material on both the two-day and one-week tests. Students may prefer repeated study because it produces short-term benefits, but they incorrectly predict that it will also result in better long-term benefits than self-testing. They mistake the fluency associated with rereading as evidence that they have successfully learned the material (Miyatsu et al., 2018).

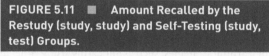

FIGURE 5.11 ■ Amount Recalled by the Restudy (study, study) and Self-Testing (study, test) Groups.

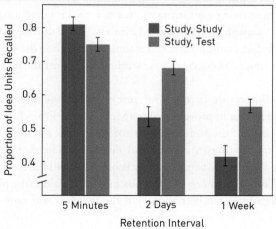

Source: "Reflections on the resurgence of the testing effect," by H. L. Roedinger III & J. D. Karpicke, 2018, *Perspectives on Psychological Science, 13*, 236–241. https://doi.org/10.1177/1745691617718873

In the 30th anniversary issue of the journal *Perspectives on Psychological Science*, the editor selected the most cited articles published in the journals of the Association for Psychological Science (Sternberg, 2018). He asked the authors why they felt their article had such a significant impact. The Roediger and Karpicke (2006) article was one of those most cited. Here is their reply:

> Of course, the testing effect was not new, but much of the prior research was conducted with word lists, and our 2006 article used more educationally relevant material. In addition, we showed that students did not predict the effect; rather, they predicted that repeated studying would help them more than repeated testing. And the idea that tests can help learning seemed novel (and implausible) to many people. So the claim that tests can serve a useful educational function besides assessment and the assignment of grades attracted attention. . . . . . . A final point, noted above, is that our experiments produced striking testing or retrieval practice effects and showed that the effect can be pronounced after a long retention interval. (Roediger & Karpicke, 2018, p. 239)

Difficulty in assessing learning is not surprising because several obstacles interfere with making accurate judgments (McDaniel & Einstein, 2020). One obstacle is that it is more convenient to assess learning when one is learning rather than wait to make a delayed assessment. Another impediment is that less effective strategies, such as rote rehearsal, occasionally work, so it's important to realize that they do not always work. A third obstacle is that students often incorrectly believe that investing more mental effort should result in better learning as a reward for their effort. A final constraint is that there are few courses on developing productive guidelines for learning.

The effectiveness of learning strategies, such as allocating study time, making delayed judgments of learning, and retesting one's memory, creates a need for designing instruction on the successful use of these strategies. McDaniel and Einstein (2020) developed a *KBCP* framework based on knowledge, belief, commitment, and planning for guiding the self regulation of learning. Table 5.1 lists the intended effects of interventions to support the four components of the KBCP framework.

The purpose of the lecture is to convey research findings to support the claim that the recommended strategies improve learning (McDaniel & Einstein, 2020). Lectures are nonetheless unproductive if the audience does not believe the strategies merit the required additional effort. Participating in a successful demonstration should aid in convincing learners. Explaining the reasons *why* a strategy is helpful should increase a commitment to using the strategy. Explaining *when* a strategy is helpful should assist planning. A delayed judgment of learning would not be necessary if the memory was only needed for a short interval.

Intervention	Component	Effects
TABLE 5.1 ■ Overview of a comprehensive intervention designed to train the self-regulated use of strategies		
Lecture: Lecture that conveys the nature of the trained strategy, its effectiveness, when to use it, and how to apply it (with practice) to realistic educational tasks	**Knowledge**	Helps students understand the strategy, the evidence behind its effectiveness, and how to apply the strategy to their educational demands
Demonstration: Concrete demonstration in which students experience the learning consequences (with explicit feedback) when they do and do not use the trained strategy	**Belief**	Helps convince students that the strategy works for them; demonstrations also help students appreciate the relationship between their strategy use and learning outcomes, thereby giving them a sense of self-efficacy over their learning outcomes
Utility-value: Intervention in which learners think through the value of using the trained strategy	**Commitment**	Helps learners appreciate the value of using the trained strategy and the value of the learning objectives, thereby increasing learners' motivation to use the strategy
Implementation: Procedure in which students form plans that force them to think through when, where, and how they will use the trained strategy	**Planning**	By associatively linking situational cues with strategy use, implementation intentions help learners follow through on their study plans

Based on "Training learning strategies to promote self-regulation and transfer: The knowledge, belief, commitment, and planning framework," by M. A. McDaniel & G. O. Einstein, 2020, *Perspectives on Psychological Science,* 15, 1363–1381.

Retrieval

Retrieval strategies involve getting information out of LTM by searching for it in memory. Recalling information from LTM sometimes occurs so rapidly that psychologists have little opportunity to study how people retrieve the information. However, occasionally retrieval succeeds only after a slow search of LTM, such as occurs in the **tip of the tongue (TOT)** phenomenon. A word is on the tip of your tongue when you know it is stored in LTM but are momentarily blocked from retrieving it.

---

tip of the tongue (TOT) A retrieval state in which a person feels he or she knows the information but cannot immediately retrieve it

There are two general experimental methods for studying the TOT state. The laboratory approach requires bringing people into the laboratory and asking them to recall words that might elicit the TOT state. The diary approach requires that people keep detailed records of what happens when faced with memory blocks in their daily lives.

The first systematic laboratory study was conducted by Roger Brown and David McNeill (1966) who gave people definitions of infrequent words and asked them to try to recall the words. For example, "What is the name of the instrument that uses the position of the sun and stars to navigate?" Some of the words produced the TOT state; that is, people were unable to immediately think of the word but were confident that they would soon recall it. Successful retrieval was often helped by using partial information related to the spelling of the word, such as its length or its initial letter. When attempting to answer the previous question, people may recall that the word starts with the letter *s* and has two syllables (*sextant*). Another study found similar results using pictures and verbal descriptions of entertainers (Read & Bruce, 1982). The most frequently reported strategy for recalling names was to make use of partial information, as reported initially by Brown and McNeill (1966).

In naturalistic studies of TOTs, subjects carry a diary to document TOT states as they occur. They are asked to record what information they could retrieve as they searched for the word and how the memory block was resolved. A review of this literature (Brown, 1991) reported a number of consistent findings—for example:

1. TOTs are reported to occur in daily life about once a week and to increase with age. Most are triggered by the names of personal acquaintances.

2. Words related both to the meaning and the spelling of the target word are retrieved, but spelling predominates. People can guess the first letter approximately 50% of the time.

3. Approximately one-half of the TOT states are resolved within one minute.

A challenge in studying the TOT effect is that it is difficult to produce. People typically retrieve the answer either immediately or not at all. However, a technique for increasing TOT states is to use questions about sex, disease, bodily functions, violence, or profanity that elicit emotional reactions (Schwartz, 2010). Examples include the following:

•   What is the last name of the serial killer in New York who went by the names "Son of Sam" and the "44-caliber killer?"

•   What is the sterilization procedure called in which a man's *vasa deferentia* are cut?

•   What was the name of the largest Nazi concentration camp in Poland?

---

naturalistic study A study of the tip-of-the-tongue state in which people record these events as they occur outside the laboratory

An emotional question was more likely to cause a TOT state for both the question and following question, suggesting that emotional arousal lasts beyond the specific question (Schwartz, 2010).

Recalling events is another example of a situation studied by psychologists, including procedures to aid retrieval. One of the most successful techniques has been the cognitive interview (CI) procedure that Fisher and Geiselman initially developed to help police detectives conduct more effective interviews. The reporting of criminal events by witnesses reflected not only their use of inefficient memory retrieval mechanisms but by the officers not carefully listening to the witness statements, keeping track of previously asked questions, and developing hypotheses about the crime. In one of the initial studies, Fisher et al. (1989) trained seven experienced detectives in Dade County, Florida, to follow the CI procedure. The detectives obtained 47% more information from the interviews following the training. In many cases, there was more than one victim or witness, so it was possible to determine whether the obtained information was consistent across the people interviewed. A high rate of consistency suggested that the obtained information was accurate.

The positive results of this and other studies on interviewing procedures resulted in the U.S. Department of Justice releasing in 1999 the first national guide for collecting eyewitness evidence (Technical Working Group for Eyewitness Evidence, 1999). Psychological researchers participated in writing the guide and later wrote about their collaboration with the justice department (Wells et al., 2000). The analysis of police interviews revealed a number of avoidable errors including (a) asking too many closed-ended questions, (b) frequently interrupting the witness, and (c) asking questions in a predetermined, inflexible order. In contrast, the new recommended procedures are to conduct the interview at a slow pace and ask a few, primarily open-ended questions (Photo 5.7). Also recommended are using memory retrieval techniques, such as reinstating the context and recalling events by using different retrieval pathways.

PHOTO 5.7 A police interview.

istockphoto.comKatarzynaBialasiewicz

cognitive interview The use of cognitively based retrieval techniques to improve recall

TABLE 5.2 ■ Elements of the cognitive interview (CI)

CI Element	Description	Processes Enhanced
Rapport	Develop rapport between respondent and interviewer	Social dynamics
Open-ended questions	Ask primarily open-ended questions	Social dynamics
Active respondent participation	Respondent to actively generate information (not merely to answer interviewer's questions)	Social dynamics
No interruptions	Do not interrupt the respondent's narration	Social dynamics
Avoid suggestive questions	Avoid asking questions that suggest a specific answer	Memory
Respondent-compatible questions	Ask questions that are compatible with respondent's currently accessible information	Memory
Close eyes	Instruct respondents to close their eyes	Cognition
Reinstate context	Reinstate the context of the original experience	Memory
Multiple retrievals	Encourage respondents to search through memory more than once	Memory
Varied retrievals	Encourage respondents to search through memory in different ways	Memory

Based on: "Expanding the cognitive interview to non-criminal investigations," by R. P. Fisher & R. E. Geiselman, 2019, in J. Dickinson, N. S. Compo, R. Carol, B. Schwartz, & M. McCauley (Eds.), *Evidence-Based Investigative Interviewing: Applying Cognitive Principles* (pp. 1–28). New York: Routledge: Taylor & Francis.

Many additional studies have refined the technique, resulting in the recommendations listed in Table 5.2 (Fisher & Geiselman, 2019). Psychologists have expanded its use to other situations, such as helping people recall internal, mental events. Fisher and Geiselman report that, although considerable progress has occurred in applying the CI procedure, there is still much to learn. They recommend that future directions should include generating new theory-based instructions, comparing individual with group interviews, and determining whether the procedure should be tailored to specific situations (Fisher & Geiselman, 2019).

The reliability of memory is one of its most important characteristics, particularly within the legal system (Brewin et al., 2020). Although early findings suggested that the confidence of an eyewitness was not an accurate measure of reliability (Kassin et al., 2001), more recent research has indicated that eyewitness confidence is a good predictor of accuracy (Wixted et al., 2018), as concluded from an extensive review of research:

We argue here that, like DNA evidence and other kinds of scientifically validated forensic evidence, eyewitness memory is reliable if it is not contaminated and if proper testing procedures are used. This conclusion applies to eyewitness memory broadly conceived, whether the test involves recognition (from a police lineup) or recall (during a police interview). From this perspective, eyewitness memory has been wrongfully convicted of mistakes that are better construed as having been committed by other actors, not by the eyewitnesses themselves (Wixted et al., 2018, p. 324).

SUMMARY

Learning can be represented as the transfer of information from STM to LTM. The distinction between STM and LTM, as well as the role of rehearsal in transferring information into LTM, was emphasized in a model proposed by Atkinson and Shiffrin. One of the findings that their model accounts for is the serial position effect: The better recall of words at the beginning of a list can be explained by their storage in LTM, and the better recall of words at the end of the list can be explained by their storage in STM.

Episodic memory contains recollections of personal experiences that help us remember the past and plan the future. Both neurological (increased connectivity of the prefrontal cortex with the hippocampus) and personality (compulsiveness) variables are likely causes of people with highly superior autobiographical memory. Semantic memory contains general knowledge, such as the sum of 7 and 8 is 15. The ability of people with severe amnesia to perform better on indirect than on direct tests of memory suggests their semantic memory is more intact than their episodic memory. Procedural memory stores actions, skills, and operations. Evidence that amnesics improve their reading speed but not their recall when rereading text indicates that their procedural memory is also more intact than their episodic memory.

Research with patients such as H. M. demonstrated that STM and LTM are accomplished in distinct regions of the brain, with the medial temporal lobes and the hippocampal complex critical to the formation of longer-term memories. Research also indicates that the right prefrontal cortex is active more during encoding, while the left prefrontal cortex is more active during retrieval. Retrieval cues guide the reinstatement of memories by connecting activation in the hippocampus to the posterior parietal cortex.

Retrieval fluency during acquisition can be a misleading indicator of learning, so delayed judgments are recommended. Self-testing is an effective method during the retention interval. Strategies for searching LTM during the tip-of-the-tongue phenomenon include using partial information, such as word length or sounds, generating plausible names, and using contextual information associated with a name. The cognitive-interview technique successfully instructs eyewitnesses how to carefully search memory to recall details about a crime.

RECOMMENDED READING

Squire and Wixted (2015) provide a general overview of LTM functions. Individual differences in LTM are explored by factor analysis (Unsworth, 2019). *Searching for Memory: The Brain, the Mind, and the Past* (Schacter, 1996) is a helpful introduction to the study of memory from a cognitive-neuroscience approach. Current behavioral, neuropsychological and neuroimaging data are compatible with the idea that episodic and semantic memory are intertwined but retain a measure of distinctiveness (Renoult et al., 2019). The desire to protect and enhance self-images favors the retention of good memories (Sedikides & Skowronski, 2020), but the recovery of repressed memories remains a controversial topic (Otgaar et al., 2019). Kredlow et al. (2018) discuss the connections among consolidation, memory disorders, and drugs. Learning from stimulus characteristics, feedback, people, and prior knowledge are four ways of learning across the life span (Wu, 2019). Miyatsu et al. (2018) analyze avoiding the pitfalls of five popular study strategies. Different instructional choices can be combined to create many options (Koedinger et al., 2013).

Getty Images/Yoshiyoshi Hirokawa

6 ACTION

LEARNING OBJECTIVES

1. Describe how action influences perception and thinking.

2. Generate combinations of physical, virtual, and mental actions with physical, virtual, and mental objects.

3. Explain how focus can shift between low-level and high-level actions.

4. Identify common principles that apply to cognitive offloading and instruction.

The chapter on action discusses a different perspective from initial theories in cognitive psychology that emphasized the mental representation of knowledge. The initial orientation considered perception and action to be peripheral, not central, components of cognitive processing. The new perspective—embodied cognition—considers perception and action to be central components of cognition (Gibbs, 2006; Wilson, 2002). This chapter continues the discussion of procedural long-term memory (LTM) and adds the motor component of the standard model

---

embodied cognition A theoretical framework in which perception and action have a central role in cognition

(Figure 6.1). Procedural LTM stores procedures for organizing actions, and the motor component executes the procedures.

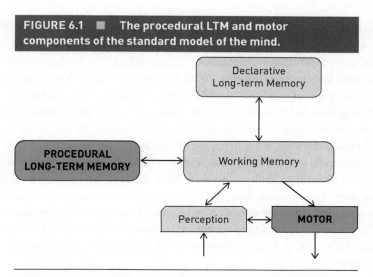

FIGURE 6.1 ■ The procedural LTM and motor components of the standard model of the mind.

Source: Based on "A standard model of the mind: Toward a common computational framework across artificial intelligence, cognitive science, neuroscience, and robotics," by J. E. Laird, C. Lebiere, & P. S. Rosenbloom, 2017, *AI Magazine*, *38*, 13–26. https://doi.org/10.1609/aimag.v38i4.2744

The embodied cognition perspective focuses on understanding cognition as an ongoing interaction with the external world. It emphasizes that much of thought is more than contemplation—it involves processes that determine possible actions. Although actions were also emphasized in the behaviorist movement described in Chapter 1, embodied cognition places action within a broader theoretical framework. This framework specifies that actions are (1) driven by goals that sometimes fail, (2) require planning and decisions among alternative actions, and (3) and involve prediction or anticipation of an intended outcome (Engel et al., 2013).

Goals, planning, and anticipation occur even for relatively simple actions, such as grasping an object (Rosenbaum et al., 2012). Consider a waiter filling water glasses that are initially placed upside down on the tables. To turn the glass upright, the waiter picks up the glass with his thumb down so he will be holding it with his thumb up after rotating it 180 degrees. Anticipation is also needed in social situations. It is polite to pass a water pitcher to another person so that person can grasp the pitcher by its handle.

The initial section of this chapter is about the interactions between actions and other components of cognition. It describes how actions influence perception, comprehension, and thinking. Actions typically act on objects, so the second section explains how physical, virtual, and mental actions act on physical, virtual, and mental objects. The third section examines how low-level actions, such as reaching for a water pitcher, become organized into high-level goals, such as filling a glass. The final section on applications discusses how actions can reduce cognitive load and support instruction.

ACTION JOINS COGNITION

Action Influences Perception

According to the standard model in Figure 6.1, cognitive components do not work in isolation but interact with each other. One consequence is that visual perception is not solely a visual process. What one sees is influenced not only by sensory information but by a person's purpose, physiological state, and emotions (Proffitt, 2006). For instance, studies have consistently found that the judged steepness of hills is influenced by physiological demands. Runners at the beginning of a race judge hills as less steep than at the end of a race, and more-fit people judge hills as less steep than those who are less fit. The advantage of this perceptual bias is that it simplifies planning. People who are tired or less fit require more energy to get up the hill.

This action-specific account of perception proposes that people perceive their surrounding environment in terms of their ability to act on it. Witt (2011) reviews extensive research documenting this effect, ranging from daily activities to superior athletic performance. Perceivers with narrow shoulders perceived doorways to be wider compared with perceivers with wide shoulders. Perceivers with a reaching tool estimated targets to be closer than perceivers who did not have the tool (Figure 6.2). Perceivers burdened with a heavy load judged distances as further and hills as steeper.

FIGURE 6.2 ■ A reaching tool makes targets seem closer.

Source: "Action's effect on perception," by J. K. Witt, 2011*Current Directions in Psychological Science*, *20*, 201–206. https://doi.org/0.1177/096372141140877

Previous successful performance makes a task appear easier. Softball players perceive the ball as larger when hitting well. Tennis players perceive the net as lower when returning balls successfully. Golfers perceive the hole as larger when playing better.

The action-specific perspective shares with Gibson's (1979) ecological approach its emphasis on the relation between perception and action. However, it differs from Gibson's theory of direct perception by demonstrating that perceivers interpret information differently in different circumstances. Witt and Riley (2014) proposed a reconciliation that makes the two perspectives more compatible. The reconciliation assumes that action-related information is not conceived of as an internal store of knowledge that relies on logical inferences but rather is detected at the time the action is anticipated. This perspective enables action-specific perception to incorporate concepts such as intention, attention, and information selection that are considered in ecological psychology.

Actions Can Be Simulated

An extensive article by Larry Barsalou (1999) at Emory University helped establish the embodied cognition framework. Barsalou argued that theories at that time were primarily amodal because they did not directly represent the perceptual experiences encountered in learning about concepts. A different theoretical approach is the perceptual symbols system proposed by Barsalou (1999), in which perceptual experiences are directly stored in LTM. A perceptual symbols system provides a modal framework that directly stores sensory experiences such as audition, vision, taste, smell, and touch. These sensory experiences can be re-experienced by mentally simulating them. For instance, try to imagine the smell, taste, and texture of a warm apple pie that was recently removed from the oven. People describe attractive foods by emphasizing words referring to taste and texture. They describe neutral foods by using words referring to visual appearance (Papies et al., 2020) .

There is evidence that people mentally simulate actions. In one experiment, college students at the University of Wisconsin had to quickly judge whether a phrase, such as "open the drawer" or "boil the air," made sense (Glenberg & Kaschak, 2002). They had to move their hand either toward or away from their body to hit a response key. Participants were faster in responding when the response required an action in the same direction as the one implied in the phrase. For example, they were faster in responding by moving their hand toward their body when verifying the statement "open the drawer" and faster when moving their hand away from their body for the statement "close the drawer." These findings are consistent with a mental simulation of the action that requires moving your arm toward your body to open a drawer and away from your body to close a drawer (Photo 6.1).

Results obtained by Stanfield and Zwaan (2001) supported the hypothesis that simulations help people comprehend the meaning of verbally described actions. For example, reading that someone put a pencil in a drawer should evoke an image of a horizontal pencil, and reading that someone put a pencil in a cup should evoke an image of a vertical pencil. Stanfield and Zwaan tested their hypothesis that visual simulations of verbal statements would include an object's

---

amodal Knowledge that is abstracted from sensory experiences

modal Knowledge is represented as sensory experiences

PHOTO 6.1 Actions such as opening a drawer can be mentally simulated.

istockphoto.com/sirawit99

orientation by asking students at Florida State University to quickly decide whether a pictured object had been mentioned in a sentence that they just read. You can obtain an approximate idea of this task by responding to whether the object in Figure 6.3 is mentioned in each of the three sentences. This demonstration is approximate because the test object did not appear until after participants read each sentence in Stanfield and Zwaan's experiment.

FIGURE 6.3 ■ Object verification task

1. She pounded the nail into the floor.
2. She painted the fence with a brush.
3. She pounded the nail into the wall.

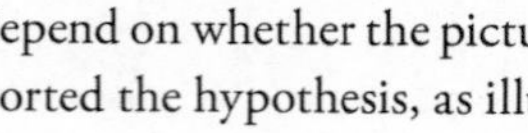

Source: "Producing gestures facilitates route learning," by W. C. So, T. H.-W. Ching, P. E. Lim, X. Cheng, & K. Y. Ip, 2014, *Plos One, 9*(e112543). https://doi.org/10.1371/journal.pone.0112543

According to the visual simulation hypothesis, the time to verify a mentioned object should depend on whether the picture matches the implied orientation in the sentence. The results supported the hypothesis, as illustrated by the distinction between the two sentences: *She pounded the nail into the floor,* versus *she pounded the nail into the wall.* The readers were faster in confirming a picture of a vertical nail following the first sentence (pounding a nail into the floor) and were faster in confirming a picture of a horizontal nail following the third sentence (pounding the nail into the wall).

Gestures Influence Comprehension

One advantage of mentally simulating actions during comprehension is that we can use these simulations as a basis for gestures. In other words, the same simulations can provide the foundation for both comprehending and producing language. This is exactly the claim made by Hostetter and Alibali (2008) in their gestures-as-simulated action framework.

As proposed in embodied theories of cognition, the link between perception and action is central. The simulations that occur during language comprehension are based on both visual and motor images. Motor imagery activates premotor areas in the brain that have the potential to spread to motor areas and create gestures. The gestures-as-simulated action framework proposes that three factors determine whether a gesture occurs. The first is the strength of the simulated action. Some simulations involve only visual imagery. The word "beautiful" will likely invoke visual imagery but not action imagery. The second factor is the height of the gesture threshold. You probably know some people who have a low threshold and use their hands frequently as they speak and others who have a high threshold and rarely gesture. The third factor is speech. Although both comprehending and producing language depend on simulations, gestures typically occur only when people produce language.

The number of gestures that speakers produce depends on the situation. For instance, if we use gestures to help people understand, then we should gesture more when talking to them face-to-face than when talking to them over the telephone. A group of researchers tested this hypothesis in a study that varied whether the listener could observe the gestures (Bavelas et al., 2008). Some participants described two pictures in a face-to-face dialogue to another person who could not see the pictures. Other participants described the pictures to another person in a telephone conversation. A third group described the pictures in a monologue to a tape recorder. The average number of gestures declined from an average of 21.8 per minute in the face-to-face conversation to 14.9 per minute in the telephone conversation to 4.3 per minute in the monologue. Speakers in the face-to-face condition were also more likely to put information in their gestures that was not in their words and refer to their gestures during the conversation. But perhaps the most surprising aspect of these findings is the large number of gestures made in a telephone conversation, suggesting that gestures aid speakers even when they know the listener cannot observe them (Photo 6.2).

This finding is consistent, nonetheless, with studies that reveal the effect of producing gestures is greater than the effect of observing gestures for comprehending speech (Dargue et al., 2019). The majority of studies used recall as a measure of comprehension, which was defined as an individual's understanding of a verbal message, such as a narrative or a set of verbal instructions. A possible explanation of the beneficial effect of producing gestures is that the speaker's gestures reduce cognitive load, enabling more resources for understanding. We will see evidence for this hypothesis later in the chapter. Other findings revealed that gestures were equally effective across a wide variety of age groups and measures of recall (Dargue et al., 2019).

PHOTO 6.2 Gestures accompany phone conversations.

istockphoto.com/fizkes

Gestures Influence Thinking

The gesture-for-conceptualization-hypothesis (Kita et al., 2017) proposes that gestures activate, manipulate, package, and explore spatio-motoric information for both speaking and thinking. This section provides examples of research to illustrate how each of the following principles applies to thinking:

1. Gestures activate and maintain spatio-motoric information.

2. Gestures manipulate spatio-motoric information.

3. Gestures package spatio-motoric information.

4. Gestures explore spatio-motoric information.

Evidence that gestures facilitate the learning of routes shows how they *activate and maintain* spatio-motoric information (So et al., 2014). Undergraduates viewed diagrams in which a red line displayed a sequence of steps to reach a destination (Figure 6.4). In the co-thought gesture condition, participants were instructed to rehearse the routes while using their hands. In the drawing condition, they drew the route. In the hand-movement-prevention condition, they visualized the route without moving their hands. In the no-rehearsal (control) condition, they performed a distracting task. As shown in Figure 6.5, the proportion of accurately recalled steps was significantly higher when using gestures during learning, even higher than drawing the route.

FIGURE 6.4   ■   The red line shows a sequence of steps during route navigation.

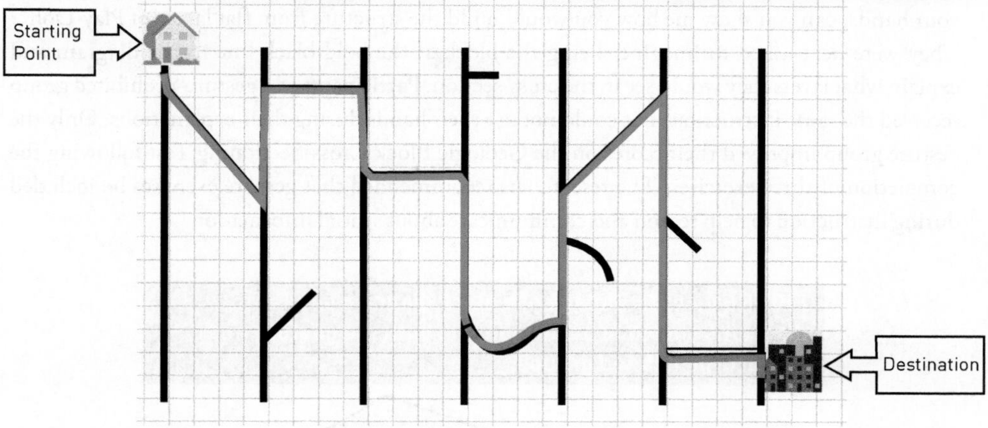

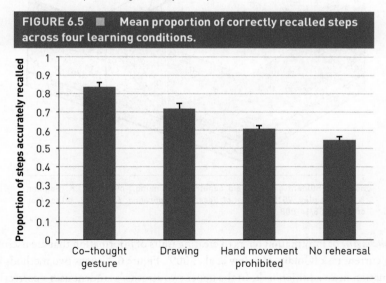

istockphoto.com.photosynthesis

Source: "Producing gestures facilitates route learning," by W. C. So, T. H.-W. Ching, P. E. Lim, X. Cheng, & K. Y. Ip, 2014, *Plos One, 9*(e112543). https://doi.org/10.1371/journal.pone.0112543

FIGURE 6.5   ■   Mean proportion of correctly recalled steps across four learning conditions.

Source: "Producing gestures facilitates route learning," by W. C. So, T. H.-W. Ching, P. E. Lim, X. Cheng, & K. Y. Ip, 2014, *Plos One, 9*(e112543). https://doi.org/10.1371/journal.pone.0112543

Gestures also enable us to demonstrate how we would *manipulate* material, as studied in an evaluation of **penetrative thinking**, defined as the ability to reason about the interior structure of an object based on what is visible on its surface. Penetrative thinking is needed to be successful in

penetrative thinking The ability to reason about the interior structure of an object based on what is visible on its surface

many scientific disciplines, particularly the geosciences. Figure 6.6 shows a block diagram used to support geoscience instruction (Atit et al., 2015). Participants in a gesture group were told "using your hands, can you show me how you would build the structure from flat layers of Play-Doh"? They were next asked to imagine slicing the block at the bold black line in the diagram and explain what layers they would see in the cross-section. Participants in a gesture-prohibited group received the same instructions but could not use their hands during their explanations. Only the gesture group improved their scores on the Geologic Block Cross-Sectioning Test following the completion of three exercises. The researchers recommended that gesture exercises be included during instruction to help reason and communicate about spatial information.

FIGURE 6.6 ■ Image of a block diagram similar to diagrams shown to participants in both the gesture and gesture-prohibited groups.

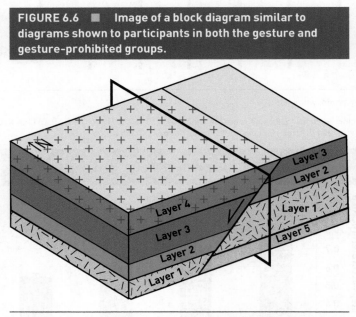

Source: "Student gestures aid penetrative thinking," by K. Atit, K. Gagnier, & T. F. Shipley, 2015, *Journal of Geoscience Education, 63*, 66–72. https://doi.org/10.5408/14-008.1

The *packaging* of information refers to creating units of information that are useful for performing a current task (Goldin-Meadow et al., 2009). Figure 6.7 shows two methods for packing information in an addition task. In the upper two screens, a student uses a correct V gesture to group two numbers (3 + 2) and a pointing gesture to demonstrate that their sum fits into the blank on the right side of the equation. In the lower two screens, a student uses a partially correct V gesture to group two numbers (5 + 7). Their sum does not fit into the blank, but the gestures illustrate that numbers can be grouped and inserted into the right side of the equation. The students required to produce correct gestures learned more than children required to produce partially correct gestures, who learned more than children required to produce no gestures.

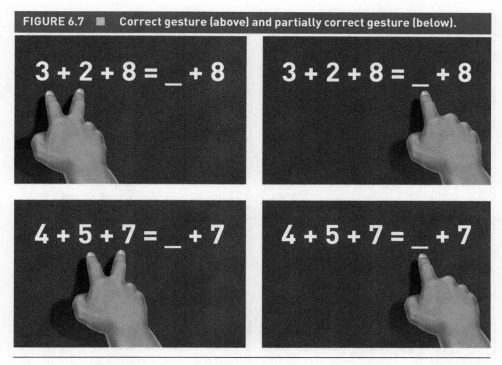

FIGURE 6.7 ■ Correct gesture (above) and partially correct gesture (below).

Source: "Action to abstraction: Gesture as a mechanism of change," by S. Goldin-Meadow, 2015, *Developmental Review, 38*, 167–184. https://doi.org/10.1016/j.dr.2015.07.007

Problem-solving initiates the last principle—the use of gestures in *exploration*. Consider a Piagetian task in which the experimenter pours the contents of one of two identical tall glasses of sand into a short, wide dish (Alibali et al., 2000). The boy in Figure 6.8 initially stated that the remaining tall glass contained more sand than the short dish. While explaining his judgment, he initially focused on the tall glass (a) but decided against it. He then explored the width and height of the dish with an up and down gesture at the side of the dish (b). He next moved his hand over the dish (c) and explored the area by spreading his hand (d). This exploration helped him generate the idea that the sand fills a larger area in the dish that could compensate for its lack of height.

A difference between gestures and action is that gestures represent the world but do not physically change it. Gestures promote understanding because they bring action into mental representations at a higher level of abstraction than manipulation. As stated by Goldin-Meadow (2015, p. 170):

> Gestures are representational and thus more abstract than direct actions on objects. It may be this comfortable middle ground, with one foot in concrete action and one foot in abstract representation, that makes gesture such a powerful tool for learning.

FIGURE 6.8 ■   Using gestures for exploration during problem-solving.

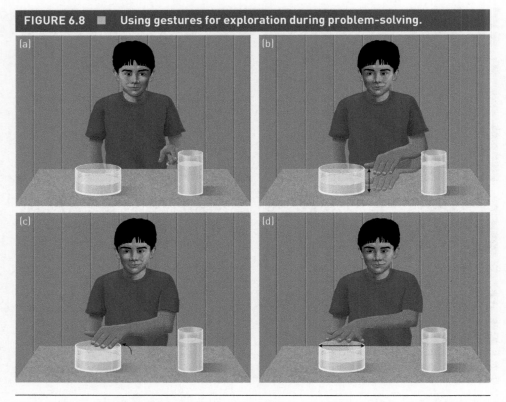

Source: "How do gestures influence thinking and speaking? The gesture-for-conceptualization hypothesis," by S. Kita, M. W. Alibali, & M. Chu, 2017, *Psychological Review, 124*, 245–266. https://doi.org/10.1037/rev0000059

COMBINING ACTIONS AND OBJECTS

Gestures occur at a higher level of abstraction than manipulation because they do not manipulate physical objects. We can use our hands to demonstrate how we would physically pound a nail into the floor, but the hammer and nail are imaginary or mental objects. Previously, we saw evidence for imagining this situation in which both the action and object are mental. These situations are examples within a taxonomy that combines physical, virtual, and mental actions with physical, virtual, and mental objects (Table 6.1). Let's explore the taxonomy in the next sections on physical, virtual, and mental actions.

Physical Actions

Many readers have some knowledge about the emphasis on physical manipulatives in Montessori schools. In her book *Montessori: The Science Behind the Genius,* Angeline Lillard (2005) discusses Montessori's work and subsequent research that has supported many of Montessori's ideas about learning and development. A review of research on what makes mathematics manipulatives effective contained four recommendations (Laski et al., 2015). The first is to use

TABLE 6.1 ■   **Combinations of physical, virtual, and mental actions and objects**

Actions	Objects		
	Physical	**Virtual**	**Mental**
Physical	Montessori Manipulatives	Wii Sports Games	Gestures
Virtual	Robotic Surgery	Virtual Experiments	Teaching the Blind
Mental	Brain-computer Robotic Interfaces	Brain-Computer Cursor Interfaces	Sports Simulations

Source: "Combining physical, virtual, and mental actions and objects," by S. K. Reed, 2018, *Educational Psychology Review, 30*, 1091–1113. https://doi.org/10.1007/s10648-018-9441-y

manipulatives consistently over a long period of time. For instance, the Montessori golden bead materials are used throughout the early elementary years to help children develop an understanding of the base-10 system. The manipulatives represent the base-10 number system by individual beads that can be assembled into 10 connected beads that form a 10 by 10 square of 100 square beads that comprise a cube of 1000 beads.

The second recommendation is to begin with concrete representations and move to more abstract representations. Figure 6.9 shows the replacement of the concrete beads with more abstract numerical tiles that can be used without the physical representation of the quantities. The third recommendation is to avoid manipulatives that have distracting irrelevant features. Because the beads are all the same color and size, children are not distracted by irrelevant attributes. The fourth recommendation is to explicitly explain the relation between a manipulative and a mathematical concept to help children make this connection.

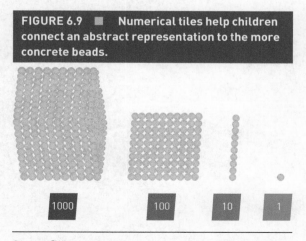

FIGURE 6.9 ■   **Numerical tiles help children connect an abstract representation to the more concrete beads.**

Source: "What makes mathematics manipulatives effective? Lessons from cognitive science and Montessori education," by E. V. Laski, J. R. Jor'dan, C. Daoust, & A. K. Murrray, 2015, *SAGE Open*, April–June, 1–8. https://doi.org/10.1177/2158244015589588

The next combination in Table 6.1 pairs physical actions with virtual objects. Physical actions on virtual objects became very popular when Nintendo launched the video game console Wii in 2006. The tracking of the Wii remote in three-dimensional space enabled players to use physical actions to control a virtual game on a screen (Sparks et al., 2009). Games included baseball, bowling, boxing, golf, and tennis. Although an innovative design, the Wii console had a higher rate of associated injuries than traditional game consoles.

Gestures offer a third combination—a physical action on a mental object. Although gestures contain many components of the actions they mimic, they also eliminate components. The force needed to lift an object is missing in a gesture that lifts nothing. However, gestures offer a potential advantage for transfer to other objects because an action such as lifting is not linked to a particular object (Goldin-Meadow, 2015).

Virtual Actions

I classify robotic surgery as performing virtual actions on physical objects because the surgeon sits at a console (enabling virtual actions) to operate on the body (a physical object). The robotic da Vinci System was designed to improve upon conventional laparoscopy surgery in which the surgeon operates while standing, using hand-held, long-shafted instruments (Photo 6.3). The da Vinci System consists of a console that the surgeon uses to control four interactive robotic arms. Three of the arms hold instruments such as scalpels and scissors. The instruments exceed the natural range of motion of the human hand while motion scaling and tremor reduction further refine the surgeon's hand movements. Performing surgical movements on the computer console requires training unique actions that differ from those used in either open or laparoscopic surgery.

PHOTO 6.3 Robotic equipment to perform minimally invasive surgery.

istockphoto.com/MARHARYTA MARKO

Surgery requires performing very skilled actions, but training in a virtual environment can be equivalent to training in a physical environment for learning concepts that do not require skilled actions. Lara Triona and David Klahr at Carnegie Mellon University-trained fourth- and fifth-grade students to design experiments to measure how far springs stretched for various combinations of springs and weights (Triona & Klahr, 2003). The springs could be long or short, wide or narrow, and thin or thick. The results showed that children who trained with virtual materials by varying only one variable at a time were as capable of designing good experiments as children who trained with physical materials. The virtual group also did as well as the physical group on a transfer task to evaluate the effect of steepness, length, surface, and type of ball on the time it would take a physical ball to roll down a physical ramp. The authors proposed that there are many advantages of computer-based laboratories, including portability, safety, cost-efficiency, and flexible, dynamic data displays (Klahr et al., 2007).

Virtual actions on mental objects occur when someone uses a virtual environment to create mental representations. A video game to teach navigation skills to the blind satisfies this requirement. Unlike sighted individuals, the blind must rely on nonvisual information to navigate the environment. An Audio-based Environment Simulator of a virtual building prepared the blind participants to subsequently navigate an actual building (Merabet et al., 2012). Exploration of the virtual building occurred through simple keystrokes while audio information described the location within the building. After training, the learners were evaluated on navigating a series of predetermined paths in the targeted physical building. They were highly successful, including finding shortcuts within the building and the shortest path to exit the building from different starting points (Connors et al., 2014).

Mental Actions

Mental actions on physical objects occur whenever someone uses thoughts to manipulate objects in the environment. The use of brain potentials to control robotic actions on physical objects requires the intervention of a robot to carry out the action between the thought and the object. Invasive sensors use surgical implants of electrodes; noninvasive sensors record brain signals from the scalp. Both approaches are based on the principle of cortical preparation that occurs before a cognitive, motor, or emotional response. Cortical preparation can be measured as a voltage shift in EEG (electroencephalographic) activity that can be used to control a physical device.

A team at the University of Palermo (Italy) used EEG recordings from the scalp to benefit amyotrophic lateral sclerosis (ALS) patients. Four ALS patients and four healthy controls learned to use the technology to control a robot to reach and grasp a glass of water. The brain computer interface (BCI) consisted of two high-level commands (grasp and give), four directional commands (forward, backward, left, right), and two turn commands. A few minutes of training was sufficient for enabling all four healthy participants and three of the four ALS patients to control the robot's actions at a high level of accuracy (Spataro et al., 2017).

The mental actions that control robots can also manipulate objects on a computer screen. However, moving a cursor occurs along two dimensions, and a single-modality

EEG signal can only exert control along a single dimension. A group at the University of Electronic Science and Technology of China found that imagining more than one signal creates more natural two-dimensional diagonal movements (Ma et al., 2017). Horizontal movement occurs by imagining the movement of either the left or right hand. Vertical movement occurs by imagining the number 1 or 2. Imagining the four combinations LEFT 1, LEFT 2, RIGHT 1, and RIGHT 2 results in greater efficiency by controlling diagonal movements of the cursor.

Mental actions on mental objects occur during visual simulations that can be used for training in many domains. In their extensive review of the role of imagery in sports Cumming and Williams (2014) discuss the variables that influence the effects of imagery training on performance. Two commonly discussed attributes are vividness and controllability. Vividness refers to the clarity and sensory richness of the image. Controllability refers to the transformation and maintenance of a generated image. For instance, the ability to mentally change the viewing angle is helpful in domains such as sports and dance.

ORGANIZING ACTIONS

Creating High-level From Low-level Actions

Jeffrey Zacks has been a leader in constructing event models of how people perceive, remember, think about, and respond to events. An article by Richmond and Zacks (2017) provides a thorough summary of work on this topic. Some of this research investigates how low-level actions become organized into high-level actions. As indicated by the checks in Figure 6.10, high-level (event model) actions begin with R holding the milk and end with Z pouring the milk. Low-level actions enable high-level actions and are described in terms of hand velocity, joints, muscle torques, and contact relations. These low-level actions support high-level actions, such as holding, getting, and pouring milk. High-level actions result in smoother changes in behavior and are more learnable. They also allow us to predict behavior by extrapolation from previous actions.

Most movement tasks involve a sequence of low-level actions that require integration to carry out complex skills (Diedrichsen & Kornysheva, 2015). A tennis serve consists of throwing the ball, taking a backswing, and accelerating the arm forward. Each of these phases involves the coordination of multiple body parts. Two stages in this coordination are the selection of particular goals and their execution through activities of the muscles. Although execution enables the performance of a complex skill, it does not support transfer to similar skills. Diedrichsen and Kornysheva (2015) therefore proposed an intermediate level between the execution and selection levels. The intermediate level enables a pianist to execute a specific chord transition within a new context and supports transfer between hands.

Gray and Lindstedt (2017) proposed that learning new methods during skill acquisition can improve performance but initially may cause a decline. An example is a shift from typing while

FIGURE 6.10 ■ Changes in high-level (left) and low-level (right) actions.

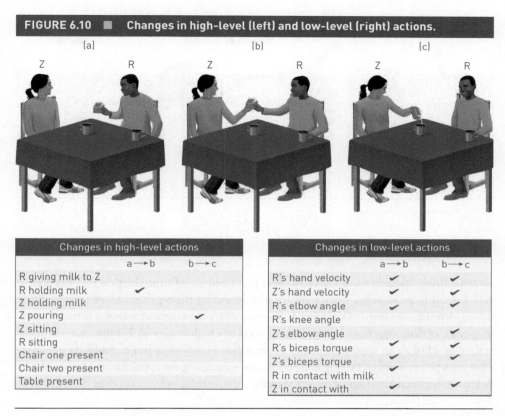

Changes in high-level actions	a→b	b→c
R giving milk to Z		
R holding milk	✓	
Z holding milk		
Z pouring		✓
Z sitting		
R sitting		
Chair one present		
Chair two present		
Table present		

Changes in low-level actions	a→b	b→c
R's hand velocity	✓	✓
Z's hand velocity	✓	✓
R's elbow angle	✓	✓
R's knee angle		
Z's elbow angle		✓
R's biceps torque	✓	✓
Z's biceps torque	✓	✓
R in contact with milk	✓	
Z in contact with	✓	✓

Source: "Constructing experience: Event models from perception to action," by L. L Richmond & J. M. Zacks, 2017, *Trends in Cognitive Sciences, 21*, 962–980. https://doi.org/10.1016/j.tics.2017.08.005

looking at the keys to typing without looking at the keys. The average speed of experienced visually guided typists is approximately 30–40 words per minute. The shift to touch-typing initially results in a decline in performance, but following a long period of training, touch typists reach an average speed of 60 to 70 words per minute (Yechiam et al., 2003). The initial dips in performance are caused by learning new methods that are either mastered or abandoned by returning to methods that have worked in the past (Gray & Lindstedt, 2017).

The development of an innovative high-jumping technique by Dick Fosbury illustrates the power of innovation in improving motor skills (Gray & Lindstedt, 2017). The traditional technique required the jumper to attempt to clear the bar with his head facing the bar while lifting one leg at a time over the bar. The "Fosbury Flop" requires the jumper to go over the bar backward while kicking both legs in the air at the end of the jump (Figure 6.11). Fosbury demonstrated the effectiveness of this new technique when he won the gold model and set an American record in the 1968 summer Olympics. The Fosbury Flop is now the most widely used method in high jumping.

FIGURE 6.11 ■ The Fosbury Flop.

Dorling Kindersley / Getty Images

Action Identification Theory

In 1987, Robin Vallacher and Daniel Wegner published an influential article that has proven very helpful in providing a framework for understanding the organization of actions. Their action identification theory (Vallacher & Wegner, 1987) represents an action at different levels of specificity that range from low-level movements to a high-level goal. For instance, the act of calling to schedule an appointment can be identified as moving a finger, touching numbers, entering a phone number, talking to a person, and scheduling the appointment. Action identification theory contains four principles to capture the interdependence between these different levels of detail (Vallacher, 2007; Vallacher & Wegner, 1987).

1. Action is maintained with respect to its consciously available identity.

2. When both a lower- and a higher-level identity are available, there is a tendency for the higher-level identity to become conscious.

3. When an action cannot be maintained at its conscious identity, there is a tendency for a lower-level identity to become conscious.

4. The principles of the theory work together to promote the level that is most appropriate or optimal for performing the action.

The first principle—maintaining an action at a specific level—is needed to account for the stability of actions. Context, however, can influence the perceived level. Solving a mathematics puzzle could be perceived as "keeping track of numbers" or "performing mental calculations" in the privacy of one's home but as "demonstrating my math skill" or "trying not to embarrass myself" in a testing situation.

The second principle—focusing on a higher level—provides meaning and implications for performing the action. Identities at a higher level have greater potential for creating one's self-concept than identities at a lower level. Creating a piece of art provides more information about the person, for example, than does a low-level identity such as moving a paintbrush.

The third principle states that switching to a lower level occurs when it is difficult to maintain an action at a higher level. A novice tennis player may devise a strategy to win the match but soon discover that a focus on basic actions, such as preparing the racket and following through with the stroke, is necessary to improve performance (Photo 6.4). For actions as diverse as video games and playing the piano, people with greater experience were more likely to perceive their actions at the more meaningful higher levels.

PHOTO 6.4 Focusing on basic actions improves performance.

JJ pixs / Alamy Stock Photo

Making the task more difficult also produces shifts in levels. An example is a study in which participants drank either from a normal coffee cup or one that was abnormally large. Participants who drank from a normal cup endorsed high-level actions, such as "getting energized" and "promoting my caffeine habit." Participants who drank from the unwieldy cup endorsed low-level actions, such as "lifting a cup to my lips" and "swallowing."

The last principle states that the first three principles work together to determine the most appropriate level of performance (Vallacher, 2007). Although people focused on low-level actions to drink from an abnormally large cup, they avoided thinking about low-level actions when they imagined rotating a spiky cup (Figure 6.12). Participants were shown different pairs of mugs and asked to describe how the left mug in each pair could be rotated to the position of the right mug. The average number of words used to describe the rotation did not differ between the smooth and spiky mugs. However, participants used fewer gestures when describing the rotation of spiky mugs (Chu & Kita, 2015). The fewer gestures reflected their avoidance of the spikes if required to physically rotate the cups.

FIGURE 6.12 ■ **Smooth versus spiky cups.**

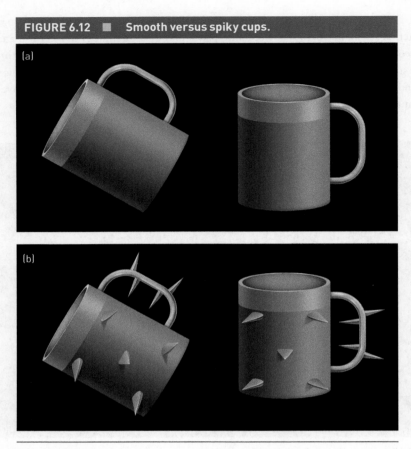

Source: "Co-thought and co-speech gestures are generated by the same action generation process," by M. Chu & S. Kita, 2016, *Journal of Experimental Psychology: Learning, Memory, and Cognition, 42*, 257–270. https://doi.org/10.1037/xlm0000168

The optimality principle of action identification theory states that over time and with repeated action, the person converges on a level that enables that individual to perform the action up to his or her capacity. However, non-optimal levels occasionally occur and not only impair performance but have been shown to promote self-consciousness and anxiety (Vallacher, 2007).

A study on persuasion demonstrates the importance of finding an optimal level (Kim & Duhachek, 2020). Construal theory (Trope & Liberman, 2010) predicts that the most effective level of persuasion depends on how we perceive the intentions of the persuader. Although there had been research on persuasive messages provided by people, there has been a lack research on persuasive messages provided by nonhumans. Robots are programmed by humans to serve us, therefore, we should find their messages more persuasive when they inform us *how* to accomplish a task (a low-level action) than *why* we should accomplish a task (a high-level action).

A robot made a recommendation, supposedly based on a list of recently purchased products (Figure 6.13), but in fact the recommended product was randomly assigned at either a low-level or high-level of construal (Figure 6.14). Participants then rated the persuasiveness of the recommendation. As predicted, they found the low-construal level (Figure 6.14A) was more effective for a typical robot that would be unaware of higher-level explanations. However, the results were reversed when told the robot was self-aware of what is happening around it. Participants who received a recommendation from the informed robot rated the high-construal message (Figure 6.14B) as more persuasive. The optimal level for persuasion in this study depended on how participants perceived the self-awareness of the messenger.

FIGURE 6.13 ■ A non self-aware (left) versus a self-aware robot (right).

An artificial intelligence robot XT-1000 is trainedto make recommendations to people based on their personal preferences. For XT-1000 to know better about your preference, please tell it up to 10 items that you have purchased recently. Please be noted that XT-1000 can make a better recommendation for you if you list as many items as you can and also describe them in detail.

An artificial intelligence robot Alex is trained to make recommendations to people based on their personal preferences. What is unique about Alex is that he is a conscious AI. That is, he is aware of his existence and he understands what is happening around him. For Alex to know better about your preferences, please tell him up to 10 items that you have purchased recently. Please be noted that Alex can make a better recommendation for you if you list as many items as you can and also describe them in detail.

Source: Kim, T. W., & Duhachek, A. (2020). Artificial intelligence and persuasion: A construal-level account. *Psychological Science, 31*, 363–380. https://doi.org/10.1177/0956797620904985

FIGURE 6.14 ■ A low-construal (left) versus a high-construal message (right).

A. Low-construal message 1

I recommend that you use Tea Tree Oil

How to use tea tree oil?
- **It is easy to use, carry, and affordable**
- Mix it with water or coconut oil and use it for various purposes
- Carry it in a spray bottle and use it for various purpose
- You can find it eaaily online or offline

B. High-construal message 1

I recommend that you use Tea Tree Oil

Why use tea tree oil?
- **Benefit and desirable effects include:**
- Sanitizing & antiseptic
- Natural deodorant & isect repellent
- Effective for nail fungus, acne, and skin inflammation

Source: From Kim, T. W., & Duhachek, A. (2020). Artificial intelligence and persuasion: A construal-level account. *Psychological Science, 31*, 363–380. https://doi.org/10.1177/0956797620904985

Neuroscience of Actions

The distinction between low-level and high-level actions indicates a distinction between mechanical actions (hitting a tennis ball) and executive actions (selecting a shot). Low-level actions depend on procedures; high-level actions depend on reasoning. Procedural memory supports low-level actions; declarative memory supports high-level actions.

The challenge is to integrate the contributions of procedural and declarative memory when both are needed. Osiurak and Heinke (2018) propose a theoretical framework shown in Figure 6.15. Tools used for manual work rely only on procedural memory because there are standard

FIGURE 6.15 ■ A unified framework for studying human tool use.

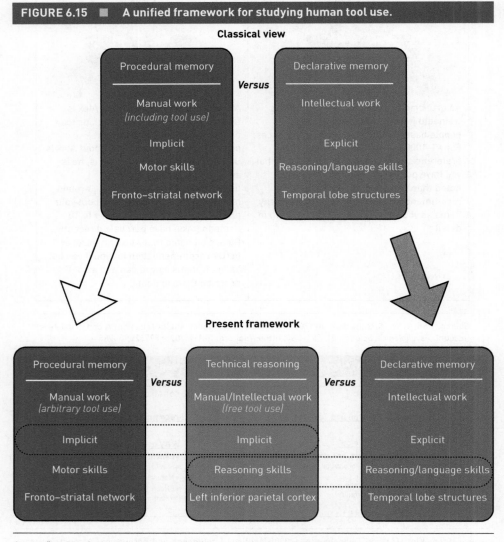

Source: "Looking for intoolligence: A unified framework for the cognitive study of human tool use and technology," by F. Osiurak & D. Heinke, 2018, *American Psychologist*, *73*, 169–185. https://doi.org/10.1037/amp0000162

procedures for using these tools. In contrast, technical reasoning relies on using tools for non-standard procedures (free tool use) and therefore requires both procedural and declarative memory. Reasoning skills are also required when one performs a task for the first time.

Try to imagine a person who has never sliced a tomato and has to select one of the three tools shown in Figure 6.16 (Osiurak et al., 2020). The person can use mechanical declarative knowledge of cutting to select the knife as the most promising tool. Mental simulation of the action supports planning and evaluation before selecting motor actions to execute the procedure. If the action is unsuccessful, there is another attempt to select an appropriate tool. The right half of Figure 6.16 illustrates a neurocognitive perspective. A region (blue) in the inferior parietal lobe (IPL) is a likely candidate for integrating the mechanical actions in another region (purple) of the inferior parietal lobe (IPL) with motor actions (yellow) in the inferior parietal sulcus (IPS).

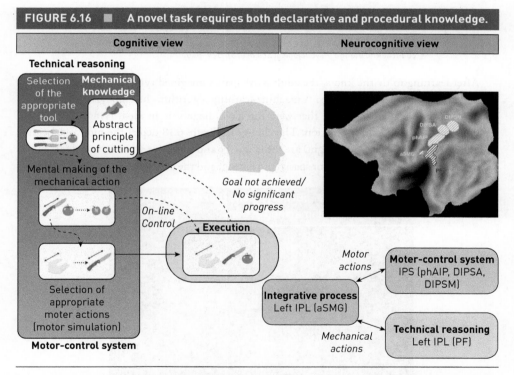

FIGURE 6.16 ■ **A novel task requires both declarative and procedural knowledge.**

Source: "Technition: When tools come out of the closet," by F. Osiurak, M. Lesourd, J. Navarro, & E. Reynaud, 2020, *Perspectives on Psychological Science, 15*, 880–897. https://doi.org/10.1177/1745691620902145

There is not only neurological evidence for the mental simulation of actions but support for the claim that, in some cases, the simulated actions can be identified from fMRI recordings (Mason & Just, 2020). The identification is aided by the fact that, unlike a declarative concept, simulating actions occurs over the time period required to perform the action. The actions in this case consisted of learning to tie seven nautical knots, such as the one shown in Figure 6.17.

FIGURE 6.17 ■ A nautical knot used to study the neural representations of imagined actions.

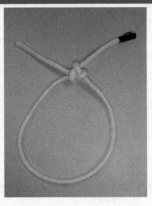

Source: Mason, R. A., & Just, M. A. (2020). Neural representations of procedural knowledge. *Psychological Science, 31*, 529–540.

After learning to tie the knots, the adult participants imagined tying each knot while the investigators took fMRI recordings. A machine-learning algorithm then analyzed the recordings to identify areas in the brain that were the most diagnostic in identifying which knot was involved in the mental simulation. The ellipses in Figure 6.18 depict the most diagnostic regions. The regions (from left to right) are the language and executive area in the frontal brain, the motor cortex, the parietal area for spatial processing, and the cerebellum.

FIGURE 6.18 ■ Brain regions that distinguished among different imagined actions.

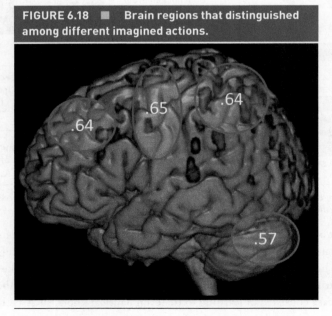

Source: From Mason, R. A & Just, M. A. (2020). Neural representations of procedural knowledge. *Psychological Science, 31*, 529-540.

Mason and Just (2020) hypothesized that the parietal area likely supported the simulated actions while the motor cortex and cerebellum supported a motor plan for execution. They recommended that future studies should include tasks that are more conceptual, such as computer programming. This recommendation would be helpful in evaluating the technical reasoning framework developed by Osiurak and his colleagues (Osiurak et al., 2020; Osiurak & Heinke, 2018).

APPLICATIONS

Cognitive Offloading

Let's now return to the concept of cognitive load introduced in Chapter 4 by examining how it can be reduced by cognitive offloading. Cognitive offloading occurs when a physical action reduces the cognitive demands of the task (Risko & Gilbert, 2016). The physical action may either directly involve the body or involve the environment. For instance, rotate this text 45° to the right. You will likely find it easier to read if you also rotate your head 45° to the right. Another example of using the body to make a task easier is the use of fingers in counting by young children. Offloading information onto the environment occurs when we enter appointments into a calendar, create a shopping list, or post sticky notes (Photo 6.5).

PHOTO 6.5 Using notes to offload information onto the environment.

istockphoto.com/diego_cervo

As illustrated in Figure 6.19, cognitive offloading onto the environment requires making a decision when to use internal processes versus external aids (Risko & Gilbert, 2016). Evaluating our memory ability and the required effort to accomplish the task influence this decision. For instance, should a driver use unaided spatial memory or a GPS device to navigate to a friend's house? GPS is typically more reliable, but it may also prevent learning unaided navigation if we rely too much on it.

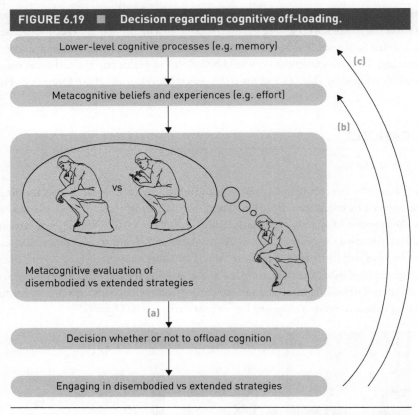

FIGURE 6.19 ■ Decision regarding cognitive off-loading.

Source: "Cognitive offloading," by E. F. Risko & S. J. Gilbert, 2016, *Trends in Cognitive Sciences*, *20*, 676–688. https://doi.org/10.1016/j.tics.2016.07.002

The overreliance on external aids was revealed in a study that provided participants with the opportunity to write numbers on a paper rather than simply remember them over a brief time period (Risko & Dunn, 2015). The research paradigm used a variant of a traditional short-term memory task that required recall of a string of auditorily presented digits. Participants knew the number of digits on each trial and, as expected, were more likely to write digits as the number increased from two to ten. They also wrote either all of the digits or none of the digits, so they would not have to decide which to record and which to remember. A surprising finding was that almost half of the participants wrote the digits even when told there would be only two digits.

Gestures use the body, rather than the environment, to offload information. Gestures are helpful during instruction because they enable teachers and students to demonstrate concepts such as size that may be difficult to state verbally. They can also facilitate reasoning by reducing the demands on working memory. Wagner et al. (2004) asked college-age adults to factor quadratic equations on a whiteboard and then explain their solutions. To determine the memory demands of the explanation task, the researchers gave the students supplementary information, such as a random string of letters, before their explanations.

Students were later able to recall more supplementary items if they gestured while explaining their solution. Gesturing reduced the memory demands, particularly when the gestures and verbal explanations were compatible.

Instruction

Instructors can aid learning by designing tasks that are supported by actions. Arthur Glenberg, a major contributor to theories of embodied cognition, and his co-investigators have tested the implications of the theory for helping young readers (Walker et al., 2017). An iPad app called *EMBRACE* (Enhanced Moved By Reading to Accelerate Comprehension of English) is designed to help English-language learners improve their comprehension of written English. It also helps them learn about science.

Figure 6.20 shows a page from a text used to teach early readers about Newton's three laws of motion. Many educators might think it too early to try to teach these concepts to children because they seem so abstract. But motion is something we experience all of the time. The key is to use embodied processing to teach children to map unfamiliar words, such as "force" and "acceleration," to actions and experiences that are familiar.

FIGURE 6.20 ■ A screen shot from EMBRACE.

Figure courtesy of Arthur Glenberg.

Source: A screen shot from EMBRACE, an iPad learning app.

When Juan ties the small dog to the cart, children can use their sensorimotor experience to simulate the dog pulling the cart. But according to Newton's second law, force = mass x acceleration, a larger force will be needed when Maria puts the logs into the cart, thereby increasing its mass. Now children can simulate the dog having a hard time providing enough force to get the cart moving—that is, to accelerate it. But, on the next page, Maria ties the horse to the cart, and the horse can apply enough force to easily move the cart.

Does this really work? Gómez and Glenberg (2020) reported on research conducted in Chile with children in the second and third grades reading the Spanish translation of the text. After reading each chapter, the children took a multiple-choice comprehension test. Children who acted out the text, either by moving the pictures on the iPad or by pantomiming, showed significantly greater comprehension compared to children who simply read the text. Also, children who acted out the text did significantly better on a vocabulary test that consisted of words such as "force" and "acceleration."

EMBRACE is an excellent example of a learning system that applies virtual actions to virtual objects. A big question for instructional design is how to choose between virtual and physical representations. To help answer this question, Martina Rau (2020) reviewed research on the effects of physical and virtual learning in science, technology, engineering, and mathematics. Her article investigates (1) what predictions different perspectives make about these two types of representations and (2) whether these predictions conflict or align with each other on issues such as physical engagement, cognitive load, and conceptual salience. For instance, Rau suggests the physical interactions can be more engaging but virtual interactions are more effective in reducing cognitive load.

A second theme in Rau's (2020) article is the design of future research to evaluate the effectiveness of blended technologies, such as displaying the effects on a computer screen while manipulating physical objects. Such research needs to identify how different learning mechanisms interact with each other to determine how to productively create blended technologies.

SUMMARY

The action-specific account of perception proposes that people perceive their surrounding environment in terms of their ability to act on it, ranging from daily activities to superior athletic performance. According to the perceptual symbol systems theory, people directly store sensory experiences in memory and can re-experience them through mental stimulation. Simulations that occur during language comprehension can result in gestures according to the gestures-as-simulation hypothesis. Gestures can then activate, manipulate, package, and explore spatial information during both speaking and thinking.

Physical, virtual, and mental actions can be combined with physical, virtual, and mental objects. Examples of physical actions on physical objects are Montessori manipulatives, on virtual objects are Wii sports games, and on mental objects are gestures. Examples of virtual actions on physical objects are robotic surgery, on virtual objects are virtual experiments, and on mental objects are teaching the blind. Examples of mental actions on physical objects are brain-computer robotic interfaces, on virtual objects are brain-computer cursor interfaces, and on mental objects are sports simulations.

High-level actions, such as holding, getting, and pouring milk, depend on low-level actions, such as movement of the joints and muscles. Modifying actions for activities as diverse as typing and high jumping requires discovering new components that initially degrade performance but can eventually result in substantial improvements. Action identification theory proposes that action is maintained with respect to its available identity, there is a bias toward a higher-level identity, a shift to a lower-level identity when necessary, and a tendency to find an optimal level of performance. Neuroscience offers support for a theoretical framework in which technical and novel actions rely on both procedural and declarative memory.

Cognitive offloading occurs when a physical action reduces the cognitive demands of the task. The physical action may either directly involve the body (such as gesturing) or incorporate the environment (such as making a list). An iPad application called EMBRACE (Enhanced Moved By Reading to Accelerate Comprehension of English) helps English-language learners improve their comprehension of written English and learn about science. The key is to use embodied processing to teach children to map unfamiliar words, such as "force" and "acceleration," to familiar actions and experiences. Future research needs to evaluate the effectiveness of blended technologies on instruction to identify how different learning mechanisms interact with each other.

RECOMMENDED READING

Action has become an increasingly important contributor to understanding the cognitive and neuropsychological aspects of cognition (Engel et al., 2013). Exploration is a unifying construct that applies across many domains, ranging from animal foraging to cultural innovation (Hills et al, 2015). Exercise, sports, and the performance arts link skill training with cognition (Tomporowski & Pesce, 2019). Knowledge of actions is useful for how we perform, simulate the actions of others, and acquire a conceptual understanding of performance (Quandt & Chatterjee, 2015). Risko and Gilbert (2016) discuss the mechanisms that trigger cognitive offloading and the consequences of this behavior.

7 MEMORY CODES

The Levels-of-Processing Theory
   Emphasis on Coding Strategies
   Implications for Verbal Rehearsal
   Supporting Evidence
   Structural, Phonemic, and Semantic Processing

Criticisms and Modifications of the Theory
   Criticisms
   Elaboration of Memory Codes
   Distinctiveness of Memory Codes

Encoding Specificity and Retrieval
   The Encoding Specificity Principle
   Interaction Between Encoding and Retrieval Operations
   Transfer Appropriate Processing

Applications
   Elaborate Memory Codes
   Distinctive Memory Codes
   Transfer Appropriate Processing

SUMMARY

RECOMMENDED READING

LEARNING OBJECTIVES

1.   Explain how the levels-of-processing theory differs from the Atkinson-Shiffrin model.

2.   Describe how criticisms of the levels-of-processing theory resulted in modifications to the theory.

3.   Distinguish between encoding specificity and transfer appropriate processing.

4.   Provide examples of how learning can be improved through memory codes and transfer appropriate processing.

The first part of this book introduced perception, working memory, declarative long-term memory (LTM), procedural LTM, and motor components of the mind. These components provide a structure but leave us with many questions. For example, why are there many different decay rates in LTM? Does verbal rehearsal always cause learning? Are some memory codes better than others? And how is knowledge organized?

The next four chapters provide some answers to these questions about the representation and organization of knowledge. Our immediate objective is to learn how memory codes differ and what the implications of these differences are for learning and retrieval. A **memory code** is the representation used to store an item in memory. Consider what memory codes might be involved if you were learning to associate pairs of words in a paired-associates task. If the words were objects such as "truck," you might form a visual image of the words. You would also probably rehearse the words and create an acoustic (phonemic) code. If the words were meaningful, you might create meaningful associations to help you learn. Atkinson and Shiffrin (1971) proposed each of these memory codes for transferring information from short-term to long-term memory. We briefly reviewed these options but will now discuss them in greater depth.

When people try to learn, they most likely form several kinds of memory codes, and psychologists have little control over what people do. So instead of asking people to learn, we often ask them to make judgments about words without telling them that they will have to recall or recognize the words after the judgment task. The purpose of the judgment task (often called an **orienting task**) is to try to control the kind of memory code formed by requesting that a person make decisions about a particular aspect of the word, such as its pronunciation or its meaning. Psychologists can then examine how well that person can recall the word as a function of the aspect emphasized.

The first section of this chapter examines a theory of memory called **levels of processing**, proposed by Craik and Lockhart (1972), which holds that success in recalling a word depends on the kinds of operations carried out while encoding the word. Criticisms and modifications of the theory are reviewed in the second section, including the proposed argument that memory codes are effective when they are distinctive and support elaboration. The third section considers the principles of encoding specificity and transfer appropriate processing to link encoding with retrieval. The final section discusses the application of three of these concepts—elaboration, distinctiveness, and transfer appropriate processing.

THE LEVELS-OF-PROCESSING THEORY

Emphasis on Coding Strategies

The levels-of-processing theory proposes that there are different ways to code material and that some memory codes are better than others. Preliminary processing is concerned with the analysis of physical features, such as lines, angles, brightness, pitch, and loudness. Later stages of analysis are concerned with pattern recognition and identification of meaning. After the stimulus is recognized, it may be further elaborated—a word, sight, or smell may trigger associations, images, or stories on the basis of the individual's past experiences. The levels-of-processing

---

memory code The format (physical, phonemic, semantic) of information encoded into memory

orienting task Instructions to focus on a particular aspect (physical, phonemic, semantic) of a stimulus

levels of processing A theory that proposes that "deeper" (semantic) levels of processing enhance memory

theory claims that analysis proceeds through a series of sensory states to levels associated with pattern recognition to semantic-associative stages.

Each level of analysis results in a different memory code—but a memory code that varies in its decay rate. The memory code and its persistence are therefore both by-products of perceptual processing. When only the physical features of a stimulus have been analyzed, the memory code is fragile and quickly decays. When the stimulus has been identified and named, the memory code is stronger and can be represented by an intermediate decay rate. Memory is best when a person elaborates the meaning of the stimulus.

The levels-of-processing theory is a theory of how we analyze a stimulus and what memory codes result from different levels of analysis. Unlike the Atkinson and Shiffrin (1968) theory, it is not concerned with the structural components or stages of memory; the two theories can therefore coexist. Craik (1979) later stated that the point of most levels-of-processing studies has been to gain a fuller understanding of memory codes operating in LTM, not to deny the distinction between short-term memory (STM) and LTM. When viewed from this perspective, the work on levels of processing extends rather than replaces a stage (component) of analysis by showing how control processes can influence the retention of material.

Implications for Verbal Rehearsal

We saw in Chapter 5 on long-term memory that the Atkinson-Shiffrin model emphasized verbal rehearsal as a means of transferring information from STM to LTM. Because most of us have used this method to learn material, the role of rehearsal in learning seems intuitively attractive. But rehearsal does not automatically result in learning, according to Craik and Lockhart. The effectiveness of rehearsal, like that of other methods of study, depends on the level at which material is processed. The reason rehearsal often results in learning is that people usually attend to the meaning of the material during rehearsal.

Another issue raised by the Atkinson-Shiffrin formulation is what happens when rehearsal is *not* used for learning. Sometimes it is used to maintain information in STM, as when we dial a telephone number. Would rehearsal result in learning if people used it simply to maintain items in STM? Does rehearsal automatically result in learning, or are there different kinds of rehearsal, only some of which promote learning? To answer these questions, Craik and Watkins (1973) asked people to perform a fairly simple task. Students were told to listen to a series of word lists and, at the end of each list, to report the last word beginning with a particular letter. The experimenter told them the critical letter before each list and assumed that they would maintain a word starting with that letter in STM until they heard another word beginning with that letter or until the list ended. The task was quite easy, and students almost always gave the correct answer at the end of the list.

The purpose of the experiment was to vary the length of time a word would have to be maintained in STM. For example, if *g* were the critical letter and the list contained, in order, the words *daughter, oil, rifle, garden, grain, table, football, anchor,* and *giraffe,* the word *garden* would be immediately replaced by *grain,* which would eventually be replaced by *giraffe.* Because there are no intervening words between *garden* and *grain*, whereas there are three intervening words between *grain* and *giraffe*, *grain* would have to be maintained in STM for a longer time than *garden*. The word *grain* should therefore be rehearsed more often than *garden*. Craik and Watkins controlled the amount of time a word would have to be maintained in STM by varying the number of intervening words from 0 to 12. If maintenance rehearsal results in learning, the probability of recalling a word at the end of the experiment should be a function of the length of time it was maintained in STM.

After hearing 27 lists of words, the students were asked to recall as many words as they could from all the lists. Craik and Watkins found that the probability of recalling a word was independent of the length of time it was maintained in STM. To consider the two extreme cases, students recalled 12% of the words that were immediately replaced in STM by the next word on the list and 15% of the words that were maintained over 12 intervening words.

The small difference between 12% and 15% shows that rehearsal does not automatically cause learning. According to the levels-of-processing view of memory, the students did not try to form a lasting memory code because they thought they would have to remember the word for only a very short time. In particular, they did not emphasize the meaning of the words. A good analogy might be reading the words in a book without thinking about what you are reading. You would be rehearsing the words in the sense that you would be covertly pronouncing them, but your thoughts might be on yesterday's football game or tonight's party. Suddenly you realize that you can't remember what you just read because you weren't thinking about what it meant.

Another example of how thought processes influence what people remember comes from the study of how professional actors learn their lines. Analysis of recall protocols following the study of a six-page script revealed that actors learned their lines through an elaborative process that emphasizes how their character affects or is affected by the other characters in the script (Noice, 1991). When forced to learn their lines through rote rehearsal, they recalled significantly less than when studying by their usual, more elaborative process (Photo 7.1). Noice concludes that "actors are expert analyzers, not expert memorizers, and one result of this in-depth analysis is that by struggling to uncover the underlying meaning of each line, the actual words are also retained without much deliberate effort to commit them to memory" (Noice, 1991, p. 456).

Let's look now at additional evidence that the way material is processed determines what kind of memory code is formed, which in turn determines how well the material is remembered. Much of this research makes use of incidental learning—our ability to remember when we are not trying to learn. For example, you likely remember what you ate for breakfast this morning even though you did not try to learn this information (Photo 7.2). Incidental learning is an important topic in psychology and provides the opportunity to create a learning task that has been widely used to study how different memory codes influence recognition and recall.

---

maintenance rehearsal Rehearsal that keeps information active in short-term memory

PHOTO 7.1 Elaborative encoding helps actors learn a script.

istockphoto.com/LightFieldStudios

PHOTO 7.2 Incidental learning creates memories without intention to learn.

istockphoto.com/evgenyatamanenko

Supporting Evidence

The influence of levels of processing on retention was nicely demonstrated in a study by Hyde and Jenkins (1969) at the University of Minnesota. Their results were published several years before Craik and Lockhart's theory and most likely influenced its development. Like most of the studies used later to test the levels-of-processing theory, Hyde and Jenkins's study used an incidental learning paradigm. In an **incidental learning task** people are given some material but are not told that they have to learn it. The experimenter then later gives them a recall or recognition test on the items presented during the experiment. In an intentional learning task, by contrast, the subjects are explicitly told to learn the material.

The first experiment in Hyde and Jenkins's study compared seven groups of subjects, but we will consider only four to simplify the discussion. One of the four groups was given an intentional learning task in which the subjects were asked to try to remember 24 words. The words consisted of 12 pairs of **primary associates**—words that are highly associated. For example, the word *red* is highly associated with the word *green*, and *table* is highly associated with *chair*. The 24 words were presented in a random order, with the restriction that primary associates could not occur next to each other in the list. After the subjects in the "intentional" group had listened to a tape recording of the 24 words, they tried to recall as many as they could, in any order.

The other three groups were incidental learning groups who were not informed that they should try to remember the words. They heard the same recording of 24 words but were asked to make a judgment about each item on the list. One group simply rated the words as pleasant or unpleasant; another group judged whether each word contained the letter *e*; and a third group estimated the number of letters in each word. The purpose of using three orienting tasks was to try to create different levels of processing. The first group would have to consider the meaning of the words. The latter two groups would have to consider the spelling of the words; the meaning of the words would be irrelevant to them. Because, according to the levels-of-processing theory, semantic processing should result in better recall than nonsemantic processing, the undergraduates who rated the pleasantness of the words should show better recall than those who considered the spelling of the words.

The results supported the prediction. The average number of words recalled was 16.3 for those students who rated pleasantness, 9.9 for those who estimated the number of letters, and 9.4 for those who judged the presence of the letter *e*. The most striking aspect of the results is that students in the pleasant-unpleasant group recalled virtually as many words as those who were told to try to learn the words (16.3 versus 16.1). In other words, incidental learning was as effective as intentional learning when the students considered the meaning of the words.

We have been assuming, along with Hyde and Jenkins, that differences in recall among the three incidental groups were caused by the possibility that the students in the pleasant-unpleasant group were more likely to attend to the meaning of the words than the students in the other two

---

incidental learning task A task that studies memories when people are not trying to learn

primary associates Words that are strongly associated with each other, as typically measured by asking people to provide associations to words

groups. Is there any direct evidence for this assumption? The fact that the list consisted of pairs of words that are semantically related provides a clue. Recognizing that words are related in meaning can make it easier to recall them. For example, the recall of *green* may remind a person that *red* was also on the list. One indication that people were attending to the meaning of the words would be if they recalled the primary associates together—*red* followed by *green* or vice versa.

Hyde and Jenkins defined the percentage of clustering as the number of associated pairs recalled together, divided by the total number of recalled words. For instance, if you recalled the words *red, table, salt, pepper,* and *green,* your clustering score would be 40% because two of the five words (*salt* and *pepper*) were recalled together as primary associates. The amount of clustering was 26% for the group that made judgments about the letter *e*, 31% for the group that estimated the number of letters, 64% for the group that was told to study the words, and 68% for the group that judged the pleasantness of the words. These results support the assumption that the groups differed in how much they used meaning to aid recall. Those groups that were the most sensitive to the meaning recalled the most words.

Structural, Phonemic, and Semantic Processing

Tests of the levels-of-processing theory have generally focused on three levels, in which the depth of processing increases from structural to phonemic to semantic coding. Table 7.1 shows examples of questions that were asked to emphasize different levels of coding. The structural coding question asks whether the word is in capital letters. Phonemic coding is encouraged by asking whether a word rhymes with another word—the question emphasizes pronunciation. Questions about whether a word is a member of a certain category or whether it fits into a sentence encourage semantic coding—a person must evaluate the meaning to answer correctly.

In a series of experiments conducted by Craik and Tulving (1975), one of the questions preceded each brief exposure of a word. Participants were informed that the experiment concerned perception and speed of reaction. After a series of question-and-answer trials based on the kinds of questions shown in Table 7.1, the subject was unexpectedly given a retention test for the exposed words. Craik and Tulving expected that memory would vary systematically with depth of processing.

Figure 7.1 shows the results from one of Craik and Tulving's experiments that used a recognition test. When students were asked which words had been presented during the initial judgment task, they recognized the most words when they had initially judged whether the word fit into a sentence (semantic processing) and the fewest words when they had initially judged whether the letters were upper- or lowercase (structural processing). Recognition accuracy was

---

clustering Percentage of occasions in which a word is followed by its primary associate during the free recall of words

structural coding A memory code that emphasizes the physical structure of the stimulus

phonemic coding A memory code that emphasizes the pronunciation of the stimulus

semantic coding A memory code that emphasizes the meaning of the stimulus

TABLE 7.1 ■	Typical questions used in levels-of-processing studies		
Level of Processing	**Question**	**Yes**	**No**
Structural	Is the word in capital letters?	*TABLE*	table
Phonemic	Does the word rhyme with *WEIGHT*?	crate	*MARKET*
Semantic	Would the word fit the sentence	*FRIEND*	Cloud
	"He met a _____ in the street"?		

Credit: From "Depth of processing and the retention of words in episodic memory," by F. I. M. Craik & E. Tulving, 1975, *Journal of Experimental Psychology: General, 104*, 268–294. https://doi.org/10.1037/0096-3445.104.3.268. Copyright 1975 by the American Psychological Association. Reprinted by permission.

at an intermediate level when the students had been asked whether one word rhymed with another (phonemic processing). The findings supported the prediction that retention would increase as processing proceeded from the structural to the phonemic to the semantic level. The same pattern of results occurred when Craik and Tulving used a recall rather than a recognition test. Questions about a word's meaning resulted in better memory than those about a word's sound or the physical characteristics of its letters (Photo 7.3).

PHOTO 7.3 Focusing on letter fonts produces a shallow level of encoding.

istockphoto.com/IrisImages

Subsequent research, however, showed that levels of processing has little impact on retention in short-term working memory (Rose et al., 2010). However, it did influence performance on a delayed recognition task of the same words in which the findings were similar to those shown in the right half of Figure 7.1. The investigators concluded that phonological processing was the predominant code used in STM, even when the orienting question emphasized structural or semantic codes. Although sufficient for short-term retention, the phonological codes were not as effective as semantic codes for long-term retention.

FIGURE 7.1 ■ **Initial decision time (response latency) and recognition performance for words as a function of the initial task.**

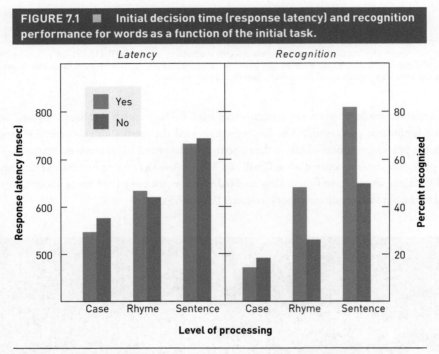

Source: "Depth of processing and the retention of words in episodic memory," by F. I. M. Craik & E. Tulving, 1975, *Journal of Experimental Psychology: General, 104,* 268–294. https://doi.org/10.1037/0096-3445.104.3.268. Copyright 1975 by the American Psychological Association.

CRITICISMS AND MODIFICATIONS OF THE THEORY

Criticisms

One of the initial challenges to the theory came from the confounding between levels of processing and the amount of time spent processing. The left half of Figure 7.1 shows the average response time required to answer the three kinds of questions. The case questions could be answered most quickly, followed by the rhyme questions, followed by the sentence questions. Perhaps the greater amount of time spent processing the words causes the better retention. This interpretation would lose support if it were possible to design a structural decision task that results in both slow responses and poor retention.

Imagine that an experimenter shows you a card with a five-letter word, such as *stoop* or *black*. Your task is to respond positively if the word consists of two consonants followed by two vowels followed by a consonant and negatively for any other sequence of consonants and vowels. As you might guess, your response times would be relatively slow. In fact, it takes about twice as long to make this kind of structural decision as to make a semantic decision about whether a word fits into a sentence. If good retention is caused by long response times, the structural processing should now result in better retention than semantic processing. However, recognition is still much better after semantic processing, proving that the level of processing, not the time spent processing, is the best determinant of retention (Craik & Tulving, 1975).

The levels-of-processing theory has had a major impact on memory research—many investigators designed studies to explicitly test its implications; others found it a convenient framework in which to discuss their results. Because much of this research was quite supportive of the theory, it wasn't until about five years after the Craik and Lockhart paper that psychologists began to question the theory (Baddeley, 1978; Eysenck, 1978; Nelson, 1977). One of the main criticisms was that it was too easy to account for differential rates of forgetting by appealing to the theory. An investigator might claim that differences in rates of forgetting were caused by differences in levels of processing, without measuring the levels of processing.

To avoid this criticism, it is necessary to be able to measure depth of processing independently of retention. The argument that depth increases from structural to phonemic to semantic processing appealed to most psychologists because it is consistent with the ordering of information-processing stages. Analyzing the physical structure of a pattern leads to retrieving its name, which in turn leads to considering its meaning by retrieving stored associations from LTM. One problem with this assumption is that, although this sequence provides a reasonable account of how information is analyzed, it is not a *necessary* sequence (Baddeley, 1978; Craik, 1979). Although Craik and Lockhart originally hoped that encoding time would provide an independent measure of depth of processing, we have seen that this measure has its limitations (Craik & Tulving, 1975).

Another difficulty with the concept of depth of processing is that, even if we had an objective ordering of the "depth" of different memory codes, it still would not tell us why some codes are more effective than others. Why are semantic codes better than phonemic codes and phonemic codes better than structural codes? Psychologists have suggested two possible answers. One is that memory codes differ in how elaborate they are, and more elaborate codes result in better memory. The other is that memory codes differ in distinctiveness, and more distinctive codes result in better memory.

Elaboration of Memory Codes

One explanation of how memory codes differ proposes that they differ in the number and types of elaborations stored in memory (Anderson & Reder, 1979). This view assumes that people store much more than simply the items presented to them—they also store additional associations that help them remember the items. Anderson and Reder have proposed that, although it is very easy to elaborate material at the semantic level, it is difficult to construct elaborations at the structural or phonemic level. Most of our associations are concerned with meaning rather than with the physical structure of letters, spelling, or pronunciation. Anderson and Reder suggest that the reason for this difference is that people usually try to remember the meaning of what they read rather than such details as what the letters looked like. As a consequence, people have learned to elaborate on the semantic content because doing so is generally more useful than elaborating on nonsemantic content.

One virtue of the elaboration hypothesis is that it provides a possible explanation of how differences can occur within a particular level of processing (Craik, 1979). Although the original levels-of-processing proposal predicted that semantic processing should be superior to nonsemantic processing, it could not account for differences in retention for two different semantic tasks. The elaboration hypothesis predicts that such differences should occur if the two tasks differ in the extent of semantic elaboration.

One method for increasing semantic elaboration is to provide a richer, more elaborate context. This approach is illustrated by one of the experiments in the 1975 Craik and Tulving study. The experiment tested for the recall of words after a semantic judgment task in which people determined whether a word would fit into a sentence frame. There were three levels of sentence complexity—simple, medium, and complex. For example:

Simple: She cooked the_____.

Medium: The ripe_____tasted delicious.

Complex: The small lady angrily picked up the red_____.

PHOTO 7.4 A complex sentence aids recall of the word "tomato."

istockphoto.com/Tim UR

After completing 60 judgments, subjects were asked to recall as many words as they could from the initial phase of the experiment. They were then shown the original sentence frames and asked to recall the word associated with each sentence. The first part of the recall task is called **noncued recall**, and the second part is called **cued recall** because students could use the sentence frames as retrieval cues. Figure 7.2 shows the proportion of words recalled as a function of sentence complexity. Sentence complexity had a significant effect on recalling words that did fit the sentence. This was true for both cued recall (CR—yes) and noncued recall (NCR—yes), although the effect was greater for cued recall. The effect of sentence complexity supported Craik and Tulving's hypothesis that more complex sentence frames would produce a more elaborate memory code and improve recall (Photo 7.4).

---

noncued recall Recall that occurs without hints or cues provided by the experimenter

cued recall Recall that occurs with hints or cues, such as providing the questions asked during the judgment phase of a task

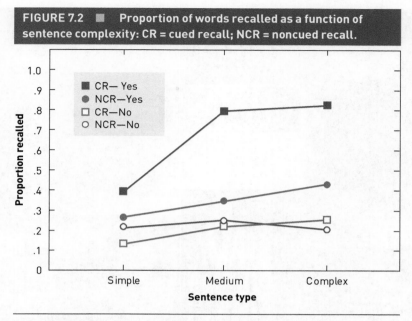

FIGURE 7.2 ■ **Proportion of words recalled as a function of sentence complexity: CR = cued recall; NCR = noncued recall.**

Source: "Depth of processing and the retention of words in episodic memory," by F. I. M. Craik & E. Tulving, 1975, *Journal of Experimental Psychology: General, 104,* 268–294. https://doi.org/10.1037/0096-3445.104.3.268. Copyright 1975 by the American Psychological Association.

The more elaborate code was ineffective, however, if the word did not fit the sentence. This finding suggests that the elaboration must be consistent with the meaning of the word to be effective. Even when elaboration is generally consistent with the meaning of a word, it can vary in effectiveness depending on how precisely it relates to the word's meaning. Imagine that you read the sentence "The fat man read the sign." Sometime later, someone shows you the same sentence with the word *fat* replaced by a blank and asks you to recall the missing word. If elaboration is effective, you might do better if you read an elaborated sentence such as

1. The fat man read the sign that was two feet high.
    or

2. The fat man read the sign warning about thin ice.

Although both sentences provide additional information, there is an important distinction between the two elaborations. The first is an **imprecise elaboration** because there is no apparent relation between the adjective *fat* and the height of the sign. The second is a **precise elaboration** because the degree of danger of thin ice depends on a person's weight (Photo 7.5).

---

imprecise elaboration Provision or generation of additional material unrelated to remembered material

precise elaboration Provision or generation of additional material closely related to remembered material

PHOTO 7.5 Consequence of weight produces a precise elaboration.

istockphoto.comTom Hayek

Stein and Bransford (1979) tested the effectiveness of precise and imprecise elaboration by comparing four groups of students in an incidental learning task. Students in the control group read ten short sentences and were told that the purpose of the experiment was to measure sentence comprehensibility. The second and third groups of students were told the same thing. They read the same ten sentences elaborated by an additional phrase that was either precisely or imprecisely related to a target word in the sentence. A fourth group of students was told to generate their own elaborations so the experimenters could measure the probability that certain phrases would be generated. At the end of the experiment, everyone was shown the unelaborated sentences and asked to recall a missing target word.

Students in the control group recalled an average of 4.2 words, compared with 2.2 words for the imprecise elaboration group, 7.4 words for the precise elaboration group, and 5.8 words for the self-generation group. The results show that elaboration is not always effective in recall because imprecise elaboration actually caused a decline in performance relative to the control group. To be effective, the elaboration should clarify the significance or relevance of a concept (such as *fat man*) relative to the context (*thin ice*) in which it occurs.

The fact that recall following **self-generation** was intermediate between that for precise and imprecise elaboration suggests that the students' elaborations contained a mixture of the two

---

self-generation Generation of items by participants in an experiment rather than the provision of these items by the experimenter

types. Two judges therefore divided the subject-generated elaborations into two groups (precise and imprecise), depending on whether the information clarified the relevance of the target words in the sentence. Students were able to recall 91% of the target words in the cases where they had generated precise elaborations and 49% in the cases where they had generated imprecise elaborations.

A second experiment revealed that instructions were effective in encouraging subjects to generate precise elaborations. Subjects in the imprecise elaboration group were asked to elaborate with the question "What else might happen in this context?" Subjects in the precise elaboration group were prompted to elaborate with the question "Why might this man be engaged in this particular type of activity?" Students in the latter group recalled significantly more target words, indicating that elaboration is particularly effective when it is directed toward understanding the potential relevance of the information presented.

Distinctiveness of Memory Codes

Memory codes can differ in distinctiveness as well as in the extent of elaboration. To remember something, we would like to make it a **distinctive item**, one that really stands out from other items that could interfere with our memory. There are several different ways in which an item can be distinctive, and here we follow a classification proposed by Schmidt (1991) that distinguishes among four different kinds of distinctiveness.

One kind of distinctiveness is called **primary distinctiveness** in which distinctiveness is defined relative to the immediate context. Imagine that you are shown a list of common words and all the words are printed in red ink, except for one word that is printed in black ink. Later you are asked to recall the words on the list. Which word do you think you would have the best chance of recalling? The results of past research indicate that you would more likely recall the word in black ink than the words in red ink. Note that the word in black ink is distinctive only because the color differs from the color of other words on the list. In general, a common word in black ink is not particularly distinctive.

Release from proactive interference (discussed in Chapter 4 on memory) is an example of improving recall by making items distinct from other items in the immediate context. People recalled more items when the material changed from words to numbers or from numbers to words than when the material stayed the same. Recall also improved when the items changed from sports events to political events or from political events to sports events. All the changes made these items more distinct from the preceding items.

In contrast, **secondary distinctiveness** is defined relative to information in our LTM rather than to information in the immediate context. One example is a characteristic of a word's spelling. A word is **orthographically distinctive** if it has an unusual shape, as determined by the

---

distinctive item An item different in appearance or meaning from other items

primary distinctiveness An item distinct from other items in the immediate context

secondary distinctiveness An item distinct from items stored in long-term memory

orthographic distinctiveness Lower case words that have an unusual shape sequencing of short and tall letters in the word. Orthographically distinctive words include *lymph, khaki*, and *afghan*. Examples of orthographically common words are *leaky, kennel*, and *airway*. The first three words have unusual shapes, and the last three have more typical shapes. Notice that a shape is unusual (distinctive) relative to all other words stored in LTM, not just to words in the immediate context of the experiment.

When people are asked to recall a list of words, half of which are orthographically distinctive and half of which are orthographically common, they recall significantly more of the distinctive words (Hunt & Elliott, 1980). It is clear that the shape of the words rather than some other factor causes the results. When the same list is presented orally rather than visually there is no difference in recall. There is also no difference in recall when the words are typed in capital letters; people do not recall *LYMPH, KHAKI*, and *AFGHAN* any better than *LEAKY, KENNEL*, and *AIRWAY*. Apparently, the different heights of lowercase letters contribute to the effect because all letters are the same height when capitalized.

A third kind of distinctiveness is called **emotional distinctiveness** and is motivated by the finding that events producing strong emotional responses are sometimes remembered well. These events include **flashbulb memories**—the vivid recollections that most people have of the circumstances surrounding their discovery of a shocking piece of news (Brown & Kulik, 1977). Events such as the assassination of President Kennedy or the explosion of the space shuttle *Challenger* (Winograd & Neisser, 1992) have been studied as examples of people's flashbulb memories.

Although Schmidt (1991) included emotional distinctiveness in his taxonomy, he admitted that it is not always clear which aspects of an emotional memory are enhanced or even whether the concept of "distinctiveness" provides an adequate explanation of the impact of emotion on memory. In addition, subsequent evidence has questioned whether emotional events (flashbulb memories) are better remembered than ordinary events. For example, Weaver (1993) compared students' memory for an emotional event (the 1991 bombing of Iraq) and an ordinary event (a routine encounter with a roommate or friend). When their memory was tested both three months and 1 year later, Weaver found no difference in the accuracy of the two memories. He did find differences in confidence—students were more confident of the accuracy of their memory about the bombing, but their confidence was unwarranted.

Phelps and Sharot (2008) reported on the neural mechanisms that mediate this feeling of confidence without an increase in accuracy. Their findings build on knowledge reported in Chapter 5 on long-term memory that the hippocampus is critical for integrating details to form episodic memories but the amygdala has a critical role in forming emotional memories. They found that the amygdala registered increased cortical activity during the recollection of emotional photos but did not show increased cortical activity during the recollection of neutral photos. The opposite findings occurred for the parahippocampus. The parahippocampus registered increased cortical activity during the recollection of neutral photos but did not show increased cortical activity during the recollection of emotional photos. People's judgment of

---

emotional distinctiveness Items that produce an intense emotional reaction

flashbulb memory A memory of an important event that caused an emotional reaction

confidence therefore uses different information. For emotional events, the *quality* of memory for a few details may matter; for neutral events, the *quantity* of contextual details may be more important.

An extensive study following the September 11, 2001 attacks on the world trade center extended the one-year retention interval studied by Weaver for the 1991 bombing of Iraq. Within a week of the 9/11 attack, a group of researchers across the United States distributed a survey that asked respondents how they learned of the attack (their flashbulb memories) and facts about the attack itself (their event memories). Respondents answered follow-up surveys approximately 1 year, 2 years, and 10 years following the destruction of the twin towers. Their responses revealed rapid forgetting of both flashbulb and event memories within the first year but did not show further change over the next 9 years (Hirst et al., 2015). The investigators suggested that the decline in the rate of forgetting for emotional events may reflect a consolidation process that makes the memories less vulnerable to interference. Reminders from media, memorials (Photo 7.6), and social interactions also likely contributed to the accuracy of their event memory and high confidence ratings over the ten years.

PHOTO 7.6 Memorials maintain memories. Here, the *Tribute in Light* memorial to 9/11 is seen over the Brooklyn Bridge in New York.

istockphoto.com/Juntaski

A fourth kind of distinctiveness is called **processing distinctiveness**. Processing distinctiveness depends on how we process the stimulus—it is therefore the result of the memory code that we create for an item rather than the characteristics of the item itself. For example, even if an item is not very distinctive, you may think of a distinctive way of remembering it. If it is distinctive, you may think of a way of processing it to make it even more distinctive. Elaboration is one possible strategy to make an item more distinctive, but the elaboration should emphasize characteristics that differentiate that item from other items (Eysenck, 1979).

---

processing distinctiveness Creation of a memory code that makes that memory distinct from other memories

An example of processing distinctiveness is that people apparently remember faces as caricatures by exaggerating the distinctive features to make the faces even more distinct. When discussing distinctive features in Chapter 2 on perception, there was the example of a study in which people more quickly identified line drawings of their friends when the line drawings were caricatures rather than accurate (Rhodes et al., 1987). Caricatures of unfamiliar faces are also better recognized in a standard recognition-memory test than the faces that were actually shown (Mauro & Kubovy, 1992). Undergraduates viewed 100 slides of faces constructed from an Identi-Kit, as illustrated by the two faces on the right in Figure 7.3. They later were shown 300 test faces and asked to indicate if each test face was exactly the same as one shown in the first series of slides. The test faces included some faces that were new, some faces that were old, and some faces that were caricatures of the old faces.

The caricatures are shown on the left side of Figure 7.3 and were created by making a distinctive feature even more distinct. The high forehead in the top face is made even higher, and the long chin of the bottom face is made longer. The interesting finding is that the caricatures were recognized significantly better than the original (old) faces. This finding is consistent with the processing distinctiveness concept—people encoded the faces into memory in a manner that made each face even more distinct than the original face.

FIGURE 7.3 ■ Two Identi-Kit faces (right) and their caricatures (left): top, high forehead; bottom, long chin.

Source: "Caricature and face recognition," by R. Mauro & M. Kubory, 1992, *Memory and Cognition, 20,* 440–443. https://doi.org/10.3758/BF03210927. Copyright 1992 Psychonomic Society.

Because both processing distinctiveness and the levels-of-processing theory emphasize the importance of creating good memory codes, it is perhaps not surprising that some psychologists have proposed that the levels-of-processing effect is caused by differences in distinctiveness. To demonstrate that distinctiveness can account for the levels-of-processing effect, it would be necessary to show that semantic codes are more distinct than phonemic codes and that phonemic codes are more distinct than physical codes. Some research has already been directed toward the first comparison. Several psychologists (Moscovitch & Craik, 1976; Eysenck, 1979) have argued that semantic codes result in better retention than do phonemic codes because semantic codes are much more distinctive than phonemic codes. They base their argument on the fact that there is a relatively small number of phonemes; thus, phonemic codes necessarily overlap with each other, whereas the domain of possible meanings is essentially limitless.

The experimental study of elaboration and distinctiveness has modified the original conception of levels of processing (Craik, 1979). Some of the original ideas have survived, however. The central idea that there are qualitative differences in memory codes, that different orienting tasks can determine which codes are emphasized, and that memory codes differ in their decay rate remains a useful conception of memory. The major shift in emphasis has been the attempt to provide a theoretical basis for these findings by determining how structural, phonemic, and semantic codes can differ in distinctiveness and elaboration.

ENCODING SPECIFICITY AND RETRIEVAL

The Encoding Specificity Principle

The change in emphasis from "levels" to "elaboration" and "distinctiveness" was accompanied by another refinement in the theory. The original theory (Craik & Lockhart, 1972) had much to say about how words were coded but little to say about how they were retrieved. Yet we saw previously that appropriate retrieval cues, such as encouraging eyewitnesses to reconstruct the context of the crime, can enhance recall. The usefulness of providing an appropriate context for facilitating retrieval is illustrated by the difference between positive and negative responses in Figure 7.1. Words that resulted in positive responses because they either formed a rhyme or fit the context of a sentence were recalled more often than words that resulted in negative responses.

The use of more complex, elaborate sentence frames facilitated recall for positive responses but not for negative responses (see Figure 7.2). This effect was particularly evident when the context was provided as a retrieval cue. Craik and Tulving (1975) interpreted this finding as support for their view that a more elaborate context is beneficial only when the test word is compatible with the context and forms an integrated unit. A complex sentence such as "The small lady angrily picked up the red_____" makes it easier to retrieve a positive response (*tomato*) but does not make it easier to retrieve a negative response (*walking*).

These results show that, under certain conditions, some retrieval cues are more effective than others. A general answer to the question of what makes a retrieval cue effective is provided by the encoding specificity principle, which has been stated as follows: "Specific encoding

---

encoding specificity principle A theory that states that the effectiveness of a retrieval cue depends on how well it relates to the initial encoding of an item

operations performed on what is perceived determine what is stored, and what is stored determines what retrieval cues are effective in providing access to what is stored" (Tulving & Thomson, 1973, p. 369).

Let's dissect this definition into two parts. The first part states that memory traces differ not only in their durability but also in the kind of information they contain. The second part states that the information that memory traces contain determines what kind of retrieval information should facilitate their recovery. The first part is essentially equivalent to the levels-of-processing framework; the second part requires a closer look at retrieval. The second part implies that it is possible to hold constant the encoding conditions of an item and still observe large differences in its recall, depending on the retrieval conditions. The encoding and retrieval conditions can interact in the sense that a cue that is effective in one situation may or may not be effective in another.

The encoding specificity principle has usually been applied to studying how the retrieval cue relates to the memory code for the stimulus. However, the encoding and retrieval conditions can apply to a broader context, such as the location in which learning occurred or even the mood of the learner. The study of **mood-dependent memory** tests the hypothesis that we are better able to recall information if our mood during retrieval matches our mood during learning (Photo 7.7). Although the evidence has generally been supportive of this hypothesis, the degree of support may depend on the particular paradigm used to test the hypothesis; for example, strongest support may come from situations in which people recall information that they generated themselves. An example of strong support for mood-dependent memory occurred when people had to recall autobiographical events that they had generated several days earlier (Eich et al., 1994). Subjects who were in the same (pleasant or unpleasant) mood during both encoding and retrieval recalled significantly more events than people who were in different moods. Tests of the encoding specificity principle have generally focused on the material that people have to recall rather than on where learning occurred or on the mood of the learner. We will now look at this research.

PHOTO 7.7 Retrieval is facilitated when the mood is the same as during encoding according to the mood-dependent memory hypothesis

istock.com/YinYang

---

mood-dependent memory Memory that is improved when people are tested under conditions that recreate their mood when they learned the material

Interaction Between Encoding and Retrieval Operations

Consider how the encoding specificity principle applies when there are two different processing levels—semantic and phonemic. Imagine that you are in an experiment and have to answer "yes" or "no" to the question "Associated with sleet?" You then see the word *hail* and answer "yes." After making a series of judgments about rhymes and associations, you are given one of the following retrieval cues:

1. Associated with *sleet*

2. Associated with *snow*

3. Rhymes with *bail*

Which of the three retrieval cues do you think would be most helpful for retrieving the word *hail*?

You would probably agree that the first cue would be most effective because it is identical to the question asked during the encoding trials. But what about the second and third cues? The second cue is similar to the original context in that, like the initial question, it emphasizes semantic associations. The third cue, by contrast, emphasizes the phonemic code and is therefore different from the original context. The encoding specificity principle predicts that the original context is the best retrieval cue, a similar context is the next best cue, and a different context is the least effective cue. The results shown in Table 7.2 support this prediction (Fisher & Craik, 1977).

Now consider what might have happened if the word *hail* had been preceded by the question "Rhymes with pail?" The same principle applies. Reproducing the exact context is the best cue, and providing a different context—a semantic association in this case—is the worst cue (see Table 7.2). The interaction between encoding and retrieval is illustrated by the fact that

TABLE 7.2 ■ **Proportions of words recalled as a function of similarity between encoding context and retrieval cue**

	Rhyme	Proportion	Associate	Proportion
Encoding context				
Example: *hail*	Rhymes with *pail*		Associated with *sleet*	
Retrieval context				
Identical	Rhymes with *pail*	0.24	Associated with *sleet*	0.54
Similar	Rhymes with *bail*	0.18	Associated with *snow*	0.36
Different	Associated with *sleet*	0.16	Rhymes with *bail*	0.22

Source: "Interaction between encoding and retrieval operations in cued recall," by R. P. Fisher & F. I. M. Craik, 1977, *Journal of Experimental Psychology: Human Learning and Memory, 3*, 701–711. https://doi.org/10.1037/0278-7393.3.6.701. Copyright 1977 by the American Psychological Association.

the effectiveness of a retrieval cue depends on how a word was coded. When its semantic characteristics were emphasized, a semantic cue was more effective than a phonemic cue. When its phonemic characteristics were emphasized, a phonemic cue was more effective than a semantic cue. In other words, the specific encoding of an item determines which retrieval cues are most effective for gaining access to what is stored—the encoding specificity principle.

Another study (Hertel et al., 1986) found that people were unable to accurately predict the relative effectiveness of retrieval cues. Subjects rated the pleasantness of 40 words in a semantic-orienting task, predicted the number of words they could recall, and then tried to recall the words. One group received semantic retrieval cues, another group received phonemic retrieval cues, and a control group received no retrieval cues. We would expect from Fisher and Craik's findings that the semantic retrieval cues would be more effective than phonemic cues—an expectation that was confirmed. Only those subjects who received semantic cues recalled significantly more words than the control group.

But the superiority of the semantic cues was not anticipated by subjects in the experiment, who predicted that the semantic and phonemic cues would be equally effective. The faulty predictions seemed to be based on overgeneralization from past experiences in which phonemic cues had been effective. For example, when our search has already been limited to a particular category, such as the names of songs, phonemic information is likely to be helpful. What subjects failed to realize was that the effectiveness of a retrieval cue depends on how the word was coded. The memory code, in this case, emphasized the semantic characteristics of the words.

A study of bilinguals illustrates how the encoding specificity theory can be applied to retrieving autobiographical knowledge. This study found that people tend to recall events from their lives that correspond to the language used in the interview. These findings generalize to classroom instruction about history, biology, chemistry, and mythology. The recall of students who were fluent in both Spanish and English was faster and more accurate when the language of the questions matched the language of the instruction (Marian & Fausey, 2006).

Transfer Appropriate Processing

A theoretical construct related to the encoding specificity principle is **transfer appropriate processing**, which emphasizes that the value of a particular learning strategy is relative to a particular goal. Transfer-appropriate processing implies that the effectiveness of learning can only be determined relative to the testing situation. If the test emphasizes phonemic information when learning a foreign language and you had been focusing on semantic information you could be in trouble.

It is relatively rare, however, that we must emphasize phonemic codes because we are generally required to recall or recognize semantic information. Transfer-appropriate processing therefore usually means semantic processing. There are different ways to process material semantically, and knowledge of the test format should help you decide how to study. If the test is a multiple-choice test, it is likely that knowledge of details will be more useful than knowledge

---

transfer-appropriate processing Encoding material in a manner related to how the material will be used later

about the general organization of the material. If the test is an essay test, it is likely that careful organization of the material will be more useful than knowledge of many details.

Evidence supports these claims (Thomas & McDaniel, 2007)). Students who were given a task that required them to focus on the details of the material did better on details than on conceptual questions. In contrast, students who were given a sentence-sorting task that encouraged relational processing of the material did better on conceptual than on detailed questions. Transfer-appropriate processing also influenced students' metacomprehension predictions. Students accurately predicted how well they would do on the test when their study preparation matched the test format. However, they did not make accurate predictions when their study preparation did not match the test format. Other studies support these findings (Thiede et al., 2011).

Another distinction between test questions is whether they emphasize factual recall or problem solving. Sometimes, an instructor asks students to recall information; at other times, students must apply the information to solve problems. The hypothesis about transfer-appropriate processing predicts that **problem-oriented acquisition** of the material is better than **fact-oriented acquisition** when people must solve problems.

Consider the following two problems:

- Uriah Fuller, the famous Israeli superpsychic, can tell you the score of any baseball game before the game starts. What is his secret?

- A man living in a small town in the United States married 20 different women in the same town. All are still living, and he has never divorced one of them. Yet he has broken no law. Can you explain?

Now imagine that you had rated a number of statements for general truthfulness earlier in an experiment. Among the statements were answers to the problems:

- Before it starts, the score of any baseball game is 0 to 0.

- A minister marries several people each week.

Somewhat surprisingly, receiving the answers in this incidental rating task was not very helpful for later solving the problems (Perfetto et al., 1983).

One interpretation of these findings is that people acquired the statements in a fact-oriented manner and therefore failed to perceive their relevance for the problem-solving task (Adams et al., 1988). Now suppose the statements were modified to encourage problem-oriented acquisition; would people be more likely to perceive their relevance? To induce problem-oriented processing, the experimenters changed the statement "A minister marries several people each week" to "It is possible to marry several people each week [pause] if one is a minister." The pause lasted

---

problem-oriented acquisition Encoding material in a manner that is helpful for its later use in solving problems

fact-oriented acquisition Encoding material in a manner that emphasizes factual knowledge without emphasizing its application

approximately two seconds and gave people a brief chance to reflect on the problem-oriented content of the statement. There were corresponding changes for nine other statements that provided answers to problems. People who received problem-oriented statements later solved 56% of the problems, compared with 36% for people who received fact-oriented statements.

To understand the distinction between encoding specificity and transfer-appropriate processing, we need to understand the similarity and difference between the two theoretical constructs. Think about this distinction and then look at Figure 7.4.

Both constructs are similar in that they emphasize that good performance depends on maximizing the similarity between the encoding and the retrieval of the material. They differ in whether the decision on how to do this is made at the encoding stage or the retrieval stage. In transfer-appropriate processing, the decision is made at the encoding stage. The retrieval conditions, such as a multiple-choice exam or an essay exam, are fixed, and you have to decide how to encode the material to prepare for the type of exam. In encoding specificity, the encoding has already occurred, and the decision requires finding effective retrieval cues to match the encoding. Transfer-appropriate processing therefore looks forward in time, from encoding to retrieval, whereas encoding specificity looks backward in time, from retrieval to encoding.

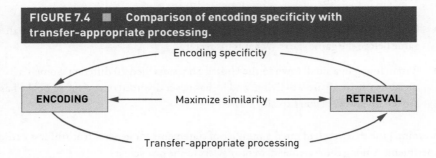

FIGURE 7.4 ■ Comparison of encoding specificity with transfer-appropriate processing.

APPLICATIONS

Elaborate Memory Codes

We have seen that an explanation of the effectiveness of semantic processing is that it supports elaborations. One of the most researched instructional methods on elaboration is self-explanation. Generating explanations for oneself helps learners make sense of new information. It encourages them to increase their understanding by discovering conceptual relationships and causal connections.

A review of research found that self-explanations were effective for a variety of outcome measures, such as the ability to make inferences, recall information, solve problems, and transfer to new tasks (Bisra et al., 2018). The review found that self-explanations benefit students at all levels of education, from elementary school to high school to undergraduate studies to professional programs. These findings suggest that generating explanations encourages students to retrieve relevant information from long-term memory and to integrate it with the new information.

Although generating self-explanations often improves learning, it is not always effective. Table 7.3 lists four constraints on its success. The first is that asking students to explain material is particularly effective for topics that have general principles. Many of the success stories have focused on learning mathematics and science. These include asking preschool children about mimicry; elementary-school children about mathematical equivalence; a range of students about biology; high school students about geometry, algebra, and probability; and undergraduates about scientific argumentation, proofs, programming, and chemistry. In contrast, self-explanations did not help students learn a topic that has exceptions to general rules, such as English grammar.

TABLE 7.3 ■ Four constraints on when prompted self-explanation aids learning	
Constraint on:	**Description**
1. Target outcomes and domains	Promotes comprehension and transfer in domains that are consistently guided by general principles or heuristics.
2. What is being explained	Best if to-be-explained content is known to be correct or incorrect rather than learners' own potentially incorrect ideas.
3. Explanation prompts	Prompts direct attention to particular information, so can reduce attention to other important information.
4. Effectiveness relative to alternative instructional techniques	Alternative instructional techniques, such as instructional explanations, solving unfamiliar problems, and retrieval practice can sometimes be equally or more effective.

Source: "Eliciting explanations: Constraints on when self-explanation aids learning," by B. Rittle-Johnson & A. M. Loehr, 2017, *Psychonomic Bulletin & Review, 24*, 1501–1510. https://doi.org/10.3758/s13423-016-1079-5

The second constraint concerns explanations based on incorrect theories. Explaining incorrect information, however, can be very effective if students know it is incorrect, such as asking them to find an error in a solution to a math problem. A third constraint requires determining whether an explanation prompt causes a student to ignore important parts of the text because the prompt shifts attention away from this material. The final constraint compares self-explanations to other instructional interventions. Other methods may occasionally be more helpful.

Distinctive Memory Codes

Encouraging distinctive memories is another method that can improve learning. An example from Chapter 2 on perception is a training method that improved children's discrimination of letters by emphasizing their distinctive features (Egeland, 1975). Making distinctions between theoretical constructs is also helpful but can be challenging. I spent many years lecturing about transfer-appropriate processing and encoding specificity before reflecting on their relationship. I then designed the diagram in Figure 7.4 to help me and others understand the distinction.

Schwartz and Bransford (1998) demonstrated the importance of making distinctions among theoretical constructs by developing instruction on contrasting cases. The method requires students to compare contrasting cases before they read a text or listen to a lecture to prepare them for understanding its content. For example, one of their experiments required students to compare encoding concepts that transfer information from short-term to long-term memory. Generating distinctions between these concepts before listening to a lecture or reading a text helped students predict the outcomes of a hypothetical experiment based on those concepts.

Another example distinguishes among the statistical concepts of mean, range, and deviation from the mean. Table 7.4 shows hypothetical data of the number of goals scored by three soccer players over a four-year span. The mean is 10 goals for each of the players.

TABLE 7.4 ■ Contrasting cases of statistical concepts	
Example 1	**Example 2**
Player A: 9, 10, 10, 11	Player B: 5, 10, 10, 15
Player B: 5, 10, 10, 15	Player C: 5, 5, 15, 15

Source: Based on "Towards a theory of when and how problem-solving followed by instruction supports learning," by K. Loibl et al., 2017, *Educational Psychology Review, 29*, 693–715. https://doi.org/10.1007/s10648-016-9379-x

The first example illustrates that the range is less for Player A (9–11) than for Player B (5–15). It also illustrates that the absolute deviations from the mean are less for Player A (1, 0, 0, 1) than for Player B (5, 0, 0, 5). We might conclude from this contrast that the differences in absolute deviations are always caused by differences in range. However, the second example illustrates that differences in absolute deviations can still occur when the range (5–15) does not differ. The absolute deviations for Player C (5, 5, 5, 5) are greater than for Player B (5, 0, 0, 5). These contrasting cases illustrate interrelationships among statistical concepts (Loibl et al., 2017).

The data in Table 7.4 are included in a review of how problem solving followed by instruction supports learning. Research supports the conclusion that this sequence is productive when the initial problem solving involves contrasting cases or the subsequent instruction builds on student solutions. Figure 7.5 illustrates successful instructional design. The initial problem solving should activate prior knowledge, such as definitions of the mean, range, and deviation. Students should be aware (or made aware) of gaps in their knowledge, such as those involving the interrelationships among statistical concepts. They should also know the relevant aspects of the examples. The specific numbers illustrate the interrelations but not that the numbers refer to soccer goals. And finally, the initial comparisons should aid subsequent learning, such as the calculation of variance to represent data.

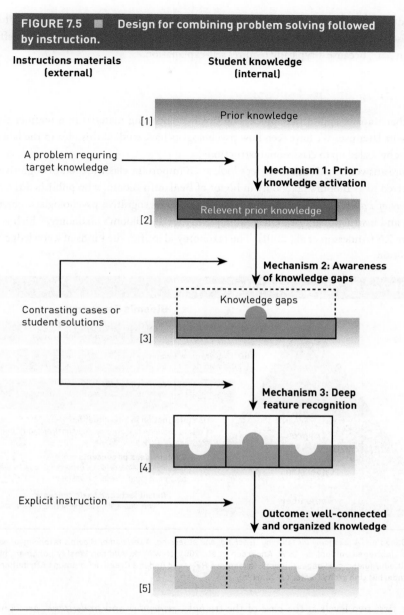

FIGURE 7.5 ■ Design for combining problem solving followed by instruction.

Source: "Towards a theory of when and how problem-solving followed by instruction supports learning," by K. Loibl et al., 2017, *Educational Psychology Review, 29*, 693–715. https://doi.org/10.1007/s10648-016-9379-x

Self-explanations and contrasting cases are two methods of instruction that build on the theoretical constructs of semantic elaboration and distinctive memory codes. However, like statistical concepts, they can be related. Evidence involving the division of fractions showed that student's self-explanations were encouraged by both prompts to self-explain and to make comparisons across examples (Sidney et al., 2015). Instruction on contrasting cases is effective, at least in part, because it typically requires self-explanation.

Transfer Appropriate Processing

Recall that transfer appropriate processing involves encoding material in a manner that will facilitate its later use. We have seen how psychologists have studied this idea in the laboratory, but can it be scaled up to classroom instruction?

Before answering this question, let's look at an important classification of cognitive skills. It is referred to as Bloom's taxonomy in honor of Benjamin Bloom, who published the book *A Taxonomy of Educational Objectives* in 1984. A group of cognitive psychologists, curriculum experts, and instructional researchers subsequently revised Bloom's taxonomy, which is shown in Figure 7.6 (Anderson et al., 2001). The taxonomy identifies the kinds of knowledge needed for cognition.

FIGURE 7.6 ■ Bloom's revised taxonomy.

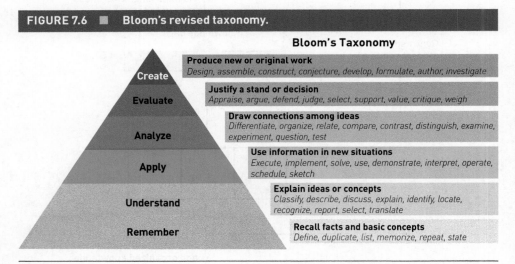

Source: Based on "A taxonomy for learning, teaching, and assessing: A revision of Bloom's taxonomy of educational objectives" (abridged edition), by L. W. Anderson et al., 2001, New York: Addison Wesley Longman. https://cft.vanderbilt.edu/guides-sub-pages/blooms-taxonomy/. Released under a Creative Commons Attributions license by the Vanderbilt University Center for Teaching.

The first two levels at the base of the triangle, *remember* and *understand*, are considered lower-level skills because they require only minimal levels of understanding. The third level—*apply*—is at an intermediate level, while *analyze, evaluate,* and *create* are higher-level skills. Bloom (1984) initially designed his taxonomy to suggest that higher-order skills depend on a mastery of lower-level skills.

The most straightforward application of the transfer appropriate processing construct to Figure 7.6 is the prediction that practice on lower-level skills should prepare students for an exam on lower-level skills and practice on higher-level skills should prepare students for an exam on higher-level skills. A more complex account is that mastering higher-level skills requires mastering lower-level skills, so practicing higher-level skills should benefit skills at all levels in the taxonomy (Jensen et al., 2014).

Jensen and his collaborators evaluated these two accounts in an undergraduate course on general biology. Students in both sections of the course received the same instruction emphasizing high-level cognitive skills. However, the quizzes and exams in one section focused on lower-level skills that required simply remembering the information while the quizzes and exams in the other section focused on higher-level skills (apply, analyze, evaluate). Figure 7.7 displays the performance of students on the final exam that consisted of questions designed to test skills at both levels. The left panel shows that students who had practiced higher-level skills did better on the low-level questions than students who had practiced lower-level skills. The right panel shows that practicing higher-level skills was also more effective in answering high-level questions. These findings support the hypothesis that practicing high-level skills can benefit skills at all levels in the taxonomy. Students who were tested throughout the semester with high-level questions acquired a deep conceptual understanding of the material and better memory for course information. The interaction between low- and high-level skills is a critical aspect of instruction and should be closely monitored across situations.

FIGURE 7.7 ■ Low-level and high-level scores on the final exam for those students who practiced on (a) lower-level and (b) higher-level skills.

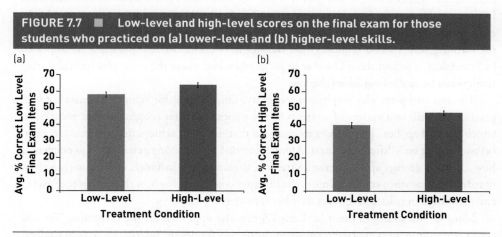

Source: "Teaching to the test...or testing to teach: exams requiring higher order thinking skills encourage greater conceptual understanding" by J. L. Jensen et al., 2014, *Educational Psychology Review, 26*, 307-329. https://doi.org/10.1007/s10648-013-9248-9

What about transferring learned knowledge and skills to daily activities? This is the task faced by therapists who supervise cognitive training of patients with acquired brain injury (Geusgens et al., 2007). Occupational therapists assist clients in a variety of learning processes, including helping clients learn or relearn skills and develop strategies to perform daily activities (Babulal et al., 2016). The challenge is to transfer these skills from the training facility to the home environment. Guesgens and colleagues in the Netherlands formulated six prerequisites for successful transfer based on a review of research. Table 7.5 lists these principles.

TABLE 7.5 ■ Six prerequisites for successful transfer of skills and strategies from occupational therapy
1. A person should be aware of his functioning before he will acknowledge that a strategy is needed to improve his functioning.
2. A person should know what transfer is and how it works.
3. Transfer should be explained during learning, as it cannot be expected to occur automatically.
4. A person should be able to judge when and where transfer can be applied.
5. A strategy or skill should be practiced in a variety of situations.
6. General knowledge should be taught, as this type of knowledge is easier to transfer than specific knowledge.

Source: Based on "Occurrence and measurement of transfer in cognitive rehabilitation: A critical review," by C. A. V. Geusgens et al., 2007, *Journal of Rehabilitative Medicine, 39,* 425–439. https://doi.org/10.2340/16501977-0092

A group at the Washington University School of Medicine subsequently elaborated on the application of these principles (Babulal et al., 2016). Self-awareness of one's limitations is necessary because a lack of self-awareness reduces motivation to engage in training. Therapists should next explain what transfer is and how it works. Explanations should focus on how situations in the home may differ from those in the training facility. Variations in the designs of kitchens have consequences for transferring skills. These explanations should continue throughout the learning sessions as a reminder that transfer does not occur automatically. As indicated in Principle 4, a person should be able to judge when and where the principles learned during therapy can be applied outside of therapy.

The last two principles emphasize generality. One method for achieving generality is to practice the skill in a variety of contexts so the patient can later recognize those contexts in which the skill applies. The authors recommend that the client achieve mastery in one context before training on a different context. Another method for achieving generality is to emphasize how a general strategy applies across a variety of situations. For instance, while discussing how to reduce fatigue when cooking a meal, the therapist could mention how the strategies of pacing and planning can reduce fatigue across other activities.

Many of the strategies listed in Table 7.5 can also apply within the classroom. Transfer across curriculum units are facilitated when the teacher frames the instruction to help students recognize which ideas do or do not transfer (Engle, 2006). For instance, there are both similarities and differences across endangered species. Birthrate and hunting may be causes for the endangerment of one species, whereas predators and lack of food may be causes for another species. Framing also made it clear to students that they were learning ideas in order to use them, creating an expectation for transfer (Engle, 2006).

SUMMARY

The levels-of-processing theory proposes that how an item is encoded determines how long it can be remembered. Qualitatively different memory codes are established by asking people to make decisions about a word's physical structure, pronunciation, or meaning. When people are unexpectedly asked to recall the words, they recall the most words following semantic process-ing and the fewest words following structural processing. Further support for the theory comes from the finding that rehearsal does not necessarily result in learning, presumably because peo-ple do not attend to the meaning of words they want to only keep active in STM.

Although the levels-of-processing theory originally proposed that retention is determined by the depth of processing (with physical, phonemic, and semantic processing, respectively, rep-resenting increasing depth), the failure to find an independent measure of depth resulted in an increasing emphasis on the elaborateness and distinctiveness of memory codes. The elaboration hypothesis claims that it is easier to retrieve more elaborate codes by creating associations at the semantic level. The distinctiveness hypothesis claims that it is easier to retrieve distinctive codes and that semantic codes are more distinctive than other codes. Studies of elaborateness and dis-tinctiveness using semantic material have found that increasing either one will improve recall.

The encoding specificity principle states that the effectiveness of a retrieval cue is determined by how well it corresponds to the characteristics of the memory trace. Although some studies have focused on the broader context of encoding, such as a person's mood during encoding and retrieval, most studies have focused on the encoding of the stimulus. Transfer-appropriate pro-cessing suggests that people should create memory codes that will correspond to how they will eventually use the material, such as in a multiple-choice, essay, or problem-solving test.

One of the most researched instructional methods based on elaboration is self-explanation. Although self-explanations typically enhance understanding, the topic, and the knowledge of the learner, the instructional focus constrains their effectiveness. Contrasting cases often improve learning by emphasizing the distinctiveness of concepts by requiring learners to com-pare the similarities and differences of related concepts. An example of instruction that evalu-ated transfer appropriate processing compared two sections of students who received quizzes on either the lower-level or higher-level skills in Bloom's revised taxonomy. Practice on the higher-level skills (apply, analyze, evaluate) improved performance on answering questions at all levels on the final exam. Research on elaboration, distinctiveness, and transfer has applica-tions to classroom instruction and rehabilitation training.

RECOMMENDED READING

A book edited by Cermak and Craik (1979) contains many excellent chapters on how the levels-of-processing concept evolved during the 1970s. Craik (2002) updates this evolvement and speculates on future directions. Although elaborative rehearsal is clearly more effective than maintenance rehearsal, students are not always aware of this difference and may there-fore not learn as much as they should (Shaughnessy, 1981). People can also improve their memories by paying more attention to the distinctiveness of items during the encoding and retrieval stages (Dodson et al., 2000). Other applied areas that can be related to the concepts of levels of processing and encoding specificity are context-dependent memory of deep-sea divers, enhancement of face recognition, and attempts to understand certain aspects of amnesia and aphasia (Baddeley, 1982). A book edited by Winograd and Neisser (1992) con-tains chapters on affect and flashbulb memories. Johnson (1983) proposed a memory model in which events can create multiple entries in a sensory, perceptual, and reflection system. The similarities—and differences—between her theory and the levels-of-processing theory are evident in her chapter. Wedlock and Growe (2017) review the evolvement of Bloom's taxonomy and argue that it needs to be adapted to a new (digital) generation of students. Examples include the design of assignments to develop critical thinking skills within business education (Zapalska et al., 2018).

Getty Images/ Danita Delimont

8 VISUAL IMAGES

LEARNING OBJECTIVES

1. Explain the implications of Paivio's dual-coding theory for learning.

2. Analyze imagery processes used to perform cognitive tasks.

3. Identify the usefulness of visual imagery in performing cognitive tasks.

4. Describe how the limitations of images affect geographical reasoning, clinical disorders, and spatial skills.

The preceding chapter on memory codes emphasized verbal knowledge. The stimuli usually consisted of items that could be easily assigned a verbal label, such as words, letters, digits, or even nonsense syllables. We might question, however, whether we assign verbal labels to everything we perceive. Some events can be hard to describe verbally, and others can simply be easier to remember as an image. Although images can exist for each of the sensory modalities, cognitive psychologists have been interested mainly in visual images. This chapter considers how visual images contribute to knowledge.

The importance of visual thinking was documented by Roger Shepard (1988) in his chapter on the imagination of the scientist. As a consequence of his own research on visual reasoning, Shepard became interested in what scientists said about the mental processes that resulted in their major achievements. Many of us have heard about Albert Einstein's thought "experiments" in which he developed a theory of relativity by imagining himself traveling in a train or alongside a beam of light. Shepard reports many other cases of how visual thinking aided the contributions of James Clark Maxwell, Michael Faraday, Hermann van Helmholtz, Sir Francis Galton, James Watt, Nicola Tesla, Sir John Herschel, Friedrich Kekule, James Watson, Richard Feynman, and Stephen Hawking. He mentions that many of these scientists had a childhood interest in physically manipulating objects and some had delayed language development.

A distinction between verbal knowledge and visual or spatial knowledge is made on intelligence tests. **Verbal knowledge** is usually measured by vocabulary questions or questions that test comprehension of written material. **Spatial knowledge** is usually measured by performance of such operations as mentally folding connected squares into a cube or mentally rotating an object to determine whether it matches another object. Scientific discoveries such as the double helix structure of DNA (Photo 8.1) have relied on the power of visual thinking.

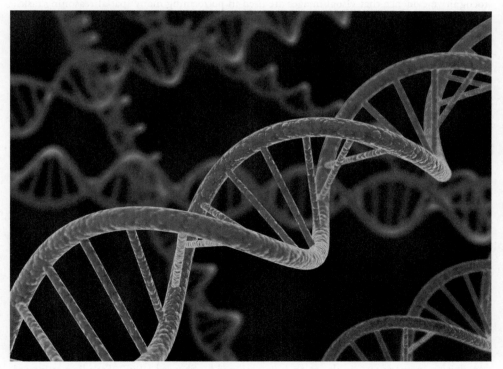

PHOTO 8.1 The double-helix structure of DNA.

istockphoto.com/OlenaT

---

verbal knowledge Knowledge expressed in language

spatial knowledge Knowledge of spatial relations that may be stored as images

The study of visual imagery has been one of the main contributions of cognitive psychology. However, psychologists ignored imagery for many years because of the influence of Watson's *Behaviorism* (1924), which was dedicated to wiping out the study of mental events. Watson argued that only behavior could be objectively studied, an argument that certainly had some merit but almost completely eliminated the study of mental processes such as visual imagery. It wasn't until the 1960s that psychologists once again began to try to understand the role of visual images in the acquisition of knowledge. Visual imagery is still difficult to study because it cannot be directly observed, but research has provided strong evidence that visual images are used in performing many tasks.

The first section of this chapter argues that forming visual images is an effective method for remembering information. However, the formation of a visual image is much easier for concrete material than for abstract material, and we will examine the implications of this finding. The second section examines how images enable us to perform cognitive operations such as visual scanning and mental rotation. The results of these experiments would be difficult to explain if we believed that all knowledge was verbal. The third section presents behavioral and neurocognitive evidence that visual images are used in performing many spatial reasoning tasks. The final section discusses the impact of images on geographical, clinical, and mathematical reasoning.

IMAGERY IN LEARNING

Memory for Pictures

One indication that visual imagery might provide an effective memory code is that people usually find it easier to recognize pictures than to recognize words. Shepard (1967) was one of the first to show that recognition accuracy for visual material is very high. Subjects in his experiment viewed 612 pictures at a self-paced rate and were later given a recognition-memory test on pairs of pictures. Each pair consisted of a picture they had previously seen and a novel picture. When they were tested two hours later, the participants were virtually perfect in identifying which member of the pair they had seen. Another group of participants, tested one week later, was still able to identify the correct picture in 87% of the pairs. When the same test was repeated using words instead of pictures, recognition accuracy wasn't as high. Participants tested immediately after seeing the words could identify which of two words had been presented in only 88% of the pairs, about the same as when pictures were tested after a week's delay.

An experiment by Standing (1973) provided further evidence of people's remarkable ability to remember pictures. One group of dedicated subjects viewed 10,000 pictures over a five-day period. Immediately after the learning session on the fifth day, the participants were given a recognition-memory test similar to the one designed by Shepard (1967). Standing estimated the number of items they must have retained in memory to reach the level of performance they attained on the test (taking into account the probability of guessing correctly). His estimate was that the participants must have remembered 6600 pictures. This estimate does not imply that the participants remembered all the details of a picture—but they did remember enough details to distinguish that picture from a novel picture.

Memory for details is also impressive, as demonstrated in a task in which observers viewed 2912 pictures for three seconds, each from 128 different scene categories that contained 1, 4, 16, or 64 examples (Konkle et al., 2010). Following a 20-minute break, the participants had to select which of two scenes they had observed (Figure 8.1). In the novel foil condition, one picture was from a category they had previously viewed (such as ocean waves, classrooms, golf courses, amusement parks) and the other picture was from a novel category. Participants were correct on 96% of these tests. In the exemplar foil condition, both pictures were from the same scene category. Accuracy depended on the number of previously viewed examples in this category, but participants could correctly identify the familiar scene on 76% of the trials, even when they had viewed 64 pictures in this category.

FIGURE 8.1 ■ **Experimental procedure and scene recognition results for scenes.**

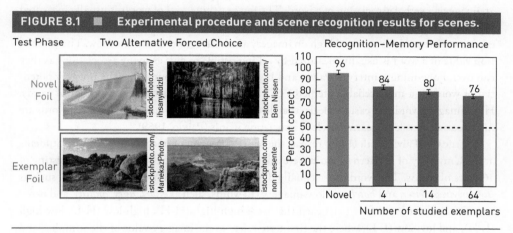

istockphoto.com/ihsanyildizli; istockphoto.com/Ben Nissen; istockphoto.com/MarieKazPhoto and istockphoto.com/non presente

Source: "Scene memory is more detailed than you think: The role of categories in visual long-term memory," by T. Konkle, T. F. Brady, G. A. Alvarez, & A. Oliva (2010). *Psychological Science, 21*, 1551–1556. https://doi.org/10.1177/0956797610385359

Paivio's Dual Coding Theory

The finding that we are good at remembering pictures suggests that we might improve our memory if we could form mental pictures (images). The work of Allan Paivio at the University of Western Ontario established that forming images does aid learning. After an extensive series of studies, Paivio (1969) argued there were two major ways a person could elaborate on material in a learning experiment. One form of elaboration emphasizes verbal associations. A word such as *poetry* can result in many associations that could help you distinguish it from other words. You might think of different styles of poetry, particular poems, or experiences in an English class. We saw in the previous chapter that verbal associations helped people recall words in the Hyde and Jenkins (1969) experiment. People who considered the meaning of the words recalled primary associates together because recalling one word reminded them of its associate.

The other form of elaboration is the creation of a visual image to represent a word. If I asked you to remember the word *juggler*, you might form an image of a person juggling three balls. If I asked you to remember the word *truth*, however, you would probably have difficulty forming an image. The first word refers to a concrete object, the second to an abstract concept. It is easy to form an image to represent a concrete object but difficult to form an image for an abstract concept. Paivio (1969) argued that the concrete-abstract dimension is the most important determinant of ease in forming an image. At the concrete end of the continuum are pictures because the picture itself can be remembered as a visual image and the person doesn't have to create an image. Pictures often result in better memory than do concrete words, which usually result in better memory than abstract words.

If visual images and verbal associations are the two major forms of elaboration, is one more effective than the other? To answer this question, we have to know how easy it is to form either an image or a verbal association of a word. The imagery potential of words is usually measured by asking people to rate on a scale how easy it is to form an image for a given word. As we might expect, concrete words are rated high on imagery and abstract words are rated low. The association value of a word is usually measured by asking people to give as many associations as they can over a one-minute interval. Paivio and his colleagues have found that the imagery potential of words is a more reliable predictor of learning than the association potential of words. High-imagery words are easier to learn than low-imagery words, but high-association words are not necessarily easier to learn than low-association words (Paivio, 1969).

A study by Paivio et al. (1968) reveals the beneficial effect of imagery on learning. Students at the University of Western Ontario were asked to learn a list of paired associates consisting of 16 pairs of words. The words were equally divided between high-imagery (H) words, such as *juggler, dress, letter,* and *hotel,* and low-imagery (L) words, such as *effort, duty, quality,* and *necessity.* The list contained four pairs each that were high-high (H-H), high-low (H-L), low-high (L-H), and low-low (L-L), where the first term refers to the imagery value of the stimulus, and the second term refers to the imagery value of the response. Examples include *juggler-dress* (H-H), *letter-effort* (H-L), *duty-hotel* (L-H), and *quality-necessity* (L-L).

Figure 8.2 shows how well the students could recall the response when given the stimulus. The powerful effect of imagery is quite evident. The H-H pairs resulted in the best recall, and the L-L pairs the worst. When only one member of the pair had a high-imagery value, recall was better when that word was used as the stimulus (H-L). The fact that H-H pairs were easiest to learn is consistent with the previously mentioned finding that interactive pictures improve the recall of brand names. When images can be created for both members of a word pair, the images can be combined to form an interactive image. For example, one can associate the word *dress* with *juggler* by forming an image of a juggler wearing a dress.

It is interesting to note that high-imagery words were easier to recall than low-imagery words, even though the learners were not told to use visual imagery. Perhaps the participants spontaneously generated images whenever they could. Support for this hypothesis was obtained

---

concrete-abstract dimension Extent to which a concept can be represented by a picture

imagery potential Ease with which a concept can be imaged

association value The number of verbal associations generated for a concept

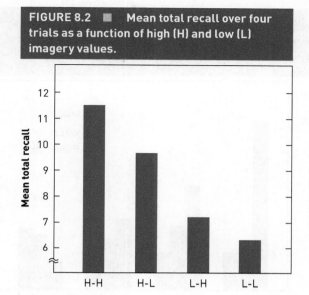

FIGURE 8.2 ■   Mean total recall over four trials as a function of high (H) and low (L) imagery values.

Source: "Imagery versus meaningfulness of nouns in paired-associate learning," by A. Paivio, P. E. Smythe, & J. C. Yuille, 1968, *Canadian Journal of Psychology, 22*, 427–441. Copyright 1968 by the Canadian Psychological Association. Reprinted by permission.

in a questionnaire completed after the learning task. The students indicated, for each of the 16 pairs on the list, which one of five strategies they had used in trying to learn that pair. Their options were "none," "repetition" (rehearsal), "verbal" (a phrase or rhyme connecting two words), "imagery" (mental pictures that include the items), and "other." The "none" and "other" options were reported infrequently. The distribution of the other three responses depended on whether the pairs consisted of high- or low-imagery words (Figure 8.3). The reported use of imagery was highest for the H-H pairs and lowest for the L-L pairs. The striking resemblance between learning (see Figure 8.2) and the reported use of imagery (see Figure 8.3) suggests that imagery is an effective learning strategy.

The reason images are effective, according to Paivio (1975), is that an image provides a second kind of memory code that is independent of the verbal code. Paivio's theory is called a **dual-coding theory** because it proposes two independent memory codes, either of which can result in recall. A person who has stored both the word *cat* and an image of a cat can remember the item if he or she retrieves either the image or the word. Evidence suggests that the two memory codes are independent in the sense that a person can forget one code without forgetting the other (Paivio, 1975). Having two memory codes to represent an item therefore provides a better chance of remembering that item than does having only a single code.

---

dual-coding theory A theory that memory is improved when items can be represented by both verbal and visual memory codes

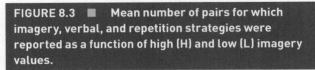

FIGURE 8.3 ■ Mean number of pairs for which imagery, verbal, and repetition strategies were reported as a function of high (H) and low (L) imagery values.

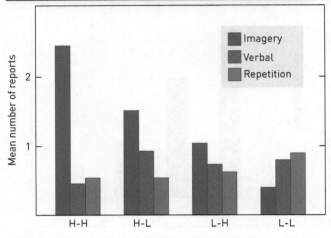

Source: "Imagery versus meaningfulness of nouns in paired-associate learning," by A. Paivio, P. C. Smythe, & J. C. Yuille, 1968, *Canadian Journal of Psychology, 22,* 427–441. Copyright 1968 by the Canadian Psychological Association. Reprinted by permission.

A criticism of dual-coding theory is that it works only in situations in which people focus on relational information, such as the associations between items in a paired-associates task (Marschark & Hunt, 1989). Subjects in Marschark and Hunt's experiment initially rated 12 concrete and 12 abstract word pairs in an orienting task. One group rated how easily the two words of each pair could be combined into an integrated unit. When they were later asked to recall the words, they recalled significantly more concrete than abstract words. Another group was told to ignore the fact that the words were presented in pairs and to rate the words individually on the ease with which each evoked a mental image. This group did not recall any more concrete words than abstract words, as would be expected from dual-coding theory.

The emphasis on relational coding is also consistent with the finding that improving the recall of brand names depended on forming an *interactive* picture that combined the product and brand name (Lutz & Lutz, 1977). For example, showing people a picture of a man with a rocket strapped on his back carrying a package helped them remember the brand name Rocket Messenger Service. If Marschark and Hunt are correct—that relational processing is necessary to achieve the benefits of concreteness—then dual-coding theory has a restricted range of applications. But the restricted range is still fairly large because many learning activities require that we learn associations between items, such as associating a brand name with a product, a word in one language with a word in another language, or a name with a face. Because images facilitate

relational information Information specifying how concepts are related recall in these situations, it is only natural that they should play a key role in suggestions for improving memory.

Mnemonic Strategies

Every so often a book appears on how to improve memory. Such a book is usually written by a person who not only has practiced *mnemonic* (memory) *techniques* but can successfully apply them to demonstrate rather remarkable acts of recall. One example, *The Memory Book*, by Lorayne and Lucas (1974), was on the best-seller list for weeks.

Although memory books always discuss several techniques for improving memory, they usually emphasize visual imagery. The author presents a mnemonic strategy in which imagery usually plays a key role and claims that use of the strategy will improve recall. The claim, however, is seldom supported by experimental data. Is there proof that the proposed strategy works? Fortunately, supportive data exist in the psychology journals.

Paivio's findings support the potential effectiveness of imagery for improving memory, but they also create a potential hurdle. If imagery works for concrete words, what happens to abstract words? This challenge faced Atkinson and Raugh (1975) when they evaluated the effectiveness of imagery for learning foreign vocabulary words, such as the Russian word *zdanie*. How does the learner create an image for *zdanie*?

The answer is that an associated word can be used to form a link between the Russian word and its English translation. The associated word is called a keyword. The keyword method divides the study of a vocabulary word into two stages. The first stage is to associate the foreign word with an English keyword, which sounds approximately like some part of the foreign word. The second stage is to form a mental image of the keyword interacting with the English translation. For example, the Russian word for *building* (*zdanie*) is pronounced somewhat like *zdawnyeh*, with the emphasis on the first syllable. Using *dawn* as the keyword, one could imagine the pink light of dawn being reflected in the windows of a building.

A striking demonstration of the keyword method occurred in the study by Atkinson and Raugh (1975) that provided learners with keywords. A good keyword should (1) sound as much as possible like a part of the foreign word, (2) be different from the other keywords, and (3) easily form an interactive image with the English translation. Table 8.1 shows a sample of 10 Russian words and their associated keywords. As an exercise in using the method, you can try to create an image linking pairs of words.

Students in Atkinson and Raugh's study tried to learn the English translations of 120 Russian words over a three-day period. The students were divided into two groups—the "keyword" group and a control group. Learners in the keyword group were taught how to use the keyword method. After the pronunciation of each Russian word, they were shown both a keyword and the English translation. The instructions said that the students should try to picture an interactive image linking the keyword and the English translation (as in Photo 8.2) or should generate a sentence

---

keyword A concrete word that sounds like an abstract word so that it can be substituted for the abstract word in an interactive image

keyword method A mnemonic strategy using keywords to improve paired-associates learning

TABLE 8.1 ■ A sample of 10 Russian words with related keywords		
Russian	**Keyword**	**Translation**
DÉLO	[Jell-O]	AFFAIR
STRANÁ	[straw man]	COUNTRY
LINKÓR	[Lincoln]	BATTLESHIP
ROT	[rut]	MOUTH
ÓSEN	[ocean]	AUTUMN
SÉVER	[savior]	NORTH
DYM	[dim]	SMOKE
DÉVUSHKA	[dear vooshka]	GIRL
PÓEZD	[poised]	TRAIN
KROVÁT	[cravat]	BED

Source: From "An application of the mnemonic keyword method to the acquisition of a Russian vocabulary," by R. C. Atkinson & M. R. Raugh, 1975, *Journal of Experimental Psychology: Human Learning and Memory, 104*, 126–133. https://doi.org/10.1037/0278-7393.1.2.126

incorporating both words if they could not form an image. The keywords were not shown to students in the control group, who were told to learn the translations in whatever manner they wished. The control group did not receive instructions on the use of keywords or mental imagery.

PHOTO 8.2 An interactive image that combines a keyword (ocean) with an English translation (autumn).

istockphoto.com/valio84sl

On the day after the three-study sessions, students in both groups were tested on the entire 120-word vocabulary. Students in the keyword group provided the correct translations for 72% of the Russian words; students in the control group did so for 46% of the words. This difference is particularly impressive considering that Russian was selected as a special challenge to the keyword method because the pronunciation of most Russian words is quite different from English pronunciation. Because many people find Russian vocabulary harder to learn than the vocabularies of other foreign languages, it is valuable to have a method that can facilitate learning.

Another application of an imagery strategy is learning to associate a name with a face. Just about everyone has had difficulty learning names at one time or another. Many authors of memory books can perform a very impressive demonstration in which they repeat back the names of all the members of an audience after hearing them only once. The method used by Lorayne involves first converting the name into a visual image and then linking the image to a prominent feature of the person's face. For example, if Mr. Gordon has a large nose, the image might be a garden (*garden* sounds like *Gordon*) growing out of his nose. A group of British psychologists found that people who were taught this strategy learned significantly more names than a control group that was not taught the strategy (Morris et al., 1978). The learning task required associating a different name (randomly selected from a telephone directory) with each of 13 photographs of male adults. After a study period of 10 seconds for each item, the imagery group could correctly name 10 of the photographs, compared with 5 for the control group. The authors admit that the use of mnemonic strategies requires some effort, and not everyone will be willing to make that effort to learn names. However, the results of imagery studies should provide encouragement to those who wonder whether the effort will be worthwhile.

IMAGERY IN PERFORMING COGNITIVE TASKS

Although psychologists have seldom questioned that images exist, some have questioned the usefulness of images as explanatory constructs. The most influential paper challenging the usefulness of images in psychological theories was written by Pylyshyn (1973). Pylyshyn argued that it was misleading to think of images as uninterpreted photographs, analogous to pictures in the head. He supported the alternative view that an image is much closer to being a description of a scene than a picture of it. The emphasis on the descriptive characteristics of images rather than their sensory characteristics is the central theme of a **propositional theory**.

Kosslyn and Pomerantz (1977) agreed with Pylyshyn that images are interpreted and organized, but they argued that we often process images in the same way that we process perceptual information. In response to Pylyshyn's paper, they summarized five experimental findings that they thought could be better explained on the basis of imagery than by nonsensory information. Two of the five findings were concerned with scanning visual images, a task studied by Kosslyn and his associates. We look first at one variable influencing scanning time—the effect of distance between objects. We then examine the other three findings on visual matching, mental rotation, and selective interference.

---

propositional theory A theory that all knowledge, including spatial knowledge, can be expressed in semantic-based propositions

Scanning Visual Images

Many explanations of performance based on visual imagery assume that an image is a spatial representation analogous to the experience of seeing an object during visual perception. Furthermore, many of the operations used in analyzing visual patterns are also used to analyze visual images (Kosslyn & Pomerantz, 1977). One such operation is **visual scanning**. The analogy between pictures and images suggests that the time it takes to scan between two objects in an image should be a function of their distance from each other. Evidence obtained by Kosslyn et al. (1978) supports this prediction.

One of their experiments required that undergraduates at Johns Hopkins University learn the exact locations of the objects shown in Figure 8.4. The map was then removed, and the students were given a series of trials that began with the name of an object. The task required that they form a mental image of the entire map and focus on the named object. Subjects then

FIGURE 8.4 ■ A fictional map used to study the effect of distances on mental scanning time.

Source: "Visual images preserve metric spatial information: Evidence from studies of image scanning," by S. M. Kosslyn, T. M. Ball, & B. J. Reiser, 1978, *Journal of Experimental Psychology: Human Perception and Performance, 4,* 47–60. https://doi.org/10.1037/0096-1523.4.1.47. Copyright 1978 by the American Psychological Association.

visual scanning A shift of attention across a visual display or image

heard the name of a second object and scanned the map in the way they had been instructed—by imagining a black speck moving in a straight line from the first object to the second. When they reached the second object, they pushed a button that stopped a clock. There are 21 possible distances among the seven objects, and the longest distance is nine times as great as the shortest distance. If distance determines the scanning time, as predicted, reaction time should be a linear function of the distance between two locations. Figure 8.5 shows how closely the prediction was supported.

These results suggest that we can mentally scan visual images in the same way that we can scan pictures. But an alternative view is that subjects in imagery tasks may be able to respond appropriately without actually using visual images (Intons-Peterson, 1983; Pylyshyn, 1981). According to this view, subjects may guess what the experimenter expects and respond so as to please the experimenter. A study by Mitchell and Richman (1980) showed that people can accurately predict how distance should influence scanning time. When the experimenters asked subjects to predict their scanning time for the different pairs of objects in Figure 8.5, predicted scanning times also increased as a linear function of distance. It is therefore possible that subjects did not actually mentally scan their visual images but simply waited longer before pushing the button as the distance increased between two objects.

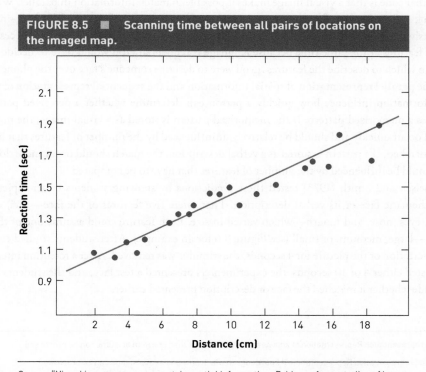

FIGURE 8.5 ■ Scanning time between all pairs of locations on the imaged map.

Source: "Visual images preserve metric spatial information: Evidence from studies of image scanning," by S. M. Kosslyn, T. M. Ball, & B. J. Reiser, 1978, *Journal of Experimental Psychology: Human Perception and Performance, 4*, 47–60. https://doi.org/10.1037/0096-1523.4.1.47. Copyright 1978 by the American Psychological Association.

This criticism can be avoided if the outcome of the experiment cannot be predicted. Reed et al. (1983) hypothesized that people may not be able to predict how the shape of patterns will influence their scanning time. For example, one of these researchers' patterns was a straight line, and another was a spiral. The rate at which people scanned a visual image of the pattern depended on its shape. An image of a straight line was scanned more quickly than an image of a spiral. However, people were unsuccessful in predicting how the different shapes would influence their scanning time. Because they couldn't predict the outcome of the experiment, their scanning times must have been produced by their actually scanning the different patterns rather than by their predictions.

Although the data of some imagery experiments might have been generated without subjects using imagery, it is highly unlikely that people could perform many spatial tasks without using imagery. Finke (1980) cites specific examples of tasks in which the expected outcome would not be obvious to subjects, usually because they were doing the task for the first time. Let's now consider some other tasks that allow us to distinguish between visual and verbal memory codes.

Sequential Versus Parallel Processing

One difference between information maintained in a visual image and information maintained as a verbal code is that a visual image makes it possible to match information in parallel. When you look at the schematic faces in Figure 8.6, you can perceive many features of the faces simultaneously. However, when you describe these same features verbally, you do not have access to all the features at the same time because language is sequential. You would have to decide the order in which to describe the features if you were to describe someone's face over the phone.

The parallel representation of spatial information and the sequential representation of verbal information influence how quickly a person can determine whether a perceived pattern matches a memorized pattern. If the memorized pattern is stored as a visual image, the match should occur quickly and should be relatively uninfluenced by the number of features that have to be matched. If a pattern is stored as a verbal description, the match should occur more slowly and should be influenced by the number of features that have to be compared.

Nielsen and Smith (1973) tested these predictions by showing students either a picture of a schematic face or its verbal description. There were five features of the face—ears, eyebrows, eyes, nose, and mouth—which varied in size. Each feature could assume one of three values—large, medium, or small (see Figure 8.6 for an example). After students studied either the description or the picture for 4 seconds, the stimulus was removed. After a retention interval that lasted either 4 or 10 seconds, the experimenters presented a test face, and the students had to decide whether it matched the face or description presented earlier.

---

parallel representation Representation of knowledge in which more than one item at a time can be processed

sequential representation Representation of knowledge in which only one item at a time can be processed

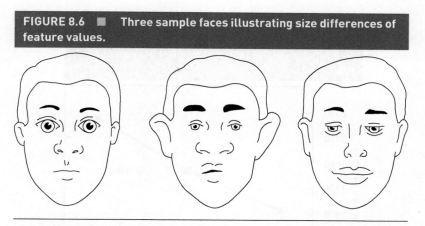

FIGURE 8.6 ■   Three sample faces illustrating size differences of feature values.

Source: "Representation and retrieval processes in short-term memory: Recognition and recall of faces," by E. E. Smith & G. D. Nielsen, 1970, *Journal of Experimental Psychology, 85*, 397–405. https://doi.org/10.1037/h0029727. Copyright 1970 by the American Psychological Association.

To test the prediction that the number of features would influence reaction time only when people compared the test face with a verbal description, Nielsen and Smith varied the number of relevant features from three to five. The students knew that they could ignore the ears and eyebrows when there were three relevant features because these features never changed, and they could ignore the ears when there were four relevant features. But they had to compare all five features when all five were relevant. Figure 8.7 shows the amount of time needed to respond that either the initial face (FF task) or the description (DF task) matched the test face. The data are from the 4-second delay, but the same pattern of results occurred for the 10-second delay. The response times indicate that matching was relatively fast and independent of the number of relevant features only when the initial item was a visual pattern.

The results imply that when a person can maintain a visual image of a pattern in STM (short-term memory), a second visual pattern can be compared with it very quickly. It's almost as if the person were superimposing the two patterns and comparing all the features simultaneously. When the features are described verbally, a match requires sequentially retrieving information from the description, such as large ears, small eyebrows, small eyes, medium nose, and large mouth. Each feature on the list is individually compared with the corresponding feature on the test face. The response time therefore increases as a function of the number of relevant features on the list. Maintaining an image in the FF task avoids a list of separate items by combining the individual features on the list into a single integrated pattern. The efficiency with which this integrated pattern can be compared with other visual patterns is an important difference between a visual image and a verbal description.

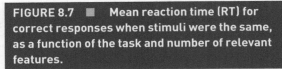

FIGURE 8.7 ■ Mean reaction time (RT) for correct responses when stimuli were the same, as a function of the task and number of relevant features.

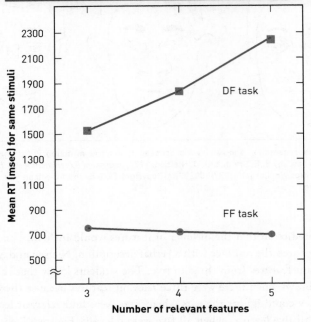

Source: From "Imaginal and verbal representations in short-term recognition of visual forms," by G. D. Nielsen & E. E. Smith, 1973, *Journal of Experimental Psychology, 101*, 375–378. https://doi.org/10.1037/h0035212. Copyright 1973 by the American Psychological Association.

Mental Transformations

Deciding whether two patterns match is considerably more difficult if they differ in orientation. The task shown in Figure 8.8 requires judging whether the two patterns in each pair are the same object (Shepard & Metzler, 1971). Pairs *a* and *b* are different orientations of the same pattern, but pair *c* consists of two different patterns. One method for determining whether two patterns are identical is to rotate one pattern mentally until it has the same orientation as the other pattern. When the patterns have the same orientation, it is easier to determine whether they match.

The pairs used by Shepard and Metzler differed in orientation from 0 degrees to 180 degrees in 20-degree steps. Half of the pairs could be rotated to match each other, and half were mirror images that did not match. Figure 8.9 shows that the time required to decide that two patterns were identical increased linearly with an increase in the number of degrees they differed in orientation, suggesting that the subjects were rotating a visual image of one of the forms until it had the same orientation as the other form. Self-reports were consistent with this

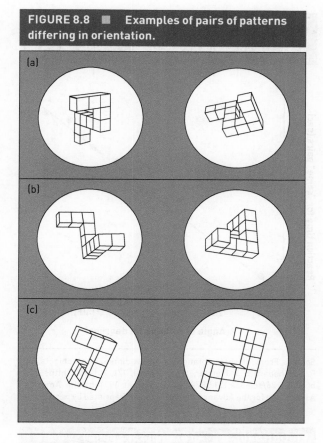

FIGURE 8.8 ■ Examples of pairs of patterns differing in orientation.

(a)

(b)

(c)

Source: From "Mental rotation of three-dimensional objects," by R. N. Shepard & J. Metzler, 1971, *Science, 171*, 701–703. https://doi.org/10.1126/science.171.3972.701. Copyright 1971 by the American Association for the Advancement of Science. Reprinted by permission.

interpretation—subjects reported that they imagined one object rotating until it had the same orientation as the other and that they could rotate an image only up to a certain speed without losing its structure. In addition, more recent neuroimaging studies provide evidence that mental rotation is a continuous transformation of spatial representations (Zacks, 2008).

The ability to mentally animate static pictures can also be useful for solving certain kinds of scientific reasoning problems (Hegarty, 2004). Look at the diagram of the pulley system in Figure 8.10 and try to determine whether the pulley on the left turns in a clockwise or a counterclockwise direction when the rope on the right side of the diagram is pulled. You probably tried to mentally animate the pulley system to answer the question. The mental animation creates a "causal chain" of events that begins with the first (right) pulley, proceeds to the second (middle) pulley, and ends with the last (left) pulley. Hegarty (1992) hypothesized that people mentally animate the pulleys in the order of this causal chain to understand how the system works.

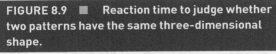

FIGURE 8.9 ■ Reaction time to judge whether two patterns have the same three-dimensional shape.

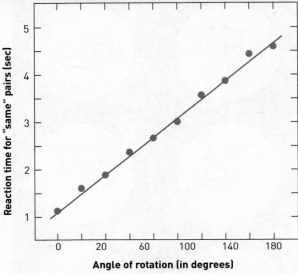

Source: From "Mental rotation of three-dimensional objects," by R. N. Shepard & J. Metzler, 1971, *Science, 171*, 701–703. https://doi.org/10.1126/science.171.3972.701. Copyright 1971 by the American Association for the Advancement of Science. Reprinted by permission.

FIGURE 8.10 ■ An example of a pulley system.

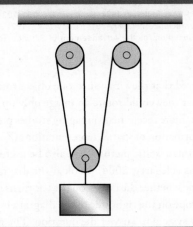

Source: From "Mental animation: Inferring motion from static displays of mechanical systems," by M. Hegarty, 1992, *Journal of Experimental Psychology: Learning, Memory, and Cognition, 18*, 1084–1102. https://doi.org/10.1037//0278-7393.18.5.1084

To test this hypothesis, she asked students to quickly respond "true" or "false" to a statement that appeared to the left of the diagram. Static statements did not mention movement, whereas kinematic statements did mention movement. If people mentally animate the pulleys to evaluate the kinematic statements, then their response times should increase as the length of the causal chain increases. This is what Hegarty found. Students verified most quickly statements about the beginning pulley and verified least quickly statements about the end pulley. Verification errors also increased from the beginning pulley to the end pulley. In contrast, neither response times nor errors varied across pulleys for the evaluation of the static statements. The location of the pulleys was important only when the verification task required animation of the pulleys in a particular order.

Interference

We have seen in earlier discussions that a major cause of forgetting is interference. Research on release from proactive interference (Wickens, 1972) has demonstrated that interference can be reduced by shifting semantic categories. Interference can also be reduced by shifting between visual and verbal material, as shown in a study by Brooks (1968). In the visual task in this study, subjects were shown a block diagram of a letter (Figure 8.11). The letter was then removed, and the subjects had to use their memory of the letter to respond "yes" to each corner that was on the extreme top or bottom and "no" to each corner that was in between. The correct answers for the example, starting at the asterisk at the lower left and proceeding in the direction of the arrow, are: yes, yes, yes, no, no, no, no, no, no, yes.

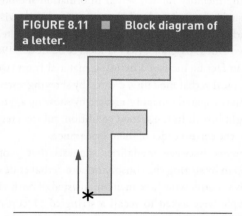

FIGURE 8.11 ■ Block diagram of a letter.

Source: From "Spatial and verbal components of the act of recall," by L. R. Brooks, 1968, *Canadian Journal of Psychology, 22*, 349–368. https://doi.org/10.1037/h0082775. Copyright 1968 by the Canadian Psychological Association.

The verbal task in Brooks's experiment required that people respond positively to each word in a sentence that was a noun. For example, people listened to the sentence "A bird in the hand is not in the bush" and then had to determine whether each word was a noun. The correct answers for the example are no, yes, no, no, yes, no, no, no, no, yes.

Brooks assumed that his subjects would rely on a verbal code to maintain the sentence in memory and a visual image to maintain the block diagram in memory. If his assumption is correct, it should be possible to *interfere selectively* with performance by using two different methods of responding. One method required that the answers be given verbally, by overtly responding "yes" or "no." A verbal response should cause a greater conflict when classifying the words of a sentence than when classifying the corners of a block diagram. Another method required that a subject point to a *Y* for each positive response and an *N* for each negative response, using a diagram in which the *Y*s and *N*s were arranged in crooked columns. Pointing to the correct letter therefore required close visual monitoring and should interfere more with the block task than with the sentence task. The selective nature of interference is revealed by the average response time required to complete each task. Classifying the words in a sentence took longer when people gave a verbal response; classifying the corners of a letter took longer when people pointed to the correct response. In other words, giving a verbal response interfered more with memory for verbal material (a sentence) than with memory for visual material (a block diagram) and vice versa.

The selective nature of interference within a modality has implications for the number of items that can be maintained in STM. When we reviewed the evidence on STM capacity in Chapter 4, we looked at research that presented items from the same modality, such as a string of letters in a memory span task or different levels of brightness in an absolute judgment task. What would happen if we designed a memory span task in which some items could be retained by using a verbal code and other items could be retained by using a visual code? According to Baddeley's (1992) working memory model, verbal information should be maintained in the articulatory loop, and visual information should be maintained in the visuospatial sketchpad. If such variety reduces interference, people should be able to recall more items.

An experiment by two Dutch psychologists (Sanders & Schroots, 1969) revealed that a person's memory span can in fact be increased by using material from two different modalities. One modality was the typical verbal modality, created by showing a string of consonants. The other modality was a visual or spatial modality, created by showing a random sequence of lights on a two-dimensional light board. In the second condition, subjects responded by pointing to the lights on the board in the correct order of their appearance.

The lack of interference between modalities suggests that people should be able to increase their memory span by storing the consonants as a verbal code and the light sequence as a visual code. Recall was better when a sequence consisted of both visual and verbal items. For example, when people were asked to recall a string of 11 consonants, they correctly recalled an average of 5.4 items. When they were asked to recall a string of 6 consonants followed by a string of 5 spatial positions, they correctly recalled an average of 8.3 items. The improvement in recall was not caused by the possibility that spatial positions were easier to recall than consonants because previous research had shown that recalling spatial positions was actually more difficult. Rather, the findings were caused by the relative lack of interference between the visual and verbal codes. These results, along with those obtained by Brooks and many other psychologists, show that using two different modalities can reduce interference and improve performance.

This research illustrates how visual images can be used to improve performance on many cognitive tasks, including preserving the spatial relations among different parts of a picture, lowering reaction times for processing spatial information, and reducing interference between visual and verbal codes. These findings are strong evidence against the claim in propositional theory (Pylyshyn, 1973) that images are not necessary for building cognitive theories. We now look at additional sources of evidence regarding the use of visual imagery.

EVIDENCE FOR IMAGES

Cognitive Neuroscience

In his book *Image and Brain: The Resolution of the Imagery Debate*, Stephen Kosslyn (1994) divided the debate over mental imagery into three phases. The first phase was the argument over whether a propositional theory could represent all types of knowledge, making it unnecessary to propose a theory based on visual images. The previous section (Imagery in Performing Cognitive Tasks) raised that issue. The second phase was whether the demand characteristics of the task could explain the results of imagery experiments. As we have seen, that issue was initially raised by the critics of Kosslyn's visual-scanning experiments. But it was the third phase—evidence from cognitive neuroscience—that Kosslyn believed silenced the critics of the theoretical importance of visual images.

Martha Farah (1988) was one of the first psychologists to gather together evidence that would make a strong case for the use of imagery in performing many cognitive tasks. She argued that supporting evidence from neuropsychology could be grouped into two broad categories: results showing (1) that visual imagery uses the same brain areas as vision and (2) that selective damage to the brain impairs visual imagery in the same manner that it impairs vision. Evidence that visual perception and visual imagery use the same areas of the brain comes from two different methods of measuring brain activity, based on either cerebral blood flow or electrophysiological activity. Both measures indicate that many tasks in which we would expect visual imagery to be involved show increased activity in that part of the brain used for visual perception—the occipital lobes, which contain the primary and secondary visual cortex (Farah, 1988).

For instance, neurological evidence supports the previously discussed usefulness of visual images in learning. In one study, different groups of participants listened to lists of concrete words under instructions to try to learn the words either by simply listening to them or by forming visual images to represent them. Recall was better for the imagery group, as would be expected from Paivio's dual-coding theory, and there was more blood flow to the occipital lobes for the imagery group (Goldenberg et al., 1987). Another study found differences in the distribution of event-related potentials for concrete and abstract words (Kounios & Holcomb, 1994), which is also consistent with dual-coding theory.

Neurological findings enable investigators to determine which tasks rely on visual imagery. Roland and Friberg (1985) measured cerebral blood flow while subjects performed one of three cognitive tasks: mental arithmetic, memory-scanning of a musical jingle, or visually imagining a walk through one's neighborhood. They found increased activity in the visual cortex for visually imagining the walk but not for the mental arithmetic or the memory-scanning task.

Figure 8.12 shows the activation of the visual cortex (V1) and lateral geniculate nucleus (LGN) for visually imagining a walk and for two other tasks (Chen et al., 1998). The fMRI measurements revealed strong activation of the visual cortex and lateral geniculate when a person viewed a flashing light pattern (8.12a), weak activation when a person imagined the flashing light pattern (8.12b), and moderate activation when a person imagined walking in his or her hometown (8.12c). The authors suggested that the greater activation from imagining a walk is caused by its familiarity relative to the novel light pattern. The larger size of the walking image could be an additional reason for its more extensive activation. The large difference in activation between viewing a light pattern (8.12a) and imagining the light pattern (8.12b) indicates the greater vividness of perceiving relative to imagining (Chen et al., 1998). Indeed, 5 of the 12 participants did not show any activation in the visual cortex and lateral geniculate nucleus when imagining the light pattern, suggesting that they did not remember the previously encountered pattern.

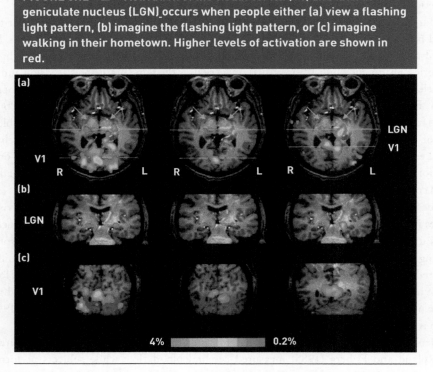

FIGURE 8.12 ■ Activation of the visual cortex (V1) and lateral geniculate nucleus (LGN) occurs when people either (a) view a flashing light pattern, (b) imagine the flashing light pattern, or (c) imagine walking in their hometown. Higher levels of activation are shown in red.

Source: From "Human primary visual cortex and lateral geniculate nucleus activation during visual imagery," by W. Chen, T. Kato, X. H. Shu, S. Ogawa, D. W. Tank, & K. Ugurbil, 1998, *Neuroreport, 9,* 3669–3674. https://doi.org/10.1097/00001756-199811160-00019

Dreams

A potential drawback of visual imagery is that we may occasionally wonder whether some event actually happened or whether we only imagined it. Johnson and Raye (1981) proposed that several kinds of cues are helpful for distinguishing between perception and imagination. First, there is *sensory information.* Perceptual events have more sensory detail than imagined events, as revealed by the difference in activation levels between Figure 8.12a and 8.12b. Second, there is *contextual information.* Perceptual events occur in an external context that contains other information. For example, perceiving a dog is typically accompanied by the perception of other objects near the dog. Imagining a dog typically consists of an image of a dog that is not surrounded by other objects.

A third cue for distinguishing between perception and imagination is memory for the *cognitive operations* that are required to generate the image. However, we occasionally produce images automatically without much conscious awareness. Dreams are of this type. They often seem very real because we are not aware of generating them. In contrast, daydreams seem less real because they are more influenced by our conscious control (Photo 8.3).

PHOTO 8.3 Day dreams are influenced by conscious control.

istockphoto.com/Cecilie_Arcurs

A group of psychologists in Belgium and Denmark reviewed research relating the vividness of imagery to various conscious experiences, including dreaming (Fazekas et al., 2020). Two aspects of vividness as a phenomenological experience are subjective intensity and subjective specificity. **Subjective intensity** is determined by how much the content of the image stands out from the perceived background. **Subjective specificity** is determined by how distinguishable the image is from other stimuli. **REM sleep** is of particular interest because it

---

Subjective intensity Determined by how much the content of the image stands out from its perceived background

Subjective specificity Determined by how distinguishable the image is from other stimuli

REM sleep (rapid eye movement) Sleep typically occurs approximately 90 minutes after falling asleep and is the primary stage of dreaming

includes complex dreaming and heightened brain activity that is accompanied by rapid eye movements. Research has revealed that REM dreams are generally rated as more intense (higher brightness and contrast) and more specific (higher clarity) than non-REM dreams Fazekas et al., 2020.

Dreams provide many new experiences, but do they have a purpose? One answer is that dreams enable the rehearsal of embodied cognition (Speth & Speth, 2018). Rather than waste our time with merely sleeping, we may practice action-based perception. The Speths hypothesized that the relative amount of motor imagery and cognitive evaluation would vary with the depth of sleep and tested their hypothesis by periodically awakening university students so they could describe their recent dream experiences. The average number of reported incidents involving motor imagery increased from 0.19 during sleep onset to 1.07 during nonREM sleep and 2.06 during REM sleep. These numbers do not include athletic motor imagery, which also increased with deeper levels of sleep. The results demonstrate that our embodied experiences persist across different levels of consciousness and become stronger on the path to REM sleep.

It is unclear whether this rehearsal of actions serves a useful function, but there is evidence that reactivation of memories during sleep improves problem solving (Sanders et al., 2019). Participants attempted to solve puzzles during the evening while each puzzle was accompanied by a different sound clip. They continued this procedure until they had accumulated six unsolved puzzles. When an electroencephalogram (EEG) recorder detected slow-wave sleep during the night, the participants received sound cues associated with half of the unsolved puzzles to determine whether activation of these puzzles would increase solutions. It did. The next morning, the problem solvers solved significantly more of the cued puzzles than the noncued puzzles.

Dream research will benefit from data mining to analyze large numbers of dreams (Holtz, 2020). Researchers at Cambridge University's Nokia Bell Labs in the United Kingdom designed an artificial intelligence system to the search for various topics. They used the largest public collection of dream reports (DreamBank) that consists of 38,000 documented dreams. The AI system partitions the dream transcripts into their most important terms according to a widely accepted dream analysis scale. Women had more friendly, upbeat dreams while men's dreams were more aggressive and negative. Teenagers often dreamed of sex. The dreams of war veterans were frequently violent. Blind people tended to dream more frequently of imaginary characters.

Limitations of Images

The emphasis throughout this chapter has been on the usefulness of visual images for learning and for performing many spatial reasoning tasks. Perhaps you find this surprising. If you are like me, you may feel that you cannot create very vivid images and perhaps even question whether you use any images at all. Let me give you a chance to form an image by asking: "Does the Star of David contain a diamond?" Try to form an image of the Star of David and examine it to answer the question. Many people have difficulty using images to identify the parts of a pattern, even after they have just seen the pattern (Reed, 1974). Because we have seen many results that show the usefulness of images, it is only fair to discuss a few limitations of images before leaving the topic.

The embedded figures task required participants to decide whether the second of two sequentially presented patterns was part of the first pattern. Figure 8.13 shows two examples that occurred as the first pattern. The bold lines (which were not bold in the experiment) depict different second patterns that were tested as parts of the first pattern. Reed (1974) proposed that figures consisting of a composition of various shapes are encoded as structural descriptions rather than as uninterpreted templates. Parts encoded into the structural description (such as a triangle for the Star of David) should be quickly and accurately identified, but parts not included in the description (such as a diamond) should be difficult to identify in an image. The findings were consistent with this hypothesis.

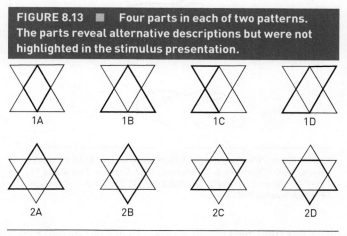

FIGURE 8.13 ■ Four parts in each of two patterns. The parts reveal alternative descriptions but were not highlighted in the stimulus presentation.

1A   1B   1C   1D

2A   2B   2C   2D

Source: Based on "Structural descriptions and the limitations of visual imagery," by S. K. Reed, 1974, *Memory & Cognition, 2*, 329–336. https://doi.org/10.3758/BF03209004

Evidence from imagery studies shows that people are quite selective in which details they maintain in their images. Let's begin with another demonstration of your ability to reinterpret a visual image. Form a visual image of the animal in Figure 8.14a. Now examine your image, without looking at the drawing in the book, and see whether you can reinterpret the figure to perceive it as a different animal. Were you successful? If not, try to reinterpret the figure in the book. If your experience was similar to the students studied by Chambers and Reisberg (1985), you should have found it much easier to reinterpret the drawing in the book than to reinterpret your image of the drawing. In fact, in one of their studies, they found that none of the 15 students in the experiment could reinterpret their image of the figure, but all 15 could reinterpret a drawing of the figure.

In a subsequent study, Chambers and Reisberg (1992) examined why people had difficulty reinterpreting their image. They hypothesized that people maintain only the more important aspects of the image; in this case, the face of the animal (that is, the front side of the head). People who perceive the pattern in Figure 8.14a as a duck should therefore have a detailed image of the left side of the pattern, and people who perceive the pattern as a rabbit should have a detailed image of the right side of the pattern. The results from a

FIGURE 8.14 ■ (a) Duck/rabbit ambiguous figure; (b) modification of the duck's bill; (c) modification of the rabbit's nose.

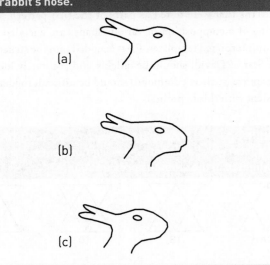

(a)

(b)

(c)

Source: From "What an image depicts depends on what an image means," by D. Chambers & D. Reisberg, 1992, *Cognitive Psychology, 24*, 145–174. https://doi.org/10.1016/0010-0285(92)90006-N. Copyright 1992 by Academic Press, Inc.

recognition-memory test confirmed this hypothesis. In one test, people were asked to indicate whether they were shown pattern Figure 8.14a (the correct choice) or pattern Figure 8.14b, which changed the front part (the bill) of the duck's face. People who had perceived the pattern as a duck did significantly better than chance on this test, but people who had perceived the pattern as a rabbit performed at chance level. The opposite results occurred when the participants had to choose between the original pattern and a pattern that modified the front part (the nose) of the rabbit's face, shown in Figure 8.14c. People who had perceived the pattern as a duck now performed at a chance level, whereas people who had perceived the pattern as a rabbit performed significantly better than chance. People therefore have difficulty reinterpreting the pattern because they are missing those details that are important for the new interpretation.

Fortunately, images can be useful in many tasks, even when we do not have a detailed memory of an object. For example, the retention of details is usually unnecessary when we use images to remember words. Your image of a penny would not have to be detailed or accurate to help you remember the word *penny*; it would only have to be detailed enough to allow you to recall the correct word when you retrieved your image.

Experimental results have shown that people who were good at recalling the names of pictures they had seen two weeks earlier did not have more detailed images than people who could not recall as many names (Bahrick & Boucher, 1968). For example, people who could recall that they had seen a cup did not necessarily remember many details of the cup in a recognition test similar to the one illustrated by Figure 8.14. The evidence suggested that people were using visual images to aid their recall, but it was necessary to remember only enough details about an object to recall its name. Visual images can therefore be incomplete if the task does not require memory for details.

Studies showing the limitations of visual images provide both good news and bad news. The bad news is that using visual images is not a universal solution for improving memory performance. The good news is that, even if people believe they have poor images, their images may still be sufficient for performing the many tasks that do not require great detail.

APPLICATIONS

Geographical Reasoning

Perhaps the most frequent use of spatial reasoning in our daily lives is navigating our environment. In his chapter on cognitive geography, Daniel Montello (2009) defines geographical reasoning as the study of cognition about space, place, and the environment. It includes cognitive processes such as perception, thinking, learning, memory, attention, imagination, language, reasoning, and problem solving. Cognitive geography considers both geographic knowledge that is directly acquired through interacting with the world and symbolic knowledge incorporated into materials such as maps. Its applications include improving spatial orientation, geographic education, map design, urban planning, and landscape design.

Barbara Tversky at Stanford and Columbia has done extensive research on the use of imagery in spatial reasoning, including how imagery can lead to memory distortions (Tversky, 2005). She cites a study that asked the question "Which city is further west—San Diego, California, or Reno, Nevada?" Research at the University of California, San Diego, revealed that even people who live in San Diego tended to answer this question incorrectly (Stevens & Coupe, 1978). To account for this and related geographical misconceptions, Stevens and Coupe proposed that spatial information is stored hierarchically. Many people incorrectly infer that San Diego must be west of Reno because California is west of Nevada. The correct answer depends on knowledge of how the coastline of California curves southeastward.

Another distortion discussed by Tversky (2005) is that people remember geographical regions as more aligned than they are; for instance, they align North America and Europe along the same horizontal axis and North and South America along the same vertical axis. Capital cities within Europe also are remembered as being more aligned along horizontal and vertical axes, as revealed by students at the University of Bologna in Italy who sketched the borders of 10 countries and marked the position of their capital cities (Costa & Bonetti, 2018). Figure 8.15A shows the correct location of the cities, and Figure 8.15B shows the average placement in the sketches. Connecting the cities reveals that the students' memories are more regular and compact than reality.

FIGURE 8.15   ■   Shapes formed by connecting European capitals in a real map (8.15A) and in a map generated by students at the University of Bologna (8.15B).

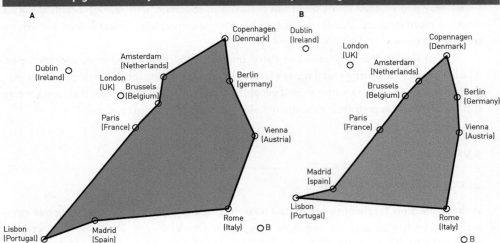

Source: From "Geometrical distortions in geographical cognitive maps," by M. Costa & L. Bonetti, 2018, *Journal of Environmental Psychology, 55*, 53–69. https://doi.org/10.1016/j.jenvp.2017.12.004

Navigating our environment is another aspect of geographical reasoning in which people differ in their ability to integrate information along a route (Weisberg & Newcombe, 2018). Figure 8.16a shows a virtual desktop environment in which participants navigated two routes by following arrows. Figure 8.16b displays a map of the routes, which was not shown to the participants. A test of the relative locations of the buildings revealed three clusters of ability (Figure 8.17). The integrators had knowledge of relative locations, both within a route and across the two routes. The nonintegrators had knowledge of relative locations within a route but made errors in determining relative locations across routes. The imprecise navigators had difficulty determining the relative locations for both routes. The data support the conclusion that forming cognitive maps of our environment is possible but not automatic or effortless.

Clinical Disorders

Visual imagery is very relevant to clinical psychology because it has a stronger link to emotion than verbal-linguistic cognition and therefore serves to maintain and amplify emotional states (Ji et al., 2019). Researchers have proposed that mental imagery can amplify the impact of cognition on emotion and mood instability in both positive and negative directions, such as occurs in bipolar disorder. The conceptual and clinical significance of imagery is also evident in many other disorders, such as mood and anxiety disorders, self-harm, suicidal tendencies, and addiction (Ji et al., 2019).

Similar conclusions were reached by Saulsman et al. (2019), who argued that mental imagery (1) is a form of cognition that generates stronger emotional responses than

FIGURE 8.16 ■ Screenshots of a desktop virtual environment (8.16a) and a map of two routes (8.16b).

a

b

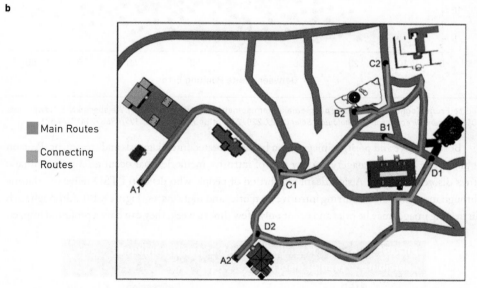

Source: From "Cognitive maps: Some people make them, some people struggle," by S. M. Weisberg & N. S. Newcombe, 2018, *Current Directions in Psychological Science, 27*, 220–226. https://doi.org/10.1177/0963721417744521

verbal-linguistic thinking; (2) is relevant to most types of psychopathology, although clients typically do not spontaneously describe images unless directly asked; and (3) has been a part of cognitive behavior therapy since its beginning but only recently has received more attention. They recommend that imagery should be applied to cognitive behavior therapy either as an enhancer of existing approaches or as an additional method that complements standard practice.

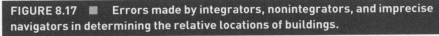

FIGURE 8.17 ■ Errors made by integrators, nonintegrators, and imprecise navigators in determining the relative locations of buildings.

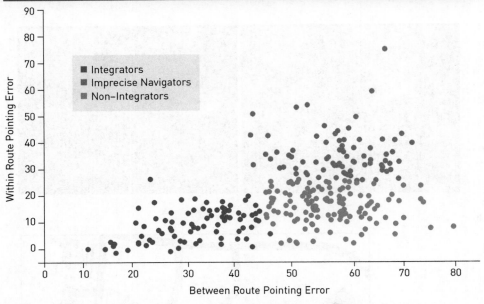

Source: From "Cognitive maps: Some people make them, some people struggle," by S. M. Weisberg & N. S. Newcombe, 2018, *Current Directions in Psychological Science, 27,* 220–226. https://doi.org/10.1177/0963721417744521

Both negative and positive imagery can be incorporated into diagnosis and treatment (Pearson et al., 2015). Negative imagery is a key part of intrusive memories that occur after posttraumatic stress disorder (PTSD). A significant proportion of people who develop PTSD relive the trauma through unwanted and recurring intrusive memories and nightmares (Figure 8.18). Although such distressing images may be brief and occur only a few times a week, they can have a profound impact.

FIGURE 8.18 ■ Negative and lack of positive imagery contribute to mental disorders.

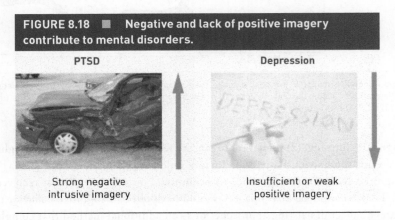

Source: From "Mental imagery: Functional mechanisms and clinical applications," by J. Pearson, T. Naselaris, E. A. Holmes, & S. M. Kosslyn, 2015, *Trends in Cognitive Sciences, 19,* 590–602. https://doi.org/10.1016/j.tics.2015.08.003

Although patients experience different reactions following trauma, intrusive memories are among their most central experiences and associated with the most severe PTSD symptoms (Singh et al., 2020). One approach to treating these image-based intrusive memories is to use imagery competing tasks. For instance, 20 patients were monitored for intrusive memories after their admission into an inpatient ward. Weekly sessions targeted specific intrusions that were followed by 25 minutes of playing a computer game (Tetris) that requires mental rotations. Reoccurrence of the targeted memories were reduced by an average of 64%, compared to an average reduction of 11% for nontargeted intrusions (Kessler et al., 2018).

A lack of positive images is also detrimental when depression limits the ability to imagine a positive future (Figure 8.18). As we learned in Chapter 5 on long-term memory, episodic memory contributes not only to our memory of the past but to our ability to imagine the future. In addition to the refinement of imagery-based techniques to target maladaptive imagery, another trend has been to develop techniques that encourage positive, adaptive imagery (Blackwell, 2021). These methods include practice in generating vivid and specific images for imagining positive future events and for carrying out steps for a healthy lifestyle. Most of these techniques are still under development and evaluation but should ultimately be integrated into routine clinical practice. Although techniques based on imagery may not be appropriate for everyone, they nonetheless have great potential for improving the practice of cognitive-based therapy (Blackwell, 2021).

Training Spatial Skills

This chapter has included a variety of spatial tasks, and it would be helpful to organize these tasks to have a better understanding of their contributions to cognition. Newcombe and Shipley (2015) identified four types of spatial abilities to distinguish between tasks that involve relations among the parts of an object (intrinsic) and tasks that involve relations among different objects (extrinsic). A second dimension indicates whether the object(s) requires transformation. Static objects do not; dynamic objects do. Table 8.2 displays the taxonomy, and Photo 8.4 shows an

PHOTO 8.4 An extrinsic dynamic task involves imagining interactions among objects.

istockphoto.com/BraunS

example. The taxonomy has proven useful for organizing research on a wide variety of experimental tasks (Reed, 2019), including mathematical ability (Xie et al., 2019) and training spatial skills (Uttal et al., 2013).

TABLE 8.2 ■ A taxonomy of spatial abilities		
Ability	**Definition**	**Example**
Intrinsic-static	Processing an object without transformation	Interpreting the components of an object
Intrinsic-dynamic	Processing an object with transformations	Manipulating the object
Extrinsic-static	Processing relationships among objects without transformations	Reading a map
Extrinsic-dynamic	Processing relationships among objects with transformation	Navigating an environment

Source: Based on "Thinking about spatial thinking: New typology, new assessments," by N. S. Newcombe & T. P. Shipley, 2015, in J. S. Gero (Ed.), *Studying visual and spatial thinking for design creativity* (pp. 179–192). New York: Springer. (https://www.springerprofessional.de/en/thinking-about-spatial-thinking-new-typology-new-assessments/4846992)

A meta-analysis of 263 effect sizes from 73 studies confirmed that all four types of spatial ability influenced mathematical reasoning (Xie et al., 2020). In addition, the review found that spatial ability influenced mathematical performance for both normal and developmentally challenged children, suggesting that training spatial ability should benefit both groups of individuals. The analysis also confirmed that all four types of mathematics (numbers, arithmetic, geometry, and logic) were influenced by spatial ability, although logical reasoning had a stronger association than numerical or arithmetic reasoning (Photo 8.5). One explanation for the larger effect of spatial ability on logical reasoning is that logical reasoning is more complex because it requires comparison, generalization, induction, deduction, and analysis, in addition to synthesis of mathematical rules and quantitative relations (Peng et al., 2019).

The importance of spatial skills has motivated researchers to design instructional programs to improve these skills. An analysis of 217 research studies found that training was successful across a wide variety of tasks, including video games, spatial tasks studied in the laboratory, and assignments in instructional courses (Uttal et al., 2013). Training was also successful for improving each of the four types of spatial skills identified by Newcombe and Shipley (2015) in Table 8.2.

Although training improves spatial skills, there had been few studies on whether training improves mathematical reasoning (Stieff & Uttal, 2015). The authors therefore advocated for systematic studies to evaluate whether performance in STEM (science, technology, engineering, and mathematics) courses are improved by training spatial skills and whether these skills generalize across courses. They also called for a need to evaluate not only *whether* spatial training is effective but *what* type of training improves STEM achievement and *when* such effects occur.

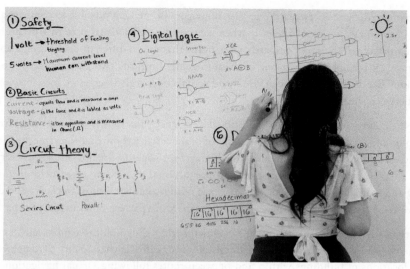

PHOTO 8.5 Spatial ability supports logical reasoning.

Photo by Jeswin Thomas on Unsplash

There has been progress on evaluating the effects of training on mathematical reasoning following the publication of Stieff and Uttal (2015) article, and the findings are promising. For instance, Lowrie et al. (2019) designed a spatial intervention program in an attempt to increase both spatial reasoning and mathematics performance. The interventions, which targeted spatial visualization and orientation, significantly improved performance on geometry and word problems relative to control groups. This and other studies are contributing answers to the questions raised by Stieff and Uttal (2015) regarding when spatial training improves performance in the classroom.

SUMMARY

The usefulness of visual images in learning is supported by research showing that people usually remember pictures better than concrete words and concrete words better than abstract ones. These results correspond to the fact that images are easiest to form from pictures and hardest to form from abstract words. Learning pairs of items is facilitated by forming an interactive image that combines the members of the pair. The dual-coding theory explains the usefulness of visual imagery in recall by proposing that a visual image provides an extra memory code that is independent of the verbal code. Visual images have been used to learn people's names and a foreign vocabulary, although it is first necessary to translate a name or foreign word into a similar-sounding concrete keyword.

A variety of evidence suggests that visual images are important to our ability to perform many spatial reasoning tasks. The time it takes to mentally scan between two objects in an image is a function of the distance between them. Visual images also make it possible to compare all the features of two patterns simultaneously when we try to match a visual pattern with an image of another pattern. When we compare two patterns that are in different orientations, a visual image makes it possible to rotate one of them mentally until the two patterns have the same orientation. The distinction between visual and verbal codes is also suggested by selective interference between the two codes.

Cognitive neuroscience provides additional evidence for when people use images. Electrophysiological and blood-flow measures of brain activity show that the same areas of the brain are used in visual perception and visual imagery. Images of dreams often seem very real because they are generated automatically. Although visual images are often helpful in many learning and spatial reasoning tasks, the images of most people are limited in clarity and detail. It is therefore difficult to use an image to find a new part in a pattern or reinterpret the pattern.

People typically simplify mental maps by remembering geographical regions and cities as aligned along the same vertical and horizontal axis. They differ in their ability to remember the relative locations of buildings within and between routes following virtual navigation. Both negative and positive images are critical for the diagnosis and treatment of clinical disorders. Negative imagery accompanies intrusive memories that occur following trauma, and positive imagery contributes to helping patients foresee a more hopeful future. Individual differences in spatial ability affect classroom performance and provide a need to develop successful training programs for improving spatial ability.

RECOMMENDED READING

Paivio (1971) discusses the experimental work during the 1960s that helped restore imagery as a major topic in experimental psychology. As described in his book *Image and the Brain: The Resolution of the Imagery Debate* (1994), Kosslyn's goal is to explain how each of a number of different subsystems interacts to determine performance across various imagery tasks. Articles by Finke (1985) and Thomas (1999) discuss the representation of information in images and the relation between imagery and perception. Psychologists continue to study the practical implications of imagery, including its role in the acquisition of spatial knowledge (Tversky, 2005, 2019). Broad overviews of research on visual thinking appear in *The Cambridge Handbook of Visuospatial Thinking* (Sha & Miyake, 2005) and in my book *Thinking Visually* (Reed, 2021). More focused articles provide excellent overviews the implications of visual imagery for clinical psychology (Blackwell, 2021; Pearson et al., 2015; Singh et al., 2020).

9 CATEGORIZATION

Concept Identification
    Discovering Rules and Attributes
    Critique of the Concept Identification Paradigm

Natural Categories
    Hierarchical Organization of Categories
    Typicality and Family Resemblances
    Person Perception

Categorization Models
    Multidimensional Scaling
    Comparing Categorization Models
    Theory-Based Categorization
    Instruction

Applications
    Dementia
    Semantic Hub Model

SUMMARY

RECOMMENDED READING

LEARNING OBJECTIVES

1. Identify the principles and limitations of the concept identification paradigm as a procedure for studying real-world categorization.

2. Explain how Rosch's categorization theory applies to objects and person perception.

3. Compare and contrast exemplar and prototype theories of categorization.

4. Summarize the semantic hub model and how it applies to semantic dementia.

This chapter and the next discuss ways in which people organize knowledge. One way to organize knowledge is to form categories. Categories consist of objects or events that we have grouped together because we feel they are somehow related. The ability to categorize enables us to interact with our environment without becoming overwhelmed by its complexity. Bruner, Goodnow, and Austin, in their influential book, *A Study of Thinking* (1956), listed five benefits of forming categories.

1. *Categorizing objects reduces the complexity of the environment*. Scientists have estimated that there are more than 7 million discriminable colors. If we responded to all of these

as unique, we could spend our entire lifetime just trying to learn the names of colors. When we classify discriminably different objects as being equivalent, we respond to them in terms of their class membership rather than as unique items (Photo 9.1).

2. *Categorizing is the means by which objects of the world are identified.* We usually feel that we have recognized a pattern when we can classify it into a familiar category such as *dog, chair,* or the letter *A*.

3. *The third achievement is a consequence of the first two—the establishment of categories reduces the need for constant learning.* We do not have to be taught about novel objects if we can classify them; we can use our knowledge of items in the category to respond to the novel object.

4. *Categorizing allows us to decide what constitutes an appropriate action.* A person who eats wild mushrooms must be able to distinguish between poisonous and nonpoisonous varieties. Eating a poisonous variety is clearly not an appropriate action (Photo 9.2).

5. *Categorizing enables us to order and relate classes of objects and events.* Although classification is by itself a useful way to organize knowledge, classes can be further organized into subordinate and superordinate relations. The category *chair*, for example, has *high chair* as a subordinate class and *furniture* as a superordinate class. The three categories form a hierarchy in which *furniture* contains *chair* as a member and *chair* contains *high chair* as a member.

PHOTO 9.1 Creating color categories from a continuous color spectrum.

istockphoto.com/Sever Orcun Edipoglu

PHOTO 9.2 Categorizing mushrooms.

Photo by Nick Grappone on Unsplash

Categories create concepts that are the building blocks of thought (Goldstone et al., 2018). We use them when we speak, reason, make inferences, and try to generalize our previous experiences. Concepts are embedded in networks where each concept's meaning depends on other concepts, perceptual processes, and language.

Psychologists have used several experimental procedures to study how people make classifications. The first section of this chapter describes a task called concept identification, in which the experimenter selects a logical rule to define a concept and the task requires discovering the rule through learning which patterns are examples of the concept. Rules use words such as "and" and "or," as illustrated by the instructions in Photo 9.3.

One limitation of this approach is that many categories cannot be distinguished on the basis of a simple rule. We can usually distinguish a dog from a cat, but it is questionable whether we use a simple rule to make this distinction. The second section discusses some characteristics of natural or real-world categories and emphasizes how we use these characteristics to organize knowledge. To recognize objects and reduce the need for constant learning, we have to be able to classify novel objects into a familiar category. The final section discusses how people do this.

---

logical rule A rule based on logical relations, such as conjunctive, disjunctive, conditional, and biconditional rules

concept identification A task that requires deciding whether an item is an example of a concept where concepts are typically defined by logical rules

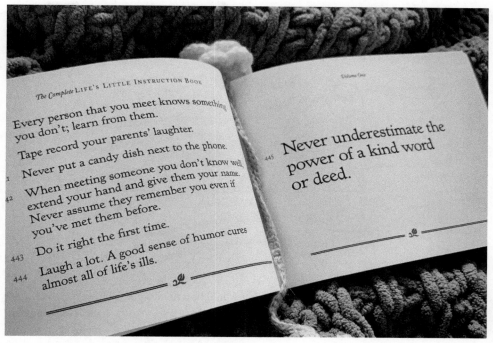

PHOTO 9.3 Instructions that include the words "and" and "or."

Photo by Gabrielle Audu on Unsplash.

CONCEPT IDENTIFICATION

Discovering Rules and Attributes

At the time Bruner, Goodnow, and Austin (1956) wrote *A Study of Thinking*, psychologists studied categorization by using the concept identification paradigm. The categories in concept identification tasks typically contain geometric patterns that vary along several dimensions—for example, shape, size, and color. The experimenter selects a rule to define the category, and the task requires discovering this rule by learning which patterns belong to the category.

Consider the **disjunctive rule** "Patterns that are *large or a circle* are members of the category." A pattern that has either of these two attributes would belong to the category. All the large patterns and all the circles would therefore be members, as shown by a plus in Figure 9.1. The nonmembers are labeled with a minus.

Bruner and his colleagues proposed that people solve concept identification problems by evaluating hypotheses. For example, you might initially hypothesize that a pattern has to be *small and square* (a **conjunctive rule**) to belong to the category. Both attributes have to be present

---

disjunctive rule A rule that uses the logical relation "or" to relate stimulus attributes, such as small or square

conjunctive rule A rule that uses the logical relation "and" to relate stimulus attributes, such as small and square

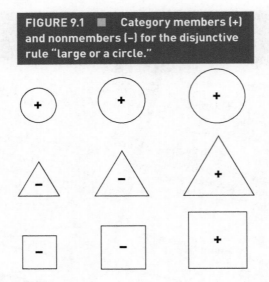

FIGURE 9.1 ■ Category members (+) and nonmembers (−) for the disjunctive rule "large or a circle."

to satisfy a conjunctive rule, so the only member would be a small square. However, you would have to abandon this hypothesis if you received contradictory information, such as learning that a small square was not a member of the category or that a large triangle was a member of the category (as shown in Figure 9.1). You would then have to formulate a new hypothesis that would be consistent with what you had learned in the experiment.

Concept identification tasks typically use many more stimuli than the ones shown in Figure 9.1, so discovering the correct rule can be very challenging. The difficulty is caused by the requirement to learn both the relevant rule (such as a disjunctive rule) and the relevant attributes (such as large, circle). One way to simplify the task would be to tell participants the relevant attributes. This task is called **rule learning** because people have to learn only the correct logical rule when they are told the relevant attributes (Haygood & Bourne, 1965). Rule-learning tasks allow researchers to study the relative difficulty of different rules, without having to be concerned about learning the relevant attributes (Bourne, 1970). A variation of this procedure—called **attribute learning**—is to tell people the rule and let them discover the appropriate attributes (Haygood & Bourne, 1965). By focusing on either rule learning or attribute learning, psychologists have learned how people formulate and evaluate hypotheses in concept identification tasks.

Critique of the Concept Identification Paradigm

Not all cognitive psychologists were satisfied with the concept identification task; some criticized it as highly artificial and unrelated to the categorization tasks we usually encounter in the

---

rule learning A concept identification task in which people are told the relevant attributes (such as small, square) but have to discover the logical rule

attribute learning A concept identification task in which people are told the logical rule (such as conjunctive) but have to discover the relevant attributes

real world. This criticism does not mean that we cannot draw any analogy between the skills needed in concept identification tasks and skills needed in other tasks.

For example, to learn the correct rule in a concept identification task, subjects must evaluate a number of hypotheses. Our inability to evaluate a large number of hypotheses simultaneously is found not only in concept-identification tasks (Levine, 1966) but also in real-world tasks such as medical diagnosis (Elstein et al., 1978). Yet real-world tasks are often different enough from concept identification tasks that we must be very careful in making generalizations.

The predominant criticism of the concept identification paradigm is that real-world categories, such as clothes, tools, and vehicles, are unlike the categories studied in the laboratory. This is not a new argument. The philosopher Wittgenstein (1953) argued that category members do not have to share identical attributes. Rather, they may have a family resemblance in which category members share some attributes with other members, but there are no or few attributes that are common to all members of the category.

A dramatic change in how psychologists viewed real-world categories had to wait until the 1970s, when Eleanor Rosch and her students at the University of California, Berkeley, began to study the characteristics of natural categories (Rosch, 1973). Her ideas and research were so important that they deserve extensive coverage. One of the characteristics of concept identification tasks that bothered Rosch is that objects in natural categories often have **continuous dimensions** rather than the discrete dimensions studied in concept identification. Colors, for example, vary along a continuum in which red gradually becomes orange, and orange gradually becomes yellow. People might therefore consider a red object and an orange object as more likely to belong to the same category than a red object and a blue object. However, colors are treated as discrete dimensions in a rule-learning task in which red, orange, and blue are attributes that are considered to be equally different from each other.

Natural categories are also **hierarchically organized**—larger categories often contain smaller categories. Thus, clothing can be partitioned into smaller categories such as pants and shirt, and shirt can be partitioned into smaller categories such as dress shirt and sports shirt. The hierarchical organization of categories was not studied in concept identification tasks, even though it is now clear that it is extremely useful in helping us organize knowledge.

Another limitation of the concept identification paradigm is that it assumed that all members of a concept are equally good members. Consider the five examples in Figure 9.1 that satisfy the disjunctive rule *large or a circle*. All five positive instances are equally good members because they all satisfy the rule. In contrast, natural categories are not composed of equally good members. If we gave people different variations of the color *red*, they would agree that some variations are more representative of the color than others (a "good" red versus an "off" red).

Even mathematical categories that can be defined on the basis of rules contain examples that differ in the **typicality** of their members. For example, a rule can be used to determine

---

continuous dimension An attribute that can take on any value along a dimension

hierarchically organized An organizing strategy in which larger categories are partitioned into smaller categories

typicality A measure of how well a category member represents that category

whether a number is even or odd. People are therefore likely to agree that even numbers can be decided by definition (Malt, 1990). They also agree that it does not make sense to rate even numbers for degree of membership (Armstrong et al., 1983). Nonetheless, people rate some even numbers (such as 4) as better examples of even numbers than others (such as 38). The better examples have fewer digits and do not contain any odd numbers.

Another example of where a rule fails to predict typicality ratings concerns the meaning of the word *water*. According to a scientific rule, water can be defined by its chemical composition as H_2O. If people use this rule, they should rate examples of water as more typical if they judge them to contain a higher percentage of H_2O (Malt, 1994). Table 9.1 shows examples of water that were judged for both typicality and percentage of H_2O. Drinking and tap water were rated most typical; followed by rain and tap water; then purified, bottled, and ice water; and finally pure, ocean, and soft tap water. Notice, however, that percentage of H_2O is not a good predictor of typicality. For example, pure, ocean, and soft tap water were rated as equally typical even though the estimated amount of H_2O ranged from 79% for ocean water to 98% for pure water.

TABLE 9.1 ■ How judged percentage of H_2O influences typicality judgments of water

Typicality	Example	Percentage of H_2O
1	Drinking water	89
2	Tap water	88
	Rain water	91
	Water fountain water	89
3	Purified water	95
	Bottled water	92
	Ice water	90
4	Pure water	98
	Ocean water	79
	Soft tap water	90

Source: Based on "Water is not H_2O," by B. C. Malt, 1994, *Cognitive Psychology, 27*, 41–70. https://doi.org/10.1006/cogp.1994.1011. Reprinted by permission of Elsevier Science.

The best examples—drinking and tap water—contain less judged H_2O than some of the other examples on the list. However, they are examples that play the most central role in our lives. This finding underscores an important point: Real-word categories and their examples are often organized according to how we use them rather than by abstract rules (Malt, 1994; Ross, 1996).

NATURAL CATEGORIES

As we saw, one characteristic of real-world or natural categories is that they are hierarchical—some categories contain other categories. For example, the category *furniture* contains *chairs*, and the category *chairs* contains *living-room chairs*. Each of these levels contains a variety of objects, but the variety decreases as the category becomes smaller. There are many kinds of furniture (beds, sofas, tables, chairs), fewer kinds of chairs (living-room chairs, dining room chairs, high chairs), and still fewer kinds of living-room chairs. The first part of this section looks at how the hierarchical organization of categories influences behavior.

Another characteristic of natural categories is that some members seem to be better representatives of the category than others. We could all agree that chairs are furniture, but what about a piano? Shirts are certainly a good example of clothing, but what about a necklace? The second part of this section examines the implications of the fact that the members of categories are not all equally good members.

Hierarchical Organization of Categories

Rosch and her colleagues studied the hierarchical organization of categories by using the three levels shown in Table 9.2 (Rosch et al., 1976). The largest categories are the **superordinate categories**, such as *musical instrument*s. They contain the **basic-level categories** (such as *drum*), which in turn contain the **subordinate categories** (such as *bass drum*). The most important of the three levels, according to Rosch, is the basic level, because basic-level categories are the most differentiated from one another, and they are therefore the first categories we learn and the most important in language (Photo 9.4).

The differentiation of categories can be measured by determining how much the members of a category share attributes with one another but have different attributes than the members of other categories. At the superordinate level, the difficulty is that members share few attributes. Examples of furniture—such as *table, lamp,* and *chair*—have few attributes in common. At the

PHOTO 9.4 Is this a musical instrument, a drum, or a bass drum?

Photo by Dominik Kempf on Unsplash.

---

superordinate category A large category at the top of a hierarchy, such as furniture, tools, and vehicles

basic-level category An intermediate category in the middle of a hierarchy, such as table, saw, and truck

subordinate category A small category at the bottom of a hierarchy, such as lamp table, jigsaw, and pickup truck

subordinate level, the difficulty is that the members share many attributes with members of similar subordinate categories. For example, a kitchen table has many of the same attributes as a dining-room table. The intermediate level of categorization—the basic level—avoids the two extremes. Members of a basic-level category, such as *chair*, not only share many attributes but also have attributes that differ from those of items in other basic-level categories, such as *lamp* and *table*.

Evidence for the differentiation of categories comes from a study in which people were asked to list the attributes of objects at different levels in the hierarchy (Rosch et al., 1976). Some people listed the attributes of superordinate objects (such as musical instruments, fruit, tools,

TABLE 9.2 ■ Examples of a subordinate, basic, and superordinate categories

Superordinate	Basic Level	Subordinates	
Musical instruments	Guitar	Folk guitar	Classical guitar
	Piano	Grand piano	Upright piano
	Drum	Kettle drum	Bass drum
Fruit	Apple	Delicious apple	McIntosh apple
	Peach	Freestone peach	Cling peach
	Grapes	Concord grapes	Green seedless grapes
Tools	Hammer	Ball-peen hammer	Claw hammer
	Saw	Hack handsaw	Crosscutting handsaw
	Screwdriver	Phillips screwdriver	Regular screwdriver
Clothing	Pants	Levi's	Double-knit pants
	Socks	Knee socks	Ankle socks
	Shirt	Dress shirt	Knit shirt
Furniture	Table	Kitchen table	Dining-room table
	Lamp	Floor lamp	Desk lamp
	Chair	Kitchen chair	Living-room chair
Vehicles	Car	Sports car	Four-door sedan car
	Bus	City bus	Cross-country bus
	Truck	Pickup truck	Tractor trailer truck

Source: "Basic objects in natural categories," by E. Rosch et al., 1976, *Cognitive Psychology, 8*, 382–440. https://doi.org/10.1016/0010-0285(76)90013-X. Copyright 1976 by Academic Press, Inc.

clothing); others listed the attributes of basic-level objects (guitar, apple, hammer, pants); still others listed the attributes of subordinate objects (classical guitar, McIntosh apple, claw hammer, Levi's).

The experimenters analyzed the data by identifying attributes that people seemed to agree were associated with the specified category. Table 9.3 shows the average number of shared attributes at each level in the hierarchy. The number of shared attributes increases from the superordinate to the subordinate level. The members of a superordinate category have very few attributes compared with those at the basic level. However, the increase in shared attributes from the basic level to the subordinate level is very small.

TABLE 9.3 ■ Number of attributes in common at each hierarchical level

Category	Raw Tallies			Judge Amended Tallies		
	Superordinate	Basic Level	Subordinate	Superordinate	Basic Level	Subordinate
Musical instruments	1	6.0	8.5	1	8.3	8.7
Fruit	7	12.3	14.7	3	8.3	9.5
Tools	3	8.3	9.7	3	8.7	9.2
Clothing	3	10.0	12.0	2	8.3	9.7
Furniture	3	9.0	10.3	0	7.0	7.8
Vehicles	4	8.7	11.2	1	11.7	16.8

Source: "Basic objects in natural categories," by E. Rosch et al., 1976, *Cognitive Psychology, 8*, 382–440. https://doi.org/10.1016/0010-0285(76)90013-X. Copyright 1976 by Academic Press, Inc.

Note: Raw tallies are attributes listed by subjects. These were modified if all seven judges thought another hierarchical level was more appropriate (judge amended columns).

The differences between levels can be illustrated by the three examples shown in Table 9.4. Only two attributes were listed for the superordinate category *clothing—you wear it* and *keeps you warm*. These same two attributes plus an additional six were listed for the basic-level category *pants*. Pants have *legs, buttons, belt loops, pockets,* and *two legs* and are made of *cloth*. One additional attribute was listed for the subordinate category *Levi's—blue*—and two additional attributes were listed for *double-knit pants—comfortable* and *stretchy*. Notice that, although the items in subordinate categories share slightly more attributes than those in basic-level categories, there is a considerable overlap of attributes for subordinate categories. Although Levi's and double-knit pants differ on a few attributes, they also share many attributes, which makes it easier to distinguish between pants and shirts than to distinguish between Levi's and double-knit pants.

Rosch tested her claim that categorization is fastest at the basic level by asking people to verify the identity of an object at each of the three levels in the hierarchy. For example, before being shown a picture of a living-room chair, people given superordinate terms were asked whether the object was a piece of furniture; people given basic terms were asked whether the object was a chair; and people given subordinate terms were asked whether the object was a living-room chair. The fastest verification times occurred for the group that verified objects at the basic level (Rosch et al., 1976). Rosch proposed that people initially identify objects at the basic level and then classify them at the superordinate level, by making an inference (a chair is a piece of furniture), or classify them at the subordinate level, by looking for distinguishing features (in this case, features that distinguish a living-room chair from other chairs). But Rosch discussed the possibility that experts might be very quick in making subordinate classifications in their area of expertise.

TABLE 9.4 ■ Examples of shared attributes at different hierarchical levels		
Tools	**Clothing**	**Furniture**
Make things	You wear it	No attributes
Fix things	Keeps you warm	
Metal		
Saw	**Pants**	**Chair**
Handle	Legs	Legs
Teeth	Buttons	Seat
Blade	Belt loops	Back
Sharp	Pockets	Arms
Cuts	Cloth	Comfortable
Edge	Two legs	Four legs
Wooden handle		Wood
		Holds people—you sit on it
Cross-cutting handsaw	**Levi's**	**Kitchen chair**
Used in construction	Blue	No additional
Hack handsaw	**Double-knit pants**	**Living-room chair**
No additional	Comfortable	Large
	Stretchy	Soft
		Cushion

Source: "Basic objects in natural categories," by E. Rosch et al., 1976, *Cognitive Psychology, 8*, 382–440. https://doi.org/10.1016/0010-0285(76)90013-X. Copyright 1976 by Academic Press, Inc.

For example, a furniture salesperson might be able to classify a living-room chair as a *living-room chair* as quickly as he or she could classify it as a *chair*. Subsequent work has confirmed this hypothesis (Tanaka & Taylor, 1991). Dog experts and bird experts, recruited from local organizations, were asked to identify colored pictures of dogs and birds at either the superordinate (*animal*), basic (*dog* or *bird*), or subordinate (such as *beagle* or *sparrow*) level.

The results replicated Rosch and her colleagues' (1976) findings when dog experts classified birds and bird experts classified dogs. Classification was fastest at the basic level. However, the results were different when dog experts classified dogs and bird experts classified birds. Their subordinate-level classifications were as fast as their basic-level classifications. The experts were so good at distinguishing between different kinds of dogs or different kinds of birds that they could identify the type of dog or type of bird as quickly as they could recognize that the picture was a dog or a bird.

The concept of an average example becomes meaningful if we think of objects from the same basic level. Although the average shape of furniture is unreasonable, the average shape of a chair is a more plausible concept. In fact, people were quite accurate in identifying the average shape of two objects from the same basic-level category—for example, the average of two chairs still looks reasonably like a chair, and the average of two shirts still looks reasonably like a shirt. Basic-level objects are sufficiently similar to each other that the average shape is identifiable. Creation of an average pattern to represent a category is therefore possible at the basic level (and at the subordinate level, where the shapes of objects in the same category are even more similar) but is not possible at the superordinate level.

Typicality and Family Resemblances

So far, we have emphasized comparing categories at different levels of generality. We will now shift our attention to comparing members within a category. Psychologists use the term *typicality* to refer to differences in how well members of a category represent that category. For example, people agree that chairs, sofas, and tables are good examples of furniture; cars, trucks, and buses are good examples of vehicles; and oranges, apples, and bananas are good examples of fruit. Table 9.5 lists 20 members for each of 6 superordinate categories, ranked from the most typical to the least typical, based on people's ratings.

Although the rank order may seem fairly obvious to us, it isn't obvious why the order exists. Why is a car a good example and an elevator a poor example of a vehicle? Both can transport people and materials. Rosch and Mervis (1975) hypothesized that good members will share many attributes with other members of the category and few attributes with members of other categories. Notice that Rosch is applying the same hypothesis she used to compare superordinate, basic, and subordinate categories to compare the typicality of members within a category.

Rosch and Mervis tested their hypothesis by asking people to list the attributes of each of the category members shown in Table 9.5. For example, for a *bicycle*, people might list that it has two wheels, pedals, and handlebars; you ride on it; and it doesn't use fuel. To test the hypothesis that the good examples of categories should share many attributes with other members of the category, it is necessary to calculate a measure of family resemblance for each item by considering how many other members share each attribute of the item.

---

family resemblance A measure of how frequently the attributes of a category member are shared by other members of the category

TABLE 9.5 ■ Typicality of members in six superordinate categories

Item	Furniture	Vehicles	Fruit	Weapons	Vegetables	Clothing
1	Chair	Car	Orange	Gun	Peas	Pants
2	Sofa	Truck	Apple	Knife	Carrots	Shirt
3	Table	Bus	Banana	Sword	String beans	Dress
4	Dresser	Motorcycle	Peach	Bomb	Spinach	Skirt
5	Desk	Train	Pear	Hand grenade	Broccoli	Jacket
6	Bed	Trolley car	Apricot	Spear	Asparagus	Coat
7	Bookcase	Bicycle	Plum	Cannon	Corn	Sweater
8	Footstool	Airplane	Grape	Bow and arrow	Cauliflower	Underpants
9	Lamp	Boat	Strawberry	Club	Brussels sprouts	Socks
10	Piano	Tractor	Grapefruit	Tank	Lettuce	Pajamas
11	Cushion	Cart	Pineapple	Tear gas	Beets	Bathing suit
12	Mirror	Wheelchair	Blueberry	Whip	Tomato	Shoes
13	Rug	Tank	Lemon	Ice pick	Lima beans	Vest
14	Radio	Raft	Watermelon	Fists	Eggplant	Tie
15	Stove	Sled	Honeydew	Rocket	Onion	Mittens
16	Clock	Horse	Pomegranate	Poison	Potato	Hat
17	Picture	Blimp	Date	Scissors	Yam	Apron
18	Closet	Skates	Coconut	Words	Mushroom	Purse
19	Vase	Wheelbarrow	Tomato	Foot	Pumpkin	Wristwatch
20	Telephone	Elevator	Olive	Screwdriver	Rice	Necklace

Source: "Family resemblances: Studies in the internal structure of categories," by E. Rosch & C. B. Mervis, 1975, *Cognitive Psychology, 7*, 573–605. https://doi.org/10.1016/0010-0285(75)90024-9. Copyright 1975 by Academic Press, Inc.

Here's a specific example: Because a car has wheels as one of its attributes, we would count the vehicles that also have wheels. Because a car has a windshield, we would count the members that have a windshield. The numerical score for each attribute can vary from 1 to 20, depending on how many of the 20 members in Table 9.5 possess that attribute. The family resemblance score for each member is obtained by adding together the numerical scores of all attributes possessed by that member. If 14 members of the category have wheels and 11 have windshields, the family resemblance score would be 25 for a car if it had only those two attributes. The actual score is of course, much higher, because we also have to add the numerical scores for all the other attributes listed for a car. The results revealed that good representatives of a category had high family resemblance scores. The correlations between the two variables were between 0.84 (for *vegetable*) and 0.94 (for *weapon*) for the six superordinate categories listed in Table 9.5.

Another way of viewing these results is to compare how many attributes are shared by the five most typical and five least typical examples in each category. The five most typical vehicles are car, truck, bus, motorcycle, and train. The five share many attributes because they possess many common parts; the subjects in the experiment were able to identify 36 attributes that belonged to all five members. The five least typical examples are horse, blimp, skates, wheelbarrow, and elevator—subjects identified only two attributes that belong to all five of the least typical members (Photo 9.5). The results were similar for the other five superordinate categories.

PHOTO 9.5 Cars share many more attributes than wheelbarrows with other types of vehicles.

Photo by Etienne Delorieux and FP Creative Ltd on Unsplash.

The fact that typical members of categories tend to share attributes with other members is also true for basic-level categories. You may have noticed that the examples of the superordinate categories shown in Table 9.5 are basic-level categories. Rosch and Mervis (1975) selected six of these examples (car, truck, airplane, chair, table, lamp) to test the same hypothesis—that the most typical members of basic-level categories should share more attributes with other members than the least typical members. For each of the six categories, the experimenters selected 15 pictures, varying from good to poor examples. They then asked groups of undergraduates to rate how well each picture represented their idea of the category. As was found for the members of superordinate categories, there was a high correlation between the typicality of a member and the number of shared attributes at the basic level.

Person Perception

The structure of natural categories, such as hierarchical organization and typicality, is also relevant for how we classify people (Cantor & Mischel, 1979). An example of a superordinate category might be people who have a strong commitment to a particular belief or cause. This category can be subdivided into religious devotees and social activists. Religious devotees can be further classified according to their particular religions, and social activists can be grouped according to their causes. Cantor and Mischel's work parallels that of Rosch and her colleagues in that it examines such issues as the number of shared attributes at different levels in the person hierarchy.

As we saw at the beginning of this chapter, categorization allows us to create a manageable view of the world, but it also has disadvantages that can be particularly troublesome when the category members are people. Exaggerating within-group similarity by creating stereotypes might not only result in erroneous assumptions about others but also make it more difficult for people to remember impressions that disconfirm their stereotypes (Cantor & Genero, 1986). In the process of organizing the world into social categories, people may perceive members of the same social category as remarkably similar and different from members of other social categories. Once having categorized a person, it is maladaptive to exaggerate the similarity among people in the category, discount disconfirming evidence, and focus on stereotypic examples of the category.

People can be categorized in many ways, but often a particular category predominates. In a 2012 interview for *New York Magazine,* Toni Morrison admitted that "I felt profoundly American, flag waving . . . but you are never out there as someone from Ohio, or even a writer because all that is clouded by the box you are put in as a Black Writer." Toni Morrison won both the Pulitzer Prize for Fiction and the Nobel Prize in Literature.

A social category that has attracted interest is generational differences. Jean Twenge has been one of the most successful authors in documenting these differences. In her book *iGen: Why Today's Super-Connected Kids Are Growing Up Less Rebellious, More Tolerant, Less Happy— and Completely Unprepared for Adulthood,* Twenge (2017) reports that this generation, born in 1995 and later, grew up with cell phones and does not remember a time before the internet. The oldest members were early adolescents when the iPhone was introduced in 2007 and high school students when the iPad arrived in 2010. As a result, the iGen generation spends less time with their friends in person because of the use of social media and texting. Twenge reports that this generation also differs from previous generations in how they behave, spend their time, and in their attitudes toward religion, sexuality, and politics.

CATEGORIZATION MODELS

At the beginning of this chapter, we learned that one advantage of categories is that they enable us to recognize novel objects. A young child who encounters a new dog for the first time can use previous knowledge of dogs to recognize the new dog. Lacking this ability to classify novel objects, the child would have to be told the identity of every new object. People are quite good at making these classifications, and psychologists are naturally interested in how they do it. Research on natural categories provides a helpful place to begin.

---

stereotype Attribute values believed to be representative of social categories

The previous sections of this chapter contrasted the early work of concept identification with Eleanor Rosch's work on natural categories. You may recall that Rosch proposed three distinctions between concept identification tasks and natural categories. One distinction is that natural categories are hierarchically organized. A second distinction is that the members of natural categories differ in typicality. A third distinction is that the attributes of natural categories are often continuous. Her research focused on the first two distinctions but not on continuous dimensions. As noted in Table 9.4, category members are differentiated by shared attributes that are discrete rather than continuous.

Some categorization models are in fact based on discrete attributes and can use shared attributes as a measure of similarity. However, other models measure similarity across continuous attributes. Continuous attributes can be plotted on a scale in which points near each other are more similar than points far from each other. A technique called multidimensional scaling is helpful in providing these measures.

Multidimensional Scaling

Multidimensional scaling often begins by asking people to judge the similarity of pairs of items. For instance, Stanford undergraduates received pairs of words from Figure 9.2 and were instructed to rate the similarity of each pair on a 4-point scale. Rips et al. (1973) then gave these ratings to a multidimensional scaling program that produced the two-dimensional plot shown in Figure 9.2. The scaled measure of similarity is the distance between two points. Goose and chicken are very similar, but chicken and robin are not.

FIGURE 9.2 ■ Multidimensional scaling solution for birds.

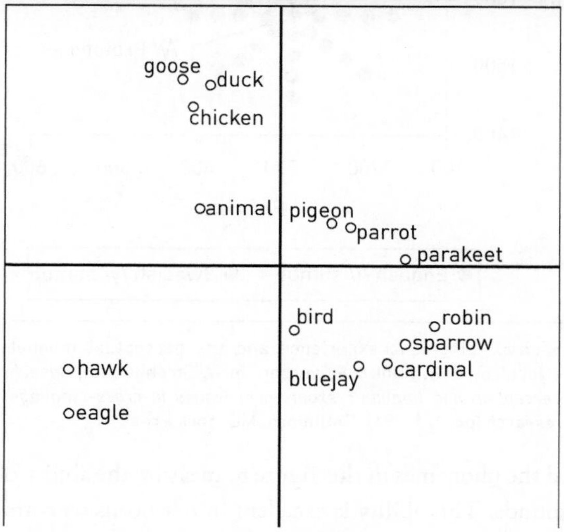

Source: From "Semantic distance and the verification of semantic relations," by L. J. Rips et al., 1973, *Journal of Verbal Learning and Verbal Behavior, 12*, 1–20. https://doi.org/10.1016/S0022-5371(73)80056-8. Copyright 1975 by Academic Press, Inc.

Multidimensional-scaling programs make three valuable contributions. First, scaled measures of similarity are better measures of similarity than the typically inconsistent similarity judgments. Second, visual displays of data reveal patterns that would be difficult to detect in a table of numbers. We can immediately see that goose, duck, and chicken form a cluster and that a robin is a more typical bird than an eagle, as depicted by their distances from the concept of a "bird." Third, an interpretation of the dimensions of the solution may reveal those attributes that most influence the ratings. The horizontal dimension in Figure 9.2 is influenced by size, as revealed by the larger birds in the left half of the figure. The vertical dimension reflects the distinction between domestic (top half) and wild (bottom half) birds.

Psychological attributes can also be used to plot the location of sensory stimuli, such as the basic sounds (phonemes) of a language. Figure 9.3 shows variations along two-pitch dimensions in the pronunciation of the American long-*e* phoneme. The category prototype is the average of these sounds and is in the center of the category. As in Figure 9.2, similar stimuli are close to each other and therefore should be difficult to discriminate.

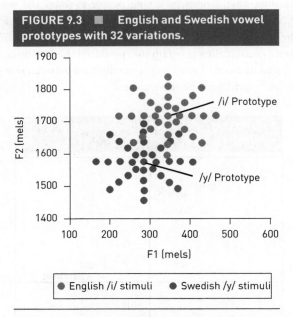

FIGURE 9.3 ■ English and Swedish vowel prototypes with 32 variations.

Source: "Linguistic experience and the perceptual magnet effect," by P. K. Kuhl & P. Iverson. In W. Strange (Ed), *Speech perception and linguistic experience: Issues in cross-language research* (pp. 121–154). Baltimore, MD: York Press.

Patricia Kuhl used the phonemes in this figure to measure the ability of infants to discriminate among similar sounds. This ability is excellent in newborns who are initially able to discriminate among phonemes in many different languages of the world (Kuhl, 1993). But infants

prototype A category example that has average attribute values soon need to recognize the similarity among sounds within the phonemic categories that make up their particular language.

Evidence for the formation of category prototypes comes from Kuhl's (1991) research demonstrating that the ability to discriminate sounds within a phonemic category (such as when different people pronounce the long-*e* sound) is worse if the category prototype is involved in the discrimination. Adults and 6-month-old infants can more easily discriminate between two nonprototypical sounds than between a prototypical and a nonprototypical sound. Kuhl (1991) uses the metaphor of a "perceptual magnet" to describe the effect. The prototypic long-*e* sound draws similar long-*e* sounds closer to it, making these variations sound more like the prototype.

This magnet effect has several interesting, counterintuitive implications. We might expect that infants become better at discriminating sounds as they grow older, but this does not occur if the sounds belong to the same phonemic category. Forming prototypes of the various phonemes reduces discrimination within a phonemic category because variations of the prototype begin to sound more like the prototype. Notice, however, that this should make it easier to recognize the phonemes by reducing variation within a category.

We might also expect that infants could better discriminate among familiar sounds in their own language than among unfamiliar sounds from a different language, but this also does not happen when the sounds belong to the same phonemic category. For example, 6-month-old Swedish infants were better than U.S. infants at discriminating between a prototypic long-*e* sound and other long-*e* sounds, even though this was an unfamiliar sound to them (Kuhl et al., 1992).

The reason is that the U.S. infants had formed a prototypic long-*e* sound and were therefore victims of the magnet effect, whereas the Swedish infants had not formed a prototypic long-*e* sound because this sound did not occur in their language. The opposite result occurred for a vowel that occurred in Swedish but not in U.S. English. American infants were now better at discriminating variations of this vowel from the category prototype. It therefore should not be a surprise that prototypes have had an important role in categorization models, as discussed in the next section.

Comparing Categorization Models

Multidimensional scaling has been very helpful in developing and evaluating models of how people categorize patterns. Figure 9.4 shows a typical task (Reed, 1972). Participants were informed that the upper row of faces represents one category (Category 1) and the bottom row represents another category (Category 2). They had to learn to classify these 10 category faces before classifying novel faces that didn't match any of the faces in Figure 9.4. Investigators compare different categorization models to determine which is most successful in predicting how people classify novel patterns.

One model, called the **average distance rule**, states that a person should compare the novel pattern with all the patterns in each category to determine the average similarity between the

---

average distance rule A classification strategy that selects the category–containing members having the greatest average similarity to the classified item

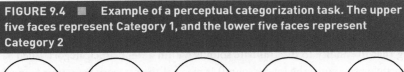

FIGURE 9.4 ■ Example of a perceptual categorization task. The upper five faces represent Category 1, and the lower five faces represent Category 2

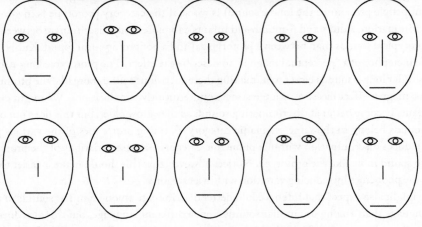

Source: "Perceptual vs. conceptual categorization," by S. K. Reed & M. P. Friedman, 1973, *Memory & Cognition, 1,* 157–163. https://doi.org/10.3758/BF03198087. Copyright 1973 by the Psychonomic Society, Inc.

novel pattern and the category patterns. If the average similarity is greater for Category 1 patterns, Category 1 should be selected; otherwise, Category 2 should be selected.

In contrast, the **prototype rule** selects the category whose prototype is the most similar to the classified item. The prototype has to be created and is usually a pattern that is the average of all other patterns in the category. The upper two faces in Figure 9.5 show the category prototypes for the two categories in Figure 9.4. The results indicated that classifiers used a prototype strategy for the categories in Figure 9.4 but used an alternative strategy for a different set of categories. The category prototypes (lower two faces in Figure 9.5) were so similar in the latter case that classifiers used a simpler strategy based on eye separation.

Theorists, of course, have continued to develop and evaluate categorization models. One general class of models that has received particular emphasis is called an **exemplar model**. An exemplar theory proposes that people base their decisions on the examples in the category rather than on information abstracted from the examples, such as a prototype. The average-distance model is an exemplar model because it assumes that a test pattern is classified by comparing its similarity to the category examples.

---

prototype rule A classification strategy that selects the category whose prototype is the most similar to the classified item

exemplar model A model that proposes that patterns are learned and categorized by comparing their similarity to category members

FIGURE 9.5 ■ Examples of category prototypes for the patterns in Figure 9.4 (above) and for an alternative set of patterns (below).

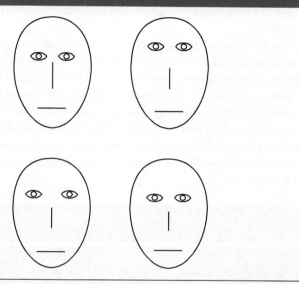

Source: "Perceptual vs. conceptual categorization," by S. K. Reed & M. P. Friedman, 1973, *Memory & Cognition, 1,* 157–163. https://doi.org/10.3758/BF03198087. Copyright 1973 by the Psychonomic Society, Inc.

The development of exemplar models has been greatly influenced by the one proposed by Medin and Schaffer (1978). They assume that people store examples of category patterns in memory and classify new patterns by comparing them with retrieved examples. The greater the similarity of the new pattern to an example stored in memory, the greater the probability that the example will be retrieved. Medin and his colleagues found that classifications were influenced by feature combinations of the examples (Medin et al., 1982). For instance, if someone has a cough and a temperature, then the diagnosis of other patients who have *both* a cough and a temperature is particularly relevant information.

A variable that influences whether people use a prototype or an exemplar classification rule is the amount of practice they have had in learning the category examples. Smith and Minda (1998) discovered that early learning results are more consistent with a prototype model because people have learned only the more prototypical patterns in the category. Eventually, however, they learn to correctly categorize all the examples in the category, which is more consistent with an exemplar model. Another influential factor is the number of examples in a category. Minda and Smith (2002) argued that exemplar models have been successful in categorization tasks that have only a small number of examples (typically five examples in one category and four in the other). This makes it possible to learn all the examples with enough practice.

Murphy (2016) concurs that exemplar models work best when a small number of exemplars are repeatedly presented in category-learning tasks. In such cases, it is likely that the individual examples are remembered, particularly when the categories are poorly structured. As more examples are added, the details of individual examples are lost or become less relevant as they are combined with new information. Murphy also argues that there is not an exemplar theory of human concepts in a broad sense. A concept in his perspective requires more than documenting its category members.

Prototype models also have limitations because a prototype represents the center of the category but not its variance. A good strategy for making inferences from categories would be to learn about the variation of category members. Research at New York University has found that younger children select idealized members but gradually shift toward selecting exemplars that cover more variation within the category (Foster-Hanson et al., 2020). Figure 9.6 is an example trial to discover whether cheetahs have tracheas. The experimenter selected the slowest cheetah in this example, so selecting the fastest cheetah as the next exemplar would provide information about diverse members. We will return to providing helpful exemplars during instruction in the Applications section.

FIGURE 9.6 ■ **An experimental trial in which a child selects a second example to learn about cheetahs.**

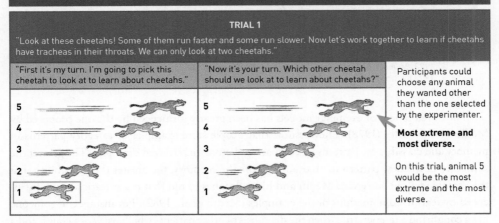

Source: From "Developmental changes in strategies for gathering evidence about biological kinds," by E. Foster-Hanson et al., 2020, *Cognitive Science, 44.* https://doi.org/10.31234/osf.io/gm96d. Covered by Creative Commons Attribution 4.0 International Public License https://psyarxiv.com/gm96d/

It is not surprising that psychologists have proposed a variety of classification strategies to describe how people categorize. It is likely that no single model will be sufficient to account for how people make classifications across a wide variety of situations. The best advice is that given by Hampton (1997) following his analysis of the strengths and weaknesses of the different models:

There is a temptation for theorists to wish to apply their own approach to all conceptual representations. It is however most unlikely that all concepts are defined or represented in the same way. What is needed for the advance of the field is for a principled account to be given of the range of representational powers that people possess, and for a matching up of different kinds of representation with different conceptual domains. (pp. 105–106)

Most categorization theorists agree with Hampton's assessment.

Theory-Based Categorization

Research on categorization has typically used rather artificial stimuli, such as schematic faces. An advantage of these stimuli is that they enable investigators to evaluate how people use the similarity of patterns to make classifications. A disadvantage of this approach is that people might use different strategies when the stimuli are more meaningful. They might use their theories about real-world categories if the task could be related to real-world categories.

A distinguishing characteristic of real-world categories is that they serve different functions that motivate a distinction between structural and functional typicality (Dieciuc & Folstein, 2019). *Structural typicality* is relatively stable, as found in the research of Rosch and Mervis (1975). It reflects the similarity of taxonomic information in long-term memory. In contrast, *functional typicality* reflects the momentary context and demands of a task. It depends on finding information in semantic memory to rapidly construct temporary conceptual structures (Dieciuc & Folstein, 2019).

PHOTO 9.6 A goal-derived category determines the contents of a backpack.

Photo by Brendon Kaida on Unsplash

For instance, although family resemblance scores are useful for predicting the typicality of members in common taxonomic categories like those listed in Table 9.5, they are not useful in predicting typicality for **goal-derived categories** (Barsalou, 1985). Goal-derived categories consist of examples that satisfy a goal, such as "make people happy when you give a birthday present." According to people's ratings, good examples of birthday presents include clothing, a party, jewelry, dinner, a watch, a cake, and a card. Notice that these examples belong to different taxonomic categories, are dissimilar to one another and do not share many attributes (Photo 9.6).

---

goal-derived category A category whose members are selected to satisfy a specified goal

Goal-derived categories are selected on the basis of some underlying principle rather than on shared attributes (Murphy & Medin, 1985). When we select weekend activities, we consider events that we enjoy; when we select things we would take from our home during a fire, we consider things that are valuable and irreplaceable, such as children and important papers. Although the similarity of attributes determines how we form many categories and judge the typicality of category members, Murphy and Medin proposed that we need to learn more about underlying principles to have a more complete understanding of categorization.

For goal-derived categories, an underlying principle is the extent to which members satisfy the goal. Barsalou (1991) has shown that goal-derived categories are organized around ideals, and the more typical members of the category are those members that best satisfy the goal. For the category *foods to eat on a weight-loss diet*, the ideal number of calories is zero, so the fewer calories a food has, the better it satisfies the goal of losing weight. Those of us who have attempted a weight-loss diet probably realize that we often like to satisfy more than one goal. We may therefore try to select foods that have minimal calories, maximal nutrition, and maximal taste to satisfy the multiple goals of losing weight, staying healthy, and enjoying food.

Murphy and Medin (1985) proposed that the importance of features depends on the role the features play in people's theories underlying the categories and hypothesized that people emphasize features that provide causal explanations. An experiment at Yale tested this hypothesis by informing undergraduates that members of a category tend to have three features; for example, blurred vision, headaches, and insomnia (Ahn et al., 2000). The students were further informed that blurred vision causes the headaches, and the headaches cause insomnia. They then rated the likelihood that an item belonged to the category if one of the features was missing. The results indicated that the judged likelihood of membership was low when the initial cause (blurred vision) was missing, higher when the intermediate cause (headache) was missing, and higher still when the terminal effect (insomnia) was missing. Identifying causes therefore is important in people's theories of categories. If the cause is missing, people think it is less likely that an item is a member of the category.

Identifying causes of symptoms is particularly important when they result in a diagnosis of what is wrong with a person. For instance, as illustrated in Figure 9.7, both bacterial pneumonia and viral pneumonia cause a fever, cough, and headache (Holyoak & Cheng, 2011). Because diagnostic categories often consist of a large number of overlapping features, it is therefore necessary to find those symptoms that distinguish between categories. This is important for treating pneumonia because bacterial pneumonia is treated with antibiotics (as shown in Figure 9.7) but viral pneumonia is treated with antiviral drugs, as is the coronavirus COVID-19 (Photo 9.7).

Another aspect of theory-based categorization is that we expect a coherent combination of features, as illustrated by the examples in Table 9.6 (Rehder & Ross, 2001). A device that operates on the surface of water, absorbs spilled oil, and is coated with spongy material is a plausible device. A device that floats in the stratosphere, absorbs spilled oil, and has a shovel seems to have

---

ideal An attribute value that relates to the goal of a goal-derived category

FIGURE 9.7 ■ Symptoms of two diagnostic categories. Solid lines show causal links and dotted lines show treatment links.

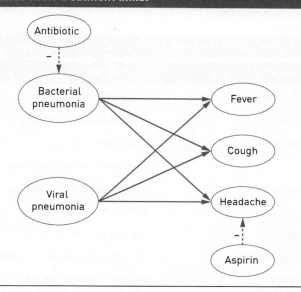

Source: "Causal learning and inference as a rational process: The new synthesis," by K. J. Holyoak & P. W. Cheng, 2011, *Annual Review of Psychology, 62,* 135–163. https://doi.org/10.1146/annurev.psych.121208.131634. Copyright 2011 by Annual Reviews. Reprinted by permission.

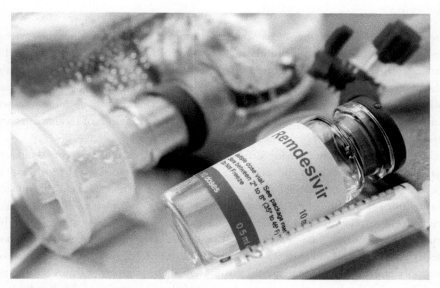

PHOTO 9.7 An antiviral drug for treating COVID-19.

the wrong combination of features. Learning to classify coherent exemplars is easier than learning to classify incoherent exemplars (Rehder & Ross, 2001). Exemplars are coherent because they fit into our organized knowledge structures called *schemas*. We discuss schemas in the next chapter on semantic organization.

TABLE 9.6 ■ Examples of coherent and incoherent category exemplars	
Coherent Exemplars	Incoherent Exemplars
Operates on surface of the water	Floats in the stratosphere
Works on absorbing spilled oil	Works on absorbing spilled oil
Coated with spongy material	Has a shovel
Operates on land	Operates on surface of the water
Works to gather harmful solids	Works to gather harmful solids
Has a shovel	Has an electrostatic filter
Floats in the stratosphere	Operates on land
Works to absorb dangerous gases	Works to absorb dangerous gases
Has an electrostatic filter	Coated with spongy material

Source: Rehder, B., & Ross, B. H. (2001). Abstract coherent categories. *Journal of Experimental Psychology: Learning, Memory, and Cognition*, 27, 1261–1275.

Instruction

In their chapter on categorization and concepts, Goldstone et al. (2018) conclude their extensive review with recommendations for future research. One of their suggestions is to extend the research to real-world concepts that often lack the controlled construction and ease of analysis of laboratory experiments. We will review an example of applying an exemplar theory to learning different types of rocks. Another issue regarding instruction involves deciding whether to present all of the examples of one category before presenting the examples of another category or to interweave the examples of both categories.

Categories typically contain many members, so which members of the category should serve as examples to help people learn other members of the category? Nosofsky et al. (2018) explored this question by applying exemplar theories to select pictures of rocks to help students learn to distinguish among different kinds, such as basalt, granite, and rhyolite. Figure 9.8 shows 12 examples of rhyolite that are represented in the multidimensional space of Figure 9.9. If an instructor wished to select 3 samples from the 12 to serve as training examples, which 3 should she select? The upper part of Figure 9.8 and left part of Figure 9.9 display 3 samples that are near the category prototype in the center of the distribution. The lower part of Figure 9.8 and right part of Figure 9.9 display 3 other samples that provide better coverage of the distribution by showing variations.

FIGURE 9.8 ■ Training samples for center stimuli (above) and coverage stimuli (below).

Rhyolite (Center Stimuli)

Rhyolite (Coverage Stimuli)

Source: "A formal psychological model of classification applied to natural-science category learning," by R. M. Nosofsky et al., 2018, *Current Directions in Psychological Science, 27*, 129–135. https://doi.org/10.1177%2F0963721417740954

Not surprisingly, learners were the most accurate in identifying the rocks on which they were trained. They excelled at classifying the central rocks in the center condition and the coverage rocks in the coverage condition (Figure 9.10). The more interesting result is that the difference between the center and the coverage samples is much smaller in the coverage condition. The exemplar model predicts this result (as shown by the white dots in Figure 9.10) because the category members are closer to one of the three training samples in the coverage condition. The coverage condition provided more information about the variation of category members.

Another instructional decision concerns whether to present all of the training examples from one category before presenting all of the training examples from another category (a **blocked presentation**) or to mix examples from the categories (an **interleaving presentation**). A meta-analysis of 59 studies revealed an overall moderate advantage for interleaving

---

blocked presentation All items of one category are presented consecutively before the items of another category are presented

interleaving presentation Category items are presented with items from at least one other category

FIGURE 9.9 ■ Locations (dotted squares) in a multidimensional space of the center and coverage training samples.

Center Condition   Coverage Condition

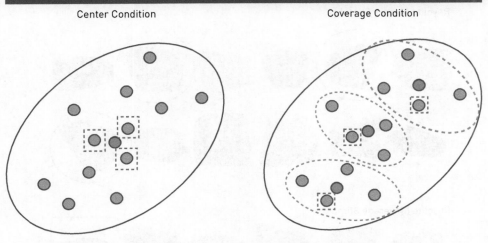

Source: "A formal psychological model of classification applied to natural-science category learning," by R. M. Nosofsky et al., 2018, *Current Directions in Psychological Science, 27*, 129–135. https://doi.org/10.1177%2F0963721417740954

FIGURE 9.10 ■ Proportion of correctly classified rocks in the center and coverage conditions.

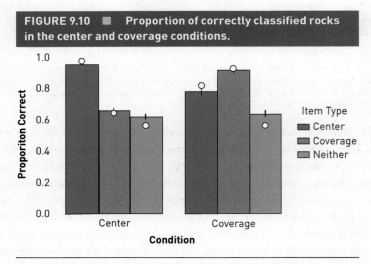

Source: "A formal psychological model of classification applied to natural-science category learning," by R. M. Nosofsky et al., 2018, *Current Directions in Psychological Science, 27*, 129–135. https://doi.org/10.1177%2F0963721417740954

instructional examples (Brunmair & Richter, 2019). An interleaving presentation emphasizes differences between items, whereas blocked presentations highlight similarities within a category. Interleaving is therefore more effective when the differences between categories are critical for learning.

Interleaving items was most effective for studies using paintings and other visual materials, such as pictures of human faces and photographs of birds and butterflies. It had an intermediate effect for studies using mathematical tasks and was ineffective for studies using expository text and words. The reviewers recommended more studies using a variety of educational materials and participants other than university students to obtain results across a broader range of situations (Brunmair & Richter, 2019).

APPLICATIONS

Ashby and Maddox (2005) propose that there are dramatic differences in the way people learn categories, depending on how the categories are constructed. Cognitive, neuropsychological, and neuroimaging results show there are qualitative differences in people's strategies that are influenced by the task. Rule-based category learning (as in Figure 9.1) depends on the frontal cortex and requires working memory and executive attention. Prototype distortion tasks that cannot be solved by rules (as in Figure 9.4) depend more on perceptual learning that uses the visual cortex. One implication of these findings is that different clinical populations can be selectively impaired in their

PHOTO 9.8 A dementia metaphor.

istockphoto.com/wildpixel

ability to learn categories. For example, Parkinson's disease patients are normal in prototype distortion tasks but are profoundly impaired in rule-based categorization (Ashby et al., 1998).

Most of this chapter has been about learning categories, but equally important is losing categories, as occurs during dementia. In the movie *The Father*, Anthony Hopkins plays an 80-year-old man who lives alone in his London flat with increasing difficulty as his memory declines. As summarized in Joe Morgenstern's review:

> The movie is a sensory free-for-all compressed into austere poetry whose most moving expression comes toward the end. "I feel as if I am losing all my leaves," Anthony says plaintively, confusedly, "the branches, and the wind, and the rain." The supporting cast includes Rüfüs Sewell, Olivia Williams, Mark Gatiss, and Imogen Poots. They're all suburb, but nothing can compete, and no one tries to, with a stirring spectacle of an old man who was once a strong tree, and is no longer. (Morgenstern, 2021, p. A10)

Dementia

According to the Dementia Society of America (www.dementiasociety.org), dementia is a descriptive term for a collection of symptoms that are caused by a number of disorders of the brain. Although memory loss is a common symptom of dementia, "dementia" is diagnosed only when functions such as memory and language skills are significantly impaired. People with dementia also have significantly impaired intellectual functioning that interferes with their normal activities and relationships. They lose their ability to solve problems and may experience personality changes, such as agitation and delusions.

Two of the most common forms of dementia are vascular dementia and Alzheimer's disease. Vascular dementia is caused by a series of small strokes that interrupts blood flow to the brain. If blood flow is stopped for more than a few seconds, the lack of oxygen can cause permanent damage. It is the second most common cause of dementia in people over age 65. The most common cause is Alzheimer's disease, named after a German psychiatrist who discovered the disease. Small abnormalities—amyloid plaques and tau tangles—in the brain are the distinguishing characteristics of this disease (Photo 9.9). The risk is greater as the person ages and if a family member has had the disease.

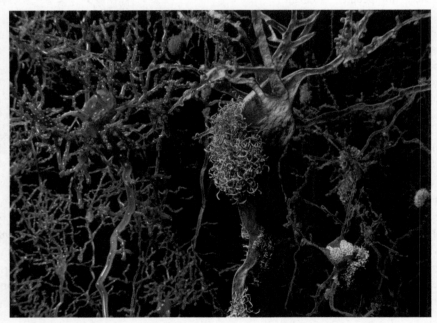

PHOTO 9.9 Impact of Alzheimer's disease on brain nerve cells.

Getty Images/JUAN GAERTNER/SCIENCE PHOTO LIBRARY

---

vascular dementia Dementia caused by a lack of oxygen to the brain

Alzheimers's disease A gradual impairment of memory that is typically identified by the formation of amyloid plaques and tau tangles in the brain

Vascular dementia and Alzheimer's disease appear to have similar underlying risk factors but are quite distinct in their effects on cognition and in their neuropathology (Kalaria, 2002). Memory and language disruptions, along with visual object agnosia, tend to be prevalent in Alzheimer's disease patients, whereas executive functions such as attention, planning, and speed of mental processing are more often disrupted in vascular dementia. These executive functions are associated with prefrontal areas of the cortex.

Risk factors for vascular dementia, such as hypertension and diabetes, are also risk factors for Alzheimer's disease because vascular dementia can accelerate its development (Takeda et al., 2020). Hypertension and diabetes adversely impact both the blood vessels that cause stroke and the growth of plaques and tangles that cause Alzheimer's disease (Figure 9.11). The treatment of hypertension during middle age is therefore important for slowing dementia in later life.

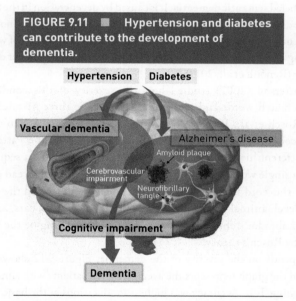

FIGURE 9.11 ■ Hypertension and diabetes can contribute to the development of dementia.

Source: From "Roles of vascular risk factors in the pathogenesis of dementia," by S. Takeda et al., 2020, *Hypertension Research*, *43*, 162–167. https://doi.org/10.1038/s41440-019-0357-9

PET scans are used to detect the presence of the amyloid plaques found in Alzheimer's disease and can now be supplemented with blood tests to identify early signs of the disease (Schindler et al., 2019). The blood tests agreed with the PET scan detections 88% of the time, and accuracy increased to 94% when the blood tests were combined with age and genetic variations. The blood test is less expensive and quicker than a PET scan, so it can be used to streamline the enrollment of individuals in research studies and with further research, could eventually be used for clinical diagnosis (Schindler et al., 2019).

Artificial intelligence is also beginning to contribute to the early diagnosis of dementia (Wang, 2020). Much of the current machine-learning research is focused on sifting through patients' electronic health records to determine which risk factors most accurately predict cognitive decline. The factors include both biological markers and changes in behavior, such as reduced social engagement. Trends over time should be particularly diagnostic.

Although it has been difficult to find treatments for dementia, an experimental Alzheimer's drug (donanemab) from Eli Lilly shows promise for slowing down the disease (Rockoff, 2021). The drug slowed the decline in memory loss by 32% over 18 months compared to a control group given a placebo. Donanemab is designed to clear the plaques and tangles that are the suspected cause of Alzheimer's disease. A follow-up study seeks to confirm the effectiveness of the drug.

Semantic Hub Model

The selective loss of categorical knowledge occurs during a progressive neurological condition that is generically labeled semantic dementia. It is caused by degeneration in the frontal-temporal region of the brain associated with long-term memory of general world knowledge. Patients with semantic dementia gradually lose their knowledge about the meaning of words and objects while often retaining other cognitive abilities, such as the ability to remember day-to-day events in episodic memory (Renoult et al., 2019).

Rogers and Patterson (2007) studied how the severity of this condition influences patients' ability to match words and pictures at each of the three hierarchical levels proposed by Rosch (Rosch et al., 1976). They examined eight patients who differed in their level of performance on the Word-Picture Matching Test. Rogers and Patterson then studied matching at different hierarchical levels by showing the patients a sequence of colored photographs with a single word printed above each. The experimenter read each word aloud and asked whether the word matched the picture. The word described the picture either at the superordinate level (animal, vehicle), the basic level (dogs, birds, cars, and boats), or the subordinate level (Labrador, robin, ferry, BMW). Would matching be the best at the basic level, as predicted by Rosch's theory?

The answer depends on the severity of the dementia. Figure 9.12 shows the findings in which each point on the graph represents the average of two patients with similar scores on the Word-Picture Matching Test. Accuracy was highest for questions at the basic level for patients with mild dementia. But as expected, performance rapidly deteriorated for basic and subordinate categories in patients with lower test scores. The exception was that identification of objects at the superordinate (General) level did not decline. The results show that although basic categories are easier to initially acquire, superordinate categories are easier to retain as semantic dementia worsens.

Rogers and Patterson (2007) used a neural network model (McClelland & Rogers, 2003) to explain why superordinate categories are better retained during dementia. We saw an early application of neural network theory (McClelland & Rumelhart, 1981) to the word superiority effect in Chapter 2. However, instead of connecting features, letters, and words, the network connects categories (robin, bird, animal) and attributes (red, sing, move). The theory assumes,

---

semantic dementia Progressive loss of knowledge about the meaning of words and objects

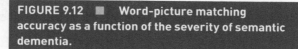

FIGURE 9.12 ■ Word-picture matching accuracy as a function of the severity of semantic dementia.

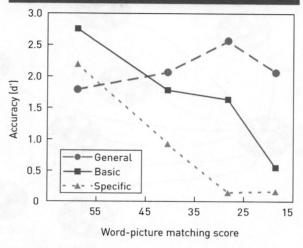

Source: "Object categorization: Reversals and explanations of the basic-level advantage," by T. T. Rogers & K. Patterson, 2007, *Journal of Experimental Psychology: General, 136*, 451–469. https://doi.org/1 0.1080%2F17470218.2012.660963. Copyright 2007 by the American Psychological Association.

as does Rosch, that categorical knowledge is represented by shared attributes at different hierarchical levels. These attributes are determined by the perceptual, motor, and language representations that are formed by our interaction with the environment and are stored in various parts of the brain.

Figure 9.13 shows a network of different attributes that are used to classify pictures at different levels in the hierarchy. The node labeled "Distributed semantic representation" serves as a semantic hub that creates a pattern of activation among the different attributes for each semantic concept.

The difficulty suffered by patients with semantic dementia is that when the anterior temporal cortex—the location of this hub—deteriorates, specific attributes in the semantic network become distorted while general properties remain more intact. Identifying a robin as a bird will therefore become more difficult than identifying a robin as an animal because general attributes, such as eating, are more intact than specific attributes such as having a beak.

The loss of specific attributes will make categorization at the subordinate level even more difficult, as shown by its rapid decline in Figure 9.11. The semantic hub model continues to be an effective theoretical framework for modeling meaning, as we will see in the next chapter on semantic organization.

semantic hub A neural network model that represents semantic relations among words

FIGURE 9.13 ■ A semantic hub model of semantic representations.

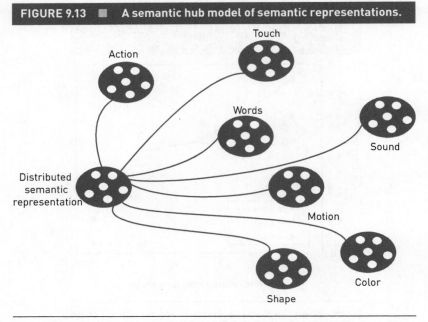

Source: "Object categorization: Reversals and explanations of the basic-level advantage," by T. T. Rogers & K. Patterson, 2007, *Journal of Experimental Psychology: General, 136,* 451–469. https://doi.org/10.1080%2F17470218.2012.660963. Copyright 2007 by the American Psychological Association.

SUMMARY

One way we organize knowledge is through categories and hierarchies made up of categories. Categories reduce the complexity of the environment and the need for constant learning and enable us to recognize objects, respond appropriately, and order and relate classes of events. The concept identification paradigm is one approach to the study of categorization. People try to learn a logical rule by forming hypotheses and receiving feedback on positive and negative instances of the concept. *Rule learning* occurs when people know the relevant attributes and therefore only have to learn the rule. *Attribute learning* occurs when people know the rule but have to learn the relevant attributes.

Real-world, or natural, categories generally cannot be distinguished by a simple rule. They are frequently hierarchically organized—for example, double-knit pants are included in the category *pants*, and pants are included in the category *clothes*. Rosch has argued that most classifications are made at the intermediate or basic level—the most general level at which a prototype can be constructed and the level at which categories are most differentiated. The members of natural categories vary in how well they represent the category in which the attributes of good members are shared with other members of the category. The concepts of hierarchical organization and category typicality also apply to person perception.

People usually categorize patterns based on their similarity to category members, and multi-dimensional scaling is helpful in representing similarities. The prototype model proposes that people create patterns that best represent the categories and then classify novel patterns by comparing them with the category prototypes. Prototype theories have been most successful in predicting how people will classify perceptual patterns consisting of feature values that vary continuously along a dimension. Exemplar theories propose that people remember specific examples rather than abstract information. Exemplar models have been most successful when people have sufficient practice to learn small categories. Theory-based models propose that people use their knowledge of the world to classify patterns. It is apparent that no single theory will work for all situations; the challenge is therefore to show how different tasks influence people's classification strategies.

Effective instruction requires selecting a good set of examples for learning category members. It also requires deciding whether to present all of the examples of one category before presenting the examples of another category or to interweave the examples of both categories. Categories are relevant for understanding the loss of knowledge from dementia. Superordinate categories are the most resistant, as explained by a semantic hub model.

RECOMMENDED READING

As implied by its title, *The Big Book of Concepts* (Murphy, 2003) presented a thorough overview of the categorization literature. Ashby and Maddox (2005) described the theoretical literature on categorization. Other reviews focus on different kinds of concepts (Medin et al., 2000) and evolutionary advantages of different categorization strategies (Klein et al., 2002). The work of Ross (1996) focuses on how our use of examples influences our classification of them. Mandler and Bauer (1988) argued that basic-level categories are not as developmentally important as Rosch's theory implies. Rogers and McClelland's (2004) book *Semantic Cognition: A Parallel Distributed Processing Approach* describes their neural network model. A group in Houston distinguished between semantic knowledge and semantic access in semantic dementia (Chapman et al., 2020). A literature review describes how object properties and categories are neurologically represented as action, perception, and emotion systems (Martin, 2016). The medial temporal lobe is critical in supporting patients' self-awareness of their diminishing cognitive abilities in neurodegenerative diseases (Chavoix & Insausti, 2017). Its decreased connectivity to the anterior-temporal system is symptomatic in early Alzheimer's disease (Berron et al., 2020). The anterior-temporal system is also a central component in semantic dementia, social behavior, and face recognition (Ding et al., 2020).

10   SEMANTIC ORGANIZATION

LEARNING OBJECTIVES

1. Describe how the truth of a semantic statement is evaluated according to different verification models.

2. Explain how a perceptual symbols model differs from amodal models.

3. Contrast stimulus-response and schema theories of knowledge organization.

4. Discuss some of the practical implications of semantic organization, including false memories, concept maps, and AI.

The need to organize knowledge is universal—it applies as much to the arts and humanities as to the sciences. Imagine that you wrote every fact you ever learned on a separate card and someone shuffled all the cards and dropped them in a gigantic pile. Now imagine that someone asked you in which city the Declaration of Independence was signed, and you had to retrieve the right card to answer the question. How would you find the card? Even worse, what if you had to write an essay on the Declaration of Independence? Because all the cards are mixed up, finding one card would provide no clues about the location of other cards on the same topic.

The desire to organize our lives is dramatically illustrated by reactions to the restrictions imposed by the pandemic that began in early 2020 (Levitz, 2021). One woman was initially grateful that she no longer had to take a 45-minute bus ride to her administrative position at Portland State University. She did not miss the commute but did miss the clear dividing lines that segmented her weekdays. Many work-from-home employees began to engage in "fake commutes" to recreate part of the commuting experience that had divided their day. One man even drove from the suburbs to downtown for a cup of coffee.

Semantic organization, including the Declaration of Independence and commuting, can be divided into taxonomic and thematic relations (Mirman et al. 2017). The matrix in Figure 10.1 illustrates this distinction. The columns are taxonomic categories. **Taxonomic relations** capture similarities based on shared features, such as *dog, horse,* and *mouse.* Taxonomic relations are often hierarchical, such as in biological taxonomies for classifying organisms. Rosch's subordinate, basic, and superordinate categories in the previous chapter are a good example of taxonomic categories. The rows in Figure 10.1 are thematic categories. **Thematic relations** capture co-occurrences in events, such as *dog, bone,* and *leash.* Commuting on a bus likely involves walking to the bus stop, engaging in some activity during the ride (reading a book for the woman on her way to Portland State), and attending to location.

FIGURE 10.1 ■ Taxonomic (columns) versus thematic (rows) categories.

DOG	BONE	LEASH
HORSE	APPLE	SADDLE
MOUSE	CHEESE	TRAP

Source: "Taxonomic and thematic semantic systems," by D. Mirman et al., 2017, *Psychological Bulletin, 143,* 499–520. https://doi.org/10.1037/bul0000092

The co-occurrence of objects in thematic relations provides a context in which objects occur. Yee and Thompson-Schill (2016) argue that semantic memory is neither context-free nor independent of specific events. Concepts are so linked to their contexts that the dividing line between a concept and its context may be impossible. Their literature review indicates that concepts are fluid, influenced not only by the environment but by individual experiences. Our interactions with objects in the world are defined by the situations in which they are embedded; so is the conceptual system in which these objects are represented (Photo 10.1).

A popular procedure for studying the taxonomic organization of semantic memory is to ask people to quickly respond *true* or *false* to statements such as "A robin is a bird" or "A canary is a building." Verification times provide the data for constructing models of taxonomic organization described in the first section of this chapter. The second section discusses the perceptual

---

Taxonomic relations Organization (often hierarchical) of concepts based on their ssimilarity

Thematic relations Organization of concepts that appear in the same context

PHOTO 10.1 Concepts co-occur within specific contexts.

istockphoto.com/monkeybusinessimages

symbols model that argues for the role of sensorimotor simulations in retrieving and verifying knowledge. The perceptual symbols model is a primary example of the embodied cognition framework discussed in Chapter 6 on action. The third section discusses organized clusters of knowledge called *schemata*. These clusters group the co-occurrences that represent thematic knowledge. The fourth section contains a few of the many applications of research on semantic organization—forming false memories, creating concept maps, and retrieving information from computers.

VERIFICATION OF SEMANTIC STATEMENTS

The verification of semantic statements has provided extensive data for building models of semantic organization. The experimenter might present a statement such as "A salmon is a bird" or "A bird is an animal" and ask the subject to respond *true* or *false* as quickly as possible. The time it takes to respond to different kinds of statements provides clues about the organization of categories.

A number of theories have been proposed to account for these findings. We will begin by contrasting the hierarchical network model of Collins and Quillian (1969, 1970) and the feature comparison model of Smith et al. (1974). The distinction between the two models can be summarized briefly with the aid of the diagram in Figure 10.2. The feature comparison model

---

feature comparison model A model proposing that items are categorized by matching the item's features to category features

assumes that instances are classified by comparing the features, or attributes, of the two nouns representing the member and the category. To verify that a robin is a bird, a person would compare the features of *robin* with the features of *bird*.

An alternative approach assumes that the relation between two categories is stored directly in memory in a **semantic network** that consists of concepts joined to other concepts by links that specify the relation between them. Networks are typically represented by diagrams in which the concepts are called *nodes* and the lines showing the relationship between two concepts are called *links*. The **hierarchical network model** is a semantic network that assumes that category information is stored directly in memory as hierarchies. The right half of Figure 10.2 shows that *robin* is an example of a *bird* and *bird* is an example of an *animal*. To make predictions, both theories require more specific assumptions. We will now examine the strengths and weaknesses of these assumptions, beginning with the hierarchical network model.

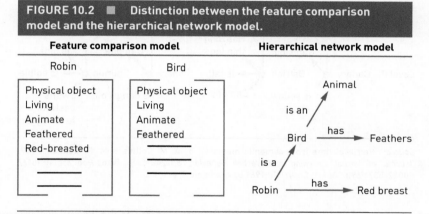

FIGURE 10.2 ■ Distinction between the feature comparison model and the hierarchical network model.

Source: "Theories of semantic memory," by E. E. Smith, 1978, in *Handbook of learning and cognitive processes* (Vol. 6)., edited by W. K. Estes. Copyright 1978 by Lawrence Erlbaum Associates.

The Hierarchical Network Model

Figure 10.3 shows how information is stored in the hierarchical network model. Each word in the network is stored with pointers (arrows) showing how it is related to other words. By following the pointers, we know that *ostrich* and *canary* are examples of birds and that *bird* and *fish* are examples of animals. We also know that a canary, an ostrich, a shark, and a salmon are animals because the pointers connect these instances with the superordinate category *animal*.

The pointers also show how features are stored at different levels in the hierarchy. Features true of all animals—such as eating and breathing—are stored at the highest level (Photo 10.2). Features that apply to basic-level categories—such as that birds have wings, can fly, and have

semantic network A theory proposing that semantic information is organized in long-term memory by linking concepts to related concepts

hierarchical network model A model proposing that items are categorized by using the hierarchical relations specified in a semantic network

FIGURE 10.3 ■ Example of a hierarchically organized memory structure.

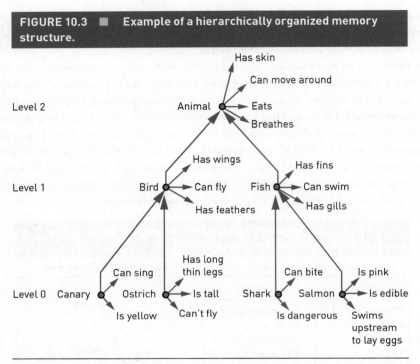

Source: "Retrieval time from semantic memory," by A. M. Collins & M. R. Quillian, 1969, *Journal of Verbal Learning and Verbal Behavior, 8,* 240–248. https://doi.org/10.1016/S0022-5371(69)80069-1. Copyright 1969 by Academic Press, Inc.

feathers—are stored at an intermediate level. Properties stored at the lowest level are true for that particular member but not for all members of the category. It is at this level that we know a canary is yellow and can sing.

One advantage of this kind of network is that it provides an economical way to store information because the information does not have to be repeated at each of the three levels. It isn't necessary to specify that eating and breathing are features of birds, fish, canaries, ostriches, sharks, and salmon because the network tells us that all are examples of *animals*, which eat and breathe. This economy of storage comes at a cost, however: Retrieval of the fact that a canary eats requires two inferences—first, that a canary is a bird and second, that a bird is an animal. In other words, it is necessary to go to the appropriate level in the hierarchy before retrieving the features stored at that level.

Although the network model was originally developed as an efficient means of storing information in a computer, it provides a number of interesting predictions if we use it as a model of human memory. Collins and Quillian (1969) used the model for that purpose by making two primary assumptions—that it takes time to move from one level in the hierarchy to another and that additional time is required if it is necessary to retrieve the features stored at one of the levels. They tested the model by asking people to respond *true* or *false* as quickly as they could to sentences like "An elm is a plant" or "A spruce has branches." The first sentence is an example of

PHOTO 10.2 Eating is stored at the animal level in the hierarchical network model.

istockphoto.com/stammphoto

a question about set relations—it asks whether one category is a member of another. The second question is a question about properties—it asks about the features of a category member.

The average reaction times to six kinds of true sentences are shown in Figure 10.4. A specific example illustrates the different points on the graph, which are the averages across many statements. The three lower points, the response times to questions about set relations, support the prediction that it takes time to move between levels in the network. To verify that "A canary is a canary" requires no change in level; "A canary is a bird" requires a one-level change; and "A canary is an animal" requires a two-level change. The graph shows that response times depend on the number of changes.

The upper three points show that it takes longer to respond to property questions. This finding is consistent with the assumption that response time should increase if it is necessary to retrieve the features stored at one of the levels in the hierarchy. Furthermore, the level in the network where the properties are stored influences response times. The network model proposes that information about singing is stored at the lowest level, information about flying is stored at the intermediate level, and information about skin is stored at the highest level. The data support this assumption and suggest that this is how property information is stored in human memory.

Another interesting prediction based on the network model concerns facilitating retrieval from memory (Collins & Quillian, 1970). Facilitation occurs when the retrieval of information is made easier because the previous question required retrieval of similar information. For example, it should be easier to verify a property of a canary if the previous question was also about a canary. The network model, however, allows us to make a more specific prediction.

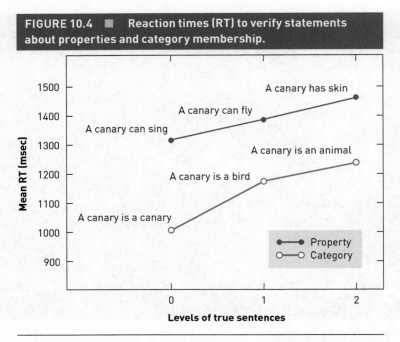

FIGURE 10.4 ■ Reaction times (RT) to verify statements about properties and category membership.

Source: From "Retrieval time from semantic memory," by A. M. Collins & M. R. Quillian, 1969, *Journal of Verbal Learning and Verbal Behavior, 8*, 240–248. https://doi.org/10.1016/S0022-5371(69)80069-1. Copyright 1969 by Academic Press, Inc.

Collins and Quillian proposed that the degree of facilitation should depend on whether one follows the same path in the network to answer the two questions. This concept can be illustrated by considering whether it would be easier to verify that "A canary is a bird" after "A canary can fly" or after "A canary can sing." The answer isn't intuitively obvious, but the network model predicts that "A canary can fly" should cause greater facilitation because the property *fly* is stored at the bird level, and *sing* is stored at the canary level. The same path is followed only when both questions require retrieving information from the bird level. The data were quite supportive of the prediction that the extent of semantic facilitation depends on using the same path as the previous question (Collins & Quillian, 1970).

The successful predictions of the reaction-time data in Figure 10.4 and the predictions about semantic facilitation are impressive accomplishments of the network model. There are two findings, however, that the model does not account for without additional assumptions. The first is that it is possible to find instances in which verification time is not a function of levels in the hierarchy. For example, it takes longer to verify that a chimpanzee is a primate than that a chimpanzee is an animal. The network model should predict the opposite because *primate*, like *bird* and *fish*, is at a lower level in the hierarchy than *animal*. The second finding is that the network model does not account for the typicality effect—the fact that more typical members

---

typicality effect The finding that the more typical members of a category are classified more quickly than the less typical category members

of categories are easier to classify than less typical ones. It is easier to verify that a canary is a bird than that an ostrich is a bird. However, because both are one level from *bird*, as is illustrated in Figure 10.3, the model does not predict the differences in response time. The feature comparison model attempted to correct these deficiencies by offering an alternative formulation.

The Feature Comparison Model

The feature comparison model proposed by E. E. Smith and colleagues (1974) seeks to account for classification times in somewhat the same way that the prototype model accounts for classifications. This model assumes that the meaning of words can be represented in memory by a list of features and that classifications are made by comparing features rather than by examining links in a network (see Figure 10.2). The features can be used to define categories, but they vary in the extent to which they are associated with a category. Smith and colleagues considered the most essential features to be defining features and the remainder to be characteristic features. **Defining features** are features that an entity must have to be a member of a category, whereas **characteristic features** are usually possessed by category members but are not necessary. The defining features for birds might include being alive and having feathers and wings; the characteristic features might include being able to fly and being within a certain size range (Photo 10.3). Because the defining features are more essential, they should play a more important role in how people make classifications.

PHOTO 10.3 Flying is a characteristic feature because not all birds fly.

istockphoto.com/vladsilver

---

defining feature A feature that is necessary to be a member of that category

characteristic feature A feature that is usually present in members of that category but is not necessary

The feature comparison model has two stages. The first stage compares all the features of two concepts to determine how similar one concept is to the other. For example, to determine whether a robin is a bird, we would compare the features of *robin* with the features of *bird*. If the comparison reveals that the two concepts are either very similar or very dissimilar, we can respond true or false immediately. The second stage is necessary when the degree of similarity is between the two extremes. The answer isn't obvious in this case, so the model proposes that we examine only the defining features to determine whether the example has the necessary features of the category. The distinction between the two stages corresponds to our experience that sometimes we make classifications very quickly on the basis of the close similarity between two concepts, and sometimes we make classifications more slowly after we evaluate the criteria for category membership.

Examples that are similar to the concept should usually be classified immediately, without consideration of their defining features during the second stage. The probability that the second stage is necessary increases as the similarity between the category concept and the example decreases. The model therefore predicts that the more typical members of a category (such as *robin, sparrow, blue jay*) should be classified more rapidly than the less typical members (*chicken, goose, duck*) because evaluating the defining features during the second stage slows the classification. Smith and colleagues (1974) found that people could classify instances that are typical of the category faster than they could classify instances that are not typical of the category.

Another advantage of the feature comparison model is that, unlike the network model, it can account for the reversal of the category-size effect. The category-size effect refers to the fact that people are usually able to classify a member into a smaller category faster than into a larger category—for example, verifying that a collie is a dog more quickly than that a collie is an animal. The network model is consistent with the category-size effect because the smaller category (*dog*) requires fewer inferences than the larger category (*animal*). Because the smaller category is a part of the larger category, it appears lower in the hierarchy and will therefore be reached sooner. Some cases, however, violate the category-size effect because the classification times are faster for the larger category. For example, people were able to verify more quickly that Scotch is a drink than that Scotch is a liquor, even though *drink* is a larger category than *liquor*.

The feature comparison model can account for violations of the category size effect because its predictions are based on similarity rather than category size. The reason it is usually easier to verify that an example belongs to a smaller category is that the similarity between the example and one's concept of the smaller category is greater than the similarity between the example and the larger category. However, there are exceptions to this rule. Sometimes there is a greater similarity between the example and a larger category. The feature comparison model predicts that in this case, people should be able to classify into the larger category more quickly than into the smaller category. Experimental results support this prediction (Smith et al., 1974). Although the feature comparison model accounts for both typicality and category-size effects, the model has some weaknesses. Let's now listen to what the critics have to say about its limitations.

---

category-size effect The finding that members of smaller categories are classified more quickly than members of larger categories

Limitations of the Feature Comparison Model

One of the problems with the feature comparison model, as one of its developers pointed out (Smith, 1978), is that it relies on similarity ratings to make most of its predictions. It's not very surprising that if people rate an example as highly similar to their concept of a category, they will be fast to verify that it belongs to that category.

Presumably, these similarity judgments are made by comparing the features of the example and the category concept, but there is little direct support for this assumption. The predictions made by the feature comparison model are therefore rather weak predictions. Its principal asset is that the major alternative—the network model—does not make even these predictions unless it uses so many additional assumptions that it can predict almost anything.

A second criticism of the feature comparison model is its proposal that all classifications require computations—that we use the features of concepts to compute their degree of similarity. Computation is an essential part of the categorization models discussed in the previous chapter where the emphasis was on classifying novel patterns. But once we have learned to associate examples with categories, is it still necessary to use features to compare the similarity of two concepts? Couldn't we use the associations among concepts, as suggested by the proponents of the network model (Collins & Loftus, 1975)? If we have learned that a robin is a bird, it would seem easier to use this information directly rather than computing the similarity between *robin* and *bird*. What information is stored directly in memory and what is computed is a very important issue that is discussed by E. E. Smith (1978). The assumption that all verifications require computing similarity seems counterintuitive.

A third criticism of the feature comparison model is the argument against necessary, or defining, features (Collins & Loftus, 1975; McCloskey & Glucksberg, 1979; Rosch & Mervis, 1975). The feature comparison model avoids this criticism to some extent by proposing that features are more or less defining and that only the more defining features are evaluated during the second stage. This implies, however, that people can identify the more defining features of categories, and we have little direct support for this assumption. Rosch and Mervis's (1975) results suggest the opposite—that the structure of categories is based not on defining features possessed by all members of the category but on a large number of features true of only some category members.

Although it may be difficult to specify defining features for some concepts, such as *fruit*, the distinction between characteristic and defining features may be helpful for explaining how children learn other concepts, such as *robber*. Consider the following two descriptions:

> This smelly, mean old man with a gun in his pocket came to your house one day and took your color television set because your parents didn't want it anymore and told him that he could have it. Could he be a robber?

> This very friendly and cheerful woman came up to you and gave you a hug, but then she disconnected your toilet bowl and took it away without permission and never returned it. Could she be a robber?

The first description contains characteristic features of a robber but not the defining features. The second description contains the defining features of a robber but not the characteristic features. A study of children in kindergarten, second, and fourth grades found that children become more sensitive to defining features as they grow older (Keil & Batterman, 1984). They become more likely to correctly respond that the mean old man is not a robber, but the friendly, cheerful woman is a robber.

One interpretation of this finding is that characteristic features are more salient and directly observable than defining features (McNamara & Miller, 1989). Characteristic features such as *mean* and *gun* are observable, whereas defining features such as *taking without permission* are more conceptual. Young children initially emphasize the directly observable features and have to learn to shift their emphasis to the more conceptual features.

In conclusion, the feature comparison model has some advantages over the hierarchical network model, but it also has some limitations. It is more promising for those concepts that we believe have defining features (Malt, 1990) and for those situations in which we use features to make a decision (Keil & Batterman, 1984; McNamara & Miller, 1989). A compromise is that at different times, we use either direct associations—links in a semantic network—or features to evaluate a concept. This flexibility is part of the theory discussed in the next section.

The Spreading Activation Model

The preceding discussion reflected both the strengths and weaknesses of the hierarchical network model and the feature comparison model. Each provided an explanation for some aspects of the data but could not explain other aspects. In an attempt to account for a greater number of findings than either of these two models, Collins and Loftus borrowed assumptions from each of the models to build a model that had greater flexibility.

Their **spreading activation model** (Collins & Loftus, 1975) is representative of semantic network models in its emphasis on concepts joined together by links that show relationships between concepts. Figure 10.5 shows how a part of human memory can be represented in a network that is somewhat analogous to the neural networks that were discussed in Chapter 2 on pattern recognition and Chapter 8 on memory codes. A change from the hierarchical network model is that the length of each link represents the degree of semantic relatedness between two concepts. Thus, the concept *red* is closely related to other colors and less closely related to red objects. Notice that the model can now account for the typicality effect because the links represent different degrees of semantic relatedness. The shorter links reveal that the more typical examples *car* and *bus* are more closely related to *vehicle* than are *ambulance* and *fire engine*.

The spreading activation model assumes that, when a concept is processed, activation spreads out along the paths of a network, but its effectiveness is decreased as it travels outward. For example, presentation of the word *red* should strongly activate closely related concepts such as *orange* and *fire* and should cause less activation of concepts such as *sunsets* and *roses*. The model therefore predicts the typicality effect because more typical members will activate the superordinate category sooner than less typical members—for example, *car* and *bus* will activate *vehicle* sooner than *fire engine* or *ambulance* will.

---

spreading activation model A model that accounts for response times by formulating assumptions about how activation spreads in a semantic network

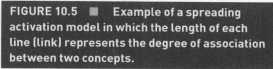

FIGURE 10.5 ■ Example of a spreading activation model in which the length of each line (link) represents the degree of association between two concepts.

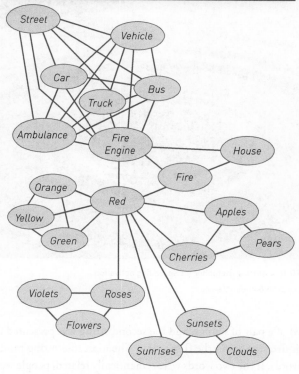

Source: "A spreading activation theory of semantic processing," by A. M. Collins & E. F. Loftus, 1975, *Psychological Review, 82*, 407–428. https://doi.org/10.1037/0033-295X.82.6.407. Copyright 1975 by the American Psychological Association.

The idea of activation spreading throughout a semantic network of interconnected concepts provides a clear picture of the semantic relations among concepts. It is easy to imagine activation decreasing in strength as it travels outward. The model also assumes that activation decreases over time or intervening activity. You can easily visualize the concept of spreading activation if you have ever thrown a rock into still water and watched the ripples spread outward until they disappear (Photo 10.4).

Although the spreading activation model can be associated with a convenient metaphor, its success depends on how well it can account for experimental results. One such result is the effect of semantic priming. Recall that priming is the facilitation in the detection or recognition of a stimulus by using prior information. An example of priming can be found in the lexical decision task studied by Meyer and Schvaneveldt (1976), which required that people judge whether a string of letters formed a word. Some of the letters did (BUTTER), and some did not (NART).

PHOTO 10.4 A visual metaphor for spreading activation.

Photo by Omar Gattis on Unsplash.

Each trial consisted of a pair of strings, and the second string was presented immediately after subjects made their decision about the first string. The most interesting results occurred when both strings were words. If the two words were semantically related, people were faster in verifying that the second string was a word than if the two words were unrelated. For example, people verified faster that the string BUTTER was a word when it was preceded by BREAD than when it was preceded by NURSE. The spreading activation model can account for these results because it proposes that the presentation of a word activates related words. BUTTER will be activated by BREAD but will not be activated by NURSE. The activation of the word makes it easier to identify, resulting in faster response times.

Limitations of the Spreading Activation Model

An advantage of semantic network models is that they are extremely flexible. It is very easy to introduce many assumptions into a model to make it consistent with many kinds of data. For example, the spreading activation model also allows for the use of feature matching (as in the feature comparison model) to verify semantic relations. The price of this advantage, however, is that it is very hard to test the model. If a model becomes so flexible that it is consistent with almost any experimental finding, it loses its predictive power. A model has predictive power only if it predicts that certain events should not occur. One can then evaluate the model by determining which events do in fact occur.

The challenge for the developers of semantic network models is not only to take advantage of their flexibility but also to place some constraints on the models to make some interesting predictions. When a network model fails to make a correct prediction, the developers usually create additional assumptions to give the model greater flexibility. Consequently, the revised model usually succeeds where the original failed, but many psychologists find the revision less satisfactory. Collins and Loftus's (1975) revision of the hierarchical network model corrected the limitations of the former but sacrificed the precise predictions that made the hierarchical network model one of the more interesting semantic network theories.

Thus, their model has considerable flexibility, but predictions can be made only with difficulty. Critics of the model (for example, McCloskey & Glucksberg, 1979; Smith, 1978) have argued that, with so many assumptions, it is not surprising that the model accounts for many empirical findings. They find the model's main weaknesses to be both the number of assumptions made and the failure to make many clearcut predictions based on it. In fact, the model was developed primarily to show how its assumptions are consistent with existing data rather than to make interesting new predictions.

However, other theorists used the spreading activation theory to make interesting new predictions. Imagine that you learned three facts about someone named Marty: (1) Marty broke the bottle; (2) Marty didn't delay the trip; and (3) Marty cooked spaghetti. Later you had to quickly respond "yes" (Marty cooked spaghetti) or "no" (Marty played tennis) to a test sentence depending on whether you previously learned the fact. Anderson (1976) successfully predicted that learning more facts about a person would increase the time to verify any one of those facts. The basis for his prediction is that (1) each fact about a person is linked to that person in a semantic network and (2) spreading activation is divided among the links. Increasing the number of links therefore decreases the amount of spreading activation along each link, increasing the time it takes to verify the connection between the person and the fact.

Now imagine that instead you had learned that (1) Marty broke the bottle, (2) Marty didn't delay the trip, and (3) Marty christened the ship. Do you see how these three facts can be integrated around a common theme? The theme is that the ship launching was on schedule because the bottle broke during the christening. Reder and Anderson (1980) proposed that, in this case, the three facts are integrated around a subnode in the semantic network, allowing for the quick verification of any of the facts. The subnode creates a cluster of knowledge that facilitates retrieval. Specifying the organization of such clusters is the objective of schema theory. We will examine it later in the chapter after considering a different theory of memory storage and semantic verification—the perceptual symbols model.

A Comparison of Models

We have spent considerable time and effort in reviewing the assumptions of the hierarchical network model, the feature comparison model, and the spreading activation model. This investment of effort is justified by the impact the theoretical constructs in these models have had on our thinking about the organization of knowledge. For instance, Rosch's (Rosch et al.,

1976) research on the implications of the hierarchical organization of knowledge continued the theme introduced in the hierarchical network model.

Table 10.1 lists the previously mentioned strengths and weaknesses of the models. There is an analogy between the development of these models and the models of selective attention in Chapter 3. The models that followed Broadbent's filter model were developed to account

TABLE 10.1 ■ A comparison of semantic verification models
The Hierarchical Network Model

Strengths

1. Provides an economical way to store information
2. Fairly accurate in predicting hierarchical verification times
3. Predicts faster verification times when reusing the same pathways

Weaknesses

1. Retrieval of hierarchical information requires inferences
2. Cannot predict faster verification times for larger categories
3. Does not predict faster verification times for more typical category members

The Feature Comparison Model

Strengths

1. Distinguishes between defining and characteristic features
2. Can predict faster verification times for larger (and smaller) categories
3. Can predict faster times for more typical category members

Weaknesses

1. Relies too much on judged similarity ratings for predictions
2. Requires a comparison of features rather than using direct associations
3. Defining features may not be clear

The Spreading Activation Model

Strengths

1. Can predict faster recognition of primed words
2. Can predict faster verification times for larger (and smaller) categories
3. Can predict faster times for more typical category members

Weaknesses

1. Relies too much on judged similarity ratings for predictions
2. Too much flexibility enables it to "predict" almost any finding

for findings that contradicted his model's assumption that speech could not bypass the filter. Likewise, the models that followed the hierarchical network model attempted to correct for its limitations in predicting category size and typicality effects.

We can also establish an analogy to the evaluation of the categorization models discussed in the previous chapter. The formulation of multiple models does not imply that one model is correct and the other models are wrong. People possess a variety of cognitive strategies for performing a task. For example, it is likely that most of us would not use the feature comparison process when we have associative links in long-term memory. Why compare the features of *dog* and *mammal* during the initial stage of the feature comparison model if we know that a dog is a mammal? However, there are cases in which we may need to pause and reflect, such as judging whether a whale is a mammal. In such cases, it seems reasonable to evaluate during the model's second stage whether a *whale* possesses the defining features of a *mammal*.

THE PERCEPTUAL SYMBOLS MODEL

The theories described thus far in this chapter are amodal because they do not directly represent the perceptual experiences encountered in learning about concepts. A dramatically different theoretical approach is the perceptual symbols system proposed by Barsalou (1999), in which perceptual experiences are directly stored in LTM. A perceptual symbols system is a modal approach because it stores sensory experiences such as audition, vision, taste, smell, and touch. It is an example of embodied cognition described in Chapter 6 on action. You may recall that embodied cognition considers perception and action to be central components of cognition (Gibbs, 2006; Wilson, 2002).

In his engaging book *Metropolis: A History of the City, Humankind's Greatest Invention* Ben Wilson writes that our interactions with the world are grounded in sensory experiences:

> I look for material in markets, souks and bazaars; in swimming pools, stadiums and parks; in street-food stalls, coffeehouse and cafés; in shops, malls and department stores. I interrogated paintings, novels, films and songs as much as official records in search of the lived experience of cities and intensity of their daily life. You have to experience the city through your senses— looking, smelling, touching, walking, reading and imagining to understand it's totality. (Wilson, 2020, pp. 8–9)

Figure 10.6 shows the distinction between the previously discussed amodal approaches and the modal approach proposed by Barsalou (1999). Amodal systems represent perceptual information indirectly as a list of features or as a list of associations in a semantic network. In contrast, perceptual symbol systems retrieve information from LTM by reenacting or simulating perceptual experiences. The strong neural basis of perceptual symbols reflects the important role that research by cognitive neuroscientists has played in shaping the model, including the reactivation hypothesis that encoding areas of the brain are reactivated during later retrieval (Danker & Anderson, 2010).

FIGURE 10.6 ■ Representation of information in amodal symbol systems (a) and perceptual symbol systems (b)

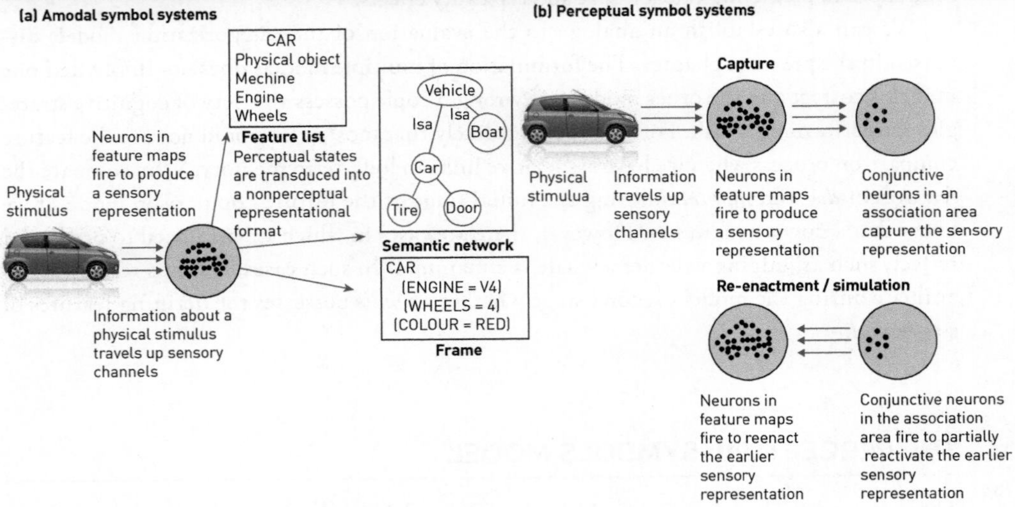

iStockphoto.com/youngID

Source: From "Grounding conceptual knowledge in modality-specific systems," by L. W. Barsalou et al., 2003, 7, 84–91 *Trends in Cognitive Sciences*. https://doi.org/10.1016/S1364-6613(02)00029-3

Semantic Verification

A perceptual-based approach is helpful for explaining a number of semantic verification findings. You can participate in one of these tasks by judging whether the vertically aligned words in Table 10.2 are semantically related. Try to make your judgment for each of the pairs as quickly as you can. Zwaan and Yaxley (2003) proposed that if people use images to help them make the decision, the position of the words should influence response times. The results supported this prediction. When the vertical alignment of the words matched the alignment in our images (ATTIC above BASEMENT), students were significantly faster in verifying semantic relatedness than when the alignments were mismatched (BASEMENT above ATTIC).

TABLE 10.2 ■ Examples of word pairs from Zwaan and Yaxley's (2003) Semantic Relatedness Study

ATTIC	LAKE	SWAN	CANDLE	TAXI	NOSE
BASEMENT	BOAT	SINK	FLAME	PEACH	MOUTH

Source: "Spatial iconicity affects semantic relatedness judgments," by R. A. Zwaan & R. H. Yaxley, 2003, *Psychonomic Bulletin & Review*, *10*, 954–958. https://doi.org/10.3758/BF03196557

Pecher et al. (2003) reasoned that if people simulate information, they should be slower when they have to shift modalities when verifying properties in a conceptual task. The task required the quick verification of properties that came from the six modalities shown in Table 10.3. People had to quickly respond "true" or "false" to statements such as a "BLENDER can be loud" and "CRANBERRIES can be tart." The statements shown in the first column of Table 10.3 are target items that were either preceded by statements from the same modality (column 2) or by statements from a different modality (column 3). The results confirmed the prediction that people would be slower in verifying properties when there was a shift in sensory modality. People were slower, for example, in verifying that a "BLENDER can be loud" when it was preceded by "CRANBERRIES can be tart" then when it was preceded by "LEAVES can be rustling."

TABLE 10.3 ■ Examples of modalities used in the target and in the preceding (context) trial

		Context trial	
Modality	**Target trial**	**Same modality**	**Different modality**
Audition	BLENDER-loud	LEAVES-rustling	CRANBERRIES-tart
Vision	BABY CLOTHES-pastel	HAIR-fair	TOAST-warm
Taste	CUCUMBER-bland	BUTTERMILK-sour	BIRD EGG-speckled
Smell	SOAP-perfumed	OLD BOOK-musty	TELEVISION-noisy
Touch	MARBLE-cool	PEANUT BUTTER-Sticky	BED SPRINGS-Squeaking
Motor	FAUCET-turned	ROCK-hurled	HIGHWAY SIGN-green

Source: "Verifying different-modality properties for concepts produces switching costs," by D. Pecher et al., 2003. *Psychological Science, 14*, 119–124. https://doi.org/10.1111/1467-9280.t01-1-01429

Pecher (2017) nonetheless subsequently raised reservations about arguing that semantic concepts necessarily depend on embodied cognition. One of her reservations, often mentioned by others (Dove, 2016), is that it is difficult to model abstract concepts within an embodied cognition framework. Another reservation, typically not mentioned by others, is that the concept itself may consist of amodal symbols even when there are links between the concept and its sensorimotor representations.

This perspective does not eliminate sensorimotor activations but considers these activations to be secondary to understanding the concept. In other words, a person can verify that "LEAVES can be rustling" without mentally simulating the sound of rustling leaves. The mental representation of the sentence may be amodal and activation spreads from this amodal representation to the sensorimotor system. Or to take an example from the chapter on action, the motor activation of the action "Open the drawer" (Glenberg & Kaschak, 2002) may occur only after a person understands the sentence. The advantage of concrete objects and actions in this view is that they enable the possibility of performing sensorimotor simulations even if semantic verification does not require them (Pecher, 2017).

An extensive literature review by Ianì (2019) documents many situations in which embodied experiences do influence memory processes. However, he also admits that there is a risk in overstating the role of sensorimotor processes in memory. Pecher (2017) and Iani (2019) concur that further investigations will contribute to a better understanding of how modal and amodal symbols combine to influence our memories in different situations. One type of memory in which sensorimotor simulations likely occur is autobiographical memory.

Autobiographical Memory

A major assumption of the perceptual symbols model is that people reenact or simulate their experiences. This assumption would seem to be particularly relevant for **autobiographical memory**, which stores personal experiences. Kubovy (2020) theorizes that our lives consist of a collection of strands that are containers of activities. Strands consist of themes, such as the relationship theme, mother theme, and work theme, that are depicted in Figure 10.7. The strands are continuous and concurrent but only one strand is in the foreground at any given time.

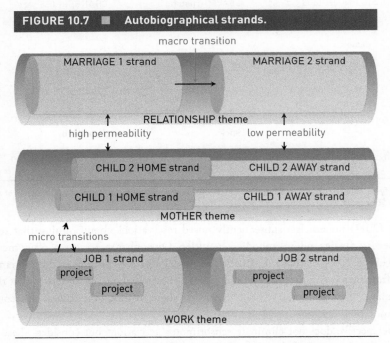

FIGURE 10.7 ■ Autobiographical strands.

Source: "Lives as collections of strands: An essay in descriptive psychology," by M.Kubovy, 2020, *Perspectives on Psychological Science, 15*, 497–515. https://doi.org/10.1177/1745691619887145

autobiographical memory Memory about our personal experiences

The strands depicted in Figure 10.7 represent Sarah, an attorney and a single mother. The microtransitions in the figure are routine alternations between strands such as when Sarah executes the work theme during the day but transitions to the mother theme during the evening. These transitions produce small changes in behavior, such as a switch to legal English when required at work. Macrotransitions produce major changes in one's life, such as leaving home, losing a job, taking a maternity leave, or getting divorced. The macrotransitions in Figure 10.7 are a change in marital status, a change in having children in the home, and a change in jobs. Kubovy (2020) uses his theoretical framework to organize research on people's lives.

Autobiographical memory shares similarities with episodic memory discussed in Chapter 5. Like episodic memory, autobiographical memory has a context. Events in our lives occur at a particular place and time. However, Rubin (2006) proposes that there are also differences between the episodic tasks studied in the laboratory and the events that occur in our lives:

- Items in episodic memory usually do not tell a story. Our lives do.

- The retention interval for items in episodic memory is typically less than one hour. Autobiographical memories may last an entire lifetime.

- Autobiographical memories consist of many modalities. Laboratory tasks typically focus on a single modality.

- Episodic retrieval has minimal emotional involvement. Autobiographical retrieval may be emotional.

Rubin (2006) persuasively argues that our autobiographical memories do not consist of abstract, homogenized information. Rather, they contain information from sensory, language, emotion, and other systems that process different kinds of information.

Research at Duke University has helped us better understand the neuropsychology of autobiographical memory. Figure 10.8 shows the major components of the brain that are involved in retrieving experiences. The prefrontal cortex (PFC) guides retrieval and monitors the feeling-of-rightness (FOR) regarding accuracy. Activation of visual imagery is prevalent in studies of autobiographical memory as revealed by greater activity in those areas of the brain that process visual images. Emotional memories are also prevalent, as revealed by the greater activation of the amygdala.

So how do these different areas of the brain combine to aid retrieval? A group of Duke investigators answered this question by tracking the brain activity of 17 young adults as they retrieved autobiographical memories in response to 80 cue words (reported by Rubin, 2006). Participants indicated that they had retrieved a memory by pressing a button and then rated it for intensity of emotion and the extent to which they relived the experience.

Figure 10.9 shows when the maximum activity occurs for three brain areas shown in Figure 10.8. Maximum activity in the prefrontal cortex occurs at the time of the button press (0 s), indicating the successful retrieval of a memory. Maximum activity in the hippocampus and amygdala occurred before the button press, suggesting that emotional content played an early role in retrieval before memories were well formed. Support for emotional content comes from

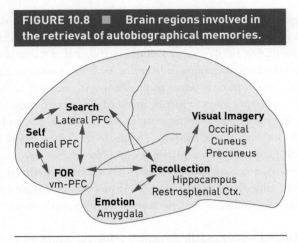

FIGURE 10.8 ■ Brain regions involved in the retrieval of autobiographical memories.

Source: "Functional neuroimaging of autobiographical memory," by R. Cabeza & P. St. Jacques, 2007, *TRENDS in the Cognitive Sciences, 11*, 219–227. https://doi.org/10.1016/j.tics.2007.02.005

the finding that activity in the amygdala correlated with the rated intensity of the emotion. In contrast, maximum activity in the visual cortex occurred after the button press and correlated with ratings of how much participants relived the experience.

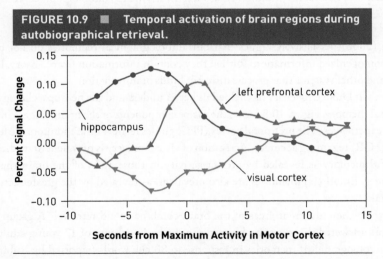

FIGURE 10.9 ■ Temporal activation of brain regions during autobiographical retrieval.

Source: "The basic-systems model of episodic memory," by D. C. Rubin, 2006 *Perspectives in Psychological Science, 1*, 277–311. https://doi.org/10.1111%2F j.1745-6916.2006.00017.x

A Neural Network Model of Semantic Integration

The research on autobiographical memory is consistent with the perceptual symbols view that our memories allow us to relive our experiences through simulations that have emotional and perceptual content. What does this mean for the many amodal theories that propose knowledge is stored more abstractly without perceptual and emotional content? A reasonable answer is that some knowledge is stored in an amodal form and other knowledge is stored in a modal form that supports simulations (Dove, 2009). A complete model of semantic organization must therefore account for the representation of both concrete and abstract information.

An important step in this direction is a neural network model that builds on the theoretical construct of a semantic hub (Rogers & Patterson, 2007) discussed in the previous chapter. As was illustrated in Figure 9.12, a semantic hub integrates the various sensorimotor properties of individual words. A major extension of this idea is to show how the meaning of abstract words can be interpreted by their association with concrete words (Hoffman et al., 2018).

Figure 10.10 lists concrete and abstract words that were learned by the neural network. Notice that the concrete words are members of categories, including ones such as vehicles, clothes, and fruits, that were studied by Rosch and Mervis (1975). The model uses the sensorimotor properties of concrete words to create the similarities illustrated in Figure 10.11. The concrete words are color-coded by category based on their close proximity in a multidimensional space. The words *train, bus, truck,* and *car,* for instance, belong to the same semantic category because of their shared sensorimotor properties.

FIGURE 10.10 ■ Concrete and abstract words learned by a network hub model.

CONCRETE		ABSTRACT		
Humans	**Animals**	problem	decision	invitation
footballer	deer	difficulty	option	meeting
hunter	pheasant			
cashier	chicken	success	leisure	sport
duchess	horse	victory	enjoyment	team
	duck			
		stain	journey	election
Vehicles	**Clothes**	blemish	distance	government
car	shoe			
truck	jacket	conservation	economics	industry
bus	boot	preservation	money	company
train	gown			
		message	measurement	production
Natural	**Fruits**	information	quantity	merchandise
Features	orange			
river	apple		instruction	
forest	lemon		direction	

Source: "Concepts, control, and context: A connectionist account of normal and disordered semantic cognition," by P. Hoffman et al., 2018, *Psychological Review, 125,* 293–328. http://dx.doi.org/10.1037/rev0000094

FIGURE 10.11 ■ Similarity of concrete and abstract words as learned by a network hub model.

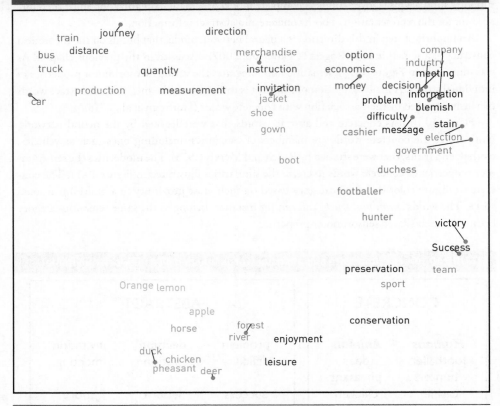

Source: "Concepts, control, and context: A connectionist account of normal and disordered semantic cognition," by P. Hoffman et al., 2018*Psychological Review*, *125*, 293–328. http://dx.doi.org/10.1037/rev0000094

Hoffman et al. (2018) further extended the semantic hub model by adding the idea that semantic relationships can also be inferred from the co-occurrence of words or objects within the same context. For instance, the abstract words *journey* and *distance* in the upper left corner of Figure 10.11 are similar to *train, bus, truck,* and *car* because they frequently appear together. The association of abstract with concrete words provides a mechanism by which abstract words can be "grounded" in meaning through their interactions with physical objects.

The similarity clusters in Figure 10.11 also capture the distinction between taxonomic and thematic relations (Mirman et al., 2017) made at the beginning of this chapter. Taxonomic relations capture similarities based on shared features, and thematic relations capture co-occurrences in events or scenarios. The network learning of both shared features and co-occurrences produced the clusters in Figure 10.11. Clusters of knowledge gain additional prominence in representing knowledge by schemas.

SCHEMA THEORY

Semantic networks provide a convenient way of organizing knowledge, but the emphasis is on showing how two nodes are related and not on showing how ideas are grouped together to form larger clusters of knowledge. A schema is a cluster of knowledge that represents a general procedure, object, percept, event, sequence of events, or social situation (Thorndyke, 1984). Schema theory refers to a collection of models, presuming that we encode such knowledge clusters into memory and use them to comprehend and store our experiences.

I mentioned during the brief historical overview in Chapter 1 that during the time period that U.S. psychologists were predominantly influenced by stimulus-response (S-R) theories, psychologists such as Bartlett in England and Piaget in Switzerland were arguing that behavior is influenced by large units of knowledge organized into schema. We will begin by looking at Bartlett's theory, as analyzed by Brewer and Nakamura (1984).

Bartlett's Schema Theory

The schema theory that Bartlett (1932) developed in his book *Remembering* has inspired many of the modern versions of schema theory. He defined a schema as an active organization of past experiences in which the mind abstracts a general cognitive structure to represent many particular instances of those experiences. Bartlett's book consists of an elaboration of schema theory and shows its application to experimental results that he had collected on memory for figures, pictures, and stories.

A fundamental assumption of Bartlett's schema theory is that all new information interacts with old information represented in the schema. This is illustrated by how people who did not share the cultural history of Native Americans recalled a story that they had read called "The War of the Ghosts." The story involved Native Americans traveling in canoes and fighting another group that turned out to be ghosts. Bartlett noticed that many of the errors people made in recall were more regular and conventional than the original material, suggesting that the material had been integrated with their prior knowledge structures.

Brewer and Nakamura (1984) point out that a number of fundamental differences exist between schema theory and the S-R approach to psychology. These include the following:

Atomistic versus molar. An S-R theory is atomistic and is based on small units of knowledge (a single stimulus). A schema is a much larger unit, showing how knowledge is combined into clusters.

Associationistic versus nonassociationistic. An S-R theory requires learning an association between a stimulus and a response. A schema provides a knowledge structure for interpreting and encoding aspects of a particular experience.

---

schema A general knowledge structure that provides a framework for organizing clusters of knowledge

Particularistic versus generic. An S-R theory shows the association between a particular stimulus and a particular response. A schema is more general and represents a variety of particular instances, much as a prototype represents the particular instances of a category.

Passive versus active. The association between a stimulus and a response can be learned in a passive manner. Invoking a schema is a more active process in which a particular experience is matched to the schema that best fits that experience.

Bartlett's ideas had little theoretical impact during his lifetime. In the United States, behaviorism and S-R psychology had a strong hold on theory construction. In England, his theory was taken more seriously but, by the early 1970s, even his own students thought the theory a failure. A dramatic turn of events occurred in 1975 when a number of prominent U.S. cognitive scientists argued that schema are needed to organize knowledge in artificial intelligence, cognitive psychology, linguistics, and motor performance. These theorists adopted the major assumptions of Bartlett's theory but were more specific about what these knowledge structures looked like. We now examine some of the contributions of these later theories.

Modern Schema Theory

Two of the strongest advocates for the importance of schema were Minsky (1975), for representing knowledge in artificial intelligence programs and Rumelhart (1980), for representing knowledge in cognitive psychology. Rumelhart argued that schema are the building blocks of cognition. According to Rumelhart, a schema theory is basically a theory about how knowledge is represented and about how that representation facilitates the use of knowledge in various ways. Schemas are used to interpret sensory data, retrieve information from memory, organize action, and solve problems.

One of the main contributions from artificial intelligence has been that programming languages allow more detailed specification of schema organization than was possible in earlier formulations (Thorndyke, 1984). Although Bartlett emphasized that schemas were organized, he was not always very specific about what the organization was. We now think of a schema as providing a skeleton structure, which can be filled out with the detailed properties of a particular instance.

Let's take a familiar routine for students: registering for courses. What kinds of knowledge would you like to have before signing up for a course? You would probably want to know what the prerequisites are, whether it meets some requirement, how many credits you will receive, when and where it meets, and perhaps who is teaching it. An advantage of having schematic knowledge is that we can sometimes rely on default knowledge—that is, likely values that enable us to make intelligent guesses in the absence of specific knowledge. For example, most lecture courses offer the same number of credits, so you could probably guess how many credits you would receive for a cognitive psychology course before looking it up. You might also have guessed that the prerequisite was introductory psychology and might even have guessed the name of the instructor if the same person usually teaches this course.

---

default knowledge Knowledge about the most likely values for the attributes of a schema

At the beginning of this section, we discussed that a schema can represent a variety of knowledge structures: procedures, objects, percepts, events, sequences of events, or social situations. People have schemas for solving different kinds of problems, recognizing faces, going shopping for groceries, and forming social stereotypes. Schemas are particularly important for text comprehension and problem solving, and we will later examine their influence on these cognitive skills. For now, we want to examine the organization of a particular type of schematic structure—our knowledge about a sequence of events. This will enable us to move from this rather abstract overview to see how cognitive psychologists do research on schematic organization.

Scripts: Representing Sequences of Events

Part of our schematic knowledge is organized around routine activities—for example, going to a restaurant, visiting a dentist, changing a flat tire, or riding a bus. Schank and Abelson (1977) used the term **script** to refer to what we know about the sequence of events that make up such routine activities. For example, a restaurant script would specify what we know about going to a restaurant. At a very general level, a restaurant script consists of standard roles, props or objects, conditions, and results. The conditions for going to a restaurant are that a customer is hungry and is able to pay for the meal. The props are tables and chairs, a menu, food, a bill, and money or a credit card. Supporting actors include waiters or waitresses and sometimes other personnel, such as bartenders or busboys. The results are that the customer has less money but is no longer hungry, whereas the owner has more money. Between the times that a customer enters and leaves, there is a fairly standard sequence of events that includes selecting a table, looking at the menu, ordering the food, eating, and paying the bill.

Because the sequence of events is quite standard, a natural way of organizing scripts is according to the temporal order in which the events occur. Imagine that you have a flat tire and need to put on the spare tire. Your memory might consist of an organized sequence of actions, beginning with what you do first and ending with what you do last. Alternatively, your memory might be organized according to the centrality or importance of the events, in which you think of the more important events before you think of the less important events. Figure 10.12 shows these two contrasting memory structures.

Figure 10.12a shows an organization in which some activities (such as removing the bad tire) are more central than others (such as putting away the jack). The more central activities are those that are particularly important in accomplishing the goal. If activities are organized according to their centrality, then people should be faster in verifying that the more central activities are included in a script. You may have noticed that the representation in Figure 10.12a is analogous to the semantic network proposed by Collins and Loftus in the previous chapter, but the shorter links represent a strong association between an activity and a script instead of a strong association between an exemplar and its category. An alternative representation, shown in Figure 10.12b, consists of activities organized according to their sequential order. If activities are reconstructed in the order in which they are performed, people should be faster in verifying that earlier activities are included in the script.

---

script Knowledge about what occurs during routine activities

FIGURE 10.12 ■ Two representations of a routine: (a) according to the centrality of component activities and (b) according to their sequential order.

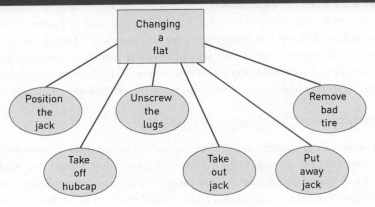

(a)

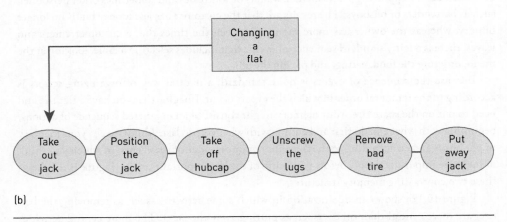

(b)

Source: "Memory for routines," by J. A. Galambos & L. J. Rips, 1982, *Journal of Verbal Learning and Verbal Behavior, 21*, 260–281. https://doi.org/10.1016/S0022-5371(82)90604-1. Copyright 1982 by Academic Press.

Galambos and Rips (1982) tested which theory was more appropriate by asking students to rank in order the activities of different scripts according to both their temporal order and their centrality. They then showed another group of subjects pairs of items that consisted of the name of a script (changing a flat) and an activity (take out jack). Students were asked to respond as quickly as possible whether the activity was included in the script. More central events were verified more quickly than less central events, but earlier events were not verified more quickly than later events. The results therefore supported the organization shown in Figure 10.12a.

However, this conclusion was challenged by Barsalou and Sewell (1985), who believed that the temporal order of events is very important in how people organize their experiences. They thought that the results would be different if they used a different experimental procedure. Instead of asking people to verify that a particular activity was part of a script, they gave people 20 seconds to name as many activities as they could that belonged to a particular script, such as doing the dishes. One group of subjects was asked "to generate actions from the most central action to the least central action" where centrality was defined in terms of the importance of the action. Another group of subjects was asked "to generate actions from the first action to the last action." The researchers hypothesized that if the events are temporally organized in memory, then it should be easier to name events in their temporal order than to name events in decreasing importance. Their findings supported this hypothesis. The average number of actions generated in 20 seconds was 8.17 when actions were listed in a temporal order and 6.10 when actions were listed according to importance. One interpretation of these conflicting findings is that both the centrality and the temporal order of events influence how we use our memory. The more central events provide the quickest access to a script, but the temporal order of events is useful for retrieving all the events that are in the script.

The complementary roles of centrality and temporal order in verifying the content of scripts is consistent with the claim that both modal and amodal codes are important in memory. For example, perceptual simulations would likely occur in temporal order. If you changed a flat tire by simulating how you did it previously, your recall would likely be based on the sequential representation in Figure 10.12b. However, the quicker verification of central events fits well with the assumptions of the amodal spreading activation model in which more central events have shorter links (Figure 10.12a).

Scripts play a dual role in cognition because both action production and event perception are organized as routine sequential behaviors (Cooper, 2019). Both are sequentially and hierarchically organized schema that are associated with goal-directed action. Scripts enable the execution and monitoring of a sequence of activities, as when you change a tire. They also provide a framework interpreting sensory input when you watch someone else change a tire. This dual role of scripts provides the link between action production and event perception (Cooper, 2019).

APPLICATIONS

As you likely suspect, semantic organization has many practical applications. Here we consider three that differ widely in their influence on people's lives. Spreading activation is usually beneficial but occasionally has bad side effects. One is triggering false memories, including harmful ones for people who are distressed or have post-traumatic stress disorder (PTSD). But semantic networks also make a positive contribution when turned into concept maps for organizing ideas presented in the classroom. Another positive contribution is the application of theories of semantic organization, such as the hierarchical network model, to build computer tools that assist us in retrieving information and reasoning from that information.

False Memories

Spreading activation within a network is typically very helpful, but a harmful side effect is that it can result in the incorrect recall of associated items (Roedinger & McDermott, 1995). Imagine that you studied a list of the following words: *table, sit, legs, seat, soft, desk, arm, sofa, wood, cushion, rest,* and *stool.* Later you are asked to recall the list. Can you think of a word that you might incorrectly recall?

Roedinger and McDermott (1995) presented undergraduates at Rice University with lists of words that were highly associated with a word that was not on the list, such as the word *chair* in the above example. Spreading activation theory predicts that activation will spread to activate the unpresented word and perhaps cause it to be incorrectly recalled. The findings confirmed this prediction. Participants recalled 65% of the words on the lists but also falsely recalled the highly associated word for 40% of the lists. They recalled the highly associated unpresented word for 55% of the lists in a second experiment in which participants studied more words.

The creation of false memories has practical applications for many situations outside the laboratory. When negative material is presented to depressed patients, they are more likely to remember related but unpresented material than people who do not suffer from depression. A meta-analysis of experiments on false memories revealed that individuals who suffer from depression or from post-traumatic stress disorder were more likely to demonstrate false memories for associated emotional material (Otgaar et al., 2017). False memories for this group did not occur more frequently for neutral or for nonassociated material.

Figure 10.13 shows a hypothetical example of a person with post-traumatic stress disorder. A list of negatively associated words will activate words in long-term memory that may generate false memories related to the unpresented word *blood.* These false memories are unlikely to occur for neutral material. Although some words in the neutral list are similar to those in the negative list, other neutral words reduce the chance of associative activation spreading to neighboring nodes that create false traumatic memories. This assumption is analogous to the biological concept of herd immunity. Neutral words reduce the spread of activation to negative words as vaccinations reduce the spread of a virus during a pandemic.

False memories are also generated when people base their recall on gist memory rather than verbatim memory (Brainerd & Reyna, 2019). Verbatim memories record the details of events (a Coke bottle on the breakfast table) and gist memories record generic meanings (a soft drink in the kitchen). Verbatim retrieval supports true memory (a Coke bottle), whereas gist retrieval supports true memories plus false memories that are consistent with the gist (a Pepsi bottle). Brainerd and Reyna label this theory "fuzzy-trace theory." Table 10.4 lists six of its principles that apply to false memories.

Many research studies have applied fuzzy-trace theory to a variety of real-world situations, including law. Brainerd and Reyna (2019) discuss three types of legal cases involving child witnesses, eyewitness identification, and police interrogations in which the principles in Table 10.3 enhance the understanding of false memories in legal settings. They advocate for informing jurors about the science of false memories to create more just verdicts.

FIGURE 10.13 ■ Hypothetical example of how false memories in PTSD are formed when emotional associative material is presented.

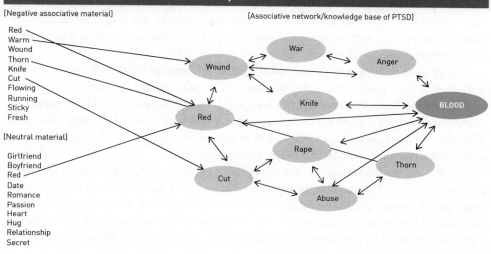

Source: "What drives false memories in psychopathology? A case for associative activation," by H. Otgaar et al., 2017*Clinical Psychological Science*, *5*, 1048–1069. https://doi.org/10.1177%2F2167702617724424

TABLE 10.4 ■ Theoretical principles of fuzzy-trace theory

Name	Description
Verbatim and gist	Subjects process the surface form and meaning of events, storing separate traces of each.
Dissociated retrieval	Recountings are based on the retrieval of both verbatim and gist traces. Some cues favor verbatim retrieval; others favor gist retrieval.
Opponent processes	Verbatim and gist retrieval both support true memory. Gist retrieval supports "false" memories of meaning-consistent events, whereas verbatim retrieval suppresses false memories.
Development	Memory for the verbatim form and semantic content of experience both improve during development. Gist improvements are more protracted with age than verbatim improvements.
Individual differences	Some individuals are more susceptible to false memory, such as individuals with poor verbatim memories or who preferentially retrieve gist.
Phantom recollection	Verbatim and gist retrieval can both produce vivid, realistic recollections that are difficult to distinguish.

Source: From "Fuzzy-trace theory, false memory, and the law," by C. J., Brainerd & V. F. Reyna, 2019, *Policy Insights From the Behavioral and Brain Sciences*, *6*, 79–86. https://doi.org/10.1177%2F2372732218797143

Concept Maps

The examples of semantic networks reviewed in this chapter depict the organization of concepts that people learn from their daily activities. Semantic networks also help students organize classroom knowledge. Such semantic networks are typically labeled **concept maps** when used as an instructional tool.

Figure 10.14 shows a concept map for organizing information on wounds from a nursing text. There are two kinds of hierarchical relations, *part* (indicated by a "p") and *type* (indicated by a "t"). *Part* indicates that a concept in a lower node is part of a concept in a higher node. The discussion of wounds is divided into two parts: the types of wounds and the process of healing. *Type* indicates that a concept in a lower node is an example of a category in a higher node. Open and closed wounds are examples of different types of wounds.

In addition, the information on wounds contains two nonhierarchical relations: *characteristics* (indicated by a "c") and *leads to* (represented by an "l"). *Characteristics* are the features or properties of a concept. A characteristic of an open wound is that there is a break in the skin. The relation *leads to* specifies that one concept leads to or causes another concept. This relation is particularly useful for describing sequential processes, such as the three phases of healing.

FIGURE 10.14 ■ **Part of a concept map that organizes information in a nursing text.**

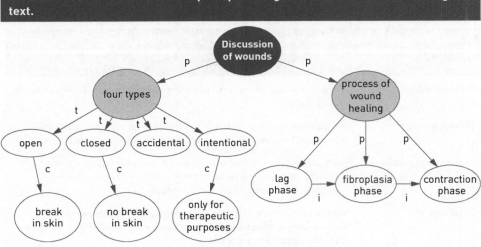

Source: "Evaluation of a hierarchical mapping technique as an aid to prose processing," by C. D. Holley et al., 1979, *Contemporary Educational Psychology*, 4, 227–237. https://doi.org/10.1016/0361-476X(79)90043-2. Copyright 1979 by Academic Press, Inc.

The effectiveness of concept maps has been extensively investigated at Texas Christian University. In a study described by Holley and Dansereau (1984), students received training on

---

concept maps An instructional procedure based on semantic networks

constructing concept maps for material in their regular courses. These students and a control group of students then studied and were later tested on a 3000-word passage from a basic science textbook. Students who constructed concept maps of this material did significantly better than the control group on short-answer and essay questions but did not do significantly better on multiple-choice questions.

This finding is consistent with the results mentioned at the end of Chapter 7 on transfer-appropriate processing. As you may recall, students who expected open questions did better on these questions than students who expected multiple-choice questions. Students who expected open questions apparently placed more emphasis on organizing their knowledge. Subsequent research on concept maps formed the basis for the following guidelines (O'Donnell et al., 2002):

1. Begin with content that is extremely familiar to students so that they do not need to search for appropriate information.

2. Use a number of well-constructed networks as initial examples.

3. Include a discussion of the different types of links and the nature of the relationships among ideas.

4. Ensure that students can recognize the corresponding relationships between information in the text and information in the networks.

A meta-analysis of research on concept maps produced a statistically significant beneficial effect when compared to alternative instructional approaches (Schroeder et al., 2018). Learning with concept maps was more effective than learning through discussions and was moderately more effective than studying outlines or lists. It was also more effective than constructing and studying texts. Concept maps were effective across a wide variety of domains and at all levels (intermediate, secondary, post-secondary) of instruction. These benefits occurred for both constructing and for studying provided concept maps, although students did better when they constructed their own maps.

Semantic Organization in AI

You have likely on many occasions depended on a computer to retrieve information or answer questions (Photo 10.5). Computers share with people the necessity of requiring effective organization of semantic knowledge to retrieve useful information (Reed & Pease, 2015). Experts in AI are kept busy designing algorithms that provide this organization.

Computer ontologies are hierarchical organizations of knowledge that are more extensive than the hierarchies created by psychologists. For instance, the Suggested Upper Merged Ontology (SUMO), is a general ontology consisting of 20,000 concepts with definitions in both English and formal logic (Niles & Pease, 2001; Pease, 2011). It covers a broad range of topics at a high level of generality by partitioning all knowledge into a large hierarchy. SUMO begins by partitioning the top entry *Entity* into *Physical* and *Abstract*—a distinction made in previous chapters.

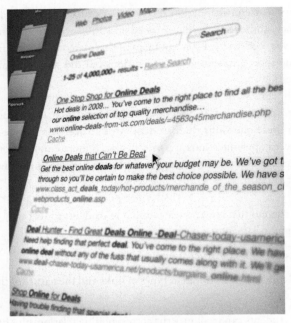

PHOTO 10.5 AI algorithms based on ontologies support computer searches.

istockphoto.com/SpiffyJ

Figure 10.15 shows the hierarchical organization of a few of SUMO's concepts in which the indentions depict levels in the hierarchy. A *Physical* entity is partitioned into *Object* and *Process*. An *Object* is a physical thing like a chair or a glass of water. A *Process* is an action that occurs over time like a lecture. The partitioning of *Process* in Figure 10.15 shows finer divisions within the hierarchy. A *Psychological Process* is one type of *Process* that includes *Perception. Seeing* and *Hearing* are subclasses of *Perception. Looking* is an intentional act of *Seeing*, and *Listening* is an intentional act of *Hearing*. When you drive you *see* many objects in front of your but should *look* at the ones that assure safe driving. When you attend a lecture you *hear* noises in the room but should try to ignore them in order to *listen* to the lecture.

FIGURE 10.15 ■ Part of the suggested upper merged ontology.
Physical Entities
Object
Process
Psychological Process
Perception
Seeing
Looking
Hearing
Listening

Source: Based on *Ontology: A practical guide*, by A. Pease, 2011, Angwin, CA: Articulate Software Press.

Ontologies share the characteristic of the hierarchical network model that categories lower in the hierarchy inherit properties from categories higher in the hierarchy. Consider the question "Is vision used in looking?" The answer to the query is "yes" because vision is included in the definition of *Seeing,* and *Looking* is a special case (subclass) of *Seeing.* These answers are derived from the formal logic that supports reasoning.

The AI concept of "frames" is analogous to the psychological construct of scripts. Frames have a different structure than ontologies because they capture co-occurrence and thematic relations among linguistic concepts rather than their taxonomic relations. The Berkeley FrameNet project provides a useful tool for representing this type of knowledge. Fillmore and Baker (2010) define frames as organized packages of knowledge that enable people to perceive, remember, and reason about their experiences. Examples include event schemas such as going to a hospital. The basic assumption is that words require a link to background frames in order to understand their meaning. FrameNet provides a tool for representing their context.

Many frames in FrameNet, such as for the word *remembering*, are relevant to cognition. The FrameNet distinction between *Remembering_experience* and *Remembering_information* captures the cognitive distinction between remembering personal experiences in episodic memory and remembering facts in semantic memory. Frames consist of core frame elements—the most essential components—and less essential non-core frame elements. Core frame elements in a person's Remembering_experience frame are the person, experience, impression, and saliency. Non-core frame elements are context, duration, manner, time, and vividness. Ontologies and frames support retrieval and reasoning in computers that parallels and aids retrieval and reasoning in humans. We will examine how context influences the interpretations of words in the next chapter on language.

SUMMARY

The hierarchical organization of categories influences the amount of time it takes to verify sentences about the members of categories. It usually takes less time to verify category membership at the basic level than at the superordinate level. For example, it is easier to verify that a canary is a bird than that a canary is an animal. The hierarchical network model also predicts that the time it takes to verify a property of an object will depend on the level in the hierarchy where the property is stored. In contrast, the feature comparison model assumes that statements are verified by using features to compute the similarity of two concepts. When there is an intermediate amount of similarity, people must evaluate only the most necessary, or defining, features of the category. The spreading activation model was proposed to correct some limitations of the hierarchical network model. Its main assumption is that activation of a concept results in activation of related concepts as activation spreads along the paths of the network.

In contrast to the previous models, the perceptual symbols model assumes that verification of semantic statements occurs through mental simulations. Support for the model comes from findings that the time to judge whether two words are associated is faster if their vertical alignment is consistent with an image, and the time to verify properties is faster if two successive properties come from the same modality. Support also comes from brain imaging techniques that reveal autobiographical memory contains both modal and amodal representations. A neural network model successfully integrates physical and abstract words by combining the sensorimotor properties of concrete words and their co-occurrence with abstract words.

The integration of knowledge into larger clusters is the primary assumption of schema theory. Emphasis on schematic structures began with the work of Bartlett and Piaget and started to have a major impact on cognitive science in the mid-1970s. In contrast to stimulus-response associations, schematic structures are molar, nonassociationistic, generic, and active. They provide a skeleton structure that can be filled out with the detailed properties of a particular instance, using default knowledge when information is missing. Scripts are one type of schema, consisting of sequences of events that make up routine activities. The temporal order of the events is useful for organizing recall, but the centrality of events determines how quickly people can access the script.

Semantic organization has many practical applications that differ widely in their influence on people's lives. Spreading activation occasionally has a negative impact by triggering false memories that are harmful for people who are distressed or have post-traumatic stress disorder. Semantic networks also make a positive contribution when turned into concept maps to help students organize ideas presented in the classroom. Another positive contribution is the application of theories of semantic organization to build computer tools that assist us in retrieving information from computers and reasoning from that information.

RECOMMENDED READING

Chi and Ohsson (2005) show how the growth and organization of knowledge can be represented in semantic networks. Hutchison (2003) provides a detailed critique of alternative models of semantic priming. Dove (2016) argues that amodal symbols enable us to acquire semantic content that goes beyond perceptual experience. Alternative models for integrating conceptual knowledge within and across modalities are investigated by McNorgan et al. (2011). Danker and Anderson (2010) review extensive support for reactivation of brain areas during retrieval but argue that reactivation does not always involve modality-specific areas of the brain. The temporal organization of event memory is positively associated with the richness of episodic detail (Diamond & Levine, 2020). Fivush (2011) reviews the development of autobiographical memory. Brainerd et al. (2008) evaluate theoretical accounts of developmental reversals in false memory. Not all traumatic memories are false, and trauma survivors occasionally intentionally recall these memories (Bellet et al., 2020). Computer science programs such as WordNet, FrameNet, and SUMO provide tools for organizing semantic information (Reed & Pease, 2015).

Getty Images/ Klaus Vedfelt

11 LANGUAGE

Three Aspects of Language
  Grammar (Forming Phrases)
  Meaning (Combining Words and Morphemes)
  Sound (Producing Phonemes)

Hierarchical Organization of Language
  Speech Errors
  Predicting While Comprehending Language
  Temporal Stages

Text Comprehension
  Local Coherence
  Influence of Context
  Global Coherence
  Memory for Text

Kintsch's Model of Text Comprehension
  Processing Assumptions
  The Construction-Integration Model
  Incorporating Prior Knowledge

Applications
  Comprehension Strategies and Assessment
  Persuasive Communications

SUMMARY

RECOMMENDED READING

LEARNING OBJECTIVES

1. Describe the distinction between phonemes and morphemes.

2. Discuss how speech errors, prediction, and temporal stages support the hierarchical organization of language.

3. Contrast local and global coherence.

4. Describe the role of short-term memory and the construction-integration and situation models in Kintsch's model of text comprehension.

5. Apply research findings to design a persuasive communication.

We are now entering Part 3 of this book. Part 1 was about the components of cognitive architecture—the perception (pattern recognition and attention), working memory, declarative long-term memory, procedural long-term memory, and motor components. Part 2 was about the representation (memory codes, images) and organization (categorization, semantic organization) of knowledge. Part 3 is about cognitive skills—language, decision making, problem-solving, and creativity. The previous chapters provide the foundation for building these cognitive skills.

The discussion of semantic organization in the previous chapter emphasized associations among words. We are now ready to consider how words can be combined to form sentences. One possible theory is that this combination occurs by associations. One could argue that, just as *robin* is associated with *bird*, the words in a sentence can be associated with each other. The problem with this view of language is that there are so many ways words can be combined that we would have to learn an infinite number of associations to form sentences. An alternative theory is that we learn grammar—a system of rules capable of producing sentences. Ideally, the rules of grammar should generate all the sentences of a language without generating any strings of words that are not sentences (Chomsky, 1957).

This brings us to a definition of language. A language is a collection of symbols and rules for combining these symbols, which can be used to create an infinite variety of messages. This definition has three critical aspects. First, language is symbolic: We use spoken sounds and written words to represent and communicate about the world around us. The symbols are arbitrary—there is no built-in relation between the look or sound of the words and the objects they represent. Second, language is generative: A limited number of words can be combined in an endless variety of ways to generate an infinite number of sentences. Third, language is structured: By following grammatical rules, we can produce grammatical sentences.

Our goal as communicators is to express meaning as sound, but this does not occur in a single step. Instead, we use an assembly line metaphor for constructing sentences from the modules shown in Figure 11.1 (Pinker, 1999). Notice that the speaker, represented at the bottom of the diagram, has beliefs and desires that she wishes to express through language. The listener, represented at the top of the diagram, listens to the sound patterns to understand the speaker. But for this to occur correctly, both the speaker and listener must be skilled at using the five modules shown in Figure 11.1. How we accomplish this is the topic of this chapter.

Let's begin with a specific example, shown in Figure 11.2. You have already learned in the previous two chapters about the usefulness of hierarchies, so it may not surprise you that language is hierarchical. At the top of the hierarchy is a sentence that can be broken down into phrases based on grammatical rules. The grammatical rules partition the sentence into a *noun phrase* ("The strangers") and a *verb phrase* ("talked to the players"). The phrases are composed of words, which can be partitioned into morphemes—the smallest units of meaning in a language. For spoken sentences, the morphemes can be further partitioned into phonemes—the basic sounds of a language.

---

grammar A set of rules for producing correct sentences in a language

language A collection of symbols and rules for combining symbols, which can express an infinite variety of messages

symbolic The use of symbols, such as spoken or written words, to represent ideas

generative The capability to produce many different messages by combining symbols in different ways

structured The organization imposed on a language by its grammatical rules

morphemes The smallest unit of meaning in a language

phonemes The basic sounds of a language

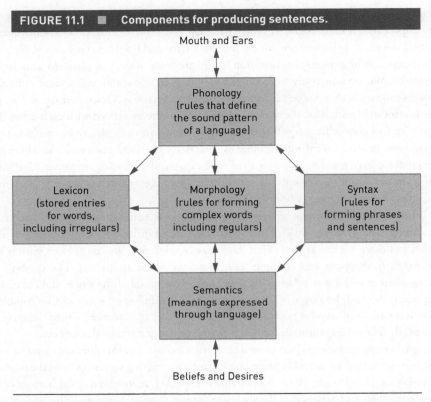

FIGURE 11.1 ■ **Components for producing sentences.**

Source: *Words and rules: The ingredients of language*, by S. Pinker, p. 23. Copyright 1999 by Steven Pinker. Used by permission.

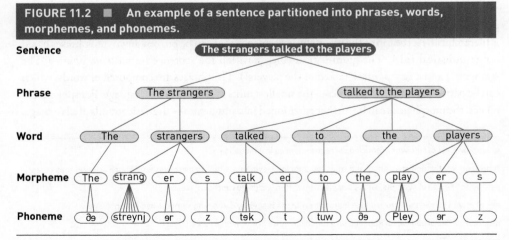

FIGURE 11.2 ■ **An example of a sentence partitioned into phrases, words, morphemes, and phonemes.**

Source: *Child development: A topical approach*, by A. Clarke-Stewart, S. Friedman, & J. Koch, p. 417. Copyright 1985 by John Wiley & Sons. Reprinted by permission of John Wiley & Sons, Inc.

The next section provides a brief overview of these three aspects of comprehending and producing sentences: grammar, meaning, and sound.

THREE ASPECTS OF LANGUAGE

Grammar (Forming Phrases)

One important influence on the development of cognitive psychology during the 1960s was the work of linguist Noam Chomsky. Prior to Chomsky's influence on psycholinguistics (the psychological study of language), psychologists had explored the possibility that people could learn a language by learning the associations between adjacent words in a sentence. According to this view, we learn to speak correctly through paired-associates learning—each word in a sentence serves as a stimulus for the word that follows it. In the sentence "The boy hit the ball," the word *the* is a stimulus for the word *boy*, and the word *boy* is a stimulus for the word *hit*. The speaker of a language would therefore have to learn which words could follow any other word in a sentence.

Chomsky (1957) argued that there are several problems with the association view of language. First of all, there are an infinite number of sentences in a language. It is therefore unreasonable to expect that people could learn a language by learning associations between all adjacent words. Consider simply a word like *the*. There are many, many words that could follow *the*, and a person might never learn all of them. When you consider all the possible words that can occur in a sentence and all the words that could possibly follow each word, you can see how this would be a very inefficient way to learn a language. Another problem with the association view is that it does not account for the relations among nonadjacent words. For example, in the sentence "Anyone who says that is lying," the pronoun *anyone* is grammatically related to the verb *is lying*, but this relation is not revealed if we consider only the relation between adjacent words. Chomsky argued that the association view ignores the hierarchical structure of sentences (Photo 11.1).

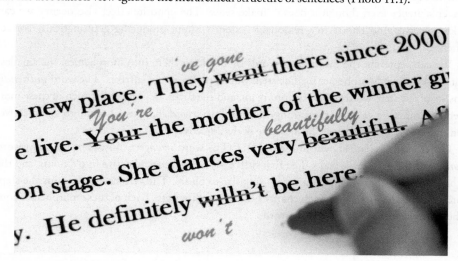

PHOTO 11.1 Language requires constructing grammatically correct phrases.
istockphotos.com/Lamaip

The hierarchy is revealed in the diagrams that you might have constructed in school. We could divide the sentence in Figure 11.2 into a noun phrase and a verb phrase. We could further subdivide the verb phrase "talked to the players" into the verb *talked* and the prepositional phrase *to the players*. The rules we use to divide a sentence into its grammatical parts form a phrase-structure grammar because they reveal how we can partition a sentence into phrases consisting of groups of words.

Chomsky (1957) argued that one limitation of a phrase-structure grammar is that it does not reveal how a sentence can be modified to form a similar sentence, such as changing an active statement into a passive statement. Consider the transformation of "The boy hit the ball" into "The ball was hit by the boy." The transformation rule in this case is

$$\text{NP1} + \text{Verb} + \text{NP2} \rightarrow \text{NP2} + was + \text{Verb} + by + \text{NP1}$$

The transformation changes the position of the two noun phrases (NP1, NP2) and inserts additional words into the passive sentence. The passive sentence begins with the second noun phrase ("the ball") and ends with the first noun phrase ("the boy"). It is also necessary to add the words *was* and *by*. Notice that the transformation rule shows how a phrase-structure description of a passive sentence can be formed from a phrase-structure description of an active sentence. The transformational grammar proposed by Chomsky in 1957 was an advance over a phrase-structure grammar because, in addition to revealing grammatical structure, it showed how sentences could be transformed.

Meaning (Combining Words and Morphemes)

A sentence that is grammatically correct isn't necessarily meaningful. Chomsky's famous example is the sentence "Colorless green ideas sleep furiously." Notice that this is a grammatically correct sentence even though it doesn't make sense. The opposite effect also occurs; we can make ourselves understood to a reasonable extent without producing grammatically correct sentences.

We can represent the meaning of words by breaking them into morphemes, the smallest units of meaning. Morphemes include stem words, prefixes, and suffixes. The word *unfriendly* consists of the stem word *friend*, the prefix *un*, and the suffix *ly*. Notice that each of these morphemes produces a change in meaning. Adding *ly* to *friend* changes a noun into an adjective. Adding *un* to *friendly* changes the meaning of the adjective.

Other examples are shown in Figure 11.2. The word *strangers* consists of the stem word *strange* and the suffixes *er* and *s*. The first suffix (*er*) converts an adjective into a noun, and the second suffix (*s*) changes the noun from singular to plural. The verb *talked* contains the stem word *talk* and the suffix *ed*, which changes the tense of the verb. Each of these morphemes contributes to the meaning of the entire word.

---

phrase-structure grammar A set of rules for partitioning a sentence into its grammatical units

transformational grammar A set of rules for transforming a sentence into a closely related sentence

One advantage of morphemes is that they allow us to generate novel words. A young child who did not know the plural of *stranger* but knew that plurals are often formed by adding an *s* to the end of a noun could generate the word *strangers*. If she did not know the past tense of *talk* but knew that the past tense is often formed by adding *ed* to the end of a verb, she could generate the word *talked*. These rules do not always work (the plural of *deer* is not *deers* and the past tense of *speak* is not *speaked*), but children eventually learn the exceptions (Pinker, 1999).

Sound (Producing Phonemes)

A first step toward producing the basic sounds (phonemes) of a language is the ability to discriminate among them. This ability is excellent in most newborns (Kuhl, 1993), as discussed in Chapter 9 on categorization. There are approximately 44 phonemes in the English language determined by the 26 letters of the alphabet. For instance, the letter *e* has two pronunciations: the long-*e* sound in *beet* and the short-*e* sound in *bet*. The letter *a* is pronounced differently in the words *father, had, call,* and *take*. Each pronunciation is represented by a different phoneme. It is also possible for two letters to combine to form a phoneme; for example, *ch* and *th*.

The correct production of sounds occasionally requires the assistance of speech therapists (Photo 11.2). There are numerous interventions for children with speech/sound disorders that range from those with relatively few mispronunciations to those with severe unintelligibility (Baker et al., 2018). The authors developed the Phonological Intervention Taxonomy to classify this instruction. At the top of their hierarchical classification are four categories that identify the goal of the intervention (such as phonological awareness and segment production), the instructional approach (spoken, visual, tactile, gestural), the context (natural or structured activities), and procedures (session frequency and duration). The purpose of the extensive taxonomy is to increase the transparency of interventions to support clinical training and research.

PHOTO 11.2 A speech therapist teaches the correct pronunciation of phonemes.

istockphotos.com/FatCamera

Although a language consists of both written and spoken words, written words are typically converted into spoken words through subvocalization. Researchers agree that reading instruction needs to incorporate both meaning and phonology, but many believe that phonics should be taught before meaning-based strategies. Systematic phonics explicitly teaches children the correspondence between letters and phonemes before emphasizing the meaning of written words. In contrast, whole language instruction emphasizes meaningful reading and teaches phonics incidentally when needed. Bowers (2020) concluded, following a meta-analysis of this research, that the "reading wars" between systematic phonics and whole language instruction is best characterized as a draw.

The coordination of the multiple processes involved in normal reading is also apparent in the diagnosis and treatment of impaired reading (dyslexia). Children begin reading with large differences in vocabulary, phonology, and orthographic skills for translating letters into sounds (Ziegler et al., 2020). Research has shown that there is not a single developmental trajectory for the development of dyslexia, so it is necessary to identify a specific set of deficits for each child. Such a personalized approach should play a critical role in the early detection of dyslexia and in the development of appropriate interventions (Ziegler et al., 2020).

HIERARCHICAL ORGANIZATION OF LANGUAGE

Speech Errors

The hierarchical diagram shown in Figure 11.2 is a convenient representation of the components in Figure 11.1, but is there evidence that people follow this hierarchical organization when producing sentences? The evidence comes from speech errors. Children and even adults make errors when speaking. These speech errors, or slips of the tongue, are unintended deviations from a speech plan (Dell, 1986).

The usefulness of the hierarchical organization shown in Figure 11.2 for representing speech errors is that the errors typically occur within but not across levels in the hierarchy (Dell, 1986). Errors can therefore be divided into *word errors, morpheme errors*, and *phoneme errors*, depending on the size of the linguistic unit involved in the error. The occurrence of errors within these linguistic units is most easily seen in exchange errors, in which two linguistic units are substituted for each other in the sentence.

Word exchanges are illustrated by the speaker saying "writing a mother to my letter" rather than "writing a letter to my mother." The exchanged words are typically members of the same syntactic category, demonstrating the constraints of grammar on speech. In this case, both *mother* and *letter* are nouns.

Morpheme exchanges are illustrated by the speaker saying "slicely thinned" rather than "thinly sliced." Morpheme errors also have categorical constraints; in this case, the two stems

---

exchange error An error in which two linguistic units are substituted for each other during sentence production

word exchange An error in which two words are substituted for each other during sentence production

morpheme exchange An error in which two morphemes are substituted for each other during sentence production *slice* and *thin* are interchanged while the suffixes *ly* and *ed* remain in their original position. Just as nouns are interchanged with other nouns or verbs interchanged with other verbs at the word level, stems are interchanged with other stems or suffixes interchanged with other suffixes at the morpheme level.

Phoneme exchanges are illustrated by the speaker saying "lork yibrary" for "York library." Once again, there are category constraints on the exchanges. In phoneme errors, initial consonants are exchanged with other initial consonants, final consonants are exchanged with other final consonants, and vowels are exchanged with other vowels. All of these examples illustrate how errors occur within the same level of the hierarchy (Dell, 1986).

Predicting While Comprehending Language

Listening to a speaker requires different skills than being a speaker, but there is substantial overlap according to the **prediction-by-production** theory (Pickering & Gambi, 2018). The theory proposes that listeners occasionally predict what speakers will say based on what they would say at that point in the conversation. Although very few words are highly predictable, many words are moderately predictable. In addition, language involves grammar, meaning, and sounds. One or more of these aspects may be predictable even when the word is not.

For instance, the meaning of words provides clues about grammatical structure (Carpenter et al., 1995; MacDonald et al., 1994; Trueswell & Tanenhaus, 1994). We use the distinction between animate and inanimate nouns to make guesses about the type of phrase that will follow the noun. This is illustrated by the difference between the following two sentences:

1. The defendant examined by the lawyer turned out to be unreliable.

2. The evidence examined by the lawyer turned out to be unreliable.

Eye movements indicate that readers slow down more in the first sentence than in the second sentence when they encounter the phrase *by the lawyer* (Trueswell & Tanenhaus, 1994). In the first sentence, readers expect the word *examined* to be the main verb followed by a noun phrase, such as in the sentence "The defendant examined the jury." However, when they read *by the lawyer*, reading slows because their expectation turns out to be incorrect. But if the sentence begins with the inanimate noun *evidence*, our expectation that *examine* is the main verb becomes unlikely because we can't imagine how evidence can examine something.

Another example is the sentence "The boy went out to the park to fly a kite." Although listeners may not be able to predict the word *fly*, they can be fairly certain from the sentence that the next word will be a verb. The noun *kite* is more predictable because it has to be an object that can fly (Photo 11.3). Listeners who correctly predict the word *kite* should find it easier to process the word *kite* than listeners who incorrectly predict the word *airplane* (Pickering & Gambi, 2018).

---

phoneme exchange An error in which two phonemes are substituted for each other during sentence production

prediction-by-production Predicting what a speaker will say based on the listener's productions

PHOTO 11.3 Sentence phrases and context support predictions.

istockphoto.com/FatCamera

Nonlinguistic information is also helpful in predicting what the speaker will say (Pickering & Gambi, 2018). Conversations often take place within a physical context that provides shared visual information. If the conversation is occurring in a park in which children are flying kites, the prediction should be fairly easy. Shared background knowledge between the listener and the speaker is also a very helpful source of nonlinguistic information. In some cases, shared background knowledge may enable the listener to literally complete the sentences of the speaker.

Pickering and Gambi (2018) propose that prediction-by-production supports comprehension but is not necessary for understanding the speaker. The drawback is that it requires time and cognitive resources to predict what the speaker will say. For this reason, it is less likely to be used by children, older adults, and non-native speakers.

Temporal Stages

Conversing with a friend and reading a book are excellent examples of cognitive activities that require online processing. The study of online processing replaces the question "How is information stored and then retrieved for later processing?" with the question "How does prior information continuously shape processing in the present moment?" (Hasson et al., 2015). The authors propose that answering the latter question requires a theory based on **process memory**, in which active traces of past information are used by neural circuits to process incoming information in the present moment. Process memory contributes to real-world cognition and

---

process memory A memory that maintains active traces of past information to process incoming information in the present moment

perception whenever information demands continuous integration rather than maintenance over delays. The authors pose many unanswered questions about how process memory works but they provide a starting point.

Figure 11.3A shows their process memory hierarchy (Hasson et al., 2015). Notice that the diagram extends the hierarchy in Figure 11.2 to include paragraphs and an entire narrative. These larger units of analysis are needed for theories of text comprehension.

FIGURE 11.3 ■ Components for understanding sentences.

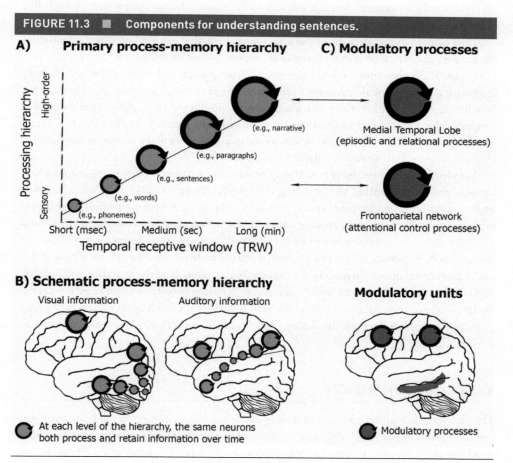

Source: "Hierarchical process memory: Memory as an integral component of information processing," by U. Hasson, J. Chen, & C. J. Honey, 2015, *Trends in Cognitive Sciences, 19*, 304–313. https://doi.org/10.1016/j.tics.2015.04.006

The temporal receptive window is a key variable in the memory framework. It is the window of time in which prior information from an ongoing stimulus can affect the processing of newly arriving information. The early stages have short temporal windows of a fraction of a

---

temporal receptive window The window of time in which prior information from an ongoing stimulus can affect the processing of newly arriving information

second, enabling them to integrate phonemes into a word. Other stages have medium temporal windows of several seconds, enabling the integration of sequences of words into sentences. Still, other areas have long temporal windows that are necessary to integrate sentences over time while comprehending narratives.

Differences were confirmed in a study that demonstrated the sensory information used to identify ambiguous phonemes has a relativity short temporal window (Caplan et al. 2021). For example, ambiguity occurs when it is difficult to determine whether the phoneme sounds like a *d* in *dime* or a *t* in *time*. Listeners were able to resolve ambiguities when a clarifying context occurred before but not after the ambiguous sound. Listening involved no direct retention of the acoustic-phonetic information that would support delayed identification.

Figure 11.3B illustrates the brain regions that both process and retain visual and auditory information. The occipital lobe plays a predominant role in visual processing and the temporal lobe plays a predominant role in auditory processing. Figure 11.3C shows that the medial temporal lobe manages and retains the narrative in episodic memory (as discussed in Chapter 5 on long-term memory). It also shows that modulatory processes in the frontoparietal network control attention (as discussed in Chapter 3 on attention).

We previously learned about modulatory processes in Chapter 4 on working memory that include inhibition, shifting, and updating (Miyake & Friedman, 2012). Updating supports readers' comprehension by maintaining relevant information in working memory; inhibition supports comprehension by suppressing irrelevant text information from entering memory; and shifting supports comprehension by flexibly allocating attention to different aspects of the text (Butterfuss & Kendrou, 2018). The authors' literature review revealed evidence for the major role of executive functions in reading comprehension, particularly in the activation and suppression of information. Prominent models of reading comprehension have nonetheless not explicitly included executive functions. There is a need to include these functions to help explain the complex interactions between the reader, the text, and the discourse situation (Butterfuss & Kendeou, 2018).

TEXT COMPREHENSION

The final stage in Figure 11.3 is understanding narratives. A large component of research on text comprehension is concerned with reading stories that describe a sequence of events. To understand the story, we need to organize information at two levels (Graesser et al., 1994). At one level, we need to establish a global coherence about the main events that occur throughout the story. We need to keep track of what is happening to the major characters (Albrecht & O'Brien, 1993) and to the events related to achieving goals (Dopkins et al., 1993). At a more detailed level, we need to establish a local coherence about the most recent events in the story. We need to integrate the ideas that we are reading with the ideas that immediately preceded those ideas.

---

global coherence Integration of major ideas that occur throughout a text

local coherence Integration of ideas within an immediate context in a text

We begin by looking at how readers integrate the details of a story to establish local coherence. We then see the important role that goals play in organizing the major events in a story to establish global coherence. Causal relations provide a means of organizing events around these goals.

Local Coherence

Understanding local coherence will be easier if we first consider Carpenter and Daneman's (1981) general model of the stages involved in sentence comprehension. The first stage in Figure 11.4 (fixate and encode the next word) involves pattern recognition. We learned in Chapter 2 on pattern recognition that a letter is easier to recognize in the context of a word than when it appears by itself. Similarly, a word is often easier to recognize in the context of a sentence.

You may have experienced difficulty in recognizing a word when reading illegible hand-writing and had to rely on the surrounding words and sentences to help you identify the word. An example of how context can influence word recognition is shown in Figure 11.5. The two sentences contain a physically identical word, yet we have little difficulty identifying the word as *went* in the upper sentence and as *event* in the lower sentence.

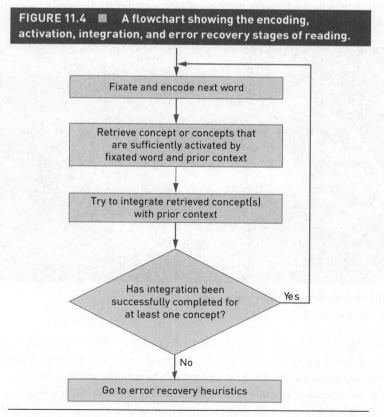

FIGURE 11.4 ■ A flowchart showing the encoding, activation, integration, and error recovery stages of reading.

Source: "Lexical retrieval and error recovery in reading: A model based on eye fixations," by P. A. Carpenter & M. Daneman, 1981, *Journal of Verbal Learning and Verbal Behavior*, 20, 137–160. https://doi.org/10.1016/S0022-5371(81)90357-1. Copyright 1981 by Academic Press, Inc.

FIGURE 11.5 ■ Dependence of letter perception on context.

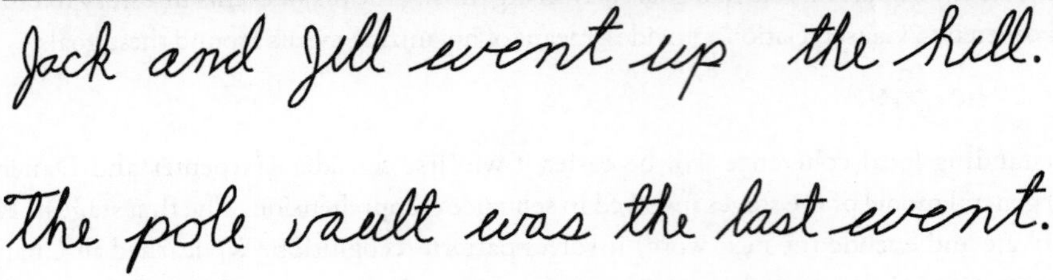

Jack and Jill event up the hill.

The pole vault was the last event.

Source: "The role of semantics in speech understanding," by B. Nash-Webber, 1975, in *Representation and understanding,* edited by D. G. Bobrow & A. Collins. https://doi.org/10.1016/B978-0-12-108550-6.50017-3. Copyright 1975 by Academic Press.

The second stage in Figure 11.4 involves retrieving the meaning of the word. Although some words have multiple meanings (Photo 11.4), one meaning may occur more frequently than the others. For the sentence "The port was a great success," you most likely associated the word *port* with ships. The less frequent meaning of *port,* a kind of drink, would be less strongly activated unless it was preceded by a context that suggested this interpretation.

PHOTO 11.4 Some words have more than one meaning.

Photo by Ross Findon on Unsplash

Both meanings would be strongly activated in the sentence "When she finally served it to her guests, the port was a great success." The ship meaning would be strongly activated because it occurs more frequently, and the drink meaning would be strongly activated because it fits the context. By studying readers' eye movements while reading sentences with ambiguous words, Duffy et al. (1988) concluded that the degree of activation of alternative meanings is influenced by prior context and by the frequency of the alternative meanings.

The selected meaning of the word is integrated with the prior context in the third stage of Carpenter and Daneman's (1981) model. If this integration is successful, the reader encodes the next word; otherwise, he or she tries to recover from the error by reinterpreting the word or the previous context.

Influence of Context

Let's now look in greater detail at how context influences the selection of a word's meaning. The reason many potentially ambiguous words do not seem ambiguous is that the intended meaning is usually clear from the preceding sentences. We might therefore expect that a clarifying context should make it as easy to comprehend ambiguous sentences as unambiguous sentences. An experiment by Swinney and Hakes (1976) supports this hypothesis.

The subjects in their experiment performed two tasks simultaneously while they listened to pairs of sentences. One task asked them to judge how closely they felt the two sentences of each pair were related. This task required comprehension of the sentences. The second task required that they press a button as soon as they heard a word beginning with a specified sound (phoneme). The rationale of this experiment is that people should be slower in responding to the phoneme whenever they are having difficulty comprehending the sentence. The following pair of sentences is a typical example:

> *Rumor had it that, for years, the government building had been plagued with problems. The man was not surprised when he found several "bugs" in the corner of his room.* (Swinney & Hakes, 1976, p. 686)

The target phoneme in this example occurs at the beginning of the word *corner*, shortly after the ambiguous word *bugs*. To determine whether the ambiguous word would delay comprehension and therefore detection of the phoneme, Swinney and Hakes compared performance on the ambiguous sentences with performance on unambiguous control sentences. The unambiguous version of the example contained the word *insects* in place of the word *bugs*. Swinney and Hakes found that subjects took significantly more time to detect the phoneme when it followed an ambiguous word than when it followed an unambiguous word.

However, sometimes the ambiguous word occurred in a context that made it clear which meaning of the word was intended:

> *Rumor had it that, for years, the government building had been plagued with problems. The man was not surprised when he found several spiders, roaches, and other "bugs" in the corner of his room.* (Swinney & Hakes, 1976, p. 686)

When the context clarified the meaning of the ambiguous word, people could comprehend the ambiguous word *bug* as quickly as they could comprehend the unambiguous word *insect*. There was no longer any difference in response times to the target phoneme.

We could interpret these results by arguing that only a single meaning of the ambiguous word is activated when the context indicates the intended meaning. This argument has considerable intuitive appeal, but research results suggest that it is wrong. In the previous chapter, we saw that when people are asked to decide whether a string of letters is a word, their decision is faster when a word is preceded by a semantically related word, such as *bread* preceded by *butter*. If people consider only a single meaning of an ambiguous word, a word such as *bug* should facilitate the recognition of either *ant* or *spy*, depending on which meaning is activated.

Swinney (1979) tested this prediction by replacing the phoneme monitoring task with a lexical decision task. He explained to the subjects that a string of letters would appear on a screen as they listened to some sentences, and they were to decide as quickly as possible whether or not each letter string formed a word. He did not mention that some of the sentences and words were related. The letter string, which appeared on the screen immediately after subjects heard the ambiguous word, was contextually appropriate, contextually inappropriate, or unrelated to the meaning of the ambiguous word. A contextually appropriate word appearing on the screen, such as *ant*, was consistent with the meaning of the ambiguous word that was suggested by the context. A contextually inappropriate word, such as *spy*, was consistent with the meaning that was not suggested by the context. An unrelated word, such as *sew*, was consistent with neither of the two meanings.

If the context causes the activation of only a single meaning, it should be easier to recognize only the contextually appropriate word (*ant*). But if both meanings of the ambiguous word are activated, the contextually inappropriate word (*spy*) should also be easier to recognize than the unrelated word (*sew*). The results showed that when the visual test word immediately followed the ambiguous word, both the contextually appropriate and the contextually inappropriate words were easier to recognize than the unrelated words. But when the test word occurred four syllables (approximately 750–1000 msec) after the ambiguous word, recognition of only the contextually appropriate word was facilitated (Figure 11.6).

Swinney's findings suggest that more than one meaning of an ambiguous word is activated, even when a prior context indicates which meaning is appropriate. If only one meaning of *bugs* were activated by the phrase "He found several spiders, roaches, and other bugs," it is not clear why it would be as easy to respond to *spy* as to *ant*. However, when the test word occurred four syllables after the ambiguous word, recognition of only the word *ant* was facilitated. It appears that, although both meanings of an ambiguous word are momentarily activated, the context allows the listener to select the appropriate meaning quickly. Selection of the appropriate meaning occurred quickly enough to prevent interference in the phoneme-detection task. As you may recall, there was a slight delay between the ambiguous word and the target phoneme. This was sufficient time to resolve the ambiguity when there was an appropriate context. An appropriate context therefore seems to allow the listener to select the appropriate meaning of a word quickly rather than to prevent more than one meaning from being activated.

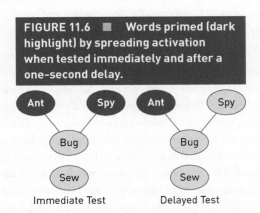

FIGURE 11.6 ■ **Words primed (dark highlight) by spreading activation when tested immediately and after a one-second delay.**

Immediate Test   Delayed Test

It would be simpler for everyone if only a single meaning (the correct one, of course) were initially activated. Although this might seem beneficial when the correct meaning is obvious, an advantage of activating multiple meanings is that the clarifying context occasionally does not occur until *after* the ambiguous word. In this case, it would be advantageous to try to keep both meanings active in short-term memory (STM) until we gain enough information to select the appropriate one.

See whether you can find the ambiguous word in the following partial sentence: "Since Ken really liked the boxer, he took a bus to the nearest . . ." If you found the ambiguous word, can you resolve the ambiguity by using the sentence context? The ambiguous word is *boxer*, and at this point, we don't have enough information to know whether Ken is interested in a fighter or a dog. The remainder of the sentence resolves the ambiguity by informing us that Ken took the bus to the nearest pet store to buy the animal. Notice, however, that unlike the previous examples in which the clarifying context preceded the ambiguous word, in this case, we had to read considerably more of the sentence following the ambiguous word before the meaning became clear (Miyake et al., 1994). Those readers who incorrectly interpreted the word *boxer* to be a fighter would need to engage in the error recovery heuristic in Figure 11.4 by reinterpreting the meaning to fit the context.

Global Coherence

A characteristic of simple narrative stories is that the structure determines how the events in the story are organized. We can study this structure at a very general level by representing a story as consisting of a setting, a theme, a plot, and a resolution (Thorndyke, 1977). The setting describes time, location, and major characters. The theme provides the general focus of the story, often a goal that the main character is trying to achieve. The plot consists of a series of actions the main character takes to try and achieve the goal. Several subgoals or intermediate goals may have to be accomplished before the main goal is reached. The resolution—the final outcome of the story—often describes whether the main character was successful in achieving the goal.

The importance that people place on goals is directly illustrated in a study on scripts. We saw in Chapter 10 that one facet of our organized knowledge is our knowledge of common activities (scripts). Bower et al. (1979) performed one of the first investigations of how people's knowledge of such routine activities helps them understand and remember information in a text. The typical events in a script provide a framework for comprehension but are themselves uninteresting because we already know about them. What is usually interesting is the occurrence of an event that is related to the script but unexpected. For example, a customer might need help translating a menu because it is in French, or the waiter might spill soup on the customer. Schank and Abelson (1977) refer to such events as obstacles because they interrupt the major goals of the script, such as ordering and eating in this case.

error recovery heuristic A strategy for correcting comprehension errors

Bower and his colleagues (1979) hypothesized that such interruptions should be remembered better than routine events. They tested this hypothesis by asking subjects to read six script-based stories about making coffee, attending a lecture, getting up in the morning, attending a movie, visiting a doctor, and dining at a restaurant. After reading all six stories and then completing an intervening task for 10 minutes, subjects attempted to recall the stories in writing. The results supported the predictions—subjects recalled 53% of the interruptions, 38% of the script actions, and 32% of the irrelevant information. The interruptions either prevented or delayed the main character from accomplishing a goal, and this aspect of the story was well remembered.

When a goal is included in a story, people use the goal to help them organize the actions described in the story. A character's attempts to achieve a goal result in the establishment of causal relations among many of the statements in a text. Work by Trabasso and his students at the University of Chicago (Trabasso & Sperry, 1985; Trabasso & van den Broek, 1985) indicated that it is these causal relations that underlie what a reader judges to be important in a text. A formal statement of a **causal relation** is that one event, *A*, is judged to be the cause of another event, *B*, if the absence of *A* implies the absence of *B*. In other words, you cannot accomplish your goal if someone eliminates the events that are necessary for achieving that goal.

An important variable in determining the judged importance of statements in a story is the number of causal connections linked to the statement. For instance, walking into your house has three causal connections (taking out the keys, unlocking the door, and opening the door) while unlocking the door has one causal connection (taking out the keys). Trabasso and Sperry (1985) found that, when subjects rated the importance of events in stories, the judged importance of an action was directly related to the number of causal connections associated with that action. The number of causal connections was also important in determining what people could recall from a story and what they would include in a summary of the story (Trabasso & van den Broek, 1985).

Causal connections also determine how quickly people can verify text information (Myers et al., 1984). These psychologists followed the general procedure used by Reder and Anderson (1980) that required quickly responding whether a test statement had occurred in a story, such as the following:

The banker

decided to see a baseball game.

arrived at the ballpark.

found a crowd buying tickets.

waited in line.*

entered to see his team score.

cheered loudly.*

---

causal relation An event that results in the occurrence of another event

The two test sentences (marked by asterisks) are preceded by causally related statements in the above example. The banker had to wait in line *because* he found a crowd buying tickets, and he cheered loudly *because* his team scored (Photo 11.5). In the control condition, these two causal statements were omitted. Myers' group found that participants were later able to verify test statements more quickly when they also read the causal statements. The causal statements required remembering more information but provided reasons for why actions occurred.

PHOTO 11.5 Scoring a run provides a cause for cheering.

istockphotos.com/adamkaz

Memory for Text

Can you think of reasons why you or others may read or listen to a text and later have difficulty recalling that information? One reason is that the text was difficult to comprehend. If you do not understand the content, you are unlikely to remember much about the content.

The influence of knowledge on the comprehension and recall of ideas was dramatically illustrated in an early study by Bransford and Johnson (1973). They asked people to read a paragraph to try to comprehend and remember it. You can get some feeling for the task by reading the following passage once and then trying to recall as much as you can.

The procedure is actually quite simple. First you arrange things into different groups. Of course, one pile may be sufficient depending on how much there is to do. If you have to go somewhere else due to lack of facilities, that is the next step; otherwise you are pretty well set. It is important not to overdo things. That is, it is better to do too few things at once than too many. In the short run, this may not seem important, but complications can easily arise. A mistake can be expensive as well. At first the whole procedure will seem complicated. Soon, however, it will become just another facet of life. It is difficult to foresee any end to the necessity for this task in the immediate future, but then one never can tell. After the procedure is completed, one arranges the materials into different groups again. Then they can be put into their appropriate places. Eventually, they will be used once more, and the whole cycle will then have to be repeated. However, that is part of life.

The paragraph describes a very familiar procedure, but the ideas are presented so abstractly that the procedure is difficult to recognize. People who read the passage recalled an average of only 2.8 ideas from a maximum of 18. A different group of subjects, who were informed after reading the passage that it referred to washing clothes, didn't do any better; they recalled only 2.7 ideas. But subjects who were told before they read the passage that it described washing clothes recalled 5.8 ideas. Although everyone is familiar with the procedure used to wash clothes, people didn't recognize the procedure because the passage was so abstract. Providing the appropriate context before the passage therefore increased both comprehension and recall.

You may be surprised by the finding that the retrieval cue "washing clothes" was ineffective when given after the passage. We can all think of situations in which a hint helped us remember. However, there has to be information in memory for a retrieval cue to be effective, and that requires comprehension. Another reason people have difficulty retrieving information is that comprehension occurs, but there is too much information to remember. A retrieval cue can be helpful in this situation.

A study by Anderson and Pichert (1978) supports the hypothesis that a shift in perspective can result in the recall of additional ideas. The participants in their study read about two boys who played hooky from school. The entire story contained 72 ideas, which had previously been rated for their importance to a prospective burglar or to a prospective homebuyer. For example, a leaky roof and damp basement would be important to a home buyer, whereas valuable possessions and the fact that no one was usually home on Thursday would be important to a burglar.

The subjects read the story from one of the two perspectives and, after a short delay, were asked to write down as much of the exact story as they could remember. After another short delay, they again attempted to recall ideas from the story. Half did so from the same perspective and half from a different perspective. The experimenters told the subjects in the same perspective condition that the purpose of the study was to determine whether people could remember things they thought they had forgotten if they were given a second chance. Subjects in the new-perspective condition were told that the purpose of the study was to determine whether people could remember things they thought they had forgotten if they were given a new perspective.

The results during the second recall attempt supported the hypothesis that a change in perspective can result in recall of additional information (Photo 11.6). Many subjects reported that the new perspective provided them with a plan for searching memory. For example, someone who shifted to the homebuyer perspective might now remember the leaky roof. In contrast, the group that did not shift perspective recalled slightly less information on its second attempt than on its first attempt.

PHOTO 11.6 Shifting perspectives helped people recall more ideas.

istockphotos.com/kali9

KINTSCH'S MODEL OF TEXT COMPREHENSION

Because comprehension and recall require the integration of ideas in the text, a model of text comprehension requires assumptions about how this integration occurs. A model developed over nearly three decades by Kintsch (1979, 2005) at the University of Colorado has provided the most comprehensive theory of text comprehension. It was constructed from previous research and continues to influence current research, as revealed in the next three sections.

Processing Assumptions

There are two inputs in the model, the reader and the text, both of which are necessary to understand comprehension. The knowledge and goals of the reader influence how the reader determines what is relevant, establishes expectations, and infers facts that are not directly stated in the text. The text itself is represented in the model by propositions. The propositions divide the text into meaningful units, which are then arranged in a network similar to the semantic networks discussed in Chapter 10.

The general characteristics of the model can be illustrated with a simple example (Kintsch, 1979). Consider the following text:

> The Swazi tribe was at war with a neighboring tribe because of a dispute over cattle. Among the warriors were two unmarried men, Kakra and his younger brother Gum. Kakra was killed in a battle. (p. 6)

---

proposition A meaningful idea that typically consists of several words

The model specifies rules for dividing the text into propositions, but we are not concerned with the details of these rules. We consider word groups that correspond approximately to the underlying propositions. Figure 11.7 shows how the first sentence is divided into word groups and how the groups are related in a network. The proposition "was at war with" is the most important proposition, and the others are joined to it. An important parameter in the model is the number of propositions that can be kept active in STM. Because STM is limited in capacity, only a few propositions can be kept active; our example assumes that the capacity limit is three propositions, as indicated by the enclosed propositions in the figure. Propositions describing the plans and goals of the characters are particularly likely to be selected (Fletcher, 1986).

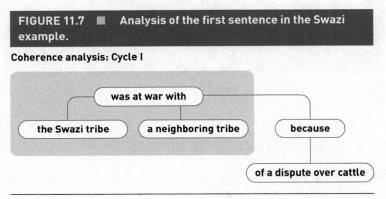

FIGURE 11.7 ■ Analysis of the first sentence in the Swazi example.

Coherence analysis: Cycle I

Source: "On modeling comprehension," by W. Kintsch, 1979, *Educational Psychologist,* *14,* 3–14. https://doi.org/10.1080/00461527909529202. Copyright 1979 by Lawrence Erlbaum Associates, Inc.

Figure 11.8 shows the propositions of the second sentence and the propositions from the first sentence that are still active in STM. The reader first tries to connect the new propositions with the old ones in STM, but the words in the second sentence don't match any of the words in STM. The reader next determines whether the new propositions can be related to any propositions in long-term memory (LTM). Kintsch proposes that the search of LTM, which he calls a reinstatement search, is one of the factors that make a text difficult to read. If information in the text can be related to ideas that are still active in STM, comprehension is easier than if the reader must first search LTM to reinstate old information in STM so it can be integrated with the new information. This assumption is consistent with the findings of Lesgold and colleagues (1979) and of Glenberg and his colleagues (1987).

The reinstatement search also fails for the example because there are no concepts that are common to the first two sentences. The model must therefore construct a new network rather than add on to the old one. It may also make an inference at this point to interrelate the two networks. The inference is that the warriors mentioned in the second sentence were members of the

---

reinstatement search The search of long-term memory to place words in short-term memory where they can be used to integrate a text

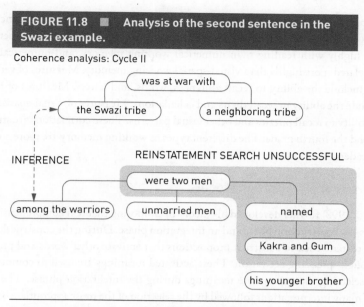

FIGURE 11.8 ■ Analysis of the second sentence in the Swazi example.

Coherence analysis: Cycle II

Source: From "On modeling comprehension," by W. Kintsch, 1979, *Educational Psychologist, 14,* 3–14. https://doi.org/10.1080/00461527909529202. Copyright 1979 by Lawrence Erlbaum Associates, Inc. Reprinted by permission.

Swazi tribe. This seems like a reasonable inference, but it is not stated directly. Kintsch's model assumes that inferences, like reinstatement searches, slow the reader and make comprehension more difficult. The evidence supports this assumption (e.g., Haviland & Clark, 1974).

The model once again selects three propositions from the second sentence to keep active in STM. Figure 11.8 shows that the three selected specify the names of the two men. The third sentence, "Kakra was killed in a battle," is easy to relate to previous information because information about Kakra is still available in STM. The new information can therefore be added directly to the network without having to search LTM or make an inference.

This example should give you an approximate idea of how the model works. The major theme of the model is that incoming information can be understood more easily when it can be integrated with information that the reader has already encountered. The easiest case is when the new information can be related to information that is still active in STM. If it cannot be related, a reinstatement search attempts to relate the new information to propositions stored in LTM. If the reinstatement search fails, a new network must be started, resulting in a memory for ideas that is not very well integrated. The result should be poorer recall, as was found by Kieras (1978) when the new sentences could not be related to previous sentences. Integration of ideas can sometimes be achieved by inference, but the need for inferences also contributes to the difficulty of the text (Britton & Gulgoz, 1991).

The critical role of STM in reading comprehension has been documented in a meta-analysis of 197 studies that resulted in a significant moderate correlation between reading and working memory capacity (Peng et al., 2019). Significant correlations occurred for the many processes involved in reading, including phonological coding, word recognition, vocabulary knowledge, reading comprehension, and listening comprehension. There were, however, differences in how different measures of working memory correlated with reading. Verbal working memory correlated more highly with reading than numerical working memory, and numerical working memory correlated more highly than visual-spatial working memory. Measures of verbal working memory include the ability to recall sentences, words, and letters. Measures of numerical memory include the ability to recall digits and calculations. Measures of visual-spatial memory include the ability to recall puzzles and other visual patterns. These correlations are stronger for reading beyond the fourth grade. The different types of working memory are more comparable in younger readers.

The Construction-Integration Model

Kintsch (1988, 1998) further developed his theory by proposing that text comprehension occurs in two phases—a construction phase and an integration phase. During the construction phrase, words of the text are used to construct propositions that activate other words and propositions in LTM through spreading activation. These activated meanings are used to comprehend the sentence by selecting the appropriate meanings during the integration phrase. The proposed activation of many interpretations followed by the selection of the most appropriate ones is consistent with research (Budiu & Anderson, 2004; Swinney, 1979).

Consider the statement "Two masked gunman made their getaway with $100,000 from the First National Bank" (Kintsch, 1998). Some of the activated meanings during the initial phase will need to be discarded as inappropriate. *Masked* can activate *Mardi gras*, and *gunman* can activate *cowboy*, in addition to the more appropriate meaning, *robber*. The ambiguous word *bank* initially activates both *river* and *money*, as we learned from Swinney's (1979) research.

The integration phase assembles the meaning of the sentence from all the activated words and propositions. Many of these are inappropriate because they do not fit the context. There are no other propositions in the sentence that indicate it describes Mardi Gras participants or cowboys, so these meanings are discarded in favor of more appropriate meanings. The sentence context is also used to discard inappropriate meanings of ambiguous words (such as *bank*). Research based on Swinney's (1979) at least 350 msec to select the appropriate meaning of an ambiguous word and discard the inappropriate meaning (Kintsch, 1998, p. 228). It takes even longer (at least 750 msec at the end of the sentence) to identify the theme of the sentence as a robbery because identifying the theme requires determining the meaning of all the words in the sentence.

The construction-integration model demonstrates that comprehension is not immediate but occurs over time (O'Brien & Cook, 2016; Singer, 2019). It is a good example of the distinction between bottom-up and top-down processing that was introduced at the beginning of this book. The construction phase illustrates bottom-up processing (Kintsch, 2005). Words in the text activate related meanings without regard to context. The integration phase illustrates top-down processing. Context is now used to determine the appropriate meaning of the words (Kintsch & Mangalath, 2011; Long & Lea, 2005).

Integration requires continual validation that the text makes sense by judging its consistency, congruence, and coherence (Singer, 2019). Much of validation is routine, such as expecting that a broken pipe will be repaired by a plumber rather than by a doctor. When integration fails, readers need to intentionally engage in the error recovery strategies (rereading, memory search) depicted in Figure 11.4. Validation fails when the reader overlooks incongruent or inaccurate information (Singer, 2019).

O'Brien and Cook (2016) proposed a model of the validation process that is based on two key theoretical constructs—a **coherence threshold** and the continuity of processing over time. A coherence threshold is the level at which a reader believes his or her understanding is good enough to move from one part of the text to the next while allowing some uncertainty to remain. The evaluation is continuous because it occurs throughout the initial activation, integration, and validation stages and then continues even after the reader has reached the coherence threshold for each stage. This continuity enables the possibility that evaluations regarding activation, integration, and validation will have a delayed impact on comprehension.

Incorporating Prior Knowledge

This chapter began by looking at how a person's prior knowledge influences text comprehension. Our prior knowledge is sufficient to understand the sentence about the robbery even though it requires both construction and integration. However, understanding academic material typically places more demands on prior knowledge. For instance, science texts differ from narratives in their demands on working memory, comprehension strategies, and use of background knowledge (Van de Broek, 2010). They often compress complex ideas into a few words, maintain an impersonal authoritative stance, and use technical words that have meanings quite different from those of daily life (Snow, 2010). The words "product," "force," and "arm" are examples when they appear in the sentence "Torque is the product of the magnitude of the force and the lever arm of the force" (Snow, 2010, p. 452).

Can we "capture" this prior knowledge and incorporate it into Kintsch's model of comprehension? In his Distinguished Scientific Award address to the annual meeting of the American Psychological Association, Kintsch (1994) focused on the role that prior knowledge plays in learning from a text.

Our emphasis thus far has been on representing the semantic relations in the text through integrating the propositions in a semantic network. But there is another, deeper level of understanding that Kintsch calls a situation model. The **situation model** is constructed by combining prior knowledge and information in the text to produce a more elaborate understanding of the situation described in the text (Photo 11.7). Rather than treating language as information to

---

coherence threshold The level at which a reader believes his or her understanding is good enough to move from one part of the text to the next

situation model Integration of prior knowledge and text information to construct an understanding of the situation described in a text

analyze syntactically and semantically, language is now viewed as a set of processing instructions on how to construct a mental representation of the described situation (Zwaan & Radvansky, 1998). You used your prior knowledge to infer that the sentence about two masked gunmen described a robbery. The use of prior knowledge becomes even more important to understand complex topics such as the circulation of blood.

PHOTO 11.7 Prior knowledge is useful for constructing situation models.

istockphotos.com/CreativaImages

Figure 11.9 shows an example for a two-sentence text fragment: "When a baby has a septal defect, the blood cannot get rid of enough carbon dioxide through the lungs. Therefore, it looks purple." The situation model in this case is represented as a diagram. It shows that, because of the septal defect, red blood carrying oxygen is mixed together with purple blood carrying carbon dioxide. Some of the purple blood is therefore recirculated back into the body without picking up oxygen in the lungs. Notice that much of the information in the situation model is derived from the reader's knowledge of the circulatory system rather than derived directly from the text.

The deeper level of understanding represented by the situation model can also be represented in the semantic networks discussed previously. In this case, the semantic network model would contain propositions that are derived both from the text and from the reader's prior knowledge. The propositions about the septal defect, color of the blood, and excess carbon dioxide come from the text, but other propositions such as the mixing of the blood depend on inferences based on prior knowledge.

FIGURE 11.9 ■ A diagrammatic situation model for the septal defect text.

TEXT:
When a baby has a septal defect, the blood cannot get rid of enough carbon dioxide through the lungs. Therefore, it looks purple.

SITUATION MODEL:

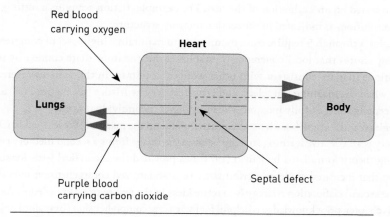

Source: "Text comprehension, memory, and learning," by W. Kintsch, 1994, *American Psychologist, 49,* 294–303. https://doi.org/10.1037/0003-066X.49.4.294. Copyright 1994 by the American Psychological Association.

APPLICATIONS

Comprehension Strategies and Assessment

We have seen in this chapter that comprehension depends on both the reader and the text. Readability depends on the text; comprehension strategies depend on the reader. Although academic material requires more inferences than narratives, whether these inferences are made depends on a reader's goals. Some participants in a comprehension study by van den Broek and his colleagues were told to imagine they were studying for an essay exam. The other participants were told to imagine that they had come upon an article of interest while browsing through a magazine (van den Broek et al., 2001). The study-goal participants produced more inferences to establish the coherence of the text and had better memory for its content. The other students were less concerned with constructing a coherent representation but made more associative ("This reminds me of the movie *Apollo 13*") and evaluative ("How strange!") comments.

Table 11.1 lists nine effective comprehension strategies based on research (Block & Duffy, 2008). The strategies should interest you for two reasons. First, they should help you comprehend and learn the material, and second, they provide an application of some of the main ideas expressed in this chapter.

The first strategy is to predict what will occur next based on an overview of the material. For example, you can study the outline provided at the beginning of each chapter in this text to learn its organization. The outline for this chapter informs you that the major sections are prior knowledge, organization of the text, Kintsch's model of comprehension, and applications. The subheadings provide additional information, such as the prior knowledge of the reader influences comprehension, retrieval, and false recognition. You may also be able to make general predictions based on an evaluation of the text. For example, fiction contains a setting, theme, plot, and resolution, as indicated in the section on story structure.

Strategies 3 through 5 require close monitoring to maintain a high level of comprehension. Monitoring assures that local coherence is established for the immediate context by selecting interpretations that are consistent with other words and phrases in the sentence. Rereading is necessary when the meaning is unclear, and error-recovery heuristics (see Figure 11.6) are occasionally needed to successfully integrate the meaning of the individual words.

Strategies 6 and 7 are elaborative strategies that build on the material. We learned in Chapter 8 that imagery is an effective learning strategy because the image forms a second memory code. The dual coding theory formulated by Paivio (1971) has provided the theoretical basis for successful instruction that increased students' performance on standardized comprehension tests (Sadoski, 2008). The second elaboration strategy is to relate ideas in the text to prior knowledge. As we have seen in this chapter, prior knowledge is helpful for increasing comprehension (Bransford & Johnson, 1973), aiding retrieval (Anderson & Pichert, 1978), and building situation models (Kintsch, 1994).

The last two strategies are needed to see the big picture. Synthesizing information establishes global coherence, showing how all of the ideas in the passage fit together. Finally, summarizing the material involves finding the main ideas and reaching conclusions.

A program called Interactive Strategy Training for Active Reading and Thinking or iSTART (McNamara et al., 2007) teaches comprehension monitoring, paraphrasing, and constructing self-explanations, inferences, predictions, and elaborations. In one study that measured prior

---

TABLE 11.1 ■ Recommended comprehension strategies

1. Predict. Size up text in advance by looking at title, text, figures, sections, pictures, and captions.

2. Evaluate. Approach a fictional text expecting to note the setting, characters, and story structure.

3. Monitor. Activate comprehension strategies to derive meaning from words, phrases, sentences, and text.

4. Question. Stop to reread and initiate comprehension processes when the meaning is unclear.

5. Fix it. Look back and reread when necessary.

6. Image. Construct meanings expressed in the text by noticing and generating mental pictures.

7. Infer. Connect ideas in the text based on personal experiences and prior knowledge.

8. Synthesize. Combine sequence of details, unique types of information, and conclusions to make meaning.

9. Summarize. Find main ideas and draw conclusions.

Source: Based on "Research on teaching comprehension," by C. C. Block & G. G. Duffy, 2008, in *Comprehension instruction: Research-based best practices*, C. C. Block & S. R. Parris (Eds.), New York: Guilford Press.

knowledge of reading strategies, iSTART training improved the quality of self-explanations and comprehension of a passage about heart disease (McNamara et al., 2006). Students who had low knowledge of reading strategies benefited most from answering questions at the more literal text level. Students who had high knowledge of reading strategies benefited most from answering questions that required more integrative inferences.

When using the program, readers initially need to represent the information in each individual sentence—a skill that requires improvement in low-skilled readers. Then readers need to understand the text at a deeper level by connecting ideas across sentences—a skill that requires improvement in high-skilled readers. For example, iSTART may ask readers to explain how a particular sentence relates to previous sentences.

McNamara's group has continued to develop and evaluate iSTART, including the incorporation of personalized learning that can adapt the selection of text to support the learner (McCarthy et al., 2020). High school students were randomly assigned to iSTART training that either assigned texts randomly or assigned texts to match the reader's skill level. Less skilled readers benefited from the adaptive text selection whereas high-skilled readers showed a slight advantage for randomly assigned texts. One explanation is that skilled readers often generate high-quality self-explanations of the text so are in less need of training.

Persuasive Communication

Another application of research on text comprehension is the design of persuasive messages. The need for persuasive health communication occurred in 2019 during the spread of measles. The website of the Center for Disease Control and Prevention informed viewers that from January 1 to May 10, 2019, 839 cases of measles had been confirmed in the United States. This was the greatest number of cases reported here since 1994. The majority of people who got measles were unvaccinated (Photo 11.8). The website reported that measles can spread when it reaches a community where groups of people are unvaccinated.

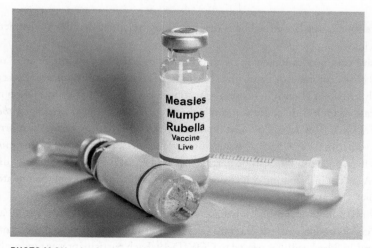

PHOTO 11.8 Vaccinations prevent the spread of measles.

istockphotos.com/AndreyPopov

Vaccinating children to prevent the spread of infectious diseases is one of four case studies reviewed in an article by Weisman and Markman (2017) at Stanford University. The study attempted to change the attitudes of those adults who believed a vaccination against measles was dangerous because it increased the risk of autism (Horne et al., 2015). Adults assigned to the Autism Correction condition read information summarizing recent research showing that vaccinations do not increase the risk of autism in children. Adults assigned to the Disease Risk condition read information summarizing the risks suffered by children who get measles. Only the participants in the Disease Risk condition changed their beliefs about vaccinations. Focusing on the dangers of a communicable disease had a positive impact on people's attitudes whereas attempting to dispel misconceptions about vaccinations was ineffective.

The other three studies reviewed by Weisman and Markman (2017) advocated (1) washing hands to prevent the spread of viral epidemics, (2) completing a full course of antibiotics to reduce antibiotic resistance, and (3) eating a variety of healthy foods to improve unhealthy diets. Based on these and other research studies, the authors recommended five guidelines for designing explanations to motivate change to healthy behavior:

1. Identify a specific target for behavior change that is clearly linked to a desired outcome, such as washing hands to prevent the spread of viral epidemics.

2. Identify the conceptual prerequisites necessary for understanding how and why engaging in this behavior would bring about the desired outcome.

3. Assess the theories currently held by the targeted audience.

4. Design educational materials to address misconceptions and gaps in people's current theories.

5. Provide just enough information to instill confidence in the causal framework of the correct theory, such as why washing hands is helpful.

The intention of the last guideline is that providing too many details can distract from the causal principles.

Persuasive communication again became critical in 2020 to convince people "to be safe" in the wake of the coronavirus pandemic. The topic of effective communication was addressed in the timely article "A scientific theory of gist communication and misinformation resistance, with implications for health, education, and policy," published in the *Proceedings of the National Academy of Sciences* (Reyna, 2020). Gist representations capture the essence of information, in contrast to verbatim details, such as exact words or numbers. A limitation of gist information, however, is its vagueness. This can be particularly problematic when the causes of diseases are unknown. A lack of information can create a void that is filled when people formulate coherent "explanations" that are inconsistent with scientific knowledge.

Misinformation is magnified when spread on social media (Pennycook et al., 2020). Through a collaboration with the Harvard Global Health Institute, investigators acquired a list of 15 true and 15 false headlines related to COVID-19. Each participant was randomly assigned to one of two conditions. In the accuracy condition, they were asked "To the best of your knowledge, is the claim in the above headline accurate?" In the sharing condition, they were asked "Would you consider sharing this story online (for example, through Facebook or Twitter?)."

Figure 11.10 shows that the truth of the headlines had a much greater impact on judgments of accuracy (left panel) than on willingness to share that information online (right panel). People placed little emphasis on perceived accuracy when deciding what to share. A follow-up study was successful in nudging people to consider accuracy by asking them to first rate the accuracy of a single headline before beginning the news-sharing task. Participants were significantly more likely to share true headlines than false headlines only if they initially evaluated the accuracy of a news headline.

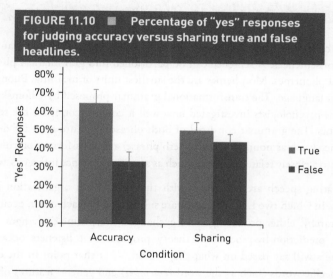

FIGURE 11.10 ■ Percentage of "yes" responses for judging accuracy versus sharing true and false headlines.

Source: From "Fighting COVID-19 misinformation on social media: experimental evidence for a scalable accuracy-nudge intervention" by G. Pennycook, J, McPhetres, Y. Zhang, J. G. Rand, 2020, *Psychological Science, 31,* 770–780. https://doi.org/10.1177/0956797620939054. Licensed under CC-BY.

These findings raise the question of how people evaluate everyday explanations (Zemla et al., 2017). Participants rated the quality of explanations that followed eight different questions, including the following:

- Why has the price of higher education skyrocketed in the United States, and who is profiting from it?

- Why are so many people up in arms over "you have to have health insurance" initiatives but okay with mandated car insurance?

- How has Switzerland managed to stay in a neutral position during times of conflict like WWII?

Each question was followed by one of three different possible explanations that differed along multiple attributes.

In addition to rating the overall quality, participants rated 20 attributes of the explanations. The attributes that correlated most strongly with overall perceived quality were the perceived truth of the explanation, its coherence, the extent to which most people would agree with the general principles, the quality of the articulation, and the ease of visualizing the principles. Perhaps surprisingly, people preferred more complex explanations that had more causal mechanisms to explain the effect. The authors proposed that the preference for complexity is due to a desire to identify enough causes to make the effect seem inevitable.

SUMMARY

A language is a collection of symbols and rules for combining symbols that can generate an infinite variety of sentences. A sentence can be partitioned into grammatical phrases, words, morphemes, and phonemes. Morphemes are the smallest units of meaning. Phonemes are the basic sounds of a language. The transformational grammar proposed by Chomsky stimulated much research as psychologists investigated how well it could account for the results of language experiments. The grammar consisted of both phrase-structure rules for describing the parts of a sentence (such as noun phrase and verb phrase) and transformation rules for changing a sentence into a closely related sentence (such as an active sentence into a passive sentence).

Errors in generating speech are consistent with the hierarchical organization of language. Exchange errors, in which two linguistic units are substituted for each other, occur at the same level in the hierarchy, either producing word exchanges, morpheme exchanges, or phoneme exchanges. The prediction-by-production theory proposes that listeners occasionally predict what speakers will say based on what they would say at that point in the conversation. For instance, specific words (such as the word *remember*) and general features of words (such as whether the sentence begins with an animate or inanimate noun) provide clues about the grammatical structure of a sentence. According to a theory based on process memory, active traces of past information are used to process incoming information in the present moment.

Understanding narratives requires establishing both global coherence about the main events that occur throughout the story and local coherence about the most recent events. A general model of sentence comprehension involves fixating and recognizing a word, retrieving conceptual meanings that are sufficiently activated by the word and the prior context, integrating one of these meanings with the prior context, testing to determine whether the integration is successful, and recovering from an error if unsuccessful. Psychologists have found that a clarifying semantic context allows the listener to quickly select the appropriate meaning of an ambiguous word following the activation of both meanings.

A model of test comprehension proposed by Kintsch focuses on how the reader attempts to relate current ideas in the text to ideas already read. Comprehension is easiest when the ideas can be related to ideas that are still available in STM. If no relations are found, the reader can search LTM to look for a relation. If no relations are found in LTM, the new material must be stored separately rather than integrated with old material. Relations can sometimes be found by making inferences, but inferences slow down comprehension.

Recommended strategies for improving comprehension include making predictions, evaluating content, creating mental pictures, constructing inferences, and synthesizing and summarizing the main ideas. Computer-based tutors such as iSTART help students learn effective strategies. Other applications involve determining the basis for persuasive communications, such as those designed to encourage people to lead healthy lives.

RECOMMENDED READING

Steven Pinker's (1994) book *The Language Instinct* provides a very readable introduction to the many facets of language. An easy introduction to the early theoretical contributions of Chomsky is a book by Lyons (1970). Some but not all children with speech-sound disorders have difficulty with speech perception (Hearnshaw et al., 2019). Keenan et al. (1977) found that their colleagues often could remember the exact words of statements that had high emotional content, although usually only the general meaning of sentences was remembered (Sachs, 1967). Gernsbacher and Faust (1991) showed that the ability to quickly suppress inappropriate meanings is an important skill in a variety of comprehension tasks. Pickering and Garrod (2007) argued that people use language production, and Elman (2009) argued that people use schema to make predictions during comprehension. Mind wandering during text comprehension occurs more frequently for difficult text and for readers with lower working memory capacity (Schurer et al., 2020). A meta-analysis of studies on instructional interventions revealed that they had an overall medium positive effect on improving metacomprehension accuracy (Prinz et al., 2020). *Embodiment and Cognitive Science* (Gibbs, 2006) contains research on embodied cognition, including its application to language. Gleitman (2005) reviews research on language and thought, and Horne et al. (2019) examine explanation as a cognitive process.

12 DECISION MAKING

Making Choices
>   Compensatory Models
>   Noncompensatory Models
>   Selecting a Strategy
>   The Adaptive Toolbox

Estimating Probabilities
>   Availability
>   Representativeness

Combining Probabilities and Values
>   Expected Value
>   Expected Utility
>   Subjective Expected Utility

Risk Dimensions
>   Importance of Risk Dimensions
>   Decision Frames
>   Perceived Risk

Applications
>   Decision Aids
>   Healthy Decisions
>   Action-Based Decision Making

SUMMARY

RECOMMENDED READING

LEARNING OBJECTIVES

1. Compare and contrast compensatory and noncompensatory decision-making models.

2. Discuss why heuristics for estimating probabilities may result in biased estimates.

3. Describe the distinction between normative and descriptive models and the usefulness of each.

4. Explain how individual risk dimensions influence decisions.

5. Provide examples of decision making in real life and the tools and strategies that could improve your own decision making.

Every day we make many decisions. Some of these are relatively unimportant. Others—such as selecting a car, a home, or a job—are important. Making decisions is often difficult because each alternative usually has many aspects, and very seldom does the best alternative excel over all others.

The first section of this chapter describes models of how people select from a set of alternatives. Examples include selecting a home, a car, or a dinner from a menu. These models do not consider probabilities because they assume that a person knows the values of relevant dimensions such as price, gas mileage, and optional equipment in the case of buying a car. The following three sections are concerned with examples of risky decision making—those in which the decision maker must consider probabilities. We examine how people make probability estimates and then use these estimates to make decisions.

The study of decision making has been influenced by both normative and descriptive models. Normative models specify what a person should do. They often provide a standard for comparing how closely actual decisions match normative decisions. Descriptive models seek to describe how people actually arrive at decisions. The relation between normative and descriptive models is a theme that occurs throughout the discussion of decision making. The final section on applications discusses decision aids, as well as making healthy and action-based decisions.

MAKING CHOICES

Compensatory Models

One reason decisions can be difficult is that alternatives usually have many attributes. If one of the attributes is not very attractive, the decision maker must decide whether to eliminate that alternative or continue to consider it because its other attributes may be very attractive. For example, a person might buy a car with low gas mileage because of the smooth ride and spaciousness of a large car. Decision-making models that allow attractive attributes to compensate for unattractive ones are called compensatory models. The spaciousness of a large car can compensate for the lower gas mileage in this case.

An additive model is a kind of compensatory model. An additive model combines the attractive and unattractive attributes to arrive at a total score for each alternative. Consider the case of Sally Smith. Sally has lived in a college dormitory for three consecutive years. It is now her senior year, and she feels that it is time to enjoy the greater freedom that an apartment can offer. She has found two rather attractive apartments and must select one, so she decides to systematically list the advantages and disadvantages of each (Table 12.1). First, she lists the attributes that will influence her decision, and then she rates each on a scale that ranges from –3 (a very negative impression) to +3 (a very positive impression). Here are her ratings:

---

normative model A model that describes what people should do

descriptive model A model that describes what people actually do

compensatory model A strategy that allows positive attributes to compensate for negative ones

additive model A strategy that adds attribute values to assign a score to each alternative

TABLE 12.1 ■ Ratings of apartment attributes		
	Apartment A	**Apartment B**
Rent	+1	+2
Noise level	−2	+3
Distance to campus	+3	−1
Cleanliness	+2	+2
	—	—
	+4	+6

PHOTO 12.1 Noise level is a relevant attribute for selecting an apartment.

istockphotos.com/lolostock

The sums of the ratings for the various attributes of the two apartments reveal that Sally's best choice is to select apartment B, which is rated higher. There are two ways of modifying the summation rule that could change the results. First, the four attributes were equally weighted in the example. If some attributes are more important to Sally than others, she will want to emphasize these attributes when making her decision. For example, she might want to emphasize distance from campus if she lives in a cold climate and has to walk to classes. If this variable is twice as important as the others, she could multiply her ratings of distance by 2 to give this dimension greater emphasis. The sum of the ratings would then be 7 for apartment A and 5 for apartment B. Second, adding the ratings of the four attributes does not account for how the attributes might interact. Although apartment A is very noisy, it is so close to campus that the library would be a convenient place to study. The high noise level is therefore not as detrimental as it would be if the apartment were the only convenient place for studying. The low rating for noise level should perhaps be modified to take into account the interaction between that dimension and distance to campus.

A model that is very similar to the additive model is called the **additive–difference model**. This model compares two alternatives by totaling the differences between their values on each attribute. The values on each attribute are shown in Table 12.2. The third column shows the value obtained by subtracting the second column from the first.

TABLE 12.2 ■ Difference in apartment attributes

	Apartment A	Apartment B	Difference
Rent	+1	+2	–1
Noise level	–2	+3	–5
Distance to campus	+3	–1	+4
Cleanliness	+2	+2	+0
—	—	—	—
	+4	+6	–2

The sum of the differences is –2, which implies that apartment A is 2 units less attractive than apartment B. The additive model implies the same conclusion—the sum of the ratings for apartment A is 2 less than the sum of the ratings for apartment B. Although the additive and the additive–difference models result in the same conclusion, the search for information is different. The additive model evaluates all attributes of one alternative before considering the next alternative. The additive–difference model compares the two alternatives attribute by attribute. If there are more than two alternatives, a given alternative is compared with the best of the preceding alternatives.

Both the additive and the additive–difference models describe a good procedure for evaluating alternatives. Both evaluate alternatives on all their attributes and allow attractive values to compensate for unattractive values. The examples show that both models provide a systematic procedure for making decisions, but are we really this systematic in making decisions? How often do we take the time to make the kind of calculations required by the models? Perhaps some other model might better describe how we actually make choices. The alternative to a compensatory model is a **noncompensatory model**, in which unattractive attributes result in eliminating alternatives.

---

additive–difference model A strategy that compares two alternatives by adding the difference in their values for each attribute

noncompensatory model A strategy that rejects alternatives that have negative attributes without considering their positive attributes

Noncompensatory Models

If we do not calculate, how do we make decisions? Tversky (1972) has proposed that we make choices by gradually eliminating less attractive alternatives. His theory is called elimination by aspects because it assumes that the elimination is based on the sequential evaluation of the attributes, or aspects, of the alternatives. If the attribute of an alternative does not satisfy some minimum criterion, that alternative is eliminated from the set of choices.

Consider Ms. Green, who is looking for a used car. If Ms. Green has only $9,000 to spend, she may first eliminate from her set of possible choices those cars that cost more than $9,000. She may also be interested in gas economy and eliminate cars that cannot travel at least 25 miles on a gallon of gas. By continuing to select attributes and rejecting those that do not satisfy some minimum criterion, she will gradually eliminate alternatives until there is only a single car remaining that satisfies all her criteria.

The final choice, based on this procedure, depends on the order in which the attributes are evaluated. If the price of the car is one of the last attributes Ms. Green evaluates, she might have eliminated all cars costing less than $9,000 early in her decision process—an undesirable situation if she has only $9,000 to spend. The model therefore proposes that the attributes differ in importance, and the probability of selecting an attribute for evaluation depends on its importance. If price is a very important attribute, it has a high probability of being selected early in the sequence.

The elimination-by-aspects model has the advantage that it does not require any calculations. The decision maker simply selects an attribute according to some probability that depends on the importance of that attribute. She then determines whether an alternative satisfies a minimum criterion for that attribute and eliminates those alternatives that do not meet the criterion.

The conjunctive model—a variant of elimination by aspects—requires that all the attributes of an alternative satisfy minimum criteria before that alternative can be selected. It differs from elimination by aspects by proposing that people finish evaluating one alternative before considering another. The first alternative that satisfies all the minimum criteria is selected. The conjunctive model is an example of what Simon (1957) has called a satisficing search. Simon argued that limited capability to evaluate many alternatives often prevents people from selecting the best alternative. Instead, they are willing to settle for a good alternative—that is, one that satisfies all the minimum criteria. Other constraints, such as limits in time or availability, may also influence us to choose a good alternative rather than wait for the best alternative. For example, we may simply become tired of looking at apartments, or an apartment we liked may be rented by the time we return, so we will choose an available alternative rather than continue searching for a better one.

---

elimination by aspects A strategy that evaluates one attribute at a time and rejects those alternatives whose attribute values fail to satisfy a minimum criterion

conjunctive model A strategy that evaluates one alternative at a time and rejects it if the value of one of its attributes fails to satisfy a minimum criterion

satisficing search A strategy that follows the conjunctive model and therefore selects the first alternative that satisfies the minimum criterion for each attribute

Selecting a Strategy

The four models we have looked at differ with respect to how people search for information. Payne (1976) took advantage of this difference in designing a procedure for finding out which strategies people use. He presented information describing the attributes of apartments, such as rent, cleanliness, noise level, and distance from campus. The information describing each apartment was printed on the back of a card, which had to be turned over to reveal its value (Figure 12.1). Subjects were allowed to turn over as many cards as they needed to make their decision. The order in which they turned over the cards should reveal how they searched for information. Payne gathered additional evidence about how they arrived at a decision by asking them to think aloud as they evaluated the information on the cards.

Payne did not expect that everyone would follow the same strategy in searching for information. His expectations were influenced by work on problem solving that showed how individuals adapted their strategies to the demands of the task. An important characteristic of people's problem-solving strategies is that they attempt to keep the demands of the task within a limited capacity. Payne argued that the strategies used by decision makers should also be adaptive to the information-processing demands of the task. One implication of this view is that the decision maker might change strategies as the demands of the task change.

FIGURE 12.1 ■ Information search task used by Payne.			
Apartment A	Low	Fair	20 min	$110
Apartment B	High	Good	30 min	$170
				Rent

Source: Reed, S.K. (2012). *Cognition: Theories and Applications 9e.* Cengage.

Payne's results supported his expectations. Students were given a variety of tasks that differed in both the number of alternatives (2, 4, 8, or 12 apartments) and the number of dimensions (4, 8, or 12 attributes). The principal finding was that the students changed strategies as the number of alternatives decreased. The search strategies and verbal protocols revealed that, when asked to evaluate many alternatives, the subjects reduced the complexity of the task by using the conjunctive or elimination-by-aspects procedure to eliminate some of the alternatives quickly. When only a few alternatives remained in the choice set, the subjects might then use one of the cognitively demanding procedures—such as the additive or additive–difference strategy—to make the final evaluation and choice.

The additive and additive–difference strategies are cognitively demanding because they require that the decision maker compute values to represent the attractiveness of each alternative. Although they allow for the careful evaluation of each alternative, their greater complexity may result in decisions that are not any better than decisions made by following a simpler strategy, such as elimination by aspects.

One way to compare the effectiveness of the different strategies is to train several groups of people to make decisions by following a particular strategy and then evaluate the quality of their decisions. Paquette and Kida (1988) used this approach to compare the relative effectiveness of the additive, additive–difference, elimination-by-aspects, and mixed strategies. The mixed strategy, based on Payne's finding that people switch strategies, initially used the elimination-by-aspects strategy followed by the additive strategy when the number of alternatives was reduced to three.

The subjects were 48 professionals who had experience evaluating a firm's financial characteristics. They were given financial data on firms and had to select the one with the highest bond rating by following the strategy taught to them during the training session. The experimenters could then evaluate the accuracy of the selections because they knew the bond rating of each firm. They found no significant differences in the accuracy of the four strategies, but the simpler elimination-by-aspects strategy required significantly less time to make a decision than the more demanding additive and additive–difference strategies. For this particular task, the elimination-by-aspects strategy was a highly efficient one (Photo 12.2).

PHOTO 12.2 The elimination-by-aspects strategy was highly efficient for analyzing financial data.

istockphotos.com/Pinkypills

The Adaptive Toolbox

The continuation of Payne's (1976) research was summarized in a book called *The Adaptive Decision Maker* (Payne et al., 1993) in which the authors argued that decision makers are guided by the dual goals of maximizing accuracy and minimizing effort, causing them to emphasize different strategies in different situations. The concept of the adaptive decision maker has continued, particularly in the work of Gigerenzer (2008) and his colleagues at the Max Planck

Institute for Human Development in Berlin, Germany. They use the metaphor of an adaptive toolbox containing a variety of heuristics that can be effectively used in different situations (Gigerenzer & Brighton, 2009).

Marewski and Link (2014) apply this concept by considering a hypothetical example of selecting a cell phone. Such selections typically require comparing several products along multiple dimensions, a potentially overwhelming task (Figure 12.2). As indicated by Payne's (1976) findings, an elimination-by-aspects strategy can reduce the choice to fewer alternatives, but even selecting between two alternatives requires selecting a decision strategy. In addition to knowledge-based strategies, there are accessibility-based strategies that depend on memory retrieval. A simple strategy that would justify spending millions of dollars on advertising is the recognition heuristic in which consumers select a brand that they recognize.

FIGURE 12.2 ■ Complex tasks lead people to adopt simplifying heuristics.

Sumsan	Sinostar	Sosida
High price (+)	Low price (−)	High price (+)
Low reliability (−)	High reliability (+)	High reliability (+)
Made in low-cost country (−)	?	Made in high-cost country (+)
Poor camera (−)	Good camera (+)	Poor camera (−)
Good battery life (+)	Poor battery life (−)	Poor battery life (−)
Dual-core (+)	Single-care (−)	Dual-core (+)
GPS integrated (+)	GPS integrated (+)	No GPS integrated (−)
Touchscreen (+)	No touchscreen (−)	No touchscreen (−)

So much information and so little time! How do I decide?

Source: "Strategy selection: An introduction to the modeling challenge," by J. N. Marewski & D. Link, 2014, *WIREs Cogn Sci, 5,* 39–59. https://doi.org/10.1002/wcs.1265

An application of the recognition heuristic helped people answer the question "Which city has more inhabitants: San Diego or San Antonio?" One hundred percent of Germans answered correctly (San Diego), compared to 62% of Americans (Goldstein & Gigerenzer, 2002). So why did the Germans appear more knowledgeable? Goldstein and Gigerenzer proposed that many Germans used the recognition heuristic: If you recognize one city but not the other, infer that it has the larger population. Americans could not use this heuristic because they likely knew the names of both cities.

ESTIMATING PROBABILITIES

Accessibility-based strategies, such as the fluency heuristic, are also used to estimate probabilities. Estimating probabilities is required for making decisions under conditions of uncertainty. There was some amount of uncertainty in the previous examples. Although the location of an apartment is not likely to change, the noise level can change as the neighbors change. Uncertainty is a major factor in many of the examples discussed in the rest of the chapter and requires that people estimate the probability that a certain event will occur.

Kahneman and Tversky (1972, 1973; Tversky & Kahneman, 1973) have shown that probability estimates are based on *heuristics* that sometimes yield reasonable estimates but often do not. Two of these heuristics are availability and representativeness. Before reading further, answer the questions in Table 12.3 to determine how you might use these heuristics.

TABLE 12.3   ■   Questions about subjective probabilities
1. How many cities that begin with the letter *F* do you think you can recall? Give your estimate before you start recalling examples.
2. Are there more words in the English language that start with the letter *K* or that have a *K* as their third letter?
3. Which is the more likely cause of death, breast cancer or diabetes?
4. If a family has three boys (B) and three girls (G), which sequence of births is more likely—BBBGGG or BGGBGB?
5. Are you more likely to find 60 boys in a random sample of 100 children or 600 boys in a random sample of 1000 children?

Availability

The availability heuristic proposes that we evaluate the probability of an event by judging the ease with which relevant instances come to mind (Tversky & Kahneman, 1973). For example, we may assess the divorce rate in a community by recalling divorces among our acquaintances. When availability is highly correlated with actual frequency, estimates should be accurate. For example, in one

uncertainty Lacking knowledge about which events will occur

availability heuristic Estimating probability by the ease with which examples can be recalled

experiment, participants were asked to estimate the number of instances they could recall from a category in two minutes. The average recall varied from 4.1 (city names beginning with the letter *F*) to 23.7 (four-legged animals). The correlation between estimation and word production was 0.93 over 16 categories. The high correlation between estimation and production revealed that subjects were quite accurate in estimating the relative availability of instances in the different categories.

Some instances, however, might be difficult to retrieve from memory even though they occur frequently. The availability hypothesis would predict that frequency should be underestimated in this case. Suppose you sample a word at random from an English text. Is it more likely that the word starts with a *K* or that *K* is its third letter? The availability hypothesis proposes that people try to answer this question by judging how easy it is to think of examples in each category. Because it is easier to think of words that begin with a certain letter, people should be biased toward responding that more words start with the letter *K* than have a *K* in the third position. The median estimated ratio for each of five letters was that there were twice as many words in which that letter was the first letter rather than the third letter in the word. The estimates were obtained despite the fact that all five letters are actually more frequent in the third position.

Slovic et al. (1976) have used the availability hypothesis to account for how people estimated the relative probability of 41 causes of death—including diseases, accidents, homicide, suicide, and natural hazards—that were combined into 106 pairs. A large sample of college students judged which member of the pair was the more likely cause of death; Table 12.4 shows how often they were correct as a function of the relative frequency of the two events.

The frequencies of accidents, cancer, and tornadoes—all of which receive heavy media coverage—were greatly overestimated (Photo 12.3). Asthma and diabetes, which receive less media coverage, were underestimated. Examination of the events most seriously misjudged provided indirect support for the hypothesis that availability, particularly as influenced by the media, biases probability estimates.

PHOTO 12.3 Tornadoes were overestimated as a cause of death.

istockphotos.com/vchal

A more selective effect of availability on probability estimates is illustrated by research on how our mood influences estimates. Emotions can have a substantial impact on the kind of information that people retrieve from LTM (long-term memory). A happy mood makes it more likely that we will recall positive events, and a sad mood makes it more likely that we will recall negative events (Blaney, 1986). The greater availability of positive events in memory should increase our estimates that more positive events will occur in the future, and the greater availability of negative events in memory should increase our estimates that negative events will occur.

Wright and Bower (1992) tested these hypotheses by inducing a happy mood or a sad mood in their subjects through hypnosis. The subjects then estimated the probability of occurrence of 24 events, some of them positive events ("I will win an important honor or award during the next year") and some of them negative events ("I will be seriously injured within the next 5 years"). The results were consistent with the prediction of the availability hypothesis. The mean estimate of a positive event occurring was 0.52 for people in a happy mood and 0.38 for people in a sad mood. The mean estimate of a negative event occurring was 0.52 for people in a sad mood and 0.37 for people in a happy mood. Notice that these results present a challenge for therapists: It may be necessary to change someone's sad mood before convincing them that the future will be brighter.

TABLE 12.4 ■ Judgments of relative frequency for selected pairs of lethal events			
Less Likely	**More Likely**	**True Ratio***	**Percentage of Correct Discrimination**
Asthma	Firearm accident	1.20	80
Breast cancer	Diabetes	1.25	23
Lung cancer	Stomach cancer	1.25	25
Leukemia	Emphysema	1.49	47
Stroke	All cancer	1.57	83
All accidents	Stroke	1.85	20
Pregnancy	Appendicitis	2.00	17
Drowning	Suicide	9.60	70
All accidents	All diseases	15.50	57
Diabetes	Heart disease	18.90	97
Tornado	Asthma	20.90	42

*1.20 means 1.20:1, and so on.

Source: "Cognitive processes and societal risk taking," by P. Slovic, B. Fischhoff, & S. Lichtenstein, 1976, in *Cognition and social behavior*, J. S. Carroll & J. W. Payne (Eds.). https://doi.org/10.1007/978-94-010-1276-8_2. Copyright 1976 by Lawrence Erlbaum Associates, Inc.

Representativeness

Representativeness is another heuristic that we use to make probability judgments. You may have used this heuristic to answer Question 4 in Table 12.3. The question asks "If a family has three boys (B) and three girls (G), which sequence of births is more likely—B B B G G G or B G G B G B?" Subjects in a study by Kahneman and Tversky (1972) estimated that the sequence of boy–girl births in the order B G G B G B was significantly more likely than the order B B B G G G, even though the two sequences are equally probable. Three boys followed by three girls appeared too orderly to have been generated by a random process.

The bias toward selecting the unorderly sequence as more probable can be explained by the representativeness heuristic (Kahneman & Tversky, 1972). Questions about probabilities typically have the general form (1) What is the probability that object A belongs to class B? or (2) What is the probability that process B will generate event A? People frequently answer such questions by evaluating the degree to which A is representative of B—that is, the degree to which A resembles B. When A is very similar to B, the probability that A originates from B is judged to be high. When A is not very similar to B, the probability that A originated from B is judged to be low.

We expect that the birth order of boys and girls should form a random pattern. A major characteristic of apparent randomness is the absence of any systematic patterns. The representativeness heuristic therefore predicts that people should judge orderly events as having low probability if they believe the events were generated by a random process. Although there are many sequences of boys and girls that are unorderly, a particular unorderly sequence (such as B G G B G B) is as difficult to obtain as a particular orderly sequence (such as B B B G G G).

One problem with basing decisions solely on representativeness is that the decisions ignore other relevant information, such as *sample size*. For example, finding 600 boys in a sample of 1000 babies was judged as likely as finding 60 boys in a sample of 100 babies, even though the latter event is much more likely. Because the similarity between the obtained proportion (0.6) and the expected proportion (0.5) is the same in both cases, people do not see any difference between them. However, statisticians tell us that it is easier to obtain a discrepancy for small samples than for large samples.

Another situation in which the representativeness heuristic can cause faulty estimates occurs when we ignore probabilities entirely by basing our decision only on the similarity between an instance and a concept (Kahneman & Tversky, 1973). Imagine that a team of psychologists has administered personality tests to 30 engineers and 70 lawyers. The following description is chosen randomly from the 100 available descriptions:

Jack is a 45-year-old man. He is married and has four children. He is generally conservative, careful, and ambitious. He shows no interest in political and social issues and spends most of his free time on his many hobbies, which include home carpentry, sailing, and mathematical puzzles. The probability that Jack is one of the 30 engineers in the sample of 100 is _____%.

Representative The extent to which an event is typical of a larger class of events

Imagine now that you have the same description but were told that 70 of the 100 descriptions came from engineers. "What is the probability that Jack is one of the 70 engineers in the sample of 100?" The average estimate was identical for both questions. People estimated the probability of Jack's being an engineer as 0.9, which reflected that the personality description matched their concept of an engineer more closely than their concept of a lawyer. But notice that there was a difference between the two cases—in the first case, there were 30 engineers in the sample of 100, and in the second case, there were 70 engineers in the sample of 100. The probability that Jack is an engineer is influenced both by the number of engineers in the sample (called the **prior probability**) and by the personality description. We should use the personality description to revise the prior probabilities rather than entirely ignore the prior probabilities.

The next chapter on problem solving mentions that heuristics are often useful but do not guarantee success. Similarly, the availability and representativeness heuristics can mislead us if we do not consider relevant information, such as how the media may influence the availability heuristic and how prior probabilities and sample size should influence the representativeness heuristic. We can learn to give more accurate estimates if we learn what variables should influence our estimates.

COMBINING PROBABILITIES AND VALUES

Estimating probabilities accurately is an important decision-making skill, but it is not sufficient for making good decisions. Consider a situation in which the United States' interests in the Middle East are threatened. The response to this situation will depend in part on the probability that the threat is a real one. But the response also depends on the perceived consequences of various courses of action that the government might take. For example, one response might be to increase military forces in the Middle East. This course of action, like other alternative actions, has both advantages and disadvantages. It is therefore necessary to assess both the probability of events and the consequences of various actions when making decisions.

When we considered the different choice models in the first section of this chapter, we assigned values to the different dimensions of each alternative in the choice set. It is also necessary to assign values in risky decision making, but in addition, we have to combine the values of the different outcomes with the probabilities that they will occur. A normative procedure for combining probabilities and values is called **expected value**. This section describes the expected value model and then shows how psychologists have modified the model to make it more descriptive of how people make risky decisions.

Expected Value

Like other normative models, expected value provides a standard of reference against which psychologists can compare how people make decisions. Psychologists have usually made this comparison by designing rather simple gambling situations in which they can inform people

---

prior probability The probability that an event will occur before obtaining additional evidence regarding its occurrence

expected value The average value, as determined by combining the value of events with their probability of occurrence

about probabilities (of winning and losing) and values (amount won or lost). The expected value is the average amount of money people can expect to win or lose each time they decide to gamble. Let's see how it is calculated.

Expected value is calculated by multiplying the value of each possible outcome by its probability and adding the products. Its use can be illustrated by a simple game. I'm going to offer you the opportunity to play the game, and you must decide whether it would be to your advantage to play. I'm going to roll a fair die. If a 6 appears, you win $5. If any of the other five numbers appear, you win nothing. It costs $1 every time you play. Should you participate?

Expected value allows you to estimate the average amount of money you can expect to win or lose on every roll of the die. You can calculate this amount if you know the probability of a win, $P(W)$; the amount of a win, $V(W)$; the probability of a loss, $P(L)$; and the amount of a loss, $V(L)$. Substituting these amounts into the equation below yields

$$\begin{aligned} \textit{Expected value} &= P(W) \times V(W) + P(L) \times V(L) \\ &= \frac{1}{6} \times \$4 + \frac{5}{6} \times -\$1 \\ &= -\$\frac{1}{6} \end{aligned}$$

The probability of a win is 1/6 and the amount of a win is $4 ($5 minus the $1 entry fee). The probability of a loss is 5/6 and the value of a loss is -$1. The expected value of this game is -$1/6, implying that you would lose an average of approximately 17¢ every time you played the game. A decision based on a normative model should be to play the game for a positive expected value and not to play the game for a negative expected value.

A problem with using expected value as a descriptive model is that it does not always predict behavior. Gambling casinos are usually crowded with people playing games that have negative expected values (Photo 12.4). People also buy insurance despite its negative expected value. Because insurance companies pay out less money in claims than they collect in premiums, a purchaser of insurance can expect to lose money. And yet the purchase of insurance can be justified on the basis that it provides protection against a large financial setback.

PHOTO 12.4 Gambling is popular even though it has negative expected value.

istockphotos.com/Bet_Noire

Expected Utility

Two changes were made in the concept of expected value to make it more descriptive of actual behavior (Payne, 1973). The first change replaced the value of an outcome by its utility. Utility is the subjective value of an outcome, or what the outcome is actually worth to an individual. If people enjoy gambling, the act of gambling has utility over and above the money that is won or lost. If you enjoy winning money and don't mind losing money, then you could formulate a positive expected utility for the game described earlier. If the utility of a win—$U(W)$—is $6 to reflect the joy of winning rather than $4, and the utility of a loss—$U(L)$—remains at -$1, the expected utility would be positive rather than negative.

The expected-utility model could also explain why people buy insurance if they are more concerned about losing a substantial amount of money at one time than about paying out the much smaller premiums each year.

Another reason why utilities or subjective values are important is that how much we value an object is influenced by how we obtained it. For example, you may have received gifts that you value more for the expressed sentiment than for the gift itself. We also value objects more if we feel we deserve them. In one experiment, students in an executive education class were given mugs that had a retail value of $6. Half of the students were informed that they were randomly selected to receive a mug; the other half were told that they received a mug because of their performance on a graded exercise. All students were then given the opportunity to trade the mug for money and were asked to indicate the amount of money they would want for the exchange. The average requested amount was $6.35 for the group who believed they earned the mug and $4.71 for the group who believed they received the mug by chance (Lowenstein & Issacharoff, 1994).

An important aspect of utility that we all struggle with is whether to select an option that we *want* to do or the option that we *should* do. The *want* option typically provides immediate benefits and the *should* option provides long-term benefits (Milkman et al., 2008). Eating pizza provides immediate gratification, but eating a salad contributes to a more healthy lifestyle.

Kahn and Dhar (2006) found that people's resolution of the want-should dilemma depends on how they resolved related decisions. People who have recently selected the *should* option now feel entitled to select the *want* option. Participants in their study were more likely to report that they would spend a tax rebate on expensive designer sunglasses (the *want* choice) than less-expensive sunglasses (the *should* choice) if they had just imagined donating $100 of their tax rebate to charity. They also found that participants who had agreed to help a foreign student understand a lecture decided to donate less to charity than participants who had not been asked to help the student.

Subjective Expected Utility

A second change in the expected-value model was to make it more descriptive by replacing probabilities with subjective probabilities. When decision makers don't know the actual

---

utility Subjective value as determined by the decision maker

subjective probability An estimated probability as determined by the decision maker

probabilities, they must use subjective probabilities, or what they think the actual probabilities are. As we learned in the previous section, subjective probabilities often differ from actual probabilities as a result of possible biases introduced by using the availability and representativeness heuristics. Such findings indicate that we should be more accurate in predicting people's decisions if we used their subjective probabilities rather than the actual probabilities.

Subjective expected utility is calculated the same way as expected value, but the actual probabilities are replaced by subjective probabilities (*SP*), and the values are replaced by utilities. The subjective probability of each outcome is multiplied by its utility, and the products are added.

$$\text{Subjective expected utility} = SP(W) \times U(W) + SP(L) \times U(L)$$

By replacing probabilities with subjective probabilities and values with utilities, the subjective expected-utility model bases its predictions on subjective information. Therefore, it should be more accurate than the expected-value model in predicting people's decisions.

Here is an example of a decision that cannot be predicted by expected value: Would you rather win $900 or have a 90% chance of winning $1000? Answer this question before answering the next one. Would you rather lose $900 or have a 90% chance of losing $1000?

You may have noticed that the expected value is the same for both choices in the first question (1.00 × $900 = $900 and 0.90 × $1000 = $900). Expected value theory would therefore predict that people should be evenly divided in their selection of the two alternatives. However, most people prefer a sure gain of $900 over the chance to gamble for $1,000. Expected value is also the same for both choices in the second question (1.00 × –$900 = –$900 and 0.90 × –$1000 = –$900). But most people now prefer the gamble because it provides them with a small (0.10) probability of not losing any money.

Kahneman and Tversky (1979) incorporated these kinds of decisions into a general theory called *prospect theory*. One of its assumptions (called loss aversion) is that people's reaction to losses is more intense than their reaction to corresponding gains. In other words, losing $900 produces more negative affect than winning $900 produces a positive affect. People therefore try to avoid the certain loss of $900, even if it means gambling for a 90% chance of losing $1,000. Kahneman (2003) reports that he and Tversky deliberatively chose a meaningless name (prospect theory) to give their theory a distinctive label in case it ever became well known. It did become well known and had a tremendous influence on economics. Kahneman's 2003 article in the *American Psychologist* describes how prospect theory influenced economic thinking—an impact that resulted in his reception of the 2002 Nobel Prize in Economics (Amos Tversky died prematurely).

---

subjective expected utility A variation of expected value that uses utilities and subjective probabilities instead of values and probabilities

loss aversion Reaction to losses is more intense than reactions to corresponding gains

RISK DIMENSIONS

The theoretical evolution from expected value to subjective expected utility is an example of how a normative model (expected value) was transformed to make it more descriptive. Discovering how people thought about risk made it easier to make accurate predictions about their choices. Like the expected value model, however, subjective expected utility assumes that people place an equal emphasis on its four components—$U(W)$, $SP(W)$, $U(L)$, and $SP(L)$. People are likely influenced by the probability of winning, the amount of a win, the probability of losing, and the amount of a loss, but they might not place equal emphasis on these four risk dimensions. This has resulted in attempts to determine whether some risk dimensions are perceived as more important than others.

Importance of Risk Dimensions

Slovic and Lichtenstein (1968) tested the hypothesis that people will be more influenced by some dimensions than others. They had subjects evaluate the attractiveness of gambles, using a special type of gamble illustrated in Figure 12.3. A duplex gamble requires that the subject spin two spinners. The first spinner determines whether he will win money, and the second spinner determines whether he will lose money. The gamble shown in Figure 12.3 has four possible outcomes: win $1 and lose $4 (a net loss of $3), win $1 and lose nothing, win nothing and lose nothing, or win nothing and lose $4. Slovic and Lichtenstein used duplex gambles to change the probability of winning and the probability of losing independently. This is not possible in a standard gamble (represented by only one spinner) because the probability of winning is equal to one minus the probability of losing. It is not possible to determine whether people are more influenced by the probability of winning or the probability of losing if the two probabilities cannot be varied independently.

Slovic and Lichtenstein used two methods to evaluate the attractiveness of gambles. One method used a simple rating scale that varied from +5 (strong preference for not playing) to –5 (strong preference for playing). The second method required that subjects indicate the largest amount of money they would be willing to pay the experimenter to play the gamble (for attractive gambles) or to not have to play the gamble (for unattractive gambles). In both cases Slovic and Lichtenstein correlated the judged attractiveness of the gambles with the four risk dimensions. The correlations should be approximately equal if people were placing an equal emphasis on all four dimensions. The results indicated that there was a large difference in the correlations. A person's highest correlation was, on average, twice the size of the lowest correlation. The responses of many people were determined by one or two risk dimensions and were unresponsive to changes in the values of the less important dimensions.

---

risk dimension A component of a gamble such as the probability of winning or the amount of a loss

duplex gamble A gamble in which the probability of winning is assigned independently of the probability of losing

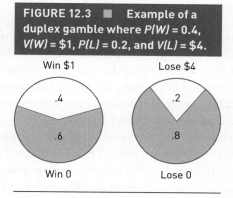

FIGURE 12.3 ■ **Example of a duplex gamble where** *P(W)* = 0.4, *V(W)* = $1, *P(L)* = 0.2, and *V(L)* = $4.

Source: "Relative importance of probabilities and payoffs in risk taking," by P. Slovic & S. Lichtenstein, 1968, *Journal of Experimental Psychology Monograph, 78* (3, Pt. 2). https://doi.org/10.1037/h0026468. Copyright 1968 by the American Psychological Association.

People's preference for a few risk dimensions over others has practical consequences. The California Lottery was able to increase lagging ticket sales by *lowering* the probability of winning. But this didn't matter because it increased the amount won, which was what ticket purchases were emphasizing (Stetz, 2002). The California example is part of a trend, according to the article. Other lotteries have also increased their jackpots and sales, by lowering the probability of winning (Photo 12.5).

PHOTO 12.5 Huge payouts drive lottery sales.

istockphotos.com/winhorse

Decision Frames

The previous research has shown that people regard some risk dimensions as more important than others. It is also possible to influence people's focus on different risk dimensions by emphasizing a particular dimension when describing the situation. In other words, the situation can be "framed" in different ways, and this framing determines how people perceive the situation. Tversky and Kahneman (1981) use the term decision frame to refer to the decision maker's conception of the decision-making situation (Photo 12.6).

The following example shows how the formulation of the problem influences the frame adopted by the decision maker (Dunegan, 1993). The subjects were 128 members of an international company that develops high-technology engineering systems. The subjects read a scenario in which a project team was requesting an additional $100,000 for a project begun several months before. Everyone read the same scenario except for the last sentence. The last sentence for half of the participants read "Of the projects undertaken by this team, 30 of the last 50 have been successful" (a positive frame). The other half read "Of the projects undertaken by this team, 20 of the last 50 have been unsuccessful" (a negative frame). Notice that the probability of successfully completing a project is 0.6 for both cases, but the positive frame mentions the 60% success rate, and the negative frame mentions the 40% failure rate. People given the positive frame allocated significantly more money to the project than people given the negative frame.

PHOTO 12.6 Decision frames influence decisions.

istockphotos.com/anyaberkut

---

decision frame Different formulations of the same problem elicit different preferences

The selection of a decision frame has important implications outside the laboratory. Although a medical treatment that results in a 75% survival rate is logically equivalent to one that results in a 25% death rate, McKenzie (2003) argued that the choice of frames can convey information, so there is a practical difference in whether a speaker selects a positive frame or a negative frame. Emphasis on a 75% survival rate is appropriate if the 75% survival represents an increase in the survival rate over an older treatment because a patient might now want to seriously consider the new treatment. In other situations, emphasis on the 25% death rate might be more appropriate such as when discussing risky surgery. Elderly men with prostate cancer could be discouraged from seeking an operation if the cancer is slow to spread and the operation is risky. Emphasizing the death rate in this situation might convince a patient that it is better to avoid surgery. Research shows that both speakers and listeners are sensitive to the choice of frames because of the information contained in the frames (McKenzie, 2003).

You can evaluate the effect of decision frames on yourself by selecting either Plan A or Plan B for two cell phone plans that differ in both the number of dropped calls and in price. Make a selection for both conditions in Table 12.5.

	——— Condition 1 ———		——— Condition 2 ———	
TABLE 12.5 ■ Cell phone plans for two conditions				
Option	**Dropped Calls per 100 Calls**	**Price per Year**	**Dropped Calls per 1000 Calls**	**Price per Month**
Plan A	4.2	$384	42	$32
Plan B	6.5	$324	65	$27

Source: From "Six of one, half dozen of the other," by K. A. Burson, R. P. Larrick, & J. G. Lynch, Jr., 2009., *Psychological Science, 20,* 1074–1078. https://doi.org/10.1111/j.1467-9280.2009.02394.x

The information is equivalent for Plans A and B across the two conditions but is scaled differently. In both conditions, Plan A drops 4.2% of the calls and costs $384 per year, and Plan B drops 6.5% of the calls and costs $324 per year. However, Condition 1 emphasizes the difference in price, and Condition 2 emphasizes the difference in dropped calls. As predicted, these differences in framing caused the majority of participants to select Plan B in Condition 1 and Plan A in Condition 2 (Burson et al., 2009).

Perceived Risk

An advantage of looking at how risk dimensions influence decisions is that it may tell us how people perceive risk. For example, perceived risk may depend on how much money could be lost, as suggested by Slovic and Lichtenstein's (1968) finding that people emphasized this dimension when they determined how much money they would bid to play a gamble.

Expected value tells us the average amount of money we can expect from a gamble but does not tell us the amount of perceived risk. This is illustrated by a question that I asked my class in which they must choose between two hypothetical gambles. In the first case, I flip a fair coin, and they win $1 if it lands heads and lose $1 if it lands tails. In the second case, I flip a fair coin, and they win $100 if it lands heads and lose $100 if it lands tails. Because the probabilities of winning and losing are identical and the amounts won and lost are identical, the expected value is zero for both gambles. If you played either gamble many times, you would expect to go home with the same amount of money you had at the beginning.

A few students chose to gamble for $100, but the vast majority chose to gamble for $1. Expected value cannot explain this result because both gambles have the same expected value. But the $100 gamble is considered more risky because it has a greater variance—there is a much greater difference between the value of a win and the value of a loss. And the outcome of my class experiment was consistent with the finding that most people do not like to take risks (Weber, 1998).

But a few people did prefer the $100 gamble, and this raises the question of whether risk taking is a stable personality trait. You probably know some people who like to take risks and others who are very conservative. However, Weber's (1998) review of the experimental evidence shows that most people, regardless of gender or culture, do not like to take perceived risks. When people make choices that are considered risky, it is usually because they do not *perceive* the choice as risky. For example, a cross-cultural study of students at major universities in the People's Republic of China, Germany, Poland, and the United States found that the Chinese respondents were more likely than the others to show preferences for risky financial options (Weber & Hsee, 1998). However, these apparent differences in risk preference were caused primarily by cultural differences in the perception of risk rather than by cultural differences in attitude toward risk. The Chinese respondents, like the others, did not like to take risks; however, they did not perceive the risky choices to be particularly risky.

Weber and Morris (2010) interpret these and other findings within a constructivist framework in which perceptions of risk are constructed judgments that vary across individuals and cultures. They assume that cultural representations are based on dynamic schemas that can vary from one occasion to the next, shifting experimental questions from "Does culture matter?" to "When does culture matter?" For instance, Chinese social networks are more dense and enduring than American social networks, so researchers need to evaluate which features of social networks impact particular decisions.

The assessment of risk dominated world headlines when an epidemic of acute respiratory syndrome (COVID-19) turned into a global pandemic between January and April, 2020. A study conducted at the University of Cambridge (United Kingdom) and the University of Groningen (Netherlands) queried nearly 7000 people in 10 countries across Europe, America, and Asia between mid-March and mid-April (Dryhurst et al., 2020). Although risk perception was high across all countries, it was significantly higher in the United Kingdom and Spain than in the other countries (Figure 12.4). There were nonetheless commonalities in the variables that influenced attitudes across countries, including worldviews, personal experience, prosocial values, and the effect of friends and family.

FIGURE 12.4 ■ **Perceived risk of COVID-19 across countries.**

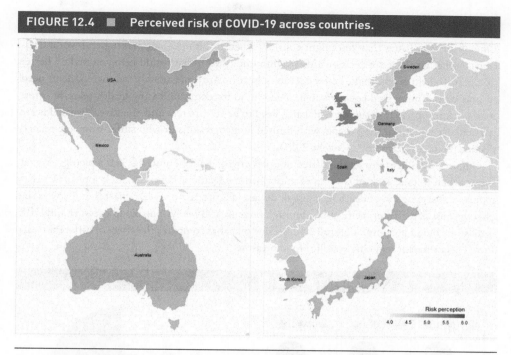

Source: "Risk perceptions of COVID-19 around the world," by S. Dryhurst et al., 2020, *Journal of Risk Research, 23*, 994–1006. https://doi.org/10.1080/13669877.2020.1758193

APPLICATIONS

Our emphasis so far has been on examining decision making within simple but well-controlled laboratory experiments. Cognitive psychologists hope their theories have some relevance to the real world, and decision making is no exception. Biased judgments can cause decision makers to undersave for retirement, marry the wrong person, and accept the wrong jobs (Milkman et al., 2009). Milkman and her coauthors propose that, in a knowledge-based economy, the knowledge worker's primary contribution is to make good decisions. As the economy becomes increasingly global, each decision can potentially impact more people.

In this concluding section, we look at how decision research is being applied to real-world situations. The first application discusses how diagrams and converting probabilities into frequencies can help people understand a medical diagnosis. The second application looks at making healthy decisions. The third application analyzes what people do in situations in which they must make a series of rapid decisions, such as in fighting a fire or a battle. Each of these applications draws on different theoretical ideas, illustrating the flexibility in theorizing that is needed to model decision making in different situations.

Decision Aids

One of the first issues that you might consider when thinking about making real-world decisions is whether there are decision aids (Kleinmuntz, 1990) that would help you make a better decision. To help people make better decisions, health-care professionals and their patients need to understand numerical concepts that are essential for communicating health-relevant information. Appropriately designed visual aids need to be transparent and effective. Visual aids are particularly beneficial for patients with limited language skills or who suffer from age-related decline (Garcia-Retamero & Cokely, 2013).

Figure 12.5 illustrates several different types of visual aids. Figure 12.5a is a pictogram that shows when to take each of si types of prescribed medication. Figure 12.5b is a pie chart that reports the proportion of death by cause of disease. Figure 12.5c is a bar chart that displays the effectiveness of different medications for high pressure (SBP is systolic blood pressure and DBP is diastolic blood pressure). Figure 12.5d is a line plot that compares the effect of different treatments over time for reducing systolic blood pressure.

FIGURE 12.5 ■ Examples of visual aids.

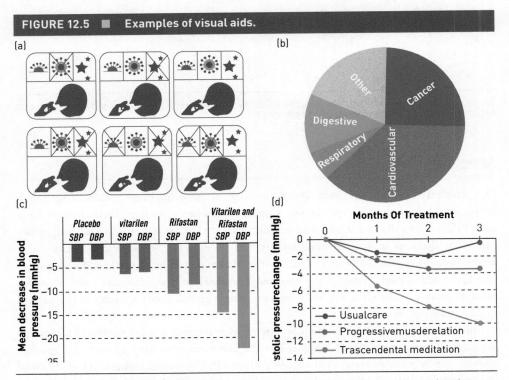

Source: From "Communicating health risks with visual aids," by R. Garcia-Retamero & E. T. Cokely, (2013). *Current Directions in Psychological Science, 22*, 392-399. https://doi.org/10.1177/0963721413491570

Decision aids become particularly critical when people need to combine multiple sources of information. We have already encountered a number of instances in which people's decisions overlooked important information. For example, in Kahneman and Tversky's (1973) experiment, people ignored the prior probability when deciding whether Jack is an engineer. They based their decision solely on the evidence contained in a biographical description.

There is a normative model called **Bayes's theorem** that enables people to combine a prior probability with new evidence to calculate a revised probability. If one knew the formula and had a calculator, it would not be too difficult to use this method. But without either, it would be surprising if people's probability estimates closely matched the normative estimates calculated from Bayes's theorem.

Consider the following problem investigated by Gigerenzer and Hoffrage (1995):

The probability of breast cancer is 1% for a woman at age 40 who participates in routine screening. If a woman has breast cancer, the probability is 80% that she will get a positive mammography. If a woman does not have breast cancer, the probability is 9.6% that she will get a positive mammography. A woman in this age group had a positive mammography in a routine screening. What is the probability that she actually has breast cancer?

The right half of Figure 12.6 shows how to solve this problem by using the formula for Bayes's theorem. The formula uses the data (D) of a positive mammography to evaluate the hypothesis (H) that the woman has breast cancer. The prior probability of having breast cancer, p(H), is 0.01. The probability of a positive mammography for a woman who has breast cancer, p(D|H), is 0.80. And the probability of a positive mammography for a woman who does not have breast cancer, p(D|-H), is 0.096. The equation at the bottom shows how to calculate the probability that the patient has breast cancer by combining the prior probability and new data. The sad face illustrates that this is difficult!

The left half of 12.6 represents the same problem expressed in frequencies rather than in probabilities. The frequencies show that in a group of 1000 women at age 40 we can expect 10 women to have breast cancer. Of these 10 women, 8 test positive on a mammography exam. Of the 990 women who do not have breast cancer, 95 test positive on a mammography exam. The smiling face indicates that the probability that the patient has breast cancer is now much simpler to calculate. One simply divides the frequency of positive test results for women who have cancer (8) by the total number of positive test results (8 + 95). This gives the same answer as the more complex formula on the right.

Gigerenzer and Hoffrage (1995) found that when problems were expressed as frequencies rather than as probabilities people provided more accurate estimates (they were not given formulas to solve the problems). In the frequency format, students were given frequencies in the problem and gave their answers in frequencies. Cosmides and Tooby (1996) also found that people did much better in using frequencies than in using probabilities and argued that the ability to encode and use frequencies is important from an evolutionary perspective.

Gigerenzer and Hoffrage concluded their article by considering the practical consequences of these findings. Instead of teaching people to use a complex formula, such as Bayes's theorem, they suggest teaching people to translate probabilities into frequencies. For example, in the mammography problem, the probability of 0.01 can be represented as 10 women in 1000,

Bayes's theorem A normative procedure for revising a probability by combining a prior probability with evidence

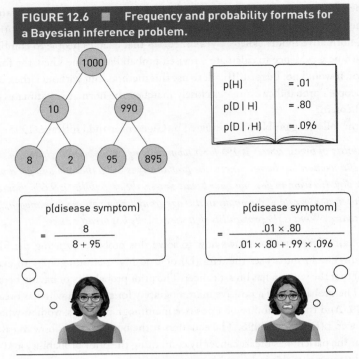

FIGURE 12.6 ■ Frequency and probability formats for a Bayesian inference problem.

$p(\text{disease symptom})$

$$= \frac{8}{8 + 95}$$

$p(\text{disease symptom})$

$$= \frac{.01 \times .80}{.01 \times .80 + .99 \times .096}$$

Source: From "How to improve Bayesian reasoning without instruction: Frequency formats," by G. Gigerenzer & U. Hoffrage, 1995, *Psychological Review, 102*, 684–704. https://doi.org/10.1037/0033-295X.102.4.684

istockphoto.com/kbeis

and the probability of 0.80 can be represented as 8 of these 10 women, as was done in Figure 12.6. Reasoning with frequencies should then be easier than reasoning with the initially specified probabilities. This has been confirmed in subsequent research that has demonstrated that reasoning with frequencies was both relatively easy to learn and remember (Sedlmeier & Gigerenzer, 2001).

Healthy Decisions

The previous chapter on language concluded with a section on persuasive communications, some of which were directed toward promoting healthy behavior. Encouraging healthy decisions is also an important application of research on decision making. Figure 12.7 displays three decision principles for changing behavior (Chapman, 2019). These principles are general and apply to many different types of decisions, in addition to those regarding health.

The first principle is to *inform* behavior by using effective methods for presenting information. Visual displays (Figure 12.5) and the use of frequencies rather than probabilities in making comparisons (Figure 12.6) are examples. Fuzzy-trace theory (Reyna & Brainerd, 1995) also offers guidance. The theory proposes that memories consist of both gist —the most essential information—and verbatim details (Reyna, 2018).

FIGURE 12.7 ■ Three decision-science principles for changing health behavior.

Inform	Incentivize	Guide
Capitalize on Presentation of Information, not Just Content	Employ Social Consequences to Motivate Behavior	Intervene on Behavior Directly, By-Passing Beliefs and Attitudes
• Framing • Order of Information • Comparison	• Behavioral Incentives • Social Norms • Social Comparisons • Prosocial Motives	• Cues and Prompts • Defaults • Recommendations • Self-Control Devices

Source: From "A decision-science approach to health-behavior change," by G. B. Chapman, 2019, *Current Directions in Psychological Science, 28*, 469–474. https://doi.org/10.1177/0963721419854102

The relevance of fuzzy-trace theory was supported by a literature review of 79 studies on using the theory to improve healthy behavior (Blalock & Reyna, 2016). As predicted, people formed distinct verbatim and gist memories, but the gist representations were retained longer than the verbatim representations. The findings from most studies also supported the prediction that, when compared to verbatim reasoning, gist-based reasoning was more often associated with the adoption of healthy behaviors. Blalock and Reyna (2016) recommended that healthcare providers should initially distinguish between gist and verbatim details and then present only the gist (essential meaning), as determined by experts.

The second principle is to *incentivize* behavior by promoting social consequences. Herd immunity is a good example in which a vaccination both protects an individual and helps protect others through lowering its rate of spread (Betsch et al., 2017). The red circles in Figure 12.8 represent infected individuals who can infect healthy individuals who are not

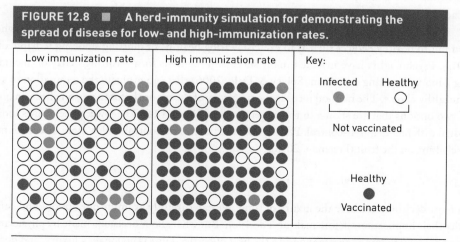

FIGURE 12.8 ■ A herd-immunity simulation for demonstrating the spread of disease for low- and high-immunization rates.

Source: From "On the benefits of explaining herd immunity in vaccine advocacy," by C. Betsch, R. Bohm, L. Korn, & C. Holtmann, 2017, *Nature Human Behavior, 1*(0056), 1–6. https://doi.org/10.1038/s41562-017-0056

vaccinated (white circles). A high immunization rate (blue circles) reduces the spread by forming a social "barrier" that helps protect those who are unvaccinated. A simulation at http://rocs.hu-berlin.de/D3/herd/ illustrates the spread of a disease for different percentages of immunization.

More than 2000 online participants learned about herd immunity through either a text-based explanation or a simulation based on Figure 12.8 (Betsch et al., 2017). The interactive simulation was more effective than the text-based presentation for increasing intention to vaccinate for participants from Western countries (Germany, Netherlands, United States). For more prosocial eastern countries (Hong Kong, South Korea, Vietnam), there was a higher intention to vaccinate, even without communicating the concept of herd immunity.

The third principle is to *guide* behavior through direct intervention. Although most people approve of organ donation, relatively few grant permission to donate their organs by signing a donor card. In an online experiment, participants in one condition were told to assume that they had recently moved to a new state where the default condition was not to be an organ donor (Johnson & Goldstein, 2003). The other condition was identical except the default condition was now to be an organ donor. Everyone was given the opportunity to confirm or change his or her status. The findings revealed that donation rates were about twice as high (82% versus 42%) when the default condition was to be an organ donor. In this case, no action was required to become an organ donor.

The order of presenting choices can also make a difference, as demonstrated by the observations recorded at a university cafeteria with a menu that included either an indulgent (lemon cheesecake) or a healthy (fresh fruit) dessert. When the dessert was presented first, approximately 2/3 of the participants who chose the lighter main dish were in the indulgent-dessert condition. They compensated for the unhealthy dessert by selecting a main dish that had lower calories. The same results occurred when participants made selections online. Those participants who were initially assigned chocolate cake as their dessert were more likely to select a healthier entrée than those participants who were assigned fruit salad as their dessert (Flores et al., 2019).

Another approach for guiding behavior is to increase self-control by rewarding people who commit to healthy choices such as to exercise, eating healthy, or quitting smoking (Chapman, 2019). Psychologists have invented many successful methods for measuring behavior, including a mouse-tracking paradigm (Spivey & Dale, 2006) that can evaluate the temptation of an unhealthy choice. The method records the trajectory of the mouse before a person clicks on one of two options that are shown in the upper panel of Figure 12.9. The lower panel shows individual differences in self-control. Participants with more self-control took a more direct course to clicking on the fruit (Freeman, 2018).

Action-Based Decision Making

In most decisions, we have the luxury of time. We can carefully examine our options and consider their implications before making a decision. But what about decisions made by physicians in emergency rooms or commanders in the heat of battle? Time is no longer a luxury, and decisions have to be made quickly before lives are lost.

FIGURE 12.9 ■ Mouse trajectories before clicking on a choice option.

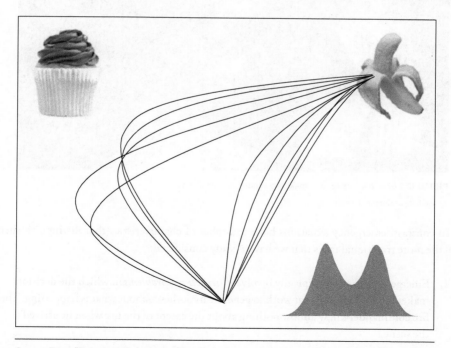

Source: From "Doing psychological science by hand," by J. B. Freeman (2018), *Current Directions in Psychological Science*, *27*, 315–323. https://doi.org/10.1177/0963721417746793

Consider the following scenario (Orasanu & Connolly, 1993). A firefighting crew arrives at a four-story apartment building, the scene of a reported fire. The commander sends his crew into the first and second stories to extinguish the fire, but they report that the fire has spread beyond the second floor. Observing smoke pouring from the eaves, the commander calls for a second unit. He also orders his crew to stop trying to extinguish the fire and to search the building for people trapped inside.

This scenario comes from the first chapter of a book called *Decision Making in Action: Models and Methods* (Klein et al., 1993). The central argument of the book is that the traditional models and methods for studying decision making are not very helpful in explaining what people do in these kinds of emergency situations (Photo 12.7). The reason is that the traditional approach has focused on only one particular type of decision making—the **decision event**. The decision event consists of a situation in which the decision maker evaluates a fixed set of alternatives according to stable criteria and differentially weights and combines these criteria to select the best alternative. Most of the tasks that we previously considered, such as selecting the best apartment, are good examples of a decision event.

PHOTO 12.7 Emergencies require making a sequence of decisions.

istockphotos.com/gorodenkoff

In contrast, emergency situations have a number of characteristics that distinguish them from the more traditional tasks that we have already considered:

1. Emergency situations typically involve *ill-structured problems* in which the decision maker has to do significant work to generate hypotheses about what is happening. The fire commander knew almost nothing about the extent of the fire when he arrived at the scene.

---

decision event Making a single decision rather than a sequence of decisions in a changing situation

2. Decision making occurs within an *uncertain, dynamic environment*. Information about what is happening is often incomplete, ambiguous, and/or of poor quality. The environment may also change quickly, as when a small fire suddenly becomes a large fire.

3. There may be *shifting or competing goals*. Goals in the previous scenario would include saving the building, the occupants, and the crew. These goals can shift as the fire grows, from saving the building to saving the occupants to saving the crew.

4. Responses to emergency situations require reacting to a sequence of events rather than to a single event. This creates *action–feedback loops* in which the decision maker has to react to the consequences of each action before determining the next action.

5. There is often considerable *time pressure*. Lack of time will typically produce less complicated reasoning strategies and perhaps high levels of personal stress.

6. There are *high stakes*. One obviously wants to avoid mistakes in life-threatening situations.

7. Often there are *multiple players*. Although there is usually a single person in charge, the leader interacts with others to solve the problem.

8. *Organizational goals* guide the decision making. Unlike the personal life decisions that we all face, medical and firefighting personnel are guided by rules set by others in the organizations.

One of the best-known models of how people make decisions in these situations is the recognition-primed decision (RPD) model proposed by Klein (1993). The starting premise is that people who make decisions in these situations are typically very experienced. They are therefore capable of responding more quickly than the less-experienced subjects tested in laboratory studies. This parallels the novice–expert differences that we will review in Chapter 14 on expertise and creativity.

Klein initially formulated the RPD model after interviewing how fire commanders made choices. Rather than evaluate many alternatives, they reported that they used their prior experience to immediately generate and modify plans in reaction to the changing situation. The model is called a *recognition-primed* model because of the emphasis it places on situation assessment and recognition of what is occurring. Once the problem is recognized, experienced decision makers can usually identify an acceptable course of action as the first one they consider rather than having to consider multiple options.

Notice that there are several reasons why this is a plausible strategy in these circumstances. First, expertise allows the decision maker to avoid considering many alternatives that would have a low probability of working. Second, there is not enough time to allow for a thorough consideration of many options. Third, Klein proposes, as did Simon (1957) many years earlier, that

---

recognition-primed decision (RPD) A decision that is quickly made following recognition of a situation

decision makers usually try to find a *satisfactory* course of action, not the best alternative. This allows them to respond more quickly than if they had to select the best strategy.

The effect of experience on situation awareness was demonstrated in a study that asked electronic warfare technicians to reconstruct from memory the location of the ships they had been tracking on a computer screen during a Navy training exercise (Randel et al., 1996). During the exercise, the screen (Figure 12.10) suddenly went blank, and the technicians were asked to reproduce the ship locations. Experts correctly drew the locations for 95% of the hostile ships, compared to 78% for intermediates and 51% for novices. They correctly located 74% of the friendly ships, compared to 53% for intermediates and 21% for novices. Both groups demonstrated the importance of locating hostile ships, but the experts were much more able to recall the locations of both hostile and friendly ships.

FIGURE 12.10 ■ Computer screen used to track ship locations.

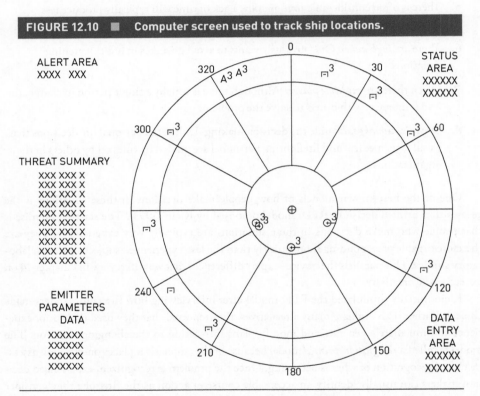

Source: From "Differences in expert and novice situation awareness in naturalistic decision making," by J. M. Randel, H. L Pugh, & S. K. Reed, 1996, *International Journal of Human-Computer Studies, 45,* 579–597. https://doi.org/10.1006/ijhc.1996.0068

A lack of situation awareness can lead to loss of life during peaceful maneuvers (Hinks, 2017; Lubold & Youssef, 2017). On the morning of June 17, 2017, the USS Fitzgerald collided with a container ship bound for Tokyo, killing seven of the crew while injuring several others. A report by the Navy concluded that its crew was unprepared for this situation in which they found themselves through a lack of preparation, ineffective command-and-control, and deficiencies in training and preparations for navigation. Another collision followed on August 21, 2017, off the coast of Singapore in which 10 crew members of the USS John S. McCain lost their lives. The Navy found there was a loss of situational awareness while responding to mistakes in one of the world's busiest shipping lanes (Photo 12.8). New directives now require Navy ships to broadcast their positions in crowded shipping lanes and make it more difficult for ships to leave port if their crews lack basic navigation skills.

PHOTO 12.8 Situation awareness is critical in crowded shipping lanes.

istockphotos.com/baona

In his book *Sources of Power: How People Make Decisions*, Klein (1998) discussed the different strategies used by experts. Successful execution of these strategies depends on the development of a variety of skills that Klein refers to as sources of power. Gigerenzer (2019) remarks that 20 years after the book's publication, it still offers directions from which current research could benefit. Klein (2015) recommended that Gigerenzer's research could benefit from a stronger focus on expertise, which has occurred. Gigerenzer (2019), in turn, recommended that theoretical terms such as "pattern matching" in Klein's theory would benefit from more detailed explanations. We will return to the topic of expert decision making in the final chapter on expertise and creativity.

SUMMARY

Making decisions usually requires evaluating at least two alternatives that differ on a number of attributes. Selecting an alternative requires the decision maker to combine this information to form an overall evaluation for each alternative. The study of how people search for information provides evidence about decision strategies. The elimination-by-aspects and conjunctive models are noncompensatory because positive attributes cannot compensate for negative attributes. The additive and additive–difference models are compensatory because positive attributes can compensate for negative attributes. Research on how people select a decision strategy has shown that people were likely to use a noncompensatory strategy when there were many alternatives and a compensatory strategy when there were few alternatives.

Risky decision making refers to decisions that are concerned with uncertainty—for example, evaluating the potential dangers of a nuclear reactor, buying insurance, and diagnosing medical problems. To make good decisions, it is necessary to make accurate estimates of probabilities. These estimates are often based on heuristics, which sometimes yield reasonable estimates but often do not. The availability heuristic proposes that we evaluate the probability of an event by judging the ease with which instances can be recalled. The representativeness heuristic states that the probability of an event is estimated by evaluating how similar it is to the essential properties of its population.

Expected value is a normative procedure for making decisions. It is calculated by multiplying the value of events by their probability of occurring and summing the products. Subjective expected utility is a modified version of this procedure in which subjective values (utilities) replace values and subjective probabilities replace probabilities. The expected-value model can be further modified by allowing for the possibility that people emphasize some components of the model more than others. For instance, the amount of a win drives the sale of lottery tickets. In addition, different formulations of gambles (decision frames) influence decisions. Perceived risk also influences choices.

Applications of decision making include the design of decision aids to help people make better decisions. Using diagrams and substituting frequencies for probabilities are examples. General principles for improving decisions are to inform behavior by effectively presenting information, incentivize behavior by employing social consequences, and guide behavior through direct intervention. In action-based decision making, it is necessary to quickly carry out a sequence of actions rather than make a single decision. The recognition-primed decision model proposes that the decision maker quickly assesses the situation, uses his or her expertise to select a course of action, and evaluates fairly immediate feedback to determine whether that action is working.

RECOMMENDED READING

Two books provide an interesting contrast in approaches to decision making. *Rational Choice in an Uncertain* World (Hastie & Dawes, 2001) discusses a deliberative approach to judgment and decision making, whereas *Educating Intuition* (Hogarth, 2001) focuses on judgments and decisions that involve little or no conscious deliberation. The edited book, *Heuristics and Biases: The Psychology of Intuitive Judgment* (Gilovich et al., 2002) contains chapters on a wide variety of topics including affect (Slovic et al., 2002) and individual differences (Stanovich & West, 2002). Another edited book, *Emerging Perspectives on Judgment and Decision Research* (Schneider & Shanteau, 2003), also contains many valuable chapters, including a summary chapter by Doherty (2003) that is particularly interesting. Neural economic models of decision-making are attracting more attention (Hakim & Levy, 2019; Parnamets et al., 2020). Other theoretical efforts integrate research on probabilistic biases with Bayesian modeling (Chater et al., 2020). Kube and Rozenkrantz (2021) review how healthy people and people with mental disorders update their beliefs. By six years of age, most children will experience regret regarding their decisions, and this emotion increases into adolescence (McCormack et al., 2020). *Decision Making in Action: Models and Methods*, edited by Klein et al. (1993), contains chapters on making multiple, action-based decisions during a brief time period.

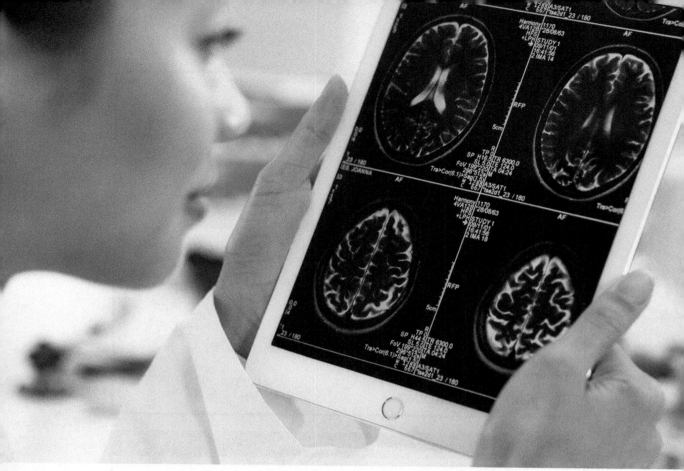

13 PROBLEM SOLVING

Classifying Problems
  Arrangement
  Inducing Structure
  Transformation

Newell and Simon's Theory
  Objectives and Method
  Theoretical Assumptions
  Means–End Analysis

General Strategies
  Subgoals
  Analogy
  Representational Transfer

Applications
  Design Problems
  Conflict Resolution

SUMMARY

RECOMMENDED READING

LEARNING OBJECTIVES:

1. Identify Greeno's three types of problems and their differences.

2. List the theoretical components that comprise Newell and Simon's theory of problem solving.

3. Discuss general strategies, also known as heuristics, for solving problems.

4. Explain why design and conflict resolution are considered examples of ill-structured problems.

Humans are not the only creatures who can solve problems, yet identifying problem solving as the most characteristically human activity emphasizes its importance in the development of civilization. This and the next chapter discuss problem solving and emphasize progress in our attempt to understand how people solve problems. This chapter establishes the basic components of a theory of problem solving.

The first section contains examples of different kinds of problems. Psychologists have been interested in the question, How general are problem-solving skills? At one extreme, the answer is that the skills are very general, and a person who is good at solving one type of problem will also be very good at solving other types. At the other extreme is the claim that skills are very specific, and a person who is good at solving one type of problem may be poor at solving other types. The claim made in the first section falls between these two extremes. The proposed classification identifies three general kinds of problems on the basis of the skills required to solve them.

The second section describes the general characteristics of a theory of problem solving proposed by Newell and Simon (1972). The theory describes how problem solving is influenced by (1) people's information-processing capabilities as determined by STM (short-term memory) and LTM (long-term memory), (2) the structure of the problem and its effect on the search for a solution, and (3) the effectiveness of different strategies and sources of information. The third section discusses general strategies, such as the use of subgoals, analogy, and diagrams. The final section applies theories to design and conflict resolution.

The problems discussed in this chapter are mainly puzzles. You may wonder why psychologists are interested in puzzles—wouldn't it be more appropriate to study the kinds of problems people encounter in school or work? One reason for studying problems such as the anagram and series-completion problems shown in Table 13.1 is that they often appear on intelligence tests. If we want to understand what intelligence tests really measure, we must take a closer look at the specific skills required to answer the questions (Carpenter et al., 1990). Another reason is that, when studying puzzles, psychologists can be less concerned about differences in people's education; everyone should have more of an "equal chance" on puzzles than on problems taken from a textbook. Fortunately, most of the issues discussed in this chapter will still be relevant when we later discuss how prior knowledge and expertise influence problem solving.

CLASSIFYING PROBLEMS

Any attempt to improve problem-solving skills raises the question of what skills are needed for different kinds of problems. Students are taught how to solve statistics problems in a statistics class and chemistry problems in a chemistry class. Have they learned any general skills in a statistics class that can make them better problem solvers in a chemistry class, or do the problems in each class require a different set of skills? The question would be easier to answer if we could classify problems according to the skills needed to solve them.

Table 13.1 shows examples of problems that have been studied by psychologists. You will better understand this chapter if you try to solve these problems before reading further. When you have finished working the problems, try to classify them according to the skills needed to solve them. We will examine one method of classification that proposes the six problems can be divided into three categories.

The proposed classification is based on the general kinds of psychological skills and knowledge needed to solve different problems (Greeno, 1978). Greeno suggested that there are three types of problems: *arrangement, inducing structure,* and *transformation*. The classification does not imply that we will be able to classify every problem into one of the three categories. Rather, it provides three ideal types to determine whether a given problem requires primarily rearrangement, inducing structure, transformation, or some combination of the three skills. We now consider examples of each type, to see how the types differ.

TABLE 13.1   ■   Examples of problems

A. Analogy

What word completes the analogy?

Merchant: Sell; Customer:

Lawyer: Client; Doctor:

B. String problem

Two strings hang from a ceiling but are too far apart to allow a person to hold one and walk to the other. On the floor are a book of matches, a screwdriver, and a few pieces of cotton. How could the strings be tied together?

C. Men and elves

Three men and three elves who have to cross a river find a boat, but the boat is so small that it can hold no more than two people. If the elves on either bank of the river or in the boat are outnumbered at any time by men, they will disappear. Find the simplest schedule of crossings that will allow everyone to cross safely. At least one person must be in the boat at each crossing.

D. Water jar

You have an 8-gallon pail and a 5-gallon pail. How could you obtain 2 gallons of water?

E. Anagram

Rearrange the letters in each row to make an English word.

RWAET

KEROJ

F. Series completion

What number or letter continues each series?

1 2 8 3 4 6 5 6

A B M C D M

Source: Reed, S.K. (2012). *Cognition: Theories and Applications 9e*. Cengage.

Arrangement

Arrangement problems present some objects and require the problem solver to arrange them in a way that satisfies some criterion. The objects usually can be arranged in many different ways, but only one or a few of the arrangements form a solution. An excellent example is the rearrangement of the letters of an **anagram** to form a word, such as rearranging the letters *KEROJ* to spell *JOKER* and *RWAET* to spell *WATER*. Solving an arrangement problem often involves much

arrangement problem. A problem that requires rearranging its parts to satisfy a specified criterion

anagram. A problem that requires rearranging a string of letters to form a word

trial and error, during which partial solutions are formed and evaluated. Greeno argued that the skills needed to solve arrangement problems include the following:

1. **Fluency in generating possibilities.** Flexibility is needed to generate many partial solutions and discard those that appear unpromising.

2. **Retrieval of solution patterns.** Ability to retrieve words from memory should be related to the ability in solving anagrams.

3. **Knowledge of principles that constrain the search.** Knowing the relative frequency with which various letters occur together should help guide the search. Because the pair JR is an unlikely combination, for example, it should be avoided when forming partial solutions.

Gestalt psychologists were particularly interested in how people solve arrangement problems. Gestalt psychology, which began as the study of perception, emphasized the structure of patterns, and consequently, it analyzed problem solving from this perspective. Many Gestalt tasks required the rearrangement of objects to find the correct relation among the parts.

A well-known example is the problem described by Kohler (1925) in his book *The Mentality of Apes*. Kohler hung some fruit from the top of a cage to investigate whether a chimpanzee or other ape could discover how to reach it. The cage contained several sticks and crates. The solution depended on finding a correct way to rearrange the objects—for example, standing on a crate and using a stick to knock down the fruit. According to the Gestalt analysis, solving the problem required the reorganization of the objects into a new structure.

Gestalt psychologists argued that discovering the correct organization usually occurred as a flash of insight. **Insight** is the sudden discovery of the correct solution following a period of incorrect attempts based primarily on trial and error or, in the case of incubation, not consciously thinking about the problem (Helie & Sun, 2010). The metaphor of the solution suddenly becoming visible is perhaps not surprising, based on the Gestalt interest in perception. The term "insight" itself emphasizes its parallel with vision, as do expressions such as "a moment of illumination" or "seeing the light." However, the inability of a single metaphor to capture all facets of the concept suggests that we should remain open to alternative ways of viewing insight.

The key factor distinguishing insight from other forms of discovery is the suddenness of the solution. In contrast to solutions that are achieved through careful planning or through a series of small steps, solutions based on insight seem to occur "in a flash." Evidence supports the argument that the correct arrangement of parts often occurs quite suddenly (Metcalfe, 1986a, 1986b). Metcalfe gave her subjects anagrams to solve, such as *ssoia, pmuoi,* and *ttnua.* They were asked to assess how close they were to solving the problem, on a scale from 1 to 10, during the course of solving the anagrams. Every 10 seconds, a tap occurred, and subjects recorded their ratings. The ratings remained very low until the discovery of the solution, implying that the correct answer suddenly appeared. In contrast, transformation problems are usually solved

---

insight. The sudden discovery of a solution following unsuccessful attempts to solve a problem

through an ordered sequence of correct steps in which people gradually progress toward the solution (Metcalfe, 1986b).

One factor that can make it difficult to find a solution to an arrangement problem occurs when a problem solver unnecessarily constrains the solution (Photo 13.1). According to this proposal, insight occurs when the problem solver removes the self-imposed constraint. You can test whether you place unnecessary constraints on the matchstick problems shown in Figure 13.1. The goal is to move a single stick to turn a false arithmetic statement into a true statement. The stick can not be discarded but can only change positions in the equation. Try to solve these problems before reading further.

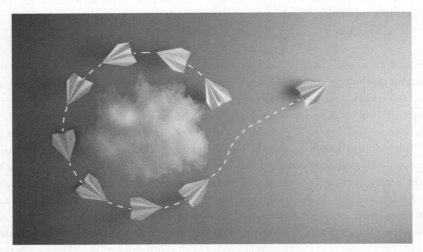

PHOTO 13.1 A solution may require removing unnecessary constraints.
istockphotos.com/Eoneren

An experiment confirmed the hypothesis that problems of type (a) would be the easiest, and problems of type (c) would be the most difficult (Knoblich et al., 1999). Type (a) problems are solved by moving a match stick in the Roman numerals, such as turning the number 4 into the number 6 to make the statement $6 = 3 + 3$. Problems of type (b) are solved by changing the arithmetic operations, such as moving a stick from the equals sign to the minus sign to make the statement $4 - 3 = 1$. Problems of type (c) create two equal signs, such as $3 = 3 = 3$. Once people realize that they can modify and create new equal signs, the three types of problems become equally easy.

Another factor that can make it difficult to find a correct arrangement is **functional fixedness**—the tendency to perceive an object in terms of only its most common use. The string problem in Table 13.1 requires finding a novel use for a tool. The screwdriver is tied to one string to create a pendulum that can be swung to the other string. Photo 13.2 shows a novel use of a tape measure.

---

functional fixedness. The tendency to use an object in a typical way

FIGURE 13.1 ■ Matchstick problems.

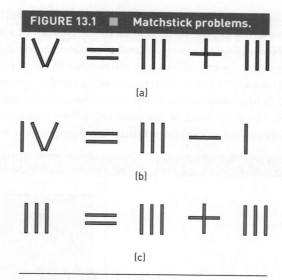

(a)

(b)

(c)

Source: "Constraint relaxation and chunk decomposition in insight problem solving," by G. Knoblich, S. Ohlsson, H. Haider, & D. Rhenius, 1999, *Journal of Experimental Psychology: Learning, Memory and Cognition, 25*, 1534–1555. https://doi.org/10.1037/0278-7393.25.6.1534.   Copyright 1999 by the American Psychological Association.

PHOTO 13.2 Novel uses overcome functional fixedness.

istockphotos.com/CatLane

The candle problem, studied by Duncker (1945), illustrates how functional fixedness can influence performance. The goal is to place three small candles at eye level on a door. Among other objects on a nearby table are a few tacks and three small boxes about the size of matchboxes. In one condition, the boxes were filled with candles, tacks, and matches. In another condition, the boxes were empty. The solution requires tacking the boxes to the door so they can serve as platforms for the candles (Figure 13.2). More subjects solved the problem when the boxes were empty (Adamson, 1952; Duncker, 1945). The use of boxes as containers rather than as platforms was emphasized when they contained objects, and so it was more difficult to recognize their novel function.

FIGURE 13.2 ■ The candle problem—initial state (a) and goal state (b).

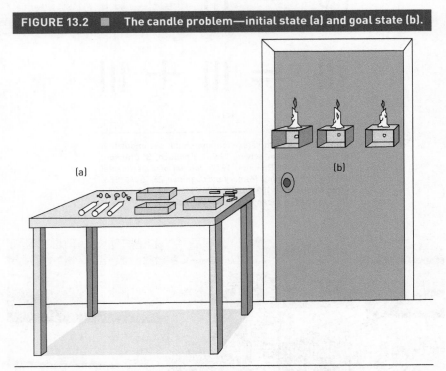

Source: Reed, S.K. (2012). *Cognition: Theories and Applications 9e*. Cengage.

Inducing Structure

Arrangement problems require the rearrangement of objects to form a new relation among them. In **inducing structure problems**, by contrast, the relation is fixed, and the problem is to discover it. Some objects are given, and the task is to discover how they are related. For example, in **series extrapolation**, problems consist of a series such as 1 2 8 3 4 6 5 6. The task is to find the next element of the series. Notice that there are two series in the example. One is the ascending

---

inducing-structure problem. A problem that requires finding a pattern among a fixed set of relations

series extrapolation. A problem that requires finding a pattern among a sequence of items to continue the sequence in the same pattern

series 1 2 3 4 5 6; the other is the descending series 8, 6, . . . So the correct answer is 4. Similarly, the answer to the letter series in Table 13.1 is *E*.

Another example of inducing structure is **analogy problems**, such as merchant: sell, customer: buy. The instructions might indicate that the analogy should be labeled true or false or the last word could be replaced by a blank, with instructions to fill in the word that best completes the analogy. Analogical reasoning is of particular interest because of its use in intelligence tests. The Miller Analogies Test, which was widely used for admission to graduate school, is composed exclusively of verbal analogies. Other ability tests, such as the Graduate Record Examination (GRE) and the Scholastic Aptitude Test (SAT), include analogies among the test items.

The psychological processes used in solving an analogy or a series-extrapolation problem involve identifying relations among the components and fitting the relations together in a pattern (Greeno, 1978). Sternberg and Gardner (1983) examined whether common components are involved in three different reasoning tasks that required inducing structure (series completion, analogy, and classification). They discovered a single reasoning variable that correlated significantly across the different tasks. In other words, students who were rapid in reasoning in one kind of induction task were also rapid in reasoning during other induction tasks. The results indicate that some common skills are involved in inducing structure across different tasks, as implied by Greeno's (1978) taxonomy.

Successful transfer across different inductive reasoning tasks confirms the generality of this skill (Bunge & Leib, 2020). A study at Berkeley evaluated pre-law students who had emphasized relational reasoning during a six-week online preparation course for the Law School Admissions Test (LSAT). The students next completed different inductive tasks that were visually distinct from the LSAT problems. For instance, the solution to the problem in Figure 13.3a involves using the numbers and color of the cards to find a rule that can be applied to the number and color of the circles. The color of the cards alternates between red and black, so black circles

FIGURE 13.3 ■ Relational reasoning tests.

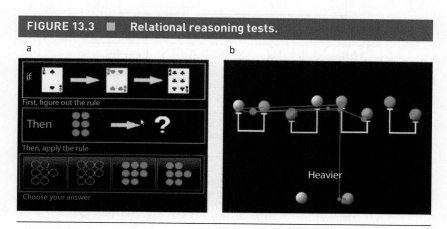

Source: From "How does education hone reasoning ability?," by S. A. Bunge & E. R. Leib, 2020, *Current Directions in Psychological Science, 29*, 167-173. https://doi.org/10.1177/0963721419898818

analogy problem. A four-term problem that requires finding the answer that completes the relation: A is to B as C is to D

should follow red circles. The numbers on the cards show an increasing sequence of even numbers, so eight circles should follow six circles.

The LSAT training improved students' accuracy on the new relational reasoning problems. A subsequent study of eye movements revealed that students were quicker in looking at the relevant relations, indicating that the training also improved the efficiency of their comparisons. Figure 13.3b shows the visual comparisons of a typical participant to determine which of two balls is heavier. The blue ball is heavier than the orange ball, which is equal in weight to the purple ball. The blue ball is therefore heavier than the purple ball. Notice that the participant does not look at the final comparison between the green and grey balls, which is irrelevant.

A particularly challenging test that requires the induction of abstract relations is the Raven Progressive Matrices Test (Raven, 1962). The instructions are to look across the rows and then down the columns to determine the rules that can be used to generate the missing pattern. You can try to solve one of these problems by determining which of the eight alternatives in Figure 13.4 is the missing pattern.

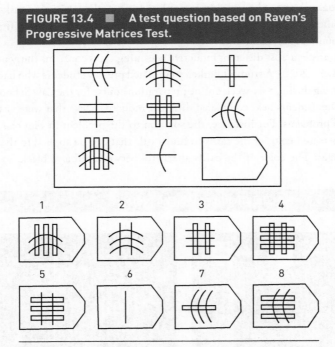

FIGURE 13.4 ■ A test question based on Raven's Progressive Matrices Test.

Source: "What one intelligence test measures: A theoretical account of the processing in the Raven Progressive Matrices Test," by P. A. Carpenter, M. A. Just, & P. Shell, 1990, *Psychological Review, 97*, 404–431. https://doi.org/10.1037/0033-295X.97.3.404. Copyright 1990 by the American Psychological Association.

People initially try to match the rectangles, curves, and lines across rows, but exact matches do not exist. For example, the two curved vertical lines in the first row do not occur in the second and third rows. Number and shape are both relevant, however, because each row contains one, two, and three vertical shapes, representing each of the three shapes, and one, two, and three horizontal shapes, representing each of the three shapes. The missing number in the bottom row is three for the horizontal shape, and the missing horizontal shape is the open rectangles. The missing number is two for the vertical shape, and the missing vertical shape is the lines. The correct answer is 5. A high score on this test depends primarily on the ability to induce abstract relations and the ability to manage many comparisons in working memory (Carpenter et al., 1990).

Spatial transformations of the figures can occasionally be used be to find a solution to simpler problems. The problem in Figure 13.5 requires selecting one of six alternatives to complete the matrix. A model developed by Kunda et al. (2013) uses spatial transformations, such as rotations and reflections, to determine similarities among the entries in the matrix. For instance, the top-left figure matches the top-right figure if reflected about the vertical axis. Applying this

FIGURE 13.5 ■ A simpler test question based on Raven's Progressive Matrices Test.

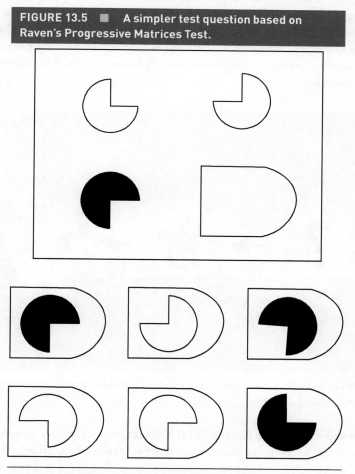

Source: "A computational model for solving problems from the Raven's Progressive Matrices intelligence test using iconic visual representations," by M. Kunda, K. McGreggor, & A. K. Goel, 2013, *Cognitive Systems Research, 22–23*, 47–66. https://doi.org/10.1016/j.cogsys.2012.08.001. Copyright 2013 by Elsevier.

spatial transformation to the bottom-left figure in the matrix produces the upper-right figure as the best of the six possible answers.

Variations of their model successfully solved between 33 and 38 of the 60 problems on the Standard Progressive Matrices test—a success rate that is typical of 9- to 11-year-old children. The main contribution of the model is its demonstration that some problems can be solved using only spatial transformations. However, other problems require forming rules (Lovett & Forbes, 2017), such as the ones stated for the problem in Figure 13.4.

Transformation

Transformation problems consist of an initial state, a goal state, and a sequence of operations for changing the initial state into the goal state (Photo 13.3). Transformation problems differ from problems of inducing structure and arrangement by providing the goal state rather than requiring solvers to produce it. An anagram problem requires finding the word that solves the anagram, and Duncker's candle problem requires finding the correct arrangement of parts that supports the candle. In contrast, a transformation problem such as the men-and-elves problem provides the goal state.

PHOTO 13.3 Transformation problems require transforming the initial state into the goal state.

istockphotos.com/Christian Horz

The men-and-elves problem (Greeno, 1974) requires transporting three men and three elves across a river under the constraint that men can never outnumber elves, either in the boat or on either side of the river. The initial state is three men, three elves, and a boat that can hold two

---

transformation problem. A problem that requires changing the initial state through a sequence of actions until it matches the goal state

people, on one side of the river. The goal state is everyone and the boat on the other side of the river. The operations consist of moving one or two persons in the boat back and forth across the river.

According to Greeno (1978), solving transformation problems primarily requires skills in planning based on a method called means–end analysis. Because a definite goal state is given in transformation problems, the problem solver can compare the current problem state with the goal state. Means–end analysis requires identifying differences that exist between the current state and the goal state and selecting actions that will reduce these differences (Photo 13.4).

PHOTO 13.4 Means-end analysis guides a series of choices to approach a goal.

istockphotos.com/YinYang

An important contribution of Bassok and Novick's (2012) chapter on problem solving is their discussion of examples in which the emphasis on organization in arrangement problems and search in transformation problems can be combined to enhance our understanding of insight. For instance, the nine-dot problem in Figure 13.6 falls squarely within the Gestalt tradition, with its emphasis on perception and insight. It requires connecting all of the dots with four straight lines, and its solution requires extending the lines outside the dots' boundary.

One model nonetheless proposes that the solution can be analyzed within a search framework using means–end analysis (MacGregor et al., 2001). The model assumes that means–end analysis progresses by counting how many unconnected dots are connected by adding each new line. According to the model, insight is evoked when there is a lack of progress from using means-end analysis, not by the perceptual organization of the array. Constraint relaxation—extending a line

---

means–end analysis. A strategy that can be used to solve transformation problems by eliminating differences between the current state and the goal state.

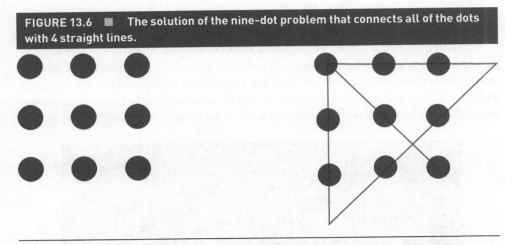

FIGURE 13.6 ■ The solution of the nine-dot problem that connects all of the dots with 4 straight lines.

Source: "Information processing and insight: A process model of performance on the nine-dot and related problems," by J. N. MacGregor, T. C. Ormerod, & E. P. Chronicle, 2001, *Journal of Experimental Psychology: Learning, Memory, and Cognition, 27*, 176–201. https://doi.org/10.1037/0278-7393.27.1.176. Copyright 2013 by the American Psychological Association.

outside the boundary of the dots—only occurs when drawing lines within the boundary connects an insufficient number of dots. The model has been extended to explain searching for a solution to the eight-coin problem, in which two coins in a starting arrangement must be moved so that each coin touches exactly three others (Ormerod et al., 2002). Solving the problem requires removing the self-imposed constraint that coins cannot be stacked on other coins.

The problems that we consider in the rest of this chapter are mostly transformation problems. This focus provides us the opportunity to study meansend analysis and alternative planning strategies. Much of what psychologists know about how people solve these problems is the result of the pioneering work of Newell and Simon at Carnegie Mellon University, as mentioned in Chapter 1. We review the major aspects of their theory of human problem solving before looking at the applications of their ideas to particular problems.

NEWELL AND SIMON'S THEORY

Objectives and Method

The initial development of Newell and Simon's theory was described in a paper titled "Elements of a Theory of Human Problem Solving" (Newell et al., 1958b), which, as we saw earlier, had an important influence on the development of information-processing theory. The paper described the first two years of a project that involved programming a digital computer to solve problems. One objective of the project was in fact to consider how programming a computer could contribute to a theory of human problem solving. The first step was to use all available evidence about human problem solving to program processes resembling those used by humans. The second step was to collect detailed data on how humans solve the same problems as those solved by the computer. The program could then be modified to provide a closer approximation of human behavior. Once success was achieved in simulating performance on a particular task, the investigators could examine a broader range of tasks, attempting to use the same set of elementary information processes and program organization in all the simulation programs. A long-term goal would be to draw implications from the theories for improving human performance.

Why does the computer play a central role in theory construction? Simon and Newell's (1971) answer is that much of our thinking is not directly observable. The covert nature of thought can make it seem magical or mysterious, leading to vague theories that obscure more than they clarify. The advantage of computer programs is that terms such as *memory* and *strategy* can be defined in precisely stated instructions for a computer. Furthermore, the requirement that the programs must work—that is, must be able to solve the problem—provides a guarantee that no steps have been left unspecified. A successful program provides a measure of sufficiency—a test that the steps in the program are sufficient for solving the problem (Photo 13.5). However, a successful program does not guarantee that a person would solve the problem the same way; it is still necessary to make detailed observations on how people solve problems and modify the program to simulate their behavior.

PHOTO 13.5 A successful computer solution proves that steps are sufficient for solving the problem.

istockphotos.com/ppart

---

simulation program. A computer program that attempts to reproduce the operations used by people to carry out various tasks

measure of sufficiency. A demonstration that the instructions in a computer program are capable of solving a problem

To obtain details about how people solve problems, Newell and Simon (1972) usually collected verbal protocols from their subjects. They told the subjects to report verbally everything they thought about as they worked on the problem. The verbal statements often provided enough details to build a computer simulation program that would solve the problem in the same way that people solved it.

The method of collecting verbal protocols and constructing a simulation program has not been widely adopted by other investigators, although the approach is slowly gaining more appeal. One deterrent is simply that this method requires a lot of work for the investigator. The investigator therefore usually studies only a few subjects and assumes that they are fairly typical in the way they solve problems. Another limitation is that the method yields many details, and it is not always clear how to summarize the results to emphasize what is most important. Failure to collect verbal protocols, however, can result in the loss of valuable information because a subject's behavior may reveal little about what he or she is thinking.

Although the particular method used by Newell and Simon has not been widely adopted, their theory of problem solving has been very influential in determining how psychologists think about human information processing in general and problem solving in particular. The theory provides a general framework for specifying how information-processing characteristics, the structure of the problem, and different sources of knowledge interact to influence behavior.

Theoretical Assumptions

An important component of Newell and Simon's theory is the identification of the basic characteristics of human information processing that influence problem solving. These characteristics are the same ones that we discussed in earlier chapters—performance on a problem-solving task is influenced by the capacity, storage time, and retrieval time of STM and LTM. The limited capacity of STM places a constraint on the number of sequential operations that can be carried out mentally. Although most people can multiply 17×8 without using paper and pencil, multiplying 17×58 is much more difficult because the number of required operations (multiplying 17×8 and 17×5, storing the products, aligning, and adding) can exceed the limit of STM. Long-term memory does not have these capacity limitations, but it takes time to enter new information into LTM. This can make it difficult to remember the steps that were used to solve a problem, causing us to repeat incorrect steps. Thus, both the limited capacity of STM and the time required to store new information in LTM can greatly influence the efficiency of a human problem solver (Atwood & Polson, 1976).

Simon and Newell's (1971) theory is concerned not only with the person but also with the task. The sequential nature of many problems raises the question of what options are available at each point in solving the problem. If many choices are available, of which only a few lead to a solution, the problem can be very difficult. However, if one has a good plan for solving the problem and can therefore ignore unpromising paths, the number of unpromising paths will have little effect on performance.

---

verbal protocol. A record of verbalized thought processes

Simon and Newell illustrate this point by referring to the problem DONALD + GERALD = ROBERT. The problem is to substitute a digit 0 to 9 for each of the ten letters to satisfy the constraint that the substitution obeys the rules of addition. The hint is $D = 5$. Therefore, $T = 0$, and a 1 has to be carried into the next column to the left. Although the number of possible choices is very large (there are 362,880 ways of assigning nine digits to nine letters), by following the rules of arithmetic and using accumulated information (such as that R must be odd), it is possible to explore relatively few promising choices. You can observe this for yourself by trying to solve the problem.

What is important, therefore, is not the number of incorrect paths but how effectively one can discover a plan that avoids the incorrect paths (Photo 13.6). To use Newell and Simon's analogy, we need not be concerned about how large the haystack is if we can identify a small part of it in which we are quite sure to find the needle. The problem itself determines the number of possible choices and paths that could be followed in searching for a solution (the **problem space**), but the problem solver determines which of these to actually explore (the **search space**).

PHOTO 13.6 A good plan avoids incorrect paths.

istockphotos.com/aydinmutlu

Figure 13.7 shows the problem space for a Tower of Hanoi puzzle that consists of three pegs and a set of rings that vary in size. The initial state (state 1) has all of the rings on the left peg, and the goal is to move the stack, one ring at a time, to the right peg (state 27) under the constraint that a larger ring can not be placed on a smaller ring. The problem space shows that it is possible to solve the problem in 7 moves although there are many other possible legal moves that make the problem challenging. The search space consists of the moves selected by the problem solver.

---

problem space. The set of choices at each step in solving the problem as determined by the problem

search space. The set of choices evaluated at each step in solving a problem as determined by the problem solver

FIGURE 13.7 ■ The Tower of Hanoi problem space.

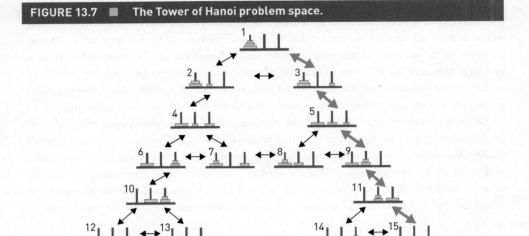

Source: "Problem solving," by M. Bassok & L. R. Novick, 2012, in K. J. Holyoak & R. J. Morrison (Eds.), *The Oxford handbook of thinking and reasoning* (pp. 413–432). New York: Oxford University Press. Reprinted by permission.

Among the sources of information that influence how a person searches a problem space are the following:

1. Previous experience with the same task or a nearly identical one

2. Previous experience with analogous tasks

3. Plans stored in LTM that generalize over a range of tasks

4. Information accumulated while solving a problem

The DONALD + GERALD = ROBERT problem is a good example of how information accumulated while solving the problem places constraints on the assignment of numbers to letters. Let's now take a look at how the other sources of information influence problem solving. We will begin by showing how means–end analysis can be used to solve transformation problems.

Means–End Analysis

The use of means–end analysis is illustrated by a computer program called the General Problem Solver (GPS) (Ernst & Newell, 1969). The program consists of general procedures that should apply across a variety of problems. A *general procedure* for solving transformation problems is to select operators that result in a problem state that is closer to the goal state. Operators are the allowed changes that can be made to solve the problem, such as moving men and elves in the boat. Getting close to the goal is accomplished by trying to reduce the differences between the current problem state and the goal state.

To follow this procedure, the GPS must be given the differences that exist between problem states and the operators that are capable of eliminating these differences. A table of connections combines these two sets of information by showing which differences can be eliminated by each of the operators. The particular operators and differences will vary across problems, but the general strategy of consulting a table of connections to determine which operators are useful for reducing differences should remain the same across problems.

In most cases, the principles used to construct GPS form a reasonable model of how people attempt to solve transformation problems. In fact, GPS was specifically used as a model of human performance on a symbol transformation task studied by Newell and Simon (1972). The problems were similar to the kind of derivations that students encounter in an introductory logic course. Students were given some initial statements, a set of 12 transformation rules, and a goal statement. The task was to use the rules to transform the initial statements to produce the goal statement. Newell and Simon identified six differences that distinguish logic statements. The table of connections specified which of these differences could be changed by each of the 12 transformation rules.

For example, a student might be asked to prove that if A implies B $(A \supset B)$, then the absence of B implies the absence of A $(-B \supset -A)$. Notice that there are two kinds of differences that distinguish the initial state $(A \supset B)$ from the goal state $(-B \supset -A)$. First, the two expressions differ in sign—there are negation signs before the A and the B in the goal state. Second, the positions of the A and the B have changed in the goal state. Students could use means–end analysis to solve this problem by applying transformation rules that changed either the sign or the position of the symbols. Newell and Simon (1972) asked their subjects to verbalize their strategies as they attempted to solve the symbol transformation problems. Students' solutions and verbal protocols revealed that many aspects of their thinking were similar to aspects of the means–end analysis used in the GPS.

GENERAL STRATEGIES

Means–end analysis is an example of a general strategy. A knowledge of general problem-solving strategies can be particularly useful because general strategies apply to many kinds of problems. For this reason, books such as Wickelgren's (1974) on how to solve problems emphasize general strategies, such as forming subgoals or working backward.

---

operator. An action that is selected to solve problems

table of connections. A table that links differences between problem states with operators for eliminating those differences

Strategies such as using means–end analysis, forming subgoals, and working backward are called **heuristics** because they are often successful but do not guarantee success. In contrast, an **algorithm** is a procedure of steps that does guarantee a solution if one follows the steps correctly. The rules for multiplication constitute an algorithm because a correct answer is guaranteed if a person correctly follows the rules. We first consider three general heuristics—forming subgoals, using analogy, and constructing diagrams—and then evaluate both their potential usefulness and their limitations as general strategies.

Subgoals

A commonly suggested heuristic for solving problems is to divide the problem into parts—that is, to formulate subgoals. **Subgoals** are problem states intermediate between the initial state and the goal state; ideally, they are on the solution path. Some problems have fairly obvious subgoals, and research has shown that people take advantage of them. A reasonable subgoal is to move the largest ring to the right peg in the Tower of Hanoi task (Figure 13.7). But how does one begin to achieve this subgoal? The answer is not obvious, and people often make the wrong choice. But as they make other moves and come closer to achieving the subgoal, the correct moves become more obvious and errors decline (Egan & Greeno, 1974).

Forming subgoals is often helpful, but it does not guarantee an easier solution. There are several limitations to keep in mind when using this method. First, it is not always obvious what are helpful intermediate problem states because some problems do not have obvious subgoals. Second, reaching a subgoal can create confusion about what to do next. Hayes (1966) found that giving people a subgoal helped them solve the part of the problem that came before the subgoal. However, some problems actually took longer to solve with a subgoal because it took a long time to figure out what to do after reaching the subgoal.

An example of a problem in which a subgoal improved performance is the missionaries-and-cannibals problem—a variation of the men and elves problem in Table 13.1. River crossing problems had been typically formulated as transporting missionaries and cannibals, a formulation that perpetuates colonizing narratives and demeaning and false stereotypes of indigenous and other colonized peoples. Increasing awareness in the field of psychology of the racial and cultural insensitivities contained in this transformation problem has resulted in moves to reformulate the language so that it does not discriminate against marginalized groups.

The classic problem requires transporting missionaries and cannibals across a river under the constraint that cannibals can never outnumber missionaries, in the boat or on either side of the river. In one version of this problem, the initial state consists of five missionaries, five cannibals, and a boat that can hold three persons, on one side of the river. The goal state consists of everyone and the boat on the other side of the river.

---

heuristic. A strategy that is often but not always helpful in solving problems

algorithm. A set of rules that will solve a problem if correctly followed

subgoal. A goal that solves part of the problem

One group of students, the control group, was simply asked to solve the problem. Another group, the "subgoal" group, was told that to solve the problem, they would have to reach a state in which there were three cannibals across the river by themselves without the boat. Students in the control group required an average of 30 moves to solve the problem, compared with an average of only 20 moves for students in the subgoal group (Simon & Reed, 1976).

To try to understand why the subgoal was so effective, Simon and I developed a simulation model of the way students in the two groups explored the search space. The goal of the model was to predict, for each of the possible legal moves, the average number of times students in each group would make that particular move. We thought students would follow a means–end strategy in which they would move as many people across the river as possible and bring as few back as possible. A model based on the means–end strategy was fairly successful in predicting their choices, but some of their moves did not follow this strategy.

Violations of the means–end strategy could be accounted for by proposing that people follow a balance strategy, which attempts to create equal numbers of missionaries and cannibals on each side of the river. The balance strategy makes it easy to avoid illegal moves because cannibals will never outnumber missionaries as long as the numbers of missionaries and cannibals are equal on both sides. The trouble with the balance strategy is that it tends to lead people away from the solution path and toward unpromising paths.

After analyzing the moves made by both groups, we proposed that the subgoal group was more likely to follow the means–end strategy, and the control group was more likely to follow the less-effective balance strategy. The fact that the subgoal—three cannibals and no missionaries—is an unbalanced state also makes it intuitively likely that students in the subgoal group would not persist in following the balance strategy.

As mentioned previously, one limitation of using the subgoal strategy is that it is not always obvious what constitutes a good subgoal. Educators can therefore help students by explicitly pointing out subgoals, as demonstrated by Catrambone (1995). Students were shown how to solve a probability problem that required finding total frequency as one of the subgoals. When this step was explicitly labeled as *Total Frequency*, students did better in transferring what they had learned to other probability problems that required finding the total frequency. The transfer problems required a different method for calculating total frequency, so it was insufficient to apply by rote the same steps shown in the example problem. Learning required understanding the example and explicitly labeling a subgoal enhanced understanding.

Analogy

Analogy is another of the major heuristics for solving problems. Analogy requires that the problem solver use the solution of a similar problem to solve a current problem. Success in using analogy depends on both recognizing the similarity between the two problems and recalling the solution of the analogous problem. Because the recall of a solution is required, analogy depends more on LTM than do means–end analysis and subgoals.

---

analogy. Solving a problem by using a solution to a related problem

One of the most famous studies of analogy involved a problem initially studied by Duncker (1945) labeled the tumor, or radiation, problem. The problem is to use radiation to destroy a tumor without destroying the healthy tissue that surrounds it. The dispersion solution requires dividing the rays so that they will have high intensity only when they converge on the tumor. Although this is a clever and practical solution that is now widely used (Photo 13.7), Duncker found that very few people solved the problem in this way.

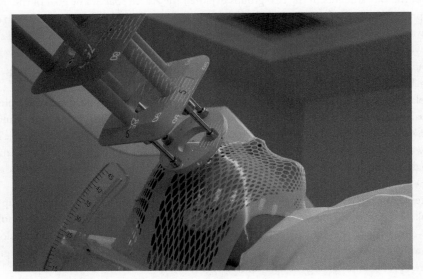

PHOTO 13.7 Man receiving radiation therapy for cancer.

istockphotos.com/Mark Kostich

Gick and Holyoak (1980) investigated whether more people would discover the dispersion solution if they were first exposed to an analogous solution. Their subjects read the attack-dispersion story before trying to solve the radiation problem. The attack-dispersion story described a solution to a military problem in which the army had to be divided to converge on a fortress. Table 13.2 shows how the solution of this problem corresponds to the solution of the radiation problem. When the instructions indicated that the story might provide hints for solving the radiation problem, most people made use of the analogy. More than half of those who read the story included the dispersion solution among their proposed solutions, compared with only 8% of those who did not read the story. But when Gick and Holyoak omitted the hint to use the story, the number of dispersion solutions greatly decreased. Their findings thus demonstrated that people could generate an analogous solution when prompted but that they did not spontaneously recognize the similarity between the two problems.

People's inability to spontaneously notice the relation between analogous problems poses a challenge for psychologists to make analogies more obvious. One reason that analogies are often not obvious is that, although the analogy preserves relations among the concepts in a problem, the concepts themselves differ (Gentner, 1983). Although the concepts (army and fortress; rays and tumor) differ in the military and radiation problems, the solutions preserve the relations of

TABLE 13.2 ■ A summary of the attack dispersion story and of a corresponding solution to the radiation problem
Attack dispersion story
A fortress was located in the center of the country. Many roads radiated out from the fortress.
A general wanted to capture the fortress with his army.
The general wanted to prevent mines on the roads from destroying his army and neighboring villages.
As a result the entire army could not attack the fortress along one road. However, the entire army was needed to capture the fortress.
So an attack by one small group would not succeed.
The general therefore divided his army into several small groups. He positioned the small groups at the heads of different roads. The small groups simultaneously converged on the fortress.
In this way the army captured the fortress.
Radiation problem and dispersion solution*
A tumor was located in the interior of a patient's body. A doctor wanted to destroy the tumor with rays.
The doctor wanted to prevent the rays from destroying the healthy tissue.
As a result the high intensity rays could not be applied to the tumor along one path.
However, high intensity rays were needed to destroy the tumor. So applying one low intensity ray would not succeed.
The doctor therefore divided the rays into several low intensity rays.
He positioned the low intensity rays at multiple locations around the patient's body.
The low intensity rays simultaneously converged on the tumor.
In this way the rays destroyed the tumor.

*Italicized propositions summarize the analogous dispersion solution.

Source: From "Analogical problem solving," by M. L. Gick & K. Holyoak, 1980, *Cognitive Psychology, 12*, 306–335. https://doi.org/10.1016/0010-0285(80)90013-4. Copyright 1980 by Academic Press, Inc. Reprinted by permission of Elsevier Science.

breaking up and converging. The solutions to both problems require breaking up a large force so that weak forces can be simultaneously applied along multiple paths.

Gick and Holyoak (1983) subsequently discovered that people were likely to form this more general schema if they read and compared two analogous stories before trying to solve the radiation problem. For example, some students read the military story and a story about forming a circle around an oil fire to use many small hoses to spray foam on the fire. Students who described the relation between these two stories were much more likely to think of the convergence solution to the radiation problem than were students who read only a single analogous story. Creating the *convergence schema* requires that people compare two analogous stories, which makes them think about the solution in general terms. Reading the two analogous stories without comparing them was not very helpful (Catrambone & Holyoak, 1989).

The advantage of a general schema, whether for a puzzle or a negotiation strategy, is that it is easier for people to recognize how particular situations are similar to each other. After an extensive review of the literature on analogy, Reeves and Weisberg (1994) concluded that there is sufficient evidence to show that we use both specific problems and more abstract schemata in analogical reasoning. One promising theory is that we begin by using the solution of specific problems, but as we apply a specific solution to other problems, we begin to form more abstract schemata (Ross & Kennedy, 1990). We will see in the next chapter that forming these more abstract schemata is an important part of acquiring expertise.

Representational Transfer

Laura Novick (1990) refers to the transfer of general methods for solving problems as representational transfer to distinguish it from the analogical transfer of specific solutions. In analogical transfer, we were concerned with the transfer of a specific solution, such as using the solution of the military problem to solve the radiation problem. In representational transfer, we are concerned with the transfer of a general method, such as using a *matrix diagram* to solve a transfer problem after being shown how to use it to solve an example problem.

Novick became interested in studying representational transfer after noticing that although many psychologists were studying the transfer of specific solutions, no one seemed to be studying the transfer of representations. Diagrammatic representations, in particular, help us represent the underlying structure of many problems. Because problem solvers often do not construct appropriate diagrams to represent problems, Novick and Hmelo (1994) examined whether students would transfer the use of an appropriate diagram from one problem to another problem that had a different solution but could be solved by using the same diagram.

Figure 13.8 shows three different kinds of diagrams. The first two should be familiar to you if you have read previous chapters in this book. A *network* consists of nodes joined by links. In the example problem, a couple had to plan a trip that involved visiting islands (nodes) joined by bridges (links). The test problem required figuring out which pairs of people (nodes) at a cocktail party shook hands (links) with each other. The example for the *hierarchy* was a categorization problem in which a mother was trying to group the words her young child knew into categories (zoo animals, farm animals, pets). The test problem involved representing different paths that a rat could take through a maze. The example for the *part–whole representation* consisted of a set membership problem in which the solver had to determine the number of children who collected only rocks, the number who collected only shells, and the number who collected both. These problems can be represented by the Venn diagram shown in Figure 13.8. The test problem was a geometry problem in which the angles of two intersecting lines could be represented as either parts or wholes.

---

analogical transfer. Use of the same solution in solving two problems

representational transfer. Use of the same format (such as a matrix) in solving two problems

Venn diagram. A diagram that shows the set relations (such as overlap) among categories

FIGURE 13.8 ■ Representational transfer of network, hierarchical, and part–whole representations.

	Network	**Hierarchy**	**Part-Whole**
Example	Bridges	Words	Shells & Rocks
Test	Handshakes	Maze	Angles
Use	Yes	Yes	No
Accuracy	Yes	No	No

Source: "Transferring symbolic representations across nonisomorphic problems," by L. R. Novick & C. E. Hmelo, 1994, *Journal of Experimental Psychology: Learning, Memory, and Cognition, 20,* 1296–1321. https://doi.org/10.1037/0278-7393.20.6.1296. Copyright 1994 by the American Psychological Association.

Novick and Hmelo (1994) compared students' ability to solve test problems under three conditions: Subjects did not previously see any examples in the control condition, saw a relevant example in the no-hint condition but were not told of its relevance, and saw and were informed about the relevant example in the hint condition. The complete lack of spontaneous transfer was shown by the lack of difference between the control and no-hint groups. When not informed that a previously studied example would be helpful, subjects did not change their representations and improve their performance.

The results for the hint group varied across the three representations. The network representation was the most successful. Students who were told to use the relevant example (bridge problem) were more likely to use a network representation to solve the handshake problem and were more successful. The results were mixed for the hierarchical representation—more people used a hierarchy to solve the maze problem, but they were not more successful. A possible reason is that people who didn't draw a hierarchy typically drew the maze, and drawing the maze was as helpful as drawing a hierarchy to represent the maze. The part–whole problem was the least successful—neither the frequency of use nor the accuracy increased for solving the geometry problem. A limitation in this case is that students were not able to identify correspondences between the shells and rocks in the example problem and the angles in the geometry problem. Figure 13.8 summarizes these findings.

You may have noticed that there are some similarities between these initial results on representational transfer and the results on analogical transfer. Spontaneous transfer of either a specific solution or a more general method was poor because of the difficulty of noticing the similarity between two problems that had different physical descriptions, such as the attack-dispersion and radiation problems (Gick & Holyoak, 1983) or the bridges and handshake problems (Novick & Hmelo, 1994). Second, even when people are told to use an analogous problem, transfer of a particular solution depends on how easily people can find correspondences between objects in one problem and objects in the other problem (Gentner, 1983). This also limited transfer of the part–whole method from the shells-and-rocks problem to the geometry problem.

There is another potential similarity between analogical and representational transfer that is suggested by Gick and Holyoak's (1983) finding that spontaneous transfer is facilitated by representing solutions at an abstract level. For spatial diagrams, this requires understanding how the diagrams differ from each other in their representation of information. Novick and Hurley (2001) hypothesized 10 properties that could be used to distinguish between a matrix, network, and hierarchy to evaluate whether people use these properties when deciding which diagram to use in solving a problem. For example, one property is how one moves about a representation. In a matrix, such as the one in the lower half of Figure 13.8, there are no links, so it doesn't make sense to talk about moving along pathways. In a hierarchical model, such as shown in Figure 10.3, there is only a single path from one node to another, as illustrated by the path from *canary* to *bird* to *animal*. In a network model, such as shown in Figure 10.5, there can be multiple paths between nodes. For example, there are multiple paths between *street* and *fire engine* by going either directly or through any one of five intermediary nodes. So one property that should influence the choice of which representation to use is whether no paths, one path, or multiple paths are needed to show the relations among the concepts.

Novick and Hurley (2001) tested their proposed properties by asking college students to select the type of diagram they thought would be most efficient for organizing information in each of 18 short scenarios and to justify their selected diagram. The results showed that students' justifications mentioned 9 of the 10 proposed properties, thus supporting Novick and Hurley's analysis. Subsequent research also revealed the importance of using diagrams in their conventional format, such as placing concepts in the nodes of a semantic network and relations in the links. Reversing this assignment increased reasoning time and lowered accuracy (Hurley & Novick, 2010).

In conclusion, the research on general strategies demonstrates that employing strategies such as subgoal formation, analogy, and construction of diagrams can be useful. However, the challenge is to know when and how to apply each of these strategies. Successful use of the strategies may therefore depend on having some amount of expertise in that problem-solving domain. In particular, many of the problems we encounter in the classroom require knowledge about that topic to solve them. Thus, both subject-matter knowledge and general strategies have to be learned if one is to become a proficient problem solver (Glaser, 1984).

APPLICATIONS

Design Problems

In his 1973 article "The Structure of Il-Structured Problems" Herbert Simon compared ill-structured problems to well-structured problems. Puzzles such as the Tower of Hanoi are good examples of well-structured problems. It is well structured because both the goal and the constraint on actions are clearly defined (Figure 13.6). An example of an ill-structured problem for Simon was designing a house in which the actions and final design slowly evolve (Simon, 1973).

Many of the characteristics of design problems (Goel & Pirolli, 1992) reflect the characteristics of ill-structured problems described by Simon. The initial, goal, and intermediate states are incompletely specified. There are no right or wrong answers, only better and worse ones. The size and complexity of the problems require decomposition into smaller problems or modules.

Constraints come from a variety of sources: physical, social, legal, and economic. The designer must request feedback and the cost of errors can be high.

Research by Goel and Pirolli (1992) required three experts to either design a post office, a bank teller machine, or technical training material. The experimental protocols revealed that not only did the experts interpret the problem situation through their personal experiences, but they would occasionally try to explicitly change the problem to more closely fit their expertise, knowledge, and experience. They would attempt to negotiate changes in the initial state and goal state that would be more easily achievable or might lead to a more effective design (Photo 13.8).

PHOTO 13.8 An architect negotiating a design.

Photo by Scott Graham on Unsplash

To provide a basis for comparison with non-design problems, Goel and Pirolli (1992) also asked undergraduates to solve well-structured problems that had been studied by Newell and Simon. A major difference between the design and non-design verbal protocols regarded the incremental development of knowledge. Abandoning an unproductive attempt in the non-design problems seldom required reusing the knowledge gained from the abandoned attempt.

In contrast, Goel and Pirolli found considerable incremental development when experts returned to a previous module within the design. For instance, the designer of a post office divided the task into four modules that included an outdoor site plan. The location of outdoor seats went through several phases that placed the seats (1) below the evergreens, (2) next to the building structure, (3) away from the building, and (4) along the borders. These findings support Simon's (1973) claim that the same information-processing framework developed for puzzles also applies to design problems. Simon proposed that design consists of a combination of using means/end analysis to guide search on well-structured subproblems and continually modifying the search by retrieving from long-term memory new constraints, new subgoals, and new design alternatives.

A difference between design and non-design tasks concerns the Gestalt concept of insight. Goel (2014) later listed two differences between classic insight problems and insight in real-world design problems. First, insight in Gestalt problems typically reveals the solution, whereas insight in the more complex design problems typically reveals only an important step toward achieving the solution. Second, insight problems are usually well structured while design problems have both well-structured and ill-structured components. As the designer progresses from the preliminary to the final design, the problem becomes more structured.

Conflict Resolution

Conflict resolution is another example of an ill-structured problem because the initial state, goal state, and connecting states cannot be clearly specified. In their *American Psychologist* article "Rethinking Intractable Conflict: The Perspective of Dynamical Systems" Vallacher, Coleman, Nowak, and Bui-Wrzosinska (2010) argued that the dynamical systems perspective provides a coherent theory of conflict resolution.

The dynamical systems perspective differs from the information-processing perspective that has been the traditional approach to modeling problem solving (Reed & Vallacher, 2020). This difference is captured by Hilpert and Marchand's (2018) distinction between component-dominant systems that are representative of information processing and interaction-dominant systems that are representative of dynamic relationships. Figure 13.9 shows their diagram of the two systems.

FIGURE 13.9   ■   The distinction between component-dominant systems (lower left) and interaction-dominant systems (lower right and upper).

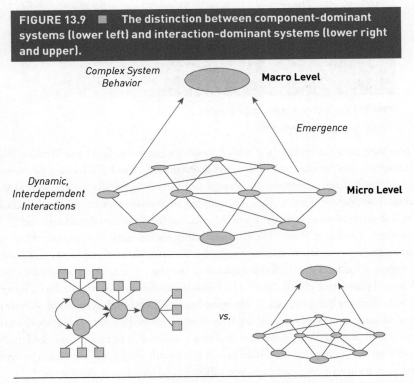

Source: "Complex systems research in educational psychology: Aligning theory and method," by J. C. Hilpert & G. C. Marchand, 2018, *Educational Psychologist, 53*, 185–202. https://doi.org/10.1080/00461520.2018.1469411

The relationships among the components in component-dominant systems are primarily sequential as depicted in the left diagram of Figure 13.10. The diagram has the structure of a problem space (such as the one in Figure 13.7) in which the solver sequentially advances from one problem state to one of the connected states. In contrast, the relationships among the components in interaction-dominant systems do not occur in a sequential order, as depicted in the upper part of Figure 13.9. The components could represent interactions among individuals, groups, or different situations. The strength and direction of the interactions change over time and context.

A key assumption of the dynamical systems perspective (Vallacher et al., 2010) is that conflict is influenced by attractors that are difficult to escape (Photo 13.9). A spatial metaphor of an attractor is a valley in a hilly landscape. The width of the valley represents the range of states that converge on the attractor. The depth of the valley represents the strength of the attractor—its resistance to change. Figure 13.10 illustrates this spatial metaphor for two attractors that correspond to (A) constructive relations and (B) destructive relations. Attractor A in this example has a wide, shallow basin. It attracts a wide range of states but the low strength of these states makes it easy to move to another attractor. Attractor B in this example has a relatively deep basin, indicating its strength, but it is relatively narrow. It attracts a smaller range of states than attractor A, but the strength of these states makes it more difficult to escape.

PHOTO 13.9 Conflicts are triggered by attractors that are difficult to escape.

istockphotos.com/Conflicts are triggered by attractors that are difficult to escape

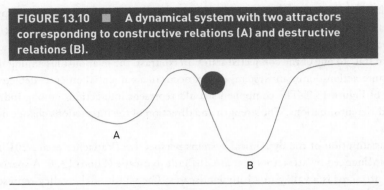

FIGURE 13.10   ■   A dynamical system with two attractors corresponding to constructive relations (A) and destructive relations (B).

A

B

Source: From "Rethinking intractable conflict: The perspective of dynamical systems" by R. R Vallacher, P. T. Coleman, A. Nowak, & L. Bui-Wrzosinska, 2010, *American Psychologist, 65*, 262–278. https://doi.org/10.1037/a0019290. Reprinted by permission.

The dynamical systems theory proposed by Vallacher and his coauthors distinguishes among several types of attractors. **Positive attractors** facilitate progress toward a positive outcome, such as reducing stress, building confidence, or resolving a conflict. **Negative attractors** impede progress toward a positive outcome. For example, a person's self-evaluative thoughts may give rise to chronically low self-esteem or a group may develop a conspiracy theory that maintains tension and mistrust toward other groups.

An understanding of attractor dynamics is beneficial because attractors are susceptible to change. One method to promote change is to disassemble the attractor so it can be more productively reassembled. Examples in the book *Groupthink* (Janis, 1982) illustrate how removing the constraint of group coherence fosters greater flexibility. A positive attractor for mutual respect and feelings among the group members may inadvertently interfere with constructive analysis. Groupthink can be overcome, however, by removing the constraint of group coherence that blocks diverse ideas. In this approach, a member of the group is appointed to be "the devil's advocate," whose role is to question or challenge proposals. The critiques may remove the initial constraint of group coherence, so the group can select among a greater variety of plans for solving the problem.

A second method for changing an attractor is to utilize a **latent attractor** that has receded to the background but can supplant the original attractor under the right set of conditions. In a system with multiple attractors, only one is manifest at a particular time. The other (latent) attractors are not present and may not even be suspected. Latent attractors are nonetheless important because they determine possible stable states to which the system could converge when conditions change. An article in *The Wall Street Journal* announced that Apple and Qualcomm had ended a long legal battle by dismissing all litigation related to their battle over patent royalties

---

positive attractor. A state in a dynamic system that facilitates progress

negative attractor. A state in a dynamic system that impedes progress

latent attractor. A state in a dynamic system that is inactive

(Mickle & Fitch, 2019). The article reported that the emergence of fifth-generation (5G) wireless speeds likely drove the agreement, as both companies would benefit through future cooperation. In such cases, the original attractor (such as patent infringements) is not disassembled but rather loses its salience in favor of an alternative frame for thinking and acting.

SUMMARY

Because there are many kinds of problems, constructing a theory of problem solving would be easier if we were able to classify problems according to the skills needed to solve them. One method of classification distinguishes among problems of arrangement, inducing structure, and transformation. Arrangement problems require the problem solver to arrange the elements of a problem in a way that satisfies some criterion. In problems of inducing structure, some elements are given, and the task is to discover how the elements are related. Transformation problems consist of an initial state, a goal state, and operations for changing the initial state into the goal state.

Much of what psychologists know about how people solve problems began with the pioneering work of Newell and Simon. Their theory specifies how the basic characteristics of the human information processor, the search space, and different strategies affect problem solving. Performance on a task is influenced by the capacity, storage time, and retrieval time of STM and LTM. It is also influenced by the problem space, which determines the number of legal moves available at each point in solving the problem. Newell and Simon depended on computer simulation models and verbal protocols for testing and developing the many details of their theory.

Four general strategies for solving problems are means–end analysis, subgoals, analogy, and diagrams. These strategies are called heuristics because, although they are often useful, none guarantees a successful solution. The means–end strategy states that the problem solver should select operators that reduce the difference between the current problem state and the goal state. Knowledge of subgoals is valuable because it reduces the size of the search space by identifying intermediate states. The use of an analogous solution is often useful, but people may not notice a potential analogy. Diagrams are beneficial for organizing information, but as is the case for analogy, it is not easy to spontaneously transfer a good representation from one problem to another.

Design problems are typically ill-structured because the initial, goal, and intermediate states are incompletely specified. The size and complexity of the problems require decomposition into smaller problems. Simon proposed that design consists of a combination of using means–end analysis to guide search on well-structured subproblems and continually modifying the search by retrieving from long-term memory new constraints, new subgoals, and new design alternatives. A dynamical systems perspective is helpful in formulating a theory of conflict resolution based on the interactions among individuals, groups, and situations. Positive, negative, and latent attractors influence the resolution of conflicts.

RECOMMENDED READING

The Oxford Handbook of Thinking and Reasoning (Holyoak & Morrison, 2012) is a good source for chapters that summarize various aspects of thinking, including a chapter on problem solving (Bassok & Novick, 2012). A comparison of ill-structured and well-structured problems provides a broad overview of both types (Reed, 2016). Sharps and Wertheimer (2000) review the contributions of Gestalt psychology, Kounis and Beeman (2014) discuss the cognitive neuroscience of insight, and Helie and Sun (2010) propose a unified theory of incubation, insight, and creative problem solving. Although the term *insight* generally implies a successful outcome, not all insights result in correct solutions (Danek & Wiley, 2017). A book edited by Detterman and Sternberg (1993) contains many chapters on the use of analogous solutions. Reed and Vallacher (2020) compare the information processing and dynamical systems perspectives on problem solving. Reviews of instructional techniques for enhancing mathematics and science learning (Richey & Nokes-Malach, 2015) and for improving self-regulated learning (van Gog et al., 2020) provide many ideas for improving education. Applications of work on problem solving have also been used to teach critical thinking (Halpern, 2014).

14   EXPERTISE AND CREATIVITY

LEARNING OBJECTIVES

1. Compare and contrast associative and dual process theories of reasoning.

2. Explain expert-defined schemas and how they can occasionally be counterproductive.

3. Describe how neurological and cognitive theories of creativity support each other.

4. Demonstrate ways to improve reasoning—including nudges and boosts—and enhance creativity.

One difference between a puzzle such as the elves and men problem in Chapter 13 and a chemistry problem on finding the concentration of a mixture is that we need considerable domain-specific knowledge to solve the latter problem. Domain-specific knowledge is knowledge about a particular subject matter. Most people could solve the standard version of the missionaries-and-cannibals problem (three missionaries, three cannibals) without previous experience on this problem, but few people could solve a mixture problem without previous classroom experience. Many problems require expertise.

---

domain-specific knowledge. Knowledge about a specific subject, such as chess or physics

In their article on expert performance, Ericsson and Charness (1994) contrast the two most dominant approaches to the study of expertise. The information-processing approach, emphasized in this book, attempts to explain exceptional performance in terms of the knowledge and skills acquired through experience. In contrast, the abilities approach focuses on the innate abilities of people that lead to exceptional performance in a particular domain. An example of this latter approach is illustrated in Howard Gardner's (1983) book *Frames of Mind: The Theory of Multiple Intelligences*. In this book, Gardner argues that exceptional performance results from a close match between an individual's intelligence profile (such as having musical, linguistic, or spatial ability) and the demands of a particular task.

Another major contributor to our knowledge of intelligence, Robert Sternberg, sought to provide a link between the literature on human abilities and on expertise. Sternberg (1998) argued that human abilities are flexible rather than fixed. In fact, the main point (and title) of his article is that abilities reflect developing expertise. An important educational implication of this view is that abilities, like expertise, can be taught. One becomes an expert in the skills needed for success on ability tests in much the same ways that one becomes an expert in doing anything else—through a combination of genetic endowment and experience.

Among the characteristics of expertise that Sternberg considered important are the following:

- Having large, rich schemas containing a great amount of declarative knowledge about a given domain

- Spending proportionately more time determining how to represent problems before searching for a solution

- Developing sophisticated representations based on structural similarities among problems

- Having schemas that contain procedural knowledge about strategies for solving the problem

- Automatizing many sequences of steps within the solution procedures

- Carefully monitoring the problem-solving strategies

We will encounter many examples of these knowledge structures and strategies in this chapter. We first look at how experience influences performance on several reasoning tasks, such as evaluating logical statements and classifying problems. The second section discusses the transition from using general search procedures to using domain-specific schema. The third section explores the relation between becoming experts at solving fairly routine problems and generating creative solutions. The final applications section summarizes techniques for enhancing creativity and distinguishes between nudges and boosts as alternative methods for improving reasoning.

EXPERTISE AND REASONING

Associative Versus Rule-Based Reasoning

Chapter 11 on language contained several examples of how the prior knowledge of the reader influences comprehension. A particularly striking example was the Bransford and Johnson (1973) study in which it was very difficult for readers to comprehend abstract ideas unless they could relate them to familiar experiences, such as washing clothes. The same argument applies to reasoning and problem solving. A task that has abstract or unfamiliar content can be very difficult compared with the same task with familiar content. This point is illustrated by varying the content of a logical reasoning task called the **four-card selection problem**.

Imagine that you are shown four cards, each containing a *D*, a *K*, a 3, or a 7 (Figure 14.1). The experimenter tells you that each card has a letter on one side and a number on the other side and then asks which cards you would have to turn over to determine the truth of the sentence, "Every card that has a *D* on one side has a 3 on the other side." Try to answer this question before reading further.

The experiment, known as the four-card selection problem, was analyzed by Wason and Johnson-Laird (1972). It is an example of a conditional reasoning task. The correct answer is that you would have to turn over the cards containing a *D* and a 7. The selection of a *D* is fairly obvious—the rule would be false if the other side of the card did not contain a 3. The rule would also be false if you turned over the card containing the 7 and found a *D* on the other side. It is not necessary to turn over the card containing the 3, although this is a common mistake. The rule does not specify what should be on the opposite side of a 3; it only specifies what should be on the opposite side of a *D*. For example, finding a *K* on one side of the card and a 3 on the other side would not make the rule false.

Experiments using this task reveal that the implications of a conditional rule are not very clear to most people. The combined results of four experiments indicated that only 5 of 128

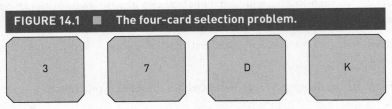

FIGURE 14.1 ■ The four-card selection problem.

Every card that has a D on one side has a 3 on the other side.

If a letter is sealed, then it has a 50-lira stamp on it.

Source: Reed, S.K. (2012). *Cognition: Theories and Applications 9e.* Cengage.

four-card selection problem. A reasoning task that requires deciding which of four cards should be turned over to evaluate a conditional rule

participants correctly turned over only the two correct cards (Wason & Shapiro, 1971). The most popular choice was to turn over the two cards mentioned in the rule—the letter *D* and the number 3 from the example.

Wason and Johnson-Laird (1972) argued that people make mistakes because they seek information that would verify the rule rather than information that would falsify it. Only the latter information is necessary. Turning over the card containing the 3 would verify the rule if a *D* were found on the other side, but it's not logically necessary to turn over this card because the rule does not specify what should be on the other side. It is necessary to turn over the 7, but people usually overlook this card because they are not seeking ways to disprove the rule.

Wason and Shapiro (1971) hypothesized that the poor performance in this task was caused in part by the abstract material. They predicted that using more realistic materials related to every-day knowledge would make the task significantly easier. The realistic rules were of the general form "Every time I go to Manchester I travel by car." The four cards contained two destinations (Manchester and Leeds) and two modes of transport (car and train). One side of the card specified the destination and the other side the transportation. Of 16 British subjects, 10 selected the two correct cards (Manchester and train) when realistic material was used, compared with only 2 of 16 subjects when abstract material was used. Participants also performed very well on a realistic postage stamp problem (Johnson-Laird, Legrenzi, & Legrenzi, 1972) that is shown in Figure 14.1.

A question raised by these findings is why people improve when they are given realistic information. Do they become better reasoners, or do they recall specific experiences from memory that eliminate the need to reason? Research by Griggs and Cox (1982) suggested that the latter explana-tion is more appropriate. To test the memory-retrieval explanation for the superiority of realistic materials, Griggs and Cox gave their subjects a rule that was familiar: "If a person is drinking beer, then the person must be over 19 years of age." This rule was the law in the state of Florida when the study was conducted. Furthermore, 76% of the subjects later reported that they had personally violated the rule more than once, and 97% of the subjects could remember specific instances of someone other than themselves violating the drinking-age rule. When given the four cards that read DRINKING A BEER, DRINKING A COKE, 16 YEARS OF AGE, and 22 YEARS OF AGE, 29 of 40 subjects made the correct selection for detecting violations of the drinking-age rule (DRINKING A BEER, 16 YEARS OF AGE), whereas none of the 40 subjects did so for the abstract version of the task ("If a card has an *A* on one side, then it has a 3 on the other side").

It is helpful to think about this research within the context of two forms of reasoning pro-posed by Sloman (2002). Table 14.1 lists the differences between reasoning that is based on associations and reasoning that is based on rules. Associative reasoning uses associations, such as the ones represented in the semantic networks of Chapter 10. Many of these associations are learned through personal experiences rather than through cultural institutions, such as schools. In contrast, causal and logical rules support strategic reasoning. The correct application of a rule is often determined by the relations among symbols rather than by the meaning of the symbols (Sloman, 2002). For example, you can apply rules to solve for *x* in the equation $11 + x = 14$ with-out knowing the meaning of *x*.

---

memory-retrieval explanation. The proposal that people solve reasoning problems about familiar situations by retrieving specific examples from their memory

TABLE 14.1 ■ Associative versus rule-based reasoning

	Associative System	Rule-Based System
Principle of operation	Similarity	Symbol manipulation
Source of knowledge	Personal experience	Language and culture
Relations	Associations	Causal and logical
Nature of processing	Reproductive	Productive
	Automatic	Strategic
Functions	Intuition	Deliberation
	Creativity	Formal analysis
	Visual recognition	Verification
	Associative memory	Strategic memory

Source: Based on "Two systems of reasoning," by S. A. Sloman, 2002, in T. Gilovich, D. Griffin & D. Kahneman (Eds.), Heuristics and biases: The psychology of intuitive judgment (pp. 379–396). Cambridge: Cambridge University Press. https://doi.org/10.1017/CBO9780511808098.024

A problem with using the distinctions shown in Table 14.1 is that it is not always easy to determine whether performance is based on associations or on rules. Nonetheless, some tasks are better candidates for rule-based reasoning, and other tasks are better candidates for associative reasoning. For example, the abstract version of the four-card selection problem (every card that has a *D* on one side has a 3 on the other side) is a good example of a task that requires rule-based reasoning. The familiar version of this task studied by Griggs and Cox (1982)—if a person is drinking beer, then the person must be over 19 years of age—is a good example of a task that could be solved by using associative reasoning. Students could use their personal experiences to solve the familiar version (Photo 14.1). The distinction between associations and rules fits within a general framework that is typically labeled **dual process theories of reasoning**.

Dual Process Theories of Reasoning

Dual process theories of reasoning have had a major impact that resulted in the award of two Nobel Prizes in Economics. Daniel Kahneman at Princeton University won the 2002 Nobel Prize in Economics for the large body of research that he had conducted with Amos Tversky, much of which was reviewed in Chapter 12. He describes their research in his 2011 book *Thinking Fast and Slow*. Richard Thaler at the University of Chicago won the 2017 Nobel Prize in Economics for his research on behavioral economics. His 2008 book *Nudge: Improving Decisions About Health, Wealth, and Happiness* with Cass Sunstein describes their contributions.

---

dual process theories of reasoning. The proposal that reasoning is based on both intuitive associations and analytic rules

PHOTO 14.1 Familiar situations support associative reasoning.

Photo by Elevate on Unsplash

Kahneman (2011) discusses two types of reasoning in *Thinking Fast and Slow*, which he labels System I and System II. I collected characteristics of these two types from a variety of sources and display them in Table 14.2.

TABLE 14.2 ■ Dual process theories of reasoning	
System I	**System II**
Associations	Rules
Intuitive	Analytic
Fast	Slow
Biases	Competencies
Nudges	Boosts

Source: Based on "Cognitive skills that you need for the 21st century," by S. K. Reed (2020b), New York: Oxford University Press.

A characteristic of System I reasoning is that it is intuitive whereas System II reasoning is analytic. For example, determine whether the following conclusion is logically valid:

All mammals can walk. Whales are mammals. Therefore, whales can walk.

The intuitive answer, based on associative reasoning, is that the conclusion is not logically valid because whales cannot walk. However, the conclusion does logically follow from the initial two statements, and the fault lies not in the logic but in the false premise that all mammals can walk.

This example is one of several discussed by Pennycook et al. (2015) to clarify the distinction between intuitive and analytical thinking. Here are two other examples that come from the Cognitive Reflection Test designed by Shane Frederick (2005). Try answering them before reading the explanation.

1. *A bat and a ball cost $1.10 in total. The bat costs $1.00 more than the ball. How much does the ball cost?*

2. *In a lake, there is a patch of lily pads. Every day, the patch doubles in size. If it takes 48 days for the patch to cover the entire lake, how long would it take for the patch to cover half of the lake?*

The intuitive answer to the bat-and-ball question is $.10, but the bat would then cost $1.10 for a total cost of $1.20. The intuitive answer to the lake question is 24 days. The correct answer is 47 days because on the 48th day the patch doubles in size from being half-filled to filling the entire lake.

Pennycook et al. (2015) argued that the emphasis on studying intuitive thinking has caused less effort devoted to studying analytic thinking. Research on the real-world consequences of analytic thought is therefore still in its infancy. The authors advocate for more research to identify the causes of analytic thinking and to investigate those aspects of our everyday lives in which analytic thinking is most consequential.

Fake news is a good example because it has become extremely prominent as a result of the rise of social media. Pennycook and Rand (2019) asked online participants to judge the accuracy of 15 factually accurate headlines (real news) and 15 inaccurate headlines (fake news). Participants also completed several items from the Cognitive Reflection Test to measure their ability to think analytically. As shown by the two distributions in Figure 14.2, deliberative thinkers who scored high on the reflection test were better at discriminating between real and fake news than intuitive thinkers who scored low on the test. A score of 0 on the *x*-axis indicates no ability to discriminate between the two sources, and higher scores indicate an increasing ability to make a distinction.

The third characteristic listed in Table 14.2 distinguishes between fast and slow responses. In his book *Thinking Fast and Slow,* Daniel Kahneman (2011) describes System I as fast and intuitive while System II is slow and analytical. Kahneman and Tversky's research challenged two ideas that Kahneman informs us were widely accepted when they began their work in the 1970s. The first is that people are usually rational and their thinking is normally sound. The second is that emotions such as fear cause departures from rationality. Their research findings revealed a different picture in which cognition causes errors when people rely too much on System I.

The bat-and-ball question serves as an example. If you made a mistake on this question, you have lots of company. Frederick and Kahneman studied this question and found that more than 50% of the students at such elite universities as Harvard, MIT, and Princeton gave the incorrect, intuitive answer (Kahneman, 2011). The students apparently placed too much faith in their intuitions to avoid the cognitive effort associated with System II reasoning.

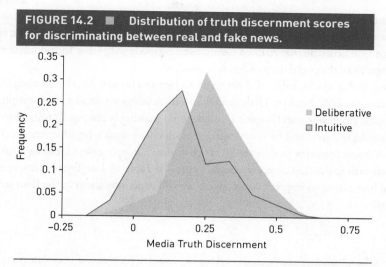

FIGURE 14.2 ■ Distribution of truth discernment scores for discriminating between real and fake news.

Source: "Lazy, not biased: Susceptibility to partisan fake news is better explained by lack of reasoning than by motivated reasoning," by G. Pennycook & D. G. Rand, 2019, *Cognition, 188*, 39-50. https://doi.org/10.1016/j.cognition.2018.06.011

Keith Stanovich (2018) at the University of Toronto constructed a detailed model of the interaction among three stages of reasoning that involve (1) accessing relevant knowledge, (2) detecting errors from System I, and (3) overriding those errors through System II reasoning. Relevant knowledge is a prerequisite for detecting System I errors. A respondent who lacks relevant knowledge for answering the question will not be able to detect a System I error. The second stage, detection of errors, is illustrated by Kahneman's (2011) analysis of the bat-and-ball problem. Students possessed the relevant knowledge—a simple arithmetic procedure for checking their answer—but failed to use it. The third stage occurs when a person realizes a System I answer is incorrect but does not know how to use System II to correct it. He may realize that the lake will not be half covered in 24 days (half of 48 days), but be unable to replace the incorrect answer with a correct answer.

The fourth dichotomy in Table 14.2 distinguishes between biases and competencies. Most decision-making strategies are based on heuristics, which were defined in the previous chapter as strategies that often work but do not guarantee success. Kahneman and Tversky studied those situations in which the strategies did not work. They identified biases that would help us make better decisions if we understood and corrected these biases.

In contrast, a group at the Max Planck Institute for Human Development in Berlin, Germany, has studied situations in which strategies (competencies) do work. Gerd Gigerenzer has directed the Institute and contributed many techniques that have proven effective. He refers to a "heuristic" in his book *Risk Savvy* (Gigerenzer, 2014) as a conscious or unconscious strategy that ignores part of the information to make better judgments. It enables us to make a decision fast but with high accuracy. The Berlin group has often labeled such heuristics "fast and frugal." An example is to imitate your peers. If you do not know what to do in an unfamiliar environment, such as which fork to use at a formal dinner party, a good strategy is simply to follow what others are doing. Another example, dicusussed in Chapter 12 on decison making, is the recognition heuristic that enabled Germans to correctly judge that the population of San Diego is larger than the population of San Antonio.

The final dichotomy in Table 14.2 contrasts nudges and boosts. Recall that nudges was the central topic of the 2008 book by Thaler and Sunstein. A **nudge** attempts to steer people toward good decisions. An example in Chapter 12 on decision making is placing an unhealthy dessert at the beginning so eaters will be encouraged to compensate with a healthier entrée (Flores et al., 2019). A **boost** attempts to educate rather than direct people toward making better decisions. Boosts seek to develop competencies so appear in Table 14.1 as Type II reasoning. Both nudges and boosts seek to improve decisions, so we will encounter them in the final section on applications.

Analogical Reasoning

People can take advantage of associative reasoning to solve problems if they can perceive how unfamiliar tasks are related to familiar tasks. They could then apply their prior knowledge to solve unfamiliar problems. Unfortunately, as discussed in the previous chapter, people find it difficult to spontaneously notice an analogy between two problems.

The failure to spontaneously notice a useful analogy is discouraging from an instructional perspective, but—as they become better problem solvers and more expert about a particular subject matter—people become more capable of perceiving how problems are related, even when they have different content. That is, they become better at classifying problems based on their solutions and are less influenced by the specific story content. A study by Silver (1981) was one of the first to demonstrate this finding.

Silver asked seventh-grade students to form groups of problems that were "mathematically related" and to explain the basis for categorizing them. He used 16 problems that could be represented by a 4 × 4 matrix. The four problems in each horizontal row were mathematically related, and the same mathematical procedure could be used to solve each. The four problems in each vertical column described a similar story content but required different procedures to solve them. For instance, the first two problems in Table 14.3 are mathematically related because the same procedure is used to solve each. The third problem has the same story content as the first but requires a different mathematical procedure.

Although Silver asked his students to classify mathematically related problems, students who had difficulty perceiving the mathematical structure of the problems might use story content as a basis of classification. Students were asked to solve 12 of the problems after they made their classification to determine whether there was any relation between the ability to classify and the ability to solve problems. Silver classified the students as good, average, or poor problem solvers on the basis of the number of problems they solved.

---

nudge. An attempt to improve choices by directing people

boost. An attempt to improve choices by educating people

TABLE 14.3 ■	A word problem and related structure
Word problem	A farmer is counting the hens and rabbits in his barnyard. He counts a total of 50 heads and 140 feet. How many hens and how many rabbits does the farmer have?
Related structure	Bill has a collection of 20 coins that consists entirely of dimes and quarters. If the collection is worth $4.10, how many of each kind of coin are in the collection?
Related content	A farmer is counting the hens and rabbits in his barnyard. He counts six coops with four hens in each, two coops with three hens in each, five cages with six rabbits in each, and three cages with four rabbits in each. How many hens and how many rabbits does the farmer have?

Source: Based on "Recall of mathematical problem information: Solving related problems," by E. A. Silver, 1981, *Journal for Research in Mathematics Education, 12*, 54–64. https://doi.org/10.2307/748658. Copyright 1981 by the National Council of Teachers of Mathematics.

The results indicated that the better problem solvers formed categories on the basis of mathematical structure, and the poorer problem solvers formed categories on the basis of story content. The good problem solvers formed an average of 3.1 categories based on mathematical structure, compared with 1.8 categories for the average problem solvers, and 0.4 category for the poor problem solvers. The opposite trend occurred for story content. The poor problem solvers formed an average of 2.3 categories based on story content, compared with 0.6 category for the average problem solvers, and 0.1 category for the good problem solvers.

Similar results were obtained when students were asked to recall information about story problems. Good problem solvers were able to recall information about mathematical structure. Poor problem solvers rarely recalled this information, even when the solutions were discussed prior to their recall. However, they could often remember details about the story content and were sometimes better than the good problem solvers at recalling these details. The results suggest that an important source of individual differences in mathematical problem solving is the ability to categorize problems initially according to the mathematical procedure needed to solve them.

Differences in the ability to categorize problems according to their mathematical structure also distinguish novices from experts in more advanced courses. Chi et al. (1982) asked eight novices and eight experts to sort 24 physics problems into categories based on the similarity of solutions. The novices were undergraduates who had recently completed a physics course. The experts were advanced doctoral degree students from the physics department. Each group formed approximately the same number of categories, but the problems in the categories differed for the two groups.

Novices tended to categorize problems on the basis of common objects, such as spring problems and inclined-plane problems. Experts tended to categorize problems on the basis of physics principles that could be applied to solve them, such as the conservation-of-energy law or Newton's second law ($F = MA$). Thus, just as in Silver's (1981) experiment with seventh-grade students, the better problem solvers were more sensitive to the formal structure of the problem (Photo 14.2).

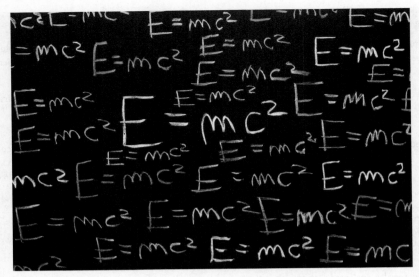

PHOTO 14.2 Experts classify physics problems based on common principles.

istockphotos.com/FotografiaBasica

EXPERTISE AND PROBLEM SOLVING

The preceding studies showed how prior knowledge influenced performance on several different kinds of reasoning tasks, including evaluating logical statements and classifying problems according to their mathematical structure and physical principles. Prior knowledge also influences how people solve more complex transformation problems, which require constructing a sequence of steps to solve the problem. Early models of problem solving (Newell & Simon, 1972) emphasized general search procedures that used heuristics such as means–end analysis to guide the search. More recent models indicate that, with practice, students can learn specific solutions that replace the less efficient general heuristics (Gick, 1986). This distinction between applying a learned solution and searching for the solution is illustrated in Figure 14.3.

Search Versus Implementation

Figure 14.3 shows three major stages in solving a problem (Gick, 1986). The problem solver first attempts to construct a representation of the problem by connecting it to prior knowledge. Certain features of the problem may activate a schema for solving the problem if the problem solver finds a connection with prior knowledge. As we saw in Chapter 10, a schema is an organized cluster of knowledge, and in this case, it is a cluster of knowledge for a particular problem type. These organized clusters of knowledge enable experts to categorize problems on the basis of mathematical structure and principles, as indicated in Photo 14.2.

In her book *Schemas in Problem Solving*, Sandra Marshall (1995) began by reviewing the historic development of schemas as a theoretical construct by tracing the ideas of Plato, Aristotle,

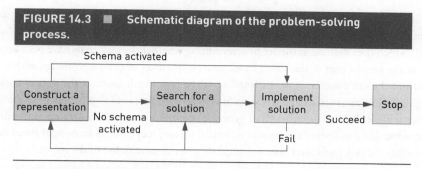

FIGURE 14.3 ■ Schematic diagram of the problem-solving process.

Source: From "Problem-solving strategies," by M. L. Gick, 1986, *Educational Psychologist*, *21*, 99–120. https://doi.org/10.1207/s15326985ep2101&2_6. Copyright by Lawrence Erlbaum Associates, Inc.

Kant, Bartlett, and Piaget. In her working definition, a schema is a memory organization that can (1) recognize similar experiences; (2) access a general framework that contains essential elements of those experiences; (3) use the framework to draw inferences, create goals, and develop plans; and (4) provide skills and procedures for solving problems in which the framework is relevant. If schema activation occurs during the construction of a problem representation, the solver can proceed directly to the third stage and implement the solution. There is very little need to search for a solution because the appropriate solution procedures are activated by recognizing the particular problem type.

A meta-analysis demonstrated the effectiveness of schema-based instruction for teaching elementary school students mathematical procedures for solving arithmetic story problems (Peltier & Vannest, 2017). Schema-based instruction requires identifying the schema, completing the corresponding schematic diagram, identifying a solution plan, carrying out the plan, and checking the answer for reasonableness. The meta-analysis revealed that schema instruction produced larger effects than other instructional interventions found in previous meta-analyses.

Searching for a solution, in contrast to schema activation, requires the use of general strategies, such as the ones discussed in the previous chapter. One strategy is means–end analysis, in which the problem solver attempts to reduce differences between the current problem state and the goal state. A second general strategy is to search for an analogous problem that might provide a useful solution. A third general strategy is planning the solution by breaking down the problem into subgoals.

Gick (1986) emphasizes, however, that general strategies can require some specific knowledge about a problem to be successful. For example, planning implies that the problem solver is looking ahead and is not simply taking one step at a time. This of course is usually not possible the first time a person encounters a problem (Sweller et al., 1983). Planning has not been emphasized in much of the research on puzzles because people usually do not have detailed knowledge about how to solve a particular puzzle. Successful models of puzzle solving have therefore been based on general strategies, such as means–end analysis (Atwood & Polson, 1976; Simon & Reed, 1976).

---

general strategy. A strategy (heuristic) that applies in many situations but does not always result in a solution

Nokes-Malach and Mestre (2013) elaborated on Gick's model in Figure 14.3 by discussing variables that influence transitions between the stages. Their key theoretical concept is "sense making," which they defined as the act of determining whether the task goals have been accomplished to the satisfaction of the solver based on coordination of prior knowledge with information from the environment and the framing of the task. An important theoretical concept within this definition is satisficing based on Simon's (1956) proposal that people generate solutions that achieve their goals rather than generate optimal solutions. Constraints on both the problem solver (such as level of expertise) and available resources (such as amount of time) determine whether the task goals have been accomplished to the satisfaction of the solver.

Limitations of Expertise

Although expert-defined schemas are usually very helpful, they can occasionally constrain innovative solutions. Robson (2019) provides numerous examples in his book *The Intelligence Trap,* including Thomas Edison and Albert Einstein. Thomas Edison refused to abandon his belief that direct current is superior to alternating current, even after one of his own engineers, Nikola Tesla, strongly argued in favor of alternating current. Albert Einstein refused to abandon his theory of general relativity after mounting scientific evidence against the theory. Both men exhibited cognitive entrenchment.

Dane (2010) defines cognitive entrenchment as a high level of stability in knowledge schemas that cause experts to be inflexible in their thinking. Cognitive entrenchment increases the likelihood of problem-solving fixation and blocks the generation of novel ideas. It restricts an expert's ability to identify optimal solutions to problems, adapt to novel situations, and generate creative ideas (Figure 14.4). Failure to adapt can result from repeated activation of schemas that makes their revision unlikely and leads to habitual behavior. For instance, one study found that expert accountants were less able to adapt to a new tax law that invalidated a previous rule concerning tax deductions.

FIGURE 14.4 ■ Consequences of cognitive entrenchment.

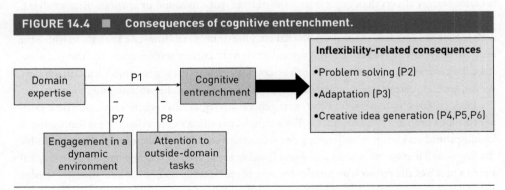

Source: Based on "Reconsidering the trade-off between expertise and flexibility: A cognitive entrenchment perspective," by E. Dane (2010), Academy of Management Review, 35, 579-603.   https://doi.org/10.5465/amr.35.4.zok579. Reprinted with permission from the publisher.

satisficing. Generating solutions that are satisfactory rather than optimal

cognitive entrenchment. Inflexible thinking that blocks novel ideas

Dane (2010) proposed two factors that can reduce cognitive entrenchment that is depicted in Figure 14.4. The first is working in a dynamic environment in which one must remain open to a wide range of possibilities and options. Dynamic environments require individuals to respond to changing conditions that can be highly collaborative, such as improvisational theater (Photo 14.3), or inherently adversarial, such as trial law. The second factor is focusing attention on tasks outside the domain in which counterexamples and exceptions can increase the flexibility of one's beliefs. An important research issue in this case is determining how the degree of similarity between the two domains influences cognitive entrenchment. There is likely to be a little conceptual overlap between nuclear physics and retail sales and therefore limited opportunities to reduce cognitive entrenchment.

PHOTO 14.3 Improvisational theater teaches flexibility.

istockphotos.com/monkeybusinessimages

Cognitive entrenchment constrains design when design fixation occurs because exploration is unintentionally limited by the designer's knowledge of prior solutions. Interviews with technology entrepreneurs revealed that they attempt to balance persistence with flexibility. Entrepreneurs have celebrated the concept of a **pivot** (Ries, 2011) in which they change direction, giving up some of their ideas to explore new opportunities. These findings have implications for design education to encourage designers to reflect on issues such as fixation and entrenchment in order to recognize how they might explore new directions (Crilly, 2018).

---

pivot. Changing direction to explore new ideas

CREATIVITY

Expertise implies that people are usually good problem solvers in their area of expertise, but expertise doesn't necessarily imply that they are creative. We think of creative problem solvers as being better than simply good problem solvers. Creativity implies that the solutions are not only correct but also novel and useful. It is helpful to consider a developmental trajectory of creativity that advances from personal creativity to everyday creativity to expert creativity to genius creativity (Kaufman, 2018). Although much of the writings on creativity focus on experts and geniuses, creativity also provides meaning to our lives. The personal benefits enable us to express ourselves and explore our own ideas, emotions, and experiences. These benefits occur even when we are not trying to impress others (Kaufman, 2018).

PHOTO 14.4 The Cat in the Hat watches Dr. Seuss.
Courtesy of the author

We nonetheless hold a special reverence for the creative solutions of experts and may believe that they are occasionally produced by a mysterious process that requires the ability of a genius. However, work by cognitive scientists suggests that creativity may be less mysterious than we expect. In fact, two books even suggest that we can apply what we already know about expertise to explain creativity.

One book, *Creativity: Beyond the Myth of Genius*, by Robert Weisberg (1993), argued that although the effects of creative ideas are extraordinary, the thought processes that produce them are not:

> Many creative products are indeed extraordinary. They are rare; they are sometimes the result of a lifetime of hard work; they can answer questions that have perplexed people for centuries; they can have far-ranging influence, beyond even the expectations of their creators. It is often assumed that if a creative product has extraordinary effects, it must have come about in extraordinary ways, but that does not necessarily follow. The creative achievement can be extraordinary because of the effect it produces, rather than because of the way in which it was brought about. (p. 10)

creativity. Creating a novel and useful product or solution

Weisberg's "myth of genius" view is based, in part, on his analysis of creative individuals, whose discoveries he felt could be explained by their use of ordinary thought processes. Ordinary thinking goes beyond past achievements, but it does so by slowly accumulating new pieces of information. There are no sudden leaps or unconscious illuminations. Weisberg uses case studies to illustrate that Watson and Crick's discovery of the structure of DNA, the Wright brothers' invention of the airplane, and Picasso's development of a new style of painting occurred through incremental processes that built on previous work. Albert Einstein is quoted as saying that the secret to creativity is knowing how to hide your sources.

You may have mixed feelings about Weisberg's view because of our admiration for highly creative individuals. Certainly, Einstein went way beyond his "sources" to give us a new understanding of the universe. Many other highly creative people, such as Frank Lloyd Wright and Dr. Seuss (Photo 14.4), seem to have had a special genius. Perhaps the resolution of the conflict between a great admiration for creative works and the desire to explain their production is contained in the preface to Boden's (2004) book, *The Creative Mind: Myths and Mechanisms*. Boden agrees that creativity is not mysterious and can be explained by the computational concepts of artificial intelligence. But providing explanations, says Boden, should allow us to appreciate the richness of creative thought better than before—even if our sense of mystery is dispelled, our sense of wonder should not be.

Inventing Products Through Imagery

Although Weisberg (1993) believes that creative discoveries can often be explained by ordinary thought processes, he admits that highly creative individuals may be exceptional in some respects. Creative individuals are not only experts in their domain but also are highly motivated. They often take paths of inquiry that others ignore, take intellectual risks, and persevere in the face of obstacles (Sternberg & Lubart, 1996).

Writings by Roger Shepard (1988) and others have indicated that many creative scientific discoveries depended on visual imagery. Einstein reported that his thought experiments, such as imagining the consequences of traveling at the speed of light, helped him formulate his special theory of relativity. Faraday claimed to have visualized force lines from electric and magnetic fields, leading to the modern theory of electromagnetic fields. Kekule reported that his discovery of the molecular structure of benzene occurred after he imagined a snake coiled in a circle.

In contrast to the biographical studies of creativity, laboratory studies have typically studied college students' performance on tasks that do not require expertise. Although this may limit generalization to the creative thinking of experts, the findings are nonetheless relevant. An example of a novel research program on creativity that grew out of previous paradigms in cognitive psychology is the work of Ron Finke (1990). Finke had been one of the main contributors to a theory of visual imagery, and he used his expertise in this area to extend imagery paradigms to the study of creativity.

Finke (1990) extended previous studies on the visual synthesis of artificial patterns (such as those by Palmer, 1977) to determine whether people could visually combine basic parts to create useful and novel products. The object parts consisted of such basic forms as a sphere, half sphere, cube, cone, cylinder, rectangular block, wire, tube, bracket, flat square, hook, wheels, ring, and handle (somewhat like the geons in Biederman's [1985] theory of pattern recognition discussed in Chapter 2). After either the experimenter or the subject selected three parts, the subjects were instructed to close their eyes and imagine combining the parts to make a practical object or device. They had to use all three parts but could vary their size, position, and orientation. The created object had to belong to one of eight categories: furniture, personal items, transportation, scientific instruments, appliances, tools or utensils, weapons, and toys or games.

Judges then scored the created objects on a 5-point scale for practicality and for originality. Strict criteria were used—the average rating for practicality had to be at least 4.5 to be classified as practical, and the average rating for originality had to be at least 4.0 to be classified as original. In one condition, subjects were allowed to select their own parts but were told the category of their invention (such as appliances). In another condition, they were allowed to invent an object that belonged to any one of the eight categories but were told which parts to use (such as half sphere, wheels, and hook). In the most restrictive condition, they were told both the parts to use and the category of their invention (use a half sphere, wheels, and a hook to make an appliance). Although the number of inventions scored as practical was approximately the same across the three conditions, the most restrictive condition resulted in the highest number of creative inventions, judged to be both practical and original. The more restrictive the task, the more difficult it was to think of an object that satisfied all the criteria and was like existing objects.

There is, however, an even more restrictive condition than assigning both the parts and category. In another experiment, people were again given the parts but didn't find out about the category until *after* they had assembled their object. Finke (1990) refers to these objects as preinventive forms because their use cannot be identified until after the object is constructed. Figure 14.5 shows how a preinventive form that was assembled from a half sphere, bracket, and hook could be used for each of the eight categories. The results demonstrated that this was the most successful condition of all for generating creative inventions.

Even in the less-constraining conditions, however, many subjects reported that they preferred to initially use a generation strategy, in which they imagined interesting combinations of parts, followed by an exploration strategy, in which they figured out how to use the invented object. Finke et al. (1992) describe these two phases in their Geneplore (generation–exploration) model shown in Figure 14.6.

In the initial phase, the inventor forms preinventive structures that are then explored and interpreted during the second phase. The preinventive structures are the precursors to the final, creative product and would be generated, regenerated, and modified throughout the cycle of invention. Finke et al. (1992) recommend that people should place greater emphasis on generating preinventive structures and then later think of possible uses. Notice that this is contrary to the usual order in which we begin with a particular use in mind—a wallet that fits in a shirt pocket or a garment that allows us to change clothes at the beach—and then try to invent something to accomplish our goal. These two paths to creativity are differentiated by whether the search begins with a problem or an idea.

---

preinventive form. Creating an object before determining its use

generation strategy. A strategy for producing preinventive forms

exploration strategy. A strategy for determining how to use a preinventive form

FIGURE 14.5 ■ Multiple interpretations of a single preinventive form (assembled from a half sphere, bracket, and hook). The interpretations are lawn lounger (furniture), earrings (personal items), water weigher (scientific instruments), portable agitator (appliances), water sled (transportation), rotating masher (utensils), ring spinner (toys), and slasher basher (weapons).

Source: From *Creative imagery: Discoveries and inventions in visualization,* by R. A. Finke, Fig. 7.24. Copyright © 1990 by Lawrence Erlbaum Associates, Inc. Reprinted by permission.

FIGURE 14.6 ■ The basic structure of the geneplore (generation-exploration) model.

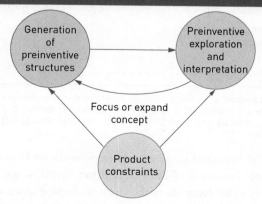

Source: From *Creative cognition: Theory, research, and applications,* by R. A. Finke, T. B. Ward, & S. M. Smith. Copyright 1992 by MIT Press. Reprinted by permission.

Problems and Ideas

Figure 14.7 captures the distinction between a problem-first and an idea-first approach to invention (Cromwell et al., 2018). The problem-first approach begins by defining the problem, then gathering information, generating new ideas, evaluating these ideas, and choosing a solution. This approach follows the traditional path to solving problems, as depicted in Figure 14.3. Thomas Edison's search for a practical light bulb is an example. His team began with a well-defined problem and then searched for materials and technology that could solve the problem.

The idea-first approach, as illustrated by the Geneplore model, begins with an idea and then explores how to make use of that idea. The "search for a solution" stage in Figure 14.3 could be replaced by "search for an application." Nintendo's sports game Wii was the application of an idea that had been developed nearly 30 years earlier in a different industry (Cromwell et al., 2018). Wii resulted from the creative application of a semiconductor that could detect three-dimensional movement.

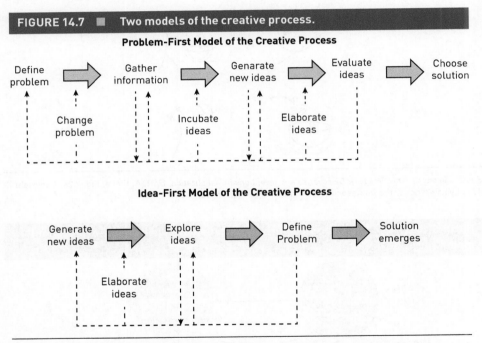

FIGURE 14.7 ■ Two models of the creative process.

Problem-First Model of the Creative Process

Idea-First Model of the Creative Process

Source: From An integrated model of dynamic problem solving within organizational constraints, by J. Cromwell, T. M. Amabile, & J.-F. Harvey, 2018, in R. Reiter-Palmon, V. L. Kennel, & J. C. Kaufman (Eds.), *Individual creativity in the workplace* (pp. 53–81). San Diego: Academic Press. https://doi.org/10.1016/B978-0-12-813238-8.00003-6

Cromwell et al. (2018) constraint-based model integrates the problem-first and idea-first perspectives (Figure 14.8). Two types of constraints Rosso (2014) shown on the horizontal dimension are imposed by either resources or the problem. *Problem* constraints include product requirements, customer preferences, and organizational needs. *Resource* constraints include limitations on time and finances. The second (vertical) dimension in Figure 14.8 is source constraints. *Internal* constraints are self-imposed such as creative skills needed to generate novel ideas and domain-relevant skills that needed for technical expertise. *External* constraints are imposed by the situation such as use of specific materials and demands of the client.

FIGURE 14.8 ■ A constraint-based model of creativity.

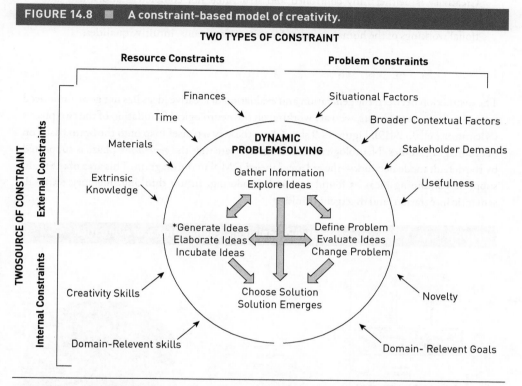

Source: From "An integrated model of dynamic problem solving within organizational constraints," by J. Cromwell, T. M. Amabile, & J.-F. Harvey, 2018, in R. Reiter-Palmon, V. L. Kennel, & J. C. Kaufman (Eds.), *Individual creativity in the workplace* (pp. 53–81). San Diego: Academic Press. https://doi.org/10.1016/B978-0-12-813238-8.00003-6

As indicated by the interaction of activities within the circle, there are multiple paths to inventing a creative product. As depicted by the problem-first model in Figure 14.7, individuals may begin by defining the problem and then moving through the stages of gathering information, evaluating ideas, and elaborating on these ideas until finding a solution. Alternatively, as depicted by the idea-first model in Figure 14.7, they may begin by generating new ideas and then exploring the ideas in the context of different problem domains until an application emerges. Problem-solving teams can benefit from combining problem solvers with both types of skills. Those members who are skilled at generating ideas can be assisted by members who are skilled at solving specific problems after the problems become clearly defined.

Let's conclude this chapter by revisiting the distinction between associative and rule-based reasoning to creativity. Associative thinking produces creative ideas that are often excessively fanciful. Rule-based reasoning tends to be realistic, but unimaginative. Sloman's (2002) argument that many tasks involve both associative and rule-based thinking applies to those tasks that require creative thinking. As pointed out by Finke (1996, p. 391):

> Creativity is neither fully controlled and structured nor completely unplanned and unstructured. Creative ideas, concepts, and images can result either from the intentional workings of the human mind or from its spontaneous, intuitive qualities.

Neuroscience of Creativity

The distinction between the generation and evaluation of creative ideas has not gone unnoticed by cognitive neuroscientists, who are working on the neurological foundation of the two phases (Kleinmintz et al., 2019). Figure 14.9 shows how these two phases map onto the brain based on neuroimaging studies. Neurological recordings indicate that the *generation* phase is supported by the default mode network—the red area labeled DMN in the diagram. This area of the brain supports combining ideas as found in mind wandering, future thinking, memory retrieval, semantic integration, and divergent thinking.

FIGURE 14.9 ■ A neurocognitive model of idea generation and evaluation.

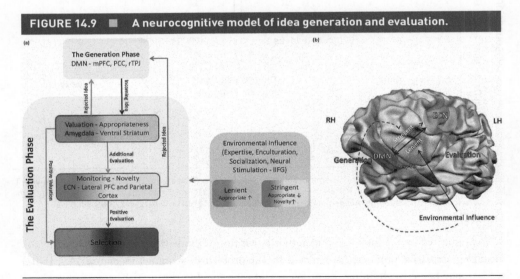

Source: From "The two-fold model of creativity: the neural underpinnings of the generation and evaluation of creative ideas," by O. M, Kleinmintz, T. Ivancovsky, & S. G. Shamay-Tsoory, 2019, *Current Opinion in Behavioral Sciences, 27*, 131–138. https://doi.org/10.1016/j.cobeha.2018.11.004

The *evaluation* phase is supported by the executive control network—the blue area labeled ECN in the diagram. This area of the brain controls the initiation and inhibition of mental processes, flexibility of working memory, planning, and error detection. A unique feature of the model is that the evaluation phase consists of three stages that vary in their leniency of accepting ideas for further evaluation. The initial *valuation* accepts appropriate ideas; *monitoring* accepts novel ideas; and *selection* makes the final choice(s) based on the initial two stages. As depicted in Figure 14.9, evaluation shifts to the executive control network (ECN) as the criteria become more stringent.

Identifying the neurological basis of creativity is also the purpose of Beaty et al. (2019) review, although these investigators place less emphasis on distinguishing between the generation and evaluation phases. They instead focus on three cognitive processes that are important during creative performance—goal-directed memory retrieval, response inhibition, and internally focused attention. A comparison of the two reviews is facilitated by the continued emphasis on the connectivity between the default network (the red area labeled DN in Figure 14.10) and the executive control network (the yellow area labeled ECN in Figure 14.10).

Goal-directed retrieval is the ability to strategically search episodic and semantic memory for task-relevant information in the default network—the area of the brain that plays an important role in the generation of ideas, according to the previous model. Response inhibition suppresses dominant concepts or ideas that interfere with generating novel responses. Both retrieving and inhibiting ideas are guided by the executive control network. Internally focused attention directs attention to self-generated thought processes to reduce sensory distractions, such as those originating in the visual network (the purple area labeled VN in Figure 14.10).

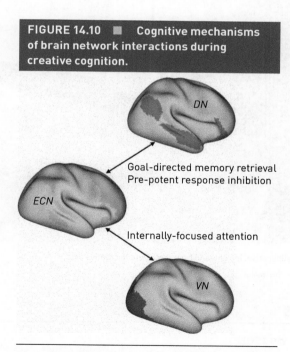

FIGURE 14.10 ■ Cognitive mechanisms of brain network interactions during creative cognition.

DN

Goal-directed memory retrieval
Pre-potent response inhibition

ECN

Internally-focused attention

VN

Source: "Network neuroscience of creative cognition: Mapping cognitive mechanisms and individual differences in the creative brain," by R. E. Beaty, P. Seli, & D. L Schacter, 2019, *Current Opinion in Behavioral Sciences, 27*, 22–33. https://doi.org/10.1016/j.cobeha.2018.08.013

A third approach, formulated by Dietrich (2019), identifies three types of creativity—a deliberate mode, a spontaneous mode, and a flow mode—that are based on established concepts in both cognitive psychology and neuroscience. In the *deliberative* mode, creative ideas are generated by a deliberate search strategy. Edison's systematic method of constructing a light bulb, Watson and Crick's disciplined approach to building a structural model of DNA, and Bach's tactics in composing hundreds of cantatas are examples of deliberation. In the *spontaneous* mode, creative ideas occur suddenly, as in Archimedes' insight that the volume of an object could be measured by displacing bath water. Insights appear to be effortless, intuitive, surprising, and accidental.

Such spontaneity may be encouraged by the *flow* mode in which creative ideas occur through unconscious, effortless motion. Dietrich (2019) bases the concept of flow on the classic theoretical concept formulated by Csikszentmihalyi (1996) in which one becomes so deeply engaged in a task that all else disappears, including the passage of time, worry of failure, and self-reflection. The essence of flow is the seamless merging of perception and action that appears to bypass higher-order thought. Deliberation, insight, and flow are not mutually exclusive. Complex creative acts such as writing a song might involve all three modes by switching between them (Photo 14.5).

PHOTO 14.5 Deliberation, insight, and flow contribute to creative acts.

istockphotos.com/DragonImages

APPLICATIONS

Nudges Versus Boosts

The final contrast in Table 14.4 compares nudges and boosts as alternative approaches to improving decisions. In their book *Nudge: Improving Decisions About Health, Wealth, and Happiness,* Thaler and Sunstein (2008) advocated an approach that they labeled "libertarian paternalism." The first word implies that people should be free to make their own choices.

The second word implies that institutions should steer people's choices in directions that will improve their lives. Libertarian paternalism will not prevent people from smoking cigarettes, eating unhealthy food, and failing to save for retirement. It will, however, attempt to nudge them in a direction that will be more beneficial.

An example of the beneficial effect of nudges is their impact on suicide-related decisions (Bauer & Capron, 2020). Although nudges have had a positive impact in many areas, only a few areas of mental health have used these techniques. Mental health should be targeted because people become worse at making rational decisions during highly emotional periods. The authors review three of their studies in which nudges were effective in encouraging at-risk patients to construct a safety plan; put a suicide prevention lifeline into their phones; and receive education on coping skills.

Government interventions using nudges have also been successful in increasing retirement savings, college enrollment, energy conservation (Photo 14.6), and influenza vaccinations (Benartzi et al., 2017). The impact of nudges on a cost-adjusted basis has often been more effective than the use of more traditional methods that depend on consumers making challenging cost/benefit calculations. The authors recommend that (1) there should be increased efforts to implement behaviorally informed policies; (2) agencies using nudges should share their data with other organizations to coordinate efforts; and (3) scientists should measure the relative effectiveness of nudges compared to other types of interventions.

PHOTO 14.6 Nudges have been successful in promoting energy conservation.
istockphotos.com/Blue Planet Studio

An alternative to nudges is boosting. Ralph Hertwig in Berlin's Max Planck Institute for Human Development and Till Grune-Yanoff in Stockholm's Royal Institute of Technology (2017) classify nudging as Type I processing because nudges do not require critical thinking. They classify boosting as Type II processing because boosting creates new procedures and mental tools to help people make better decisions. The goal of boosting is to create competencies through enhancing skills, knowledge, and decision tools. Boosts require active cooperation and investment in time, effort, and motivation. Individuals must decide whether to engage or not to engage in a boost. Table 14.4 summarizes differences between boosts and nudges.

TABLE 14.4 ■ Seven dimensions on which nudging and boosting approaches to public policy can be distinguished		
Dimension	**Nudging**	**Boosting**
Intervention target	Behavior	Competences
Roots in research programs and evidence	Show decision maker as systematically imperfect and subject to cognitive and motivational deficiencies	Acknowledge bounds but identify human competencies and ways to foster them
Causal pathways	Harness cognitive and motivational deficiencies in tandem with changes in the external choice architecture	Foster competencies through changes in skills, knowledge, decision tools, or environment
Assumptions about cognitive architecture	Dual-system architecture	Cognitive architectures are malleable
Empirical distinction criterion (reversibility)	Once intervention is removed, behavior reverts to preintervention state	Implied effects should persist after successful intervention is removed
Programmatic ambition	Correct momentous mistakes in specific contexts: "local repair"	Equip individuals with domain-specific or generalizable competences
Normative implications	Might violate autonomy and transparency	Necessarily transparent and requires cooperation—an offer that may or may not be accepted

Source: From "Nudging and boosting: steering or empowering good decisions," by R. Hertwig & T. Grune-Yanoff (2017), Perspectives on Psychological Science, 12, 973-986. https://doi.org/10.1177/1745691617702496

The different implications of nudges and boosts for behavioral change are illustrated by their application to judging the accuracy of information obtained from social media (Lorenz-Spreen et al., 2020). Figure 14.11a shows three dimensions that influence transparency of these messages and their potential for manipulation. The transparency of the obtained information diminishes when it is inferred rather than directly stated, is aimed at a collective group rather than at an individual, and is old rather than recent.

An additional influence on judged accuracy is perceived versus actual group size (Figure 14.11b). People who belong to small social networks of like-minded people are more likely to receive biased information that supports the opinions of those individuals. Believing the network is larger gives a false impression that these views represent a majority opinion. The example illustrates that a person believes that four of six people share his views based on his direct links to those people. In reality, only five of 13 people in the network share his view when indirect links are included.

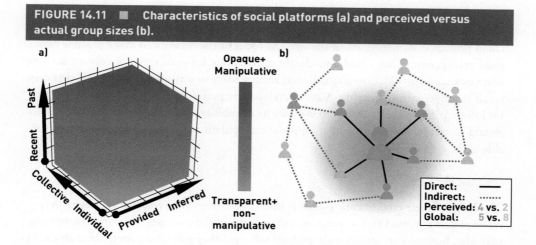

FIGURE 14.11 ■ Characteristics of social platforms (a) and perceived versus actual group sizes (b).

Source: "How behavioral sciences can promote truth, autonomy and democratic discourse online," by P. Lorenz-Spreen, S. Lewandowsky, C. R. Sunstein, & R. Hertwig, 2020, *Nature Human Behavior.* https://doi. org/10.1038/s41562-020-0889-7

Social networks provide an avenue for spreading misinformation as indicated by people's evaluation of 15 true and 15 false headlines regarding COVID-19 (Pennycook et al., 2020). Responders made a judgment about the headline's accuracy and whether they would be willing to share it on online media such as Facebook or Twitter. The responders were capable of discriminating between true and false headlines but were nonetheless willing to share both types of information (Figure 14.12).

FIGURE 14.12 ■ Percentage of "yes"responses that true and false headlines were accurate and whether responders would consider sharing that information.

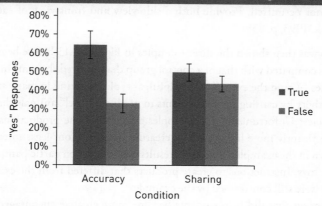

Source: From "Fighting COVID-19 misinformation on social media: experimental evidence for a scalable accuracy-nudge intervention," by G. Pennycook, J,McPhetres, Y. Zhang, J. G. Lu, & D. G. Rand, 2020, *Psychological Science, 31,* 770-780. https://doi.org/10.1177/0956797620939054. Licensed under CC-BY.

Both nudges and boosts offer solutions for evaluating information on the internet. Nudges can help by providing aids for identifying possible biases. Social media platforms could provide information about the size and focus of the network to make possible biases more transparent. They could also clearly differentiate between types of content such as ads, news, and posts by supporters. Boosts require users to play a more active role that may result in longer-lasting benefits. A skill developed by professional fact-checkers is to search for information on multiple sites to evaluate its credibility. Additionally, social media users should educate themselves about attempts at manipulation in order to become less vulnerable to these methods.

Enhancing Creativity

The design of these experimental studies is an extension of previous research paradigms in cognitive psychology, modified to emphasize the novelty of the creations. Take the case of using examples. Examples are important in problem solving—they provide the source of analogies in analogical problem solving. They also can be the source of creative ideas, but there is a subtle difference in how we use examples to solve routine problems and how we use examples to produce creative solutions. When we search for an analogous problem to solve a routine problem, we try to maximize the similarity between the example and test problem to minimize the differences in the two solutions. When we use an example to produce something creative, we want to make changes in the example to produce a novel product or solution.

If we are not careful, examples can have a constraining effect on creativity. This is illustrated in a task in which people were given the following instructions:

> Imagine a planet just like Earth existing somewhere in the universe. It is currently uninhabited. Your task is to design new creatures to inhabit the planet. Within the allotted 20 minutes draw as many new and different creatures of your own creative design as you are able. Duplication of creatures now extinct or living on the planet Earth are not permitted. Provide both a side view and front view of each creature. (Smith et al., 1993, p. 839)

One group was then shown the three examples in Figure 14.13 before beginning the task. Their work was compared with that of a control group that received the same instructions without the examples. Would the examples be helpful, as typically found in many studies, or would they stifle creativity by causing the participants to produce "novel" animals that closely resembled the examples? Unfortunately, the examples constrained the productions. The examples group was significantly more likely to draw creatures that had four legs, antennae, and a tail, like those shown in the examples. The same results occurred when participants were instructed to create novel toys. Instructions to create products that differed from the examples had little effect—people were still constrained by the examples.

An intervention that did help students become more creative encouraged them to think about examples more abstractly (Ward et al., 2004). The instructions asked participants to think about a planet that was very different from Earth and generate new animals either by

FIGURE 14.13 ■ Example creatures, along with their labels and descriptions.

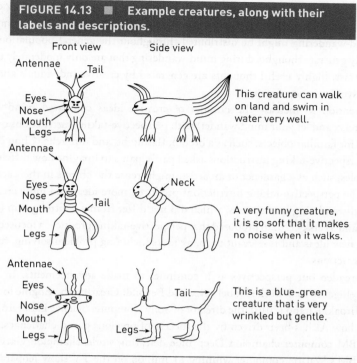

Source "Constraining effect of examples in a creative generation task," by S. M. Smith, T. B. Ward, & J. S. Schumacher, 1993, *Memory & Cognition, 21*, 837–845. https://doi.org/10.3758/bf03202751. Copyright 1993 by the Psychonomic Society, Inc.

thinking (1) about animals on earth or (2) about attributes the animals would need to adapt to the new imagined environment. Students who thought about the imagined environment were less likely to include typical animal properties, such as eyes, ears, noses, and legs. Considering a new environment led to more abstract ways of thinking about the assignment, which resulted in greater novelty in completing the task.

Another approach that may have the potential for enhancing creativity is to encourage mind-wandering. We learned that the default mode network in Figure 14.8 supports combining ideas, as has been found in a variety of situations including mind-wandering (Kleinmintz et al., 2019). An online survey of professional physicists and writers (Gable et al., 2019) indicated that creative ideas do occur during mind wondering, defined as thoughts that occurred when not actively pursuing their profession. The participants completed an email questionnaire each night during a two-week period that asked them to describe their most meaningful creative idea of the day. They also asked whether at that time were actively pursuing their project, working on another work-related project, or doing something unrelated to work. Approximately 30% of their reported creative ideas occurred when the physicists and writers were thinking about something unrelated to their work.

A limitation of mind-wandering, however, is that it is likely to benefit only individuals who are highly creative. Fox and Beaty (2019) proposed a speculative model of how the novelty and utility of mind-wandering might be distributed throughout the general population. Normal adults typically generate thoughts during mind-wandering that are only moderately useful and novel. In contrast, highly useful thoughts are generated by creative individuals and harmful thoughts by psychiatric populations.

An intervention to increase the number of creative ideas compared mind-wandering instructions (relax and let your mind wander) with perspective-taking instructions on a task to find new uses for familiar objects, such as a broom, flashlight, and umbrella (Chou & Tversky, 2020). The perspective-taking instructions asked participants to imagine how different people in different roles, such as a gardener or an artist, might reuse the objects in their activities. In two studies, the perspective-taking instructions produced more ideas and more creative ideas than the mind-wandering instructions, which did not differ from a control group (see Figure 14.14). Chou and Tversky (2020) proposed that perspective-taking produces a focused approach to generating new ideas and is relevant to many tasks including problem solving, forecasting, and social interactions.

AI will broaden our perspectives as it continues to make advancements. In his article "Artificial Intelligence to Win the Nobel Prize and Beyond: Creating the Engine for Scientific Discovery" Hiroaki Kitano (2016), the director of Sony Computer Science Laboratories, began by reviewing how AI has been driven by the success of previous grand challenges. Examples include the IBM computer champion Deep Blue defeating world champion Gary Kasparov in 1997and IBM's Watson computer winning $1 million on the TV show Jeopardy in 2011. Although these victories surpassed human efforts, Kitano (2016) recommended a new collaborative grand challenge to develop an AI system to assist in scientific discovery that is worthy of a Nobel Prize in the biomedical sciences.

Kitano (2016) listed fundamental difficulties that overwhelm the cognitive capabilities of researchers. The first is an overload of information. The amount of data is accumulating at a faster and faster pace based on a variety of new measurements. The publication of biomedical research is far beyond the capabilities of scientists to read these articles. A second problem is that papers frequently involve ambiguity, inaccuracy, and missing information. Readers therefore have to fill in gaps based on their own knowledge, resulting in an arbitrary interpretation of the content. A third problem is cognitive bias that occurs for both authors and their readers. AI can provide valuable assistance in helping scientists overcome these obstacles.

I hope that this book has provided you with a broad perspective on cognition that you will find useful in your daily life and career. Best wishes for success in both endeavors.

SUMMARY

Our ability to reason and solve problems is influenced by the familiarity of the material. For example, correctly evaluating the implications of a logical rule depends on whether the semantic content of the rule is abstract ("If a card has a *D* on one side, then it has a 3 on the other

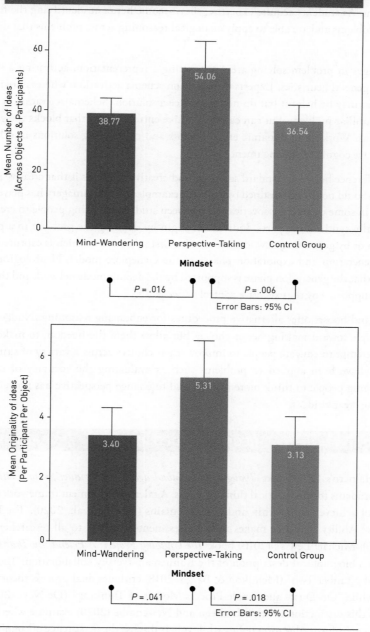

FIGURE 14.14 ■ **Number of ideas and creative ideas generated following mind-wandering, perspective-taking, and neutral (control) instructions.**

Source: "Changing perspective: Building creative mindsets," by Y.-Y. Chou & B. Tversky, 2020, *Cognitive Science*, 44(4), e12820. https://doi.org/10.1111/cogs.12820

between these two examples illustrates differences between associative and rule-based reasoning and more generally between System I and System II reasoning. System I reasoning is associative, intuitive, fast, and biased. System II reasoning is rule based, analytic, slow, and competent. As students acquire expertise, they become better at identifying the formal structure of problems and are able to apply analogical reasoning across problems that differ in story content.

Three stages in problem solving are constructing a representation, activating a schema, and applying general heuristics. Experts often rely on schema activation, whereas novices use heuristics that may be helpful but do not guarantee a solution. Schema activation is effective for solving familiar problems but can cause cognitive entrenchment that blocks the generation of novel ideas. Working in dynamic environments and considering solutions in other domains helps reduce cognitive entrenchment.

A big difference between standard solutions and creative solutions is that creative solutions are novel so should not be constrained by previous examples. Mental imagery has played an important role in some creative discoveries and has been studied by asking people to create products by mentally synthesizing parts. Individuals begin by defining the problem in a problem-first approach or by generating new ideas in an idea-first approach—which is captured by the successive generation and exploration phases of the Geneplore model. Neurological recordings indicate that the generation phase is supported by the default mode network and the evaluation phase is supported by the executive control network.

Nudges and boosts offer alternative procedures for enhancing reasoning. Nudges attempt to push people toward making better choices but allow them the freedom to make the choice. Boosts attempt to educate people to improve their choices across a variety of situations. Both methods have been applied to problems such as evaluating the accuracy of social media. Encouraging people to think more broadly and to change perspective has proven effective in increasing creative ideas.

RECOMMENDED READING

Diane Halpern's (2014) text *Thought and Knowledge: An Introduction to Critical Thinking* teaches students to apply critical thinking skills. A talent development framework aids the integration of achievements within and across domains (Preckel et al., 2020). The International Cognitive Ability Resource makes ability assessments available to all researchers (Revelle et al., 2020). Michael Lewis's (2016) book *The Undoing Project: A Friendship That Changed Our Minds* is a biographical description of the Kahneman-Tversky collaboration. The article "The Mythical Number Two" (Melnikoff & Bargh, 2018) critiques dual-process theory as oversimplified while "On Dual- and Single-Process Models of Thinking" (De Neys, 2021) analyzes whether this distinction is helpful. Green and Newcombe (2020) examine whether cognitive training can inform education policy while others discuss the persistence of cognitive interventions (Bailey et al., 2020). The book *Explaining Creativity* (Sawyer, 2006) gives an introductory overview of this topic. Chapters in a book edited by Markman and Wood (2009) focus on innovative design. Case studies, such as Leonardo da Vinci's plans for flying machines, provide another source of data for analyzing the creative process (Guss et al., 2021). Work in artificial intelligence has contributed a computational model of the Alternative Uses Test (Oleteanu & Falomir, 2016). Embedding the creative process within a self-regulated learning framework will guide future assessment and research (Rubenstein et al., 2018). Increases in the amount of research on mind-wandering require a classification of its variations (Murray et al., 2020).

GLOSSARY

absolute judgment task. Identifying stimuli that vary along a single, sensory continuum

acquisition. Storage of information in long-term memory

activation rule. A rule that determines how inhibitory and excitatory connections combine to determine the total activation of a concept

acute stress. Symptoms that quickly develop but usually do not last long

additive model. A strategy that adds attribute values to assign a score to each alternative

additive–difference model. A strategy that compares two alternatives by adding the difference in their values for each attribute

alerting network. Maintains sensitivity to incoming stimuli

algorithm. A set of rules that will solve a problem if correctly followed

allocation of capacity. When a limited amount of capacity is distributed to various tasks

Alzheimers's disease. A gradual impairment of memory that is typically identified by the formation of amyloid plaques and tau tangles in the brain

amodal. Knowledge that is abstracted from sensory experiences

anagram. A problem that requires rearranging a string of letters to form a word

analogical transfer. Use of the same solution in solving two problems

analogy problem. A four-term problem that requires finding the answer that completes the relation: A is to B as C is to D

analogy. Solving a problem by using a solution to a related problem

anterograde amnesia. Inability to form new memories

apperceptive agnosia. An inability to combine visual features into contours, surfaces, and objects

arousal. A physiological state that influences the distribution of mental capacity to various tasks

arrangement problem. A problem that requires rearranging its parts to satisfy a specified criterion

artificial intelligence. The study of how to produce computer programs that can perform intellectually demanding tasks

association value. The number of verbal associations generated for a concept

associative agnosia. Ability to combine visual features into a whole object but an inability to recognize that object

attenuation. A decrease in the perceived loudness of an unattended message

attribute learning. A concept identification task in which people are told the logical rule (such as conjunctive) but have to discover the relevant attributes

auditory information store. In Sperling's model, this store maintains verbal information in short-term memory through rehearsal

autobiographical memory. Memory about our personal experiences

automatic processing. Performing mental operations that require very little mental effort

availability heuristic. Estimating probability by the ease with which examples can be recalled

average distance rule. A classification strategy that selects the category containing members having the greatest average similarity to the classified item

basic-level category. An intermediate category in the middle of a hierarchy, such as table, saw, and truck

Bayes's theorem. A normative procedure for revising a probability by combining a prior probability with evidence

blocked presentation. All items of one category are presented consecutively before the items of another category are presented

boost. An attempt to improve choices by educating people

bottleneck theory. A theory that attempts to explain how people select information when some information-processing stage becomes overloaded with too much information

capacity theory. A theory proposing that we have a limited amount of mental effort to distribute across tasks, so there are limitations on the number of tasks we can perform at the same time

caricature. An exaggeration of distinctive features to make a pattern more distinctive

category-size effect. The finding that members of smaller categories are classified more quickly than members of larger categories

causal relation. An event that results in the occurrence of another event

central executive. A component of Baddeley's working memory model that manages the use of working memory

characteristic feature. A feature that is usually present in members of that category but is not necessary

chronic stress. Emotional response to pressure suffered for a long period of time

chunks. A cluster of items that has been stored as a unit in long-term memory

clustering. Percentage of occasions in which a word is followed by its primary associate during the free recall of words

coding. Semantic elaboration of information to make it easier to remember

cognitive architecture. An integrated system of cognitive components for modeling cognition

cognitive entrenchment. Inflexible thinking that blocks novel ideas

cognitive interview. The use of cognitively based retrieval techniques to improve recall

cognitive psychology. The study of the mental operations that support people's acquisition and use of knowledge

cognitive science. The multidisciplinary study of cognition through such fields as psychology, philosophy, artificial intelligence, neuroscience, linguistics, and anthropology

coherence threshold. The level at which a reader believes his or her understanding is good enough to move from one part of the text to the next

compensatory model. A strategy that allows positive attributes to compensate for negative ones

concentration. Investing mental effort in one or more tasks

concept identification. A task that requires deciding whether an item is an example of a concept, where concepts are typically defined by logical rules

concept maps. An instructional procedure based on semantic networks

concrete-abstract dimension. Extent to which a concept can be represented by a picture

conjunctive model. A strategy that evaluates one alternative at a time and rejects it if the value of one of its attributes fails to satisfy a minimum criterion

conjunctive rule. A rule that uses the logical relation "and" to relate stimulus attributes, such as small and square

consolidation. The process of stabilizing a memory trace following the initial acquisition

contextual effect. The influence of the surrounding context on the recognition of patterns

continuous dimension. An attribute that can take on any value along a dimension

control process. A strategy that determines how information is processed

creativity. Creating a novel and useful product or solution

cued recall. Recall that occurs with hints or cues, such as providing the questions asked during the judgment phase of a task

decay theory. Proposal that information is spontaneously lost over time, even when there is no interference from other material

decision event. Making a single decision rather than a sequence of decisions in a changing situation

decision frame. Different formulations of the same problem elicit different preferences

declarative memory. Memory for facts and concepts

deep neural networks. Networks that learn by adjusting thousands of connections in multiple layers

default knowledge. Knowledge about the most likely values for the attributes of a schema

defining feature. A feature that is necessary to be a member of that category

descriptive model. A model that describes what people actually do

direct memory test. A test that asks people to recall or recognize past events

disjunctive rule. A rule that uses the logical relation "or" to relate stimulus attributes, such as small or square

distinctive feature. A feature present in one pattern but absent in another, aiding one's discrimination of the two patterns

distinctive item. An item different in appearance or meaning from other items

domain-specific knowledge. Knowledge about a specific subject, such as chess or physics

dual process theories of reasoning. The proposal that reasoning is based on both intuitive associations and analytic rules

dual-coding theory. A theory that memory is improved when items can be represented by both verbal and visual memory codes

duplex gamble. A gamble in which the probability of winning is assigned independently of the probability of losing

elimination by aspects. A strategy that evaluates one attribute at a time and rejects those alternatives whose attribute values fail to satisfy a minimum criterion

embodied cognition. A theoretical framework in which perception and action have a central role in cognition

emotional distinctiveness. Items that produce an intense emotional reaction

encoding specificity principle. A theory that states that the effectiveness of a retrieval cue depends on how well it relates to the initial encoding of an item

enduring disposition. An automatic influence to which people direct their attention

episodic buffer. A component of Baddeley's working memory model that combines visual and verbal codes

episodic memory. Stores specific events, including when and where they occurred

error recovery heuristic. A strategy for correcting comprehension errors

event-related potential (ERP). A diagnostic technique that uses electrodes placed on the scalp to measure the duration of brain waves during mental tasks

exchange error. An error in which two linguistic units are substituted for each other during sentence production

excitatory connection. A positive association between concepts that belong together, as when a vertical line provides support for the possibility that a letter is a *K*

executive attention network. Monitors and resolves conflicts

exemplar model. A model that proposes that patterns are learned and categorized by comparing their similarity to category members

exhaustive search. A search that continues until the test item is compared with all items in the memory set

expected value. The average value, as determined by combining the value of events with their probability of occurrence

exploration strategy. A strategy for determining how to use a preinventive form

fact-oriented acquisition. Encoding material in a manner that emphasizes factual knowledge without emphasizing its application

family resemblance. A measure of how frequently the attributes of a category member are shared by other members of the category

feature comparison model. A model proposing that items are categorized by matching the item's features to category features

feature theory. A theory of pattern recognition that describes patterns in terms of their parts, or features

filter model. The proposition that a bottleneck occurs at the pattern recognition stage and that attention determines what information reaches the pattern recognition stage

flashbulb memory. A memory of an important event that caused an emotional reaction

four-card selection problem. A reasoning task that requires deciding which of four cards should be turned over to evaluate a conditional rule

functional fixedness. The tendency to use an object in a typical way

functional magnetic resonance imaging (fMRI). A diagnostic technique that uses magnetic fields and computerized images to locate mental operations in the brain

general strategy. A strategy (heuristic) that applies in many situations but does not always result in a solution

generation strategy. A strategy for producing preinventive forms

generative. The capability to produce many different messages by combining symbols in different ways

geons. Different three-dimensional shapes that combine to form three-dimensional objects

global coherence. Integration of major ideas that occur throughout a text

goal-derived category. A category whose members are selected to satisfy a specified goal

grammar. A set of rules for producing correct sentences in a language

heuristic. A strategy that is often but not always helpful in solving problems

hierarchical network model. A model proposing that items are categorized by using the hierarchical relations specified in a semantic network

hierarchically organized. An organizing strategy in which larger categories are partitioned into smaller categories

human information processing. The psychological approach that attempts to identify what occurs during the various stages (attention, perception, short-term working memory) of processing the stimulus

ideal. An attribute value that relates to the goal of a goal-derived category

imagery potential. Ease with which a concept can be imaged

imaging. Creating visual images to make material easier to remember

imprecise elaboration. Provision or generation of additional material unrelated to remembered material

incidental learning task. A task that studies memories when people are not trying to learn

indirect memory test. A test that does not explicitly ask about past events but is influenced by memory of those events

inducing-structure problem. A problem that requires finding a pattern among a fixed set of relations

inhibitory connection. A negative association between concepts that do not belong together, as when the presence of a vertical line provides negative evidence that a letter is a *D*

insight. The sudden discovery of a solution following unsuccessful attempts to solve a problem

interactive activation model. A theory proposing that both feature knowledge and word knowledge combine to provide information about the identity of letters in a word

interference theory. Proposal that forgetting occurs because other material interferes with the information in memory

interleaving presentation. Category items are presented with items from at least one other category

keyword. A concrete word that sounds like an abstract word so that it can be substituted for the abstract word in an interactive image

keyword method. A mnemonic strategy using keywords to improve paired-associates learning

language. A collection of symbols and rules for combining symbols, which can express an infinite variety of messages

latent attractor. A state in a dynamic system that is inactive

late-selection model. Proposal that the bottleneck occurs when information is selected for memory

levels of processing. A theory that proposes that "deeper" (semantic) levels of processing enhance memory

limited-capacity perceptual channel. The pattern recognition stage of Broadbent's model, which is protected by the filter (attention) from becoming overloaded with too much perceptual information

local coherence. Integration of ideas within an immediate context in a text

logical rule. A rule based on logical relations, such as conjunctive, disjunctive, conditional, and bi-conditional rules

long-term memory (LTM). Memory that has no capacity limits and lasts from minutes to an entire lifetime

long-term potentiation. Strengthening of synapses that result from the simultaneous activation of presynaptic and postsynaptic neurons

loss aversion. Reaction to losses is more intense than reactions to corresponding gains

maintenance rehearsal. Rehearsal that keeps information active in short-term memory

means–end analysis. A strategy that can be used to solve transformation problems by eliminating differences between the current state and the goal state.

measure of sufficiency. A demonstration that the instructions in a computer program are capable of solving a problem

memory code. The format (physical, phonemic, semantic) of information encoded into memory

memory set. A set of items in short-term memory that can be compared against a test item to determine whether the test item is stored there

memory span. The number of correct items that people can immediately recall from a sequence of items

memory-retrieval explanation. The proposal that people solve reasoning problems about familiar situations by retrieving specific examples from their memory

mental effort. The amount of mental capacity required to perform a task

meta-analysis. A quantitative method to systematically evaluate the combined results of previous research

metacognition. Awareness of how our cognitive processes can improve information-processing strategies

modal. Knowledge is represented as sensory experiences

momentary intention. A conscious decision to allocate attention to certain tasks or aspects of the environment

mood-dependent memory. Memory that is improved when people are tested under conditions that recreate their mood when they learned the material

morpheme exchange. An error in which two morphemes are substituted for each other during sentence production

morphemes. The smallest unit of meaning in a language

multimode theory. A theory proposing that people's intentions and the demands of the task determine the information-processing stage at which information is selected

multiple trace theory. Episodic memories continue to be more dependent on the hippocampus than semantic memories

naturalistic study. A study of the tip-of-the-tongue state in which people record these events as they occur outside the laboratory

negative attractor. A state in a dynamic system that impedes progress

neocortex. Layers of the cerebral cortex that are involved in higher-order brain functions, such as perception, cognition, motor commands, and language

neural network model. A theory in which concepts (nodes) are linked to other concepts through excitatory and inhibitory connections to approximate the behavior of neural networks in the brain

nodes. The format for representing concepts in a semantic network

noncompensatory model. A strategy that rejects alternatives that have negative attributes without considering their positive attributes

noncued recall. Recall that occurs without hints or cues provided by the experimenter

normative model. A model that describes what people should do

nudge. An attempt to improve choices by directing people

operator. An action that is selected to solve problems

orienting network. Selects information from different sensory inputs

orienting task. Instructions to focus on a particular aspect (physical, phonemic, semantic) of a stimulus

orthographic distinctiveness. Lower case words that have an unusual shape

parallel distributed processing (PDP). When information is simultaneously collected from different sources and combined to reach a decision

parallel processing. Carrying out more than one operation at a time, such as looking at an art exhibit and making conversation

parallel representation. Representation of knowledge in which more than one item at a time can be processed

partial-report procedure. A task in which observers are cued to report only certain items in a display of items

pattern completion. A partial activation of a memory trace activates associated information

pattern recognition. The stage of perception during which a stimulus is identified

penetrative thinking. The ability to reason about the interior structure of an object based on what is visible on its surface

perceptual confusion. A measure of the frequency with which two patterns are mistakenly identified as each other

pharmacotherapy. Medical treatment by using drugs

phoneme exchange. An error in which two phonemes are substituted for each other during sentence production

phonemes. The basic sounds of a language

phonemic coding. A memory code that emphasizes the pronunciation of the stimulus

phonological loop. A component of Baddeley's working memory model that maintains and manipulates acoustic information

phrase-structure grammar. A set of rules for partitioning a sentence into its grammatical units

pivot. Changing direction to explore new ideas

plan. A temporally ordered sequence of operations for carrying out some task

positive attractor. A state in a dynamic system that facilitates progress

positron-emission tomography (PET). A diagnostic technique that uses radioactive tracers to study brain activity by measuring the amount of blood flow in different parts of the brain

precise elaboration. Provision or generation of additional material closely related to remembered material

prediction-by-production. Predicting what a speaker will say based on the listener's productions

preinventive form. Creating an object before determining its use

primacy effect. The better recall of words at the beginning of a list

primary associates. Words that are strongly associated with each other, as typically measured by asking people to provide associations to words

primary distinctiveness. An item distinct from other items in the immediate context

prior probability. The probability that an event will occur before obtaining additional evidence regarding its occurrence

proactive interference. Forgetting that occurs because of interference from material encountered before learning

problem space. The set of choices at each step in solving the problem as determined by the problem

problem-oriented acquisition. Encoding material in a manner that is helpful for its later use in solving problems

procedural memory. Memory for actions, skills, and operations

process memory. A memory that maintains active traces of past information to process incoming information in the present moment

processing distinctiveness. Creation of a memory code that makes that memory distinct from other memories

proposition. A meaningful idea that typically consists of several words

propositional theory. A theory that all knowledge, including spatial knowledge, can be expressed in semantic-based propositions

prototype. A category example that has average attribute values

prototype rule. A classification strategy that selects the category whose prototype is the most similar to the classified item

recency effect. The better recall of words at the end of a list

recognition-primed decision (RPD). A decision that is quickly made following recognition of a situation

rehearsal. Repeating verbal information to keep it active in short-term memory or to transfer it into long-term memory

reinstatement search. The search of long-term memory to place words in short-term memory where they can be used to integrate a text

relational information. Information specifying how concepts are related

release from proactive interference. Reducing proactive interference by having information be dissimilar from earlier material

REM sleep (rapid eye movement). Sleep that typically occurs approximately 90 minutes after falling asleep and is the primary stage of dreaming

representational transfer. Use of the same format (such as a matrix) in solving two problems

Representative. The extent to which an event is typical of a larger class of events

retention. Maintaining information in long-term memory

retrieval. Recalling information from long-term memory

retrieval fluency. The ease with which an item can be recalled

retroactive interference. Forgetting that occurs because of interference from material encountered after learning

retrograde amnesia. Partial loss of previous memories

risk dimension. A component of a gamble such as the probability of winning or the amount of a loss

rote learning. Learning by repetition rather than through understanding

rule learning. A concept identification task in which people are told the relevant attributes (such as *small, square*) but have to discover the logical rule

satisficing. Generating solutions that are satisfactory rather than optimal

satisficing search. A strategy that follows the conjunctive model and therefore selects the first alternative that satisfies the minimum criterion for each attribute

scan component. The attention component of Sperling's model that determines what is recognized in the visual information store

schema. A general knowledge structure that provides a framework for organizing clusters of knowledge

script. Knowledge about what occurs during routine activities

search space. The set of choices evaluated at each step in solving a problem as determined by the problem solver

secondary distinctiveness. An item distinct from items stored in long-term memory

self-generation. Generation of items by participants in an experiment, rather than the provision of these items by the experimenter

self-terminating search. A search that stops as soon as the test item is successfully matched to an item in the memory set

semantic coding. A memory code that emphasizes the meaning of the stimulus

semantic dementia. Progressive loss of knowledge about the meaning of words and objects

semantic hub. A neural network model that represents semantic relations among words

semantic memory. Stores general knowledge not associated with a particular context

semantic network. A theory proposing that semantic information is organized in long-term memory by linking concepts to related concepts

sequential representation. Representation of knowledge in which only one item at a time can be processed

serial position effect. The ability to recall words at the beginning and end of a list better than words in the middle of the list

serial processing. Carrying out one operation at a time, such as pronouncing one word at a time

series extrapolation. A problem that requires finding a pattern among a sequence of items to continue the sequence in the same pattern

shadowing. An experimental method that requires people to repeat the attended message out loud

short term memory. A temporary memory store that is limited in both capacity and duration

simulation program. A computer program that attempts to reproduce the operations used by people to carry out various tasks

situation model. Integration of prior knowledge and text information to construct an understanding of the situation described in a text

spatial knowledge. Knowledge of spatial relations that may be stored as images

spontaneous retrieval. A retrieval that occurs without making a conscious effort to recall information

spreading activation model. A model that accounts for response times by formulating assumptions about how activation spreads in a semantic network

stereotype. Attribute values believed to be representative of social categories

stimulus-response (S-R). The approach that emphasizes the association between a stimulus and a response, without identifying the mental operations that produced the response

Stroop effect. The finding that it takes longer to process a stimulus when it has conflicting attributes

structural coding. A memory code that emphasizes the physical structure of the stimulus

structural theory. A theory that specifies how the features of a pattern are joined to other features of the pattern

structured. The organization imposed on a language by its grammatical rules

subgoal. A goal that solves part of the problem

subjective expected utility. A variation of expected value that uses utilities and subjective probabilities instead of values and probabilities

subjective intensity. Is determined by how much the content of the image stands out from its perceived background.

subjective probability. An estimated probability as determined by the decision maker

subjective specificity. Is determined by how distinguishable the image is from other stimuli

subordinate category. A small category at the bottom of a hierarchy, such as lamp table, jigsaw, and pickup truck

subsidiary task. A task that typically measures how quickly people can react to a target stimulus to evaluate the capacity demands of the primary task

superordinate category. A large category at the top of a hierarchy, such as furniture, tools, and vehicles

symbolic. The use of symbols, such as spoken or written words, to represent ideas

table of connections. A table that links differences between problem states with operators for eliminating those differences

targeted memory reactivation. The presentation of stimuli during sleep to reactivate and consolidate memories

taxonomic relations. Organization (often hierarchical) of concepts based on their similarity

template. An unanalyzed pattern that is matched against alternative patterns by using the degrees of overlap as a measure of similarity

temporal receptive window. The window of time in which prior information from an ongoing stimulus can affect the processing of newly arriving information

thematic relations. Organization of concepts that appear in the same context

threshold. The minimal amount of activation required to become consciously aware of a stimulus

tip of the tongue (TOT). A retrieval state in which a person feels he or she knows the information but cannot immediately retrieve it

transcranial magnetic stimulation (TMS). A brain stimulation technique in which electrical pulses produced by a magnetic field causes neurons to fire in a focused region of the brain

transfer-appropriate processing. Encoding material in a manner related to how the material will be used later

transformation problem. A problem that requires changing the initial state through a sequence of actions until it matches the goal state

transformational grammar. A set of rules for transforming a sentence into a closely related sentence

typicality. A measure of how well a category member represents that category

typicality effect. The finding that the more typical members of a category are classified more quickly than the less typical category members

uncertainty. Lacking knowledge about which events will occur

utility. Subjective value as determined by the decision maker

vascular dementia. Dementia caused by a lack of oxygen to the brain

Venn diagram. A diagram that shows the set relations (such as overlap) among categories

verbal knowledge. Knowledge expressed in language

verbal protocol. A record of verbalized thought processes

visual agnosia. An impairment in the recognition of visual objects

visual information store (VIS). A sensory store that maintains visual information for approximately one-quarter of a second

visual scanning. A shift of attention across a visual display or image

visuospatial sketchpad. A component of Baddeley's working memory model that maintains and manipulates visual/spatial information

whole-report procedure. A task that requires observers to report everything they see in a display of items

word exchange. An error in which two words are substituted for each other during sentence production

word superiority effect. The finding that accuracy in recognizing a letter is higher when the letter is in a word than when it appears alone or is in a nonword

working memory. The use of short-term memory as a temporary store of information to accomplish a particular task

REFERENCES

Adams, L. T., Kasserman, J. E., Yearwood, A. A., Perfetto, G. A., Bransford, J. D., & Franks, J. J. (1988). Memory access: The effects of fact-oriented versus problem-oriented acquisition. *Memory & Cognition, 16,* 167–175.

Adamson, R. E. (1952). Functional fixedness as related to problem solving: A repetition of three experiments. *Journal of Experimental Psychology, 44,* 288–291.

Advokat, C. D., Comaty, J. E., & Julien, R. M. (2019). *Julien's primer of drug action: A comprehensive guide to the actions, uses, and side effects of psychoactive drugs.* Worth Publishers.

Ahn, W. K., Kim, N. S., Lassaline, M. E., & Dennis, M. J. (2000). Causal status as a determinant of feature centrality. *Cognitive Psychology, 41,* 361–416.

Albrecht, J. E., & O'Brien, E. J. (1993). Updating a mental model: Maintaining both local and global coherence. *Journal of Experimental Psychology: Learning, Memory, and Cognition, 19,* 1061–1070.

Alderman, J. S., Marquis, S. J., & Sabatos-DeVito, M. G. (2010). Letters in words are read simultaneously, not in left-to-right sequence. *Psychological Science, 21,* 1799–1801.

Alibali, M. W., Kita, W., & Young, A. (2000). Gesture and the process of speech production: We think, therefore we gesture. *Language and Cognitive Processes, 15,* 593–613.

Amer, T., Campbell, K. L., & Hasher, L. (2016). Cognitive control as a double-edged sword. *Trends in Cognitive Sciences, 20,* 905–915.

Anderson, J. R. (1976). *Language, memory, and thought.* Erlbaum.

Anderson, J. R. (1982). Acquisition of cognitive skill. *Psychological Review, 89,* 369–406.

Anderson, J. R. (1983). *The architecture of cognition.* Harvard University Press.

Anderson, J. R. (1990). Analysis of student performance with the LISP tutor. In N. Frederiksen, R. Glaser, A. Lesgold, & M. G. Shafto (Eds.), *Diagnostic monitoring of skill and knowledge acquisition* (pp. 27–50). Erlbaum.

Anderson, J. R., Boyle, C. F., & Reiser, B. J. (1985). Intelligent tutoring systems. *Science, 228,* 456–462.

Anderson, J. R., Corbett, A. T., Koedinger, K. R., & Pelletier, R. (1995). Cognitive tutors: Lessons learned. *Journal of the Learning Sciences, 4,* 167–207.

Anderson, J. R., & Reder, L. M. (1979). An elaborative processing explanation of depth of processing. In L. S. Cermak & F. I. M. Craik (Eds.), *Levels of processing in human memory* (pp. 385–404). Erlbaum.

Anderson, L. W., Krathwohl, D. R., Airasian, P. W., Cruikshank, K. A., Mayer, R. E., Pintrich, P. R., & Wittrock, M. C. (2001). *A taxonomy for learning, teaching, and assessing: A revision of Bloom's taxonomy of educational objectives (abridged addition).* Addison Wesley Longman.

Anderson, M. C., Bjork, E. L., & Bjork, R. A. (2000). Retrieval-induced forgetting: Evidence for a recall-specific mechanism. *Psychonomic Bulletin & Review, 7*(3), 522–530. https://doi.org/10.3758/bf03214366

Anderson, R. C., & Pichert, J. W. (1978). Recall of previously unrecallable information following a shift in perspective. *Journal of Verbal Learning and Verbal Behavior, 17,* 1–12.

Anderson, R. E. (1984). Did I do it or did I only imagine doing it? *Journal of Experimental Psychology: General, 113,* 594–613.

Anderson, S. J., & Conway, M. A. (1993). Investigating the structure of autobiographical memories. *Journal of Experimental Psychology: Learning, Memory, and Cognition, 19,* 1178–1196.

Anderson, S. J., & Conway, M. A. (1997). Representations of autobiographical memories. In M. A. Conway (Ed.), *Cognitive models of memory* (pp. 217–246). MIT Press.

Arguin, M., & Saumier, D. (2004). Independent processing of parts and of their spatial organization in complex visual objects. *Psychological Science, 15,* 629–633.

Armstrong, S. L., Gleitman, L. R., & Gleitman, H. (1983). What some concepts might not be. *Cognition, 13,* 263–308.

Ashby, F. G., Alfonso-Reese, L. A., Turken, A. U., & Waldron, E. M. (1998). A neuropsychological theory of multiple systems in category learning. *Psychological Review, 105,* 442–481.

Ashby, F. G., & Maddox, W. T. (2005). Human category learning. *Annual Review of Psychology, 56,* 149–178.

Ashcraft, M. H., & Krause, J. A. (2007). Working memory, math performance, and math anxiety. *Psychonomic Bulletin & Review, 14,* 243–248.

Asperholm, M., Hogman, N., Rafi, J., & Herlitz, A. (2019). What did you do yesterday? Analysis of sex differences in episodic memory. *Psychological Bulletin, 145,* 785–821.

Aston-Jones, G., & Cohen, J. D. (2005). An integrative theory of locus coeruleus-norepinephrine function: Adaptive gain and optimal performance. *Annual Review of Neuroscience, 28,* 403–450. https://doi.org/10.1146/annurev.neuro.28.061604.135709

Atkinson, A. P., Thomas, M. S. C., & Cleeremans, A. (2000). Consciousness: Mapping the theoretical landscape. *TRENDS in Cognitive Sciences, 7,* 84–91.

Atkinson, R. C. (1972a). Ingredients for a theory of instruction. *American Psychologist, 27,* 921–931.

Atkinson, R. C. (1972b). Optimizing the learning of a second-language vocabulary. *Journal of Experimental Psychology, 96,* 124–129.

Atkinson, R. C., & Raugh, M. R. (1975). An application of the mnemonic keyword method to the acquisition of a Russian vocabulary. *Journal of Experimental Psychology: Human Learning and Memory, 104,* 126–133.

Atkinson, R. C., & Shiffrin, R. M. (1968). Human memory: A proposed system and its control processes. In K. W. Spence & J. T. Spence (Eds.), *The psychology of learning and motivation* (Vol. 2, pp. 89–195). Academic Press.

Atkinson, R. C., & Shiffrin, R. M. (1971). The control of short-term memory. *Scientific American, 225,* 82–90.

Atwood, M. E., & Polson, P. G. (1976). A process model for water jar problems. *Cognitive Psychology, 8,* 191–216.

Awh, E., Jonides, J., Smith, E. E., Schumacher, E. H., Koeppe, R. A., & Katz, S. (1996). Dissociation of storage and rehearsal in verbal working memory: Evidence from PET. *Psychological Science, 7,* 25–31.

Babulal, G. M., Foster, E. R., & Wolf, T. J. (2016). Facilitating transfer of skills and strategies in occupational therapy practice: Practical application of transfer principles. *Asian Journal of Occupational Therapy, 11,* 19–25.

Baddeley, A. D. (1978). The trouble with "levels": A reexamination of Craik and Lockhart's framework for memory research. *Psychological Review, 85,* 139–152.

Baddeley, A. D. (1982). Domains of recollection. *Psychological Review, 89,* 708–729.

Baddeley, A. D. (1992). Is working memory working? The fifteenth Bartlett lecture. *Quarterly Journal of Experimental Psychology, 44A,* 1–31.

Baddeley, A. D. (2000). The episodic buffer: A new component of working memory? *Trends in Cognitive Sciences, 4,* 417–423.

Baddeley, A. D. (2001). Is working memory still working? *American Psychologist, 56,* 851–864.

Baddeley, A. D., & Andrade, J. (2000). Working memory and the vividness of imagery. *Journal of Experimental Psychology: General, 129,* 126–145.

Baddeley, A. D., Gathercole, S., & Papagno, C. (1998). The phonological loop as a language learning device. *Psychological Review, 105,* 158–173.

Baddeley, A. D., & Hitch, G. (1974). Working memory. In G. H. Bower (Ed.), *The psychology of learning and motivation* (Vol. 8, pp. 17–90). Academic Press.

Baddeley, A. D., Hitch, G. J., & Allen, R. J. (2019). From short-term store to multicomponent working memory: The role of the modal model. *Memory & Cognition, 47*(4), 575–588.

Baddeley, A. D., Papagno, C., & Vallar, G. (1988). When long-term learning depends on short-term storage. *Journal of Memory and Language, 27*, 586–595.

Baddeley, A. D., & Warrington, E. K. (1970). Amnesia and the distinction between long and short-term memory. *Journal of Verbal Learning and Verbal Behavior, 9*, 176–189.

Bahrick, H. P., & Boucher, B. (1968). Retention of visual and verbal codes of the same stimuli. *Journal of Experimental Psychology, 78*, 417–422.

Bahrick, H. P., & Hall, L. K. (1991). Lifetime maintenance of high school mathematics content. *Journal of Experimental Psychology: General, 120*, 20–33.

Bailey, D. H., Duncan, G. J., Cunha, F., Foorman, B. R., & Yeager, D. S. (2020). Persistence and fade-out of educational intervention effects: Mechanisms and potential solutions. *Psychological Science in the Public Interest, 21*, 55–97.

Baker, E., Williams, A. L., McLeod, S., & McCauley, R. (2018). Elements of phonological interventions for children with speech sound disorders: The development of a taxonomy. *American Journal of Speech-Language Pathology, 27*, 906–935.

Bargh, J. A., & Chartrand, T. L. (1999). The unbearable automaticity of being. *American Psychologist, 54*, 462–479.

Barrett, L. F., Tugade, M. M., & Engle, W. (2004). Individual differences in working memory capacity and dual-process theories of the mind. *Psychonomic Bulletin, 130*, 553–573.

Barrouillett, P., Portart, S., & Camos, V. (2011). On the law relating processing to storage in working memory. *Psychological Review, 118*, 175–192.

Barsalou, L. W. (1985). Ideals, central tendency, and frequency of instantiation as determinants of graded structure in categories. *Journal of Experimental Psychology: Learning, Memory, and Cognition, 11*, 629–654.

Barsalou, L. W. (1991). Deriving categories to achieve goals. In G. H. Bower (Ed.), *The psychology of learning and motivation* (Vol. 27, pp. 1–64). Academic Press.

Barsalou, L. W. (1999). Perceptual symbol systems. *Behavioral and Brain Sciences, 22*, 557–660.

Barsalou, L. W. (2003). Situated simulation in the human conceptual system. *Language and Cognitive Processes, 18*, 513–562.

Barsalou, L. W., & Sewell, D. R. (1985). Contrasting the representation of scripts and categories. *Journal of Memory and Language, 24*, 646–665.

Barsalou, L. W., Simmons, W. K., Barbey, A. K., & Wilson, C. D. (2003). Grounding conceptual knowledge in modality-specific systems. *TRENDS in Cognitive Sciences, 7*, 84–91.

Bartlett, F. C. (1932). *Remembering: A study in experimental and social psychology*. Macmillan.

Bassok, M., & Novick, L. R. (2012). Problem solving. In K. J. Holyoak & R. J. Morrison (Eds.), *The Oxford handbook of thinking and reasoning* (pp. 413–432). Oxford University Press.

Battich, L., Fairhurst, M., & Deroy, O. (2020). Coordinating attention requires coordinated senses. *Psychonomic Bulletin & Review, 27*, 1126–1138.

Bauer, B. W., & Capron, D. W. (2020). How behavioral economics and nudges could diminish irrationality in suicide-related decisions. *Perspectives in Psychological Science, 15*, 44–61.

Bavelas, J., Gerwing, J., Sutton, C., & Prevost, D. (2008). Gesturing on the telephone: Independent effects of dialogue and visibility. *Journal of Memory and Language, 58*, 495–520.

Beaty, R. E., Seli, P., & Schacter, D. L. (2019). Network neuroscience of creative cognition: Mapping cognitive mechanisms and individual differences in the creative brain. *Current Opinion in Behavioral Sciences, 27*, 22–30.

Bellet, B. W., Jones, P. J., & McNally, R. J. (2020). Self-triggering? An exploration of individuals who seek reminders of trauma. *Clinical Psychology Science, 8*(4), 739–755.

Belyusar, D., Reimer, B., Mehler, B., & Coughlin, J. F. (2016). A field study on the effects of digital billboards on glance behavior during highway driving. *Accident Analysis and Prevention, 88*, 88–96. https://doi.org/10.1016/j.aap.2015.12.014

Benartzi, S., Beshears, J., Milkman, K. L., Sunstein, C. R., Thaler, R. H., Shankar, M., Tucker-Ray, W. Congdon, W. J, & Galing, S. (2017). Should governments invest more in nudging? *Psychological Science, 28*, 1041–1055.

Benjamin, A. S., & Bjork, R. A. (1996). Retrieval fluency as a metacognitive index. In L. M. Reder (Ed.), *Implicit memory and metacognition* (pp. 309–338). Erlbaum.

Bentall, R. P. (1990). The illusion of reality: A review and integration of psychological research on hallucinations. *Psychological Bulletin, 107*, 82–95.

Berron, D., van Westen, D., Ossenkoppele, R., Strandberg, O., & Hansson, O. (2020). Medial temporal lobe connectivity and it's associations with cognition and early Alzheimer's disease. *Brain: A Journal of Neurology, 143*, 1233–1248.

Betsch, C., Bohm, R., Korn, L., & Holtmann, C. (2017). On the benefits of explaining herd immunity in vaccine advocacy. *Nature Human Behavior, 1*(56), 1–6.

Biederman, I. (1985). Human image understanding: Recent research and a theory. *Computer Vision, Graphics, and Image Processing, 32*, 29–73.

Biederman, I., & Cooper, E. E. (1991). Priming contour-deleted images: Evidence for intermediate representations in visual object recognition. *Cognitive Psychology, 23*, 393–419.

Biederman, I., Yue, X., & Davidoff, J. (2009). Representation of shape in individuals from a culture with minimal exposure to regular, simple artifacts. *Psychological Science, 20*, 1437–1442.

Bisra, K., Liu, Q., Nesbit, J. C., Salimi, F., & Winne, P. H. (2018). Inducing self-explanation: A meta-analysis. *Educational Psychology Review, 30*, 703–725.

Blackwell, S. E. (2021). Mental imagery in the science and practice of cognitive behavior therapy: Past, present, and future perspectives. *International Journal of Cognitive Therapy, 14*, 160–181.

Blalock, S. J., & Reyna, V. F. (2016). Using fuzzy-trace theory to understand and improve health judgments, decisions, and behaviors: A literature review. *Health Psychology, 2016*, 781–792.

Blaney, P. L. (1986). Affect and memory: A review. *Psychological Bulletin, 99*, 229–246.

Block, C. C., & Duffy, G. G. (2008). Research on teaching comprehension. In C. C. Block & S. R. Parris (Eds.), *Comprehension instruction: Research-based best practices* (pp. 19–37). Guilford Press.

Bloom, B. S. (1984). *Taxonomy of educational objectives*. Boston: Allyn and Bacon.

Blum, H. (1973). Biological shape and visual science (part 1). *Journal of Theoretical Biology, 38*, 205–287.

Boden, M. A. (2004). *The creative mind. Myths and mechanisms* (2nd ed.). Routledge.

Bornstein, B. H., & Greene, E. (2011). Jury decision making: Implications for and from psychology. *Current Directions in Psychological Science, 20*, 63–67.

Botvinick, M. M., Braver, T. S., Barch, D. M., Carter, C. S., & Cohen, J. D. (2001). Conflict monitoring and cognitive control. *Psychological Review, 108*(3), 624–652. https://doi.org/10.1037/0033-295x.108.3.624

Bourne, L. E., Jr. (1970). Knowing and using concepts. *Psychological Review, 77*, 546–556.

Bourne, L. E., Jr., Ekstrand, B. R., Lovallo, W. R., Kellogg, R. T., Hiew, C. C., & Yaroush, R. A. (1976). Frequency analysis of attribute identification. *Journal of Experimental Psychology: General, 105*, 294–312.

Bower, G. H. (1970). Organizational factors in memory. *Cognitive Psychology, 1*, 18–46.

Bower, G. H., Black, J. B., & Turner, T. J. (1979). Scripts in memory for text. *Cognitive Psychology, 11*, 177–220.

Bower, G. H., Clark, M., Winzenz, D., & Lesgold, A. (1969). Hierarchical retrieval schemes in recall of categorized word lists. *Journal of Verbal Learning and Verbal Behavior, 8*, 323–343.

Bower, G. H., & Winzenz, D. (1970). Comparison of associative learning strategies. *Psychonomic Science, 20*, 119–120.

Bowers, J. S. (2020). Reconsidering the evidence that systematic phonics is more effective than alternative methods of reading instruction. *Educational Psychology Review, 32*, 681–705.

Boyd, R., & Richerson, P. J. (2005). *The origin and evolution of cultures*. Oxford University Press.

Brainerd, C. J., & Reyna, V. F. (2019). Fuzzy-trace theory, false memory, and the law. *Policy Insights From the Behavioral and Brain Sciences, 6*, 79–86.

Brainerd, C. J., Reyna, V. F., & Ceci, S. J. (2008). Developmental reversals in false memory: A review of data and theory. *Psychological Bulletin, 134*(3), 343–382. http://dx.doi.org/10.1037/0033-2909.134.3.343

Brainerd, C. J., Reyna, V. F., & Zember, E. (2011). Theoretical and forensic implications of developmental studies of the DRM illusion. *Memory & Cognition, 39*, 365–380.

Brandimonte, M. A., & Gerbino, W. (1993). Mental image reversal and verbal recoding: When ducks become rabbits. *Memory & Cognition, 21*, 23–33.

Bransford, J. D., & Johnson, M. K. (1973). Considerations of some problems of comprehension. In W. G. Chase (Ed.), *Visual information processing* (pp. 383–438). Academic Press.

Brennan, S. E. (1985). The caricature generator. *Leonardo, 18*, 170–178.

Brewer, W. F., & Dupree, D. A. (1983). Use of plan schemata in the recall and recognition of goal-directed actions. *Journal of Experimental Psychology: Learning, Memory, and Cognition, 9*, 117–129.

Brewer, W. F., & Nakamura, G. V. (1984). The nature and function of schemas. In R. S. Wyer & T. K. Srull (Eds.), *Handbook of social cognition* (pp. 118–160). Erlbaum.

Brewin, C. R., Andrews, B., & Mickes, L. (2020). Regaining consensus on the reliability of memory. *Current Directions in Psychological Science, 29*(2), 121–125.

Britton, B. K., & Graesser, A. C. (Eds.). (1996). *Models of understanding text*. Erlbaum.

Britton, B. K., & Gulgoz, S. (1991). Using Kintsch's computational model to improve instructional text: Effects of repairing inference calls on recall and cognitive structures. *Journal of Educational Psychology, 83*, 329–345.

Britton, B. K., Van Dusen, L., Glynn, M., & Hemphill, D. (1990). The impact of inferences on instructional text. In A. C. Graesser & G. H. Bower (Eds.), *Inferences and text comprehension* (pp. 53–70. Academic Press.

Broadbent, D. E. (1954). The role of auditory localization in attention and memory span. *Journal of Experimental Psychology, 47*, 191–196.

Broadbent, D. E. (1957). A mechanical model for human attention and immediate memory. *Psychological Review, 64*, 205–215.

Broadbent, D. E. (1958). *Perception and communication*. Pergamon Press.

Broca, P. (1865). Sur le siege de la faculté du langage articulé. *Bulletin de la Société d'Anthropologie, 6*, 377.

Broekkamp, H., & Van Hout-Wolters, B. H. A. M. (2007). Students' adaptation of study strategies when preparing for classroom tests. *Educational Psychology Review, 19*, 401–428.

Brooks, L. R. (1968). Spatial and verbal components of the act of recall. *Canadian Journal of Psychology, 22*, 349–368.

Brown, A. S. (1991). A review of the tip-of-the-tongue experience. *Psychological Bulletin, 109*, 204–223.

Brown, E., Deffenbacher, K., & Sturgill, W. (1977). Memory for faces and the circumstances of encounter. *Journal of Applied Psychology, 62*, 311–318.

Brown, R., & Kulik, J. (1977). Flashbulb memories. *Cognition, 5*, 73–99.

Brown, R., & McNeill, D. (1966). The "tip-of-the tongue" phenomenon. *Journal of Verbal Learning and Verbal Behavior, 5*, 325–337.

Bruner, J. S., Goodnow, J. J., & Austin, G. A. (1956). *A study of thinking.* Wiley.

Brunmair, M., & Richter, T. (2019). Similarity matters: A meta-analysis of interleaved learning and it's moderators. *Psychological Bulletin, 145*, 1029–1952.

Buchin, Z., & Mulligan, N. W. (2017). The testing effect under divided attention. *Journal of Experimental Psychology: Learning, Memory and Cognition, 43*, 1934–1947.

Buckhout, R. (1974). Eyewitness testimony. *Scientific American, 231*, 23–31.

Buckhout, R., Eugenio, P., Licitra, T., Oliver, L., & Kramer, T. H. (1981). Memory, hypnosis, and evidence: Research on eyewitnesses. *Social Action and the Law, 7*, 67–72.

Budiu, R., & Anderson, J. R. (2004). Interpretation based processing: A unified theory of semantic sentence comprehension. *Cognitive Science, 28*, 1–44.

Bunge, S. A., & Leib, E. R. (2020). How does education hone reasoning ability? *Current Directions in Psychological Science, 29*, 167–173.

Burgoyne, A. P., & Engle, R. W. (2020). Attention control: A cornerstone of higher-order cognition. *Current Directions in Psychological Science, 29*(6), 624–630.

Burke, D. M., & Light, L. L. (1981). Memory and aging: The role of retrieval processes. *Psychological Bulletin, 90*, 513–546.

Burson, K. A., Larrick, R. P., & Lynch, J. G., Jr. (2009). Six of one, half dozen of the other. *Psychological Science, 20*, 1074–1078.

Bussey, T. A., & Loftus, G. R. (2007). Cognitive science and the law. *TRENDS in the Cognitive Sciences, 11*, 111–117.

Butterfuss, R., & Kendeou, P. (2018). The role of executive functions in reading comprehension. *Educational Psychology Review, 30*(801), 826.

Cabeza, R., & Jacques, P, St. (2007). Functional neuro imaging of autobiographical memory. *TRENDS in the Cognitive Sciences, 11*, 219–227.

Caccamise, D., Snyder, L., & Kintsch, E. (2008). Constructivist theory and the situation model. In C. C. Block & S. R. Parris (Eds.), *Comprehension instruction: Research-based best practices* (pp. 80–97). Guilford Press.

Cantor, N., & Genero, N. (1986). Psychiatric diagnosis and natural categorization: A close analogy. In T. Milton & G. Klerman (Eds.), *Contemporary directions in psychopathology: Toward the DSMIV (pp. 233–256).* Guilford.

Cantor, N., & Mischel, W. (1979). Prototypes in person perception. In L. Berkowitz (Ed.), *Advances in experimental social psychology* (Vol. 12, pp. 3–52). Academic Press.

Cantor, N., Smith, E. E., French, R., & Mezzich, J. (1980). Psychiatric diagnosis as prototype categorization. *Journal of Abnormal Psychology, 89*, 181–193.

Caplan, S., Hafri, A., & Trueswell, J. C. (2021). Now you hear me, later you don't: The immediacy of linguistic computation in the representation of speech. *Psychological Science, 32*(3), 410–423.

Caramazza, A., & Shelton, J. R. (1998). Domain specific knowledge systems in the brain: The animate-inanimate distinction. *Journal of Cognitive Neuroscience, 10*(1), 1–34.

Carlson, K. A., & Russo, J. E. (2001). Biased interpretation of evidence by mock jurors. *Journal of Experimental Psychology: Applied, 7*, 91–103.

Carpenter, P. A., & Daneman, M. (1981). Lexical retrieval and error recovery in reading: A model based on eye fixations. *Journal of Verbal Learning and Verbal Behavior, 20*, 137–160.

Carpenter, P. A., Just, M. A., & Shell, P. (1990). What one intelligence test measures: A theoretical account of the processing in the Raven Progressive Matrices Test. *Psychological Review, 97*, 404–431.

Carpenter, P. A., Miyake, A., & Just, A. (1995). Language comprehension: Sentence and discourse processing. *Annual Review of Psychology, 46*, 91–120.

Carroll, D. W. (1986). *Psychology of language.* Brooks/Cole.

Carroll, J. M., Thomas, J. C., & Malhotra, A. (1980). Presentation and representation in design problem solving. *British Journal of Psychology, 71,* 143–153.

Catrambone, R. (1995). Aiding subgoal learning: Effects on transfer. *Journal of Educational Psychology, 87,* 5–17.

Catrambone, R., & Holyoak, K. J. (1989). Overcoming contextual limitations on problem-solving transfer. *Journal of Experimental Psychology: Learning, Memory, and Cognition, 15,* 1147–1156.

Cermak, L. S., & Craik, F. I. M. (Eds.). (1979). *Levels of processing in human memory.* Erlbaum.

Chambers, D., & Reisberg, D. (1985). Can mental images be ambiguous? *Journal of Experimental Psychology: Human Perception and Performance, 11,* 317–328.

Chambers, D., & Reisberg, D. (1992). What an image depicts depends on what an image means. *Cognitive Psychology, 24,* 145–174.

Chapanis, A. (1965). *Man machine engineering.* Brooks/Cole.

Chapman, C. A., Hasan, O., Schultz, P. E., & Martin, R. C. (2020). Evaluating the distinction between semantic knowledge and semantic access: Evidence from semantic dementia and comprehension-impaired stroke aphasia. *Psychonomic Bulletin & Review, 27*(4), 607–639.

Chapman, G. B. (2019). A decision-science approach to health-behavior change. *Current Directions in Psychological Science, 28,* 469–474.

Chase, W. G., & Ericsson, K. A. (1982). Skill and working memory. In G. H. Bower (Ed.), *Psychology of learning and motivation* (Vol. 16, pp. 1–58). Academic Press.

Chase, W. G., & Simon, H. A. (1973). Perception in chess. *Cognitive Psychology, 4,* 55–81.

Chater, N., Zhu, J.-Q., Spicer, J., Sundh, J., Leon-Villagra, P., & Sanborn, A. (2020). Probabilistic biases meet the Bayesian brain. *Current Directions in Psychological Science, 29,* 506–512.

Chavoix, C., & Insausti, R. (2017). Self-awareness and the medial temporal lobe in neurodegenerative diseases. *Neuroscience & Biobehavioral Reviews, 78,* 1–12.

Chen, W., Kato, T., Shu, X. H., Ogawa, S., Tank, D. W., & Ugurbil, K. (1998). Human primary visual cortex and lateral geniculate nucleus activation during visual imagery. *Neuroreport, 9,* 3669–3674.

Cheng, P. W., Holyoak, K. J., Nisbett, R. E., & Oliver, L. M. (1986). Pragmatic versus syntactic approaches to training deductive reasoning. *Cognitive Psychology, 18,* 293–328.

Cherry, C. (1953). Some experiments on the recognition of speech with one and with two ears. *Journal of the Acoustical Society of America, 25,* 975–979.

Chevalier, P., Kompatsiari, K., Ciardo, F., & Wykowska, A. (2020). Examining joint attention with the use of humanoid robots—A new approach to study fundamental mechanisms of social cognition. *Psychonomic Bulletin & Review, 27,* 217–236.

Chi, M. T. H., Glaser, R., & Rees, E. (1982). Expertise in problem solving. In R. J. Sternberg (Ed.), *Advances in the psychology of human intelligence* (Vol. 1). Erlbaum.

Chi, M. T. H., & Ohsson, S. (2005). Complex declarative learning. In K. J. Holyoak & R. G. Morrison (Eds.), *The Cambridge handbook of thinking and reasoning* (pp. 371–400). Cambridge University Press.

Chiesi, H. L., Spilich, G. J., & Voss, J. F. (1979). Acquisition of domain-related information in relation to high and low domain knowledge. *Journal of Verbal Learning and Verbal Behavior, 18,* 257–273.

Chipman, S. E. F. (2016). An introduction to cognitive science. In S. E. F. Chipman (Ed.), *Oxford handbook of cognitive science* (pp. 1–14). Oxford University Press.

Chomsky, N. (1957). *Syntactic structures.* Mouton.

Chomsky, N. (1965). *Aspects of the theory of syntax.* MIT Press.

Chou, Y.-Y., & Tversky, B. (2020). Changing perspective: Building creative mindsets. *Cognitive Science, 44*(4), e12820.

Chu, M., & Kita, S. (2015). Co-thought and co-speech gestures are generated by the same action generation process. *Journal of Experimental Psychology: Learning, Memory, and Cognition, 42*, 257–270.

Chun, M. M., Golomb, J. D., & Turk- Browne, N. B. (2011). A taxonomy of external and internal attention. *Annual Review of Psychology, 62*, 73–101.

Clowes, M. (1969). Transformational grammars and the organization of pictures. In A. Graselli (Ed.), *Automatic interpretation and the organization of pictures* (pp. 43–78). Academic Press.

Colias, M. (2020, December 28). Hands-free driving accelerates. *The Wall Street Journal*, p. B3.

Collins, A. M., & Loftus, E. F. (1975). A spreading activation theory of semantic processing. *Psychological Review, 82*, 407–428.

Collins, A. M., & Quillian, M. R. (1969). Retrieval time from semantic memory. *Journal of Verbal Learning and Verbal Behavior, 8*, 240–248.

Collins, A. M., & Quillian, M. R. (1970). Facilitating retrieval from semantic memory: The effect of repeating part of an inference. *Acta Psychologica, 33*, 304–314.

Connors, E. C., Chrastil, E. R., Sanchez, J., & Merabet, L. B. (2014). Virtual environments for the transfer of navigation skills in the blind: A comparison of directed instruction vs. video game based learning approaches. *Frontiers in Human Neuroscience, 8*, 223.

Conrad, R. (1964). Acoustic confusions in immediate memory. *British Journal of Psychology, 55*, 75–84.

Conrad, R. (1972). Speech and reading. In J. F. Kavanagh & I. G. Mattingly (Eds.), *Language by ear and by eye: The relationships between speech and reading*. MIT Press.

Conway, M. A., Cohen, G., & Stanhope, N. (1991). On the very long-term retention of knowledge acquired through formal education: Twelve years of cognitive psychology. *Journal of Experimental Psychology: General, 120*, 395–409.

Conway, M. A., Loveday, C., & Cole, S. N. (2016). The remembering-imagining system. *Memory Studies, 9*, 256–265.

Cook, A. E., & Gueraud, S. (2005). What have we been missing? The role of general world knowledge in discourse processing. *Discourse Processes, 39*, 265–278.

Cook, A. E., Gueraud, S., Was, C. A., & O'Brien, E. J. (2007). Foregrounding effects during reading, revisited. *Discourse Processes, 44*, 91–111.

Cooke, S. F. (2006). Plasticity in the human central nervous system. *Brain, 129*(7), 1659–1673. https://doi.org/10.1093/brain/awl082

Cooper, J. M., Vladisavljevic, I., Medieiros-Ward, N., Martin, P. T., & Strayer, D. L. (2009). Near the tipping point of traffic stability: Investigation of driving while conversing on a cell phone in simulated highway traffic of varying density. *Human Factors, 51*, 261–268.

Cooper, R. P. (2019). Action production and event perception as routine sequential behaviors. *Topics in Cognitive Science, 13*(1), 63–78.

Cooper, R. P., & Shallice, T. (2010). Cognitive neuroscience: The troubled marriage of cognitive science and neuroscience. *Topics in Cognitive Science, 2*, 398–406.

Corbetta, M., & Shulman, G. L. (2002). Control of goal-directed and stimulus-driven attention in the brain. *Nature Reviews. Neuroscience, 3*(3), 201–215. https://doi.org/10.1038/nrn755

Cosmides, L., & Tooby, J. (1996). Are humans good intuitive statisticians after all? Rethinking some conclusions from the literature on judgment under uncertainty. *Cognition, 58*, 1–73.

Costa, M., & Bonetti, L. (2018). Geometrical distortions in geographical cognitive maps. *Journal of Environmental Psychology, 55*, 53–69.

Cowan, N. (1988). Evolving conceptions of memory storage, selective attention, and their mutual constraints within the human information processing system. *Psychological Bulletin, 104*, 163–191.

Cowan, N. (1995). *Attention and memory: An integrated framework*. Oxford University Press.

Cowan, N., Wood, N. L., Wood, P. K., Keller, T. A., Nugent, L. D., & Keller, V. (1998). Two separate verbal processing rates contributing to shortterm memory span. *Journal of Experimental Psychology: General, 127,* 141–160.

Craik, F. I. M. (1970). The fate of primary memory items in free recall. *Journal of Verbal Learning and Verbal Behavior, 9,* 143–148.

Craik, F. I. M. (1979). Levels of processing: Overview and closing comments. In L. S. Cermak & F. I. M. Craik (Eds.), *Levels of processing in human memory.* Erlbaum.

Craik, F. I. M. (1982). Selective changes in encoding as a function of reduced processing capacity. In F. Klix, J. Hoffmann, & E. Van der Meer (Eds.), *Cognitive research in psychology* (pp. 152–161). DVW.

Craik, F. I. M. (2002). Levels of processing: Past, present . . . and future? *Memory, 10,* 305–318.

Craik, F. I. M., & Lockhart, R. S. (1972). Levels of processing: A framework for memory research. *Journal of Verbal Learning and Verbal Behavior, 11,* 671–684.

Craik, F. I. M., & Rabinowitz, J. C. (1983). Age differences in the acquisition and use of verbal information: A tutorial review. In H. Bouma & G. Bowwhuis (Eds.), *Attention and performance X.* Erlbaum.

Craik, F. I. M., & Tulving, E. (1975). Depth of processing and the retention of words in episodic memory. *Journal of Experimental Psychology: General, 104,* 268–294.

Craik, F. I. M., & Watkins, M. J. (1973). The role of rehearsal in shortterm memory. *Journal of Verbal Learning and Verbal Behavior, 12,* 599–607.

Crilly, N. (2018). 'Fixation' and 'the pivot': Balancing persistence with flexibility in design and entrepreneurship. *International Journal of Design Creativity and Innovation, 6,* 52–65.

Cromwell, J., Amabile, T. M., & Harvey, J.-F. (2018). An integrated model of dynamic problem solving within organizational constraints. In R. Reiter-Palmon, V. L. Kennel, & J. C. Kaufman (Eds.), *Individual creativity in the workplace* (pp. 53–81). Academic Press.

Csikszentmihalyi, M. (1996). *Creativity.* Harper Penguin.

Cumming, J., & Williams, S. E. (2014). The role of imagery in performance. In S. M. Murphy (Ed.), *The Oxford handbook of sport and performance psychology* (pp. 213–232). Oxford University Press.

Dane, E. (2010). Reconsidering the trade-off between expertise and flexibility: A cognitive entrenchment perspective. *Academy of Management Review, 35,* 579–603.

Danek, A. H., & Wiley, J. (2017). What about false insights? Deconstructing the aha! experience along its multiple dimensions for correct and incorrect solutions separately. *Frontiers in Psychology, 7,* 1–14.

Danker, J. F., & Anderson, J. R. (2010). The ghosts of brain states past: Remembering reactivates the brain regions engaged during encoding. *Psychological Bulletin, 136,* 87–102.

Dargue, N., Sweller, N., & Jones, M. P. (2019). When our hands help us understand: A meta-analysis into the effects of gesture on comprehension. *Psychological Bulletin, 145,* 765–784.

Davis, R., Shrobe, H., & Szolovits, P. (1993). What is a knowledge representation? *AI Magazine, 14,* 17–33.

de Bruin, A. B. H., Roelle, J., Carpenter, S. K., Baars, M., & EFG-MRE. (2020). Synthesizing cognitive load and self-regulation theory: A theoretical framework and research agenda. *Educational Psychology Review, 32,* 903–915.

de Groot, A. D. (1965). *Thought and choice in chess.* Mouton.

de Groot, A. D. (1966). Perception and memory versus thought: Some old ideas and recent findings. In B. Kleinmuntz (Ed.), *Problem solving: Research, method, and theory* (pp. 19–50). Wiley.

Dehaene, S. (2020). *How we learn: Why brains learn better than any machine . . . for now.* Viking.

Dell, G. S. (1986). A spreading activation theory of sentence production. *Psychological Review, 93,* 283–321.

Detterman, D. K., & Sternberg, R. J. (Eds.). (1993). *Transfer on trial: Intelligence, cognition, and instruction*. Ablex.

Deutsch, J. A., & Deutsch, D. (1963). Attention: Some theoretical considerations. *Psychological Review, 70*, 80–90.

Deutsch, J. A., Deutsch, D., & Lindsay, P. (1967). Comments on "Selective attention: Stimulus or response." *Quarterly Journal of Experimental Psychology, 19*, 362–367.

Diamond, N. B., & Levine, B. (2020). Linking detail to temporal structure in naturalistic-event recall. *Psychological Science, 31*(12), 1557–1572.

Dieciuc, M. A., & Folstein, J. R. (2019). Typicality: Stable structures and flexible functions. *Psychonomic Bulletin & Review, 26*, 491–505.

Diedrichsen, J., & Kornysheva, K. (2015). Motor skill learning between selection and execution. *Trends in Cognitive Sciences, 19*, 227–233.

Dietrich, A. (2004). The cognitive neuroscience of creativity. *Psychonomic Bulletin and Review, 11*, 1011–1026.

Dietrich, A. (2019). Types of creativity. *Psychonomic Bulletin & Review, 26*, 1–12.

Ding, J., Chen, K., Liu, H., Huang, L., Chen, Y., Lv, Y. ... Lambon Ralph, M. A. (2020). A unified neurocognitive model of semantics language social behaviour and face recognition in semantic dementia. *Nat Commun, 11*(1). http://dx.doi.org/10.1038/s41467-020-16089-9

Dodson, C. S., Koutstaal, W., & Schacter, D. L. (2000). Escape from illusion: Reducing false memories. *TRENDS in Cognitive Sciences, 4*, 391–397.

Doebel, S. (2020). Rethinking executive function and its development. *Perspectives in Psychological Science, 4*, 942–956.

Doherty, M. E. (2003). Optimists, pessimists, and realists. In S. L. Schneider & J. Shanteau (Eds.), *Emerging perspectives on judgment and decision research* (pp. 643–679). Cambridge University Press.

Domingos, P. (2015). *The master algorithm: How the quest for the ultimate learning machine will remake our world*. Basic Books.

Dopkins, S., Klin, C., & Myers, J. L. (1993). Accessibility of information about goals during the processing of narrative texts. *Journal of Experimental Psychology: Learning, Memory, and Cognition, 19*, 70–80.

Dove, G. (2009). Beyond perceptual symbols: A call for representational pluralism. *Cognition, 110*, 412–431.

Dove, G. (2016). Three symbol ungrounding problems: Abstract concepts and the future of embodied cognition. *Psychonomic Bulletin & Review, 23*, 1109–1121.

Dryhurst, S., Schneider, C. R., Kerr, J., Freeman, A. L. J., Recchia, G., van der Bles, A. M., Spiegelhalter, D., & van der Linden, S. (2020). Risk perceptions of COVID-19 around the world. *Journal of Risk Research, 23*, 994–1006.

Dudai, Y. (2004). The neurobiology of consolidations, or, how stable is the engram? *Annual Review of Psychology, 55*(1), 51–86. https://doi.org/10.1146/annurev.psych.55.090902.142050

Duffy, S. A., Morris, R. K., & Rayner, K. (1988). Lexical ambiguity and fixation times in reading. *Journal of Memory and Language, 27*, 429–446.

Duncker, K. (1945). On problem solving. *Psychological Monographs, 58*(5, Whole No. 270), i–113.

Dunegan, K. J. (1993). Framing, cognitive modes, and image theory: Toward an understanding of a glass half full. *Journal of Applied Psychology, 78*, 491–503.

Dunlosky, J., Badali, S., Rivers, M. L., & Rawson, K. A. (2020). The role of effort in understanding educational achievement: Objective effort as an explanatory construct versus effort as a student perception. *Educational Psychology Review, 32*, 1163–1175.

Dunlosky, J., & Nelson, T. O. (1994). Does the sensitivity of judgments of learning (JOLs) to the effects of various study activities depend on when the JOLs occur? *Journal of Memory and Language, 33*, 545–565.

Egan, D., & Greeno, J. G. (1974). Theory of rule induction: Knowledge acquired in concept learning, serial pattern learning, and problem solving. In L. Gregg (Ed.), *Knowledge and cognition*. Erlbaum.

Egeland, B. (1975). Effects of errorless training on teaching children to discriminate letters of the alphabet. *Journal of Applied Psychology, 60*, 533–536.

Eich, E., Macaulay, D., & Ryan, L. (1994). Mood dependent memory for events of the personal past. *Journal of Experimental Psychology: General, 123*, 201–215.

Elliot, A., Murayama, K., Kobeisy, A., & Lichtenfeld, S. (2015). Potential-based achievement goals. *Br J Educ Psychol, 85*(2), 192–206. http://dx.doi.org/10.1111/bjep.12051

Elman, J. L. (2009). On the meaning of words and dinosaur bones: Lexical knowledge without a lexicon. *Cognitive Science, 33*, 1–36.

Elstein, A. S., Shulman, L. S., & Sprafka, S. A. (1978). *Medical problem solving*. Harvard University Press.

Emberson, L. L., Lupyan, G., Goldstein, M. H., & Spivey, M. J. (2010). Overheard cell-phone conversations: When less speech is more distracting. *Psychological Science, 21*, 1383–1388.

Engel, A. K., Maye, A., Kurthen, M., & Konig, P. (2013). Where's the action? The pragmatic turn in cognitive science. *Trends in Cognitive Sciences, 17*, 202–209.

Engle, R. A. (2006). Framing interactions to foster generative learning: A situative explanation of transfer in a community of learners classroom. *The Journal of the Learning Sciences, 15*, 451–499.

Engle, R. W. (2018). Working memory and executive attention: A revisit. *Perspectives on Psychological Science, 13*, 190–193.

Engle, R. W., Kane, M. J., & Tuholski, W. (1999). Individual differences in working memory capacity and what they tell us about controlled attention, general fluid intelligence, and functions of the prefrontal cortex. In A. Miyake & P. Shah (Eds.), *Models of working memory: Mechanism of active maintenance and executive control* (pp. 102–134). Cambridge University Press.

Engle, R. W., & Oransky, N. (1999). The evolution from short-term to working memory: Multistore to dynamic models of temporary storage. In R. J. Sternberg (Ed.), *The nature of cognition* (pp. 514–555). MIT Press.

Erickson, T., & Mattson, M. (1981). From words to meaning: A semantic illusion. *Journal of Verbal Learning and Verbal Behavior, 20*, 540–552.

Ericsson, K. A. (1985). Memory skill. *Canadian Journal of Psychology, 39*, 188–231.

Ericsson, K. A., & Charness, N. (1994). Expert performance: Its structure and acquisition. *American Psychologist, 49*, 725–747.

Ericsson, K. A., & Kintsch, W. (1995). Long-term working memory. *Psychological Review, 102*, 211–245.

Ericsson, K. A., & Polson, P. G. (1988). An experimental analysis of the mechanisms of a memory skill. *Journal of Experimental Psychology: Learning, Memory, and Cognition, 14*, 305–316.

Ernst, G. W., & Newell, A. (1969). *GPS: A case study in generality and problem solving*. Academic Press.

Evans, G. W., & Schamberg, M. A. (2009). Childhood poverty, chronic stress, and adult working memory. *Proceedings of the National Academy of Sciences, 106*(16), 6545–6549. https://doi.org/10.1073/pnas.0811910106

Eysenck, M. W. (1978). Levels of processing: A critique. *British Journal of Psychology, 69*, 157–169.

Eysenck, M. W. (1979). Depth, elaboration, and distinctiveness. In L. S. Cermak & F. I. M. Craik (Eds.), *Levels of processing in human memory*. Erlbaum.

Eysenck, M. W., & Keane, M. T. (1990). *Cognitive psychology: A student's handbook*. Erlbaum.

Fallshore, M., & Schooler, J. W. (1995). Verbal vulnerability of perceptual expertise. *Journal of Experimental Psychology: Learning, Memory, and Cognition, 21*, 1608–1623.

Fan, J., McCandliss, B. D., Fossella, J., Flombaum, J. I., & Posner, M. I. (2005). The activation of attentional networks. *NeuroImage, 26*(2), 471–479.

Farah, M. J. (1988). Is visual imagery really visual? Overlooked evidence from neuropsychology. *Psychological Review, 95*, 307–317.

Farah, M. J. (2004). *Visual agnosia* (2nd ed.). MIT Press.

Fazekas, P., Nemeth, G., & Overgaard, M. (2020). Perceptual representations of the vividness of stimulus-triggered and stimulus-independent experiences. *Perspectives on Psychological Science, 15,* 1200–1213.

Fenker, D. B., Waldmann, M. R., & Holyoak, K. J. (2005). Accessing causal relations in semantic memory. *Memory & Cognition, 33,* 1036–1046.

Fillmore, C. J., & Baker, C. F. (2010). A frames approach to semantic analysis. In B. Heine & H. Narrog (Eds.), *The oxford handbook of linguistic analysis* (pp. 313–340). Oxford University Press.

Fincher-Kiefler, R. (2001). Perceptual components of situation models. *Memory & Cognition, 29,* 336–343.

Finke, R. A. (1980). Levels of equivalence in imagery and perception. *Psychological Review, 87,* 113–132.

Finke, R. A. (1985). Theories relating mental imagery to perception. *Psychological Bulletin, 98,* 236–259.

Finke, R. A. (1990). *Creative imagery: Discoveries and inventions in visualization.* Erlbaum.

Finke, R. A. (1996). Imagery, creativity and emergent structures. *Consciousness and Cognition, 5,* 381–393.

Finke, R. A., Ward, T. B., & Smith, S. M. (1992). *Creative cognition: Theory, research, and applications.* MIT Press.

Fischhoff, B., & Bar-Hillel, M. (1984). Focusing techniques: A shortcut to improving probability judgments? *Organizational Behavior and Human Performance, 34,* 175–194.

Fischler, I., Rundus, D., & Atkinson, R. C. (1970). Effects of overt rehearsal processes on free recall. *Psychonomic Science, 19,* 249–250.

Fisher, D., Laurie, N., Glaser, R., Connerney, K., Pollatsek, A., Duffy, S., & Brock, J. (2002). The use of a fixed-base driving simulator to evaluate the effects of experience and PC-based risk awareness training on drivers' decisions. *Human Factors, 44,* 287–302.

Fisher, K. M., Wandersee, J. H., & Moody, D. E. (Eds.). (2000). *Mapping biology knowledge.* Kluwer Academic.

Fisher, R. P., & Craik, F. I. M. (1977). Interaction between encoding and retrieval operations in cued recall. *Journal of Experimental Psychology: Human Learning and Memory, 3,* 701–711.

Fisher, R. P., & Geiselman, R. E. (2019). Expanding the cognitive interview to non-criminal investigations. In J. Dickinson, N. S. Compo, R. Carol, B. Schwartz, & M. McCauley (Eds.), *Evidence-based investigative interviewing: Applying cognitive principles* (pp. 1–28). Taylor & Francis.

Fisher, R. P., Geiselman, R. E., & Amador, M. (1989). Field test of the cognitive interview: Enhancing the recollection of actual victims and witnesses of crime. *Journal of Applied Psychology, 74,* 722–727.

Fiske, S. T., Cuddy, A. J. C., & Glick, P. (2007). Universal dimensions of social cognition warmth and competence. *Trends in Cognitive Sciences, 11,* 77–83.

Fivush, R. (2011). The development of autobiographical memory. *Annual Review of Psychology, 62,* 559–582.

Fletcher, C. R. (1986). Strategies for the allocation of short-term memory during comprehension. *Journal of Memory and Language, 25,* 43–58.

Flores, D., Reimann, M., Castano, R., & Lopez, A. (2019). If I indulge first, I will eat less overall: The unexpected interaction effect on indulgence and presentation order on consumption. *Journal of Experimental Psychology: Applied, 25,* 162–176.

Folk, C. L., Remington, R. W., & Johnston, J. C. (1992). Involuntary covert orienting is contingent on attentional control settings. *Journal of Experimental Psychology: Human Perception and Performance, 18,* 1030–1044.

Forstmann, B. U., Wagenmakers, E., Eichele, T., Brown, S., & Serences, J. T. (2011). Reciprocal relations between cognitive neuroscience and formal cognitive models: Opposites attract? *Trends in Cognitive Sciences, 15*, 272–278.

Foster-Hanson, E., Moty, K., Cardarelli, A., Ocampo, J. D., & Rhodes, M. (2020). Developmental changes in strategies for gathering evidence about biological kinds. *Cognitive Science, 44*(5), e12837.

Fox, K. C. R., & Beaty, R. E. (2019). Mind wandering and creative thinking: Neural, psychological, and theoretical considerations. *Current Opinion in Behavioral Sciences, 27*, 123–130.

Franconeri, S. L., & Simons, D. J. (2003). Moving and looming stimuli capture attention. *Perception & Psychophysics, 65*(7), 999–1010. https://doi.org/10.3758/bf03194829

Frankland, P. W., & Bontempi, B. (2005). The organization of recent and remote memories. *Nature Reviews Neuroscience, 6*, 119–30.

Franklin, B. (1887). *Complete works* (Vol. 4). Putnam.

Freeman, J. B. (2018). Doing psychological science by hand. *Current Directions in Psychological Science, 27*, 315–323.

Friedman, N. P., & Miyake, A. (2000). Differential roles for visuospatial and verbal working memory in situation model construction. *Journal of Experimental Psychology: General, 129*, 61–83.

Gable, S. L., Hopper, E. A., & Schooler, J. W. (2019). When the Muses strike: Creative ideas of physicists and writers routinely occur during mind wondering. *Psychological Science, 30*, 396–404.

Galambos, J. A., & Rips, L. J. (1982). Memory for routines. *Journal of Verbal Learning and Verbal Behavior, 21*, 260–281.

Garcia-Retamero, R., & Cokely, E. T. (2013). Communicating health risks with visual aids. *Current Directions in Psychological Science, 22*, 392–399.

Gardner, H. (1983). *Frames of mind: The theory of multiple intelligences*. Basic Books.

Gardner, H. (1985). *The mind's new science: A history of the cognitive revolution*. Basic Books.

Garner, W. R. (1974). *The processing of information and structure*. Erlbaum.

Gathercole, S. E. (1997). Models of verbal short-term memory. In M. A. Conway (Ed.), *Cognitive models of memory* (pp. 13–45). MIT Press.

Gegenfurtner, K. R., & Sperling, G. (1993). Information transfer in iconic memory experiments. *Journal of Experimental Psychology: Human Perception and Performance, 19*, 845–866.

Geiselman, R. E., Fisher, R. P., MacKinnon, D. P., & Holland, H. L. (1985). Eyewitness memory enhancement in the police interview: Cognitive retrieval mnemonics versus hypnosis. *Journal of Applied Psychology, 70*, 401–412.

Gentner, D. (1983). Structure-mapping: A theoretical framework for analogy. *Cognitive Science, 7*, 155–170.

Gentner, D. (2019). Cognitive science is and should be pluralistic. *Topics in Cognitive Science, 11*, 884–891.

Gentner, D., Lowenstein, J., Thompson, L., & Forbus, K. D. (2009). Reviving inert knowledge: Analogical encoding supports relational retrieval of past events. *Cognitive Science, 33*, 1343–1382.

Gernsbacher, M. A. (1993). Less skilled readers have less efficient suppression mechanisms. *Psychological Science, 4*, 294–298.

Gernsbacher, M. A. (1997). Two decades of structure building. *Discourse Processes, 23*, 265–304.

Gernsbacher, M. A., & Faust, M. E. (1991). The mechanism of suppression: A component of general comprehension skill. *Journal of Experimental Psychology: Learning, Memory and Cognition, 17*, 245–262.

Geusgens, C. A. V., Winkens, I., van Heugten, C. M., Jolles, J., & van den Heuvel, W. J. A. (2007). Occurrence and measurement of transfer in cognitive rehabilitation: A critical review. *Journal of Rehabilitative Medicine, 39*, 425–439.

Geyer, L. H., & De Wald, C. G. (1973). Feature lists and confusion matrices. *Perception & Psychophysics, 14*, 479–482.

Gibbs, R. W. (2006). *Embodiment and cognitive science*. Cambridge University Press.

Gibson, E. J. (1969). *Principles of perceptual learning and development*. Prentice-Hall.

Gibson, E. J., Osser, H., Schiff, W., & Smith, J. (1963). An analysis of critical features of letters, tested by a confusion matrix. In In *A basic research program on reading* (pp. 1–20). U. S. Office of Education.

Gibson, J. J. (1979). *The ecological approach to visual perception*. Houghton-Mifflin.

Gick, M. L. (1986). Problem-solving strategies. *Educational Psychologist, 21*, 99–120.

Gick, M. L., & Holyoak, K. J. (1980). Analogical problem solving. *Cognitive Psychology, 12*, 306–355.

Gick, M. L., & Holyoak, K. J. (1983). Schema induction and analogical transfer. *Cognitive Psychology, 15*, 1–38.

Gigerenzer, G. (2008). Why heuristics work. *Perspectives in Psychological Science, 3*, 20–29.

Gigerenzer, G. (2014). *Risk savvy*. Penguin/Viking.

Gigerenzer, G. (2019). Expert intuition is not rational choice. *American Journal of Psychology, 132*, 475–478.

Gigerenzer, G., & Brighton, H. (2009). Homo Heuristicus: Why biased minds make better inferences. *Topics in Cognitive Science, 1*, 107–143.

Gigerenzer, G., & Hoffrage, U. (1995). How to improve Bayesian reasoning without instruction: Frequency formats. *Psychological Review, 102*, 684–704.

Gilhooly, R. H., Logie, R. H., Wetherick, N. E., & Wynn, V. (1993). Working memory and strategies in syllogistic-reasoning tasks. *Memory & Cognition, 21*, 115–124.

Gilovich, T., Griffin, D., & Kahneman, D (Eds.). (2002). *Heuristics and biases: The psychology of intuitive judgment*. Cambridge University Press.

Glaser, R. (1984). Education and thinking: The role of knowledge. *American Psychologist, 39*, 93–104.

Gleitman, L. (2005). Langauge and thought. In K. J. Holyoak & R. G. Morrison (Eds.), *The Cambridge handbook of thinking and reasoning* (pp. 633–662). Cambridge University Press.

Glenberg, A. M., & Kaschak, M. P. (2002). Grounding language in action. *Psychonomic Bulletin & Review, 9*, 558–565.

Glenberg, A. M., Meyer, M., & Lindem, K. (1987). Mental models contribute to foregrounding during text comprehension. *Journal of Memory and Language, 26*, 69–83.

Glucksberg, S., & McCloskey, M. (1981). Decisions about ignorance: Knowing that you don't know. *Journal of Experimental Psychology: Human Learning and Memory, 7*, 311–325.

Goel, A. K., & Davies, J. (2020). Artificial intelligence. In R. J. Sternberg (Ed.), *Cambridge handbook of intelligence* (2nd ed., pp. 602–625). Cambridge University Press.

Goel, V. (2014). Creative brains: Designing in the real world. *Frontiers in Human Neuroscience, 8*(241), 1–14.

Goel, V., & Pirolli, P. (1992). The structure of design problem spaces. *Cognitive Science, 16*, 395–429.

Goldenberg, G., Podreka, I., Steiner, M., & Willmes, K. (1987). Patterns of regional cerebral blood flow related to memorizing of high and low imagery words: An emission computer tomography study. *Neuropsychologia, 25*, 473–486.

Goldin-Meadow, S. (2015). From action to abstraction: Gesture as a mechanism of change. *Developmental Review, 38*, 167–184.

Goldin-Meadow, S., Cook, S. W., & Mitchell, Z. A. (2009). Gesturing gives children new ideas about math. *Psychological Science, 20*, 267–272.

Goldin-Meadow, S., & Wagner, S. M. (2005). How our hands help us learn. *TRENDS in Cognitive Sciences, 9*, 234–241.

Goldstein, D. G., & Gigerenzer, G. (2002). Models of ecological rationality: The recognition heuristic. *Psychological Review, 109*, 75–90.

Goldstone, R. L., Kersten, A., & Carvalho, P. F. (2018). Categorization and concepts. In S. Thompson-Schill (Ed.), *Steven's handbook of experimental psychology and cognitive neuroscience* (Vol. 3, pp. 275–317). John Wiley & Sons.

Gómez, L., & Glenberg, A. M. (2020). Embodied classroom activities for vocabulary acquisition. In S. L. Macrine & J. Fugate (Eds.), *Movement matters: How embodied cognition informs teaching and learning*. The MIT Press.

Gonthier, C. (2021). Charting the diversity of strategic processes in visuospatial short-term memory. *Perspectives in Psychological Science, 16*(2), 294–318.

Gopher, D., & Kahneman, D. (1971). Individual differences in attention and the prediction of flight criteria. *Perceptual and Motor Skills, 33*, 1335–1342.

Gorodetsky, M., & Fisher, K. M. (1996). Generating connections and learning in biology. In K. M. Fisher & M. R. Kibby (Eds.), *Knowledge acquisition, organization, and use in biology* (pp. 135–154). Springer.

Graesser, A. C., Kassler, M. A., Kreuz, R. J., & McLain-Allen, B. (1998). Verification of statements about story worlds that deviate from normal conceptions of time: What is true about Einstein's Dreams? *Cognitive Psychology, 35*, 246–301.

Graesser, A. C., McNamara, D. S., & Kulikowich, J. M. (2011). CohMetrix: Providing multilevel analyses of text characteristics. *Educational Researcher, 40*, 223–234.

Graesser, A. C., Singer, M., & Trabasso, T. (1994). Constructing inferences during narrative text comprehension. *Psychological Review, 101*, 371–395.

Grahek, I., Everaert, J., Krebs, R. M., & Koster, E. H. W. (2018). Cognitive control in depression: Toward clinical models informed by cognitive neuroscience. *Clinical Psychological Science, 6*, 464–480.

Grandin, T., & Johnson, C. (2005). *Animals in translation*. Harcourt.

Gray, W. D., & Lindstedt, J. K. (2017). Plateaus, dips, and leaps: Where to look for inventions and discoveries during skill performance. *Cognitive Science, 41*, 1838–1870.

Green, C. S., & Newcombe, N. S. (2020). Cognitive training: How evidence, controversies, and challenges inform education policy. *Policy Insights From the Behavioral and Brain Sciences, 7*, 80–86.

Greene, R. L. (1986). Sources of recency effects in free recall. *Psychological Bulletin, 99*, 221–228.

Greeno, J. G. (1974). Hobbits and orcs: Acquisition of a sequential concept. *Cognitive Psychology, 6*, 270–292.

Greeno, J. G. (1978). Natures of problem solving abilities. In W. K. Estes (Ed.), *Handbook of learning and cognitive processes* (Vol. 5, pp. 239–270). Erlbaum.

Griggs, R. A., & Cox, J. R. (1982). The elusive thematic-materials effect in Wason's selection task. *British Journal of Psychology, 73*, 407–420.

Gunter, B., Clifford, B. R., & Berry, C. (1980). Release from proactive interference with television news items: Evidence for encoding dimensions within televised news. *Journal of Experimental Psychology: Human Learning and Memory, 6*, 216–223.

Guss, C. D., Ahmed, S., & Dorner, D. (2021). From da Vinci's flying machines to a theory of the creative process. *Perspectives on Psychological Science*.

Haber, R. N. (1969). R. N. Haber (Ed.), *Introduction. Information-processing approaches to visual perception*. Holt, Rinehart & Winston.

Hakim, A., & Levy, D. J. (2019). A gateway to consumers' minds: Achievements, caveats, and prospects of electoencephalography-based prediction in neuromarketing. *Wiley Interdisciplinary Reviews: Cognitive Science, 10*, e1485.

Halpern, D. F. (2014). *Thought and knowledge: An introduction to critical thinking* (5th ed.). Psychology Press.

Hampton, J. A. (1997). Psychological representation of concepts. In M. A. Conway (Ed.), *Cognitive models of memory* (pp. 81–110). MIT Press.

Hanley, J. R., & Chapman, E. (2008). Partial knowledge in a tip of the tongue state about two and three word proper names. *Psychonomic Bulletin & Review, 15*, 156–160.

Haque, S., Vaphiades, M. S., & Lueck, C. J. (2018). The visual agnosias and related disorders. *Journal of Neuro-Ophthalmology, 38*, 379–392.

Harris, L. R., Blakemore, C., & Donaghy, M. (1980). Integration of visual and auditory space in the mammalian superior colliculus. *Nature, 288*(5786), 56–59. https://doi.org/10.1038/288056a0

Hasher, L., & Zacks, R. T. (1979). Automatic and effortful processes in memory. *Journal of Experimental Psychology: General, 108*, 356–388.

Hasher, L., & Zacks, R. T. (1984). Automatic processing of fundamental information: The case of frequency of occurrence. *American Psychologist, 39*, 1372–1388.

Hasson, U., Chen, J., & Honey, C. J. (2015). Hierarchical process memory: Memory as an integral component of information processing. *Trends in Cognitive Sciences, 19*, 304–313.

Hastie, R., & Dawes, R. M. (2001). *Rational choice in an uncertain world*. SAGE.

Hastie, R., & Pennington, N. (2000). Explanation based decision making. In T. Connolly, H. R. Arkes, & K. R. Hammond (Eds.), *Judgment and decision making: An interdisciplinary reader* (2nd ed., pp. 212–228). Cambridge University Press.

Haviland, S. E., & Clark, H. H. (1974). Whats new? Acquiring new information as a process of comprehension. *Journal of Verbal Learning and Verbal Behavior, 13*, 512–521.

Hayes, J. R. (1952). Memory span for several vocabularies as a function of vocabulary size. In Acoustics Laboratory, Massachusetts Institute of Technology (Ed.), *Quarterly progress report* (pp. 338–352).

Hayes, J. R. (1966). Memory, goals, and problem solving. In B. Kleinmuntz (Ed.), *Problem solving: Research, method, and theory*. Wiley.

Hayes, J. R., & Simon, H. A. (1977). Psychological differences among problem isomorphs. In N. J. Castellan, D. B. Pisoni, & G. R. Potts (Eds.), *Cognitive theory* (Vol. 2, pp. 21–41). Erlbaum.

Hayes-Roth, B., & Hayes-Roth, F. (1977). Concept learning and the recognition and classification of examples. *Journal of Verbal Learning and Verbal Behavior, 16*, 321–338.

Haygood, R. C., & Bourne, L. E., Jr. (1965). Attribute and rule learning aspects of conceptual behavior. *Psychological Review, 72*, 175–195.

Healy, A. F. (1980). Proofreading errors on the word "The": New evidence on reading units. *Journal of Experimental Psychology: Human Perception and Performance, 6*, 45–57.

Hearnshaw, S., Baker, E., & Munro, N. (2019). Speech perception skills of children with speech sound disorders: A systematic review and meta-analysis. *Journal of Speech, Language, and Hearing Research, 62*, 3771–3789.

Hebb, D. O. (1949). *The organization of behavior: A neuropsychological theory*. Wiley and Sons.

Hegarty, M. (1992). Mental animation: Inferring motion from static displays of mechanical systems. *Journal of Experimental Psychology: Learning, Memory, and Cognition, 18*, 1084–1102.

Hegarty, M. (2004). Mechanical reasoning by mental simulation. *TRENDS in the Cognitive Sciences, 8*, 280–285.

Heidbreder, E. (1961). *Seven psychologies*. Appleton-Century-Crofts.

Helie, S., & Sun, R. (2010). Incubation, insight, and creative problem solving: A unified theory and a connectionist model. *Psychological Review, 117*, 994–1024.

Hennessey, B. A., & Amabile, T. M. (2010). Creativity. *Annual Review of Psychology, 61*, 569–598.

Hertel, P. T., Anooshian, L. J., & Ashbrook, P. (1986). The accuracy of beliefs about retrieval cues. *Memory & Cognition, 14*, 265–269.

Hertwig, R., & Grune-Yanoff, T. (2017). Nudging and boosting: Steering or empowering good decisions. *Perspectives on Psychological Science, 12,* 973–986.

Hessels, R. S. (2020). How does gaze to faces support face-to-face interaction? A review and perspective. *Psychonomic Bulletin & Review, 2020,* 856–881.

Hills, T. T., Todd, P. M., Lazer, D., Redish, A. D., Couzin, I. D., & Group, C. S. R. (2015). Exploration versus exploitation in space, mind, and society. *Trends in Cognitive Sciences, 19,* 46–54.

Hilpert, J. C., & Marchand, G. C. (2018). Complex systems research in educational psychology: Aligning theory and method. *Educational Psychologist, 53,* 185–202.

Hinkelmann, K., Moritz, S., Botzenhardt, J., Riedesel, K., Wiedemann, K., Kellner, M., & Otte, C. (2009). Cognitive impairment in major depression: Association with salivary cortisol. *Biological Psychiatry, 66*(9), 879–885. https://doi.org/10.1016/j.biopsych.2009.06.023

Hinks, J. (2017, November 2). Two U.S. warships had deadly crashes this year. Here's what the navy says went wrong. *Time*. time.com/5006790/pacific-navy-collisions-avoidable/

Hirst, W., Phelps, E. A., Meksin, R., Vaidya, C. J., Johnson, M. K., Mitchell, K. J., Buckner, R. L., Budson, A. E., Gabrieli, J. D. E., Lustig, C., Mather, M., Ochsner, K. N., Schacter, D., Simons, J. S., Lyle, K. B., Cuc, A. F., & Olsson, A. (2015). A ten-year follow-up of a study of memory for the attack of September 11, 2001: Flashbulb memories and memories for flashbulb events. *Journal of Experimental Psychology: General, 144,* 604–623.

Hoffman, D. D. (1998). *Visual intelligence.* Norton.

Hoffman, P., McClelland, J. L., & Lambon Ralph, M. A. (2018). Concepts, control, and context: A connectionist account of normal and disordered semantic cognition. *Psychological Review, 125,* 293–328.

Hogan, J. P. (1997). *Mind matters: Exploring the world of artificial intelligence.* Random House.

Hogarth, R. M. (2001). *Educating intuition.* University of Chicago Press.

Holbrook, M. B. (1975). A comparison of methods for measuring interletter similarity between capital letters. *Perception & Psychophysics, 24,* 529–533.

Holley, C. D., & Dansereau, D. F. (1984). Networking: The technique and the empirical evidence. In C. D. Holley & D. F. Dansereau (Eds.), *Spatial learning strategies* (pp. 81–108). Academic Press.

Holley, C. D., Dansereau, D. F., McDonald, B. A., Garland, J. C., & Collins, K. W. (1979). Evaluation of a hierarchical mapping technique as an aid to prose processing. *Contemporary Educational Psychology, 4,* 227–237.

Hollon, S. D. (2020). Is cognitive therapy enduring or anti-depressant medication iatrogenic? Depression as an evolved adaptation. *American Psychologist, 75,* 1207–1216.

Holst, V. F., & Pezdek, K. (1992). Scripts for typical crimes and their effects on memory for eyewitness testimony. *Applied Cognitive Psychology, 6,* 573–587.

Holtz, R. L. (2020, September 15). New research on what dreams reveal. *The Wall Street Journal,* p. A13.

Holyoak, K. J. (2005). Analogy. In K. J. Holyoak & R. G. Morrison (Eds.), *The Cambridge handbook of thinking and reasoning* (pp. 117–142). Cambridge University Press.

Holyoak, K. J., & Cheng, P. W. (2011). Causal learning and inference as a rational process: The new synthesis. *Annual Review of Psychology, 62,* 135–163.

Holyoak, K. J., & Morrison, R. G (Eds.). (2005). *The Cambridge handbook of thinking and reasoning.* Cambridge University Press.

Horne, Z., Muradoglu, M., & Cimpian, A. (2019). Explanation as a cognitive process. *Trends in Cognitive Sciences, 23,* 187–199.

Horne, Z., Powell, D., Hummel, J. E., & Holyoak, K. J. (2015). Countering anti-vaccination additudes. *PNAS Proceedings of the National Academy of Sciences of the United States of America, 112*(33), 10321–10324.

Horton, W. S., & Rapp, D. N. (2003). Out of sight, out of mind: Occlusion and the accessibility of information in narrative comprehension. *Psychonomic Bulletin & Review, 10,* 104–110.

Hostetter, A. B., & Alibali, M. W. (2008). Visible embodiment: Gestures as simulated action. *Psychonomic Bulletin & Review, 15,* 495–514.

Hu, X., Cheng, L. Y., Chiu, M. H., & Paller, K. A. (2020). Promoting memory consolidation during sleep: A meta-analysis of targeted memory reactivation. *Psychological Bulletin, 146,* 218–244.

Hubel, D. H., & Wiesel, T. N. (1962). Receptive fields, binocular interaction, and functional architecture in the cat's visual cortex. *Journal of Physiology, 160,* 106–154.

Hubel, D. H., & Wiesel, T. N. (1963). Receptive fields of cells in the striate cortex of very young visually inexperienced kittens. *Journal of Neurophysiology, 26,* 994–1002.

Hummel, J. E., & Holyoak, K. J. (1997). Distributed representations of structure: A theory of analogical access and mapping. *Psychological Review, 104,* 427–466.

Humphreys, M. S., & Bain, J. D. (1983). Recognition memory: A cue and information analysis. *Memory & Cognition, 11,* 583–600.

Hunt, E., Pellegrino, J. W., & Yee, P. L. (1989). Individual differences in attention. In G. H. Bower (Ed.), *The psychology of learning and motivation* (Vol. 24, pp. 285–310). Academic Press.

Hunt, R. R., & Elliott, J. M. (1980). The role of nonsemantic information in memory: Orthographic distinctiveness effects on retention. *Journal of Experimental Psychology: General, 109,* 49–74.

Hurley, S. M., & Novick, L. R. (2010). Solving problems using matrix, network, and hierarchy diagrams: The consequences of violating construction conventions. *The Quarterly Journal of Experimental Psychology, 63,* 275–290.

Hutchison, K. A. (2003). Is semantic priming due to association strength or feature overlap? A microanalytic review. *Psychonomic Bulletin & Review, 10,* 785–813.

Hyde, T. S., & Jenkins, J. J. (1969). The differential effects of incidental tasks on the organization of recall of a list of highly associated words. *Journal of Experimental Psychology, 82,* 472–481.

Hyman, I. E., & Pentland, J. (1996). The role of mental imagery in the creation of false childhood memories. *Journal of Memory and Language, 35,* 101–117.

Ianì, F. (2019). Embodied memories: Reviewing the role of the body in memory processes. *Psychon Bull Rev, 26*(6), 1747–1766. doi:10.3758/s13423-019-01674-x

Intons-Peterson, M. J. (1983). Imagery paradigms: How vulnerable are they to experimenter's expectations? *Journal of Experimental Psychology:. Human Perception and Performance, 9,* 394–412.

Jacobs, R. A., & Bates, C. J. (2019). Comparing the visual representations and performance of humans and deep neural networks. *Current Directions in Psychological Science, 28,* 34–39.

Jacoby, L. L., & Dallas, M. (1981). On the relationship between autobiographical memory and perceptual learning. *Journal of Experimental Psychology: General, 110,* 306–340.

Jahn, G. (2004). Three turtles in danger: Spontaneous construction of causally relevant spatial situation models. *Journal of Experimental Psychology: Learning, Memory, & Cognition, 30,* 969–987.

James, L. E., & Burke, D. M. (2000). Phonological priming effects on word retrieval and tip-of-tongue experiences in young and older adults. *Journal of Experimental Psychology: Learning, Memory, and Cognition, 26,* 1378–1391.

James, W. (1890). *The principles of psychology* (2 vols.). Holt.

Janis, I. L. (1982). *Groupthink.* Houghton Mifflin.

Jarecki, J., Tan, J. H., & Jenny, M. A. (2020). A framework for building cognitive process models. *Psychonomic Bulletin & Review, 27,* 1218–1229.

Jensen, J. L., McDaniel, M. A., Woodward, S. M., & Kummer, T. A. (2014). Teaching to the test...or testing to teach: Exams requiring higher order thinking skills encourage greater conceptual understanding. *Educational Psychology Review, 26*, 307–329.

Ji, J. L., Kavanagh, D. J., Holmes, E. A., MacLeod, C., & Di Simplicio, M. (2019). Mental imagery in psychiatry: Conceptual & clinical implications. *CNS Spectrum, 24*, 114–126.

Johnson, E. J., & Goldstein, D. (2003). Do defaults save lives? *Science, 302*, 1338–1339.

Johnson, M. K. (1983). A multiple-entry, modular memory system. In G. H. Bower (Ed.), *The psychology of learning and motivation* (Vol. 17, pp. 81–123). Academic Press.

Johnson, M. K. (2009). Memory and reality. *American Psychologist, 61*, 757–771.

Johnson, M. K., Hashtroudi, S., & Lindsay, D. H. (1993). Source monitoring. *Psychological Bulletin, 114*, 3–28.

Johnson, M. K., & Raye, C. L. (1981). Reality monitoring. *Psychological Review, 88*, 67–85.

Johnson, M. K., Raye, C. L., Wang, A. Y., & Taylor, T. T. (1979). Fact and fantasy: The roles of accuracy and variability in confusing imaginations with perceptual experiences. *Journal of Experimental Psychology: Human Learning and Memory, 5*, 229–240.

Johnson, S. (1967). Hierarchical clustering schemes. *Psychometrika, 32*, 241–254.

Johnson-Laird, P. N. (1989). Analogy and the exercise of creativity. In S. Vosniadou & A. Ortony (Eds.), *Similarity and analogical reasoning* (pp. 313–331). Cambridge University Press.

Johnson-Laird, P. N., Legrenzi, P., & Legrenzi, M. S. (1972). Reasoning and a sense of reality. *British Journal of Psychology, 63*, 395–400.

Johnston, W. A., & Dark, V. J. (1986). Selective attention. *Annual Review of Psychology, 37*, 43–75.

Johnston, W. A., & Heinz, S. P. (1978). Flexibility and capacity demands of attention. *Journal of Experimental Psychology: General, 107*, 420–435.

Jonides, J., & Yantis, S. (1988). Uniqueness of abrupt visual onset in capturing attention. *Perception & Psychophysics, 43*(4), 346–354. https://doi.org/10.3758/bf03208805

Just, M. A., & Carpenter, P. A. (1980). A theory of reading: From eye fixations to comprehension. *Psychological Review, 87*, 329–354.

Just, M. A., & Carpenter, P. A. (1987). *The psychology of reading and language comprehension.* Allyn & Bacon.

Kaan, E., & Swaab, T. Y. (2002). The brain circuitry of syntactic comprehension. *Trends in Cognitive Sciences, 8*, 350–356.

Kahn, U., & Dhar, R. (2006). The licensing effect in consumer choice. *Journal of Marketing Research, 43*, 259–266.

Kahneman, D. (1973). *Attention and effort.* Prentice-Hall.

Kahneman, D. (2003). Experiences of collaborative research. *American Psychologist, 58*, 723–730.

Kahneman, D. (2011). *Thinking fast and slow.* Farrar, Straus and Giroux.

Kahneman, D., Ben-Ishai, R., & Lotan, M. (1973). Relation of a test of attention to road accidents. *Journal of Applied Psychology, 58*, 113–115.

Kahneman, D., & Frederick, S. (2005). A model of heuristic judgment. In K. Holyoak & R. G. Morrison (Eds.), *The Cambridge handbook of thinking and reasoning* (pp. 267–294). Cambridge University Press.

Kahneman, D., & Tversky, A. (1972). Subjective probability: A judgment of representativeness. *Cognitive Psychology, 3*, 430–454.

Kahneman, D., & Tversky, A. (1973). On the psychology of prediction. *Psychological Review, 80*, 237–251.

Kahneman, D., & Tversky, A. (1979). Prospect theory: An analysis of decisions under risk. *Econometrica, 47*, 263–291.

Kahneman, D., & Tversky, A. (1984). Choices, values, and frames. *American Psychologist, 39*, 341–350.

Kalaria, R. (2002). Similarities between Alzheimer's disease and vascular dementia. *Journal of the Neurological Sciences*, *203-204*, 29–34. https://doi.org/10.1016/s0022-510x(02)00256-3

Kalat, J. W. (2004). *Biological psychology* (8th ed.). Wadsworth.

Kalyuga, S., Rikers, R., & Paas, F. (2012). Educational implications of expertise reversal effects in learning and performance of complex cognitive and sensorimotor skills. *Educational Psychology Review*, *24*, 313–337.

Kane, M. J., Hambrick, D. Z., Tuholski, S. W., Wilhelm, O., Payne, T. W., & Engle, R. W. (2004). The generality of working memory capacity: A latent variable approach to verbal and visuospatial memory span and reasoning. *Journal of Experimental Psychology: General*, *133*, 189–217.

Kanizsa, G. (1979). *Organization in vision: Essays on Gestalt perception*. Praeger.

Karpicke, J. D., Butler, A., & Roediger, H. L. (2009). Metacognitive strategies in student learning: Do students practice retrieval when they study on their own? *Memory*, *17*, 471–479.

Kassai, R., Futo, J., Demetrovics, Z., & Takacs, Z. K. (2019). A meta-analysis of the experimental evidence on the near- and far-transfer effects among children's executive function skills. *Psychological Bulletin*, *145*, 165–188.

Kassin, S. M., Tubb, V. A., Hosch, H. M., & Memon, A. (2001). On the "general acceptance" of eyewitness testimony research. *American Psychologist*, *56*, 405–416.

Kaufman, J. C. (2018). Finding meaning with creativity in the past, present, and future. *Perspectives on Psychological Science*, *13*, 734–749.

Keenan, J. M., MacWhinney, B., & Mayhew, D. (1977). Pragmatics in memory: A study of natural conversation. *Journal of Verbal Learning and Verbal Behavior*, *16*, 549–560.

Keil, F. C. (2006). Explanation and understanding. *Annual Review of Psychology*, *57*, 227–254.

Kehyayan, A. (2018). Reducing intrusive memories of trauma using a visuospatial interference intervention with inpatients with posttraumatic stress disorder (PTSD). *Journal of Consulting and Clinical Psychology*, *86*, 1076–1090.

Keil, F. C., & Batterman, N. (1984). A characteristicto defining shift in the development of word meaning. *Journal of Verbal Learning and Verbal Behavior*, *23*, 221–226.

Kelley, T. D., McNeely, D. A., Serra, M. J., & Davis, T. (2020). Delayed judgments of learning are associated with activation of information from past experiences: A neurobiological examination. *Psychological Science*, *32*(1), 96–108.

Keppel, G., & Underwood, B. (1962). Proactive inhibition in short-term retention of single items. *Journal of Verbal Learning and Verbal Behavior*, *1*, 153–161.

Kessler, H., Holmes, E. A., Blackwell, S. E., Schmidt, A. C., Schweer, J. M., Bucker, A., & Kehyayan, A. (2018). Reducing intrusive memories of trauma using a visuospatial interference intervention with inpatients with posttraumatic stress disorder (PTSD). *Journal of Consulting and Clinical Psychology*, *86*, 1076–1090.

Kieffer, M. J., & Christodoulou, J. A. (2019). Automaticity and control: How do executive functions and reading fluency interact in predicting reading comprehension? *Reading Research Quarterly*, *55*, 147–164.

Kieras, D. E. (1978). Good and bad structure in simple paragraphs: Effects on apparent theme, reading time, and recall. *Journal of Verbal Learning and Verbal Behavior*, *17*, 13–28.

Kim, T. W., & Duhachek, A. (2020). Artificial intelligence and persuasion: A construal-level account. *Psychological Science*, *31*(4), 363–380.

Kintsch, W. (1979). On modeling comprehension. *Educational Psychologist*, *14*, 3–14.

Kintsch, W. (1988). The use of knowledge in discourse processing: A construction-integration model. *Psychological Review*, *95*, 163–182.

Kintsch, W. (1994). Text comprehension, memory, and learning. *American Psychologist, 49,* 294–303.

Kintsch, W. (1998). *Comprehension: A paradigm for cognition.* Cambridge University Press.

Kintsch, W. (2005). An overview of top-down and bottom-up effects in comprehension: The CI perspective. *Discourse Processes, 39,* 125–128.

Kintsch, W., & Mangalath, P. (2011). The construction of meaning. *Topics in Cognitive Science, 3,* 346–370.

Kintsch, W., & Van Dijk, T. A. (1978). Toward a model of text comprehension and production. *Psychological Review, 85,* 363–394.

Kintsch, W., & Vipond, D. (1979). Reading comprehension and readability in educational practice and psychological theory. In L. G. Nilsson (Ed.), *Perspectives on memory research* (pp. 329–365). Erlbaum.

Kita, S., Alibali, M. W., & Chu, M. (2017). How do gestures influence thinking and speaking? The gesture-for-conceptualization hypothesis. *Psychological Review, 124,* 245–266.

Kitano, H. (2016). Artificial intelligence to win the Nobel prize and beyond: Creating the engine for scientific discovery. *AI Magazine, 37,* 39–49.

Klahr, D., Triona, L. M., & Williams, C. (2007). Hands on what? The relative effectiveness of physical vs. virtual materials in an engineering design project by middle school children. *Journal of Research in Science Teaching, 44,* 183–203.

Klapp, S. T., Marshburn, E. A., & Lester, P. T. (1983). Short-term memory does not involve the "working memory" of information processing: The demise of a common assumption. *Journal of Experimental Psychology: General, 112,* 204–264.

Klatzky, R. L. (2009). Giving psychological science away: The role of applications courses. *Perspectives on Psychological Science, 4,* 522–530.

Kleiman, G. M. (1975). Speech recoding in reading. *Journal of Verbal Learning and Verbal Behavior, 14,* 323–339.

Klein, G. (1998). *Sources of power: How people make decisions.* The MIT Press.

Klein, G. (2015). A naturalistic decision making perspective on studying intuitive decision making. *Journal Applied Research in Memory and Cognition, 4,* 164–168.

Klein, G. A. (1993). A recognition-primed decision (RPD) model of rapid decision making. In G. A. Klein, J. Orasanu, R. Calderwood, & C. E. Zsambok (Eds.), *Decision making in action: Models and methods* (pp. 138–147). Ablex.

Klein, G. A., Orasanu, J., Calderwood, R., & Zsambok, C. E. (Eds.). (1993). *Decision making in action: Models and methods.* Ablex.

Klein, S. B., Cosmides, L., Tooby, J., & Chance, S. (2002). Decisions and the evolution of memory: Multiple systems, multiple functions. *Psychological Review, 109,* 306–329.

Kleinmintz, O. M., Ivancovsky, T., & Shamay-Tsoory, S. G. (2019). The two-fold model of creativity: The neural underpinnings of the generation and evaluation of creative ideas. *Current Opinion in Behavioral Sciences, 27,* 131–138.

Kleinmuntz, B. (1990). Why we still use our heads instead of formulas: Toward an integrative approach. *Psychological Bulletin, 107,* 296–310.

Klin, C. M., & Drumm, A. P. (2010). Seeing what they read and hearing what they say: Readers' representation of the story characters' world. *Psychonomic Bulletin & Review, 17,* 231–236.

Knoblich, G., Ohlsson, S., Haider, H., & Rhenius, D. (1999). Constraint relaxation and chunk decomposition in insight problem solving. *Journal of Experimental Psychology: Learning, Memory and Cognition, 25,* 1534–1555.

Knowlton, B. J., & Foerde, K. (2008). Neural representations of nondeclarative memories. *Current Directions in Psychological Science, 17,* 107–111.

Koedinger, K. R., Booth, J. L., & Klahr, D. (2013). Instructional complexity and the science to constrain it. *Science, 342,* 935–937.

Kohler, W. (1925). *The mentality of apes.* Harcourt.

Konen, C. S., Behrmann, M., Nishimura, M., & Kastner, S. (2011). The functional neuro-anatomy of object agnosia: A case study. *Neuron, 71*(1), 49–60. https://doi.org/10.1016/j.neuron.2011.05.030

Konkle, T., Brady, T. F., Alvarez, G. A., & Oliva, A. (2010). Scene memory is more detailed than you think: The role of categories in visual long-term memory. *Psychological Science, 21*, 1551–1556.

Kopfermann, H. (1930). Psychologische Untersuchunen uber die Wirkung zweidimen-sionaler Darstellungen Korperlicher Gebilde. *Psychologische Forschung, 13*, 293–364.

Koriat, A., Bjork, R. A., Sheffer, L., & Bar, S. K. (2004). Predicting one's own forgetting: The role of experience-based and theory-based processes. *Journal of Experimental Psychology: General, 133*, 643–656.

Kornell, N., & Bjork, R. A. (2007). The promise and perils of self-regulated study. *Psychonomic Bulletin & Review, 14*, 219–224.

Kosslyn, S. M. (1975). Information re-presentation in visual images. *Cognitive Psychology, 7*, 341–370.

Kosslyn, S. M. (1994). *Image and brain: The resolution of the imagery debate.* MIT Press.

Kosslyn, S. M., Ball, T. M., & Reiser, B. J. (1978). Visual images preserve metric spatial information: Evidence from studies of image scanning. *Journal of Experimental Psychology: Human Perception and Performance, 4*, 47–60.

Kosslyn, S. M., & Pomerantz, J. R. (1977). Imagery, propositions, and the form of internal representations. *Cognitive Psychology, 9*, 52–76.

Kounios, J., & Holcomb, P. J. (1994). Concreteness effects in semantic processing: ERP evidence supporting dual-coding theory. *Journal of Experimental Psychology: Learning, Memory, and Cognition, 20*, 804–823.

Kozyreva, A., Lewandowsky, S., & Hertwig, R. (2020). Citizens versus the internet: Confronting digital challenges with cogni-tive tools. *Psychological Science for the Public Interest, 21*, 103–156.

Kredlow, M. A., Eichenbaum, H., & Otto, M. W. (2018). Memory creation and modification: Enhancing the treatment of psychological dis-orders. *American Psychologist, 73*, 269–285.

Kristjansson, A., & Egeth, H. (2019). How fea-ture integration theory integrated cognitive psychology, neurophysiology, and psychophys-ics. *Attention, Perception, & Psychophysics, 82*, 7–23.

Kroll, N. E. A., Schepeler, E. M., & Angin, K. T. (1986). Bizarre imagery: The misremembered mnemonic. *Journal of Experimental Psychology: Learning, Memory, and Cognition, 12*, 42–53.

Kube, T., & Rozenkrantz, L. (2021). When beliefs face reality: An integrative review of belief updating in mental health and ill-ness. *Perspectives in Psychological Science, 16*, 247–274.

Kubovy, M. (2020). Lives as collections of strands: An essay in descriptive psychol-ogy. *Perspectives on Psychological Science, 15*, 497–515.

Kuhl, P. K. (1991). Human adults and human infants show a "perceptual magnet effect" for the prototypes of speech categories, monkeys do not. *Perception & Psychophysics, 50*, 93–107.

Kuhl, P. K. (1993). Infant speech perception: A window on psycholinguistic development. *International Journal of Psycholinguistics, 9*, 33–56.

Kuhl, P. K., & Rivera-Gaxiola, M. (2008). Neural substrates of language acquisition. *Annual Review of Neuroscience, 31*, 511–534.

Kuhl, P. K., Williams, K. A., Lacerda, F., Stevens, K. N., & Lindblom, B. (1992). Linguistic experience alters phonetic percep-tion in infants by 6 months of age. *Science, 225*, 606–608.

Kuhn, G., Amlani, A. A., & Rensink, R. A. (2008). Towards a science of magic. *Trends in Cognitive Sciences, 12*, 349–354.

Kunda, M., McGreggor, K., & Goel, A. K. (2013). A computational model for solving problems from the Raven's Progressive Matrices intelli-gence test using iconic visual representations. *Cognitive Systems Research, 22–23*, 47–66.

Kvavilashvili, L. K., & Mandler, G. (2004). Out on one's mind: A study of involuntary semantic memories. *Cognitive Psychology*, *48*, 47–94.

LaBerge, D. L. (1990). Attention. *Psychological Science*, *1*, 156–162.

LaBerge, D. L., & Samuels, S. J. (1974). Toward a theory of automatic information processing in reading. *Cognitive Psychology*, *6*, 292–323.

Laird, J. E. (2012). *The soar cognitive architecture*. MIT Press.

Laird, J. E., Lebiere, C., & Rosenbloom, P. S. (2017). A standard model of the mind: Toward a common computational framework across artificial intelligence, cognitive science, neuroscience, and robotics. *AI Magazine*, *38*, 13–26.

Landauer, T. K., McNamara, D. S., Dennis, S., & Kintsch, W. (2007). *Handbook of latent semantic analysis*. Erlbaum.

Lashley, K. S. (1950). In search of the engram. In *Society of Experimental Biology Symposium, No. 4: Psychological mechanisms in animal behavior* (pp. 454–480). Cambridge University Press.

Laski, E. V., Jor'dan, J. R., Daoust, C., & Murrray, A. K. (2015). What makes mathematics manipulatives effective? Lessons from cognitive science and Montessori education. *SAGE Open*, *5*(2), 1–8.

Laughery, K. R. (1969). Computer simulation of short-term memory: A component decay model. In G. H. Bower & J. T. Spence (Eds.), *The psychology of learning and motivation* (Vol. 3, pp. 135–200). Academic Press.

LePort, A. K., Stark, S. M., McGaugh, J. L., & Stark, C. E. L. (2017). A cognitive assessment of highly superior autobiographical memory. *Memory & Cognition*, *25*, 276–288.

Lesgold, A. M., Roth, S. F., & Curtis, M. E. (1979). Foregrounding effects in discourse comprehension. *Journal of Verbal Learning and Verbal Behavior*, *18*, 291–308.

Lesgold, A., & Shafto, M. (Eds.). (1990). *Diagnostic monitoring of skill and knowledge acquisition* (pp. 27–50). Erlbaum.

Levine, D. N., Warach, J., & Farah, M. J. (1985). Two visual systems in mental imagery: Dissociation of "what" and "where" in imagery disorders due to bilateral posterior cerebral lesions. *Neurology*, *35*, 1010–1018.

Levine, M. (1966). Hypothesis behavior by humans during discrimination learning. *Journal of Experimental Psychology*, *71*, 331–338.

Levitz, J. (2021, January 12). The office commute is gone, so workers make one up. *The Wall Street Journal*, p. A1.

Levy, B. A. (1978). Speech processing during reading. In A. M. Lesgold, J. W. Pellegrino, S. D. Fokkema, & R. Glaser (Eds.), *Cognitive psychology and instruction* (pp. 123–151). Springer.

Lewis, M. (2016). *The undoing project: A friendship that changed our minds*. Penguin.

Lillard, A. S. (2005). *Montessori: The science behind the genius*. Oxford, UK: Oxford University Press.

Lin, L., Stamm, K., & Christidis, P. (2018). *How diverse is the psychology workforce?* https://www.apa.org/monitor/2018/02/datapoint

Lindsay, D. S., & Read, J. D. (1994). Psychotherapy and memories of childhood sexual abuse: A cognitive perspective. *Applied Cognitive Psychology*, *8*, 281–338.

Liu, X., Crump, M. J. C., & Logan, G. D. (2010). Do you now where your fingers have been? Explicit knowledge of the spatial layout of the keyboard in skilled typists. *Memory & Cognition*, *38*, 474–484.

Loftus, E. F. (1975). Leading questions and the eyewitness report. *Cognitive Psychology*, *7*, 560–572.

Loftus, E. F. (1993). The reality of repressed memories. *American Psychologist*, *48*, 518–537.

Loibl, K., Roll, I., & Rummel, N. (2017). Towards a theory of when and how problem-solving followed by instruction supports learning. *Educational Psychology Review*, *29*, 693–715.

Long, D. L., & Lea, R. B. (2005). Have we been searching for meaning in all the wrong places? Defining the "search after meaning" principle in comprehension. *Discourse Processes*, *39*, 279–298.

Long, G. M., & Toppino, T. C. (2004). Enduring interest in perceptual ambiguity: Alternating views of reversible figures. *Psychological Bulletin, 130,* 748–768.

Lorayne, H., & Lucas, J. (1974). *The memory book.* Ballantine.

Lorenz-Spreen, P., Lewandowsky, S., Sunstein, C. R., & Hertwig, R. (2020). How behavioral sciences can promote truth, autonomy and democratic discourse online. *Nature Human Behavior, 4,* 1102–1109.

Lovett, A., & Forbes, K. (2017). Modeling visual problem solving as analogical reasoning. *Psychological Review, 124,* 60–90.

Lowenstein, G., & Issacharoff, S. (1994). Source dependence in the valuation of objects. *Journal of Behavioral Decision Making, 7,* 157–168.

Lowrie, T., Logan, T., & Hegarty, M. (2019). The influence of spatial visualization training on students' spatial reasoning and mathematics performance. *Journal of Cognition and Development, 20,* 729–751.

Lubold, G., & Youssef, N. A. (2017, November 2). Deadly navy collisons were avoidable. *Wall Street Journal,* p. A8.

Lundeberg, M. A., & Fox, P. W. (1991). Do laboratory findings on test expectancy generalize to classroom outcomes? *Review of Educational Research, 61,* 94–106.

Lutz, K. A., & Lutz, R. J. (1977). Effects of interactive imagery on learning: Applications to advertising. *Journal of Applied Psychology, 62,* 493–498.

Lyons, J. (1970). *Chomsky.* Collins.

Ma, T., Li, H., Deng, L., Yang, H., Lv, X., Li, P., Li, F., Zhang, R., Liu, T., Yao, D., & Xu, P. (2017). The hybrid BCI system for movement control by combining motor imagery and moving onset visual evoked potential. *Journal of Neural Engineering, 14,* 1–12.

MacDonald, M. C., Pearlmutter, N. J., & Seidenberg, M. S. (1994). Syntactic ambiguity resolution as lexical ambiguity resolution. In C. Clifton, K. Rayner, & L. Frazier (Eds.), *Perspectives in sentence processing* (pp. 123–153). Erlbaum.

MacGregor, J. N., Ormerod, T. C., & Chronicle, E. P. (2001). Information processing and insight: A process model of performance on the nine-dot and related problems. *Journal of Experimental Psychology: Learning, Memory, and Cognition, 27,* 176–201.

MacKay, D. G. (1966). To end ambiguous sentences. *Perception & Psychophysics, 1,* 426–435.

Mackenzie, C. S., Wiprzycka, U. J., Hasher, L., & Goldstein, D. (2009). Associations between psychological distress, learning, and memory in spouse caregivers of older adults. *The Journals of Gerontology: Series B, 64B*(6), 742–746. https://doi.org/10.1093/geronb/gbp076

MacLeod, A. K. (2016). Prospection, well-being, and memory. *Memory Studies, 9,* 266–274.

Malcolm, G. L., Groen, I. I. A., & Baker, C. I. (2016). Making sense of real-world scenes. *Trends in Cognitive Sciences, 20,* 843–856.

Malpass, R. S., & Devine, P. G. (1981). Guided memory in eyewitness identification. *Journal of Applied Psychology, 66,* 343–350.

Malt, B. C. (1990). Features and beliefs in the mental representation of categories. *Journal of Memory and Language, 29,* 289–315.

Malt, B. C. (1994). Water is not H2O. *Cognitive Psychology, 27,* 41–70.

Mandler, G. (1967). Organization and memory. In K. W. Spence & J. T. Spence (Eds.), *The psychology of learning and motivation* (Vol. 1, pp. 327–372). Academic Press.

Mandler, G. (1980). Recognizing: The judgment of previous occurrence. *Psychological Review, 87,* 252–271.

Mandler, J. M., & Bauer, P. J. (1988). The cradle of categorization: Is the basic level basic? *Cognitive Development, 3,* 247–264.

Marewski, J. N., & Link, D. (2014). Strategy selection: An introduction to the modeling challenge. *Wiley Interdisciplinary Reviews: Cognitive Science, 5,* 39–59.

Marian, V., & Fausey, C. M. (2006). Language-dependent memory in bilingual learning. *Applied Cognitive Psychology, 20,* 1025–1047.

Markman, A. B., & Gentner, D. (2001). Thinking. *Annual Review of Psychology, 52*, 223–247.

Markman, A. B., & Wood, K. L. (Eds.). (2009). *Tools for innovation.* Oxford University Press.

Markman, A. B., Wood, K. L., Linsey, J. S., Murphy, J. T., & Laux, J. P. (2009). Supporting innovation by promoting analogical reasoning. In A. B. Markman & K. L. Wood (Eds.), *Tools for innovation* (pp. 85–103). Oxford University Press.

Marschark, M., & Hunt, R. R. (1989). A reexamination of the role of imagery in learning and memory. *Journal of Experimental Psychology: Learning, Memory, and Cognition, 15*, 710–720.

Marsh, R. L., & Bower, G. H. (1993). Eliciting cryptomnesia: Unconscious plagiarism in a puzzle task. *Journal of Experimental Psychology: Learning, Memory, and Cognition, 19*, 673–688.

Marsh, R. L., Landau, J. D., & Hicks, J. L. (1996). How examples may (and may not) constrain creativity. *Memory & Cognition, 24*, 669–680.

Marshall, S. P. (1995). *Schemas in problem solving.* Cambridge University Press.

Martin, A. (2016). GRAPES–Grounding representations in action, perception, and emotion systems: How object properties and categories are represented in the human brain. *Psychonomic Bulletin & Review, 23*, 979–990.

Martindale, C. (1991). *Cognitive psychology: A neural network approach.* Wadsworth.

Mason, R. A., & Just, M. A. (2020). Neural representations of procedural knowledge. *Psychological Science, 31*(6), 529–540.

Mauro, R., & Kubovy, M. (1992). Caricature and face recognition. *Memory & Cognition, 20*, 433–440.

McCabe, J. (2011). Metacognitive awareness of learning strategies in undergraduates. *Memory & Cognition, 39*, 462–476.

McCarthy, K. S., Watanabe, M., Dai, J., & McNamara, D. S. (2020). Personalized learning in START: Past modifications and future design. *Journal of Research on Technology in Education, 3*, 301–321.

McClelland, J. L., Botvinick, M. M., Noelle, D. C., Plaut, D. C., Rogers, T. T., Seidenberg, M. S., & Smith, L. B. (2010). Letting structure emerge: Connectionist and dynamical systems approaches to cognition. *Trends in Cognitive Sciences, 14*, 348–356.

McClelland, J. L., & Rogers, T. T. (2003). The parallel distributed processing approach to semantic cognition. *Nature Reviews Neuroscience, 4*, 310–322.

McClelland, J. L., & Rumelhart, D. E. (1981). An interactive-activation model of context effects in letter perception: Part 1. An account of basic findings. *Psychological Review, 88*, 375–407.

McClelland, J. L., Rumelhart, D. E., & The PDP Research Group. (1986). *Parallel distributed processing: Explorations in the microstructure of cognition.* MIT Press.

McCloskey, M. (1991). Networks and theories: The place of connectionism in cognitive science. *Psychological Science, 2*, 287–295.

McCloskey, M., & Glucksberg, S. (1979). Decision processes in verifying category membership statements: Implications for models of semantic memory. *Cognitive Psychology, 11*, 1–37.

McCormack, T., Feeney, A., & Beck, S. R. (2020). Regret and decision making: A developmental perspective. *Current Directions in Psychological Science, 29*, 346–350.

McDaniel, M. A. (2007). Applying cognitive psychology to education. *Psychonomic Bulletin & Review, 14*, 185–186.

McDaniel, M. A., & Einstein, G. O. (1986). Bizarre imagery as an effective memory aid: The importance of distinctiveness. *Journal of Experimental Psychology: Learning, Memory, and Cognition, 12*, 54–65.

McDaniel, M. A., & Einstein, G. O. (2020). Training learning strategies to promote self-regulation and transfer: The knowledge, belief, commitment, and planning framework. *Perspectives on Psychological Science, 15*(6), 1363–1381.

McDaniel, M. A., Howard, D. C., & Einstein, G. O. (2009). The read-recite-review study strategy. *Psychological Science, 20*, 515–522.

McDermott, K. B., Buckner, R. L., Petersen, S. E., Kelley, W. M., & Sanders, A. L. (1999). Set-and code-specific activation in the frontal cortex: An fMRI study of encoding and retrieval of faces and words. *Journal of Cognitive Neuroscience, 11*(6), 631–640. https://doi.org/10.1162/089892999563698

McGaugh, J. L. (2017). Highly superior autobiographical memory. In J. Stein (Ed.), *Reference module in neuroscience and biobehavioral psychology* (pp. 1–9). Elsevier.

McKenzie, C. R. M. (2003). Rational models as theories—not standards—of behavior. *TRENDS in Cognitive Sciences, 7,* 403–406.

McKoon, G., & Ratcliff, R. (1990). Dimensions of inference. In A. C. Graesser & G. H. Bower (Eds.), *Inferences and text comprehension.* Academic Press.

McKoon, G., & Ratcliff, R. (1992). Inference during reading. *Psychological Review, 99,* 440–466.

McKoon, G., & Ratcliff, R. (1998). Memory-based language processing: Psycholinguistic research in the 1990s. *Annual Review of Psychology, 49,* 25–42.

McKoon, G., Ratcliff, R., & Dell, G. S. (1986). A critical evaluation of the semantic-episodic distinction. *Journal of Experimental Psychology: Learning, Memory, and Cognition, 12,* 295–306.

McNamara, D. S (Ed.). (2007). *Reading comprehension strategies: Theories, interventions, and technologies.* Taylor & Francis.

McNamara, D. S., & Healy, A. F. (2000). A procedural explanation of the generation effect for simple and difficult multiplication problems and answers. *Journal of Memory and Language, 43,* 652–679.

McNamara, D. S., & Magliano, J. (2009). Toward a comprehension model of comprehension. In B. H. Ross (Ed.), *Psychology of learning and motivation* (Vol. 51, pp. 297–384). Elsevier.

McNamara, D. S., O'Reilly, T., Best, R., & Ozura, Y. (2006). Improving adolescents' reading comprehension strategies with iSTART. *Journal of Educational Computing Research, 34,* 141–171.

McNamara, D. S., O'Reilly, T., Row, M., Boonthum, C., & Levinstein, I. B. (2007). iSTART: A web-based tutor that teaches self-explanation and metacognitive reading strategies. In D. S. McNamra (Ed.), *Reading comprehension strategies: Theories, interventions, and technologies* (pp. 397–420). Erlbaum.

McNamara, T. P., & Miller, D. L. (1989). Attributes of theories of meaning. *Psychological Bulletin, 106,* 355–376.

McNorgan, C., Reid, J., & McRae, K. (2011). Integrating conceptual knowledge within and across representational modalities. *Cognition, 118,* 211–233.

Medin, D. L., Altom, M. W., Edelson, S. M., & Freko, D. (1982). Correlated symptoms and simulated medical classification. *Journal of Experimental Psychology: Learning, Memory, and Cognition, 8,* 37–50.

Medin, D. L., Lynch, E. B., & Solomon, K. O. (2000). Are there kinds of concepts? *Annual Review of Psychology, 51,* 121–147.

Medin, D. L., & Schaffer, M. M. (1978). Context theory of classification learning. *Psychological Review, 85,* 207–238.

Melby-Lervag, M., Redick, T. S., & Hulme, C. (2016). Memory training does not improve performance on measures of intelligence or other measures of far transfer: Evidence from a meta-analytic review. *Perspectives on Psychological Science, 11,* 512–534.

Melnikoff, D. E., & Bargh, J. A. (2018). The mythical number two. *Trends in Cognitive Sciences, 22,* 280–293.

Merabet, L. B., Connors, E. C., Halko, M. A., & Sanchez, J. (2012). Teaching the blind to find their way by playing video games. *Plos One, 7*(9), e44958.

Meredith, M. A., & Stein, B. E. (1986). Visual, auditory, and somatosensory convergence on cells in superior colliculus results in multisensory integration. *Journal of Neurophysiology, 56*(3), 640–662. https://doi.org/10.1152/jn.1986.56.3.640

Merritt, P. S., Cobb, A. R., & Cook, G. I. (2012). Sex differences in the cognitive effects of tobacco abstinence: A pilot study. *Experimental and Clinical Psychopharmacology, 20*(4), 258–263. https://doi.org/10.1037/a0027414

Metcalfe, J. (1986a). Feeling of knowing in memory and problem solving. *Journal of Experimental Psychology: Human Perception and Performance, 6*, 58–66.

Metcalfe, J. (1986b). Premonitions of insight predict impending error. *Journal of Experimental Psychology: Learning. Memory, and Cognition, 12*, 623–634.

Meyer, D. E., & Schvaneveldt, R. W. (1976). Meaning, memory structure, and mental processes. *Science, 192*, 27–33.

Mickle, T., & Fitch, A. (2019, April 17). Apple, qualcomm end legal feud. *The Wall Street Journal.*

Middlebrooks, C. D., Kerr, T., & Castel, A. D. (2017). Selectively distracted: Divided attention and memory for important information. *Psychological science, 28*(8), 1103–1115. https://doi.org/10.1177/0956797617702502

Mihal, W. L., & Barett, G. V. (1976). Individual differences in perceptual information processing and their relation to automobile accident involvement. *Journal of Applied Psychology, 61*, 229–233.

Mikels, J. A., & Reuter-Lorenz, P. A. (2019). Affective working memory: An integrative psychological construct. *Perspectives on Psychological Science, 14*, 543–559.

Milkman, K. L., Chugh, D., & Bazerman, M. H. (2009). How can decision making be improved? *Perspectives on Psychological Science, 4*, 379–383.

Milkman, K. L., Rogers, T., & Bazerman, M. H. (2008). Harnessing our inner angels and demons: What we have learned about want/should conflicts and how that knowledge can help us reduce short-sighted decision making. *Perspectives on Psychological Science, 3*, 324–338.

Miller, G. A. (1951). *Language and communication.* McGraw-Hill.

Miller, G. A. (1956). The magical number seven, plus or minus two: Some limits on our capacity for processing information. *Psychological Review, 63*, 81–97.

Miller, G. A. (2003). The cognitive revolution: A historical perspective. *TRENDS in Cognitive Sciences, 7*, 141–144.

Miller, G. A., Galanter, E., & Pribram, K. (1960). *Plans and the structure of behavior.* Holt, Rinehart & Winston.

Minda, J. P., & Smith, J. D. (2002). Comparing prototype-based and exemplar-based accounts of category learning and attentional allocation. *Journal of Experimental Psychology: Learning, Memory, & Cognition, 28*, 275–292.

Minsky, M. (1975). A framework for the representation of knowledge. In P. Winston (Ed.), *The psychology of computer vision.* McGraw-Hill.

Mirman, D., Landrigan, J.-F., & Britt, A. E. (2017). Taxonomic and thematic semantic systems. *Psychological Bulletin, 143*, 499–520.

Mitchell, D. B., & Richman, C. L. (1980). Confirmed reservations: Mental travel. *Journal of Experimental Psychology: Human Perception and Performance, 6*, 58–66.

Mitchell, K. J. (2018). *INNATE: How the wiring of our brains shapes who we are.* Princeton University Press.

Miyake, A. (2001). Individual differences in working memory: Introduction to the special section. *Journal of Experimental Psychology: General, 130*, 163–168.

Miyake, A., & Friedman, N. P. (2012). The nature and organization of individual differences in executive functions four general conclusions. *Current Directions in Psychological Science, 21*, 8–14.

Miyake, A., Just, M. A., & Carpenter, P. A. (1994). Working memory constraints on the resolution of lexical ambiguity: Maintaining multiple interpretations in neutral contexts. *Journal of Memory and Language, 33*, 175–202.

Miyatsu, T., Nguyan, K., & McDaniel, M. A. (2018). Five popular study strategies: Their pitfalls and optimal implementations. *Perspectives on Psychological Science, 13*, 390–407.

Montaldi, D., Spencer, T. J., Roberts, N., & Mayes, A. R. (2006). The neural system that mediates familiarity memory. *Hippocampus*, *16*(5), 504–520. https://doi.org/10.1002/hipo.20178

Montello, D. R. (2009). Cognitive geometry. In R. Kitchen & N. Thrift (Eds.), *International encyclopedia of human geography* (Vol. 2, pp. 160–166). Oxford Elsevier Science.

Moray, N. (1959). Attention in dichotic listening: Affective cues and the influence of instructions. *Quarterly Journal of Experimental Psychology*, *11*, 56–60.

Morgenstern, J. (2021, February 26). 'Father': Who are you? who am I? *The Wall Street Journal*, p. A10.

Morris, P. E., Jones, S., & Hampson, P. (1978). An imagery mnemonic for the learning of people's names. *British Journal of Psychology*, *69*, 335–336.

Morris, R., & Chakrabarty, A. (2019). Addressing autonomy in conceptual design. *AI Magazine*, *40*, 3–16.

Morrison, J. H., & Foote, S. L. (1986). Noradrenergic and serotoninergic innervation of cortical, thalamic, and tectal visual structures in old and new world monkeys. *The Journal of Comparative Neurology*, *243*(1), 117–138. https://doi.org/10.1002/cne.902430110

Moscovitch, M., & Craik, F. I. M. (1976). Depth of processing, retrieval cues, and uniqueness of encoding as factors in recall. *Journal of Verbal Learning and Verbal Behavior*, *15*, 447–458.

Mulligan, N. W. (1998). The role of attention during encoding in implicit and explicit memory. *Journal of Experimental Psychology. Learning, Memory, and Cognition*, *24*(1), 27–47. https://doi.org/10.1037//0278-7393.24.1.27

Murphy, G. (2003). *The big book of concepts*. MIT Press.

Murphy, G. L. (2016). Is there an exemplar theory of concepts? *Psychonomic Bulletin and Review*, *23*, 1035–1042.

Murphy, G. L., & Medin, D. L. (1985). The role of theories in conceptual coherence. *Psychological Review*, *92*, 289–316.

Murray, S., Krasich, K., Schooler, J. W., & Seli, P. (2020). What's in a task? Complications in the study of the task-unrelated-thought variety of mind wondering. *Perspectives on Psychological Science*, *15*, 572–588.

Musen, G., Shimamura, A. P., & Squire, L. R. (1990). Intact text-specific reading skill in amnesia. *Journal of Experimental Psychology: Learning, Memory, and Cognition*, *6*, 1068–1076.

Myers, J. L., O'Brien, E. J., Balota, D. A., & Toyofuku, M. L. (1984). Memory search without interference: The role of integration. *Cognitive Psychology*, *16*, 217–242.

Myers, N. E., Stokes, M. G., & Nobre, A. C. (2017). Prioritizing information during working memory: Beyond sustained internal attention. *Trends in Cognitive Sciences*, *21*, 449–461.

Nadel, L., & Moscovitch, M. (1997). Memory consolidation, retrograde amnesia and the hippocampal complex. *Current Opinion in Neurobiology*, *7*(2), 217–227. https://doi.org/10.1016/s0959-4388(97)80010-4

Nairne, J. S. (2002). Remembering over the short-term: The case against the standard model. *Annual Review of Psychology*, *53*, 53–81.

Nash-Webber, B. (1975). The role of semantics in automatic speech understanding. In D. G. Bobrow & A. Collins (Eds.), *Representation and understanding* (pp. 351–382). Academic Press.

Naveh-Benjamin, M. (1988). Recognition memory of spatial location information: Another failure to support automaticity. *Memory & Cognition*, *16*, 437–445.

Neisser, U. (1967). *Cognitive psychology*. Appleton-Century-Crofts.

Nelson, T. O. (1977). Repetition and depth of processing. *Journal of Verbal Learning and Verbal Behavior*, *16*, 151–171.

Nelson, T. O., Dunlosky, J., Graf, A., & Narens, L. (1994). Utilization of metacognitive judgments in the allocation of study during multitrial learning. *Psychological Science*, *5*, 207–213.

Nelson, T. O., & Narens, L. (1990). Metamemory: A theoretical framework and some new findings. In G. H. Bower (Ed.), *The psychology of learning and motivation* (Vol. 25). Academic Press.

Nelson, T. O., & Smith, E. E. (1972). Acquisition and forgetting of hierarchically organized information in longterm memory. *Journal of Experimental Psychology, 95,* 388–396.

Newcombe, N. S., & Shipley, T. P. (2015). Thinking about spatial thinking: New typology, new assessments. In J. S. Gero (Ed.), *Studying visual and spatial thinking for design creativity* (pp. 179–192). Springer.

Newell, A. (1990). *Unified theories of cognition.* Harvard University Press.

Newell, A., Shaw, J. C., & Simon, H. A. (1958a). Chess-playing problems and the problem of complexity. *IBM Journal of Research and Development, 2,* 320–335.

Newell, A., Shaw, J. C., & Simon, H. A. (1958b). Elements of a theory of human problem solving. *Psychological Review, 65,* 151–166.

Newell, A., & Simon, H. A. (1972). *Human problem solving.* Prentice-Hall.

Nickerson, R. S., & Adams, M. J. (1979). Long-term memory for a common object. *Cognitive Psychology, 11,* 287–307.

Nielsen, G. D., & Smith, E. E. (1973). Imaginal and verbal representations in short-term recognition of visual forms. *Journal of Experimental Psychology, 101,* 375–378.

Niles, I., & Pease, A. (2001). Toward a standard upper ontology. In C. Welty & B. Smith (Eds.), *Proceedings of the 2nd international conference on Formal Ontology in Information Systems (FOIS-2001)* (pp. 2–9). Association for Computing Machinery.

Noice, H. (1991). The role of explanations and plan recognition in the learning of theatrical scripts. *Cognitive Science, 15,* 425–460.

Nokes-Malach, T. J., & Mestre, J. P. (2013). Toward a model of transfer as sense-making. *Educational Psychologist, 48,* 184–207.

Norman, D. A. (1968). Toward a theory of memory and attention. *Psychological Review, 75,* 522–536.

Nosofsky, R. M. (1991). Tests of an exemplar model for relating perceptual classification and recognition memory. *Journal of Experimental Psychology: Human Perception and Performance, 17,* 3–27.

Nosofsky, R. M., & Johansen, M. K. (2000). Exemplar based accounts of "multiple-system" phenomena in perceptual organization. *Psychological Bulletin & Review, 7,* 375–402.

Nosofsky, R. M., Sanders, C. A., & McDaniel, M. A. (2018). A formal psychological model of classification applied to natural-science category learning. *Current Directions in Psychological Science, 27,* 129–135.

Novick, L. R. (1990). Representational transfer in problem solving. *Psychological Science, 1,* 128–132.

Novick, L. R., & Bassok, M. (2005). Problem solving. In K. J. Holyoak & R. G. Morrison (Eds.), *The Cambridge handbook of thinking and reasoning* (pp. 321–350). Cambridge University Press.

Novick, L. R., & Hmelo, C. E. (1994). Transferring symbolic representations across nonisomorphic problems. *Journal of Experimental Psychology: Learning, Memory, and Cognition, 20,* 1296–1321.

Novick, L. R., & Hurley, S. M. (2001). To matrix, network, or hierarchy: That is the question. *Cognitive Psychology, 42,* 158–216.

Nunez, R., Allen, M., Gao, R., Rigoli, C. M., Relaford-Doyle, J., & Semenuks, A. (2019). What happened to cognitive science? *Nature Human Behavior, 3,* 782–791.

O'Brien, E. J., & Cook, A. E. (2016). Coherence threshold in the continuity of processing: the RI-Val model of comprehension. *Discourse Processes, 53,* 326–338.

O'Donnell, A. M., Dansereau, D. F., & Hall, R. H. (2002). Knowledge Maps as Scaffolds for Cognitive Processing. *Educational Psychology Review, 14,* 71–86.

Ohlsson, S. (2011). *Deep learning: How the mind overrides experience.* Cambridge University Press.

Oleteanu, A.-M., & Falomir, Z. (2016). Object replacement and object composition in a creative cognitive system. Towards a computational solver of the Alternative Uses Test. *Cognitive Systems Research, 39,* 15–32.

Olivers, C. N. L. (2007). The time course of attention: It is better than we thought. *Current Directions in Psychological Science, 16*, 11–15.

Orasanu, J., & Connolly, T. (1993). The reinvention of decision making. In G. A. Klein, J. Orasanu, R. Calderwood, & C. E. Zsambok (Eds.), *Decision making in action: Models and methods* (pp. 3–20). Ablex.

O'Reilly, T., & McNamara, D. S. (2007). Reversing the reverse cohesion effect: Good texts can be better for strategic, high-knowledge readers. *Discourse Processes, 43*, 121–152.

Ormerod, T. C., MacGregor, J. N., & Chronicle, E. P. (2002). Dynamics and constraints in insight problem solving. *Journal of Experimental Psychology: Learning, Memory, and Cognition, 28*, 791–799.

Osiurak, F., & Heinke, D. (2018). Looking for intoolligence: A unified framework for the cognitive study of human tool use and technology. *American Psychologist, 73*, 169–185.

Osiurak, F., Lesourd, M., Navarro, J., & Reynaud, E. (2020). Technition: When tools come out of the closet. *Perspectives on Psychological Science, 15*, 880–897.

Otgaar, H., Howe, M. L., Patihis, L., Merckelbach, H., Lynn, S. J., Lilienfeld, S. O., & Loftus, E. F. (2019). The return of the repressed: The persistent and problematic claims of long-forgotten trauma. *Perspectives on Psychological Science, 14*, 1072–1095.

Otgaar, H., Muris, P., Howe, M. L., & Merckelbach, H. (2017). What drives false memories in psychopathology? A case for associative activation. *Clinical Psychological Science, 5*, 1048–1069.

Paivio, A. (1969). Mental imagery in associative learning and memory. *Psychological Review, 76*, 241–263.

Paivio, A. (1971). *Imagery and verbal processes.* Holt, Rinehart & Winston.

Paivio, A. (1975). Coding distinctions and repetition effects in memory. In G. H. Bower (Ed.), *Psychology of learning and motivation* (Vol. 9, pp. 179–214). Academic Press.

Paivio, A. (2008). Looking at reading comprehension through the lens of neuroscience. In C. C. Block & S. R. Parris (Eds.), *Comprehension instruction: Research-based best practices* (pp. 101–113). Guilford Press.

Paivio, A., Smythe, P. E., & Yuille, J. C. (1968). Imagery versus meaningfulness of nouns in paired associate learning. *Canadian Journal of Psychology, 22*, 427–441.

Paller, K. A., Creery, J. D., & Schechtman, E. (2021). Memory and sleep: How sleep cognition can change the waking mind for the better. *Annual Review of Psychology, 72*, 123–150.

Pan, Z., Grovu, R. C., Cha, D. S., Carmona, N. E., Subramaniapillai, M., Shekotikhina, M., Rong, C., Lee, Y., & McIntyre, R. S. (2017). Pharmacological treatment of cognitive symptoms in major depressive disorder. *CNS & Neurological Disorders Drug Targets, 16*(8), 891–899. https://doi.org/10.2174/187152731666617 0919115100

Papies, E. K., Barsalou, L. W., & Rusz, D. (2020). Understanding desire for food and drink: A grounded-cognition approach. *Current Directions in Psychological Science, 29*(2), 193–198.

Paquette, L., & Kida, T. (1988). Effect of decision strategy and task complexity on decision performance. *Organizational Behavior and Human Decision Processes, 41*, 128–142.

Parasuraman, R. (2011). Neuroergonomics: Brain, cognition, and performance at work. *Current Directions in Psychological Science, 20*, 181–186.

Parker, E. S., Cahill, L., & McGaugh, J. L. (2006). A case study of unusual autobiographical memory. *Neurocase, 12*, 35–49.

Parnamets, P., Shuster, A., Reinero, D. A., & Van Bavel, J. J. (2020). A value-based framework for understanding cooperation. *Current Directions in Psychological Science, 29*(3), 227–234.

Pashler, H. (1994). Graded capacity-sharing in dual task interference? *Journal of Experimental Psychology: Human Perception and Performance, 20*, 1–13.

Pashler, H. E. (1998). *The psychology of attention*. MIT Press.

Pashler, H., Rohrer, D., Cepeda, N. J., & Carpenter, S. K. (2007). Enhancing learning and retarding forgetting: Choices and consequences. *Psychonomic Bulletin & Review, 14*, 187–193.

Payne, J. W. (1973). Alternative approaches to decision making under risk. *Psychological Bulletin, 80*, 439–453.

Payne, J. W. (1976). Task complexity and contingent processing in decision making: An information search and protocol analysis. *Organizational Behavior and Human Performance, 16*, 366–387.

Payne, J. W., Bettman, J. R., & Johnson, E. J. (1992). Behavioral decision research: A constructive processing perspective. *Annual Review of Psychology, 43*, 87–131.

Payne, J. W., Bettman, J. R., & Johnson, E. J. (1993). *The adaptive decision maker*. Cambridge University Press.

Pearson, J., & Keogh, R. (2019). Redefining visual working memory: A cognitive-strategy, brain-region approach. *Current Directions in Psychological Science, 28*, 266–273.

Pearson, J., Naselaris, T., Holmes, E. A., & Kosslyn, S. M. (2015). Mental imagery: Functional mechanisms and clinical applications. *Trends in Cognitive Sciences, 19*, 590–602.

Pease, A. (2011). *Ontology: A practical guide*. Articulate Software Press.

Pecher, D. (2017). Curb your embodiment. *Topics in Cognitive Science, 10*, 501–517.

Pecher, D., Zeelenbreg, R., & Barsalou, L. W. (2003). Verifying different- modality properties for concepts produces switching costs. *Psychological Science, 14*, 119–124.

Pellegrino, J. W., Chudowsky, N., & Glaser, R. (2001). *Knowing what students know*. National Academy Press.

Peltier, C., & Vannest, K. J. (2017). A meta-analysis of schema instruction on the problem-solving performance of elementary school students. *Review of Educational Research, 20*, 1–22.

Peng, P., Wang, T., Wang, C., & Lin, X. (2019). A meta-analysis on the relation between fluid intelligence and reading/mathematics: Effects of task, age, and social economic status. *Psychological Bulletin, 145*, 189–236.

Pennington, N., & Hastie, R. (1988). Explanation based decision making: The effects of memory structure on judgment. *Journal of Experimental Psychology: Learning, Memory, and Cognition, 14*, 521–533.

Pennington, N., & Hastie, R. (1991). A cognitive theory of juror decision making: The story model. *Cardozo Law Review, 13*, 519–557.

Pennycook, G., Fugelsang, J. A., & Koehler, D. J. (2015). Everyday consequences of analytic thinking. *Current Directions in Psychological Science, 24*, 425–432.

Pennycook, G., McPhetres, J., Zhang, Y., Lu, J. G., & Rand, D. G. (2020). Fighting COVID-19 misinformation on social media: Experimental evidence for a scalable accuracy-nudge intervention. *Psychological Science, 31*, 770–780.

Pennycook, G., & Rand, D. G. (2019). Lazy, not biased: Susceptibility to partisan fake news is better explained by lack of reasoning than by motivated reasoning. *Cognition, 188*, 39–50.

Perfetti, C. A., Beverly, S., Bell, L., Rodgers, K., & Faux, R. (1987). Comprehending newspaper headlines. *Journal of Memory and Language, 26*, 692–713.

Perfetto, G. A., Bransford, J. D., & Franks, J. J. (1983). Constraints on access in a problem solving context. *Memory & Cognition, 11*, 24–31.

Peterson, L. R., & Peterson, M. J. (1959). Short-term retention of individual verbal items. *Journal of Experimental Psychology, 58*, 193–198.

Peterson, M. A., & Rhodes, G. (Eds.). (2003). *Perception of faces, objects, and scenes: Analytic and holistic processes*. Oxford University Press.

Phelps, E. A. (2004). Human emotion and memory: Interactions of the amygdala and hippocampal complex. *Current Opinion in Neurobiology, 14*(2), 198–202. https://doi.org/10.1016/j.conb.2004.03.015

Phelps, E. A., & Sharot, T. (2008). How (and why) emotion enhances the subjective sense of recollection. *Current Directions in Psychological Science, 17,* 147–152.

Pickering, M. J., & Gambi, C. (2018). Predicting while comprehending language: A theory and review. *Psychological Bulletin, 144,* 1002–1044.

Pickering, M. J., & Garrod, S. (2007). Do people use language production to make predictions during comprehension? *TRENDS in the Cognitive Sciences, 11,* 105–110.

Pinker, S. (1994). *The language instinct.* William Morrow.

Pinker, S. (1997). *How the mind works.* Norton.

Pinker, S. (1999). *Words and rules.* Harper-Collins.

Plass, J. L., Moreno, R., & Brunken, R. (Eds.). (2010). *Cognitive load theory.* Cambridge University Press.

Pollatsek, A., Fisher, D. L., & Pradhan, A. (2006). Identifying and remedying failures of selective attention in younger drivers. *Current Directions in Psychological Science, 15,* 255–259.

Pollatsek, A., & Rayner, K. (1989). Reading. In M. I. Posner (Ed.), *Foundations of cognitive science* (pp. 401–436). MIT Press.

Pollatsek, A., Romoser, M. R. E., & Fisher, D. L. (2012). Identifying and remediating failures of selective attention in older drivers. *Current Directions in Psychological Science, 21,* 3–7.

Polson, P. G., & Jeffries, R. (1985). Instruction in general problem-solving skills: An analysis of four approaches. In J. W. Segal, S. F. Chipman, & R. Glaser (Eds.), *Thinking and learning skills* (Vol. 1, pp. 417–458). Erlbaum.

Polya, G. (1962). *Mathematical discovery* (Vol. 1). Wiley.

Posner, M. I., DiGirolamo, G. J., & Fernandez-Duque, D. (1997). Brain mechanisms and cognitive skills. *Consciousness and Cognition, 6,* 267–290.

Posner, M. I., & Keele, S. W. (1968). On the genesis of abstract ideas. *Journal of Experimental Psychology, 77,* 353–363.

Posner, M. I., & Petersen, S. E. (1990). The attention system of the human brain. *Annual Review of Neuroscience, 13*(1), 25–42. https://doi.org/10.1146/annurev.ne.13.030190.000325

Posner, M. I., & Rothbart, M. K. (1994). Constructing neuronal theories of the mind. In C. Koch & J. Davis (Eds.), *Large scale neuronal theories of the brain* (pp. 183–199). MIT Press.

Posner, M. I., & Rothbart, M. K. (2005). Influencing brain networks: Implications for education. *TRENDS in Cognitive Sciences, 9,* 99–103.

Posner, M. I., & Rothbart, M. K. (2007). Research on attention networks as a model for the integration of psychological science. *Annual Review of Psychology, 58*(1), 1–23. https://doi.org/10.1146/annurev.psych.58.110405.085516

Posner, M. I., & Snyder, C. R. R. (1975). Attention and cognitive control. In R. L. Solso (Ed.), *Information processing and cognition: The Loyola Symposium* (pp. 58–85). Erlbaum.

Postle, B. R. (2006). Working memory as an emergent property of the mind and brain. *Neuroscience, 139,* 23–38.

Postman, L., & Phillips, L. W. (1965). Short term temporal changes in free recall. *Quarterly Journal of Experimental Psychology, 17,* 132–138.

Preckel, F., Golle, J., Grabner, R., Jarvin, L., Kozbet, A., & Worrell, F. C. (2020). Talent development in achievement domains: A psychological framework for within-and cross-domain research. *Perspectives in Psychological Science, 15,* 691–722.

Pretz, J. E. (2008). Intuition versus analysis: Strategy and experience in complex everyday problem solving. *Memory & Cognition, 36,* 554–566.

Prinz, A., Golke, S., & Wittwer, J. (2020). To what extent do situation-model-approach interventions improve relative metacomprehension accuracy? Meta-analytic insights. *Educational Psychology Review, 32,* 917–949.

Proffitt, D. R. (2006). Embodied perception and the economy of action. *Perspectives on Psychological Science, 1,* 110–121.

Ptak, R., Lazeyras, F., Di Pietro, M., Schnider, A., & Simon, S. R. (2014). Visual object agnosia is associated with a breakdown of object-selective responses in the lateral occipital cortex. *Neuropsychologia, 60,* 10–20.   https://doi.org/10.1016/j.neuropsychologia.2014.05.009

Pylyshyn, Z. W. (1973). What the mind's eye tells the mind's brain: A critique of mental imagery. *Psychological Bulletin, 80,* 1–24.

Pylyshyn, Z. W. (1981). The imagery debate: Analogue media versus tacit knowledge. *Psychological Review, 88,* 16–45.

Quandt, L. C., & Chatterjee, A. (2015). Rethinking actions: Implementation and association. *WIREs Cognitive Science, 6,* 483–490.

Radvansky, G. A., & Copeland, D. E. (2001). Working memory and situation model updating. *Memory & Cognition, 29,* 1073–1080.

Radvansky, G. A., & Zacks, R. T. (1991). Mental models and fact retrieval. *Journal of Experimental Psychology: Learning, Memory, and Cognition, 17,* 940–953.

Rahwan, I., Cebrian, M., Obradovich, N., Bongard, J., Bonnefon, J.-F., Breazeal, C., Crandall, J. W., Christakis, N. A., Couzin, I. D., Jackson, M. O., Jennings, N. R., Kamar, E., Kloumann, I. M., Larochelle, H., Lazer, D., McElreath, R., Mislove, A., Parkes, D. C., Pentland, A. S., . . . Wellman, M . (2019). Machine behavior. *Nature, 568,* 477–486.

Randel, J. M., Pugh, H. L., & Reed, S. K. (1996). Differences in expert and novice situation awareness in naturalistic decision making. *International Journal of Human-Computer Studies, 45,* 579–597.

Rasch, B., Buchel, C., Gais, S., & Born, J. (2007). Odor cues during slow-wave sleep prompt memory consolidation. *Science, 315,* 1426–1429.

Rau, M. A. (2020). Comparing multiple theories about learning with physical and virtual representations: Conflicting or complementary effects? *Educational Psychology Review, 32,* 297–325.

Raven, J. C. (1962). *Advanced progressive matrices, Set II.* H. K. Lewis. (Distributed in the United States by the Psychological Corporation, San Antonio, TX)

Raz, N., & Levin, N. (2017). Neuro-visual rehabilitation. *Journal of Neurology, 264,* 1051–1058.

Read, J. D., & Bruce, D. (1982). Longitudinal tracking of difficult memory retrievals. *Cognitive Psychology, 14,* 280–300.

Redelmeier, D. A., & Tibshirani, R. J. (1997). Association between cellular telephone calls and motor vehicle collisions. *The New England Journal of Medicine, 336,* 453–458.

Reder, L., & Kusbit, G. (1991). Locus of the Moses illusion: Imperfect encoding, retrieval, or match? *Journal of Memory and Language, 30,* 385–406.

Reder, L. M., & Anderson, J. R. (1980). Partial resolution of the paradox of interference: The role of integrating knowledge. *Cognitive Psychology, 12,* 447–472.

Reder, L. M., & Ross, B. H. (1983). Integrated knowledge in different tasks: The role of retrieval strategy on fan effects. *Journal of Experimental Psychology: Learning, Memory, and Cognition, 9,* 55–72.

Reed, S. K. (1972). Pattern recognition and categorization. *Cognitive Psychology, 3,* 382–407.

Reed, S. K. (2016). The structure of ill-structured (and well-structured) problems revisited. *Educational Psychology Review, 28,* 691–716.

Reed, S. K. (2018). Combining physical, virtual, and mental actions and objects. *Educational Psychology Review, 30,* 1091–1113.

Reed, S. K. (2019). Building bridges between AI and cognitive psychology. *AI Magazine, 40,* 17–28.

Reed, S. K. (2020a). Searching for the big pictures. *Perspectives on Psychological Science, 15,* 817–830.

Reed, S. K. (2020b). *Cognitive skills that you need for the 21st century.* Oxford University Press.

Reed, S. K. (2021). *Thinking visually* (2nd ed.). Routledge.

Reed, S. K., Ernst, G. W., & Banerji, R. (1974). The role of analogy in transfer between similar problem states. *Cognitive Psychology, 6,* 436–450.

Reed, S. K., & Friedman, M. P. (1973). Perceptual vs. conceptual categorization. *Memory & Cognition, 1,* 157–163.

Reed, S. K., Hock, H., & Lockhead, R. (1983). Tacit knowledge and the effect of pattern configuration on mental scanning. *Memory & Cognition, 11,* 137–143.

Reed, S. K., & Johnsen, J. A. (1975). Detection of parts in patterns and images. *Memory & Cognition, 3,* 569–575.

Reed, S. K., & Pease, A. (2015). A framework for constructing cognition ontologies using WordNet, FrameNet, and SUMO. *Cognitive Systems Research, 33,* 122–144.

Reed, S. K., & Vallacher, R. R. (2020). A comparison of information processing and dynamical systems perspectives on problem solving. *Thinking & Reasoning, 26,* 254–290.

Reeves, L. M., & Weisberg, R. W. (1994). The role of content and abstract information in analogical transfer. *Psychological Bulletin, 115,* 381–400.

Rehder, B., & Ross, B. H. (2001). Abstract coherent categories. *Journal of Experimental Psychology: Learning, Memory, and Cognition, 27,* 1261–1275.

Reicher, G. M. (1969). Perceptual recognition as a function of meaningfulness of stimulus material. *Journal of Experimental Psychology, 81,* 275–280.

Reitman, J. S. (1974). Without surreptitious rehearsal, information in shortterm memory decays. *Journal of Verbal Learning and Verbal Behavior, 13,* 365–377.

Reitman, J. S., & Bower, G. H. (1973). Storage and later recognition of exemplars of concepts. *Cognitive Psychology, 4,* 194–206.

Renoult, L., Irish, M., Moscovitch, M., & Rugg, M. D. (2019). From knowing to remembering: The semantic-episodic distinction. *Trends in Cognitive Sciences, 23,* 1041–1056.

Revelle, W., Dworak, E., & Condon, D. (2020). Cognitive ability in everyday life: The utility of open source measures. *Current Directions in Psychological Science, 29,* 358–363.

Reyna, V. F. (2018). When your rational biases are smart: A fuzzy-trace theory of complex decision making. *Journal of Intelligence, 6(29),* 1–16.

Reyna, V. F. (2020). A scientific theory of gist communication and misinformation resistance, with implications for health, education, and policy. *PNAS Proceedings of the National Academy of Sciences of the United States of America, 118,* e1912441117.

Reyna, V. F., & Brainerd, C. J. (1995). Fuzzy-trace theory: An interim synthesis. *Learning and Individual Differences, 7,* 1–75.

Rhodes, G., Brennan, S., & Carey, S. (1987). Identification and ratings of caricatures: Implications for mental representations of faces. *Cognitive Psychology, 19,* 473–497.

Rhodes, M. G., & Castel, A. D. (2008). Memory predictions are influenced by perceptual information: Evidence for metacognitive illusions. *Journal of Experimental Psychology: General, 137(4),* 615–625.

Rhodes, M. G., & Tauber, S. K. (2011). The influence of delaying judgments of learning on metacognitive accuracy: A meta-analytic review. *Psychological Bulletin, 137,* 131–148.

Richardson-Klavehn, A., & Bjork, R. A. (1988). Measures of memory. *Annual Review of Psychology, 39,* 475–543.

Richey, J. E., & Nokes-Malach, T. J. (2015). Comparing four instructional techniques for promoting robust knowledge. *Educational Psychology Review, 27,* 181–218.

Richmond, L. L., & Zacks, J. M. (2017). Constructing experience: Event models from perception to action. *Trends in Cognitive Sciences, 21,* 962–980.

Ries, E. (2011). *The lean startup: How constant innovation creates radically successful businesses.* Penguin UK.

Rips, L. J. (2001). Necessity and natural categories. *Psychological Bulletin, 127,* 827–852.

Rips, L. J., Shoben, E. J., & Smith, E. E. (1973). Semantic distance and the verification of semantic relations. *Journal of Verbal Leaning and Verbal Behavior, 12,* 1–20.

Risko, E. F., & Dunn, T. L. (2015). Storing information in the world: Metacognition and cognitive offloading in a short-term memory task. *Consciousness and Cognition, 36,* 61–74.

Risko, E. F., & Gilbert, S. J. (2016). Cognitive offloading. *Trends in Cognitive Sciences, 20,* 676–688.

Ritter, F. E., Tehranchi, F., & Oury, J. D. (2019). ACT-R: A cognitive architecture for modeling cognition. *Wiley Interdisciplinary Reviews: Cognitive Science, 10,* e1488.

Ritter, S., Anderson, J. R., Koedinger, K. K., & Corbett, A. (2007). Cognitive Tutor: Applied research to mathematics education. *Psychonomic Bulletin & Review, 14,* 249–255.

Rittle-Johnson, B., & Loehr, A. M. (2017). Eliciting explanations: Constraints on when self-explanation aids learning. *Psychonomic Bulletin & Review, 24,* 1501–1510.

Robins, R. W., Gosling, S. D., & Craik, K. H. (1999). An empirical analysis of trends in psychology. *American Psychologist, 54,* 117–128.

Robson, D. (2019). *The intelligence trap: Why smart people make dumb mistakes.* W. W. Norton & Company.

Rock, P. L., Roiser, J. P., Riedel, W. J., & Blackwell, A. D. (2013). Cognitive impairment in depression: A systematic review and meta-analysis. *Psychological Medicine, 44*(10), 2029–2040. https://doi.org/10.1017/s0033291713002535

Rockoff, J. D. (2021, January 12). Lilly Alzheimer's drug helped patients in small trial. *The Wall Street Journal,* p. A3.

Roediger, H. L. (1990). Implicit memory: Retention without remembering. *American Psychologist, 45,* 1043–1056.

Roediger, H. L., & Butler, A. C. (2011). The critical role of retrieval practice in long-term retention. *Trends in Cognitive Sciences, 15,* 20–26.

Roediger, H. L., III., & Karpicke, J. D. (2006). Test-enhanced learning: Taking memory tests improves long-term retention. *Psychological Science, 17,* 249–255.

Roediger, H. L., III., & Karpicke, J. D. (2018). Reflections on the resurgence of the testing effect. *Perspectives on Psychological Science, 13,* 236–241.

Roediger, H. L., III., & McDermott, K. B. (1995). Creating false memories: Remembering words not presented in lists. *Journal of Experimental Psychology: Learning, Memory, and Cognition, 21,* 803–814.

Rogers, T. T., & McClelland, J. L. (2004). *Semantic cognition: A parallel distributed processing approach.* MIT Press.

Rogers, T. T., & Patterson, K. (2007). Object categorization: Reversals and explanations of the basic-level advantage. *Journal of Experimental Psychology: General, 136,* 451–469.

Roland, P. E., & Friberg, L. (1985). Localization of cortical areas activated by thinking. *Journal of Neurophysiology, 53,* 1219–1243.

Roll, I., Aleven, V., McLaren, B. M., & Koedinger, K. R. (2011). Improving students' help-seeking skills using metacognitive feedback in an intelligent tutoring system. *Learning and Instruction, 21,* 267–280.

Rosanova, M., Casarotto, S., Pigorinni, A., Canali, P., Casali, A. G., & Massimini, M. (2012). Combining transcranial magnetic stimulation with electroencephalography to study human cortical excitability and effective connectivity. *Neuromethods, 67,* 435–457.

Rosch, E. (1973). Natural categories. *Cognitive Psychology, 4,* 328–350.

Rosch, E. (1975). Cognitive representations of semantic categories. *Journal of Experimental Psychology: General, 3,* 192–233.

Rosch, E., & Mervis, C. B. (1975). Family resemblances: Studies in the internal structure of categories. *Cognitive Psychology, 7,* 573–605.

Rosch, E., Mervis, C. B., Gray, W. D., Johnsen, D. M., & Boyes-Braem, P. (1976). Basic objects in natural categories. *Cognitive Psychology, 8,* 382–440.

Rose, N. S. (2020). The dynamic processing model of working memory. *Current Directions in Psychological Science, 29*(4), 378–387.

Rose, N. S., Myerson, J. L., Roediger, L., & Hale, S. (2010). Similarities and differences between working memory and long-term memory: Evidence from the levels-of-processing span task. *Journal of Experimental Psychology: Learning, Memory, and Cognition, 365,* 471–483.

Rosenbaum, D. A., Chapman, K. M., Weigelt, M., Weiss, D. J., & van der Wel, R. (2012). Cognition, action, and object manipulation. *Psychological Bulletin, 138,* 924–946.

Rosso, B.D. (2014). Creativity and constraints: Exploring the role of constraints in the creative processes of research and developmental teams. *Organization Studies, 35,* 551–585.

Ross, B. H. (1984). Remindings and their effects in learning a cognitive skill. *Cognitive Psychology, 16,* 371–416.

Ross, B. H. (1996). Category learning as problem solving. In D. L. Medin (Ed.), *The psychology of learning and motivation* (Vol. 35, pp. 165–192). Academic Press.

Ross, B. H., & Kennedy, P. T. (1990). Generalizing from the use of earlier examples in problem solving. *Journal of Experimental Psychology: Learning, Memory, and Cognition, 16,* 42–55.

Rubenstein, L. D., Callan, G. L., & Ridgley, L. M. (2018). Anchoring the creative process within a self-regulated learning framework: Inspiring assessment methods and future research. *Educational Psychology Review, 30,* 921–945.

Rubin, D. C. (Ed.). (1996). *Remembering our past.* Cambridge University Press.

Rubin, D. C. (2006). The basic-systems model of episodic memory. *Perspectives in Psychological Science, 1,* 277–311.

Ruddell, R. B., & Unrau, N. J. (Eds.). (2004). *Theoretical models and processes of reading* (5th ed.). International Reading Association.

Rudoy, J. D., Voss, J. L., Westerberg, C. E., & Paller, K. A. (2009). Strengthening individual memories by reactivating them during sleep. *Science, 326,* p. 1079.

Rumelhart, D. E. (1980). Schemata: The building blocks of cognition. In R. Spiro, B. Bruce, & W. Brewer (Eds.), *Theoretical issues in reading comprehension* (pp. 33–58). Erlbaum.

Rumelhart, D. E., Hinton, G. E., & McClelland, J. L. (1986). A general framework for parallel distributed processing. In D. E. Rumelhart, J. L. McClelland, & the PDP Research Group (Eds.), *Parallel distributed processing: Explorations in the microstructure of cognition* (Vol. 1, pp. 45–76). Bradford.

Rumelhart, D. E., & McClelland, J. L. (1982). An interactive-activation model of context effects in letter perception: Part 2. The contextual enhancement and some tests and extensions of the model. *Psychological Review, 89,* 60–94.

Runco, M. A. (2004). Creativity. *Annual Review of Psychology, 55,* 657–687.

Rundus, D. (1971). Analysis of rehearsal processes in free recall. *Journal of Experimental Psychology, 89,* 63–77.

Saariluoma, P. (1992). Visuospatial and articulatory interference in chess players' information intake. *Applied Cognitive Psychology, 6,* 77–89.

Sachs, J. S. (1967). Recognition memory for syntactic and semantic aspects of connected discourse. *Perception & Psychophysics, 2,* 437–442.

Sack, A. T., van de Ven, V. G., Etschenberg, S., & Linden, D. E. (2005). Enhanced vividness of imagery as a trait marker of schizophrenia. *Schizophrenia Bulletin, 31,* 1–8.

Sacks, O. (1985). *The man who mistook his wife for a hat.* Gerald Duckworth.

Sadoski, M. (2008). Dual coding theory: Reading comprehension and beyond. In C. C. Block & S. R. Parris (Eds.), *Comprehension Instruction: Research-based best practices* (pp. 38–49). Guilford Press.

Salerno, J. M., & Diamond, S. S. (2010). The promise of a cognitive perspective on jury deliberation. *Psychonomic Bulletin & Review, 17,* 174–179.

Samson, P. J. (2010). Deliberate engagement of laptops in large lecture classes to improve attentiveness and engagement. *Computers in Education, 20*(2), 22–37.

Sana, F., Weston, T., & Cepeda, N. J. (2013). Laptop multitasking hinders classroom learning for both users and nearby peers. *Computers & Education, 62*, 24–31. https://doi.org/10.1016/j.compedu.2012.10.003

Sanders, A. F., & Schroots, J. J. F. (1969). Cognitive categories and memory span: III. Effects of similarity on recall. *Quarterly Journal of Experimental Psychology, 21*, 21–28.

Sanders, K. E. G., Osburn, S., & Paller, K. A. (2019). Targeted memory reactivation during sleep improves next-day problem-solving. *Psychological Science, 30*, 1616–1626.

Santangelo, V., Cavallina, C., Colucci, P., Santori, A., Macri, S., McGaugh, J. L., & Campolongo, P. (2018). Enhanced brain activity associated with memory access in highly superior autobiographical memory. *Proceedings of the National Academy of Sciences, 115*(30), 7795–7800.

Saulsman, L. M., Ji, J. L., & McEvoy, P. M. (2019). The essential role of mental imagery in cognitive behavior therapy: What is old is new again. *Australian Psychologist, 54*(4), 1–8.

Saunders, G., & Klemming, F. (2003). Integrating technology into a traditional learning environment. *Active Learning in Higher Education, 4*(1), 74–86.

Sawyer, R. K. (2006). *Explaining creativity: The science of human innovation*. Oxford University Press.

Schacter, D. L. (1987). Implicit memory: History and current status. *Journal of Experimental Psychology: Learning, Memory, and Cognition, 13*, 501–518.

Schacter, D. L. (1996). *Searching for memory: The brain, the mind, and the past*. Basic Books.

Schacter, D. L. (2001). *The seven sins of memory*. Houghton Mifflin.

Schacter, D. L., & Madore, K. P. (2016). Remembering the past and imagining the future: Identifying and enhancing the contribution of episodic memory. *Memory Studies, 9*, 245–255.

Schank, R., & Abelson, R. (1977). *Scripts, goals, and understanding*. Erlbaum.

Scheiter, K., Ackerman, R., & Hoogerheide, V. (2020). Looking at mental effort appraisals through a metacogntive lens: Are they biased? *Educational Psychology Review, 32*, 1003–1027.

Schindler, S. E., Bollinger, J. G., Ovod, V., Mawuenyega, K. G., Li, Y., Gordon, B. A., Holtzman, D. M., Morris, J. C., Benzinger, T. L. S., Xiong, C., Fagan, A. M., & Bateman, R. J. (2019). High-precision plasma β-amyloid 42/40 predicts current and future brain amyloidosis. *Neurology, 93*, e1647–e1659.

Schmidt, S. R. (1991). Can we have a distinctive theory of memory? *Memory & Cognition, 19*, 523–542.

Schneider, S. L., & Shanteau, J. (2003). *Emerging perspectives on judgment and decision research*. Cambridge University Press.

Schneider, V. I., Healy, A. F., & Gesi, A. T. (1991). The role of phonetic processes in letter detection: A reevaluation. *Journal of Memory and Language, 30*, 294–318.

Schneider, W., & Graham, D. J. (1992). Introduction to connectionist modeling in education. *Educational Psychologist, 27*, 513–530.

Schneider, W., & Shiffrin, R. M. (1977). Controlled and automatic human information processing: I. Detection, search, and attention. *Psychological Review, 84*, 1–66.

Schroeder, N. L., Nesbit, J. C., Anguiano, C. J., & Adesope, O. O. (2018). Studying and constructing concept maps: A meta-analysis. *Educational Psychology Review, 30*, 431–455.

Schurer, T., Opitz, B., & Schubert, T. (2020). Working memory capacity but not prior knowledge impact on readers' attention and text comprehension. *Frontiers in Education, 5*, 1–12.

Schwanenflugel, P. J., & Shoben, E. J. (1985). The influence of sentence constraint on the scope of facilitation for upcoming words. *Journal of Memory and Language, 24*, 232–252.

Schwartz, B. L. (2002). *Tip-of-the-tongue states: Phenomenology, mechanism, and lexical retrieval*. Erlbaum.

Schwartz, B. L. (2010). The effects of emotion on tip-of-the-tongue states. *Psychonomic Bulletin & Review, 17*, 82–87.

Schwartz, B. L., & Metcalfe, J. (2011). Tip-of-the-tongue (TOT) states: Retrieval, behavior, and experience. *Memory & Cognition*, *39*, 737–749.

Schwartz, D. L., & Bransford, J. D. (1998). A time for telling. *Cognition and Instruction*, *16*, 475–522.

Schweickert, R., Guentert, L., & Hersberger, L. (1990). Phonological similarity, pronunciation rate, and memory span. *Psychological Science*, *1*, 74–77.

Schweizer, S., Satpute, A. B., Atzil, S., Field, A. P., Hitchcock, C., Black, M., Barrett, L. F., & Dalgleish, T. (2019). The impact of affective information on working memory: A pair of meta-analytic reviews of behavioral and neuroimaging evidence. *Psychological Bulletin*, *145*, 566–609.

Scoville, W. B., & Milner, B. (1957). Loss of recent memory after bilateral hippocampal lesions. *Journal of Neurology, Neurosurgery, and Psychiatry*, *20*(1), 11–21. https://doi.org/10.1136/jnnp.20.1.11

Sedikides, C., & Skowronski, J. J. (2020). In human memory, good can be stronger than bad. *Current Directions in Psychological Science*, *29*, 86–91.

Sedlmeier, P., & Gigerenzer, G. (2001). Teaching Bayesian reasoning in less than two hours. *Journal of Experimental Psychology: General*, *130*, 380–400.

Seidenberg, M. S. (1993). Connectionist models and cognitive theory. *Psychological Science*, *4*, 228–235.

Seidenberg, M. S., Waters, G. S., Sanders, M., & Langer, P. (1984). Pre and postlexical loci of contextual effects on word recognition. *Memory & Cognition*, *12*, 315–328.

Sejnowski, T. J. (2018). *The deep learning revolution*. The MIT Press.

Sejnowski, T. J., & Rosenberg, C. R. (1987). Parallel networks that learn to pronounce English text. *Complex Systems*, *1*, 145–168.

Seli, P., Kane, M. J., Smallwood, J., Schachter, D. L., Maillet, D., Schooler, J. W., & Smilek, D. (2018). Mind-wandering as a natural kind: A family-resemblances view. *Trends in Cognitive Sciences*, *22*, 479–490.

Seli, P., Risko, E. F., Smilek, D., & Schachter, D. L. (2016). Mind-wandering with and without intention. *Trends in Cognitive Sciences*, *20*, 605–617.

Semb, G. B., & Ellis, J. A. (1994). Knowledge taught in school: What is remembered? *Review of Educational Research*, *64*, 253–286.

Seufert, T. (2020). Building bridges between self-regulation and cognitive load—An invitation for a broad and differentiated approach. *Educational Psychology Review*, *32*, 1151–1162.

Sha, P., & Miyake, A. (Eds.). (2005). *The Cambridge handbook of visuospatial thinking*. Cambridge University Press.

Sharps, M. J., & Wertheimer, M. (2000). Gestalt perspectives on cognitive science and on experimental psychology. *Review of General Psychology*, *4*, 315–336.

Shaughnessy, J. J. (1981). Memory monitoring accuracy and modification of rehearsal strategies. *Journal of Verbal Learning and Verbal Behavior*, *20*, 216–230.

Shepard, R. N. (1967). Recognition memory for words, sentences, and pictures. *Journal of Verbal Learning and Verbal Behavior*, *6*, 156–163.

Shepard, R. N. (1988). The imagination of the scientist. In K. Egan & D. Nadaner (Eds.), *Imagination and education* (pp. 153–185). Teachers College Press.

Shepard, R. N., & Metzler, J. (1971). Mental rotation of three-dimensional objects. *Science*, *171*, 701–703.

Shields, G. S., Bonner, J. C., & Moons, W. G. (2015). Does cortisol influence core executive functions? A meta-analysis of acute cortisol administration effects on working memory, inhibition, and set-shifting. *Psychoneuroendocrinology*, *58*, 91–103. https://doi.org/10.1016/j.psyneuen.2015.04.017

Shiffrin, R. M. (1988). Attention. In R. C. Atkinson, R. J. Hernstein, G. Lindzey, & R. D. Luce (Eds.), *Stevens' handbook of experimental psychology* (pp. 731–811). Wiley.

Shiffrin, R. M., & Schneider, W. (1977). Controlled and automatic human information processing: II. Perceptual learning, automatic attending, and a general theory. *Psychological Review, 84,* 127–190.

Shipstead, Z., Harrison, T. L., & Engle, R. W. (2016). Working memory capacity and fluid intelligence: Maintenance and disengagement. *Perspectives on Psychological Science, 11,* 771–799.

Shulman, H. G. (1971). Similarity effects in short-term memory. *Psychological Bulletin, 75,* 399–415.

Sidney, P. G., Hattikudur, S., & Alibali, M. W. (2015). How do contrasting cases and self-explanation promote learning? Evidence from fraction division. *Learning and Instruction, 40,* 29–38.

Silver, E. A. (1981). Recall of mathematical problem information: Solving related problems. *Journal for Research in Mathematics Education, 12,* 54–64.

Simon, H. A. (1957). *Models of man.* Wiley.

Simon, H. A. (1973). The structure of ill-structured problems. *Artificial Intelligence, 4,* 181–201.

Simon, H. A. (1974). How big is a chunk? *Science, 183,* 482–488.

Simon, H. A., & Gilmartin, K. (1973). A simulation of memory for chess positions. *Cognitive Psychology, 5,* 29–46.

Simon, H. A., & Kaplan, C. A. (1989). Foundations of cognitive science. In M. I. Posner (Ed.), *Foundations of cognitive science.* MIT Press.

Simon, H. A., & Newell, A. (1971). Human problem solving: The state of the theory in 1970. *American Psychologist, 26,* 145–159.

Simon, H. A., & Reed, S. K. (1976). Modeling strategy shifts in a problem-solving task. *Cognitive Psychology, 8,* 86–97.

Simut, R. E., Vanderfaeillie, J., Peca, A., Van de, Perre., G, & Vanderborght, B. (2016). Children with autism spectrum disorders make a fruit salad with Probo, the social robot: An interaction study. *Journal of Autism Developmental Disorders, 46,* 113–126.

Singer, J. L (Ed.). (1990). *Repression and dissociation: Implications for personality theory, psychopathology, and health.* University of Chicago Press.

Singer, M. (2019). Challenges in processes of validation and comprehension. *Discourse Processes, 56,* 465–483.

Singh, L., Espinosa, L., Ji, J. L., Moulds, M. L., & Holmes, E. A. (2020). Developing thinking around mental health science: The example of intrusive, emotional mental imagery after psychological trauma. *Cognitive Neuropsychiatry, 25,* 348–363.

Sloman, S. A. (1999). Rational versus Arational models of thought. In R. J. Sternberg (Ed.), *The nature of cognition* (pp. 557–586). MIT Press.

Sloman, S. A. (2002). Two systems of reasoning. In T. Gilovich, D. Griffin, & D. Kahneman (Eds.), *Heuristics and biases: The psychology of intuitive judgment* (pp. 379–396). Cambridge University Press.

Sloman, S. A., & Rips, L. J. (Eds.). (1998). *Similarity and symbols in human thinking.* MIT Press.

Slovic, P., Finucane, M., Peters, E., & Gregor, D. G. (2002). The affect heuristic. In T. Gilovich, D. Griffin, & D. Kahneman (Eds.), *Heuristics and biases: The psychology of intuitive judgment* (pp. 397–420). Cambridge University Press.

Slovic, P., Fischhoff, B., & Lichtenstein, S. (1976). Cognitive processes and societal risk taking. In J. S. Carroll & J. W. Payne (Eds.), *Cognition and social behavior.* Erlbaum.

Slovic, P., & Lichtenstein, S. (1968). Relative importance of probabilities and payoffs in risk taking. *Journal of Experimental Psychology Monograph, 78*(3 Pt. 2), 1–18.

Smith, E. E. (1978). Theories of semantic memory. In W. K. Estes (Ed.), *Handbook of learning and cognitive processes* (Vol. 6, pp. 1–56). Erlbaum.

Smith, E. E. (1995). Concepts and categorization. In E. E. Smith & D. N. Osherson (Eds.), *An invitation to cognitive science* (Vol. 3, pp. 3–34). MIT Press.

Smith, E. E., Adams, N., & Schorr, D. (1978). Fact retrieval and the paradox of interference. *Cognitive Psychology, 10*, 438–464.

Smith, E. E., & Nielsen, G. D. (1970). Representation and retrieval processes in short-term memory: Recognition and recall of faces. *Journal of Experimental Psychology, 85*, 397–405.

Smith, E. E., Shoben, E. J., & Rips, L. J. (1974). Structure and process in se-mantic memory: A featural model for semantic decision. *Psychological Review, 81*, 214–241.

Smith, J. D., & Minda, J. P. (1998). Prototypes in the mist: The early epochs of category learning. *Journal of Experimental Psychology: Learning, Memory, and Cognition, 24*, 1411–1436.

Smith, M. E. (1983). Hypnotic memory enhancement of witnesses: Does it work? *Psychological Bulletin, 94*, 387–407.

Smith, S. M., Ward, T. B., & Schumacher, J. S. (1993). Constraining effects of examples in a creative generation task. *Memory & Cognition, 21*, 837–845.

Smyth, M. M., & Scholey, K. A. (1994). Interference in immediate spatial memory. *Memory & Cognition, 22*, 1–13.

Snow, C. E. (2010). Academic language and the challenge of reading for learning about science. *Science, 328*, 450–452.

Snyder, A. Z., Abdullaev, Y. G., Posner, M. I., & Raichle, M. E. (1995). Scalp electrical potentials reflect regional cerebral blood flow responses during processing of written words. *Proceedings of the National Academy of Sciences USA, 92*, 1689–1693.

So, W. C., Ching, T. H.-W., Lim, P. E., Cheng, X., & Ip, K. Y. (2014). Producing gestures facilitates route learning. *Plos One, 9*, e112543.

Sokolowski, H. M., Hawes, Z., & Lyons, I. M. (2019). What explains sex differences in math anxiety? A closer look at the role of spatial processing. *Cognition, 182*, 193–212.

Son, L. K., & Metcalfe, J. (2000). Metacognitive and control strategies in study-time allocation. *Journal of Experimental Psychology: Learning, Memory, and Cognition, 26*, 204–221.

Sparks, D., Chase, D., & Coughlin, L. (2009). Wii have a problem: A review of self-reported Wii related injuries. *Informatics in Primary Care, 17*, 55–57.

Spataro, R., Chella, A., Allison, B., Giadina, M., Sorbello, R., Tramonte, S., Guger, C., & La Bella, V. (2017). Reaching and grasping a glass of water by locked-in ALS patients through a BCI-controlled humanoid robot. *Frontiers in Human Neuroscience, 11*, 1–10.

Spence, C., Nicholls, M. E. R., & Driver, J. (2000). The cost of expecting events in the wrong sensory modality. *Perception & Psychophysics, 63*, 330–336.

Sperling, G. (1960). The information available in brief visual presentations. *Psychological Monographs, 74*(11), 1–29.

Sperling, G. (1963). A model for visual memory tasks. *Human Factors, 5*, 19–31.

Sperling, G. (1967). Successive approximations to a model for short-term memory. *Acta Psychologica, 27*, 285–292.

Speth, C., & Speth, J. (2018). A new measure of hallucinatory states and a discussion of REM sleep dreaming as a virtual laboratory for the rehearsal of embodied cognition. *Cognitive Science, 42*, 311–333.

Spivey, M. J., & Dale, R. (2006). Continuous dynamics in real-time cognition. *Current Directions in Psychological Science, 15*, 207–211.

Squire, L. R., & Alvarez, P. (1995). Retrograde amnesia and memory consolidation: A neurobiological perspective. *Current Opinion in Neurobiology, 5*(2), 169–177. https://doi.org/10.1016/0959-4388(95)80023-9

Squire, L. R., & Knowlton, B. J. (1994). Memory, hippocampus, and brain systems. In M. Gazzaniga (Ed.), *The cognitive neurosciences* (pp. 825–837). MIT Press.

Squire, L. R., & Wixted, J. T. (*2015*, Winter). Remembering. *Daedalus, the Journal of the American Academy of Arts and Sciences, 2015*, 53–66.

Squire, L. R., & Zola, S. M. (1996). Structure and function of declarative and nondeclarative memory systems. *Proceedings of the National Academy of Science, 93*, 13515–13522.

Squire, L. R., & Zola, S. M. (1997). Amnesia, memory and brain systems. *Philosophical Transactions of the Royal Society of London B, 352*, 1663–1673.

Srna, S., Schrift, R. Y., & Zauberman, G. (2018). The illusion of multitasking and its positive effect on performance. *Psychological Science, 29*(12), 1942–1955.

Standing, L. (1973). Learning 10,000 pictures. *Quarterly Journal of Experimental Psychology, 25*, 207–222.

Stanfield, R. A., & Zwaan, R. A. (2001). The effect of implied orientation derived from verbal context on picture recognition. *Psychological Science, 12*, 153–156.

Stanovich, K. E. (1990). Concepts in developmental theories of reading skill: Cognitive resources, automaticity, and modularity. *Developmental Review, 10*, 72–100.

Stanovich, K. E. (2018). Miserliness in human cognition: The intersection of detection, override and mindware. *Thinking & Reasoning, 24*, 423–444.

Stanovich, K. E., & Stanovich, P. J. (2010). A framework for critical thinking, rational thinking, and intelligence. In D. Preiss & R. J. Sternberg (Eds.), *Innovations in educational psychology: Perspectives on learning, teaching and human development* (pp. 195–237). Springer.

Stanovich, K. E., & West, R. F. (1983). On priming by a sentence context. *Journal of Experimental Psychology: General, 112*, 1–36.

Stanovich, K. E., & West, R. F. (2002). Individual differences in reasoning: Implications for the rationality debate? In T. Gilovich, D. Griffin, & D. Kahneman (Eds.), *Heuristics and biases: The psychology of intuitive judgment* (pp. 421–440). Cambridge University Press.

Staresina, B., & Wimber, M. (2019). A neural chronometry of memory recall. *Trends in Cognitive Sciences, 23*, 1071–1085.

State v Henderson. (New Jersey Supreme Court, 2011, August 24). https://casetext.com/case/state-v-henderson-578

Stein, B. S., & Bransford, J. D. (1979). Constraints on effective elaboration: Effects of precision and subject generation. *Journal of Verbal Learning and Verbal Behavior, 18*, 769–777.

Sternberg, R. J. (1998). Abilities are forms of developing expertise. *Educational Researcher, 27*, 11–20.

Sternberg, R. J. (2018). Which articles make a difference? Introduction to the special 30th APS anniversary issue of Perspectives on Psychological Science. *Perspectives on Psychological Science, 13*, 127–129.

Sternberg, R. J., & Gardner, M. K. (1983). Unities in inductive reasoning. *Journal of Experimental Psychology: General, 112*, 80–116.

Sternberg, R. J., & Lubart, T. L. (1996). Investing in creativity. *American Psychologist, 51*, 677–688.

Sternberg, S. (1966). High-speed scanning in human memory. *Science, 153*, 652–654.

Sternberg, S. (1967a). Retrieval of contextual information from memory. *Psychonomic Science, 8*, 55–56.

Sternberg, S. (1967b). Two operations in character recognition: Some evidence from reaction time measurements. *Perception & Psychophysics, 2*, 45–53.

Stetz, M. (2002, March 20). Lottery fans drawn to bigger prizes. *The San Diego Union-Tribune*.

Stevens, A., & Coupe, H. P. (1978). Distortions in judged spatial distances. *Cognitive Psychology, 10*, 526–550.

Stevenson, R. L. (1993). The strange case of Dr. Jekyll and Mr. Hyde. In Bell (Ed.), *Robert Louis Stevenson: The complete short stories* (Vol. 2, pp. 102–164). Mainstream.

Stieff, M., & Uttal, D. (2015). How much can spatial ability improve STEM achievement? *Educational Psychology Review, 27*, 607–615.

Strayer, D. L., & Drews, F. A. (2007). Cell-phone-induced driver distraction. *Current Directions in Psychological Science, 16*, 128–131.

Strayer, D. L., & Fisher, D. L. (2016). SPIDER: A framework for understanding driver distraction. *Human Factors*, *58*, 5–12.

Strayer, D. L., & Johnston, W. A. (2001). Driven to distraction: Dualtask studies of simulated driving and conversing on a cellular telephone. *Psychological Science*, *12*, 462–466.

Strobach, T. (2020). The dual-task practice advantage: Empirical evidence and cognitive mechanisms. *Psychonomic Bulletin & Review*, *27*, 3–14.

Stroop, J. R. (1935). Studies of interferences in serial verbal reactions. *Journal of Experimental Psychology*, *18*, 643–662.

Sulin, R. A., & Dooling, D. J. (1974). Intrusion of a thematic idea in retention of prose. *Journal of Experimental Psychology*, *103*, 255–262.

Sutherland, N. S. (1968). Outlines of a theory of visual pattern recognition in animals and man. *Proceedings of the Royal Society*, *171*, 297–317.

Sweller, J. (1988). Cognitive load during problem solving: Effects on learning. *Cognitive Science*, *12*, 257–285.

Sweller, J. (2003). Evolution of human cognitive architecture. In B. Ross (Ed.), *The psychology of learning and motivation* (Vol. 43, pp. 215–266). Academic Press.

Sweller, J., Mawer, R. F., & Ward, M. R. (1983). Development of expertise in mathematical problem solving. *Journal of Experimental Psychology: General*, *112*, 639–661.

Sweller, J., van Merrienboer, G. J., & Paas, F. (2019). Cognitive architecture and instructional design: 20 years later. *Educational Psychology Review*, *31*, 261–292.

Sweller, P., & Chandler, P. (1994). Why some material is difficult to learn. *Cognition and Instruction*, *12*, 185–233.

Swinney, D. A. (1979). Lexical access during sentence comprehension: Reconsideration of some context effects. *Journal of Verbal Learning and Verbal Behavior*, *18*, 645–659.

Swinney, D. A., & Hakes, D. T. (1976). Effects of prior context upon lexical access during sentence comprehension. *Journal of Verbal Learning and Verbal Behavior*, *15*, 681–689.

Swinney, D. A., & Osterhout, L. (1990). Inference generation during auditory language comprehension. In A. C. Graesser & G. H. Bower (Eds.), *Inferences and text comprehension*. Academic Press.

Takacs, Z. K., & Kassai, R. (2019). The efficacy of different interventions to foster children's executive function skills: A series of meta-analyses. *Psychological Bulletin*, *145*, 653–697.

Tanaka, J. W., & Taylor, M. (1991). Object categories and expertise: Is the basic level in the eye of the beholder? *Cognitive Psychology*, *23*, 457–482.

Tang, Y.-Y., Hölzel, B. K., & Posner, M. I. (2015). The neuroscience of mindfulness meditation. *Nature Reviews Neuroscience*, *16*(4), 213–225.

Tang, Y.-Y., Ma, Y., Wang, J., Fan, Y., Feng, S., Lu, Q., Yu, Q., Sui, D., Rothbart, M. K., Fan, M., & Posner, M. I. (2007). Short-term meditation training improves attention and self-regulation. *Proceedings of the National Academy of Sciences*, *104*(43), 15152–15156.

Tang, Y.-Y., & Posner, M. I. (2009). Attention training and attention state training. *TRENDS in Cognitive Sciences*, *14*, 13, 222–227.

Taverniers, J., Van Ruysseveldt, J., Smeets, T., & von Grumbkow, J. (2010). High-intensity stress elicits robust cortisol increases, and impairs working memory and visuo-spatial declarative memory in Special Forces candidates: A field experiment. *Stress*, *13*(4), 324–334. https://doi.org/10.3109/10253891003642394

Technical Working Group for Eyewitness Evidence. (1999). *Eyewitness evidence: A guide for law enforcement* [Booklet]. United States Department of Justice, Office of Justice Programs.

Teteris, E., Fraser, K., Wright, B., & McLaughlin, K. (2012). Does training learners on simulators benefit real patients? *Advances in Health Sciences Education*, *17*, 137–144.

Thaler, R. H., & Sunstein, C. R. (2008). *Nudge: Improving decisions about health, wealth, and happiness*. Penguin Books.

Thiede, K. W., Wiley, J., & Griffen, T. D. (2011). Test expectancy affects metacomprehension accuracy. *British Journal of Educational Psychology*, 81, 264–273.

Thomas, A. K., & McDaniel, M. A. (2007). Metacomprehension for educationally relevant materials: Dramatic effects of encoding-retrieval interactions. *Psychonomic Bulletin & Review*, 14, 212–218.

Thomas, N. J. T. (1999). Are theories of imagery theories of imagination? An active perception approach to conscious mental content. *Cognitive Science*, 23, 207–245.

Thompson, C. P., Skowronski, J. J., Larsen, S. F., & Betz, A. (1996). *Autobiographical memory: Remembering what and remembering when.* Erlbaum.

Thompson, W. L., Slotnick, S. D., Burrrage, M. S., & Kosslyn, S. M. (2009). Two forms of spatial imagery: Neuroimaging evidence. *Psychological Science*, 20, 1245–1253.

Thorndyke, P. W. (1977). Cognitive structures in comprehension and memory of narrative discourse. *Cognitive Psychology*, 9, 77–110.

Thorndyke, P. W. (1984). Applications of schema theory in cognitive research. In J. R. Anderson & S. M. Kosslyn (Eds.), *Tutorials in learning and memory* (pp. 167–191). Freeman.

Tomporowski, P. D., & Pesce, C. (2019). Exercise, sports, and performance arts benefit cognition via a common process. *Psychological Bulletin*, 145, 929–951.

Townsend, J. T. (1971). Theoretical analysis of an alphabetic confusion matrix. *Perception & Psychophysics*, 9, 40–50.

Trabasso, T., & Sperry, L. L. (1985). The causal basis for deciding importance of story events. *Journal of Memory and Language*, 24, 595–611.

Trabasso, T., & van den Broek, P. (1985). Causal thinking and the representation of narrative events. *Journal of Memory and Language*, 24, 612–630.

Trabasso, T., & Wiley, J. (2005). Goal plans of action and inferences during comprehension and narratives. *Discourse Processes*, 39, 129–164.

Treisman, A. M. (1960). Contextual cues in selective listening. *Quarterly Journal of Experimental Psychology*, 12, 242–248.

Treisman, A. M., & Geffen, G. (1967). Selective attention and cerebral dominance in responding to speech messages. *Quarterly Journal of Experimental Psychology*, 19, 1–17.

Treisman, A. M., & Gelade, G. (1980). A feature integration theory of attention. *Cognitive Psychology*, 12, 97–136.

Treisman, A. M., & Schmidt, H. (1982). Illusory conjunctions in the perception of objects. *Cognitive Psychology*, 14, 107–141.

Triona, L. M., & Klahr, D. (2003). Point and click or grab and heft: Comparing the influence of physical and virtual instructional materials on elementary school students' ability to design experiments. *Cognition and Instruction*, 21, 149–173.

Trope, Y., & Liberman, N. (2010). Construal-level theory of psychological distance. *Psychological Review*, 117, 440–463.

Trueswell, J. C., & Tanenhaus, M. K. (1994). Toward a lexicalist framework for constraint-based syntactic- ambiguity resolution. In C. Clifton, K. Rayner, & L. Frazier (Eds.), *Perspectives in sentence processing* (pp. 155–179). Erlbaum.

Trueswell, J. C., Tanenhaus, M. K., & Kello, C. (1993). Verb-specific constraints in sentence processing: Separate effect of lexical preference from garden paths. *Journal of Experimental Psychology: Learning, Memory, and Cognition*, 19, 528–553.

Tulving, E. (1972). Episodic and semantic memory. In E. Tulving & W. Donaldson (Eds.), *Organization of memory* (pp. 381–403). Academic Press.

Tulving, E. (1985). How many memory systems are there? *American Psychologist*, 40, 385–398.

Tulving, E. (2002). Episodic memory: From mind to brain. *Annual Review of Psychology*, 53, 1–25.

Tulving, E., & Thomson, D. M. (1973). Encoding specificity and retrieval processes in episodic memory. *Psychological Review*, 80, 352–373.

Tversky, A. (1972). Elimination by aspects: A theory of choice. *Psychological Review, 79,* 281–299.

Tversky, A., & Kahneman, D. (1973). Availability: A heuristic for judging frequency and probability. *Cognitive Psychology, 5,* 207–232.

Tversky, A., & Kahneman, D. (1981). The framing of decisions and the psychology of choice. *Science, 211,* 453–458.

Tversky, B. (1981). Distortions in memory for maps. *Cognitive Psychology, 13,* 407–433.

Tversky, B. (2005). Visuospatial reasoning. In K. J. Holyoak & R. G. Morrison (Eds.), *The Cambridge handbook of thinking and reasoning* (pp. 209–240). Cambridge University Press.

Tversky, B. (2019). *Mind in motion: how action shapes thought.* New York: Basic Books.

Twenge, J. (2017). *iGen: Why today's super-connected kids are growing up less rebellious, more tolerant, less happy—and completely unprepared for adulthood.* Atria Books.

Umanath, S., & Coane, J. H. (2020). Face validity of remembering and knowing: Empirical consensus and disagreement between participants and researchers. *Perspectives on Psychological Science, 15*(6), 1400–1422.

Unsworth, N. (2019). Individual differences in long-term memory. *Psychological Bulletin, 145,* 79–139.

Uttal, D. H., Newcombe, N. S., Meadow, N. G., Tipton, E., Hand, L. L., Alden, A. R., & Warren, C. (2013). The malleability of spatial skills: A meta-analysis of training studies. *Psychological Bulletin, 139,* 352–402.

Vallacher, R. R. (2007). Action identification theory. In R. F. Baumeister & R. F. Vohs (Eds.), *Encyclopedia of social psychology* (pp. 7–9). SAGE.

Vallacher, R. R., Coleman, P. T., Nowak, A., & Bui-Wrzosinska, L. (2010). Rethinking intractable conflict: The perspective of dynamical systems. *American Psychologist, 65,* 262–278.

Vallacher, R. R., & Wegner, D. M. (1987). What do people think they're doing? Action identification and human behavior. *Psychological Review, 94,* 3–15.

Van Assche, E., Duyck, W., Hartsuiker, R. J., & Diependaele, K. (2009). Does bilingualism change native-language reading. *Psychological Science, 20,* 923–927.

Van Dantzig, S., Pecher, D., Zeelenberg, R., & Barsalou, L. W. (2008). Perceptual processing affects conceptual processing. *Cognitive Science, 32,* 579–590.

Van de Broek, P. (2010). Processing texts in science education: Cognitive processes and knowledge representation. *Science, 328,* 453–456.

Van den Broek, P., Lorch, R. F., Linderholm, T., & Gusafson, M. (2001). The effect of readers' goals on inference generation and memory for texts. *Memory & Cognition, 29,* 1081–1087.

Van Dijk, T. A., & Kintsch, W. (1983). *Strategies of discourse comprehension.* Academic Press.

Van Dillen, L. F., Heslenfeld, D. J., & Koole, S. L. (2009). Turning down the emotional brain: An fMRI study of the effects of cognitive load on the processing of affective images. *Neuroimage, 45,* 1212–1219.

Van Dillen, L. F., & van Steenbergen, H. (2018). Turning down the hedonic brain: Cognitive load reduces neural responses to high-calorie food pictures in the nucleus accumbens. *Cognitive, Affective, and Behavioral Neuroscience, 18,* 447–459.

van Gog, T., Hoogerheide, V., & van Harsel, M. (2020). The role of mental effort in fostering self-regulated learning with problem-solving tasks. *Educational Psychology Review, 32,* 1055–1072.

Verdonk, C., Trousselard, M., Canini, F., Vialatte, F., & Ramdani, C. (2020). Toward a refined mindfulness model related to consciousness and based on ERP. *Perspectives in Psychological Science, 15*(4), 1095–1112.

Vergunst, F., Tremblay, R. E., Nagin, D., Algan, Y., Beasley, E., Park, J., Galera, C., Vitaro, F., & Cote, S. M. (2019). Association between childhood behaviors and adult employment earnings in Canada. *JAMA Psychiatry, 76,* 1044–1051.

Verkampt, F., & Ginet, M. (2010). Variations of the cognitive interview: Which one is the most effective in enhancing children's testimonies? *Applied Cognitive Psychology, 24,* 1279–1296.

Verschooren, S., Schindler, S., De Raedt, R., & Pourtois, G. (2019). Switching attention from internal to external information processing: A review of the literature and empirical support of the resource sharing account. *Psychonomic Bulletin & Review, 26*, 468–490.

Vidyasagar, T. R., & Pammer, K. (2009). Dyslexia: Deficit in visuospatial attention, not in phonological processing. *Trends in Cognitive Sciences, 14*, 317–324, 57–63.

Vitali, M. R., & Romance, N. R. (2007). A knowledge-based frame-work for unifying content-area reading comprehension and reading comprehension strategies. In D. S. McNamara (Ed.), *Reading comprehension strategies: Theories, interventions and technologies* (pp. 73–104). Taylor & Francis.

Vosniadou, S., Pnevmatikos, D., Makris, N., Lepenioti, D., Eikospentaki, K., Chountala, A., & Kyrianakis, G. (2018). The recruitment of shifting and inhibition in on-line science and mathematics tasks. *Cognitive Science, 42*, 1060–1886.

Wade, K. A., Garry, M., Nash, R. A., & Harper, D. N. (2010). Anchoring effects in the development of false childhood memories. *Psychonomic Bulletin & Review, 17*, 66–72.

Wagner, S. M., Nusbaum, H., & Goldin-Meadow, S. (2004). Probing the mental representation of gesture: Is handwaving spatial? *Journal of Memory and Language, 50*, 395–407.

Walker, C. H., & Yekovich, F. R. (1987). Activation and use of script-based antecedents in anaphoric reference. *Journal of Memory and Language, 26*, 673–691.

Walker, E., Adams, A., Restrepo, M. A., Fialko, S., & Glenberg, A. M. (2017). When and how interacting with technology-enhanced storybooks helps dual language learners. *Translational Issues in Psychological Science, 3*, 66–79.

Wang, S. S. (2020, November 4). Finding early clues of dementia. *The Wall Street Journal*, p. R7.6.

Wang, T., Yue, T., & Huang, X. T. (2016). Episodic and semantic memory contribute to familiar and novel future thinking. *Frontiers in Psychology, 7*, 1746.

Ward, T. B., Patterson, M. J., & Sifonis, C. M. (2004). The role of specificity and abstraction in creative idea generation. *Creativity Research Journal, 16*, 1–9.

Warrington, E. K., & Weiskrantz, L. (1968). New method of testing longterm retention with special reference to amnesic patients. *Nature, 217*, 972–974.

Warrington, E. K., & Weiskrantz, L. (1970). Amnesic syndrome: Consolidation or retrieval? *Nature, 228*, 628–630.

Wason, P. C., & Johnson-Laird, P. N. (1972). *Psychology of reasoning: Structure and content.* Harvard University Press.

Wason, P. C., & Shapiro, D. (1971). Natural and contrived experience in a reasoning problem. *Quarterly Journal of Experimental Psychology, 23*, 63–71.

Watson, J. B. (1924). *Behaviorism.* Norton.

Watson, P., Pearson, D., & Chow, M. (2020). Capture and control: Working memory modulates attentional capture by reward-related stimuli. *Psychological Science, 30*(8), 1174–1185.

Watson, P., Pearson, D., Chow, M., Theeuwes, J., Wiers, R. W., Most, S. B., & Le Pelley, M. E. (2019). Capture and control: Working memory modulates attentional capture by reward-related stimul. *Psychological Science, 30*, 1174–1185.

Waugh, N. C., & Norman, D. A. (1965). Primary memory. *Psychological Review, 72*, 89–104.

Weaver, C. A., & III. (1993). Do you need a flash to form a flashbulb memory? *Journal of Experimental Psychology: General, 122*, 39–46.

Weber, E. U. (1998). Who's afraid of a little risk? New evidence for general risk aversion. In J. Shanteau, B. A. Mellers, & D. A. Schum (Eds.), *Decision research from Bayesian to normative systems: Reflections on the contributions of Ward Edwards.* Kluwer Academic.

Weber, E. U., & Hsee, C. (1998). Cross-cultural differences in risk perception, but cross-cultural similarities in attitudes towards perceived risk. *Management Science, 44*, 1205–1217.

Weber, E. U., & Morris, M. W. (2010). Culture and judgment and decision making: The constructivist turn. *Perspectives on Psychological Science, 5,* 410–419.

Wedlock, B. C., & Growe, R. (2017). The technology-driven student: How to apply Bloom's revised taxonomy to the digital generations. *Journal of Education & Social Policy, 7,* 25–34.

Weisberg, R. W. (1993). *Creativity: Beyond the myth of genius.* Freeman.

Weisberg, R. W. (2009). On "out-of-the-box" thinking in creativity. In A. B. Markman & K. L. Wood (Eds.), *Tools for innovation* (pp. 23–47). Oxford University Press.

Weisberg, R. W. (2018). Insight, problem-solving, and creativity: An integration of findings. In F. Valle-Tourangeau (Ed.), *Insight: On the origins of new ideas* (pp. 191–215). Routledge.

Weisberg, S. M., & Newcombe, N. S. (2018). Cognitive maps: Some people make them, some people struggle. *Current Directions in Psychological Science, 27,* 220–226.

Weisman, K., & Markman, E. M. (2017). Theory-based explanation as intervention. *Psychonomic Bulletin & Review, 24,* 1555–1562.

Weiss, H. M., & Merlo, K. L. (2020). Affect, attention, and episodic performance. *Current Directions in Psychological Science, 29,* 433–459.

Wells, G. L., Malpass, R. S., Lindsay, R. C., Fisher, R. P., Turtle, J. W., & Fulero, S. M. (2000). From the lab to the police station: A successful application of eyewitness research. *American Psychologist, 55,* 581–598.

Wells, G. L., & Olson, E. A. (2003). Eyewitness testimony. *Annual Review of Psychology, 54,* 277–295.

Wernicke, C. (1874). *Der aphasische symptom-encomplex.* Franck U. Weigart.

Wharton, W., Hirshman, E., Merritt, P., Stangl, B., Scanlin, K., & Keriger, L. (2006). Lower blood pressure correlates with poorer performance on visuospatial attention tasks in younger individuals. *Biological Psychology, 73,* 227–234.

Wickelgren, W. A. (1974). *How to solve problems.* Freeman.

Wickens, C. D., & Kramer, A. (1985). Engineering psychology. *Annual Review of Psychology, 36,* 307–348.

Wickens, D. D. (1972). Characteristics of word encoding. In A. W. Melton & E. Martin (Eds.), *Coding processes in human memory.* Winston.

Wickens, D. D., Born, D. G., & Allen, C. K. (1963). Proactive inhibition and item similarity in short-term memory. *Journal of Verbal Learning and Verbal Behavior, 2,* 440–445.

Widhalm, M. L., & Rose, N. S. (2019). How can transcranial magnetic stimulation be used to causally manipulate memory representations in the human brain? *Wiley Interdisciplinary Reviews: Cognitive Science, 10,* e1469.

Wilder, J., Feldman, J., & Singh, M. (2011). Superordinate shape classification using natural shape statistics. *Cognition, 119,* 325–340.

Wilson, B. (2020). *Metropolis: A history of the city, humankind's greatest invention.* Doubleday.

Wilson, M. (2002). Six views of embodied cognition. *Psychonomic Bulletin & Review, 9,* 625–636.

Wingen, G. A. van., Geuze, E., Caan, M. W. A., Kozicz, T., Olabarriaga, S. D., Denys, D., Vermetten, E., & Fernández, G. (2012). Persistent and reversible consequences of combat stress on the mesofrontal circuit and cognition. *Proceedings of the National Academy of Sciences, 109*(38), 15508–15513.

Winograd, E., & Neisser, U. (1992). *Affect and accuracy in recall: Studies of "flashbulb" memories.* Cambridge University Press.

Wirth, J., Stebner, F., Trypke, M., Schuster, C., & Leutner, D. (2020). And interactive layers model of self-regulated learning and cognitive load. *Educational Psychology Review, 32,* 1127–1149.

Witt, J. K. (2011). Action's effect on perception. *Current Directions in Psychological Science, 20,* 201–206.

Witt, J. K., & Riley, M. A. (2014). Discovering your inner Gibson: Reconciling action-specific and ecological approaches to perception-action. *Psychonomic Bulletin & Review, 21,* 1353–1370.

Wittgenstein, L. (1953). *Philosophical investigations* (G. E. M. Anscombe, Trans.). Blackwell.

Wixted, J. T., Mickes, L., & Fisher, R. P. (2018). Rethinking the reliability of eyewitness memory. *Perspectives on Psychological Science, 13*, 324–335.

Wolfe, J. M. (2018). Ann Treisman (1935–2018). *Current Biology, 28*, R329–R341.

Wright, W. F., & Bower, G. H. (1992). Mood effects on subjective probability assessment. *Organizational Behavior and Human Decision Processes, 52*, 276–291.

Wu, L. L. (1995). *Perceptual representation in conceptual combination* [Unpublished dissertation, University of Chicago].

Wu, R. (2019). Learning what to learn across the lifespan: From object to real world skills. *Current Directions in Psychological Science, 28*, 392–397.

Wykowska, A. (2021). Robots as mirrors of the human mind. *Current Directions in Psychological Science, 30*, 34–40.

Xie, F., Zhang, L., Chen, X., & Xin, Z. (2019). Is spatial ability related to mathematical ability: A meta-analysis. *Educational Psychology Review, 32*, 113–155.

Xie, F., Zhang, L., Chen, X., & Xin, Z. (2020). Is spatial ability related to mathematical ability: A meta-analysis. *Educational Psychology Review, 32*, 113–155.

Yarkoni, T., Poldrack, R. A., Van Esssen, D. C., & Wager, T. D. (2010). Cognitive neuroscience 2.0: Building a cumulative science of human brain function. *Trends in Cognitive Sciences, 14*, 489–496.

Yechiam, E., Erev, I., Yehene, V., & Gopher, D. (2003). Melioration and the transition from touch-typing training to everyday use. *Human Factors, 45*, 671–684.

Yee, E., & Thompson-Schill, S. L. (2016). Putting concepts into context. *Psychonomic Bulletin & Review, 23*, 1015–1027.

Yerkes, R. M., & Dodson, J. D. (1908). The relation of strength of stimulus to rapidity of habit-formation. *Journal of Comparative Neurology and Psychology, 18*, 459–482.

Yoon, S. A., Ericsson, K. A., & Donatelli, D. (2018). Effects of 30 years of disuse on exceptional memory performance. *Cognitive Science, 42*, 884–903.

Zacks, J. M. (2008). Neuroimaging studies of mental rotation: A meta-analysis and a review. *Journal of Cognitive Neuroscience, 20*, 1–19.

Zapalska, A., McCarty, M. D., Young-McLear, K., & White, J. (2018). Design of assignments using the 21st century bloom's revised taxonomy model for development of critical thinking skills. *Problems and Perspectives in Management, 16*, 291–305.

Zarkadi, T., Wade, K. A., & Stewart, N. (2009). Creating fair lineups for suspects with distinctive features. *Psychological Science, 20*, 1448–1453.

Zemla, J. C., Sloman, S., Bechlivanidis, C., & Lagnado, D. A. (2017). Evaluating everyday explanations. *Psychonomic Bulletin & Review, 24*, 1488–1500.

Zheng, Z., Zhao, H., Swanson, A. R., Weitlauf, A. S., Warren, Z. E., & Sarkar, N. (2018). Design, development, and evaluation of a non-invasive autonomous robot-mediated joint attention intervention system for young children with ASD. *IEEE Transactions on Human-machine Systems, 48*, 125–135.

Ziegler, J. C., Perry, C., & Zorzi, M. (2020). Learning to read and dyslexia: From theory to intervention through personalized computational models . *Current Directions in Psychological Science, 29*, 293–300.

Zuckerman, H., Pan, Z., Park, C., Brietzke, E., Musial, N., Shariq, A. S., Iacobucci, M., Yim, S. J., Lui, L. M. W., Rong, C., & McIntyre, R. S. (2018). Recognition and Treatment of Cognitive Dysfunction in Major Depressive Disorder. *Frontiers in Psychiatry, 9.* https://doi.org/10.3389/fpsyt.2018.00655

Zurif, E. B., Caramazza, A., Meyerson, R., & Galvin, J. (1974). Semantic feature representation for normal and aphasic language. *Brain and Language, 1*, 167–187.

Zwaan, R. A., & Radvansky, G. A. (1998). Situation models in language comprehension and memory. *Psychological Bulletin, 123*, 62–185.

Zwaan, R. A., & Yaxley, R. H. (2003). Spatial iconicity affects semantic relatedness judgments. *Psychonomic Bulletin & Review, 10*, 954–958.

SUBJECT INDEX

15-object test, 46

ability, 43–46, 72–73, 82, 97, 102–3, 109–10, 141, 159, 240, 243–46, 264–65, 275–76, 278, 325, 342, 393, 399, 423, 428, 430–31
absolute deviations, 206
absolute judgment and memory span, 118
abstraction, 37, 161
    higher level of, 161–62
abstract words, 218, 220–21, 233, 245, 305–6, 318
accidents, 76, 79, 103, 363–64
accuracy, 37, 74, 148, 165, 196–97, 277–79, 349, 360, 413, 446–47, 452
acoustic information, 101
    manipulating, 118
acquisition, 2, 4, 13, 82–83, 122–23, 140–42, 149, 216, 222, 246
action-based decision making, 354, 380
action identification theory, 168, 170, 179
actions, 16–17, 40–41, 133, 151–79, 280–81, 299, 301–2, 308–9, 311, 335–37, 366, 380, 382–84, 386–87, 414
    alternative, 153, 366
    appropriate, 249
    central, 311
    direct, 161
    familiar, 179
    imagined, 174
    mechanical, 172–73
    simulated, 157, 173, 175
    simulating, 157, 173
    skilled, 165
activation, 11, 39, 113–15, 234, 236, 294–96, 301, 303, 312, 317, 330–32, 334, 342–43
    associative, 312–13
    simultaneous, 137
    spreading, 295–97, 311–12, 318, 334, 342
activities
    central, 309
    daily, 57, 154, 178, 209, 314
    increased, 233–34

    mental, 67, 72, 82, 100
    routine, 71, 309, 318, 335
additive model, 355, 357
age, 132, 146, 276–77, 313, 377, 387, 425–26
age groups, 157, 377
alerting network, 52, 55, 68, 82
algorithms, 15, 174, 316, 408
allocation of attention, 57, 67, 105
allocation of capacity, 67, 112
Alzheimer's disease, 276–78
ambiguity, 330, 334–35, 450
amnesia, 128, 132–33, 149, 211, 132–33
amodal symbol systems, 300
AMPA, 137
amygdala, 134–35, 138, 196, 303–4
anagram, 391–93, 391, 400
analogy, 224, 253, 298–99, 390–92, 397, 408–10, 412, 414, 419, 430, 448
analysis, 183–84, 244, 268, 272, 340–41, 401, 406–9, 419, 429, 432–33, 437
    information-processing, 6
    of recall protocols, 185
    of rehearsal processes in free recall, 127
    semantic, 68–70
anterograde amnesia, 134
antibiotics, 270–71, 348
anticipation, 153
antidepressants, 115–16, 118
anxiety, 3, 58–59, 68, 115–18, 170
apperceptive agnosia, 45–46, 48
arithmetic, mental, 233–34
arousal, 56, 67–68
arrangement problems, 392–94, 396, 401, 419
artificial intelligence, 2, 7–8, 13–17, 21, 28, 42, 53, 87, 308, 450, 453
ASD (Autism Spectrum Disorder), 81
associations, 183, 187, 191, 211, 217–18, 220, 293, 295, 299, 305–8, 321, 323, 425–27
    semantic, 201
    strong, 309
    verbal, 217–18
associative agnosia, 45–46
Asthma, 363–64
Atkinson-Shiffrin Model, 122–23, 128, 182, 184

NAME INDEX